The Transformation of the Classical Heritage

Peter Brown, General Editor

ART AND CEREMONY
IN LATE ANTIQUITY

ART AND CEREMONY

SABINE G. MacCORMACK

IN LATE ANTIQUITY

UNIVERSITY OF CALIFORNIA PRESS
Berkeley · Los Angeles · London

University of California Press
Berkeley and Los Angeles, California

University of California Press, Ltd.
London, England

© 1981 by
The Regents of the University of California
Printed in the United States of America
First Paperback Printing 1990

1   2   3   4   5   6   7   8   9

Library of Congress Cataloging in Publication Data

MacCormack, Sabine.
  Art and ceremony in late antiquity.

  (The Transformation of the classical heritage;
1)
  Bibliography: p. 379
  Includes index.
  1. Emperor worship, Roman.   2. Rites and
ceremonies—Rome.   3. Roman emperors—Succession.
4. Laudatory poetry, Latin—History and criticism.
5. Rome—History—Empire, 284–476.   I. Title.
II. Series: Transformation of the classical
heritage; 1.
DG124.M33   937'.06   78-62864
ISBN 0-520-06966-8

FOR CATHERINE

Ἔστι μοι κάλα πάις χρυσίοισιν ἀνθέμοισιν
ἐμφέρην ἔχοισα μόρφαν, Κλέις ἀγαπάτα,
αντὶ τᾶς ἔγωύδὲ Λυδίαν παῖσαν ὀυδ᾽ ἐράνναν·

SAPPHO

CONTENTS

CONTENTS

PLATES

THE FIGURE OF THE EMPEROR

ADVENTUS

ACCESSION

GRATIARUM ACTIO

I owe the original training in the field covered by this book to my teacher at Frankfurt University, Hadwig Hörner, whose refined and cultured understanding of the classical languages has been a lasting inspiration. At Oxford, I learnt about using these languages as a historian from Peter Brown. I would like to recall here Gervase Mathew—not so much his words, much though they have meant to me, but what on this earth he was, a deep quietness and "laughter in the next room." Oswyn Murray introduced me to the English tradition of classical scholarship, and many happy hours have been spent talking about late antiquity with Robert Markus. Dumbarton Oaks was the haven which its founders intended it to be. I had time there to learn to appreciate and enjoy Ken Holum's patient erudition and insight.

I am grateful to John Matthews for help which he was always prepared to offer when this book was in thesis form. Earlier versions of the manuscript were also read by Joscelyn Toynbee, Peter Brown, Averil Cameron, Roger Collins, and Sister Charles Murray. Their comments helped to eliminate numerous errors and omissions and brought about substantive changes in arrangement and content. It is a pleasure to remember both what I learnt from these comments, and the personal contacts to which they gave rise. My especial gratitude goes to Oliver Nicholson, who not only read and commented on large parts of the book, but also supervised the acquisition of the photographs. The final manuscript gained much in clarity and consistency from Leonie Gordon's perspicacious and careful editing. To her and to the staff of the University of California Press I would like to express my very warm thanks.

Geoffrey MacCormack encouraged me to begin and continue research when it seemed unimaginable that it would ever lead to published results. I am very deeply indebted to his generous confidence in my work. I have learnt more than I can record from all whom I have taught, many of whom have become friends. Christopher Wallis in particular has contributed to this book and to my thinking in ways which I cannot easily define, but which I know to be fundamental. Finally, it would not have been possible to pursue my research without the peace and true refuge which for many years I found in the Bodleian Library, and found again in the library at Dumbarton Oaks, where books became not only a source of knowledge but a pointer to wisdom:

> felix qui potuit rerum cognoscere causas,
> atque metus omnis et inexorabile fatum
> subiecit pedibus strepitumque Acherontis avari.
> fortunatus et ille deos qui novit agrestis
> Panaque Silvanumque senem Nymphasque sorores.

I would like to thank Linacre College, Oxford, St. Anne's College, Oxford, and the Craven Committee for supporting my work at a time when such support was essential for its continuance. A most generous award from the Twenty-Seven Foundation covered the cost of the photographs and of typing the final script. The Research Institute of the University of Texas at Austin paid for assistance in preparing the Greek and Latin citations for print, and in making the index.

S.G.M.

THE WORLD OF THE PANEGYRISTS

Public speaking was part and parcel of life in any city of the Roman Empire, and for many men of culture it was also a career. Aristotle had distinguished three types of speeches: political or advisory, juridical, and speeches for the entertainment and pleasure of the audience. Panegyrics—speeches in praise of individuals or gods, of cities or countries—counted among this latter group; within it, the panegyrics which were of the greatest practical importance were those of emperors.

Although numerous speeches praising an emperor have survived, we can catch only one glimpse of a late Roman man on the point of delivering such a speech, and that one glimpse is misleading. Augustine, installed as a teacher of rhetoric in Milan in 385, was not enjoying his job. The panegyric which he was about to deliver struck him as a polished exercise in lying.

> How unhappy I felt . . . on that day, when I was preparing to declaim the emperor's praises, and to lie about many matters; and for doing it, I would gain favour from persons of discrimination.[1]

Walking through Milan, Augustine saw in a lane a beggar whose state of inebriated bliss highlighted his own sense of the futility of worldly endeavour. For it seemed that the beggar had attained that very joy of happiness here and now, *laetitia temporalis felicitatis*, which had eluded Augustine, and which at the same time constituted a potent slogan of late Roman politics. In his panegyric, Augustine would therefore doubtlessly have striven to ascribe it, in the face of disquieting facts—Gaul in the hands of a usurper, the Danubian frontier insecure, the emperor at Constantinople of uncertain goodwill—to the prevailing political situation of the court of Milan.[2]

Augustine's prejudice still lies heavily over the study of the panegyric literature of late antiquity. The combination of a highly artificial and traditionalist style with the exaltation of the imperial majesty seems to bring together, in one genre, precisely those two features of the later empire which have caused most uneasiness to the modern scholar. Fulsome praise of an autocrat is distasteful, while the products of what is often considered to be a small and backward-looking elite are doubly suspect—suspect both because the panegyrist, as Augustine claimed, was committed, by the nature of his task, to distorting the truth, and because, in any case, his choice of a highly traditionalist literary style appeared to carry him far away from the 'realities' of the late Roman political scene.[3] Treated, therefore, as a singularly unfortunate amalgam of preciosity and propaganda, late Roman panegyric has suffered a fate reserved for the study of propaganda in most periods, compounded by a lack of empathy quite peculiar to students of late classical literature: that is, the interpretation of panegyrics has swung between the excessively grandiose and the dismissive.

Some scholars have hoped to reconstruct from the panegyrics a single, coherent theory of imperial power, or a single portrait of the ideal emperor.[4] Others have used the same material with exemplary diligence to cast an uncertain light on precise details of the shifting policies of the imperial court at precise moments of crisis.[5] Both groups of scholars have used this material with ill-disguised feelings of frustration. Somehow, the evidence was not giving them what they had sought. But, in a sense, they had courted this disillusionment, for they had assumed that, in handling panegyrics, they were handling a body of 'evidence,' which was to act as a mirror for them—a mirror that should ideally reflect without distortion the reality that lay outside its surface. They have been led to conclude that, in the later Roman Empire, as in Byzantium, much of reality can be glimpsed only through a 'distorting mirror,' and that, of these distorting mirrors, the most warped was panegyric. Yet it is worthwhile noting, as a fact in the history of late Roman and Byzantine scholarship, that advances in our understanding of late antiquity have usually happened when the rigid antithesis between 'reality' and 'distortion' has been modified.

The most notable advance of all has taken place in our understanding of late Roman art as a whole, and of the fate of the classical elements in it.[6] Less noticeable, but equally decisive, has been the re-evaluation of the role of the traditionalist elements in late antique culture. Far from being dismissed as so many 'fossilized' remnants of the past and as so many wilful 'distortions' of the 'reality' of the late Roman present, many institutions and cultural forms inherited from the classical past have been seen to have maintained a positive function in the late Roman world, even to have gained a strange new vigour and to have shown unexpected sensitivity to their changed environment. The old forms could be regrouped to express new themes.

To trace this *pseudomorphosis* of late classical culture has remained the *ars artium* of late antique scholarship.[7] It is therefore important that a study of change and continuity in this period should begin with the search for a lever with which to shift the intractable boulder of late antique panegyric into different positions, so that it can be viewed from angles other than conventional ones. We must, therefore, situate the panegyrists of the late third and early fourth centuries in their world. That is, we must study the milieu in which panegyrics were composed, and indicate the concrete circumstances in which they were delivered. For, behind the surviving texts of Latin panegyrics there lay the formation of a specific intellectual environment, the adaptation of this environment to the needs of the court, the careful and deliberate choice of particular means of expression which had been made available by the literary tradition, and their overall orchestration to communicate a precise message at a precise time. These diverse aspects of panegyrics must be examined as a whole.

What emerges from such a study is not a static picture. Seen against the background of late antiquity as a whole, the Tetrarchy stands out as a rare moment of equilibrium. It was not, as the conventional chronological divisions of late Roman history books seem to imply, the starting point for a future continuous tradition. In the history of panegyric, as in many other aspects, it was, rather, an age of achievements which were not maintained in the course of the fourth century. The curtain rises on the Tetrarchy and reveals a situation where intimate and ceremonious relations existed between the emperor and certain towns of Gaul.[8]

The schools of these towns produced rhetors whose panegyrics were outstanding for their certainty of touch, their choice of topics, their manipulation of information and for their discreet and skilful application of a living pagan imagery. These panegyrics were a sophisticated and delicate means of political communication almost unprecedented in the ancient world. For, the panegyrists were not merely an elite which defined itself by preserving the ancient culture, men "from whom words proceed without the blemish of stylistic imperfections";[9] nor was their training merely one which rendered them *capable de tout*. Long study of the classics had given them an impressive reserve of images and turns of phrase which were hallowed by usage and were the common property of every member of their audience. Furthermore, the exacting discipline of the rhetorical schools, which may seem so dry to us, enabled them to remain in control of this inert but potentially charged mass of material, and therefore to deploy it at will.[10]

This ability to organise a mass of material, to hold it in the mind and to bring it out with clarity—and not the remote inaccessibility of an elitist culture—was what distinguished a man who had received the traditional rhetorical education. As St. Clement told St. Peter in a legend circulating in this period: *Narrandi ordinem et lucidius quae res expedit proferendi eruditio nobis contulit liberalis.*[11] As a result, the very rigidity of the rhetorical training, with its strict rules governing the sequence and subdivisions of topics, maintained rather than confined the flexibility of the classical tradition within which the panegyrists grew up. It was by such a discipline that what might strike the modern observer as a single, fossilized lump of classical imagery was cut up into fine fragments, like glittering *tesserae*, from which mosaics of widely differing patterns might be made.

When our period begins, therefore, in the reign of Diocletian, a continuous tradition of Greco-Roman eulogistic oratory stood behind the panegyrists. Rather than weighing upon them, however, this long tradition, absorbed through the educational routines of the rhetorical schools and summarised in handbooks, ensured that the panegyrics of the Tetrarchy marked a new departure in their clarity of presentation and in their discreet relevance to living political issues. The panegyrics can take their place not merely as so much 'evidence,' but as factors in their own right in a crucial moment of definition in late Roman society. They were active elements in forming the views of contemporaries of their own society—a society where the role of the emperor, though predominant, was nevertheless balanced by the roles of gods and men.

Let us begin with the handbooks that have survived. In the later third and fourth centuries A.D. two comprehensive treatises on eulogistic discourses were composed by the rhetor Menander.[12] The περὶ ἐπιδεικτικῶν, attributed to Dionysius of Halicarnassus, probably dates from the late second or the third century.

The principles of composition which were laid down in these treatises were the same as those in earlier works, but, particularly in the work of Menander, they were worked out in greater detail and with an abundance of examples. At times one can almost hear the teacher of rhetoric addressing his class, first stating the principle in question in the abstract, then applying it in practice. Menander was certainly well aware of all the quandaries in which a panegyrist might find himself and was resourceful in suggesting solutions. The treatises were schoolbooks, designed to prepare the young orator for what was, in late antiquity, one of his chief functions as a public speaker: the praise of emperors, generals and governmental dignitaries.

The treatises, therefore, outlined speeches for different types of official occasions, such as arrivals, departures, marriages and the presentation of wreaths—the last applicable to the *aurum coronarium* offered to Roman emperors. There was also a basic scheme for the *basilikos logos*, the royal address, which could be adapted according to the occasion. Apart from pointing out some general methods, such as comparisons and careful and clear subdivisions of the speech, so that the listener might follow more easily, the basic scheme outlined the order in which topics had to follow one another. After an introduction the orator was to praise briefly the home country, the family, the birth and education of the subject; if any of these was likely to cause embarrassment, it was to be left out. In the main part of the speech, the deeds, divided under the rubrics of war and peace, were to be praised in detail and the author was to point out how in his deeds the subject of the panegyric practised the different virtues.

Menander, however, still wrote for a classroom. The panegyric of Pliny, which headed the late fourth-century edition of the *Panegyrici Latini*, also belonged to a more secluded world, with far less clearly-defined priorities.[13] The panegyrics of late antiquity were a development of, and in some senses an improvement on, the panegyric by Pliny. They were, it is true—if one is to judge them by the standards of classical Latin literature—inferior to Pliny's and certainly to Cicero's, from the literary and the linguistic point of view. Where Pliny tried to create methods of expression and literature, the fourth-century panegyrists used the expressions made available to them by the authors of the past, especially Cicero. They did not aim to create literature for its own sake.[14] Also, their speeches were less comprehensive as a record, much shorter and less factual. However, these characteristics were in many respects an advantage, for they served to differentiate panegyrics more clearly from historiography and turned them from pure eulogy into an instrument of propaganda. Such panegyrics had to be concise, systematic and comprehensive, but simple. Narrative detail and linguistic and structural complexity yielded to clarity.

These principles did not exclude the rules of Menander, but in many ways they modified what had been said about amplification. The late Roman panegyrists observed Menander's rules, but they did so very selectively. Among the omissions were not only those parts of eulogistic speeches which had to be passed over because, as Menander himself said, they could not always apply or would strain the credulity of the audience, but also matters which could perfectly well have been said but were nonetheless left out. The late Roman panegyrists were deliberately not writing history, and most of them did not aim at completeness, even as regarded the emperor's good qualities. Rather, they deployed their skills to interpret a particular situation for a particular purpose, place and time.

Although not to be confused with historical writing, the substance of a late antique panegyric did concern itself with the deeds and virtues of the emperor, whether these manifested themselves within or outside a ceremonial occasion. However, by a subtle change of balance which crept into the method of composing panegyrics in the course of our period, a panegyric dating from the beginning of the period looks very different from a panegyric from its end. For, while in the late third and early fourth centuries the deeds and virtues of the emperor not only made up the substance of panegyric but also determined the arrangement of each particular speech, the arrangement of later panegyrics could equally well be determined by the course of a certain ceremonial occasion. We see the emperor in these later panegyrics less as an individual with particular characteristics and more as the focal point of a complex courtly ritual.

This change in the nature of the panegyrics was highlighted by one of the ceremonies we will discuss, the ceremony of accession. Thanks to its great antiquity, the ceremony of *adventus*—the traditional rite of welcome for a ruler—figured as a regular ingredient in late antique panegyrics. Arrival could illustrate the emperor's virtues. Accession, by contrast, did not develop as a ceremony until the fourth century, and so escaped the textbook rules of panegyric. First, accession was not counted among the items which could be praised in the panegyric, and second, the textbooks did not describe a special type of panegyric to celebrate an accession which would have matched panegyrics for arrival and funerary eulogies. This was so even though the emperor's virtues, which could be and were cited as being a reason for his accession, were habitually discussed.

It needed a change of emphasis in the composition of panegyrics—away from deeds and virtues, and toward the description of ceremonial—for full stock to be taken of accession ceremonies in the framework of a panegyric. This was done by Corippus in his panegyric of 566 A.D. on Justin II. Corippus discarded the rhetorical form of panegyric, the customary sequence of topics and their subdivisions. Also, his narrative technique was different from that of other panegyrists. He used direct speech to report acclamations and addresses, and employed similes and the vocabulary of poetry to describe his scenes. Earlier, these techniques were used by Claudian and Sidonius, who, like Corippus, wrote their panegyrics in verse. Verse panegyric emerged as a suitable medium for the description of the ceremony of accession because the epic form on which it could draw[15] allowed for reporting the verbal interchanges which an accession involved, and for descriptive elaboration of ceremonial actions which could not strictly be classified as deeds or virtues. These features of verse panegyrics were anticipated in some panegyrics in prose.

A prose panegyric which comes very close to verse form is that by Cassiodorus on the Gothic royal couple Vitigis and Matasuntha, which is in part a highly colourful description of the queen in her regalia.[16] This panegyric demonstrates just how far a prose panegyric could go in discarding the conventions of panegyric strictly speaking, although earlier panegyrics did contain passages of a similar character. Thus, developments within the genre of panegyric itself—the tendency of panegyric, even when written in prose, towards description rather than narrative and analysis—led up to Corippus' manner of treating Justin's accession.

But the transition from the description of imperial deeds and virtues to the description of imperial ceremonial was not merely a matter of literary form, but proof of a significant change in outlook. The textbooks instructing orators how to construct their panegyrics frequently used as the basis of their disquisitions an analysis of the personality in terms of virtues of the soul on the one hand and virtues external to the soul on the other,[17] the latter leading to the praise of such imperial gestures as generosity—largitio. These rhetorical treatises analysing the constituent parts of the personality drew on a very broad philosophical literature which treated virtues and vices and the right way to live in terms of the tenets of the various philosophical schools. The late Latin rhetorical treatises, by contrast, give very cursory instruction in the matter of the virtues. Among other finer points which were passed over, the distinction between virtues of the soul and virtues external to the soul disappeared or was merely repeated mechanically.[18] This lack of interest was paralleled by the disappearance of the philosophical schools with the exception of the Neoplatonist schools of Athens and Alexandria. The personality was no longer a matter of concern in the way that it had been earlier. Given this development, it becomes clear why the later panegyrics had much less to say on imperial virtues and why even in

Claudian the topic was dropped, to be gradually replaced by the *ek-phrasis* of deeds in terms of ceremonies.

In such a framework, the *topos* of panegyric came to coincide with the actual content of ceremonies. The obvious example here is *adventus*, where the basic ceremonies of welcome were so ancient, and so well known, that any description of them, however coloured by local detail, contained familiar points which were, at least potentially, literary *topoi*. Similarly, imperial funerals developed their own set of *topoi* and com-monplaces. For instance, the solemn procession of the imperial funerary cortège was spontaneously described as an *adventus* by two authors of quite different outlook, Gregory Nazianzen and Ambrose.[19]

Likewise with accession: by the time Corippus came to write about the accession of Justin II, he could draw on a large collection of com-monplaces which at the same time described elements of the ceremony. Of Justin II as an individual we thus hear very little. This gradual change in the content of panegyrics can be observed throughout the period here studied. At the beginning of the period stand the Tetrarchic pan-egyrics, in which ceremonies were a topic mentioned as incidental to, or as a part of, other topics. Thereafter, narrations of ceremonial actions in their own right became more elaborate, initially in Eusebius and The-mistius, and later in Claudian.

In panegyrics, from the late fourth century onwards, themes such as imperial death and accession were clothed in a complex ceremonial and in a many-layered descriptive imagery which served to elucidate the ceremonial. With that, ceremonial actions were capable of becoming lit-erary commonplaces, much as the imperial virtues had been earlier. But, whereas for the virtues we turn to the rhetorical textbooks to learn the principles by which they were to be organized in a panegyric, for ceremonies we turn to historians like Ammianus who reported imperial ceremonies as they occurred, and to the sixth-century appendix of Con-stantine Porphyrogenitus' *De Ceremoniis*.[20] There we find as accurate a guide for imperial ceremonies as we did for imperial virtues in the rhe-torical textbooks of earlier late antiquity.

Panegyric can thus be understood as one element among many in the evolution of imperial ceremonial. In this ceremonial, the surviving pan-egyric was not a detached 'mirror' reflecting events outside itself; it was the speech of an actor in a play—in the permanent quasi-liturgical drama by which late antique men sought to articulate the modes of con-tact between the emperor, his subjects and his invisible but ever-present companions: the gods, and later, God.

Gibbon perceived this aspect of late Roman life clearly: "By a philosophic observer the system of the Roman government might have been mistaken for a splendid theatre, filled with players of every character and degree, who repeated the language, and imitated the passions, of their original model."[21] If the art of panegyric is to be fully understood, it must be set among the "players" in this "splendid theatre."

First, and most important, what was the play? Gibbon and later scholars had few doubts on this: "Like the modesty affected by Augustus, the state maintained by Diocletian was a theatrical representation; but it must be confessed that, of the two comedies, the former was of a more liberal and manly character than the latter. It was the aim of the one to disguise, and the object of the other to display, the unbounded power which the emperors possessed over the Roman world."[22]

It is partly the aim of this study to show that so unilateral a view of the imperial ceremonial, and of the role of panegyric within it, is misleading. Precisely because of the formal nature of the "splendid theatre," the "players" in it could express more freely and more continuously than we would ever first expect those checks and balances which made the exercise of imperial power in late antiquity intimately dependent on a doctrine of *consensus* which, as we shall often have occasion to see, was an all the more operative force for being taken for granted. Thus the delivery of a panegyric on an imperial occasion and in a formal ceremonial setting was not merely a method of making propaganda; it was also a token of legitimate rule and a form of popular consent, demonstrated by the presence of an audience.

Second, this play was performed far more regularly than the surviving evidence would indicate. Those panegyrics which survive are no more than fragments of a continuous frieze of imperial occasions.[23]

Third, the panegyrics were part of a "splendid theatre" in a manner far more integral than even Gibbon realised. The vast ceremoniousness of late Roman life was the point at which the study of art and literature could converge, for both were facets of that ever-present *tertium quid*— the effort of late Roman men to express themselves in such a way as to absorb both eyes and ears. In Byzantium and in the Christian liturgy, this was to emerge as one of the richest and most lasting aspects of post-classical civilisation.[24]

Because ceremonial was so fundamental a factor in late antique life, its actual importance is almost too great to be perceived. It has been studied at length, and with increasing sympathy, in the life of the imperial court, in the rhythm of the great cities of the empire, in the rituals of the Christian church.[25] Like many such facts, however, the role of ceremonial has been taken for granted more often than it has been applied in a consistent manner to the understanding of a large body of late Roman evidence. The history of artistic and literary forms of expression in late antiquity has seldom been joined together without the one aspect insensibly sinking into the inferior position of merely providing illustrative footnotes for the other. If, however, both artistic and literary forms of expression can be shown to have been joined within a single "splendid theatre" by the elaboration of imperial ceremonial, then each can also maintain a separate and equal role as a "player" in a common play.

Seen in this light, the panegyric will not merely 'reflect' a visual and ceremonial setting by providing valuable but essentially piecemeal evidence for imperial architecture or court etiquette; the panegyric will itself be seen to have drawn its cogency from the context in which it was delivered. The art of the panegyrist—and, by implication, what the historian can fairly expect a panegyric to tell him—will be assessed in terms of the skill with which the orator could relate to and exploit this context—how he could highlight it at some moments, and pass it over as obvious to his audience at others. Above all, the art of the panegyrist will be assessed by the degree to which he could open himself up to that process of osmosis between sound and vision which was such a constant strand in the sensibility of ancient men, so as to evoke a visual experience in his words, as he opted, from the wide choice of means of expression at his disposal, for the one image which was most congruent with the experience of his audience.

The panegyrists, especially those of the Tetrarchy, show plainly that these were the aims of panegyric. Their cogency comes very largely from the ease with which they moved in a situation where literary and visual imagery was finely articulated on clearly delimited ceremonial occasions. Their equilibrium set a standard for the remaining centuries of late antiquity. It was a standard which late antique men accepted and had themselves established. Therefore, deviations from it faithfully reflect moments of confusion and breakdown.

Before we turn to the 'performance' of our various players at different ceremonial moments in different periods of late antiquity, we should examine briefly a few of the points at which the ceremonial setting and its visual elements permeated the work of the panegyrist.

Many points of contact are obvious enough. A splendid architectural setting or the unrolling of a ceremonial could provide immediate material for the speaker and at times, one must suspect, such visual excuses were for the orator a welcome diversion from the need to express himself on more delicate issues. Panegyric and description, or *ekphrasis*, were often on the point of converging and were so with increasing frequency in the course of late antiquity.[26]

Less obvious, but as important, was the ever-present influence of verbal imagery which had exact visual equivalents in the art and coinage of the age. What was at stake here was nothing as simple as a direct 'influence' of art on literature. Direct influences of that sort were exceptionally common in late antiquity. More importantly, literary men were alert to the existence of artefacts and expected their readers to draw wide-reaching religious or political conclusions from what they saw. Of this world of images, a mere fragment survives compared with what must have met the eyes of every late Roman man in every city of the empire. To take one example: one type of artefact that must have been vital for the elaboration of the imperial ceremonial has entirely vanished. This is the great painted *tableaux* which were carried in procession or were exhibited in the hippodrome as part of the ceremonies of the imperial triumph. Yet, we happen to know that the iconography of one such *tableau* provoked comment, and that this comment focused upon the implications of precisely those issues that were being raised in what scholars might wrongly suppose was the 'unreal' and 'sheltered' world of the panegyrists.

> Perses, prefect in ["New"] Rome brought the good fortune of the Roman Empire into contempt and mockery. He set up many small billboards in the middle of the Stadion, and wanting to express the imperial deeds in a picture, he made a laughing stock of his message and secretly held up what he had written to ridicule by means of the picture. For the picture showed nothing of the courage of the emperor, the strength of the soldiers or the course of an open and just war—merely a hand as if it was coming out of the clouds, with the inscription: 'The Hand of God chases away the barbarians.'[27]

Such *tableaux* have not survived. All that is available for the historian are the diminutive and highly simplified *tableaux* of the imperial coinage. This coinage should not be underrated. Like the panegyrics, its value as evidence has been dismissed because too much has been expected of it. Coins do not 'make' propaganda in their own right, nor can they be treated as evidence to 'reveal' policies. Their contribution was more humble, but all the more effective for being continuous and all-pervasive. For, what contemporaries saw on their coins was a reservoir of simple, clearly intelligible images of 'good happenings' connected with the empire: a *laetitia . . . felicitatis* that could be held in the palm of the hand (see plates 9, 11, 23, 44–51, 58–60).

What the historian can see is equally precious: legends which clearly indicate the subject of the image. Moreover, these legends often echo what was said at greater length in panegyric, while the images delineate episodes such as a panegyrist would describe for his audience. A panegyric thus drew together multifarious events, ideas and hopes which were pinpointed on the coinage in one coherent and cogent whole, one solemn exegesis. The coinage, in its turn, could become a lasting reminder of such an exegesis—*verba volant, nomismata manent*.[28]

Yet, even to speak of artefacts as separate from literature, though necessary for purposes of exposition, is misleading. We are not dealing with anything as unilateral as the 'influence' of the one on the other, or the 'reflection' of the one in the other. We are dealing with a convergence and a collaboration that is as intimate as a mode of perception. A ceremonial would not have been complete in late antiquity without some verbal expression. Likewise, a literary work intended for such a ceremony would not have been successful if it had not taken into itself the quality of a series of *tableaux*. To say that a panegyric of late antiquity was full of *clichés* is nothing less than the truth, as long as we use the word *cliché* not for an outworn literary device, but in the French meaning of the term—a lantern slide—and as long as we are prepared to see the panegyric as in some ways resembling a lecture with lantern slides, in which the author projected before his audience a skilfully-chosen succession of readily recognisable images of *laetitia . . . felicitatis*.

Thus, an enquiry which began with a lonely and harassed rhetor has given access to a "splendid theatre" where art and literature can be seen as united in a single communication. This, in itself, might be of some help in understanding and in delimiting more accurately the role of panegyric in late antiquity. It would, however, provide the scholar with a tool of little use outside a world of courtly ceremonial which might still strike him as no less enclosed and grandiose for being coherent.

Studies of propaganda and ceremonial can breed a sense of claustrophobia and of remoteness from reality. The following chapters hope to relieve this impression. We have suggested that the panegyrists who will provide our main literary evidence throughout this study approached the world with finer tools of expression and perception, and were more open to a communication which could mobilise eyes as well as ears, than has been allowed for. What needs to be stressed as the corollary to this suggestion is that the world in which the panegyrists lived was often one of headlong change and movement. There was nothing static in the "splendid theatre." Rather, the great events of the imperial court—a death or an accession—were usually times of upheaval which called for explanation. Because of this, work on the well-regulated ceremonial life of the Byzantine court, though often an inspiration for late Roman studies, is irrelevant to the study of late antiquity until its final phases. For, the more we follow the origins of Byzantine ceremonial in late antiquity, the more alien Byzantium itself must appear, and the more profound the transmutation of the classical inheritance that lies between the reigns of Diocletian and Constantine Porphyrogenitus.

We shall therefore be dealing throughout with occasions where the various devices of communication we have outlined were exploited to make sense of change. Thus, we are dealing with 'moments' rather than with a permanently established ritual. Each of these moments, scattered over three centuries of dramatic political and religious change, was a time when ceremonies such as the imperial *adventus*, the imperial funeral, or varied forms by which the imperial majesty gained at accession was manifested to the subjects, could be occasions for tacit stock-taking. In their ceremonies, in the clusters of associations which they brought to ceremonies, late antique men had an opportunity to express, and to express faithfully, in their own, slow-moving language, changes in the Roman Empire which the historian sees with the foreshortening effect of hindsight.

What we will be trying to do, in some ways, is to see the course of late Roman history through late Roman eyes. We will be seeing how developments in politics and religion, of whose eventual outcome we are now aware, were first perceived and communicated by contemporaries. But instead of seeing these developments in terms of contemporary comments on unique historical events, such as the conversion of Constantine, the sack of Rome, or the reconquest of Justinian, we have chosen ceremonies. That is, we have chosen events which everybody knew were bound to recur: emperors arrived, died and took up power, and a whole constellation of associations and expectations formed around such events. The shifts in these associations and expectations, the ways in which they were expressed in art and ceremonial, were all the more revealing for occurring within a continuum of recurrent occasions.

Inevitably, such an approach must beg the reader's pardon for overlaps and repetitions. The same authors and artefacts are relevant to more than one occasion, and behind each occasion lies a development whose broader outlines may be plain to most students, but whose relevance in detail needs to be highlighted. Many well-known events and processes of late Roman history will pass more than once under the scrutiny of more than one lense. One well-known feature of the reign and attitudes of Constantine may be made more clearly visible through the study of representations of his *adventus*, other features by descriptions of his accession and funeral.

To conflate these various features of any given reign in the interests of tidiness would be to neglect the main concern of this study—to differentiate clearly the occasions and the tools which late Romans used to make sense of the world around them. Although at different points in time, panegyrists did deal with the same person or situation, different aspects of a reign or personality would emerge in the type of 'stock-taking' which was allowed for in the theatre of late antique imperial ceremonial.

At the same time, however, the basic questions asked were strikingly constant. An emperor's arrival, his funeral and his accession would each in its own way provide opportunities for giving answers to the same questions: how did the emperor stand with his subjects, and how did he stand with his gods or God? The basic themes of late antique life— one of the most persistent being that of the relation between man and the divine (see plates 8, 12–13, 15 with 41, 22, 26–29, 36, 45–46, 59)— recur at each ceremonial occasion; they must, therefore, recur at each stage of our enquiry.

One can only hope that the picture built up in this way of the thought-world of late antique men is cumulative, not merely repetitive. If, on the other hand, we wish to dismiss out of hand the literary and artistic endeavours which surrounded such moments as 'unreal,' or as irrelevant to the course of late Roman history, then we must be prepared to abandon the effort to enter into the minds of men in the past, and to cut off our sympathy for the manner in which the inheritors of a great and complex tradition grappled with a future to which they were as blind as we are to our own.

I · ADVENTVS

PART·I

THE CLASSICAL TRADITION
OF *ADVENTUS* IN ACTION

1. ARRIVAL AND PRESENCE OF THE EMPEROR

Of all the ceremonies involving the emperor, that of *adventus* seems the most fraught with truism. Given the rudimentary communication system of the Roman Empire, the constant movement, and hence the frequent arrival of the emperor, it would seem an event so obviously necessary as to require little comment. An imperial arrival would be preceded by a spasm of administrative activity.[1] It was bound to be a solemn event, from which it was unwise to absent oneself, and from which profit might be gained by a man of ready wit. When the person who arrived was an emperor whose legitimacy was as yet unestablished or, as in the last days of Roman rule in the Near East, a foreign conqueror, it was even more incumbent on the local community to go through the proper protocol of welcome.

The results, also, were predictable. At best, a moment of direct, and therefore firm, government would fall like a ray of sunlight on the locality. When the 'divinity' of Maximin Daia 'shone down' on Stratonicea, brigandage came to a momentary halt in the mountains of Caria.[2] For towns on the frontier, the arrival of an emperor meant a blessed moment of safety. As Athanasius said,

> As when a great king has entered some great city and dwelt in one of the houses in it, such a city is then greatly honoured and no longer does any enemy or bandit come against it, but rather it is treated with regard because of the king who has taken up residence in one of its houses. So also is the case with the King of all.[3]

The remark finds grim confirmation in the embassy of the cities of Gaul to Valentinian I, when the emperor thought of turning his attention from Gaul to the Balkans. His advisers, on that occasion, were "supported by deputations from famous cities, who begged that he should not leave unprotected in such hard and doubtful times cities which by his presence he could save from the greatest dangers."[4]

Yet it would be wrong to assume that, just because the arrival of an emperor might strike the modern historian as a straightforward event, it meant the same to contemporaries. To them it was not straightforward. It was an occasion to which they brought a variety of associations, some of the greatest antiquity. The arrival of an emperor threw into high relief their expectations about the availability to man of figures of power in general, divine as well as human. The imagery of the imperial *adventus* reached back to descriptions of divine arrival in a Homeric Hymn.[5] At the same time, Christian thought on the 'presence' of Christ in the Eucharist, throughout late antiquity and often in circles close to the imperial court, applied to the ritual of consecration an imagery taken, in turn, from imperial ceremonial.[6] Furthermore, the moment of contact between the arriving emperor and the community brought a spotlight to bear on late antique ideas concerning those elements of *consensus*—expressed in terms of meeting and welcoming—on which the imperial power rested, both in theory and in practice.

These, and many other associations were recurrently and ceremoniously mobilised in imperial *adventus*. An event which happened far more often than did imperial death or accession was bound to achieve a more fixed form and to awaken more stable expectations. *Adventus* remained the ceremonial *par excellence* of late antiquity, and for that reason is the starting point of our enquiry. We shall see how, as a result of these associations, the "splendid theatre" of an imperial arrival, at first sight so obvious, became the high moment at which shifting views of the imperial power, and the relations of the emperor to men and gods alike, could find expression in art and literature.

In following the expression of some of these associations throughout the centuries, in tracing the shifts of emphasis within the ceremony itself—a double-faced ceremony, which could stress either the moment when the travelling emperor 'arrived' or the moment when the emperor symbolically gave to the city the almost numinous security of his 'presence,' and either the moment when the emperor appeared in his majesty or mixed with his subjects on familiar terms—we can catch some of that ineluctable evolution in late Roman attitudes to the empire that takes us from the pagan towns of Gaul to the Christian Constantinople of the emperor Heraclius.

We begin with an impressive continuity, both in the religious and in the secular associations of *adventus*. The topic of divine arrivals and departures was discussed in the third century A.D. in the treatise περὶ ἐπιδεικτικῶν by the rhetor Menander.[7] Menander gave instructions as to how an orator should handle orations of calling upon a god for his coming and bidding him farewell. He illustrated what was to be said on such occasions by reference to Homer, Sappho, Alkman, Bacchylides and Plato; in other words, he saw in this field a direct continuity between the Greek pre-classical and classical past and the practice of the rhetor's art in his own time. The religious content of cults and of their expression in literature and philosophy changed immeasurably even during the period from which Menander chose his examples, but the formal and ceremonial expression of cult was sufficiently stable to allow a rhetorical tradition to develop, which in its turn gave expression to cult and ceremonial.[8]

On the human level, as distinct from the divine, a formulation of myth that illustrates what could be conveyed by arrival is Aeschylus' account of the homecoming of Agamemnon.[9] Clytemnestra's preparations for her husband's death were highlighted by her arrangements for his ceremonious arrival. She caused him to step on a purple carpet,[10] token of Agamemnon's destruction of Troy, but also token of acquiescing in honours accepted only by barbarian rulers[11]—a poignant observation at the time of the Persian Wars—and of claim to a supra-human station.[12] The continuity and stability of at least some aspects of the ceremonial of arrival as applied to human beings are borne out by the fact that it was precisely the two charges of claiming divine status and honours only accepted by barbarian rulers that were raised against some emperors in connection with, among other matters, the ceremonial of arrival.[13]

At the same time, it emerges from the arrival of Agamemnon, as described by Aeschylus, that the ceremony was a microcosm of the characters and their interactions, which were worked out in the play as a whole.[14] This is also the message of the rhetorical handbooks: the welcoming speech was a means of establishing a relationship between him who was welcomed and those who welcomed him. The community at large expressed itself by acclamations, and these were expanded upon in the orator's speech. In the words of Ps. Dionysius of Halicarnassus in his Τέχνη ῥητορικής of the late second century A.D.:

> Isocrates says . . . that good men must cultivate their ability to make addresses. As he himself says, this consists of addressing those who

are being welcomed. . . . This manner of address is appropriate when
those who wield power and dominion come into our presence, and particularly those who come to the nations and our cities as the emissaries
of kings; by means of such a speech we can hope to bring it about that
they think with affection of us. . . . This task falls on you on behalf of
everyone, and just as some law and obligation obtains as soon as the
dignitary enters the first gate, as the saying goes, namely that the cities
should in common acclaim the entry, so it is right that one of the best
men according to education and culture should make an address, and
speak with an official voice, and in a speech made on behalf of all.[15]

Here and in Menander, it is clear that the panegyric served to formulate a relationship between those welcoming and him who was arriving.[16] But while Ps. Dionysius merely refers to creating a good atmosphere, Menander is much more specific, and instructs the orator how
he might make the subject of the panegyric aware of past misrule without incriminating any earlier ruler[17]—a piece of advice which was put
into practice in several panegyrics. The rhetor, Menander points out,
had to welcome the magistrate (ἄρχων) or emperor (βασιλεύς) as a star
from on high[18] or as a ray of the sun[19] and express the sense of renewal
brought about by the arrival. The image of the star was also used in the
Homeric Hymn to Apollo, by Aristophanes and by the Athenians welcoming Demetrius Poliorcetes.[20] The imagery of the ruler coming as a
star from on high in this context of past misrule was not merely a pictur-
esque way of expressing oneself, but a practical and therefore all the
more powerful method of pointing out the importance of the arrival and
its desired and potential results:

    After the preface you continue with what is to be said about the
    subjects. This is twofold. If they have fared ill under the preceding
    ruler, you give examples and elaborate their misfortunes, while not,
    however, speaking any ill of the preceding ruler, but you simply speak
    about the misfortune of the subjects. Then you go on, saying that when
    night and darkness have covered everything, he himself [who has ar-
    rived] is beheld like the sun dispelling all evil.[21]

Menander's example for the epilogue of a panegyric of welcome shows
how the ceremony of *adventus* provided a crucial meeting point between
any community and its ruler:

    [You say], for instance, 'We have all gone out to meet you for your
    welcome, with our whole families, children, old men and men in their
    prime, the priestly families, the city council and the people at large. We
    were all glad in our hearts [and expressed it] with acclamations calling
    you our saviour and wall, a most radiant star, and children called you
    their nourisher and the saviour of their parents. And if it were possible

for the cities to send forth a voice and to take the appearance of women as in plays, they would say: "Oh, for the exaltedness of your governance, the sweetness of the day on which now has come to us a light more radiant than the sun." Now it seems to us that we look upon a bright day out of some darkness. Shortly we will erect statues, shortly, poets, orators and rhetors will sing your virtues and hand them down to the whole of mankind. Let the theatres be opened, let us hold festivals.'[22]

Here, as also in panegyrics and elsewhere, the people are enumerated in groups according to age on the one hand, and to official status on the other, and these were also the groupings according to which they would appear in a welcoming procession.[23] The ruler thus encountered an orderly and organised body of citizens, headed by their dignitaries, with whom business could be transacted. At the same time, the enumeration serves to indicate that everyone was present, that this body of people was in a position to express that *consensus omnium* which was fundamental to most classical and late antique theories about legitimate government.[24] The orator played a crucial role in this expression of consent, for, as Ps. Dionysius said together with some panegyrists, in his speech the orator spoke on behalf of all.[25] This formalised, consensual element in the ceremony is also conveyed in the Greek technical term for it, ἀπάντησις, which was sometimes employed in panegyrics of welcome and occurs in the New Testament description of Christ's entry into Jerusalem and of His second coming.[26]

Menander highlights the actual ceremony of arrival: he mentions two types of oration for the occasion, the *epibaterios* and the *prosphonetikos*.[27] The former was intended for the occasion when ruler and subjects first encountered each other. The subjects would leave their city to welcome the ruler at some distance beyond the walls and would solemnly conduct him into the city; upon arrival there, the *prosphonetikos* was to be delivered. However, the Latin panegyrics seem to indicate that usually there was in fact only one formal speech of welcome. A panegyric to Constantine describes his arrival in Autun,[28] and here it can be seen clearly that the ceremony consisted of a short welcome outside the city and a more elaborate one within it.

The twin elements of consent and the transaction of business conveyed in the ceremony of *adventus* made this ceremony one of the most characteristic expressions of late antique public life, the means whereby a population formulated its corporate identity, in both good times and ill. Thus, in one of the last glimpses we have of Syria under Byzantine rule, the people of various towns organised themselves according to the

time-honoured ceremonial of *adventus* to welcome their new rulers, the
Arabs, one of whom, with an outsider's sharpness of perception, was
able to define what the ceremonial meant at that moment of crisis:

> I was one of those who went with abu-ʿUbaidah to meet ʿUmar as he
> was coming to Syria. As ʿUmar was passing, he was met by the singers
> and tambourine players of the inhabitants of Adhriʿât with swords and
> myrtle. Seeing that, ʿUmar shouted, 'Keep still, stop them.' But abu-
> ʿUbaidah replied, 'This is their custom (or some other word like it),
> Commander of the Believers, and if thou shouldst stop them from do-
> ing it, they would take that as indicating thy intention to violate their
> covenant.' 'Well, then,' said ʿUmar, 'let them go on.'[29]

At Hims, after the battle of the Yarmûk, the Arabs were welcomed in
similar fashion: "When by Allah's help the unbelievers were defeated
and the Moslems won, [the people] opened the gates of their cities,
went out with singers and music-players who began to play and paid
the *kharâj*."[30]

We see from these accounts that much of the ceremonial of welcoming developed from common sense. Citizens going out of their city to
welcome a distinguished visitor, calling out to him and offering up
prayers, were performing rather obvious actions that could happen independently and spontaneously throughout the late antique Mediterranean world. At the same time, the panegyrics show that these spontaneous actions were clothed in a language of ceremonial actions which
could be shared between subjects and ruler.

Such was the background to the event of an imperial *adventus*. Out
of the wide spectrum of associations, which in the course of time had
accumulated around the *adventus* ceremony, the panegyrists and artists
of late antiquity were free to make their own choice for each occasion.
Of the examples known to us, different themes received emphasis at
different times, and in following these differences, we can trace the outlines of an evolution in the meaning of the imperial office.

2. THE TETRARCHY AND AFTERMATH: THE *ADVENTUS* OF THE EMPEROR AS *DEUS PRAESENS*

The ceremonial of arrival highlighted an interaction of characters, of
two different sets of people, those who did the welcoming and him who
was welcomed. At the same time the ceremony highlighted the visible
presence and activity of him who was welcomed, for which the Romans
used the term *deus praesens*. This term reflects the religious undertones
of actions, such as offering incense and pouring libations, which formed

part of some *adventus* ceremonies. An ingredient which became increasingly crucial in late antiquity was the singing of hymns by the welcomers. These finally turned into the late antique and Byzantine acclamations which were recited on such occasions.[31]

The element in the ceremony of *adventus* whereby the person being welcomed was welcomed as a superhuman being emerged particularly clearly under the Tetrarchs, because Tetrarchic propaganda in art and panegyric sought to explain how in different ways divine and imperial dominion were interdependent.[32] Accordingly, Tetrarchic panegyrists deliberately overlooked the old Roman dichotomy and tension between the concept of an emperor who modelled himself after the public image of Augustus to be *primus inter pares*, and the emperor who would aspire after some approximation to the divine, between an emperor who would preserve some republican ideal, and an emperor who would not.[33]

One of the vehicles for expounding this dichotomy or its suspension was the ceremony of *adventus*. Under the Tetrarchs, the ceremony was therefore explained in such a way as to highlight one aspect in particular, namely the arrival of the *deus praesens*, the emperor able to aid and protect his subjects because he was present and available.[34] The Athenians had expressed this aspect of arrival before Demetrius Poliorcetes:

> Other gods indeed are a great distance away
> Or have no ears,
> Or they do not exist or take no notice of us.
> But you we see present,
> Not made of wood or stone, but truly.

Similar feelings were articulated in the East, concerning Caesar, when he was called θεὸς ἐπιφανής.[35]

What was at issue in a Tetrarchic *adventus* ceremony was expressed most clearly in the panegyric to Maximian, entitled *Genethliacus*.[36] Here, *adventus* is universalised into a cosmic and an imperial, not merely an urban, event.[37] The arrival of Diocletian and Maximian in Milan in 291[38] is described as an example of imperial *pietas*, meaning, here, the loyalty which the emperors had for each other. The *pietas* in question was not a personal quality practised in the course of a lifetime, but a virtue which was part of an imperial destiny, a *genesis imperatoria*:[39]

> Other virtues and good qualities evolve with age: fortitude is strengthened with increasing years, moderation is handed down by the precepts of morality, justice is learnt by knowing the law, and finally, wisdom, who appears to be the queen of all things, is taught by studying the conduct of men and the outcome of events. Only piety

and felicity come into being when a man is born, for these are the innate qualities of souls and the gifts of destiny.[40]

It was initially in this way that the *adventus* of the emperors in Milan—
which was also their *adventus* towards each other—acquired a wider
significance than that of a mere historical event:

> A certain impatience occasioned by your piety broke forth, so that no
> distance, no difficult territory, no inclemency of the seasons could hold
> you back or delay you from coming into each other's presence.[41]

The imperial *pietas* was the foundation on which the atmosphere of
imperial *adventus* was built up, an atmosphere of the supernatural penetrating into the natural order.

> It was some divine impetus by which you suddenly came to one
> place from opposite cardinal points . . . and some people could indeed
> believe that which is worthy of your majesty, that the two luminaries of
> the universe lent you their chariots of the night and the day. Yet, let us
> set aside these fables of the foolish and speak the truth: it was your
> piety, most holy Emperor, that gave wings to your progress.[42]

Here, another factor has emerged: the suddenness of the advent, and
hence the suddenness of the vision[43] produced by that advent, which
was to be built upon in the sequel of the panegyric. From there, the orator returns to the supernatural, to a hint, as it were, of the golden age:
the emperors, although suffering great hardships,[44] were yet exempt
from hardship, from the course of nature. During their journey across
the Alps in winter,

> the power of your majesty protected you against the rigours of place
> and climate, and while other men and regions were hard pressed by
> frost, you alone were accompanied on your path by gentle winds and
> the breath of spring, the clouds were pierced and the sun shone upon
> you.[45]

The association of such imagery with the emperors was highlighted
by the Christian polemicist Lactantius. This former rhetorician appears
to have deliberately inverted the images of imperial 'good happenings'
to create in the *de mortibus persecutorum* a panegyric *à rebours*. Witness
the pleasure with which he recounts the hardships of Diocletian's winter journey over the Apennines after an unsuccessful visit to Rome:

> He set out at the worst time of winter and from the cold and rain
> contracted a light but lingering disease, so that, ailing, he travelled
> most of the road in a litter.[46]

As for the panegyrist of 291, he heightens the significance of imperial
advent by introducing a divine precedent for the journey of the em-

perors to Milan. He compares the latter to Hercules' journey to Italy
when he brought the spoils of Spain, the herds of Geryon.[47] To the theme
of imperial advent and victory, the panegyrist thus adds the story of divine events in the form of the myth of Hercules, and he also contrasts a
story of human events, that of Hannibal's crossing of the Alps in winter.[48] He thus creates a pattern of intelligibility by expressing the meaning and comprehensibility of contemporary events in terms of both religious cult and past history.

The panegyrist slips spontaneously and naturally from one stage of
the narrative into the next, supported by the rhetorical methods he
learnt as a student, the real issue being, however, that these methods
had trained him, not merely to describe an imperial *adventus*, but to perceive it in such a way as to communicate that fundamental Tetrarchic
theme, the imperial epiphany. The climax of the narrative describes the
actual *adventus*, which, as in Menander, is twofold: there is first the initial encounter of emperors and subjects, and then the meeting within
the city walls:

> Now for the first time your holiness radiated from the eastern and
> western peaks of the Alps, and all Italy was covered in a more lumi-
> nous light; all who watched this were affected by both wonder and
> doubt, asking themselves what gods were rising[49] on those mountain
> peaks, and descending on such steps from heaven. And when you
> were recognised more closely at hand, all the fields were filled, not
> merely with men hastening forward to behold you but also with herds
> of animals which left their remote pastures and forests. The farmers
> ran towards each other, and announced to all their villages what they
> had seen. Altars were lit, incense was placed on them, wine was poured
> in libation, victims were slain and all were warmed with joy and danced
> to acclaim you, and hymns of praise and thanks were sung to the im-
> mortal gods. People invoked, not the god familiar from hearsay, but
> Iuppiter close at hand, visible and present, they adored Hercules, and
> him not a stranger, but the emperor.[50] (See plate 44.)

Here is the first overt step of the approximation of gods and emperors as welcomed by the people of Italy. In the second stage of *adventus*, that within the city of Milan, this approximation is made clear in a
different way, when the palace is likened to a temple:

> What a sight did your piety grant to us, when in the palace of Milan
> you were both beheld by those who were given admission to adore
> your sacred countenances, and when of a sudden by the fact of your
> holy presence being twofold you bewildered our custom of venerating
> one divinity at a time! . . . And this secret worship rendered to you, as
> it were within the innermost sanctuary[51] stunned and amazed the
> minds of those to whom their rank granted access. And when, crossing

the threshold, you drove together through the city, the very roofs, so I
am told, were almost set in motion, when children and old people either rushed out into the open, into the squares, or else leaned out of
the upper windows of buildings. All shouted with joy, indeed without
any fear of you, and showed it openly with their gestures: 'Can you see
Diocletian? Can you see Maximian? They are two, yet they are together! How amicably they converse with each other! How quickly
they are passing!' None in their eagerness were equal to looking on you
as much as they desired . . . none were able to see enough of either of
you.[52]

In the encounter between emperors and subjects in Milan, the religious intensity of the vision of the imperial advent in Italy and the imperial presence in Milan both culminate in the actual historical event of
the emperors' being greeted within the city and are toned down to a
practical level. This is the importance of the term *deus praesens*: such a
personage is exalted, the object of vision, yet tangible, the recipient of
speeches, and, as the panegyric states, of acclamations, and comment
from the man in the street.

The meeting of Diocletian and Maximian in Milan was of no overriding historical importance; as an historical event, it was only one of the
many imperial arrivals which constitute the present theme. However,
the interpretation and formulation of such arrivals in panegyric and ceremonial lifted them out of the realm of the ordinary, and gave them a
significance other than the merely factual. In such a context, the emperors were described as able to change the seasons, of being, in this
direct and explicit sense, rulers of the cosmos and initiators of a new
golden age, both of which themes formed, as we shall see, regular
strands in imperial art.

One of the reasons why imagery of this kind could be so pronounced
in connection with the arrival in Milan is precisely that it was in itself a
fairly neutral event. The panegyric discloses, as happens often elsewhere, that such an event acquired significance because it fitted into a
wider pattern of meaning and reality. It was not that the panegyrist applied haphazardly to an unimportant occasion the *topoi* he had learnt at
school; it was rather that he had been trained by his culture—a culture
in which important themes could be articulated by and incorporated
into imperial propaganda—to be able to see the significance of events in
a particular way. We are not dealing so much with flattery and eulogy—
although this is also the case—as with a trained method of perception.

When the historical occasion to which this method of perception was
applied was more definite, or, one could say, more important in itself,

the expression of the method of perception shifted slightly. On such occasions, panegyric and historiography could meet more intimately, in
that panegyric could comprise historical narrative as one of its strands,
as Menander allowed in his instructions for the praise of the deeds of
the subject of the panegyric.[53] The panegyric of 297 utilises such an instruction: here Constantius' reconquest of Britain and *adventus* in
London are celebrated. In this oration, the themes familiar from the
panegyric of 291 are hinted at, but they are less prominent. In other
words, they are supported by the historical narrative, rather than, as in
291, standing in the place of historical narrative, and at the same time
the emphasis is less on arrival than on welcoming, so that epiphany and
the description of divinity play a lesser part.

> As soon as you approached that shore as the long desired avenger
> and liberator, a triumphal procession came to meet you, and the Brit-
> ons, dancing with joy, came before you with their wives and children,
> paying worship not only to you, whom they beheld as one fallen from
> the heavens, but also to the sails and oars of that ship which had con-
> veyed your holiness; and they were ready to acknowledge your arrival
> by prostrating themselves before you. It is not surprising that they
> were transported with such joy when after so many years of most ab-
> ject captivity . . . they were at last recreated as free men and Romans,
> in the true light of empire. For, apart from your well-known clemency
> and piety, which are celebrated with one voice by the nations, they saw
> on your very face the signs of all the virtues.[54]

The virtues are a promise, as the panegyrist goes on to say, of the
future felicity of the Britons. Thus the arrival of the *deus praesens*, of him
who is beheld as though fallen from heaven—that is, utterly unexpected—is an epiphany with practical meanings. The act of welcoming
is an expression of allegiance, and thereafter, as Menander said, suffer-
ings will be relieved.

The account in the panegyric of 310 of Constantine's arrival in Britain,
preceding his proclamation by his father's soldiers, provides both an
epilogue to the Tetrarchic theory of arrival and an outlook on the future.
On the one hand, this arrival was a Tetrarchic divine and imperial ceremony; on the other, it was the first stage of a ceremony of accession of
the kind that became current in the fifth-century Christian empire. According to the panegyrist:

> You were called forward for the salvation of the state by divine de-
> cree even at the time when your father was crossing to Britain, and
> when your sudden arrival shone upon the fleet already setting sail. It
> seemed that you had been transported not by the public post, but by
> some divine vehicle.[55]

There is again the imagery of light, the supernatural impinging on the natural order, an imagery which was still used when, in 311, Constantine arrived in Autun and granted the city a remission of tax at a time of hardship:[56]

> You were so gracious as to illumine the city [of Autun] which lived in the abundance only of expecting you. . . . Immortal gods, what a day shone upon us . . . when you entered the gates of this city, which was the first token of our salvation, and when the gates, curved inwards and flanked by twin towers, seemed to receive you in a kind of embrace.[57]

The orator then describes the multitude who came out to meet Constantine, expectant of future happiness:

> We decorated the streets leading to the palace, although only poorly, yet we carried forth for your welcoming the standards of all the colleges, and the images of all our gods, accompanied by the clear sounds of some few instruments.[58]

The very form of the welcome is here made to express what, according to Menander, the orator could also describe in his speech: the hardship of the subjects, but without attribution of any blame. Finally, the completion of the ceremony, Constantine's welcome by the *curia* of Autun:[59]

> We saw your moistened eyes expressing your compassion. Through your countenance healing tears came to us and . . . we wept with joy. For, just as the fields, thirsting after a long drought, are made fertile by rain solicited by prayers, so your tears watered our breasts with rejoicing, since, although it is wrong to be glad of your weeping, yet our gratitude overcame our sense of reverence for you and those tears were tokens of piety, not sorrow.[60]

Here again is the two-fold ceremony of welcome beyond and within the city, and the terminology of light, epiphany and salvation, without reference now to pagan sacred story. The whole is then transformed in tone at the end of the ceremony into a human, this-worldly, yet delicate scene.

A certain disciplining of perception lies at the root of these rhetorical accounts of *adventus*, yet the availability of a rhetorical structure and a set of *topoi* did not make them either over-complex or commonplace. The form of the panegyric is sober and restrained; there are no digressions and what is to be said is conveyed in a clear and straightforward manner, without being submerged in ornament and technique. This feature in the panegyrics of the Tetrarchy and the early reign of Constantine in the West links them to the sculptures and coins of the same pe-

riod, which likewise worked in a deliberate idiom and technique which
had been fully mastered.

The multiplicity and many-layered nature of this idiom and technique are well illustrated in the Arras medallion, minted in Trier and
commemorating Constantius I's arrival in Britain in 296.[61] (See plate 9.)
This multiple also provides a bridge from visual art into panegyric, for
the legend which the image illustrates is REDDITOR LUCIS AETERNAE, recalling not merely the terminology of the panegyric on the event, but
the imagery of light used in general to describe imperial epiphanies during the Tetrarchy. The image itself shows Constantius armed, mounted
and riding towards the right, holding a spear; before him kneels LON
(dinium) outside her city gate, stretching out her arms to welcome him.
Below is one of the ships in which Constantius arrived, while the crowds
of Britons in the panegyric are replaced on the coin by the personification of London.

How did the components of this image come to be fitted together, or
rather, how did they come to acquire a coordinated meaning? The answer to this question will provide a means for surveying the history of
some images of *adventus* in Roman art.

To begin with, Londinium: she recalls the words of Menander: "We
have all gone out to meet you . . . and if it were possible for cities to
acquire a voice and take the appearance of women as in plays, they
would [speak]." [62] Personifications and *Tychai* of cities had a long history
in ancient art and literature, the origins of which were entirely spontaneous, like the Greek practice of viewing divine presence in terms of
arrival.[63] Thus, for instance, the inscription recording a treaty between
Corcyra and Athens in 375–374 B.C.[64] is headed by personal representations of the two communities, with Athena standing for Athens. When,
however, a city did not have such a noteworthy founding deity, *Tyche*
could become a much more powerful notion, as she did, for instance, in
the case of Antioch. During the Hellenistic period, city *Tychai* entered
the idiom of the visual arts and thence passed into Roman imperial art,
where provinces, as well as cities, came to be personified.[65]

The coinages depicting Hadrian's travels employ this idiom of city
Tychai and provinces, represented either alone, or else as shaking hands
with the arriving emperor or in the act of kneeling before and being
raised by him, to express the idea that the imperial coming inaugurated
a renewal, a period of happiness. For the second group of images, the
legends incorporate the term *adventus*, arrival and encounter, which the
image itself conveys. Here, then, is the iconographic ancestor of kneeling Londinium (for Rome and Constantinople, see plate 57).

Maximian's campaign in Africa of 296–297 A.D., referred to briefly in the panegyric of 307,[66] is recorded on the coinage of Carthage precisely in the iconographic terms for the portrayal of cities and provinces which were authoritatively formulated under Hadrian.[67] The first set of issues, FELIX ADVENTUS AUGG NN for all four Tetrarchs, showed the figure of Africa.[68] The legend SALVIS AUGG ET CAESS FEL KART with the figure of Carthage began in 298 and continued until 306–307.[69] Similarly, gold multiples from Trier celebrating Constantine's arrival of 296 show Constantius standing upright, raising a kneeling Britannia.[70] (See plate 9.)

While the image of these last issues is formulated in the familiar *adventus* terminology, the legend is PIETAS AUGG. This combination of concepts accords with the panegyric of 291, which describes *adventus* as an act of imperial *pietas*. A variant of this image, the standing emperor encountering the kneeling province, occurred also under Carausius, but on the coin portraying Carausius, the province of Britain was standing like the emperor, holding hands with him, the legend being the unique EXPECTATE VENI.[71] This legend recaptures very precisely the tone of the Tetrarchic concept of *adventus* as articulated in the panegyrics: *adventus* is the epiphany of a saviour. Here, as on the PIETAS AUGG issue celebrating Constantius' reconquest of Britain, the emperor is shown armed and standing, not, as on the Arras medallion, mounted, while the Hadrianic *adventus* issues had shown the emperor standing and togate, never mounted and never armed.

This change in imperial costume and attitude, which had been effected by the late third century, points to the transformation of the emperor from a mainly civilian to a mainly military personage, and this is documented in many other aspects of imperial rule.[72] (See plates 2–3, 7.) The pictorial antecedent of the mounted emperor appears on coinage as early as Augustus, showing the imperial princes mounted,[73] and more directly in the military DECURSIO of Nero.[74] It was under Trajan that this military image entered the *adventus* vocabulary.[75] It had become the rule, then, rather than the exception, by the mid-third century.[76] An aureus of Maximian ADVENTUS AUGUSTORUM applies this military *adventus* image to a meeting of two Tetrarchs—possibly the meeting in Milan which was described in the panegyric of 291—by representing two mounted emperors facing each other with arms raised in greeting.[77]

The galley on the Arras medallion, which evokes Constantius' passage across the Channel, while being a parallel to the panegyric of 297 conceptually, likewise has an iconographic antecedent in Gordian III's TRAIECTUS AUG issues, showing a galley with oarsmen which announced, in 242, Gordian's projected expedition to the East.[78]

As for the city gate of the Arras medallion, such gates figured in the *adventus* ceremonial itself. According to the orator of 312, the very gates of Autun, with their protruding towers, seemed to hold Constantine in an embrace. A gate of this type appears on a gold multiple minted at Trier in 312, AUGG GLORIA.[79] A bronze multiple of Marcus Aurelius, ADVENTUS AUG,[80] shows the emperor about to pass through a triumphal gateway. But the coinage, vehicle for abbreviated concise images, usually omits the gate and concentrates on persons.

Thus, the Arras medallion illustrates how a multifarious set of images loosely linked by the theme of arrival could be brought together into a unified whole to convey the message of Tetrarchic victory and epiphany, the interpenetration of the natural and the supernatural orders, and, on a more subdued level within the actual image, the interpenetration of reality with allegory, which was one of the important themes of Roman imperial art.[81]

But in general, the numismatic imagery of *adventus* during the Tetrarchy does not repeat the very pronounced panegyric theme of imperial and divine epiphany. This theme, however, is represented elsewhere on the coinage: in the numerous issues, after the reform, dedicated to Iuppiter and Hercules, with legends such as IOVI CONSERVATORI AUGG and HERCULI CONSERVATORI AUGG.[82] In other words, the coinage, because of the restrictions governing this medium of communication, had to fragment and divide themes whereas the panegyrics did not. Still, in the sum total of themes treated, the two media are consistent with each other.

One of the elements which the panegyrics stressed in the experience of imperial *adventus* was that of vision, of seeing the imperial countenance, on which were expressed, as the panegyrist of 297 said, the emperor's virtues.[83] Tetrarchic portraiture conveys this aspect of the imperial personality, and therefore, on the coinage and in sculpture, draws together many of the elements articulated in Tetrarchic arrivals; it also defines more clearly what was to be understood by a Tetrarchic arrival and by Tetrarchic rule. Tetrarchic portraiture is more realistic and more restrained than the portraiture of the third century up to Gallienus (see plate 1). Gone are the flowing locks, the upward glance, the idealised features of the divinely inspired ruler in the tradition, ultimately, of Lysippus' Alexander.[84] Instead there emerged, after Gallienus, a style of portraiture which was characterised by soldierly precision and realism, which was applied even where Diocletian, on a bronze multiple, is shown in heroic nudity, laureate and holding a sceptre, IOVIO DIOCLETIANO AUG,[85] and on the very frequent issues showing Maximian with the lionskin of Hercules drawn over his head.[86] (See plate 44.)

In sculpture in the round, the Venice Tetrarchs expound this soldierly idiom.[87] (See plate 3.) Two pairs of emperors in military dress approach and embrace each other. Both the walking movement of the approach and the suspension of movement of the embrace are rendered in these sculptures: we see the *concordia* of the emperors as described by the panegyrist of 291. The faces of the emperors look lined and careworn, yet dignified and majestic; the eyes gaze straight ahead, hair and beards are closely cropped. There are no allusions to divine portraiture at all. We see simply the physical presence of the emperors, emperors facially and in stature very similar to each other, for, as the panegyrics explained, they were made similar by their destiny, by their imperial office on the one hand, and by the performance of the resulting obligations, the *cura* of empire, of which the panegyrists speak, on the other. An aspect of the exercise of this *cura* is the imperial presence, the presence of the *praesens deus* with his subjects, which was the culminating point of *adventus*, and which often was an outcome, according to the panegyrists, of labours to which ordinary mortals would have been unequal.

At this stage, the portraiture of the divinely inspired, heavenward-glancing ruler was superseded. The emperors needed not to glance to heaven, for they had their *pietas* and their *felicitas* within them.[88] Accordingly, the divine and human spheres, while intermingling in the ways that have been described, remained nonetheless distinct. The often uneasy fusion of the two that was represented in the person of the divinely inspired, heavenward-glancing ruler, together with the exaltation and idealisation of the individual emperor which this fusion implies, was no longer relevant.

Thus the almost prosaic style of Tetrarchic portraiture[89] (see plate 2) does square with the imperial epiphanies of the panegyrics. The Tetrarchs overcame the fundamental *impasse* of late second- and early third-century imperial theology, which sought to define how the emperor's divinity could be depicted in portraiture for example, without actually transforming the emperor into a god. What the pre-Tetrarchic period lacked was a precise vocabulary for defining the emperor's relationship to the gods, and to his subjects. Such a vocabulary was created by the Tetrarchic panegyrists: the emperors followed in the footsteps of Iuppiter and Hercules, who were their *conservatores*, and Imperial nomenclature reiterated this fact.

On that basis, it became possible to interpret, and make sense of, imperial activity on earth, and this is precisely what the panegyrists did in describing imperial *adventus* as a pragmatic historical event, which was at the same time the outcome of imperial *pietas*, *pietas* being an inborn quality of the soul, a gift of destiny. This was one way of linking the natural and the supernatural orders. At the same time, the panegyrists, while aware of the supernatural elements of the imperial arrival as clothed in ceremonial and language at one stage of the ceremonial, were yet able to formulate the other stage as factual and matter-of-fact. In short, imperial *pietas* was the ground for the supernatural aspect of arrival, and both *pietas* and supernatural arrival culminated and ended with arrival in an actual city.

This is also the message of the narrative treatment of imperial *adventus* under the Tetrarchs that survives on the arch of Galerius.[90] (See plate 10.) The relief depicts both the emperor's departure, *profectio*, from one city, represented by its city gate, and his arrival at another. The handling of the theme is factual. The emperor, enthroned on a carriage, is welcomed by citizens coming out of their city gate, while the local deity, in a temple, extends a hand in greeting. This is an historical, narrative image which reflects in some detail the panegyric account of Constantine's arrival in Autun in 310. The narrative of the relief relates the facts of imperial arrival. By contrast, a relief on the same face of the arch[91] (see plate 10) depicts in a wider context the other aspect of imperial arrival described in the panegyrics, namely the revelation, the epiphany of the emperors, and the resulting correlation of the natural and supernatural orders. Diocletian and Maximian, attended by Galerius and Constantius, are seen enthroned on heaven and earth, surrounded by the personifications of land and sea, and by the Dioscuri and other gods. Their empire is universal and, as the panegyrics express it in the context of *adventus*, is capable of incorporating within it the order and ordering of nature.[92] This is the effect of imperial *pietas* and *felicitas*.

We have here, on the arch and in Tetrarchic panegyrics, a clearly defined theory of the ultimately divine nature of imperial power, such as had not been available earlier.[93] This theory, which left the human person of the emperor intact, allowed artist and panegyrist alike to portray the concrete impact of the emperor in terms of carefully selected vignettes of real life which were expounded in a framework of religion and myth. The fine balance of fact and exegesis which was achieved in Tetrarchic imperial theory is all the more clearly revealed when we see it in the process of disruption during the reign of Constantine.

3. CHANGE AND CONTINUITY IN *ADVENTUS* IN THE FOURTH CENTURY

i. Constantine in Rome, 312 A.D.: Pagan and Christian *adventus*

The focal point for the celebration of imperial triumphs and accessions in the late third century was still Rome, and the tradition went

back to republican and early imperial times. At the culminating moment
of triumph the victorious general deposited his wreath in the temple of
Iuppiter on the Capitol. Even after this pagan ceremony had been abandoned, Themistius continued to call Rome the "mother city of trophies,"
μητρόπολις τῶν τρωπαίων.[94]

Accession required the consent of the Senate. In the course of the
third century, this consent became increasingly a matter of form, but it
did help to maintain certain links between the emperor and Rome. Emperors would accordingly visit Rome upon being proclaimed by the
army, as Trajan who became emperor when in Germany had done. The
association of accession with Rome came to be expressed in a highly sophisticated language of symbols, and in that each imperial victory re-
affirmed and justified accession, triumph and accession were related issues in late antiquity, both, furthermore, formulated in the idiom of
adventus. The panegyric of 307 on Constantine and Maximian points to
the connection between triumph and, if not accession precisely stated,
then the justification of imperial rule:

> You [Maximian] conquered, subdued and transplanted elsewhere the
> most warlike tribes of Mauritania, confident though they were of the
> protection afforded them by the natural barrier of inaccessible moun-
> tains. At your first entry [into Rome] the Roman people received you
> with such joy and in such numbers that the crowds, desiring to carry
> you into the lap of Capitoline Iuppiter on their very eyes, almost pre-
> vented your entry into the gates of the city. And again, in your twen-
> tieth year [of empire] when you were consul for the eighth time, Rome
> wished to hold you, as it were, in her embrace.[95]

Thus the city of Rome is associated with Maximian's return to power, a
second accession, justified, as was the first, by victory and triumph.[96]
The orator here expresses triumph in the terminology of adventus.

In 312, political and military facts forced into prominence this aspect
of adventus, rooted as it was in past tradition and theory. In view of his
Christian vision, Constantine refused, or hesitated to make the customary triumphal sacrifice on the Capitol.[97] However, since the vocabulary
of adventus had long been available to describe an imperial triumph, the
panegyrist who greeted Constantine in Trier in 313 could spontaneously
describe Constantine's entry into Rome as an adventus, and at the same
time could relate adventus to the victory over Maxentius,[98] who was portrayed in the conventional terminology of the tyrant.[99] This panegyrist
was not informed about the details of Constantine's entry into Rome[100]—
in view of the unusualness of the occasion, this may have been a deliberate omission by the court—but was able to utilise the traditional

vocabulary for arrival at a time when triumph was in the process of being definitively transposed into *adventus*. Like Nazarius in 321, the panegyrist of 313 described the two stages of *adventus*: the welcoming, and Constantine's arrival within the city and encounter with the Senate and the people.[101] This much the traditional idiom could provide.

But a note of embarrassment, the hint of a hiatus, only too typical of the Constantinian era, is detectable, and this not only in the panegyric of 313. The panegyric of 321 also is dry and lacks any analysis of the impact of imperial doings in other than a most down-to-earth style.[102] The meaning of the events which panegyrists described had changed. While some aspects of Constantinian policy depended on and were derived directly from the Tetrarchy,[103] this did not apply to *adventus*. For the ceremony of *adventus* underwent a fundamental change under Constantine; one might even say that it became one of the means of differentiating Constantine from his Tetrarchic predecessors. This point is highlighted when we examine the depiction of Constantine's entry into Rome in 312 on his arch.

On the arch of Constantine this entry is represented beneath the tondo showing Sol on his *quadriga* rising out of the ocean.[104] (See plate 13.) What is the meaning of this association? An introduction to the imagery is provided by the Ticinum medallion and its third-century numismatic ancestry, beginning with Gallienus.[105] (See plate 11.) From the mid-third century, Sol could be not only the companion and protector of the emperor, but his divine prototype, so far as imperial dominion, and in particular imperial advent, were concerned.[106] It was the closeness of Constantine to Sol, a closeness bordering on physical resemblance to the god, that was stressed in the art and panegyrics of this time.

When Constantinian portraiture departed from the norms set down by the portraiture of the Tetrarchy, it was ultimately Gallienic portraiture that provided a precedent.[107] (See plates 1, 4.) Some background for this change in styles in imperial portraiture is provided by the Latin panegyrics on Constantine, which regularly emphasised the emperor's physical beauty[108] as an expression of his inner virtues and his proximity to the divine. Thus the panegyrist of 310[109] was able to describe a vision Constantine had of Apollo, whose identity had by this time merged with that of Sol,[110] in the following terms:

> I believe, Constantine, that you saw your own Apollo accompanied by Victoria, who was offering you laurel crowns which each carry the prophecy of thirty years [of rule]. For this is the extent of human life, which is your share beyond the longevity of Nestor. But why do I say, 'I believe'? You saw him and recognised yourself in his aspect, to whom,

according to the divine songs of seers, belong all the kingdoms of the world. This, I think, has now at last come to pass, since you are, like he, young and glad,[111] health-giving, and most beautiful, our emperor.[112]

Here Constantine experienced, according to his panegyrist, a divine epiphany which was transposed into an epiphany of himself as world ruler. This is what is represented on the Ticinum medallion of 313 (see plate 11). On the obverse, INVICTUS CONSTANTINUS AUG, appear the jugate busts of Sol radiate and Constantine laureate, carrying a shield on which is depicted the *quadriga* of Sol rising out of the ocean above Oceanus and Tellus.[113] On the reverse, FELIX ADVENTUS AUGG NN,[114] Constantine is shown in the usual vocabulary of late antique *adventus*, mounted, and raising his right hand in greeting. The emperor is accompanied by Victoria, who, holding high a laurel wreath, leads Constantine's horse, as the panegyrist of 310 had visualised it. Behind follows a soldier bearing a standard, thus giving a more precise military and victorious setting to the *adventus*.

On the arch of Constantine, the image of Sol rising from the ocean, although not as tightly interwoven with the image of the emperor as on the Ticinum medallion, is associated nonetheless with the relief of Constantine's triumphal entry into Rome in 312, which shows the imperial procession between the Porta Flaminia and Domitian's elephant arch.[115] (Plate 13.) There are no welcoming people. Winged Victoria, flying over the emperor's carriage, indicates her theme, but unlike the triumphator, Constantine sits in a carriage, rather than standing in a triumphal chariot.

The triumph had gained an important part of its meaning, a meaning that drew heavily on Roman republican history and religion,[116] by approximating the emperor to Iuppiter. The tondo of Sol prohibits any such meaning. With that, a fundamental theme of the Tetrarchy—the association of the emperors with Iuppiter and Hercules, with all that could result from this, in the interpretation, for instance, of victory—was dismissed. Instead, Constantine is linked to Sol-Apollo, not only theoretically but also in his appearance. The juxtaposition with Sol transforms Constantine's entry into a cosmic event, a meaning which is heightened when we examine the panel matching the *adventus* on the other side of the arch. Here Constantine's *profectio* from Milan is dominated by a tondo showing Luna in her *biga* setting into the sea.[117] (See plate 12.)

An analogy to this cosmic framework appears on the Parabiago plate where Cybele and Attis are surrounded by a series of cosmic figures including the rising sun and the setting moon, who, like the sun and moon on the arch, determine the time as break of day, metaphor for the *oriens Augusti*. We see here the same method of correlating divine and imperial events that was used under the Tetrarchs, but while the method is the same, the content has changed: the guardian deities of the Tetrarchs, Iuppiter and Hercules, have been supplanted by Sol. And while the images of Sol could be translated into Christian terms, Iuppiter and Hercules remained until the end gods of the pagans.[118]

The *adventus* and *profectio* reliefs are placed on the sides of the arch, thus providing transitions between the themes displayed on the two fronts. Facing away from the city is a pair of reliefs depicting warfare, that is, the siege of Verona and the battle of the Milvian Bridge. These two panels which expound the emperor's military virtues are balanced, on the city side, by panels showing his virtues as a civilian, as a ruler of cities. The legionary eagles, as Claudian expressed it,[119] have given way to the lictors. On the city side, the emperor is shown standing on the Rostra in a scene of *adlocutio* and enthroned in one of the imperial fora distributing largesse.[120] (See plates 14–15.)

These two reliefs, with their specifically civilian, urban emphasis, depict the second stage of *adventus*, the personal encounter between ruler and subjects, which is a regular feature in panegyric. The arch thus shows the ceremony of *adventus* with its two aspects, as we encountered it also under the Tetrarchy. The interpretation of the ceremony, however, had changed. While the idiom of the arch is still pagan, it also expresses the fact that Constantine had departed radically from Tetrarchic religious imagery. Where, however, Constantine's Latin panegyrists after 312 showed some uncertainty as to how to handle the new situation, the sculptors of the arch produced a finely balanced and coherent statement of new policies.

But ultimately, it was Eusebius, bishop of Caesarea, who supplied, long after the event, a theoretical and doctrinal interpretation of Constantinian *adventus*. In Eusebius' account, pagan sacred story and the precedents of earlier Roman history were replaced by Christian sacred story. The victory of Constantine over Maxentius was likened to the victory of Israel, led by Moses, over the Egyptians, and the song of triumph by Moses and Israel on that occasion was applied to Constantine's victory and put into his mouth.[121]

Here the content of the exegesis of imperial deeds was thus new, but the method of juxtaposing the emperor's deeds with precedents in divine or sacred history had also been used by the Tetrarchic panegyrists. The crossing of the Red Sea was in the early fourth century one of the themes of salvation which Western Christians represented on their sarcophagi, in a context, that is, in which Biblical history was regularly employed to illustrate the individual's salvation from death. These sarcophagi are closely related to the rendering of the battle of the Milvian Bridge on the arch of Constantine. Here Maxentius' soldiers are shown, exactly as described in the panegyric of 313, swallowed up in the waters of the Tiber in the same way as the Egyptians on the sarcophagi are swallowed up in the Red Sea.[122]

The similarity between the sarcophagi and this panel on the arch does not constitute a Christian influence on the latter, but, echoed as this similarity later was by Eusebius' exegesis of the meaning of Constantine's victory over Maxentius, it is nonetheless deeply significant, for it is a first visual example of a fusion between Biblical story and imperial deeds which in the early fourth century was as yet only potential, but which was to have a long history in both East and West.

Eusebius' Christian reinterpretation of Constantinian portraiture was equally far-reaching and profound, although, like his reinterpretation of *adventus*, it was essentially simple. As we have seen, Constantinian portraiture—the rendering of the imperial face which was beheld in *adventus*—turned its back on the portraiture of the Tetrarchy and reverted to the style of the divinely inspired ruler with floating hair, looking to heaven. Eusebius made of this the image of a Christian emperor:

> How great was the power of divine faith that motivated his soul may be learnt from the fact that he himself ordered his image to be imprinted on gold coins, looking upwards eagerly, in the way of one praying to God. . . . [See plate 47.] He was also represented standing upright by means of images raised over the entrance to the palace in some cities, looking up to heaven and stretching out his hands in the posture of prayer.[123]

But the message of the Tetrarchy was not entirely lost, for Christianity ultimately provided the barrier between the divine and the human spheres which had become blurred during the third-century empire and earlier, and which the Tetrarchs had re-established. Later Constantinian portraiture formed the model for imperial portraiture during the fourth and early fifth centuries, with the result that imperial portraiture became an expression of the fact that it was now the office of the emperor, rather than his person, that was approximated to the position of God.

Post-Constantinian portraiture generally shows the imperial face, rather than the face of an individual, whereas in the third century and earlier it had been each individual emperor in his own right who was idealised (see plates 1, 4–5, 8, 46–50). It was by this means that the third-century *impasse* of the divinely inspired ruler—a ruler whose identity would defy such means as were available for differentiating divinity from humanity—was resolved, and here elements of the Tetrarchy's theory of empire found their way into the Christian empire.

Eusebius' Christian interpretation of the originally pagan portrait of the divinely inspired ruler brought together what had been, until he wrote, divergent strands of imperial theory. Here, as in his rendering of *adventus*, he made the first consistent and coherent attempt at replacing the pagan religious images of the state with Christian imagery in such a way that the latter could directly emerge from the former.

He was able to do this because, like the Tetrarchic panegyrists, he extended the terrestrial contemporary event into other spheres—into the historical victory of Moses and the Israelites, and into the cosmic victory of Christ. It was some time before this imagery could firmly take root,[124] but in that process Eusebius' contribution was fundamental.[125]

ii. Constantius II in Rome in 357 A.D.: Triumph Transformed into an Urban Roman *adventus*

When we compare *adventus* under the Tetrarchs and under Constantine, we see that the ceremony was an event in which the emperor's relation to the divine could be submitted to careful scrutiny, admitting a variety of interpretations. At the same time, arrival, if it was in Rome, had a particular historical dimension for, by coming to Rome, the emperor added a further example to a long series of significant homecomings, of which Claudian was still aware when, in 404 A.D., he began his panegyric on Honorius' sixth consulship and arrival in Rome with the lines:

> Our ancestors vowed golden temples to Homecoming Fortune for the return of their leaders and this goddess could never more rightly claim a noble temple for her services than when both the Consulship and Rome have their proper majesty restored to them.[126]

By restoration of proper majesty is meant arrival of the emperor in Rome. This historical dimension of arrival in Rome could find very specific expression if the arrival were also a triumph, when the emperor's homecoming would culminate in the sacrifice to Capitoline Iuppiter, which Constantine probably did not offer in 312. The precedent which Constantine set had lasting results: no subsequent emperor performed this exclusively Roman sacrifice. The symbolic impact of Constantine's omission of the sacrifice was heightened with the foundation of Constantinople.[127] But paradoxically, the foundation of Constantinople enhanced the status of Rome, for it reopened the issue of the role of an imperial capital—or now of two imperial capitals—vis-à-vis the capital cities of the provinces.[128]

Accordingly, arrival in Rome, and later in Constantinople, was thought to be in some way different from arrival elsewhere. *Adventus* in Rome and Constantinople could provide an occasion to express the ideal relationship between the emperor and a representative group of his subjects. This element was seriously overshadowed in Rome under Constantine, but re-emerged with particular clarity in the reign of Constantius II. The *adventus* of Constantius II in Rome in 357 offered an occasion both for taking up the issue of the status of Rome along with that of Constantinople, within the empire, and for defining the person and image of the emperor himself.

Constantius made a triumphal entry into Rome in 357 to celebrate his vicennalia and his victories over Magnentius and Decentius and over the Alamanni.[129] For this event, Themistius, then a senator of Constantinople, composed an oration which he delivered before Constantius in Rome.[130] This oration touches upon Constantius' entry in general terms, its chief themes being, however, the relationship between the emperor and his capitals,[131] and imperial benefactions to the two cities. In other words, the oration discusses the second stage of *adventus*, after the emperor had arrived and when, by means and as a result of the arrival, a certain state of coexistence between ruler and subjects had been attained. Themistius visualised himself as offering to Constantius a wreath of victory, the gift of his city, just as the Athenians had offered wreaths to Demetrius (cf. plate 19). But the wreath was more than an object: "She herself [Constantinople] is your wreath entire, and your offering."[132] And the occasion was more than a festival at which wreaths were offered, as they had been at Delphi, Olympia, and Athens:

> Rather, in the city who is the ruler of cities, the city who is the second ruler over us wreathes the ruler of men, and Constantinople makes Rome the witness of your honour, Rome, who alone is more exalted than the city who does honour to you.[133] (Cf. plate 57.)

Themistius is very explicit in this oration about the special importance of Rome for empire and emperor, but he formulates it in terms of the interdependence of Rome and Constantinople.[134] Rome is the site, the θέατρον of the arrival, but the gift for arrival, the triumphal wreath, is given by Constantinople, so that two fundamental ingredients of the ceremony of *adventus* become dissociated from each other, but in such a way that the old meaning of the ceremony is not destroyed. The arrival expresses and creates a set of relationships, the relationships between the emperor and his two capitals, the latter seen not so much as groups of people but as concepts, abstractions. As such Rome and Constantinople were shown in late antique art.[135] (See plate 57.)

The arrival of Constantius in Rome in 357, according to Themistius, was in no way to be understood as a Roman triumph, nor was it an arrival merely in geographical terms; rather, the geographical arrival had become the foundation of a theoretical expression of the nature of imperial dominion. It was in this framework of the interpretation of an ancient ceremony as it related to events of the time that Themistius as a philosopher[136] explicitly found for himself the role of expounder of the nature of empire. It was a role which the Tetrarchic, and to a lesser degree the Constantinian, Latin panegyrists also filled, although they did not directly explain that this was so, but simply spoke on the basis of that link between official ceremonial and rhetorical training which could be operative in explaining *adventus*. Under Constantius II the content of the ceremony of *adventus* was different from the Tetrarchic content, but the formulation of the ceremony, as the expression and establishment of a relationship between ruler and ruled, remained sufficiently stable to provide a visible continuity.

In terms of how the ceremony was enacted, Ammianus' account of Constantius' arrival of 357 gives a detailed picture highlighting this continuity. Also, Themistius' themes of emperor and capital, and the expression of a relationship between them, are articulated in Ammianus, but in a totally different, much more pragmatic idiom. This idiom can be documented firstly in Ammianus' definition of the type of event that Constantius' arrival in Rome represented, and secondly in his description of the event in itself and of Rome.[137]

Ammianus saw Constantius' entry as an attempt to gain a triumph and stated his own view that there were no grounds for triumph since Constantius had merely won a civil war. However, Ammianus' narrative discloses that no triumph took place, but merely a ceremonial arrival. What becomes clear from Ammianus' account is that arrival, when it took place in Rome, the "mother city of trophies" of Themistius, had the special significance of expressing imperial victory. The fourth century was the time when on the coinage imperial titles such as UBIQUE VICTOR had become frequent. They expressed on a general level what *adventus* in Rome expressed on a particular level: the universal victoriousness of the emperor, a theoretical quality upon which concrete historical victories were based; not, as formerly, the other way round.[138] Victory, like *pietas* under the Tetrarchy, was an innate imperial quality, and just as under the Tetrarchy *adventus* had been one of the vehicles for expressing imperial *pietas*, so under Constantius, Theodosius and Honorius, *adventus*, especially in Rome, became the vehicle for expressing within the walls of the city imperial victory, both universal and particular.

The difference between Ammianus and Themistius was not merely between the 'sober and alert' historian and the idealising panegyrist; rather, each stood in a tradition that looked for different qualities in an emperor. Themistius built up his portrait of Constantius by rejecting the validity of precisely those warlike qualities which Ammianus found regrettably lacking in Constantius.[139] Themistius, the pagan court philosopher of the fourth-century Christian empire, formulated a theoretical model which could be applied to the civilian emperors of the fifth and sixth centuries, in particular to Justinian. This became one strand in Byzantine imperial theory; the other was that of the warlike emperor, reiterated for instance by Synesius. It was by means of this latter strand that Ammianus formulated his critique of Constantius.

Adventus as a relationship with the community was well illustrated by the events of 357, as related by Ammianus. The imperial procession, it appears, was formed at Ocriculum and shortly afterwards Constantius encountered first the Senate, then the people of Rome who had come to welcome him. Next, Ammianus describes the imperial procession, its military splendour, with Constantius sitting in a golden carriage,[140] just as Constantine was shown on his arch (plate 13). That is, Constantius did not come in the attitude of the old Roman triumphator. There follows Constantius' acclamation by the people inside Rome,[141] with a description of his dignified bearing during the ceremony as a whole.

That was the end of the arrival. The relationship of emperor and citizens had been established, the emperor was present, and his conduct changed: in the circus and while seeing the sights of Rome, he behaved as a citizen, was integrated into the community.[142] Constantius' change of conduct, dignified, immobile, remote, during the *adventus* ceremony, and relaxed and friendly after he had entered Rome, was explicable within a purely urban Roman tradition.[143] However, a change of conduct was also an inherent part of the ceremony of arrival, wherever it took place. The panegyric of 291 describes first the divine exaltedness of Diocletian and Maximian, and then stresses how, once they were within the walls of Milan, they were seen intimately, close at hand. At Autun, Constantine was welcomed as a saviour, but when he came face to face with the city *curia*, the panegyrist emphasized his kindness and humanity.

In short, the ceremony of *adventus* in Rome, just as elsewhere, provided a vocabulary for the encounter of different types of persons, and for their convergence into one group. This, in itself, provided the ceremonial model for other forms of relationship between the emperor and his subjects. The same delicate balance of awesome entry, "like an angel of heaven," and unself-conscious familiarity marked Constantine's conduct towards the bishops at the council of Nicaea.[144]

In art, this balance is illustrated on the Arch of Constantine. In the *adventus* ceremony, only the imperial procession is shown, pointing to the isolation and dignity of the emperor, and also taking some account of the novelty of the entry of 312. But when in Rome, Constantine, in the *adlocutio* and *largitio* panels, is shown surrounded by people: the integration and convergence have taken place (plates 13–15).

The feeling of the remoteness and dignity of the emperor, as conveyed in one part of Ammianus' narrative, is very well rendered on a *largitio* dish of Constantius II in the Hermitage, showing him mounted on a horse with jewelled reins, nimbate, wearing an embroidered tunic and holding a spear, in the idiom of the *adventus* imagery of the coinage.[145] (Plate 16.) Before the horse, drawn on a slightly smaller scale than the emperor, Victoria delicately trips along. In her left hand she holds a palm branch and in her right she raises up a wreath towards Constantius, recalling Themistius' wreath-giving imagery. A barbarian bodyguard, also drawn slightly smaller than the emperor, follows behind, carrying a lance and a round shield with a Chi Rho design. Below the hind legs of the horse a shield lies on the ground—a trace of the fallen enemy sometimes shown on the coinage.

On the surface, the ingredients of this imperial image are the same as those of the Ticinum medallion (plate 11): both show the emperor preceded by Victoria and a *pedisequus*. But there the similarity ends. On the medallion, Constantine is shown on the obverse as the counterpart of Sol. Here there is no such implication: the emperor is alone and majestic, but he remains the emperor. Instead of a resolute, forward movement along a horizontal groundline, as on the medallion, the silver dish shows the emperor and his companions as almost stationary, and there is no groundline.

The straightforward and clear-cut profile view of the medallion has changed into a more subtle and complicated three-quarter frontality.[146] The whole composition is turned in on itself: Victoria, supposedly moving in the same direction as the emperor, yet looks the other way. But neither she nor the soldier looks directly at the emperor, as some of the followers of Galerius and Constantine did on their arches. Their eyes are discreetly lowered in the presence of majesty. The emperor himself looks out beyond his companions, and also, in a sense, beyond the viewer of the image. The image portrays a reality where those who accompany the emperor serve merely as a background and exist on a different plane. This representation refers to no specific place or occasion.[147] Victory and arrival are to be understood here as something other than distinct, identifiable historical events.

In Ammianus' account, the emperor moves in the procession as if completely untouched by what surrounds him. He does not turn his head to see the multitude, and does not hear their shouts in his honour. Constantius, in the context of the *adventus* Ammianus describes, had become an image, a statue. Thus, it is not inappropriate that the earliest imperial image of the Christian empire that can be said to have the qualities of an icon is the *largitio* bowl of Constantius. The characteristics that give this image the features of an icon, a sacred image, are these: within the picture, the emperor is dissociated from the other figures by his greater physical stature, by his frontality, by the fact that his figure partly covers the others.[148] Only the emperor and his immediate following are shown, in the same way as later Christ or the *Theotokos* were depicted enthroned between angels and saints. The image thus shows a world disconnected from the world of every day. Nonetheless, like an icon, it establishes a link between the subject of the image and the onlooker, and it does this chiefly by means of depicting Constantius' serious, somewhat stylised, impersonal yet personal face: large eyes looking out of the image at the onlooker. There was no need here to depict a welcoming crowd; it was the image that, when formulated like this, in itself became capable of welcome, and therefore could suggest to the beholder the *adventus* ceremony as a whole.

At this point we may look back to the Venice Tetrarchs (plate 3) to point out that in that work precisely these icon-like features had also found expression. The style of the portrait of the *largitio* bowl derived from the Constantinian style of Imperial portraiture, but the theoretical, doctrinal difficulties that this style could produce earlier—in that it was a direct descendant of the pre-Christian portrait of the divinised ruler— had been transcended. We can now see again, and more clearly, by looking back over the development of *adventus* as a whole and by juxtaposing the bowl and the Venice Tetrarchs, that in this transcendence, which was achieved lastingly in the Christian empire, the pagan Tetrarchs had provided a crucial stage.

It is as well to look back over the strands that have concerned us so far. Every *adventus* of which we know sums up the expectations of the subjects for their emperor. Prosaically, they met the emperor in a ceremony which remained stable throughout this period, for all its differing elements and associations, in stage-managing a delicate blend of majesty and intimacy. Less prosaically, in seeing the emperor, the subjects had occasion to reflect on the exact quality of his relation to the divine, as shown on his face. Although this was conveyed in a wide variety of styles, from the Tetrarchy to Constantius II, none of these portrait styles should be isolated simply as portraits; they offer glimpses of the emperor in the midst of a ceremony in which all these issues were crystallised. Furthermore, in troubled times, to go out to meet an emperor was to accept him as emperor, as we shall now see in the case of Julian.

iii. *Salutare Sidus.* Julian: Pagan *adventus* Restated, and *adventus* as Accession

The image of the coming ruler as a star, as a vision of light, had been much stressed in the Tetrarchy and earlier. It plays an important role in accounts of the accession of Julian. One of the ways in which Vergil foreshadowed the destiny of Rome, as rising out of fallen Troy, was his description of the supernatural radiance that appeared over the head of Ascanius, future king of Alba Longa, while a star pointed the way to Mount Ida, a place of withdrawal and safety.[149] This passage is a crucial turning point in Book Two of the *Aeneid*. But the revelation of kingship in terms of light, while an image of poetry, could also have a political tone. Thus, the image of the coming ruler as a star was used to acclaim Caligula at his accession, which Suetonius related as an *adventus*:

> So he attained the empire and fulfilled the desire of the Roman people or rather, of mankind, for he was the emperor who was most eagerly expected by most of the provincials and the army . . . and also by the people of Rome. . . . Therefore, when he set out from Misenum, although in the garb of mourning, and following the funerary procession of Tiberius, he nonetheless moved altars and victims, and burning torches, and was surrounded by dense crowds who rejoicingly came to meet him and acclaimed him with auspicious names, such as 'star, darling, dear child, and son.'[150]

Of Constantine's arrival in Britain, an *adventus* which at the same time signified his accession,[151] a panegyrist used the telling phrase: "Your sudden coming shone upon us."[152] (Cf. plate 9.) In short, the imagery of accession and arrival, seen as a supernatural event and expressed in terms of a vision of light, was current in antiquity and late antiquity. This was so not only in literature, but increasingly in imperial art, where, from the Tetrarchy onwards, the emperor could be shown nimbate.

The most telling late antique instances of accession formulated as *adventus* in pagan terms occurred under Julian, whose accession was spontaneously visualised, according to Ammianus in particular, as an epiphany, the appearance of one sent by the gods,[153] as one coming into the world like a health-giving star. Ammianus' accounts are in perfect accord with what was said of *adventus* in panegyric. This is an indication, initially, that he may have used panegyrics as source material.[154] But more importantly, the consistency of Ammianus' accounts of Julian's arrivals indicates that late antique people were indeed trained to perceive the event of arrival in a certain way, to see some significance in it. We have before us, in short, not just a ceremonial, but a method of perceiving and understanding it which was communicated consistently within different genres of literature.

According to Ammianus, Julian viewed his becoming Caesar as a tragic destiny,[155] and Ammianus tells of his first days as Caesar in sombre tones. But this climate suddenly changed when the populace of Vienne welcomed its new ruler:

> When he came to Vienne and entered the city, people of all ages and ranks came together to receive him with honour as one who had been hoped for and desired; and when he was seen at a distance, the whole populace and people from the neighbourhood, acclaiming him as a kind and good emperor, joyfully walked before him, together singing his praises, for they were very glad to see royal splendour in a legitimate emperor. From his coming they expected a remedy to be found for their common woes, and they thought that some health-giving genius was shining on their difficulties. Then a blind old woman who, after asking who had entered, found out that it was the Caesar Julian, exclaimed that he would restore the temples of the gods.[156]

This arrival has the usual features: the two stages of arrival and presence and what is hoped for from the latter, highlighted by the prophecy of the old woman. Accession in the fourth century, as indicated by Julian's proclamation as Caesar, and then as Augustus, was a military ceremonial. The ceremony in which the cities of the empire could express their consent to these military imperial elections was *adventus*. This *adventus* had to be reiterated city by city, each severally expressing consent, as is made clear by Julian's reaction to his reception in Sirmium after his usurpation. He hoped that the other cities would welcome him similarly; it could not be taken for granted.

> Julian advanced with rapid steps, and, as he was approaching the suburbs, a crowd of soldiers and people of all kinds equipped with many lights and flowers accompanied him to the palace, making auspicious vows for the future and calling him Augustus and lord. Thus

Julian, glad of the outcome and the omen, with his hopes for the future confirmed, thought that, after the example of this populous and famous metropolis, he would be welcomed in the other cities also as a health-giving star; on the next day, amidst the rejoicing of the people, he held chariot races.[157]

The people and garrison of Sirmium ratified for themselves the outcome of the military election at Paris, just as the people of Vienne had ratified the nomination of Julian as Caesar. Such ratifications were not regarded as mere ceremonial by-products of political events, but as political events in themselves. This is why Symmachus' panegyric on Maximus could, after the event, be understood as more than an unfortunate indiscretion, for in this panegyric Symmachus could be regarded as having expressed to Maximus the allegiance of the Senate and people of Rome.[158] Such was the function of panegyrics. Like the *adventus* ceremony, they expressed consent to arrangements that had been made, but they were arrangements which, until ratified by such consent, had to remain tentative.

Another *adventus* pointing to accession is related by Ammianus when he tells of Julian's arrival in Constantinople. This account is to be taken together with Mamertinus' panegyric on January 1st, 362, shortly after this arrival. Ammianus explicitly links the arrival of Julian in Constantinople with his accession, the arrival in Constantinople being an important climax to Julian's imperial progress from West to East:

> [Julian] hastened [from Philippopolis] yet more exalted, in some chariot, as it were, of Triptolemus, which, because of its swiftness is, in the ancient tales, imagined to have been drawn by winged serpents of the air. In this way, feared by land and sea, and held up by no delay, he entered Heraclea. . . . When this became known at Constantinople, all ages and sexes poured forth as though they were going to see someone sent down from heaven. So he was received . . . with the respectful attendance of the Senate and the universal acclaim of the people; being accompanied by rows of citizens and soldiers, he was escorted as though in a line of battle, and the eyes of all were turned on him not just with a fixed gaze,[159] but with great wonder. For, it seemed closer to a dream that a young man, short of stature but distinguished by great deeds, should, after the bloodstained destruction of kings and nations, after a progress of unheard-of speed from city to city, increasing in wealth and strength wherever he went, have seized all places more easily than rumour flies, and should at last have taken up the empire with the assent of heaven.[160]

In a sense, the people and Senate of Constantinople could not but accept this *fait accompli*. Nonetheless, this is not what happened according to the late antique manner of perceiving *adventus* and accession. For, *adventus* remained a ceremony of persuasion, integration and consent, in which spontaneous action could be clothed in a familiar ceremonial. The formal welcome of the *de facto* emperor was obligatory. Nonetheless, to be accepted as valid, as not extorted by a tyrant, it had to have an air of spontaneity. Thus Libanius in his speech of welcome to Julian in Antioch stressed precisely the spontaneity of welcome:

> If all mankind had been afflicted with a common disease of the eyes and by the kindness of some divinity had suddenly recovered their sight, [the cities welcoming Julian] could not have been more glad. Fear did not constrain them to simulate their gladness, but in the soul of each one the rejoicing flowered . . . [and] the shouting of those who were glad rose to heaven from everywhere, from cities and fields, from houses and theatres, mountains and plains, and I might say, from those sailing on rivers and lakes, and on the high sea.[161]

It was a spontaneous, inspired *consensus universorum*, highlighted by Libanius' parable of recovering eyesight. Both the spontaneity and the universality of the reception of Julian in the empire after his military accession were also stressed by his panegyrist Mamertinus. From the public, civilian point of view, Julian's accession consisted not of the moment of acclamation, or the moment of inner struggle for inspiration and lucidity that Julian himself described;[162] such a comprehension of the moment of accession still lay in the future, and that moment came to be crystallised in the ceremony of accession.

In the fourth century, imperial accession could still be a process rather than a single event, a continuous ratification of the initiating event of military accession, which could not exist without its civilian ratification,[163] the process of ratification being from time to time seized upon and highlighted by an imperial *adventus*. This is what Mamertinus spoke about when explaining how and why Julian became emperor:

> After having suppressed Alamannia in the very act of rebellion, Julian who shortly before had with his victorious army crossed regions, rivers and mountains of names unknown, had passed through the most distant kingdoms of ferocious tribes, and had flown over the heads of kings trodden underfoot, appeared unexpectedly, in the midst of Illyricum. We, the blessed companions of that journey, saw how the people of the towns were amazed and doubted what they saw. But no different, I think, was the amazement of those who first received the Palladium when it fell from heaven.[164] Not without a great sense of awe did virgins, children, women, women trembling with old age, and old men behold the emperor. . . . The greatness of the miracle quite undid the voices of those who rejoiced.[165]

Then he spoke of the voyage along the Danube:

> What a progress of splendour was that voyage, when the right bank of that noble river was crowded with a continuous flow of men and women, people of all ranks, of soldiers and citizens, and on the left could be seen the barbarian world on its knees making abject prayers.[166]

On that journey Julian restored the fortunes of cities, in particular of Athens and Eleusis, but also of the empire at large,[167] and in this context Mamertinus makes of Julian a new Triptolemus, an idea which was later taken up by Ammianus.[168] Mamertinus avoids mentioning any specific arrivals but portrays arrival and accession as the activity of ruling; the tasks of the emperor were fulfilled as he progressed through the empire.[169] Nonetheless, arrival in Constantinople could have a special significance:

> This city [Constantinople], new in name but most ancient in nobility, is your home. Here you were born and here you arose like some health-giving star for mankind.[170]

However, for Julian this theme of the emperor and his capital could not be fully worked out in its fourth-century framework even at a practical level, for Julian was opposed to making Constantinople a capital, at what he regarded as the expense of the other cities of the East, while at a theoretical, philosophical level, Athens, not Rome or Constantinople, was the ultimate point of reference. Hence Mamertinus' perspective of universal *adventus* was in accord with Julian's policy as emperor. The topic was taken up in a very similar form by Libanius in 362,[171] but Libanius culminates differently:[172]

> What they say Asclepius did for Hippolytus, that you yourself performed for the body of our world.[173] You raised the dead to life and the name of kingship has, as formerly, gained a practical meaning.

In a less elevated style, the Antiochenes meant something similar when, as Julian was arriving in Antioch, they met him. Ammianus says:

> When [Julian] came near to the city he was received like some divinity with public prayers, and was surprised at the clamour of the great multitude which acclaimed him as a health-giving star shining on the East.[174]

The images of light, of the star, the shining upon mankind, of beholding, are applied to Julian's arrivals with unusual consistency and regularity.

From this point of view, and from the point of view of the connection made between Julian's arrivals and pagan sacred story, these accounts are reminiscent of Tetrarchic imperial arrival; but only distantly, because the illustrating sacred stories are of a different origin and significance, and because the perception of light, of epiphany, is more fragmentary and is nowhere as fully explained as it had been under the Tetrarchy. However, if the specific imagery of *adventus*, as articulated under Julian, remained incomplete, the emphasis placed on this ceremonial as an urban consent to imperial accession endured beyond his short reign.

In the fifth century the military ceremony of accession became an urban ceremony. Furthermore, *adventus* as a display of victory on the one hand, and of imperial benefactions on the other, as we see it under Julian, also continued. But those pagan religious aspects in *adventus* which half emerged again under him, in the imagery of the saviour coming like a star, were to become, in Claudian's hands, part of a courtly, not a religious, culture, and were ultimately almost completely submerged in the Christian empire.

So we find in the paganism of the mid-fourth century a renewed ability to formulate precisely the link between empire and emperor on the one hand, and between the emperor and the divine on the other.[175] In comparison to Julian's lucid perception of his position,[176] the Christian formulations of the same period, although they contained the ground upon which precise and clear thinking was to be founded in the future, still seem confused and evasive.

4. THE EMPEROR AND HIS CITY

i. Arrivals of Theodosius and Honorius

Julian's reign was incomplete; his own image of the imperial office was idiosyncratic and a little baffling to contemporaries. This makes all the more impressive the certainty of touch with which his *adventus* was seized upon in so many cities and articulated with such unusual zest and consistency. The element in *adventus* which made the ceremony a continuous progress and an acknowledgement of sovereignty recurred under Theodosius. But with Theodosius there was the additional feature of *adventus* in both Rome and Constantinople, the two capital cities of the empire, whereby a relationship between emperor and capital was established, such as has been encountered already with Constantius II. At the same time, Christianity was now sufficiently established as the religion of the empire to put firmly into the past those aspects of *adventus* which had enabled it to orchestrate the revelation of a *praesens deus*. Imperial majesty was henceforth to be expressed by different means.

In describing Theodosius' triumphal celebration of his victory over Maximus and Victor, Pacatus in his panegyric refers to Theodosius' arrival in Haemona and later passes on to his arrival in Rome. The arrival

in Haemona was a preliminary one, for it anticipated the more important arrival in Rome. Thus the whole of Theodosius' campaign could be
rendered as a long triumphal *adventus*. Pacatus describes how the people of Haemona came to meet Theodosius and their sense of relief at his
coming:

> Crowds of dancers came to meet you and everywhere resounded
> songs and applause. One choir sang the triumph for you and the other
> one sang the funerary chant . . . for the tyrant. One choir called for the
> departure of the conquered, the other for the frequent return of the vic-
> tors. . . . No one was hindered by consideration of you or themselves;
> the spontaneity of joy became a friendly violation of decorum. Need I
> describe how the freed nobility solemnly came to meet you outside the
> walls, the senators distinguished by their white garments, the venera-
> ble priests wearing their purple headdress? Need I mention the gates
> crowned with blooming branches? . . . You had not yet completed the
> war, yet already you celebrated your triumph.[177]

The promise in this *adventus* of a successful outcome of Theodosius' war
against Maximus is fulfilled with Theodosius' *adventus* in Rome:

> The events which occurred in Rome, the day on which you entered
> the city, what you did in the curia and on the rostra, how you followed
> your procession of triumphal carts sometimes on a chariot, sometimes
> on foot, and how you were distinguished by this two-fold entry, tri-
> umphing on the one hand in war and on the other triumphing over
> pride; how you showed yourself as emperor to the commonalty, and as
> senator to individuals . . . how, having dismissed your military guards,
> you were in fact more securely guarded by the affection of the people:
> let these events be praised by the language and voice of those who, in
> the rejoicing which is common to all, can rightly praise what is most
> important and can justly praise what concerns them directly.[178]

This *adventus* at the same time forms the epilogue to Pacatus' panegyric and represents a high point in his experience of the emperor and
of Rome, where he had gone to deliver his oration:

> What a blessed pilgrimage have I had! . . . [On my homecoming,]
> with how many listeners will I be surrounded when I say: 'I saw Rome,
> I saw Theodosius, and I saw both together; I saw him who is an em-
> peror's father, an emperor's avenger, and an emperor's saviour.'[179]

Here the movement of the ceremony had come to rest in the act of
beholding Theodosius and Rome. Triumph, now in effect transformed
into *adventus*, culminated in the relationship that was to be formed between the emperor and his capital. This was a theme which became very
prominent in Claudian's descriptions of Honorius' arrival in Rome in
404.

Claudian, as a great poet, with his imagination formed and trained in
the Latin poetry of the past and in the rhetorical schooling he received,
presents a personal, even an enigmatic picture of imperial *adventus* in
the late fourth and early fifth centuries—personal in that he applies his
own vision to contemporary events, enigmatic in that what he says
seems so little in accord with the post-Theodosian Christian empire.[180]
Adventus to Claudian could be a divine theme which he articulated by
means of the imagery of pagan religion, drawing for this imagery on a
period in literature and artistic achievement when religion and art, worship and personal culture had been inseparable:

> Madness divine has driven earthly perception
> From my breast, my heart is inspired by Apollo.
> The temple before my eyes shakes in its foundations,
> And from its threshold spreads a radiant light
> Which gives witness to the advent of the god.[181]

In Claudian's poetry the question of how religion and culture were
to be differentiated was not asked, and was therefore not answerable.
Claudian could accordingly articulate the propaganda of a Christian
court in a pagan idiom. In a sense, he did not commit the court to either
paganism or Christianity;[182] rather, he created an artistic language of his
own, related though this was to the language of earlier Latin poets. It is
therefore necessary to understand how Claudian viewed *adventus* in itself, and then how this view can be integrated into a late antique context.

Claudian describes three arrivals of Honorius: Honorius' coming to
the West in 392, his consular *adventus* in Milan in 398, and his consular
adventus in Rome in 404. In the two earlier instances,[183] *adventus* was one
theme among several in his writings, while the whole panegyric of 404
was devoted to Honorius' arrival in Rome.

The themes of the *adventus* of 404 are triumph on the one hand, and
the relation between emperor and Rome on the other,[184] so that here
emerge again the strands of *adventus* that were prominent under Constantine, Constantius and Theodosius. As for the triumph, it is formulated in the Constantinian sense: it is a *pompa*,[185] in which the theme of
triumph is combined with that of consulship in the structure of the
poem.[186] This melding of themes is highlighted by the interspersed narrative of Alaric's defeat, so that the ceremonial climax of victory—*adventus* formulated as triumph and consulship—is related to an historical
setting, to historical fact.

But this is only one strand in the structure of the poem, the other
being the mythological setting of victory. In order to create this setting,

Claudian incorporated into his narrative the figure of Eridanus, who
represented also the river Po, guardian of the borders of Italy, and the
father of Phaethon, whose fate could have been a warning example to
Alaric before he invaded Italy.[187] There is no separation between history
and myth, however, for, just as Roma, a figure of myth and imagination, can address Honorius, the visible emperor,[188] so Eridanus, figure
of myth, speaks to Alaric,[189] the only too factual enemy.

In short, we have here a very skilful handling of the theme of *adventus* on several levels which, as during the Tetrarchy, are capable of inter-
penetrating each other, thereby enhancing and extending visible and
historical reality and giving it universal significance and comprehensibility. Reality becomes comprehensible because it can be set into the
framework of Roman history and Graeco-Roman myth. History makes
sense because it is continuous, and one of the ways of highlighting such
continuity is the use of the ceremony of *adventus*.

These topics, the interpenetration of different modes of reality, the relating of contemporary history to past experience and myth, and the
perception of continuity among them are also disclosed in the other
main theme of Claudian's *Sixth Consulship*, that of the emperor and
Roma (cf. plate 56).

The actual *adventus* is brought about initially by Roma's request to see
her emperor and by the dialogue between Roma and Honorius.[190] But
the *adventus* of Honorius in Rome is not merely an *ad hoc* event; it also
has a theoretical, doctrinal rightness about it, which Claudian discusses
in four introductory themes to the poem as a whole,[191] which point to
Honorius' *adventus*. He opens with the significance of Fortuna Redux.
That is, he points to *adventus* and consulship in their Roman Republican and Augustan context—the emperor and the consul's home are in
Rome.

Next, he says the same thing in astrological terms: Honorius is the
sidus imperii[192] (we may recall Julian's being welcomed as a star) which,
when the emperor is in Rome, is in its own seat, *propria sede*.[193] Then, the
adventus of Honorius is visualised in terms of Apollo's coming to Delphi,
when the spring of Castalia speaks again and the laurel is again the tree
of prophecy. This theme is then related to Rome and Honorius:

> Behold how the sanctity of the Palatine hill is enhanced
> And rejoices in the presence of its god, granting oracles
> Greater than those of Delphi to suppliant nations,
> And it commands its laurels to flourish, ready for the standards of
>   Rome.[194]

Finally Rome is described as though the *adventus* were already taking place, and this evocation of the topography of Rome is reiterated in the context of the actual ceremony at the end of the poem.[195]

The *adventus*, then, takes place in the contexts of both triumph and the interdependence of Rome and emperor. Claudian's illustrations of these contexts, which have been discussed so far, explain the meaning of the actual ceremony. This consists of the progress of Honorius from Ravenna,[196] the preparations in Rome,[197] and Honorius' entry: a vast crowd receives him,[198] and Honorius and his entourage are described.[199] Once within the city, the first stage of *adventus* having been accomplished, Honorius meets the senators and mounts the Palatine, his home.[200] He presides in the circus,[201] and performs consular New Year ceremonies.[202]

> How greatly does the presence of the empire's guardian genius enhance the people's majesty; how greatly does the majesty of the one reflect the other.[203]

These words introduce Claudian's description of Honorius in the circus presiding over the accustomed *laetitiae*, and performing the consular ceremonies of the New Year. The words sum up the interdependence of emperor and people, emperor and Rome, which the ceremony of *adventus* could orchestrate. The ceremony culminates in achieving, in visible terms, in the emperor's visible presence, that tightly-knit unity between emperor and subjects which was the goal of so much late antique imperial theory.

Honorius' *adventus* in Rome of 392 also takes the form of a progress[204] and of a welcome in Rome by an eager crowd.[205] Both progress and welcome—this time in Milan—again figure in 398,[206] when Claudian lays special stress on the splendour of Honorius' jewel-clad figure.[207] The aspect of the emperor is described in a simile:

> Now, what garments, what miracles of spendour
> Have we not seen, when, clad in the robe of Italy
> You passed through Liguria more exalted than is your custom
> And when you were carried amidst the cohorts clad in white,
> And picked soldiers bore upon their shoulders
> A starry burden. Thus in Memphis are gods brought out
> Before the people. The image leaves its shrine.[208]

Here, then, the emperor does not merely stand still and unperturbed by the surrounding tumult of rejoicings, as Constantius had done, but he himself has, as it were, become the image. Claudian's simile, even if interpreted in the most casual way possible, is most significant. The ceremony of *adventus* in late antiquity had become a stylisation, an expression in literary and visual art, of an originally spontaneous experience. The experience could still be spontaneous, but it was, from a very early stage, capable of formalisation, stylisation, of an interpretation which universalised it in different ways.

In the expression of *adventus*, rhetoric and visual art worked hand in hand, and Claudian's simile highlights this fact from one particular point of view: the person of the emperor could be compared to the artefact, the work of art, and according to Ammianus, could deliberately behave in such a way as to become like the artefact, the work of art. There is thus a connection between Claudian's Honorius and the statuesque emperors of imperial art on the obelisk base of Theodosius and the column base of Arcadius in Constantinople (plates 17–21).

ii. The Eternal Presence

Once the emperor is united with his capital, *adventus*, the ceremony of movement and arrival, has come to rest. It is in this coming to rest that we can follow the ceremony to its next phase. In so doing, we cross one of the watersheds separating the late antique from the early Byzantine worlds. For, a ceremonial, once perceived as highlighting the momentary and dramatic impingement of the imperial presence on the local community, is transformed into its opposite—a ceremonial that communicates the worldwide dominion of the emperor, exercised from the still centre of the imperial presence. The opening phases of this development are implied in the language of Pacatus; it becomes plain in the art of the Theodosian age. *Adventus* imagery on the coinage became very rare during the fourth century, and it is necessary to ask why this was so. Partly it was because the repertoire of themes in imperial art during the fourth century decreased drastically,[209] but also, and more importantly, the change reflected the way in which the ceremony of *adventus* had altered in meaning.

From a military ceremony of movement enacting in particular localities the universal presence of the emperors[210]—a political and military necessity for the Tetrarchs—the first stage of *adventus*, which had stressed arrival *per se*, became less practically conditioned and less military. What came to be emphasised was not so much the movement or the progress of the emperor, but rather his presence. This tendency had been adumbrated on the *largitio* bowl of Constantius: already the mounted emperor was, as it were, stationary, and the movement turned in on itself. The imperial presence was epitomised in the second stage of the ceremony of *adventus*, that of the coexistence between emperor and subjects, and in the visual arts in the fourth century a terminology for this imperial presence was formulated: stationary, enthroned emperors.[211] This entirely superseded the earlier themes of the emperor in movement.

A major example among depictions of the imperial presence is the obelisk base of Theodosius in Constantinople, showing the imperial family presiding over scenes in the hippodrome, just as, in the panegyrics, once arrival had been effected, the emperor presided in the circus.[212] The obelisk base is linked by its Latin inscription to Theodosius' defeat of Maximus:

> Once reluctant to obey the exalted lords,
> I am commanded to carry the palm over the vanquished tyrants
>   [Maximus and Victor];
> All things yield to Theodosius and to his everlasting offspring;
> Thus am I conquered and subdued in thirty days,
> Am raised under Proclus [Proculus] the judge into the high air.[213]

The scene on the obelisk base that relates most intimately to Theodosius' arrivals of 389 (although not strictly historically, for at this period imperial art almost totally abandoned historical representation) is the submission of barbarians, among whom are Iranians on the north west side.[214] (Plate 17.) Three emperors, Theodosius, Valentinian II, Arcadius and the prince Honorius, sit enthroned in the Kathisma, flanked by senators, courtiers and soldiers, while below from the right approach Northern barbarians and one African, and from the left three Iranians, all bearing gifts. The locale is Constantinople, so that these are not the Iranians who, according to Claudian, came to Rome.[215] Rather, neither the Iranians nor their Western counterparts are historical personages at all but stereotypes of imperial ideology which convey the message of the emperor's universal dominion. A theme which, on the arch of Galerius, was still relatively realistically depicted—the reception of a foreign embassy—had here become a stereotype[216] and would remain one in the art of the fifth to the sixth centuries, just as Claudian visualised it in his *mise-en-scène* of imperial triumph transformed into *adventus*: "They laid down their crowns and bowed the knee before you."[217]

The four imperial personages shown in the relief were never in Constantinople together after the outset of the campaign against Maximus, so that from this point of view the relief is not historical either. What is depicted is the imperial presence—the emperors made present through their images—together with a typological imperial event—the arrival of the embassy—which defines, from a theoretical standpoint, the nature of imperial rule. The image makes permanent the second stage of *adven-*

tus, the presence of the emperor in his city, be it Rome, or, as here, Constantinople.[218]

The companion panel to the submission scene shows the same four figures in the Kathisma, watching a chariot race, this being another expression of imperial victory (see plate 18). Victory is depicted non-historically, without reference to a particular occasion; the occasion is only hinted at in the inscription.[219] The other two sides of the obelisk base do show an historical event—the erection of the obelisk and its inauguration. Three figures appear in the Kathisma, in the front row, and they are personages who were at that time in Constantinople, one of them being Arcadius.[220]

The obelisk base of Theodosius marks an important moment in imperial art in Constantinople, in that it picked up a method of representation utilised already on the Arch of Constantine in the *largitio* and *adlocutio* panels.[221] (See plates 14–15.) Frontality is the decisive visual feature in these reliefs, and as a result, the emperors are stationary and majestic. The emperor might still participate, as we have seen, in ceremonies of arrival, where he moved, but in visual art movement increasingly disappeared, and with that there disappeared one of the chief links that existed between the expression of *adventus* in literature and its expression in visual art: insofar as *adventus* was described in literature as movement, it was no longer represented visually. But on the other hand, imperial art represented the second stage of *adventus*, the presence of the emperor in a city, all the more convincingly and insistently. For the time being *adventus* as a military ceremony of arrival, and of arrival at times of emergency and need in the provinces of the empire, had had its day.

Such is also the message of another Constantinopolitan monument, the column base of Arcadius.[222] The column, following the model of the two triumphal columns of Rome,[223] depicted the expulsion of the Goths from Constantinople, while on three sides of the base were shown scenes expounding the joint consulship of Arcadius and Honorius in 402 A.D. Drawings made while the monument was still standing reveal that these scenes contained throughout the element of encounter between emperors and subjects, and of emperors and conquered enemies, which was also a feature of *adventus*. But once again the viewer here faced emperors still and majestic. Each of the three sculpted sides had four bands of relief, one beneath the other. On the east side (plate 19), in the band second from the top, the two emperors emerge from a columned porch, each followed by an *armiger*. The emperors are clothed in togas, and each holds a *mappa* in his raised right hand, an eagle sceptre in his left. To the right stand two *togati* and seven lictors, and to the left one *togatus*, one *chlamydatus* and another seven lictors. All these figures are seen frontally. The *chlamydatus* on the left is probably the pretorian prefect who accompanied the emperor when he transacted business with the Senate.[224] The lictors in the imperial consular procession are mentioned in Claudian's panegyrics.

The register below shows two groups of senators seen frontally, moving towards the centre, each headed by a senator carrying a crown.[225] At the extreme left and right stand Roma and Constantinopolis, each under an arch. Crowns were a customary gift to the emperor by the Senate, as well as by the cities of the provinces, on the occasions of imperial victories, anniversaries, and consulships. Symmachus brought such *aurea munuscula* as representative of the Roman Senate to Gratian and Valentinian I for the latter's quinquennalia in 369, and Synesius offered a crown to Arcadius on behalf of his home city, Cyrene.[226]

These two registers show the emperors in the act of meeting the Senate. A consular *adventus* was an urban senatorial event, "when armour gives way to the toga";[227] accordingly, the emperors are here togate. The bottom register, divided into three parts by columns, shows weapons and armour, with two barbarian women in an attitude of mourning. To left and right Nikai write on shields. These reliefs show the imperial consuls in the ceremonial setting of their office; the senators, and the Eastern and Western empires in the guise of Roma and Constantinopolis (cf. plates 56–57), make their due offerings. The bottom register sets these scenes into the wider context of victory and of events in the empire, as Claudian does in his poems. The message of these reliefs was, however, essentially different from Claudian's, for in the top register two Nikai in flight hold up a rectangular panel with a cross which is flanked by two attendant figures. Left and right of these Nikai Hesperus and Phosphorus, each with a torch, fly upwards. The sign by which Constantine had been victorious was by this time thought to have been the cross.[228] The top panel thus transforms the message of the other three, which could, without it, have been pagan, into a Christian one.

Imperial art achieved the transition from paganism to Christianity with a certain ease, by superimposing one concept over another, or, simply, by joining concepts. The new religion was expressed by adding to the old imagery without destroying it. In literature, such a Christianisation of the pagan imperial past came about much more slowly; its first fully articulate exponent was Corippus, in the later sixth century.[229]

Hesperus and Phosphorus flanking the cross, like Sol and Luna on the arch of Constantine, indicate that the setting of the scene is a cosmic universal one.[230] This universal imagery is more striking on the west side of the base (plate 21), where in the top register the Nikai holding up the cross in a wreath are flanked by Helius and Selene on their chariots, both raising their hands and preceded by Hesperus and Phosphorus. The second register shows the emperors as victors; they wear military dress, and are attended, on the left, by a *togatus*, a *chlamydatus* and soldiers, all standing frontally. Below, Germans, left, and Persians, right, emerging from an archway and led by Nikai, each with a kneeling woman, bring gifts, recalling the submission scene of the obelisk base. In the centre stand a trophy and two kneeling Nikai holding up the Chi Rho in a wreath, flanked by armour. In the fourth register, captives, trophies and captured armour emphasise imperial victoriousness.

The south side (plate 20) shows the homage of the provinces to the emperors in an iconographical scheme parallel to the other two, except that here, for a technical reason, the captured arms appear in the top register. Below this, two flying Nikai flanked by trophies and arms hold up the Chi Rho in a wreath. In the third register stand the two emperors in military dress, each holding a Nike on a globe; between them kneel two bound barbarians; on the right are four *chlamydati* and soldiers, and on the right, five *chlamydati*, a *togatus* and soldiers. Below, female personifications of the provinces or cities of the empire wearing mural crowns are led towards the centre by two Nikai, to offer their homage to the emperors; in the centre kneels a woman.[231] The cities formulated as women, as personifications, as Menander had suggested, are coming to meet the emperors who, in the register above, arrive triumphant.

We have come a long way, in these reliefs, from the Tetrarchic images of *adventus* with which we began. This Tetrarchic imagery, both in art and in panegyric, of empire-wide movement, no longer fit the circumstances of the early fifth century, when emperors lived in capitals and delegated military operations to generals. Nor was civilian government by now the face-to-face operation, the direct encounter between ruler and ruled, which the Tetrarchic panegyrists and Julian's advocates had envisaged and praised. There had occurred a deep and long-term change in perspectives of portraying the emperor. Synesius, who took a hostile view of this phenomenon, described it very accurately: the emperor no longer campaigned at the head of his troops, no longer met his subjects directly, no longer legislated from personal knowledge and experience. Instead the emperor remained in his palace, adorned in jewelled robes, "keeping your lairs like lizards, scarcely peeping out at all to enjoy the

sun's warmth, lest being men you should be detected as such by men." [232]
This is the critical counterpart to Claudian's description of the splendour of Honorius' consular processions.

If one seeks to define the change that took place in terms of visual art, it may serve to look back to the Arch of Constantine. Here the imperial procession of a particular *adventus* is shown in a precise location; similarly, the *largitio* and *adlocutio* panels are placed in clearly recognisable Roman localities (plates 14–15). On the column base, on the other hand, precise locality is not depicted at all, while neither the obelisk base nor the column base refers to imperial deeds in as particularised a fashion as does the arch of Constantine. Imperial deeds are represented on the arch as going from the specific to the universal. The *adventus* of the emperor ties in with the rising of Sol.

On the column base, and to a lesser extent on the obelisk base, on the other hand, the representation begins with the universal, the non-specific and the non-historical, and stops there. The viewer is accordingly left outside the image, and is not, as in earlier imperial art, drawn to participate in it by the gestures and glances of the figures. Instead, the viewer of the column base and the obelisk base is invited to comprehend the image by the familiar symbolism of triumph, consulship and the offering of gifts to the emperor, which all point to imperial qualities, especially victory. He is also invited to comprehend the image by its layout, by the symmetry and frontality of the main figures and the composition in registers, the latter serving to convey the content of the images in a hierarchy descending from God via the emperor to the emperor's subjects. [233]

These images, although anchored in an actual occurrence—the consulship of Arcadius and Honorius in 402—are nonetheless non-historical, for they do not record this event *per se* so much as a schematisation of it. Arcadius and Honorius did not meet either as consuls or as emperors, and the representation of them together is therefore to be viewed as conveying a certain theory of empire, that is, a theory of imperial unity, but this at a time when unity was factually and politically ineffective. [234]

Thus, the imperial presence, that of Honorius in Constantinople, was not in this instance historically or geographically conditioned. [235] The representations of the column base take the viewer away from what actually happened so as to show a certain type of event. This type of event was rooted in the *adventus* ceremonial of the fourth century, in that the reliefs show the outcome or culmination of *adventus*, the second stage of this ceremony. Each of the three encounters that are depicted—with the senators of Rome and Constantinople, with the provinces, and with the subject nations—has its analogies in depictions of earlier imperial arrivals. But whereas these latter concerned actual events, the events depicted on the column base were not as strictly founded on fact. Instead, the representations of the column base took one ingredient of the earlier imperial *adventus* ceremonial, the second stage of *adventus*, and transformed it into a *tableau* of imperial presence.

The earlier symbolism of *adventus* was founded on imperial deeds, the deeds of peace and war, as the classification of Menander and others expressed it, whereas the column base alludes to no deeds and instead expounds qualities. The keynote of each set of reliefs is given in a symbol of Christian victory, which served to define and introduce the victory of the emperor, for victory is the *leitmotif* of all these compositions. These Constantinopolitan representations did not demand of the viewer that he attribute to them a specific time and place. Iuppiter's prophecy in the *Aeneid*,

> *his ego nec metas rerum nec tempora pono*
> *imperium sine fine dedi*

had found concrete if paradoxical expression in late Roman imperial ceremonial and art, in the emperor's eternal presence.[236]

PART · II

DISRUPTION AND RESTATEMENT OF *ADVENTUS*

5. SECULAR AND CHRISTIAN ARRIVALS

The effectiveness of imperial arrival as a means of explaining the empire and the activity of the emperor depended very largely on a rhetorical tradition; that is to say, on a distinct method of perception.[237] The instructions given in rhetorical textbooks were applied in panegyrics, and the message of panegyrics treating *adventus* was regularly reflected in imperial art. Rhetorical theory about *adventus*, its application in panegyric, and the expression of *adventus* in art were thus coordinated phenomena. These phenomena all depended on the actual performance of the ceremony in question. The performance of the ceremony of *adventus* and its subsequent expression in art and literature required a certain degree of political stability and order in the empire, and in particular, a carefully organised regional and local bureaucracy which, in coordination with the central bureaucracy, could organise the various *adventus* ceremonies as they were performed, for instance, for the Tetrarchy and Julian.

Such stability and order had broken down by the time Sidonius wrote his three panegyrics. All three were produced for occasions on which the theme of *adventus* had been very prominent: the consular arrival and accession of Avitus in Rome in 456, the arrival of Majorian in Lyon in 459, and the consulship and accession of Anthemius in 468.[238]

The panegyric of Majorian, functionally, is a counterpart to the panegyric of Constantine of 311, in which the orator thanks the emperor for his tax remissions. In this context he describes Constantine's visit to Autun of the preceding year, with the resulting benefits to the city, as the *adventus* of a saviour. This *adventus* had been preceded by the request of another orator for Constantine to visit Autun.[239] We see here at work a very delicate mechanism for preparing imperial arrival: the preliminary agreements between the two parties to the ceremony. Something similar took place before Sidonius held his panegyric on Majorian, who was the successor to Sidonius' relative Avitus. This in itself created a difficult situation, rendered more difficult by the fact that the people of Lyon—a city which had only recently been recaptured from the Visigoths—wished to rid themselves of their imperial garrison, and obtain a remission of taxation.

In this situation, Petrus, Majorian's *magister epistolarum* and a friend of Sidonius, acted as go-between by arranging the imperial arrival and the delivery of the panegyric.[240] The text of the panegyric contains the request for help,[241] preceded by a brief encomium of Petrus,[242] the crucial mediator. The situation had all the ingredients for the description of an imperial *adventus*, for Majorian did enter the city. It is therefore significant that Sidonius did not describe an *adventus*; more so when one sees, from the content of the panegyric, how little he knew about Majorian at the time of writing it.[243] *Adventus* would have been an ideal means of concealing gaps in knowledge.

What occurred was a change in perception of the nature of imperial dominion, and in this perception *adventus* no longer played the crucial role that it had played, for instance, in the panegyrics of Sidonius' model, Claudian. Sidonius still saw the emperor as a saviour, *spes unica rebus*,[244] but his coming is referred to in the single word *venisti*.[245] Avitus' accession was followed by a journey from Gaul to Rome, and was officially ratified by his taking up the consulship of the following year. Anthemius' succession was preceded by a journey from Constantinople to Rome and followed by his first consulship. Fifty years earlier such events had been among the fundamental themes of *adventus*, but they were this no longer for Sidonius. Instead, his panegyrics took the form of an epic and mythological narrative in which *adventus* was not mentioned, let alone expounded.

The panegyric of Ennodius on Theodoric shows that Sidonius' omission of the theme of *adventus* was not a mere personal idiosyncrasy; it reflects the breakdown of a tradition.[246] For, the analytical methods of the rhetors, the organisation, that is, of a panegyric around a selection of specific themes, had enabled them to compress their message by focusing on a single great occasion, such as an *adventus*. The rhetors had sought to highlight certain aspects of imperial deeds and virtues, rather than render them in continuous narrative.[247] However, Ennodius used the analytical method to a very limited degree only, so that overall his panegyric is a narrative, rather than an analysis concentrating on episodes such as *adventus*.

Accordingly, when describing Theodoric's war against Odovacer and advent in Italy, Ennodius omitted the theme of *adventus*, even though Theodoric was formally received in Ravenna,[248] whereas Pacatus, for instance, had formulated Theodosius' war against Maximus analytically rather than as a straight narrative, by using the terminology of *adventus* and triumph. Behind Pacatus's treatment of this theme stood the precedents of the Constantinian and ultimately the Tetrarchic panegyrics.

The relationships and the theories of government which could be brought together in the theme of *adventus*—the integration with each other of ruler and subjects, civilians and soldiers—find expression elsewhere in Ennodius' panegyric: he comments on the successful coexistence of Italians and Goths, on Theodoric's humaneness and accessibility, on his dignified appearance, and on the admiration felt for him by his subjects. However, these topics, once assembled together in the ceremony of *adventus* and in its portrayal in literature and art, are scattered and diffused throughout Ennodius' panegyric and have therefore lost the collective impact they formerly had. The ceremony survived, but the associations surrounding it had either fallen silent or found expression through other means.[249]

The shift in emphasis and in the meaning of imperial *adventus* was accompanied chronologically by the development of Christian visualisations of the different types of arrivals of Christ and of arrivals of bishops and of relics. In the late fourth century Egeria described the liturgical reenactment of Christ's entry into Jerusalem which took place in that city on Palm Sunday[250]—an urban ceremony in which all the faithful, young and old, were expected to take part. Whether the bishop, who in this celebration played the part of Christ, rode on a donkey, as Christ had done, remains uncertain, but it is possible, since Athanasius, on his return from exile rode into Alexandria on a donkey, and his eulogist Gregory Nazianzen drew a deliberate parallel between him and Christ.[251] As emerges from Gregory's account, this welcome of Athanasius was an urban ceremony on an imperial scale, an *adventus*, for which the patterns of conduct by all participants had been laid down in imperial ceremonial. But the ceremonial was now enacted within a Christian, ecclesiastical context.

If relics were to be received, this also was done in the framework of imperial *adventus*. One such occasion, particularly magnificent because Arcadius and the empress Eudocia took part in it, was the translation of the relics of St. Thomas to that saint's martyrium outside Constantinople. Two sermons of Chrysostom describe the translation and deposition—reflecting the two stages of *adventus*—of these relics.[252] This translation was merely one of many similar occasions, one of which, the reception of the relics of St. Stephen in the Great Palace, is represented on the Trier ivory.[253] In the West also, the translation and advent of relics were formulated in the ceremonial of imperial *adventus*, and the saint would become the protector of his city,[254] as once the emperor had been.

Within such a context, an iconography of Christ's entry into Jerusalem was developed on Christian sarcophagi.[255] An early version, showing Christ mounted on the donkey with its foal trotting alongside and a child spreading a cloak in Christ's path, appears on a sarcophagus from S. Agnese of the early fourth century.[256] Somewhat later, the donkey gradually acquired the look of a horse and Christ, instead of holding a scroll, held the reins of his mount, his attitude and manner of entry becoming thereby more imperial. The closest approximation in art of the entry into Jerusalem to imperial *adventus* appears on the cover to the Etschmiadzin Gospels, in which Christ is welcomed by the personification of Jerusalem wearing, like the cities and provinces in imperial art, a mural crown.[257] Christ's entry into Jerusalem is a New Testament theme, but the manner of communicating this theme became imperial in the fourth century, when it was depicted in visual art in the iconography of imperial arrivals.

We have seen that in an imperial context, a particular historical *adventus* could be related to and could become a universal imperial presence, could be made to reach beyond the facts of history. In similar fashion, in Christianity Christ's historical entry into Jerusalem was described by the same technical term ἀπάντησις as was his second coming.[258] In visual art, these two arrivals, the historical and the eschatological, are conjoined on the sarcophagus of Junius Bassus, dated by its inscription in the year 359 A.D.[259] (See plate 25.) The sarcophagus has two registers of five scenes each. The central scene of the lower register shows Christ entering Jerusalem mounted on a horse-like donkey, being welcomed by a boy spreading a cloak before him. The central scene of the top register shows Christ enthroned above the personification of the sky—exactly like Diocletian on the arch of Galerius (plate 10; see also 41–42)—between Peter and Paul. The juxtaposition of these two scenes, one above the other, and the central place they both occupy in the iconographical scheme of the sarcophagus as a whole indicate that the content of each was clearly understood to be related to the other, and both scenes are rendered in iconographies familiar from imperial art.[260]

The sarcophagus of Junius Bassus demonstrates that by the mid-fourth century Christianity had become capable of absorbing a fundamental theme of imperial propaganda, of public relations, within its own orbit. It was not merely a matter of looking at Christian images, but, as the liturgy of Jerusalem described by Egeria and the entry of Athanasius into Alexandria indicate, it was a matter of performing an urban ceremonial in which heretofore only the emperor had been capable of filling the central role.

The absorption by Christianity of the network of ideas and relationships crystallised in the *adventus* ceremonial went even further, for it was now Christ at his birth who could be greeted as the rising sun, or He who Rises,[261] so that the imagery which, on the Arch of Constantine, was applied to the emperor could, after the fourth century, be applied to Christ. In art, however, the nativity of Christ was rendered not in the imagery of the rising sun; rather, in accordance with the New Testament, Christ was shown as a child with his mother, but not without an important addition from Roman imperial art. The three wise men bringing their offerings were rendered in the iconography which, in Roman imperial art, was used to portray Persians or Persian ambassadors making their submissions to the emperors.[262] Claudian referred to such an episode in the context of the arrival of Theodosius and Honorius in Rome in 389, and the submission of Persians is represented on the obelisk base of Theodosius (plate 17). On Christian sarcophagi the Magi offering gifts are a frequent theme,[263] which in the West was canonised in a very imperial rendering on the wall of S. Apollinare Nuovo.[264]

The themes of imperial *adventus* were redistributed, placed into different settings in the renderings of the different arrivals of Christ, and old thoughts were reformulated in new contexts. Christianity did not merely utilise the imperial idiom of *adventus*; it penetrated and reshaped it. As a result, in the West, the two worlds, the Christian and the imperial, drew apart. An entire study could be devoted to the elements of continuity between the *adventus* of the invisible 'presence' of the saint in the works of Gregory of Tours and that of the palpable *praesens deus* of the pagan Tetrarchs. In a sense, the ceremony sank back, in the West, into the bedrock of religious associations on which it had rested since archaic Greek times.

But when we look at the functions of the ceremony, the *adventus* of a saint to his shrine or of a bishop to his city in Merovingian Gaul was still perceived as a high moment in which it was possible to precipitate that ever-elusive elixir of Late Roman politics, the *consensus universorum*.

6. THE OLD AND THE NEW IN EARLY BYZANTIUM

i. The Arrival of the Imperial Images: Anthemius and Anastasius

Continuity was also expressed in another aspect of *adventus*: the arrival of the imperial images. The imperial images, exactly like the emperor in person, were met formally, were acclaimed and were then displayed in public places. What made possible the application of the same set of ceremonial actions to both the emperor and his image was the classical and late antique theory of the connection between an image and its prototype,[265] a theory which in the Roman Empire was also expressed in long-standing political practice as a means of confirming and securing the allegiance of the civilian and military subjects of the emperor.[266]

The imperial images had always been received with a degree of formality, but it was only with the Tetrarchy that a set ceremonial became obligatory and officially recognised.[267] An instance of the enactment of this ceremonial is the proclamation of Maximus in Alexandria in 386 A.D.:

> The emperor Theodosius conceded that Maximus should be emperor and should be shown together with himself in the [imperial] images, and he made Maximus worthy of being acclaimed emperor. . . . To this effect, Theodosius also sent Cynegius, the quaestor of the palace, to Egypt with orders to cause everyone to forswear the worship of the gods, and to put locks on the temples. The Alexandrians were to receive the image of Maximus, and to erect it in public, and Cynegius was to proclaim to the people that Maximus had become co-emperor.[268]

According to Zosimus, the issue here was not merely the erection of the images of a co-emperor, but the replacement of pagan cult by these images. Thus there is an underlying notion that in some way the imperial images partook of the nature of the sacred.[269] This idea was also articulated by a Coptic preacher, who used the imperial image as an object lesson for a proper comprehension of the image of the *Theotokos*, its power and sanctity. An image of this kind could be regarded as standing for the presence of the person represented:

> If the image of the emperor of this world when painted is set up in the midst of the market-place, becoming a protection to the whole city, and if violence is committed against anyone, and he goes and takes hold of the image of the emperor, then no man will be able to oppose him, even though the emperor is naught but a mortal man; and he is

taken to a court of law. Let us therefore, my beloved, honour the *eikon*
of Our Lady, the veritable queen.[270]

It has been seen how in the West the classical tradition of compre-
hending and interpreting imperial arrivals disintegrated. In the East circumstances also changed. The great military arrivals and the arrivals
to mark accession which were so prominent in the fourth century no
longer took place once the emperor was resident in Constantinople and
rarely led campaigns in person. In effect, for a time the arrival of the
imperial images in the East supplanted the arrival of the emperor, and
the *Book of Ceremonies*[271] records the protocol of the arrival of the images
of Anthemius in Constantinople, of the same emperor whose *adventus*
in the West Sidonius omitted to comment upon. The protocol of the arrival of the images of Anthemius in Constantinople is set into the framework of instructions for receiving ambassadors from the Western Empire, where great care is taken that the officials of the West should be
honoured in the same way as their counterparts in the East.

In 467, the Roman legate Heliocrates, who was conveying the images
of Anthemius and his letters, was admitted to the presence of the senior
emperor, Leo. The silentiaries received the image and Diaferentius,
praefectus urbi in Constantinople, followed by Dioscorius, ex-prefect of
Constantinople, pronounced panegyrics on both emperors. This ceremonial was not unlike the arrival of an emperor, which was also followed by a panegyric: on the occasion of receiving Anthemius' images
the panegyric for both emperors ratified the fact that Anthemius was
the legitimate emperor. The panegyric validated the reception of the image, just as it validated the *adventus* of the emperor in person. Next Leo
ordered that the joint images of himself and Anthemius should be sent
out and received with joy throughout the empire, the images expressing the unity of the Eastern and Western empires. A joyful reception—
which, after a preliminary reception in the consistorium, was regarded
as being spontaneous and obligatory at the same time—thus figured in
the reception of the imperial images as much as of the emperor himself.

The Book of Ceremonies gives a courtly, official perspective on the reception of imperial images. How such a reception was conceived of
from the point of view of a city of the empire when the imperial image
was received is made clear by Procopius of Gaza[272] in a panegyric pronounced when an image, most probably a statue, of Anastasius was
erected in his home town. The occasion for setting up the image cannot
have been Anastasius' accession. Although it is not clearly specified, the
image appears to have been erected as a thanksgiving for a benefaction

by the emperor, most probably a remission of taxation, for in the *pro-oemium*, reflecting in accurate detail the precepts of Ps. Dionysius, Procopius says:

> Already, most mighty Emperor, the entire city thinks of you, and rejoices in your trophies, and having learnt by experience what is blessedness, she tries in every way not to seem to fall behind in her offerings [to you], but is unable to compete with a recompense for your achievements. And she admires her benefactor all the more for his benefactions, since his deeds excel her attempts at recompense. This adornment indeed is fitting for the emperor, to conquer, first his enemies, then his subjects, the former by force of arms and the latter by the multitude of his benefactions, and both by his virtues. Our city, having received her benefactor himself by [receiving] his image, like some eager lover, is raised up by the sight and arouses her citizens both young and old; the father points out [the emperor] to his son, the old man to the young, and they rejoice together at the sight. As for myself, perhaps it seems that I have come to such a state of pride over the other [citizens] and am so confident that I stand up even in the middle of the theatre and dare to speak and will not stop even if someone objects. However, this is not so; rather the whole city is moved to make some just recompense for the benefits she has received—yet since she realises that there is not time for each man to speak for himself, the community, by the agreement of all, is content with the voice of the rhetor. For he is chosen for his ability to speak on behalf of the city, and with one voice he expresses the thought of all.[273]

In the peroration Procopius returns to the topic of the statue:

> The cities are resplendent, each exalted over the other; they have taken on a splendour common to all when erecting images of you, in return for your benefactions . . . your images are honoured by orations and contests of orations, and with that the Muses honor you. But what shall we now inscribe on those images? What is appropriate? Perhaps this: 'The city to her benefactor, thanks to whom I now raise my head with pride and am a city.' May it come about that . . . the cities because of their good fortune make wreaths, dedicate inscriptions, and sing hymns. May the sons of poets and rhetors, dedicating their words to you, be always eloquent and delight in your trophies.[274]

This is an expression of that same tradition of *adventus* in the framework of which Constantine was welcomed in Autun of 310, and which articulated very clearly and deliberately an urban consciousness and sense of identity. The position of the rhetor, in Procopius' panegyric, is expressed in terms similar to those used by Menander, while the giving of wreaths is a regular feature in the contexts of *adventus*, accession, and imperial anniversaries.

The account in *De Ceremoniis* of the reception of imperial images in Constantinople provides a unique insight into how the court, as distinct from the population of a city, handled a ceremonial of this type. By comparing this account with panegyric narratives of *adventus* and the oration by Procopius of Gaza, it emerges that the principal stages of the ceremony, whether held in a courtly or an urban milieu, coincide. The reception of Anthemius' image at court was preceded by the arrangements for his proclamation to which Sidonius refers, just as the *adventus* of the emperor or his image in a city was preceded by preparations which can be traced in some panegyrics.

As regards the appearance of the image of Anastasius which was erected in Gaza—most probably a statue—the closest approximation in date is perhaps the Barletta statue, portraying a diademed emperor in military dress, holding a globe and long sceptre or standard which is now missing.[275] (Plate 7.) This work came to Italy from the eastern Mediterranean in the thirteenth century. It stands in the tradition of the cuirassed emperor of which there are many earlier examples,[276] as well as countless late antique numismatic parallels. The emperor is depicted as the leader of an army, and therefore as victorious. This at any rate is what is spelt out on the consular diptych of Probus, where the left wing shows Honorius in almost identical attitude and attire, and the standard which he holds in his right hand is inscribed IN NOMINE XPI VINCAS SEMPER (plate 6).

Not all imperial images were as grand in scale as the Barletta statue. Imperial images carried by the army and displayed in court rooms were both smaller and simpler. The latter are depicted in the Rossano gospels: images showing, frontally, the busts of two emperors stand next to the judgement seat of Pilate.[277] Another series of imperial images survives on the consular diptychs, where, suggesting the hierarchy of dominion we also encountered on the column base of Arcadius, in the top register the imperial images in the form of busts on *clipei* are shown above the enthroned consul.[278] Accordingly the recipients of the diptych with the image of the consul also received the image of the emperor. This may be regarded as an *adventus* of images in an individualised, rather than in a communal, urban milieu.

For the consular diptychs document a set of personal relationships which differed from the public relationships embodied in the sending out and erection of imperial images in the cities of the empire. In the latter relationship, as in an imperial *adventus*, the emperor was officially and formally incorporated into a communality, into the population of a city. The gift of a consular diptych was no less an official action—the kind of gifts that could be given when persons entered on magistracies was a topic for legislation[279]—but it was an official action taking place between two individuals within the official hierarchy. If the emperor was shown on a diptych, the relationship between him and the consul in question was also an individualised, personal one. From the ceremonial point of view, the consul would be one of those to whom, during an *adventus* ceremony, rank accorded direct access to the emperor.[280]

Among the surviving official diptychs of the empire, the diptych showing Honorius and the Barberini diptych[281] (plate 22) are something of an exception, in that the emperor himself is represented as the main theme of the image, moreover not as consul. Both are imperial images, but not of the kind that were sent out to the cities of the empire. Insofar as they represent the emperor in his imperial function, however, they are of an official nature. The Barberini diptych probably represents the emperor Anastasius.[282]

Iconographically, it is related to the column base of Arcadius (plates 19–21), for like the column base it represents a hierarchy, Christ in heaven, the emperor on earth, and subject nations, by means of a division into registers: the emperor, wearing diadem and armour, is mounted, leaning on his spear, and is shown in a complicated three-quarter frontality; from the right Victoria, with one foot on a globe, holds out a wreath to him; Tellus, seated, supports his foot and a bearded barbarian in Iranian dress holds his spear from behind while raising his left hand towards the emperor.

This image contains the ingredients of the traditional imagery of *adventus* still used on the coinage of the fourth century, where Tellus beneath the mounted emperor can be traced.[283] However, although the main ingredients of the image are familiar from the iconography of *adventus*, the message conveyed is not that of a ceremony of movement or advance, for any movement is arrested by the backward turn of the horse and by the frontality of the emperor, while, on the left, the consul of the year, in a stationary pose, holds a figure of Victoria towards the emperor. What is shown, once more, is not so much an imperial coming as an imperial presence, a state of tranquillity.

In the top register appears Christ, on a *clipeus*, with the sun, the moon, and a star, holding a cross-sceptre and making the gesture of power;[284] the *clipeus* is supported on clouds and held by two angels. This also is an image of tranquillity, a stationary frontal image, even though it carries an allusion to Christ's second coming on the clouds of heaven, and is juxtaposed to the coming of the emperor on earth, by an association of ideas which is analogous to the juxtaposition of Christ's second coming and the entry into Jerusalem on the sarcophagus of Junius Bassus (plate 25). In this context, as on the column base of Arcadius, the emperor's *adventus*, or rather, presence, is clearly expressed as a terrestrial one occurring in the visible universe, within the context of terrestrial space and time. This is so even though space and time are not identified in the image as they had been, for instance, on the arches of Galerius and Constantine.

On earth, the presence of the emperor through his images and through the activity of ruling was universal, but this was only on earth. Imperial arrival and presence could no longer be described as they had been during the Tetrarchy, as events of cosmic scope, as an interpenetration, defined according to the nature of imperial rule, of the natural and supernatural orders. On the Barberini diptych Christ and the emperor are separated by their positions in the image as a whole, as well as by their activity, and by those same means are defined the position and dignity of the emperor on earth. But both Christ and the emperor are figures of majesty, and what they have in common is their motionless tranquillity.[285]

The only figures shown on the Barberini diptych as busy, moving, occupied are the subject nations in the bottom register. They are beckoned forward by Victoria, and are weighed down with offerings, displayed not in frontality, like Christ and the emperor, but in profile. These subject nations—Indian and Persian—illustrate, in generalised terms, the effect of imperial victory. Procopius of Gaza in his prologue and epilogue also refers to it in terms of the emperor's trophies, in which the cities rejoice; later some particulars of imperial victory are given in the main part of the panegyric.

There is an intimate connection between the arrival and presence of the emperor in person (as depicted on the representations of *adventus* discussed earlier and as alluded to on the Barberini diptych) on the one hand, and the arrival and presence of the imperial image as described by Procopius of Gaza on the other. The technical term ἀπαντᾶν is used for the welcome of both the emperor and his image.[286] Also, whether it is the image that arrives, or the emperor in person, a face-to-face encounter between ruler and subject takes place. This encounter was articulated by Procopius of Gaza when he applied to the beholding of the image the sentiment generally applied to the beholding of the emperor himself: "The father points out the emperor to his son, the young to the old." Mamertinus had said about Diocletian and Maximian in Milan: "All shouted with joy and without any fear of you openly pointed at you with their hands";[287] and about Constantine the panegyrist of 313 said:

"Blessed were they who saw you close at hand, and those at a distance called your name." [288]

The Latin panegyrists, in describing imperial *adventus*, had described the creation of a relationship between the emperor and a body of citizens. Procopius of Gaza articulated a similar relationship, but did so by reference to an imperial image.

ii. The Triumph of Justinian

The process of replacing the arrival of the emperor in person by that of his image was accentuated by the fact that the Eastern emperors of the fifth century rarely left Constantinople. This was a trend which continued in the sixth century: Justinian did not travel in the empire and himself fought no campaigns.[289] Nonetheless, under him the theory and iconography of arrival and triumph found important applications, which are reported by Procopius.

In the *Aedificia*, a work which is a form of panegyric, Procopius described the ceiling mosaic of the Chalke, the vestibule to the imperial palace in Constantinople,[290] which was completed after 540. The mosaic depicted an imperial triumph. An essential presupposition for understanding the image which Procopius described is that Justinian, like Constantius II, was supplanted in actual warfare by his generals, but in the act of triumph, the generals were supplanted by the emperor. Victory belonged to the emperor, and therefore Belisarius could celebrate his victorious return from the Vandal war only as the emperor's delegate and subordinate.

Constantius II was still close enough to the military emperors of the earlier fourth century to enter Rome as a general, and he did actually arrive in Rome from elsewhere. Not so Justinian and his consort Theodora; they did not, in the mosaic Procopius describes, appear as military personages, but merely arrived, or rather appeared, in the hippodrome. As a result, what could be depicted was not the former movement of *adventus*, but something still and stationary, in harmony with imperial tranquillity, or, in other words, the second stage of *adventus*, the theme of which is the imperial presence in a city. This is an urban theme, where the emperor related to his subjects in a non-military, civilian capacity. Were this presence and triumph not civilian, the people of Constantinople could not have participated so directly in it. The participation in imperial acts by the populace of the city in which the emperor resided, be it the earlier provincial capitals, Rome, or now, Constantinople, was one of the fundamental strands of public life in late antiquity, highlighted as it was in *adventus*.

However, the nature of popular participation in imperial acts changed in early Byzantium, and this is very clear in Procopius' description of the Chalke mosaic and in what he says of the triumph of Belisarius. The people are present at spectacles which are set before their eyes, but they do not in any way determine and influence these spectacles, as the people of Rome, for instance, had, according to Claudian, influenced the arrivals of Honorius. In visual terms, this may have meant that the people were represented as a closed, undifferentiated mass as depicted already on the city scenes of the arch of Constantine; not as a group, as they could still be depicted on the arch of Galerius.[291] The Chalke mosaic, according to Procopius, looked as follows:

> On either side, there is war and battle, and many cities are being captured in Italy and Libya. And the emperor Justinian is victorious through Belisarius his general, and the general returns to the emperor with his entire army unharmed and gives him spoils, kings and kingdoms, and all things which are most esteemed among men. In the centre stand the emperor and the empress Theodora, both seeming to rejoice, and they celebrate the festival of victory over the kings of the Vandals and Goths who come into their presence as prisoners and to be led into bondage. Around them stand the senators, all rejoicing. This is indicated by the *tesserae*, which show a glad bloom on their faces. Thus they rejoice and smile at the emperor while bestowing on him god-like honours for the magnitude of his achievements.[292]

This was an image of motionless imperial majesty: Justinian and Theodora stood still in the centre, while around them, perhaps in two bands in the dome of the Chalke, were grouped the Senate and Belisarius with his army, an iconographical scheme which is also found in the two baptisteries in Ravenna and in the Rotunda at Salonika.[293] It was only at some distance from the imperial pair, "on either side," that the uproar and chaos of war and battle could be represented, a principle which is also observed on the Barberini diptych. Thus nothing disturbed the imperial serenity and the celebration of victory in Constantinople.

The representation, as described by Procopius, had a high degree of realism, in that it incorporated historical personages and even portrayed their mood, the gladness which was regularly commented on in descriptions of *adventus* and triumph.[294] Nonetheless, the image ignored fact, for no joint triumph over Vandals and Ostrogoths was ever celebrated. Like the column base of Arcadius, the mosaic depicted, not an historical fact, but a fundamental universal truth about the empire: triumph and victory expressing an imperial characteristic which existed regardless of the outcome of particular wars. The mosaic in the Chalke illustrated how and what imperial art under Justinian selected and adapted from available facts, for Procopius also described the triumph over the Vandals and the arrival of Belisarius with Vitigis in Constantinople.[295]

Here, in a work of history, the position of Procopius the narrator is different from his position in the *Aedificia*. In the latter he describes a picture much in the way that earlier panegyrists had described imperial arrivals in terms of what one saw, and in terms of emotion expressed by the imperial subjects, in terms also of the integration of groups in society with their ruler. Possibly the gesture made by the senators to convey to Justinian the ἰσοθέους τιμάς was the offering of wreaths as depicted on the column base of Arcadius.[296] However that may be, the centralised manner of composition of the mosaic, as Procopius describes it, points very clearly to the theme of integrating the people of Constantinople into imperial victory and of allowing them to participate in it.

This participation becomes apparent also in Procopius' historical accounts of triumph, but here Procopius' role is not merely descriptive and evocatory, but also analytical and critical. He adds to his narrative of the Vandal triumph aspects which set it outside the field of panegyric, even though the ceremony as described is related to what could be said of it in panegyric,[297] and, equally importantly in this context, to what was to be seen by the populace of Constantinople, whether in an image, as in the Chalke, or in a ceremonial enacted before their eyes.

The actual event, however, was different from what was represented in the Chalke. Belisarius was not permitted to celebrate a Gothic triumph. As for the Vandal triumph, Procopius begins his account of it with an historical *mise-en-scène*, emphasising that for the first time in six centuries someone other than the emperor had triumphed. But situations had changed:[298]

> [Belisarius did not triumph] in the ancient manner, but on foot walked from his house to the hippodrome and then from the barriers to the place where the imperial throne is. And there was the booty. . . . And there were slaves in the triumph, including Gelimer himself, his shoulders covered with some purple cloth, and all his kin. . . . When Gelimer entered the hippodrome and saw the emperor seated on a high seat and the people standing on either side, and when he realised as he looked around into what evil he had fallen, he did not weep or cry out, but never stopped repeating the words of the Hebrew scriptures: 'Vanity of vanities, all is vanity.' And when he reached the imperial seat his

purple garment was taken away and he was constrained to fall down
and prostrate himself before the emperor Justinian and Belisarius also
did this, for he was like Gelimer, a suppliant of the emperor.

Belisarius makes a triumphal entry into the Hippodrome of Constantinople, which has replaced the Capitol and Forum of Rome, the
former settings of triumph and arrival. But the triumphal nature of this
entry is qualified by Belisarius' *proskynesis*, which removes the distinction between the subjects of the emperor and his enemies, once drawn
so carefully in imperial art and panegyric.

Procopius' descriptions of triumph in the hippodrome can be related
to the submission scene on the obelisk base of Theodosius and to the
column base of Arcadius where the emperors receive the offerings of
their subjects and their enemies. In early Byzantium, imperial art and
panegyric once again moved in a continuum, providing a stable means
of expressing contemporary events.[299] Writers and artists, whose perceptions were trained to interpret the relationship between emperor
and subjects, still communicated their message within the literary and
artistic genres which their own time made available to them. But when
we look back to the late third and fourth centuries, we see that there
were deep changes in the expression of imperial arrival and imperial
presence. Of these the most fundamental was perhaps that imperial action and imperial personality—or, as a late antique person would have
said, imperial virtues—were translated into ceremonial and were universalised in it. On the one hand, ceremonial interposed between emperor and subjects, kept them distinct and separate. This was made
clear in different ways in the Chalke mosaic and in the triumph of Belisarius. On the other hand, ceremonial provided a crucial means of
communication.[300]

Thus, roughly eight years after the upheaval of the Nika riot, it was
again possible in the Chalke mosaic to convey triumph in an idiom
which was related to earlier imperial art, without at the same time losing
the contemporary impact of the scene being represented. For, unlike
earlier imperial 'scenes,' this one needed no specific time; it was not part
of history. Instead, the Chalke mosaic epitomised from the celebrations
that did take place a general statement which could be applied to the
emperor at any time. Thus, art absorbed the timelessness of a stable,
continuous ceremonial, a ceremonial where meanings no longer shifted
between divergent, even mutually exclusive, interpretations.

On the side of continuity, however, the imperial art and architecture
of Constantinople recaptured an important aspect of Roman imperial
art and architecture: it defined and reinforced the ceremonial topogra-

phy of the capital.[301] In imperial Rome, Capitol and Forum had been focal points of the imperial presence in the city; for sixth-century Constantinople, these focal points were S. Sophia and the hippodrome. In the hippodrome, the spectators, as Gelimer noted, participated in the imperial triumph by their presence, by being able to watch this spectacle, and also by their acclamations. The hippodrome was an image, according to Corippus, of the cosmos,[302] in which the colours of the four factions represented the seasons. It was therefore a fitting scene for an empire-wide triumph in which the spoils of the world, of Jerusalem and Rome,[303] were assembled.

However, the hippodrome was not merely a loose image for the cosmos, but a very urban, very Constantinopolitan meeting place, a new focus for imperial ceremonial which, in this setting, became a Constantinopolitan ceremonial. In Themistius, the role of Constantinople as a capital was still expressed in terms of classical personifications of cities, and was also to a certain extent still speculative. But already on the obelisk base and the column base of Arcadius, the emperor is shown as being resident in Constantinople, for several generations of emperors had by then lived there. Thus the Justinianic expressions of triumph could take this residence of the emperor in his capital as given and build on it.

Indicative of this development is Procopius' view of the meaning conveyed by Justinian's equestrian statue in the Augustaeum.[304] The horse seems to advance, while the emperor in the ancient imagery looks like:

> . . . that autumn-star. He directs his glance towards the rising sun, taking, I think, his course against the Persians. In his left hand he holds a globe, by which the sculptor indicates that all land and sea serve him, but he has neither sword nor spear or any other weapon, but on his globe there is a cross, by which alone he has acquired the empire and victory in war. And extending his right hand to the rising sun and spreading out his fingers he orders the barbarians in that direction to remain at home and to advance no further.[305]

In Procopius' view, this is an imperial *profectio*, conveyed by the forward urge of the horse, yet the emperor does not leave his capital, but by his presence in Constantinople, physically and in his portrait, he defends his empire. An old iconography, that of the mounted triumphant emperor, riding, usually, over a fallen enemy,[306] had been used in a new context, where movement had become localised in one place, in Constantinople.

Similarly, the old iconography of *adventus*, of the mounted emperor led by Victoria, who in this case holds a trophy, was used again, after a long interval, on Justinian's gold medallion, probably of 534, the year of the Vandal triumph:[307] SALUS ET GLORIA ROMANORUM (plate 23). Next to the mounted emperor is a star, that familiar image of *adventus*. No Constantinopolitan setting is shown here, but what the medallion indicates is that the iconography of *adventus* in its fourth-century form could still be relevant. In the context of deep change, it was still possible to see continuity, whether this was in applying an ancient iconography to sixth-century circumstances, or in relating the triumph and advent of Belisarius, transferred as they had been to Justinian and Theodora, in Constantinople, to the ceremonial of imperial Rome.[308]

7. *ADVENTUS* AS ACCESSION

In the late third and early fourth centuries, *adventus* was still basically a ceremony of the ancient world. It was, its precise ritual notwithstanding, a very loose ceremony, for a great multiplicity of meanings, which had their origins in the past of Greece and Rome, could be expressed in it, depending on the demands of the situation. This diversity of interpretation was no longer possible in sixth-century Constantinople, although the ceremony itself survived.[309] So did the idea that on certain occasions a manifestation of the imperial presence was called for. An instance was the triumph of Justinian and Theodora as depicted in the Chalke. Another instance of *adventus* in a new guise, but still recognisable, is Corippus' account of the accession of Justin II in his *Laus Justini*.

This work is theoretically a panegyric, but has many characteristics of epic narrative. The treatment of themes takes place in strict chronological order, and there is no longer the analysis and assessment of imperial deeds or virtues which had formerly provided the panegyrist with his Ariadne's thread. Instead, coherence in Corippus is based on the sequence of events in ceremonial, and it is the ceremonial more than anything Justin II did or was that gives rise to excursus and exegesis.[310] Corippus narrates the imperial accession for which, by 568, a full Constantinopolitan ceremonial had been developed, and he precedes this by an account of an imperial advent in the palace and the showing forth of the emperor in the hippodrome.

In Corippus' account, there are the old ingredients of *adventus*, but they have regrouped themselves within the city of Constantinople. The imperial procession which in the fourth century could still cover hundreds of miles moves within the city walls only, so that, just as it is described in the *Book of Ceremonies*, the emperor arrives not in Constantinople as a whole, but at S. Sophia, at the Holy Apostles, at Blachernae and at numerous other places, in each of which there were certain actions to be performed. In some of these we can still recognise aspects of the *adventus* of the ancient world, even when the evidence comes from as hostile and uncomprehending a witness as Liutprand of Cremona.[311]

Adventus within the city, then, is Corippus' theme, and initially, *adventus* at the palace:

> Justin went to the palace, dutifully accompanied by the Senate. His beloved consort followed on, although not escorted by the usual applause, for it was in the middle of the night that they passed through the safely-kept city. . . . When the revered emperor reached the threshold of the imperial palace, the crowing of cocks proclaimed the glad day and gave the alarm for his enthusiastic welcome. The excubitors who guard the sacred palace were the first to wish Justin and Sophia, as they entered, an auspicious reign.[312]

The public *adventus* of the emperor—although all takes place within the walls of Constantinople—occurs in the morning, when a Virgilian Fama[313] spreads the news of Justin's accession through the city:

> A huge voice arose and joy burst forth, a noise from the earth beneath rose up into the air, and everywhere the citizens were pleased to act in gentle concord. Fama on chattering wings gladly flew through the imperial city and aroused the people heavy with sleep, drove them forth, and urged them from their houses. Joyfully she heaped words upon words when announcing [the event].[314]
> 'Arise, arise!' she shouts, and reproves delay. . . . The people make haste, leave their houses empty, they run rejoicing through all the streets, and rumours mixed with fear, since they are not yet confirmed, rush about, as one citizen makes enquiries of all the others whom he meets.[315]

The concourse of people in the streets of Constantinople and their excitement are reminiscent of earlier accounts of *adventus*. But in these earlier accounts, the crowd had directly encountered the emperor and his train. Now, by contrast, the emperor meets his people in the hippodrome, which Corippus goes on to describe and expound:

> The Senate of old sanctioned the spectacles of the new circus in honour of the New Year's sun, and they believed that by some ordering of the world there were four horses of the sun, which were symbols of the four seasons in the recurring years. Thus, the senators of old laid down that there should be in the likeness of the seasons as many charioteers, and as many colours, and they created two opposing parties, just as the coldness of winter strives against the fire of summer. [Each colour in the circus matches one of the seasons.][316] The huge circus itself, or the

full circle of the year, is closed within a well-turned elongated round, embracing the two turning points at equal distances and the open expanse of sand which stretches out in the centre.[317]

This ceremony was not observed rightly by our earliest ancestors, for they, in their error, believed that the sun was God. But after the creator of the sun had deigned to be beheld under the sun, and had accepted the form of mankind from a virgin, the games of the sun were abolished; the honour and the games were transferred to the Latin emperors, and the enjoyment of the circus came to the new Rome.[318]

There follows the acclamation of the new emperor:

[To this place] everyone went, boys, young men and old men; the crowd acclaimed [the emperor], all speaking with one voice[319] and one mind. One name is pleasing to all. . . .

The people were brought together from all sides by love of their lord. . . . 'May you conquer, Justin,' they sing, and the huge uproar grows. . . . The sound arouses all. All the elements favour Justin, all rejoice with him. Called together by the clamour the senators come together. Light fills the sacred palace. . . . God has given clear signs and proved that He Himself has placed the noble crown of empire on Justin's head.[320]

This last passage clearly expresses the spontaneous *consensus universorum* going hand in hand with the will of God, which together brought about the accession of the emperor. Ammianus mentions this same combination of factors, *consensus* and divine election, when he tells of Julian's advent in Constantinople. In Corippus there are also some of the other features of *adventus*: the assembly of the multitude, their eagerness to see the emperor, the acclamations. But what is absent in Corippus is the movement, which was so pronounced in earlier arrivals, and as a result no clear distinction can be made between a first and second stage of *adventus*. Moreover, the encounter of emperor and subjects is transferred to the stage-set of the hippodrome, where any personal contact, like that between Constantine and the senators of Autun, the culmination of the *adventus* of 310, is made impossible. Contact has been formalised by its setting, and also by the singing of regular acclamations which were applicable on a wide number of occasions.

Setting and acclamations thus gain a new and precise significance which is alien to the earlier *adventus* ceremonies, except when they took place in Rome, where the surroundings imposed a particular meaning on the ceremony.[321] Accordingly, Corippus interprets the meaning of the hippodrome with a clear sense of discontinuity and continuity between the pagan and the Christian empires, and this interpretation affects the significance of Justin's appearance before the people. Justin appears in a cosmic setting, but whereas on the column base of Arcadius this cosmic setting is only very loosely associated with Constantinople, in Corippus it is precisely localised in the hippodrome of *nova Roma*. Thus Justin's appearance in the hippodrome can be visualised in terms of the representation on Theodosius' obelisk base, with the cosmic dimension added. This cosmic dimension was not restricted to the hippodrome, but came to be extended to other parts of Constantinople.[322]

The empire-wide universal *adventus* of the Tetrarchs, Julian's city-by-city *adventus* at his accession, were transformed into Justin's appearance in the hippodrome—itself the world—of the πόλις βασιλευοῦσα. Justin, as Julian had done at Sirmium, and as Constantine, Constantius II and Honorius had done after their arrivals in Rome, presided at chariot races. Presiding at the races had been one of the culminating points of an imperial *adventus* of movement and an imperial action;[323] as such it fittingly survived among the preliminaries of Justin's accession, preliminaries which derived from the late antique ceremony of *adventus*.

Circumstances changed the meaning of *adventus*, and the change in both circumstances and meaning affected the form of the ceremony, so that gradually the convergence, which had existed under the Tetrarchy and in the fourth century as a whole, between the form of the ceremony and its representation in art and literature, disintegrated. Corippus is an example of this development, for the parts of the ceremonial of the imperial appearance which he describes are no longer linked, as they had been earlier, into a coherent whole. The elements which he mentions— Fama, the concourse of citizens, the emperor in the hippodrome—are all possible aspects of *adventus*, but in Corippus they do not interact as they had done in earlier panegyric, because he provides little exegesis of the ceremonial actions which he describes. There is no interweaving, for instance, of imperial deeds and sacred story as there had been in the Tetrarchic panegyrists and in Eusebius. In Corippus, the ingredients of *adventus* are left to speak for themselves, each in turn, rather than being highlighted or omitted by a panegyrist using ceremonial to communicate a particular view of the emperor and his subjects. Communication of this sort had passed from panegyrist to the ceremonial itself.

Panegyric could therefore become a stage-by-stage narrative of ceremonial, while the ceremonial could be left, if need be, to speak for itself. Thus, George of Pisidia, in his poem on the advent of Heraclius in Constantinople in 610,[324] which also marked that emperor's accession, mentions the ceremonial hardly at all, and the ideas and actions of *adventus* appear in the poem only as a set of distant echoes. George sees and comments upon the effects of imperial arrival: overcoming the enemies

of the empire[325] and tyranny,[326] and saving the state.[327] He also conveys
the effect of the imperial presence, the effect of seeing the emperor:

> He who gave you greatness of heart so that you may do all things with-
> out toil, will show you how to direct affairs out of the storm into the
> peace which you have, so that, freed from all troubles, we may engrave
> in our hearts as in an image, the beauty of your soul: [In our hearts] we
> will document your lasting graciousness, showing forth what a blessed
> flower has been hidden in such a thicket of thorns.[328]

This, however, is a personal, individualised, even poetic statement,
which is very different from the official, stable idiom of imperial *adventus*
and presence in the earlier panegyrics. The emperor does not, here, act
out of an official, public position, but he serves the state as an act of personal kindness—χάρις—and he undertakes the hardships of the journey from Africa as a personal task.[329]

There was no longer any clear framework or pattern such as had been
provided earlier by the regular occurrence of commonly comprehensible *adventus* ceremonies, in which imperial virtues and actions could be
brought to bear on each ceremony and could thus be understood. This
absence of framework affected equally what could be expected of the
emperor as a person, and what could be expected of the empire as an
institution. The two no longer interlocked in the classical and late antique manner; rather, the emperor came upon, impinged upon the empire as the chosen of God:

> My speech is insufficient to express your [being] for the Word of God
> has elected you, and has placed you above the impermanence of
> words.[330]

In George of Pisidia's poem on Heraclius' arrival in Constantinople,
arrival is no longer a means of correlating emperor and subjects so as to
shed light on various aspects of imperial activity. Rather, George of
Pisidia uses Heraclius' arrival to work on one of his chief themes: the
hierarchy of God, emperor and subjects, where the subjects, in themselves, remain inert. In that harsh and ultimate perspective, the delicate
nuances of a continuously shifting, adjustable relationship between emperor and subjects disintegrated.

Looking back, it is possible to see this process at work in Sidonius and
Ennodius in the West, and in the East, under Justinian. In the triumph
of Justinian as viewed by Procopius, the people are integrated into an
imperial event by acting as spectators; they do not directly participate as
the subjects in earlier *adventus* ceremonies had done. The triumph
makes a declaration about the nature of imperial rule under which sub-

jects and barbarians, Belisarius and Gelimer, are ultimately all the same.

Justinian dictated his triumph to his subjects. At no point could they have taken the lead, as had been possible earlier, for at no point would the emperor's conduct change so as to make him approachable and available, as he had been in the second stage of *adventus* in the fourth century. *Civilitas* was no longer an imperial virtue. The acclamations of the people at Justin's accession would not serve to define or redefine their relationship with the emperor; these acclamations were now fixed. Furthermore, the setting of Justin's appearance, the hippodrome, prevented any direct and personal encounter between emperor and subjects, such as had taken place in earlier *adventus* ceremonies.

Nonetheless, as George of Pisidia, in particular, shows, the emperor of early Byzantium did not necessarily have to be depersonalised or made inhuman; there is a new and fine sensitivity in George of Pisidia's interpretation of Heraclius' God-inspired soul and personality. What disappeared, rather, was the classical terminology, still current in late antiquity, of describing personality in terms of a set of philosophically defined virtues and of deeds, which had been the chief instrument of analysis in late antique panegyric.

The imperial portraiture of the later fourth and fifth centuries, especially on the coinage, consisted of a set of variants on an imperial stereotype. There were exceptions, where a personality might be seen within the stereotype. Such is the marble head of Arcadius from Constantinople: large, sensitive, almost tender eyes looking forth from under the heavy diadem and crown of hair (plate 5). The imperial portrait rendered a canon of virtues. To the Arcadius portrait one could attach the imperial titles used in the law codes: *clementia nostra, solicitudo nostra*. In the major portraits of Justinian, on the gold medallion (plate 23) and in San Vitale (plate 63), the imperial stereotype had disappeared, together with the canon of virtues to be rendered in portraiture.

The medallion captures a face, eyes glancing to the right, at a particular moment; it is not a generalised portrait. Similarly, in San Vitale Justinian and Theodora are portrayed as distinct individuals, and the artist's technique is strictly subordinated to what these faces convey as individual faces. These portraits are in visual art precursors to George of Pisidia's view of Heraclius: the emperor is exalted, he is in communion with the divine voῦς, he is set apart from his subjects by a carefully rendered ceremonial. Yet by virtue of the very changes in ceremonial which have been traced, he comes closer to being comprehensible as a human being.

What disappeared in the ceremony of *adventus* were those aspects of it which would express the deeds and virtues of the emperors in a classical and late antique context, the virtues and deeds of an emperor whose personality in one way or another could intermingle with the divine. The majesty of the early Byzantine emperor as expressed in triumph and *adventus* was thus a contradictory quality. While it removed the emperor further from his subjects than would have been possible in any earlier rendering of the ceremony, it also brought him closer toward a humanity, which he shared with his subjects, than any earlier emperor had ever been.

8. THE RETURN OF HERACLIUS AFTER THE PERSIAN WAR AND THE ADVENT OF THE TRUE CROSS IN JERUSALEM

In George of Pisidia's poem on the return of the Cross to Jerusalem,[331] the perspective that may be gained on *adventus* is, once again, diffuse and broken up, for *adventus* is not rendered as a single coherent theme; nor, although the idea of *adventus* recurs throughout the poem, is it the theme by which the poem is held together. The theme which does hold the poem together is, rather, the link which is established between the emperor and the cross, the instrument of the emperor's victory,[332] where Constantine can be evoked.[333] But in fact much more than this is at issue. The Cross was not only the object recovered from the Persians, and the cross found by Helena,[334] but also a concept, the concept of the burning cross,[335] whereby, in a holy war,[336] the fire of the Zoroastrians was destroyed. This concept was not the same as the object of the Cross, which was at the time of the war in Persian keeping, although the recovery of the object could highlight the existence of the concept.

The emperor's personal association with the Cross, together with his association with Christ, is a theme which from the early fifth century was worked out in visual art.[337] In imperial art a particularly telling depiction of this association survives in the cross given by Justin II and Sophia to the Pope,[338] containing a fragment of the true Cross and inscribed:

LIGNO QUO CHRISTUS HUMANUM SUBDIDIT HOSTEM DAT ROMAE IUSTINUS OPEM ET SOCIA DECOREM. (See plate 24.)

On the reverse side the cross has in the centre the Lamb and on either side, Justin and Sophia *orantes*, while on the upper and lower branches are two images of Christ the Pantocrator. This depiction is an extension of the formula used for the imperial images on some consular diptychs, where the imperial pair are shown on either side of Christ.[339] The figure of the Cross on which these images are set was a new ingredient in this traditional formula of the fifth-century Christian empire.

The cross of Justin and Sophia is an example of what happened very frequently in late antiquity; this is that an idea which was subsequently worked out in literature made its first appearance in visual art. The cross of Justin and Sophia not only represents a hierarchy of Christ and emperor; this could be taken for granted by the sixth century.[340] More importantly, it illustrates a unity of purpose between Christ and emperor. The cross, the principle whereby Christ conquered death, was also the principle whereby the emperor ruled the empire and could conquer his enemies. In his poem celebrating the restoration of the True Cross to Jerusalem by Heraclius, George of Pisidia says:

> The cross, thanks to you,[341] was seen by the enemy to be a new Ark, and more than the Ark; for the Ark afflicted the enemy in taking the place of missiles, but the force of the wood [of the cross] sent against the enemy living missiles. Thus it is that the Parthians destroy the Persians with fire and the Scythian destroys the Slav and is in turn destroyed; they bleed from internecine war and have much difficulty in joining together in one single battle. But you yourself keep silence, bearing crown and sceptre, like the umpire surrounded by athletes; you have wrestled against many, but have now concluded the battle. Now the combatants look to you for a sign in the midst of contests whose outcome is uncertain. And when you give the sign, then the combat is successful . . . and you smile at the sight of barbarians who pressed upon you, seeing them now as your subjects.[342]

With this, the poet turns to the cross, as the instrument of Christ's victory:

> Such good news was brought to us at a welcome moment, a moment which itself conveyed victory, when [Christ], who for us made life anew, went forth against the tyrants of death and gave life to the corpse of Lazarus. Indeed, it was fitting that the new revelation of the cross should coincide with the resurrection of the dead.[343]

George of Pisidia now comes to one of the traditional themes of *adventus*, which he uses as a conclusion to the poem, namely the joy with which the people of the capital anticipate the coming of their ruler:

> The whole City gathered together, like sand, like a stream, like boundless waves which rise up in the face of each other. For she was eager, like a deer, thirsty and heated in the chase, to drink at once of the moisture of your words.[344]

This passage refers to the desired advent of Heraclius in Constantinople after his advent in Jerusalem, where he had restored the cross. In that latter advent, the themes of emperor and cross are very tightly knit together, as is stated at the outset of the poem, where George of Pisidia describes the welcome of the emperor and the cross on Golgotha, the welcome defined by the old term ἀπάντη:

> Oh Golgotha, dance; again the entire creation
> Honours you and calls you God-receiving.
> For the emperor coming from Persia
> Shows forth the cross which is raised upon you.
> Acclaim him with words of song.
> But since the stones have no words,
> Prepare new palm branches
> For the welcome of the new bearer of victory.[345]

Later, George of Pisidia describes the welcome given to the cross itself:

> The cross has come, and has been royally welcomed with supplications, prayers, tears and night-watches, with harmonious verses and well-tuned instruments, since it has granted a great triumph to the emperor, that the enemy should desire and yet more fear [to possess it]. For it did not wish to dwell among the barbarians, even though formerly, in order to punish sin, it went as a stranger into a foreign land. But it returned and calls its children from their dwelling of shadow and falsehood, and since it has granted pardon and redeems once again, it is worshipped and glorified all the more.[346]

The concept of the cross as the instrument of imperial rule and victory had also been noted by Procopius when describing Justinian's equestrian statue. What George of Pisidia did in the light of contemporary circumstances was to highlight and expound fully one point in the network of ideas which made this concept viable. Contemporary circumstances made up the *adventus* themes of the poem, and these circumstances were unique. Hence the terminology and formulae of *adventus* appear in an unfamiliar manner, as though somewhat distorted. Nonetheless, *adventus* could still serve as a framework for new ideas and events when it came to formalising these ideas and events so as to include the emperor's subjects.[347]

In a more strictly imperial sense also, the ceremony of *adventus* did not disappear but was reformulated in a new setting and reinterpreted in the light of partly new and partly old ideas. *Adventus* in Byzantium was recreated in its military aspect, when after six years of warfare in Iran, Heraclius returned to Constantinople. The *adventus* ceremony enacted on that occasion had a number of features which seem strangely old-fashioned and antiquarian. Heraclius came to Constantinople with four elephants, which, amidst general rejoicing, he brought out in a triumphal procession during the races in the hippodrome.[348] Elephants had figured in several Roman triumphs and were depicted among the spoils which Galerius gained from Iran on his arch. By the fourth century elephants had almost become a *topos* of Roman victory and triumph, and as such they figured on the Barberini diptych (plate 22) and related monuments.[349]

In parading his captured elephants, Heraclius was therefore not merely providing an entertainment that lay ready to hand, but was conforming to a very old tradition of enacting a Roman victory under the eyes of the citizens of the capital. Similarly, it was in accord with ancient custom that on the occasion of his return Heraclius should make his son Constantine consul, and should nominate Heraclius II Caesar.[350] Moreover, the ritual as a whole, which was performed on this occasion, was, in its form, late antique: the people left Constantinople carrying lights and olive branches to meet the emperor, and brought him back into the city "with acclamations and glory."[351]

Not so late antique, however, was the interpretation made of the events which Theophanes extracted from a now lost work of George of Pisidia:

> The emperor, having for six years fought against Persia, in the seventh made peace and with great rejoicing returned to Constantinople, demonstrating thereby some sacred meaning. For God created the whole world in six days and called the seventh a day of rest. Thus the emperor also for six years endured many toils and rested on the seventh, when he returned to the city with peace and rejoicing. And the people of the city, when they learnt of his approach, with great longing went out to Hiera to welcome him, together with the patriarch, and with the Emperor Constantine, the son of Heraclius. They carried olive branches and lights and praised Heraclius with rejoicing and tears. Then the son of Heraclius stepped forward and fell at his feet and embraced him and both moistened the ground with their tears. The people, seeing all this, began singing hymns of thanksgiving to God and thus they brought back the emperor with joy and entered the city.[352]

In the context of the old ceremonial of arriving and entering a city, Theophanes, following George of Pisidia, was able to integrate contemporary events not only into Biblical history, but also into the ordering and creation of the universe in Old Testament terms. That is, while the actions of the ceremony of *adventus* survived, the tradition in which these actions had been formulated did not. There is no reference here, as there had been, for example, in Ammianus, Claudian, and Procopius, to earlier imperial arrivals and triumphs; rather, a Christian interpretation, such as Eusebius had been the first to make, dominates the event. The old association of two particular aspects of arrival—that of movement and that of being present and at rest—with one another has disintegrated, for Theophanes in his interpretation writes not so much about arrival itself, as about being at rest, about action which, like the creation, has been completed and consummated.

This distinguishes Heraclius' arrival sharply from the arrivals of the Tetrarchs and the fourth-century emperors, which the panegyrists had set into the context of continuous and continuing imperial activity. On the other hand, Heraclius' arrival and coming to rest contain something akin to Justinian's stationary triumph in the hippodrome, for in both the ideal that is aspired to is imperial splendour and tranquillity, not imperial action.

What is important about Theophanes' interpretation of Heraclius' arrival is that he was able to give to the event a full doctrinal and religious interpretation. He did in a Christian idiom what the Tetrarchic panegyrists had done in a pagan idiom: he interpreted a particular event on a cosmic scale. The cosmos had changed in the interval between the Tetrarchs and Heraclius, but in the early seventh century it was still, or rather again, possible to make the emperor the focal point of one's understanding of it. The arrival of Heraclius was the culminating point of a long war, the visible culminating point, so far as the citizens of Constantinople were concerned. Like earlier imperial arrivals, it was the method of bringing before the emperor's subjects the effects of imperial activity by means of an encounter between emperor and subjects. In this respect, the arrival of Heraclius was one of a long chain of arrivals, occurring throughout the Roman and early Byzantine Empire.

Other aspects of Theophanes' view of Heraclius' arrival, however, differentiated him radically from earlier narrators of imperial arrivals. Theophanes' view of Heraclius' arrival was the view of an early mediaeval chronicler; the author and his public were no longer interested in the kind of analysis of imperial actions and virtues which was so prominent in the fourth-century panegyrics and in Ammianus. In chronicles, as in the epic panegyric of Corippus on Justin, description and analysis of personality and even of ceremonial were replaced by narrative of ceremonial and other events. The impact of an individual on the course of history had been one of the major themes of classical historiography and panegyric; this theme was quietly dropped. At a time when the *adventus* ceremonial, by which formerly an individual like the emperor could be integrated among different groups of his subjects, had ceased being open to the variegated interpretations and uses which it displayed in late antiquity, the impact of an individual on history likewise was no longer debated, was no longer defined and adjusted from one occasion to the next. Instead, the ceremonial was taken for granted, and could be left to speak in its own right.

We have entered a world of definitions, and a defined world, where the task of definition and self-definition could be relinquished because, in a sense, it had been completed. Further aspects of this process of definition will occupy us in the following pages.

II · CONSECRATIO

PART · I

CONFLICTS ABOUT THE
AFTERLIFE
OF THE EMPEROR

1. THE AFTERLIFE OF THE STATESMAN AND
EMPEROR IN GREECE AND ROME

Having considered the numerous strands of meaning which could find expression in imperial arrivals, we come now to the death of emperors and the steps that their subjects took to deal with this event. The ceremonial of *adventus* at its different stages of development showed a society capable of integration *vis-à-vis* its gods and rulers and within its own different parts. Within this ceremonial, from post-Homeric times until Heraclius and later, different forms were created in order to express different states of affairs in a harmonious and comprehensible manner. The close correlation between the actual ceremony and the delivery of panegyrics on the one hand, and that between the ceremony and representations of it in art, especially in the earlier period, on the other hand, well express this harmony.

Consecratio, the divinisation of Roman emperors, may be regarded, in some respects, as the counterpart of *adventus,* for whereas *adventus* was concerned with overcoming distance, *consecratio,* and the ancient beliefs which underlay it, was concerned with the overcoming of time and, in the Byzantine outcome of this Roman ceremony, with the correlation of divine and human dominion. But, unlike *adventus, consecratio* did not reveal a set of integrated harmonious ideas, but rather a set of conflicts, which were resolved only in Christian Byzantium.

In *consecratio,* the association between ceremony and panegyric was much looser. The ancient Roman *laudatio funebris* never became an in-

strumental part of the *consecratio* procedures, although it remained a
regular part of funerals until the second century.[1] Thus, in *consecratio*
there did not exist the intimate and detailed interpretation of each occasion which could occur in late antique *adventus*, where the panegyrist
would address the emperor before the same people who had welcomed
him, so that the oration could become a conscious means of communication between ruler and subjects. Hence, while in *adventus* Christianity
contributed to the loss of important elements which lay at the root of the
ability to act corporately in the societies, especially the urban societies of
the ancient and late classical world, where *consecratio* was concerned,
Christianity resolved a set of ancient and deeply rooted conflicts. These
conflicts found expression both in what was meant by the funeral and
consecratio of emperors and in the ways in which *consecratio* was expressed visually.

We will begin by discussing the origins of imperial *consecratio* and
then go on to its imagery and the further development of the concept
and its accompanying ceremonial.

Compared with *adventus*, *consecratio* in imperial Rome was a recent
invention. It was the public formalisation, so far as the emperor was affected, of a series of very diverse beliefs concerning the afterlife, which
were current at different levels, religious and philosophical, in Greece
and Rome.

The experience of death is common to all human beings, but ways of
dealing with it vary. Thus, the concern over what happened to the dead
was a deep and continuing one in the ancient and mediaeval world,
while in Islam, for instance, the dead are beyond all reach removed from
the living.[2] What we can know about the death of emperors concerns
less the actual event, and more the ways in which the event was interpreted in law and ceremonial. It was inherent in the position of the emperor that this should be so, that we should hear little of the personal
impact of grief over an emperor's death, and of the inner disrupting that
any death caused. Mark Antony's speech over the dead Caesar in
Shakespeare:

> Friends, Romans, countrymen, lend me your ears
> I come to bury Caesar, not to praise him[3]

where personal grief is aroused and articulated, is very different from
what actually happened in the ancient world and in Byzantium. In the
passage from the ancient world to Byzantium, we witness a change in
how imperial deaths were absorbed. For, we start in Rome with legisla-
tive decision-making about the dead emperor and end in Constantino-

ple with a ceremony, that of funerals, in which every human being had to participate at some time, but which, when performed for emperors, had a distinctive interpretation.

Almost from the beginning, coming to terms with the death of emperors was a process which revolved around two interdependent poles: on the one hand, there was concern over the status of the emperor after death, and on the other, the emperor's status after death was an important, often crucial factor in establishing a legitimate succession. The dead emperor's *consecratio* and funeral supplied one of the few methods—at times the only one—of providing his successor with a legitimate, publicly ratifiable, succession. This aspect of Roman imperial theory was, of course, articulated in the framework of pagan religion, but it ran so deep that it entered Christian Byzantium; with it came many a pagan way of seeing the world, which passed over this watershed between the pagan and the Christian empires.

We glimpse the changes and continuities that were at issue in this process through the eyes of only a few observers, but their detailed accounts are enough to show that we are dealing with a continuous tradition and at the same time with changes of sentiment, which in turn reflect changes in the theory of government.

Many people in the Hellenistic world held the view that kings and statesmen were in some way set apart from the rest of mankind by their fortune, by their virtues, or by being the chosen of the gods. Many thought that this special status should find some kind of expression.[4] The most obvious expression took the form of honours, and even cults like those accorded to gods, which were granted to such individuals in their lifetime. Most of the Roman conquerors of the Eastern Mediterranean tended to view these honours and cults with suspicion and unease, even when addressed to one of their own number, and found that, whatever their exalted status might have been in the Greek East, the egalitarianism of late republican politics prevented them from importing such status to Italy and Rome.[5]

But during the first century B.C. and earlier, the dividing lines between Greek and Roman ideas on glory and fame loosened, and Cicero, who had himself refused to receive divine honours when proconsul in Asia Minor,[6] produced one of the most refined and influential statements of the special position of the statesman in his *Dream of Scipio* at the end of *De republica*. Here, Scipio Africanus the Younger recounted to his friends a dream in which he saw his grandfather in a blessed place amid the stars of heaven and heard from him about his own future destiny:

> Truly, there is in heaven a place set apart for all who preserved, aided
> and increased their fatherland; there, they are blessed and enjoy eter-
> nity. For nothing occurs on this earth more acceptable to the greatest
> god who rules the entire universe than associations and federations of
> men brought together by law. These we call cities, and their rulers and
> preservers descend from here, and return hither after death.[7]

This formulation crystallised a long tradition of ancient thought
about immortality, the rewards of justice and the approximation between man and the divine. And it contributed to both pagan and, as we
shall see, Christian redefinitions of these issues in subsequent times.
Macrobius and Eulogius Favonius who commented on the *Dream of
Scipio* in late antiquity both noted a connection between the Dream and
the story told of the life after death by Er in Plato's *Republic*.[8] At this time
the political rivalries which had made the divinisation of individuals a
controversial matter in Rome had been superseded by four centuries of
imperial government. How immortality was to be attained, however,
was still a matter of debate, although it was now a debate between
pagans and Christians.

In such a context, Plato's story of the afterlife, which he tells through
the mouth of one returned from the dead, and Cicero's *Dream of Scipio*
could, by a pagan, be drawn together as expounding the same process
of the statesman's attainment of immortality. However, this process, as
visualised by pagan commentators on Cicero, no longer had the political
impact it had formerly exerted; rather, the political impact of the form of
immortality that was available to the emperor had come to be formulated by the rites of imperial funeral, and these were, by the late fourth
century, Christian rites.

Whatever the nature and origin of ancient beliefs about the afterlife,
they all had one feature in common and this was the isolation, or rather
dissociation from his fellows, of the individual as regarded his ultimate
destiny, and his relationship with the divine. This was expressed very
clearly by Cicero.[9] To overcome this dissociation various living people
came together in the processes of mourning and funeral. For a great
man of the Roman Republic, this would be a state funeral such as was
described by Polybius.[10] The republican state funeral provided the model
for the later funerals of emperors.

The funerary procession in which the effigies of the ancestors of the
deceased worn by actors and an image of the deceased himself were displayed was a means of preserving the memory of the dead among the
living. In itself, this implied no statement about any beliefs in an after-

life. The dead remained among the living by virtue of their achievements, and on this fact was based the *laudatio funebris*, a form of panegyric, in which the dead man's deeds and the deeds of his ancestors were recounted by a relative. A decision or judgement was made about the dead man's worth, which, after Caesar, was formulated and formalised with regard to emperors in the antithesis *consecratio-damnatio memoriae*.[11]

At the time of Caesar's death there arose two new issues, which Polybius did not treat. In the first place, a judgement of the deceased could no longer be made by any form of tacit consent among the Senate such as Polybius seems to have assumed existed. The spontaneous popular judgement of Caesar, which after his death was mobilised by his supporters, was not regarded as sufficient by Octavian, who therefore, in 42 B.C., initiated the *senatus consultum* for Caesar's official *consecratio*,[12] almost two years after his funeral.

In the second place, *consecratio* was not, like the earlier procedure described by Polybius, merely a judgement about the dead man's deeds, but also a judgement about his status *vis-à-vis* the divine and *vis-à-vis* immortality. This issue had already emerged in Caesar's lifetime, in connection with a statue of him on the Capitol. This showed him with the *oikoumene*, and in the inscription Caesar was referred to as ἡμίθεος.[13] Thus, Caesar's *consecratio* was not merely a validation of his *acta*; it also sanctioned the divine status that had been attributed to him while he was alive.[14] *Consecratio* was therefore of very real practical and philosophical importance. From a practical point of view, the *consecratio* of Caesar not only activated ideas of Roman imperial unity and a sense of identity for the subjects of the empire, but it also recapitulated and made present earlier thinking about the origins of Rome, about the divinisation of Aeneas and Romulus.[15] The *consecratio* of Caesar therefore created a new awareness of the Roman past as it was applicable to present and future, and this endured until the end of the Empire in the West.[16]

On a theoretical and philosophical level, the *consecratio* of Caesar made it possible to relate the concepts of immortality which were articulated in Plato's *Republic*, and thereafter in Cicero's *De republica* and in the commentary of Macrobius on the *Dream of Scipio* to practical politics. It was this relevance of speculation on the afterlife of the statesman and ruler which, in late antiquity, made it possible for most Christians to accept—although with many reservations and restatements—some special position for the emperor in heaven. In doing so, the Christians, in

their views of the imperial afterlife, abandoned the reservations about
the emperor's status after death which were formulated in the *consecratio*
procedures.

The *senatus consultum* of *consecratio* was a political as well as a religious procedure, its form being related to the *consecratio*, the setting
aside of an object for sacred use.[17] But whereas in the case of objects set
aside for sacred use the *pontifices* were the agents of *consecratio*, in the
case of the emperor the agent very fittingly was the Senate, for the senators, theoretically, if not in practice, were the emperor's peers and were
most competent to judge his deeds. The *consecratio* of Caesar set a crucial precedent, since his successors, the Roman emperors, were also to
be consigned to the company of the gods or to oblivion by means of *consecratio* or *damnatio memoriae*.

The *consecratio* of the emperor was a formal act, performed by the
Senate, either after the emperor's funeral or, at a later date, before it. By
this act the emperor was made divine and was accorded a temple and
priests.[18] *Consecratio* exalted the individual on whom it was bestowed by
making that individual divine. But divinity was attained by the human
verdict of the Senate, and in that the *consecratio* procedure exposed the
recipient to senatorial scrutiny and evaluation, it was a "last expression
of Roman freedom,"[19] freedom to be understood here in the republican
Roman sense as meaning free political competition among an aristocracy of equals. By passing their verdict on the deceased emperor, the
senators asserted their right to judge and evaluate imperial deeds.

The official and political nature of *consecratio* should not, however, de-
ceive the student as to its religious undertones. For, *consecratio* could
crystallise and make tangible hopes for the afterlife which were held by
many people. The eagle, which in imperial art conveyed the departed
emperor to heaven, was derived from Syrian tombstones,[20] thus applying to the emperor specifically a more widely-held expectation of immortality. Conversely, imperial immortality could be extended to others.
This is the message of the funerary monument at Igel near Trier, where
the apotheosis of Hercules is represented; the hero ascends to heaven in
a chariot assisted by Minerva (plate 32). The Secundinii, the creators of
the monument, here applied one of the main iconographic schemes of
imperial divinisation, ascent by chariot, to themselves; and they went
further even than this, by choosing Hercules, one of the traditional
models and patron deities of emperors.[21]

The difficulty and complexity of the concepts involved in the divinisation of a human being led very quickly and easily to panegyrical exploi-
tation of *consecratio*, as, for instance, in the otherwise finely conceived

account of Caesar's *consecratio* by Ovid,[22] who, to praise Augustus, inserted the comment: "So that Augustus be not born of mortal seed, it had to be that Caesar was made a god."[23] Subsequently Ovid stated the problem of *consecratio* in a nutshell, when speaking of the future *consecratio* of Augustus: "May that day be long distant and later than our own age, when, leaving the earth which he rules, Augustus our head attains heaven, and listens to our prayers though absent."[24]

A contrast may here be made with the *deus praesens* of *adventus*. *Consecratio*, a problem overtly concerned with honouring the dead, was in fact, *inter alia*, a way in which the living came to terms with death, disruption, and breaches in continuity. Imperial *consecratio* was thus a compromise, a method of expressing different, and at times divergent, ideas about death and its effects. Besides, the death of an emperor and the disruption and discontinuity it caused represented, from the point of view of the subjects, an inconvenience which one hoped to defer as long as possible.[25] Divinising the emperor was, in the circumstances, the best one could do. Seen from the point of view of the emperor's successor, however, the issue looked different: an accession was an event to be greeted with pleasure, and the *consecratio* of the predecessor was a mere by-product of it. Thus there came into existence a very multifarious imagery of *consecratio*—multifarious both in origin and in content—an imagery which lacked the clarity and harmony of the *adventus* imagery, since the aims which produced the imagery of *consecratio* were so diffuse.

The earliest *consecratio* issues of the official coinage were more indistinct in their imagery and legends than the later ones. It was only in the second century that the legend CONSECRATIO, sometimes replaced by AETERNITAS and a few others, became regular. CONSECRATIO was first used for Marciana,[26] and next for Hadrian.

Although the imperial *consecratio* coinage, throughout the period of its existence, emphasized different aspects of the procedure at different times, there were some motifs which did recur and which were used as components of commemorative issues as late as the Second Tetrarchy. These are the temple and altar of the *divus*, and the eagle, which could be visualized as carrying the soul of the departed emperor to the gods.[27] The commemorative coinage issued by the emperor Traianus Decius for selected emperors of the past took up the altar and eagle imagery. Each *divus* commemorated by Decius on obverses with legends of the type DIVO AUGUSTO, DIVO VESPASIANO, had two reverse types both reading CONSECRATIO. One depicted an eagle with outspread wings, the other an altar.[28] These motifs expounded the strictly Roman significance of *consecratio*, in that the effect of the *senatus consultum* of consecrating an emperor had been to grant him divine status, the achievement of which is alluded to by the eagle, and a cult, as is indicated by the altar. These are the most general, non-specific examples in the repertoire of images of *consecratio*, which survived into the fourth century because their very lack of precision made them adaptable to changing circumstances.

Other iconographies were more complex in origin and content. Such was the image of Caesar and the *oikoumene* on the Capitol, referred to above. Images of this kind may have served as a prototype of late antique depictions of the emperor enthroned on a globe or over the sky, which subsequently entered Christian art.[29] (See plates 10, 41, 25, 42.)

Another complex and allegorical image of *consecratio* showed the emperor actually carried to the above by an eagle. This notion of the ascent of the *divus* on the wings of an eagle appeared initially on imperial gems of the first century A.D. Although Roman viewers of such representations might have placed the eagle into the mythological and iconographical framework of Iuppiter—and might have added the further factor that the eagle represented victory and triumph—the origins and significance of the eagle in this particular context may nonetheless be looked for elsewhere, that is, in the Eastern Mediterranean. For, on a sculpted plaque from the ancient Semitic sanctuary of Baalbek, the divinities of which had been transformed into a Greco-Roman triad, a solar deity is depicted being carried upwards by two eagles (plate 26). Such imagery was not restricted to gods, however, for versions of it also figured on Syrian tombstones to convey the idea of the immortality of the deceased individual.[30]

In Roman monumental art, the earliest surviving example of the eagle as the bearer of the *divus imperator* appears in the vault of the arch of Titus, which was dedicated to him posthumously. The bust of the emperor is seen behind the soaring eagle as if through a window in the coffering of the vault. But it was only with the *consecratio* of Hadrian that the eagle bearing the emperor to heaven appeared regularly on official images, that is, on the coinage.[31] The eagle carrying the *divus* up to heaven was only one of several roles in which this bird appeared on *consecratio* issues. There was the eagle holding in its claws Iuppiter's thunderbolt,[32] the eagle standing on a globe—this being one of the most frequent versions[33]—the eagle standing on a sceptre,[34] and the eagle without any attributes.

A *consecratio* medallion of Antoninus Pius[35] shows Antoninus on the back of an eagle with the personification of Campus Martius waving below. This may be regarded, in general terms, as an abbreviation of the representation of the *consecratio* of Antoninus and Faustina on the base of the column of Antoninus in the Vatican. On this monument, the imperial couple are shown borne aloft by a winged genius, who carries in his left hand a globe with the moon, a star and the zodiac.[36] An eagle flies up on either side. Below, seated at the right, Roma raises her right hand in salutation, and to the left reclines the figure of Campus Martius holding his obelisk for identification (plate 28).

Antoninus and Faustina died at different times, yet are here shown ascending to the sky together. This throws some light on the meaning of representations of this nature. They were not intended to state a simple fact, for factually, the relief is incorrect. Rather, the relief, like other expressions of *consecratio* by means of images, served to initiate a train of thought in the beholder. The image set the scene for the train of thought: it shows Rome and the Campus Martius, both carefully and unmistakably identified by attributes. At its most elementary, this was a geographical definition, but it also evoked an event, the state funeral. The importance and interest of much of Roman imperial art lies in the fact that it could anchor ideas of this sort in a known and definable setting—here the geographical definition—and that it could take facts as a starting point, without being encumbered by them.[37]

However, on the *consecratio* relief of Antoninus and Faustina, the train of thought is simultaneously approached from a different angle: the winged genius who carries up the imperial couple, unlike all the other figures, is shown in complete frontality. It is thereby dissociated from the glances and movements which relate all the other figures to each other, and signifies the removal of the imperial couple to heaven. The interrelation of the figures to each other, which had so far been characteristic of Roman imperial art, had been broken.

The relief thus represents an aspect of that Roman conflict in ideas about divinisation, *consecratio*, which we discussed earlier. On the one hand, the dead remained with the living, no longer merely through effigies carried in funerary processions, as in Polybius, but also now through the cult established for consecrated emperors. On the other hand, the dead were removed on the wings of an eagle, or, as here, by a cosmic genius, to a beyond which ultimately defied definition, as Cicero had already sensed. The frontality of the genius is a manifestation of an overall change in style in Roman imperial art, a decreased concern with naturalism. This stylistic change had a particular significance concerning concepts about immortality and divinisation, for the emperor is depicted as removed from his subjects.

The Antoninus and Faustina relief betrays a certain Roman self-consciousness and reluctance concerning divinisation which was not expressed as clearly elsewhere: that of sending off the imperial couple and at the same time keeping them within the geographical framework of the city of Rome. The Antonine monument of Ephesus shows, without doubt, definition, or hesitation, the ascent of an emperor, probably Trajan[38] (see plate 29) in the chariot of Sol. He is accompanied by a flying Victoria and is about to mount the solar chariot. Sol with Virtus leads the procession. Beneath the chariot reclines the figure of Tellus, who holds a cornucopia, with a child. A parallel representation shows the ascent of 'Plotina' as Diana–Luna, accompanied by a flying Vesperus. She is shown in the act of mounting a chariot drawn by two stags, preceded by Night.[39] Below reclines Oceanus holding an oar.

The method of representation is similar to that of the relief with the *consecratio* of Antoninus and Faustina. The personifications of land and sea set the 'geographical' scene, like Campus Martius. Instead of Rome, there are Victoria, Sol, Virtus, on the one hand, and Luna and Hesperus on the other. The difference between the two works is that one has the city of Rome as its setting, the other the *oikoumene*. One could perhaps even say that the one, with its specific frame of reference, represents a Roman form of *consecratio*, and the other, with its universalised frame of reference, an Eastern divinisation. The Roman relief is restrictive in the ideas it conveys, for the personifications, while helping to define what is being shown, at the same time limit it, whereas the Ephesian relief, with its cosmic gods, places the scene into a cosmic setting.

In part, the Ephesian relief is a version of an iconography which frequently appeared on the imperial coinage, showing the pyre, crowned by a chariot to convey the ascent of the emperor, as described by Dio and Herodian.[40] The chariot (for emperors it was mostly a *quadriga*) on top of the funerary pyre appears regularly, beginning with issues for Antoninus Pius.[41] As with issues showing the funerary eagle bearing up the emperor, the pyre and chariot coins became rarer in the third century. Constantine's Trier solidus of 310–313,[42] (see plate 35) for DIVUS CONSTANTIUS, showing on the reverse a pyre surmounted by a radiate emperor in a chariot, was a revival of this iconography.

The imagery of the imperial ascent on the eagle or in the chariot of Sol on the coinage and in official art reflects loosely the funerary ceremony and the effects of *consecratio* as envisaged in imperial funerals. The disappearance of this imagery in the later third century points to changed views about *consecratio*, an issue to which we will return. Another factor contributes to explaining the disappearance of these images, which in turn helped to redefine notions of *consecratio*: cremation went out of fashion in the ancient world from the early second century.[43] It took some time before imperial ceremonial absorbed this change, for Septimius Severus was still cremated both in reality and in effigy. But the Tetrarchs, like the Byzantine emperors, were buried.

Unlike the imagery of *adventus*, the imagery of *consecratio* was diverse, if not diffuse, and could not easily merge into a composite which would express *consecratio* in its totality. In a sense, there never was a totality, for, while the ceremony of *adventus* developed coherently, stage by stage, in *consecratio* there occurred a number of abrupt changes which illustrated how, when it came to interpreting imperial deaths in a public setting, various concepts remained at odds with each other until the fourth century.

Beginning with Caesar, *consecratio* took place after the funeral. At the funeral, the soul was thought to rise from the pyre. In the case of Augustus, a witness swore that he had seen this happen,[44] and after the funeral of Caesar, a comet appeared, which was thought to be his soul and which was duly shown on the coinage over his head, with legends DIVUS IULIUS.[45] Now, it has been seen that *consecratio* may be partly understood as an expression of the genuine reluctance of the Roman aristocracy to deify a human being. If deification were to happen, it had to be in such a way that the Senate, not the human being in question, would make the decision. Disapproval of certain emperors—Nero, Domitian, Commodus—in Roman historiographical tradition was not founded primarily on their political and military performance. In Domitian's case, for instance, the latter was not as discreditable as Tacitus would have us believe.[46] Rather, it was based on their attempted self-exaltation to a divine level.

This feature could determine whether a certain ruler was a tyrant just as much as could a flaw in his title or actual misconduct. Despite Roman or senatorial reluctance to countenance a divine emperor, however, there was a considerable popular and empire-wide urge to make the emperor divine, which was expressed, for example, in art and showed emperors 'consecrated' before their death.[47] This urge received increasing official sanction, beginning with the cult of Roma and Augustus in the East, and procedures which were labelled as tyrannical under one emperor were accepted, out of habit, under the next.[48] Emperors would thus have to become divine at some point, and one way of limiting imperial divinity was to allow this to happen only after death, by means of official *consecratio*. Accordingly, the ideal of Cicero's divinised statesman, and the more concrete ideal of the ruler conceived of, for instance, as the θεὸς ἐπιφανής or *praesens deus* of *adventus*, were scrutinised and made concrete by a very pragmatic political procedure, which was expressed by the order of events following upon an imperial death. In the earlier part of the first century, the order of events whereby an emperor attained divinity was death, state funeral on the Campus Martius, and *consecratio* by *senatus consultum*.

This order had changed by the later second century. In 193 in the case of Pertinax according to Dio, and in 211 in the case of Septimius Severus according to Herodian, a different form was observed. Pertinax was murdered in Rome and received no official funeral. His memory was rehabilitated by Severus, who claimed to be his successor, adopted his name, and initiated the *senatus consultum* of his *consecratio*;[49] also, a wax effigy of him was given a state funeral on the Campus Martius. Preceding that, the effigy was laid out in triumphal garb on a platform next to the Rostra and treated as though it were a person sleeping. Then the senators, their wives and Severus himself appeared in mourning, Severus pronounced the *laudatio funebris*, and the effigy, together with the images of great men, was conducted to the Campus Martius in a procession in which moved detachments of the army, magistrates, and other personages of note. Severus and Pertinax' relatives gave the effigy the last kiss. Magistrates and knights, cavalry and infantry "represented elaborate warlike and civilian performances around the pyre."[50] Then the pyre, on top of which was the golden chariot of Pertinax, was lit and an eagle escaped from it, "and in this manner Pertinax was made immortal." (Cf. plates 35–36.)

Severus died in Britain[51] and his remains were brought back to Rome in an alabaster urn by Geta and Caracalla. They received a formal welcome and those who greeted them also performed the *proskynesis* before the urn. Herodian's account of the state funeral is a rough parallel to that of Dio. The effigy was treated as a sick man, visited by doctors and finally pronounced to be dead. It then lay in state on the Forum, was mourned for and taken to the Campus Martius, where the pyre had been prepared, loaded with aromatic herbs. The knights performed the πυρρικὸς δρόμος and chariots with the effigies of Roman generals and emperors circled round the pyre. The pyre was then lit, and "an eagle is released which rises into the air with the fire, and which, the Romans believe, takes the soul of the emperor from earth to heaven."[52]

Neither Dio nor Herodian mentions a *senatus consultum* whereby *consecratio* was achieved; this is, however, described elsewhere[53] as preceding the funeral, and still appears on some CONSECRATIO coins of Valerian II.[54] The order of events portrayed by Dio and Herodian was thus death, funeral, and state funeral where the *senatus consultum* for *consecratio* was assumed to have taken place already. In short, the *consecratio* by *senatus consultum* had taken place before the state funeral, in which the ascent of the emperor's soul was expressed by the symbols of the escape of the eagle and the chariot crowning the pyre.

Whatever procedure was adopted, *consecratio* did not occur at death, but at some point afterwards. When the *senatus consultum* had come to precede the funeral, the funeral could become instrumental in the achievement of *consecratio* in a way that it had not been earlier. But even in the case of Augustus someone swore that he had seen the emperor's soul arise from the pyre. The procedure whereby the *senatus consultum* preceded the funeral recognised the existence of this type of belief and sought to comply with it; that is, it sought to state the divinisation of the emperor through official channels, before popular enthusiasm would attribute divinity to the emperor spontaneously, as had happened in the case of Caesar. Hence the *senatus consultum* of the earlier empire, which followed the funeral, was less efficacious as an act of government. It could pronounce only on something which had happened already, whereas the *senatus consultum* before the funeral could contribute to the event of *consecratio*. This difference in function of the *senatus consultum* was, I suggest, the reason for the change in its timing.

In other words, during the second century there occurred a renewed attempt to achieve some sort of constitutional control over the divinity of the emperor. Such constitutional control could be efficacious as long as the Senate remained in touch with, and—to however small a degree—in control of the emperor, and as long as Rome was not only the recognised capital of the Empire but also the official burial place of the emperors. During the third century, however, these traditional links between the emperor on the one hand, and Rome and the Senate on the other, were disrupted.

The result as regarded *consecratio* was that *consecratio* was no longer in any significant, practical sense an expression of senatorial approval of a deceased emperor. Rather, another aspect of it, latent from the time when Augustus became *divi filius*, became predominant: an emperor would divinise his recognised predecessor and acknowledge the divinisation of earlier emperors as a declaration of his own legitimacy and policy, which often meant a dynastic policy. This aspect of *consecratio* emerged already in Pliny,[55] and more consistently on the third-century *consecratio* coinages—in particular the *consecratio* coinage of Traianus Decius issued for the occasion of the millennium of the foundation of Rome, where he commemorated selected emperors of the past.[56] *Con-*

secratio became an act of *pietas* on the part of an emperor's successor and thus lost its religious and objective validity. This fact was a crucial precondition to the Tetrarchic approach to the issues involved in *consecratio*.

2. THE TETRARCHY: THE DISRUPTION AND RESTATEMENT OF THE ROMAN TRADITION OF *CONSECRATIO*

The duration of the public and official life of a Roman emperor was delimited by two salient events: his accession, the *dies natalis* of his rule, and his *consecratio*. The changing emphasis placed on one or the other of these two events, and the manner in which they balanced each other, constantly redefined the emperor's relationship to the divine and thereby defined the nature of his own divinity. At his accession, the emperor might be presented as the chosen of the gods, as one who already enjoyed a special relationship with the gods, or else he might be chosen for his *virtus*, by a human choice. These two features could be linked and interrelated; they did not exclude each other. If the emperor was chosen by the gods, his actions would be performed *instinctu divinitatis*,[57] and his reign would reveal why and how he had been chosen by the gods.

The other way in which the special status of the emperor might be stated occurred at the moment of his death: he became a god and companion of the gods by his *consecratio*. Yet *consecratio* was not always an isolated moment; it could be preceded during the reign by a gradual assimilation into divine status, expressed chiefly in portraiture.[58] In the first and second centuries the pattern of an emperor's life had dictated that he be chosen by the people and, in some way, by the gods (which might coincide with adoption by his predecessor or with being the son of his predecessor), rule and be rewarded for his toils with *consecratio* after his death.[59] This pattern changed in the third, and especially the fourth, centuries: emperors who were already the chosen of the gods had no need of *consecratio* and the human approval which it implied, because to an increasing degree a supra-human status became theirs at the moment of accession.

The change became very clear during the Tetrarchy. The Tetrarchy presented an entirely new set of circumstances which helped to transform *consecratio* into a different concept. Diocletian, like Aurelian, claimed to rule by the highest authority a ruler could have: he had been chosen by God.[60] Whether or not any connection could be established between him and any predecessor was therefore quite irrelevant, and *consecratio* was not, in the First Tetrarchy, a factor which contributed to the establishment of a legitimate succession. Diocletian's claim to empire was dissociated from that of any predecessor. It therefore was not a pious duty for him to issue a commemorative coinage, or to make arrangements for a predecessor's state funeral, official recognition and *consecratio* in Rome, as Severus had done; nor could it be of any political advantage. This is implicit in the very names these two emperors chose for themselves for, whereas Severus on the coinage called himself L. Septimius Severus Pertinax or *divi Marci filius* . . . ,[61] Diocletian and his colleagues made no such claims.

The nature of Diocletian's title to rule rendered superfluous any claims which could be made by means of the *consecratio* of a predecessor, since nothing could be added to his status by human intervention or approval.[62] The emperor was already *conspicuus et praesens Iuppiter*, or *imperator Hercules*.[63] This claim, made at the accession, overrode all earlier precautions which had been taken to limit the approximation to the divine of the emperor in his lifetime.[64] Thus the arch of Galerius showed Diocletian and Maximian during their lifetime enthroned above earth and sky, in a position of divinity.[65] (Plate 10)

Accordingly, during the Tetrarchy, an entire set of options whereby the emperor's divine status could be defined and described positively or negatively from the religious and political point of view, as well as from the successor's point of view, were closed. During the Tetrarchy, the emperor was all he could be during his life; death could add nothing.

Although the Tetrarchic system did not long outlive the retirement of Diocletian,[66] this reformulation of the position of the emperor lastingly influenced what could be meant by *consecratio* when *consecratio* became an issue again in the context of Constantine's accession. The connection to be made between the *consecratio* of a preceding, and the accession of a succeeding, emperor is familiar from earlier interpretations of *consecratio*, where it was used pragmatically as a claim to legitimacy. Two Constantinian panegyrics explore this theme. Nonetheless, the meaning of *consecratio* had changed, for the ascent of Constantius was dissociated completely from any action either on the part of the Senate or of Constantine. *Consecratio* was no longer seen as an official action, because it now arose out of the relation between the emperor and the divine throughout his reign, to which no human agency could make any further contribution.

> You are blessed in your empire, and more blessed thereafter, god-like Constantius, because for a certainty you hear these things and see

them: you whom the sun, with his chariot barely visible, as he was setting and returned again to his not far distant point of rising, received in
heaven as he was about to ascend [on his course]. In what joy do you
participate now when a man, who at the same time is your son's father,
father-in-law and emperor, introduces this son of yours, who first made
you a father, to your empire.[67] More than any of the divine emperors
this is the immortality which is your very own, this immortality which
we see: your son is similar to you in appearance, in spirit, and in the
power of empire.[68]

The emperor, according to this panegyric, was *ad deorum concilia
translatus*,[69] in the chariot of Sol, and this happened, not in Rome, as
might have been suggested by the funerary ceremony which used to
take place there, but in a remote part of the empire, far from the gaze of
the vulgar.

The panegyric of 310 goes a step further: it reveals the *consecratio* of
Constantius as a divine mystery, and dispenses with any imagery to
suggest how Constantius actually reached heaven; there is no solar
chariot, no pyre, no eagle. The imagery of the panegyric verges on metaphor and is intended to convey a truth which cannot be stated in terms
other than those of revelation:

> The day would end sooner than my speech, if I were to rehearse all
> the deeds of your father. That last expedition which he made was not,
> as is commonly believed, undertaken for trophies from Britain, but
> rather, he went to the very end of the earth when the gods were already
> calling him. The man who had performed so many and such great
> deeds . . . [desired] something which he did not want to tell to any-
> one. When he was about to go to the gods he looked out on Oceanus,
> the father of the gods from which the fiery stars of heaven gain new
> light, so that when, [departing] thence to enjoy eternal light,[70] he
> should already see from that place an almost unending daylight. For in
> truth the abodes of the gods stood open for him and he was received in
> the assembly of the dwellers in heaven, with Iuppiter himself holding
> out his right hand.[71] Moreover, when he was straightway asked on
> whom he would bestow the empire, he decreed as befitted Constantius
> the Righteous; for clearly you were elected by the choice of your father,
> [our] emperor. And while truth commands us to say this, it is also, as I
> see, most welcome to your piety. But why should we take account only
> of your private affection, when this was the decree of all the gods,
> which had been given effect a long time ago, although it was then con-
> firmed in a full assembly?[72]

The panegyrist here propounds a theology of empire; as he so often
repeats, he allows his listeners to share in truths not commonly known.
Thus he was the first to state that Constantine descended from Claudius

Gothicus—this likewise in an atmosphere of mystery, of letting the listeners into a secret.[73]

Concepts of *consecratio* itself had become more exalted because it had now been dissociated from a decision of the Senate, from the *pietas*—or whatever other motive—of the successor, and from any vagaries of history. Constantius was *divus* in his own right; and both the panegyrics which discuss his ascent to the above could take this for granted in a way which had not been possible earlier, when the Roman traditions and conflicts of *consecratio* were still dominant. Apart from this, however, the atmosphere conveyed in the two panegyrics differs.

The orator of 307 states, or rather assumes, the divinity of Constantius without feeling any need for apology or explanation. The image of the solar ascent which he chose to express imperial divinity was one that would be thoroughly familiar both from imperial art and from popular notions of immortality.[74] He then proceeds to reinforce this notion of immortality by another, more down-to-earth one, which was mentioned in a different form by Ovid and by Trajan's panegyrist, Pliny—namely, the continued presence on earth of Constantius' image, his son Constantine.[75]

Again the issues of *consecratio* and accession are related, although, of course, according to this panegyric Constantine owed his empire not only to his descent from Constantius, but also to the intervention of his father-in-law Maximian. Thus, while paying lip service to the Tetrarchy, the orator in fact welcomes the re-emergence of a *domus divina*.[76] Constantius was a link in the imperial succession, in the dynasty, the existence of which his divinity helped to justify. This attitude also emerges in the panegyric of 310, which recalls, on the one hand, the preceding centuries of imperial Rome, when a means whereby an emperor could justify his rule had been the *consecratio* of his predecessor. On the other hand, it foreshadows the succession of sons after fathers and ideas concerning legitimacy in the fourth century and later.

The attitude of the orator of 310 is less political, less factual than that of the orator of 307, and as a result his claims are both more fluid and more far-reaching. He also tells of a *domus divina*, but it goes back to Claudius Gothicus. He also links Constantine's right to rule with the empire of his now divine father, *manifeste enim sententia patris electus es*. But this is only one aspect of Constantine's title. As for Constantius' immortality, the orator omits the standard phrase about being called to the councils of the gods, and refers instead to *lux perpetua* and the *superum templa*, which Constantius reached when contemplating Oceanus, the procreator of the gods, from whom the stars of heaven gain new light. The emperor's immortality and divinity are fitted into a cosmology, a theory of the nature of the world.

The panegyric of 310 also exemplifies the changes which had occurred in the concept of *consecratio*. As in the panegyric of 307, *consecratio* is dissociated from any human agency, and there is no reluctance on the part of the orator to exalt Constantius as a human being who reached divinity. Thus Constantine, unlike earlier emperors, can in no way be glorified as having contributed anything at all to his father's divinity. Constantine enjoys his father's reflected glory, but his father's divinity is not dependent on a posthumous cult instituted by his son. Already in the emperor's lifetime anything to do with his person is sacred, and the palace is described as a temple.[77] To this *consecratio* cannot add, for, according to this panegyric, *consecratio* is simply the fulfilment of the emperor's ultimate destiny, and is to be taken for granted.

Because Constantius reached heaven *Iove ipso dexteram porrigente*, by the consent of the gods, not the consent of humans, the dynastic claim arising from his divinisation was more pronounced than it had been in the case of earlier emperors. The divine approval which Constantius attained at death could at once be extended not only to his successor, who was praised as being like him,[78] but also to his descendants at large. The panegyrist gave graphic expression to this state of affairs by saying that Constantius chose his successor in the presence of the gods in heaven,[79] not in the presence of human beings on earth.

Thus we see that certain aspects of *consecratio* were reintroduced in a new and more clear-cut form after Diocletian, but as a result of Diocletian's reformulation of the position of the emperor in this life—so clearly expressed in Tetrarchic ceremonies of *adventus*—*consecratio* underwent a change which endured: the verdict of humans ceased to matter. Thereby ended the need for interpretation and evaluation of the ceremonies of imperial funerals which earlier had confounded any consistent and continuous view of the status an emperor should have before and after his death.

Despite this fundamental change and discontinuity in the way in which an emperor's life and afterlife should be realised and imagined, *consecratio*, in the early fourth century, provided a very clear instance of continuity as well as of change, in that, at a practical, pragmatic level it retained one of its old functions: it helped to explain and justify the next imperial accession, such as Constantine's, which, in terms of the Tetrarchic *status quo*, was a usurpation. This more traditional, conservative view of *consecratio* was expressed, to the exclusion of any other view, in the panegyric of 313. Here Constantine is said to have surpassed the glories of his peerless divinised parent so that any other comparison would be unworthy of him; here also, Constantius is visualised in heaven rejoicing over the deeds of his son and successor.[80]

This dichotomy of change and continuity further emerges in the major extant visual medium in which *consecratio* was communicated during the Tetrarchy and aftermath, the coinage. Diocletian had issued no commemorative coins, but the concepts of *consecratio* which were expressed in panegyrics after the collapse of the First Tetrarchy, in the West were illustrated on a voluminous commemorative coinage, produced for Constantine and Maxentius.

While the panegyrics claim that Constantine was elected emperor by the gods, they also emphasise the importance of the dynasty of Constantius, or, even more so, that of Claudius Gothicus,[81] in flat contradiction to Diocletian's Tetrarchy. This dynastic element is also stressed on the Constantinian coinage.

Commemorative issues were revived by Constantine for Constantius I and appeared in all the mints over which he gained control up to 318, beginning at Londinium, 307–310.[82] Obverse legends refer to *divus Constantius*,[83] while one group of reverses features CONSECRATIO. The design of these reverses, showing the funerary pyre surmounted by the radiate emperor on a chariot, is unique for this period, and constitutes an anachronism because Constantius was buried (cf. plate 35). Reverses reading CONSECRATIO also appeared at Lugdunum in 306–308 A.D., but here an eagle with outspread wings, or standing on an altar, is shown.[84] Other commemorative issues for Constantius by Constantine read on the reverse MEM[ORIA] DIVI CONSTANTI, and show an eagle with outspread wings standing at a square altar enclosure, or on a domed shrine with closed doors.[85] Other reverses read MEMORIA FELIX and show altars of various sorts, with one or more eagles.[86] One exception from Lugdunum,[87] MEMORIA FELIX, has an eagle standing in a tetrastyle temple with a wreath in the pediment, and another eagle at the apex.[88]

MEMORIA legends in these issues far outnumber legends reading CONSECRATIO, and only one of the images which formerly suggested how the ascent to the above was achieved is reproduced, namely the pyre and chariot type from Trier. Thus, the images of the coinage reflect the panegyrists' lack of interest in the mechanics of *consecratio* and in the human determination of it. All the other designs on the Constantinian commemorative issues—with the exception of one group which will be

discussed below—show the temple or altar with eagles. They assume
the *consecratio* and make a loose reference to the cult of the divinised
emperor about which, however, nothing is said in the panegyrics.[89] The
MEMORIA legends are something of a new departure in the context of
commemorative issues, but not entirely new, since earlier commemorative issues for Claudius Gothicus from Rome, which have no precedent
or parallel elsewhere, have reverses reading MEMORIAE AETERNAE, with a
lion, or more frequently an eagle.[90]

In due course, from 317 A.D., Constantine issued commemorative
coins for Claudius himself. These issues, like those for Constantius, recall the original commemorative coinage for Claudius.[91] Such borrow-
ings from the commemorative coinage of Claudius suggest that the pyre
and chariot type, of which there are no other examples during this period, was derived from the same source.[92]

The evidence of the panegyrics, taken with that of the coinage,
shows how the idea of *consecratio* could be used as a propaganda weap-
on, as a claim for legitimacy. The perfect numismatic example of this
comes, however, not from Constantine but from Constantine's rival
Maxentius, who issued commemorative coinages in the mints of Rome
and Ostia, 309–312 A.D.[93] The reverse type is common to all, AETERNAE
MEMORIAE, showing a domed shrine or mausoleum surmounted by an
eagle, with one face of its double door ajar (see plate 39). The obverses
display Maxentius' kinsmen. Apart from his son Romulus, who died in
309,[94] there are Maximian, who died in 310,[95] Galerius, who died in 311,[96]
and Constantius.[97] This series falls into two groups: it was begun for
Romulus and then extended to the other *divi* on a systematic basis, as
can be seen from the phrasing of the obverse legends. All these issues
were based on kinship or kinship by marriage.

The iconography of the reverses—the temple with door ajar surmounted by the eagle—is unique to these issues of Rome and Ostia. An
echo, of a shrine with closed doors, appeared at Thessalonica, then controlled by Licinius, for Galerius, MEM DIVI MAXIMIANI, and at Ticinum,
then controlled by Maxentius, for Constantius.[98] This iconography of
the temple of the departed, or ἡρῷον,[99] with a door ajar points to beliefs about the afterlife which are represented in greater detail on a set
of third-century sarcophagi. These show either a gateway with double doors where one wing is slightly open, and on either side the four
seasons,[100] or else such a gateway with a deceased couple standing at
either side[101] (plate 38) making gestures of farewell or prayer and ecstasy, and contemplating the life after death which they are to enter. An
early third-century cinerary urn in the Vatican shows two victories

beneath palm trees opening a similar gateway with double doors.[102] (Plate 37)

The symbolism of the four seasons points most clearly to the afterlife as part of the cycle of nature, while victories and *orantes* explain the nature of the afterlife as an overcoming of death.[103] The pagan Velletri sarcophagus of the earlier second century A.D. has the motif of the slightly open door as part of a cycle of scenes illustrating life and afterlife. On one side of the enthroned rulers of the underworld, Hercules takes Alcestis through a door, which stands ajar, back to Admetus on earth, while on the other, Protesilas and Hermes are about to accompany Laodamia into the underworld through an open door.[104] Here it is clear that the open door indicates a passage both to and from the world of the dead. For this reason, the iconography could be adopted by Christians. It appears on an ivory plaque depicting Christ's tomb with an open door; this door points to the resurrection of Christ, that unique passage from life to death and into life eternal.[105] (See plate 40.)

How, then, are we to understand Maxentius' AETERNAE MEMORIAE coinage, where perhaps the building that is represented was initially the temple of *divus* Romulus on the Forum,[106] the image being adopted subsequently for the other *divi* also? It is not so much the cult and temple of the *divus* that is referred to, dependent as they were on human agency, but his continued existence, not to say his presence, which did not depend on cult. From the earthly, imperial point of view, such a presence, the presence of the divinised kinsmen which Maxentius claimed, was of far greater value to the ruling emperor than the obligation, *pietas*, of performing his deceased predecessor's cult.

In the panegyrics and again on the coinage of the Second Tetrarchy, the notion of *consecratio* was reinforced, but in a new form. A panegyrist might refer to Constantius watching his son from heaven. That is partly what the imagery intended, but this was not so very new. What was new was the method whereby the difficult issue of whether a human being, alive or dead, should receive a cult was bypassed and thereby resolved on the Roman coinages. From this, the way lay open for the concept of the Christian emperor in heaven with God, exercising a continued presence on earth, as propounded by Eusebius.

The predominance of the MEMORIAE and REQUIES over CONSECRATIO legends shows from another angle how the emphasis had changed. *Consecratio*, formerly a public act and ceremony which could be performed or omitted, had now become a right that belonged to the emperor by virtue of his being emperor. The old terminology and imagery of the coinage had not described this new state of affairs and were therefore dropped. The term *requies* is particularly interesting, since in the panegyrics[107] it is a state—contrasted by *cura*—which the senior emperors within the Tetrarchy had earned as a result of their labours, being assisted now by the junior emperors, the Caesars. Life after death was a continuance of that state of tranquillity[108] which the well-deserving emperor achieved in life and continued to enjoy after death.

It is worth noting, however, that on the coinage only one new image—the shrine with door ajar—was produced to describe the changed significance of *consecratio*. Whereas the coinage very faithfully mirrors what the panegyrics say about the dynastic relevance of *consecratio*, *consecratio* itself remained a quality largely unidentified by numismatic images other than very conventional ones. According to the coinage— with the one exception of the issues of Maxentius—the concept of *consecratio* which prevailed in the early fourth century was the traditional utilitarian device, used to claim legitimacy. The difference between the commemorative coinage of the early fourth century and that of earlier periods is that in the latter a variety of ideas, frequently conflicting, about *consecratio* could and did find frequent expression. In late antiquity it was mainly in the panegyrics that *consecratio* received a heightened significance, achieved by dissociating it from the traditional Roman limitations which had been imposed on the concept of the divine emperor.

The official *consecratio* of the emperor originated as a Roman idea which was, during the first and second centuries, usually expressed in a visual idiom relating it to the city of Rome and Roman ceremonies. In the panegyrics of Constantine, the emperor's ascent to the above had become dissociated from this idiom, a development which was also borne out on the coinage. Furthermore, the coinage also suggests that *consecratio* and the Tetrarchic variant which developed out of it were important chiefly in the West. The complex numismatic propaganda war which was carried on in the West by means of issues dedicated to the various *divi* in the early fourth century had only very slight parallels in the East. Apart from the above-mentioned issue to Galerius in Thessalonica, there were only two issues for him from Siscia, one from Cyzicus, and six from Alexandria.[109] In fact, throughout the imperial period *consecratio* issues were much more frequent in the West, particularly in Italy and Gaul, than in the East.[110] The reason for this is that the divinity of rulers, whether before or after death, was a *fait accompli* in the East long before Caesar and Augustus. The East had no need of *consecratio*, whether as an exaltation of the emperor or as a means of restricting imperial claims to divinity, and the policy of Eastern and Western mints was adapted accordingly.[111]

The commemorative coinage of the early fourth century was a thoroughly Western phenomenon, with which the panegyrics do not entirely match—another indicator, perhaps, of the difficulties in conceiving the status of the pagan emperor which *consecratio* highlighted. What the panegyrics of 307 and 310 have to say about *consecratio* had heretofore been carefully suppressed in the West. These panegyrics therefore spell out very clearly what was new in those concepts of the emperor which had become prominent under Diocletian.

3. THE CHRISTIAN VIEW OF THE EMPEROR'S AFTERLIFE IN THE EAST: EUSEBIUS ON CONSTANTIUS I AND CONSTANTINE

The ceremonies and ideas which formed the background to *consecratio*, or the emperor's ascent to heaven, produced a view of the ascent which, in the Western context which has so far dominated our consideration of *consecratio*, could be used to reinforce the impression of continuity between succeeding emperors, and to give the ruling emperor an aura of legitimacy. This continuity and legitimacy could be expressed in two ways: on the one hand, *consecratio* could be understood as an expression of the *pietas* of the ruling emperor, who conferred *consecratio*. This was the case, for instance, in Ovid and Pliny,[112] and presupposed a man-made *consecratio*. On the other hand, *consecratio* could be used to confer a certain status on the ruling emperor, to claim legitimacy and to contribute to the establishment of a dynasty. This was the case whether *consecratio* was conferred by human agency or not. We have seen how during the second tetrarchy *consecratio*, which came to the departed emperor as of right, was used as a claim to legitimacy and to help the establishment of a *domus divina*. One such family lasted, that of Constantius; the other, that of Maxentius, did not.

Approaching, as we now do, Greek and Christian notions of imperial death and afterlife, we face not only a difference in the nature of the literary sources, but also a different outlook,[113] which was only partially conditioned by Christianity.[114]

Eusebius was a Christian, and as such he had no vested interest in imperial divinisation, although he did have an interest in the status after death of Constantine, his hero. Both aspects of this attitude become clear when one juxtaposes Eusebius' accounts of the death of Constantius and the death of Constantine. In the former case, Eusebius' aim was the familiar one of justifying the accession of Constantius' son and successor:

> Indeed, in every sense God was [Constantine's] helper; and he had before ordained that he should be present in readiness to succeed his father. . . . Taking his farewell from his sons and daughters who stood around him in a circle, [Constantius] in his own palace, on the imperial couch, bequeathed the empire, according to the law of nature, to his eldest son and died. . . . Constantine, adorned in his father's purple, proceeded from his father's palace, and presented to all a renewal, as it were, in his own person, of his father's life and reign. He then conducted the funeral procession . . . and performed the last rites . . . while all were united in honouring this thrice-blessed prince with acclamations and praises. And while with one mind and voice they glorified the rule of the son as a living again of him who was dead, they immediately proclaimed their new emperor with auspicious shouts as Autokrator and Augustus. Thus the memory of the deceased emperor received honour from the praises bestowed upon his son, while the latter was pronounced blessed in being the successor of such a father.[115]

Here the death of Constantius and the accession of Constantine, the themes of Constantine's election by God and by his father run parallel; they do also in the panegyric of 310, and even in Pliny's panegyric of Trajan, where the adoption of Trajan by Nerva, that is, Trajan's designation as successor, directly precedes Nerva's death.[116] Eusebius, in other words, describes a ceremonial of imperial death and accession in which no major change had taken place since the early second century concerning the order in which events were to follow one another. The way in which Eusebius differs from the Latin panegyrists, however, is that he stresses the ceremonial rather than Constantius' divine status as the means of expressing Constantine's legitimacy.

The formalisation and elaboration of imperial ceremonial was a gradual process, but during the Tetrarchy and in the Christian empire it became a sign of the times to be commented upon. Contemporaries in late antiquity thought that the Tetrarchs, Constantine and his successors unduly elaborated court ceremonial. Such statements were made not because an elaborate court-ceremonial had suddenly come into existence, but because the existing ceremonial had acquired a heightened meaning. People had become aware of it, and although the ceremonial had existed for generations, they were now prepared to give it a meaning.[117] The panegyrist of 291 did so when describing the *proscynesis* performed before Diocletian and Maximian in the Palace of Milan, and so did Eusebius when writing of the death of Constantius. That death and the accompanying ceremonial were the means of explaining Constantine's legitimacy as emperor.

Eusebius' emphasis on imperial ceremonial was, however, more than a general sign of the times; it betrayed the self-consciousness and uncertainty of the propagandist of the Christian empire. The Christian empire came into existence through the direct assistance of God, according to Eusebius. This statement is made through a variety of assertions, mainly in connection with Constantius' victories.[118] But apart from this, it also needed to be demonstrated that the Christian empire was the right kind of empire, and Eusebius did this by describing the ceremonial of the Christian empire, in connection mainly with the erection of churches and the holding of church-councils,[119] but also in connection with the time-honoured formalities of passing on power from one emperor to the next. He stated that Constantine was the legitimate emperor because his father passed on his own empire to him in a form which would be recognisable by and acceptable to all. In the case of Constantius I, the divinity of the emperor after his death was a side issue, to which Eusebius makes no reference. Eusebius' aim as regarded the ceremonial was similar when he discussed the death of Constantine and the succession of his sons, but more was at stake here. For, what also needed explaining was the position of the Christian emperor when confronted by his god. There had to be some replacement for, or alternative to, the pagan imperial ascent to heaven.

Firstly, the ceremonial of the imperial funeral, the baptism of Constantine, the journey of his body from Nicomedia to Constantinople, the lying in state in the palace, the proclamation of Constantine's sons by the army and Constantine's funeral are described by Eusebius in that order, and in considerable detail,[120] while elsewhere he states that Constantine designated his sons to succeed him. Here are to be met again elements of the ceremonial which have been encountered in the narrative of Herodian and Dio, and in Eusebius' own account of the death of Constantius.

Constantine's death was marked by universal mourning by both soldiers and citizens. Then the soldiers laid his body in a golden sarcophagus which was covered by the imperial purple and taken to Constantinople. During the lying in state in the palace, the body was adorned in imperial splendour with the purple and diadem, and the same honours were paid to it as Constantine had received in his lifetime.[121] According to Eusebius, Constantine was unique in receiving such honours, but in fact this was not the case: "Those who approached the new emperors [Caracalla and Geta] also came forward and bowed before the urn [containing the ashes of Septimius Severus]." [122]

While Constantine was lying in state in the palace, the soldiers spontaneously conferred the empire on his three sons,[123] Constantine having already bequeathed it to them, "like some ancestral dominion." [124] Eusebius then comes to the burial of Constantine. The body was escorted to the Church of the Apostles by Constantius II with the army. The army and Constantius II, who was only a catechumen, then withdrew and the Christian ministers performed the actual funeral.[125]

The ceremonial of the imperial obsequies covered the period between the death of one emperor and the accession of the next. Eusebius is particularly clear on this point. He says that Constantius I designated Constantine as his successor and then died. After the funeral the soldiers acclaimed Constantine. Next, when Constantine died, his body was honoured as though he were still alive, and meanwhile his sons were proclaimed as emperors by the soldiers, "as though the great emperor were still alive for them." [126] After this, Constantius II celebrated the funeral.

Eusebius' statements that events after Constantine's death took place as though he were still alive, and that he received the same honours in death as in life, have parallels in earlier accounts which bring to light with greater clarity the reason for this procedure. According to Suetonius, the announcement of Augustus' death was delayed until Agrippa Postumus had been murdered.[127] Similarly:

> The death of Claudius was not revealed until all arrangements had been completed for Nero's succession. As a result, people made vows for his safety as though he still lived, and a troupe of actors were summoned to the palace under the pretence that he had asked to be diverted by their performance.[128]

This fiction, that the emperor was still alive, became part of the ceremonial of the imperial funeral to cover the period which elapsed between the death of one emperor and the succession of the next. Eusebius does not pretend that Constantine was still alive, but asserts that the impact made by him in his life was such that he controlled events even after his death. This notion was expressed in the ceremonial, which ultimately arose out of events such as those described by Suetonius. The fiction of the survival of the emperor and the ceremonial which was built on it were used as a claim for legitimacy by the succeeding emperor. Thus Severus could pose as the avenger and successor of Pertinax, and the succession of the sons of Constantine was given an official appearance of orderliness and legitimacy which in fact it did not have.

The procedures for *consecratio* in Rome and the funerary ceremonial at Byzantium were designed to provide an impression of direct continuity between one emperor and the next. The continuity between the reign of Constantine and those of his sons is also emphasised by Libanius in his panegyric on Constantius II and Constans, which draws extensively on Eusebius:

> When, as it seemed good to God, the father of these emperors had set the world to rights and went away in order to rejoin him who had sent him down, the magnitude of this event did not disturb the peace of the empire.[129]

Secondly, the meaning and content of the ceremonial of imperial funerals: Constantine's ascent to heaven was, according to Eusebius, achieved without human intervention, like the ascent of Constantius I in the panegyrics of 307 and 310. As in these panegyrics, Eusebius views the entire universe as populated by the imperial family. While the earth is governed by Constantine's sons, who are images of their father and impersonate him, Constantine himself lives in communion with God on the arch of heaven, where he is rewarded by God for his long labours as are the souls of the saints:[130]

> For, to whatever quarter I look, whether it is towards the east or the west, or whether it is on the entire earth or the very heaven, everywhere I see the blessed emperor being present with his sons.[131]

> And now when I extend my understanding to the very vault of heaven, I behold even there his thrice-blessed soul abiding with God.[132]

Constantine's communion with God is elsewhere referred to in philosophical terms which presuppose a monotheistic religion, but not necessarily Christianity: ". . . joining to God that part of himself which was capable of apprehending and loving him."[133]

The ascent of that part of the soul which is νοερός and φιλόθεος differentiates Eusebius' view of *consecratio* from the version which has been met in the panegyrics of the second tetrarchy. Constantius, according to the panegyric, had simply been admitted *ad deorum concilia*,[134] or *receptus concessu caelitum*.[135] As has been seen, the panegyric of 310 places the description of Constantius' ascent in a cosmic setting, a pagan interpretation of the universe. This pagan universe could also accommodate the immortality and communion with God which Eusebius attributed to Constantine, and which was not specifically Christian. Nonetheless, Eusebius' view of the immortality of the emperor differs crucially from that expressed in the panegyrics. Eusebius wrote from a philosophical and theological point of view, while the panegyrics were practical and political. The panegyrists of 307 and 310, although the view of *consecratio* which they expressed differs from Pliny's in the respects which have been pointed out, yet spoke in the same idiom, even, sometimes, using the same phrases.[136] What was envisaged was that the emperor rose to some pagan Olympus which could be evoked, as in the panegyric of 310, in the language of mythology, and this defined the milieu as a pagan one.

Such terminology was avoided by Eusebius, who employed instead the language of philosophy, which could be pagan or Christian. Phrases such as *ad deorum concilia translatus, in consessu caelitum*, and the image of the chariot of Sol,[137] could be only pagan, whereas the ἀψῖδες οὐράνιαι[138] needed not be. However, within his philosophical vocabulary, Eusebius maintained a certain ambiguity. For instance, in referring to the honours which Constantine received after his death, Eusebius comes very close to implying a cult, although, of course, sacrifice, which was the formal definition of pagan worship, is not mentioned.[139] Eusebius does indeed emphasise that Constantine was the first Christian emperor, and his account of Constantine's ascent to heaven should be understood in this context, but the description of the heavenly status of Constantine itself remains open-ended, although it set one crucial precedent. In Eusebius, as in some later theorists of empire, the emperor is exempted from the last judgement.[140] He enters heaven directly to rule with God, as it was later expressed, by virtue of his imperial dominion, and such had also been the outcome of the *senatus consultum* of *consecratio*. It is true that the ascent of the Christian emperor is matched by similar sentiments in numerous Christian epitaphs,[141] but what for the ordinary Christian had to remain a pious hope[142] for the emperor could be stated as fact.[143]

What differentiates the views of Eusebius from earlier pagan and Latin views of *consecratio* can perhaps be summed up as follows. In Western, pagan terms, *consecratio* raised the two issues of the succession and of the status of the departed emperor. These two, although connected, remained independent points: once the departed pagan emperor was consecrated, the problem of continuity between father and son, or if not this, of continuity between one emperor and his successor, was settled and finished with. The problem was conceived in terrestrial terms; divine status was conferred by human verdict. In Eusebius, and to a certain extent in the panegyrics of 307 and 310, the problem of continuity was no longer viewed entirely in terrestrial terms: continuity between one emperor and the next, between father and son—although the question of terrestrial dominion was still involved—became an explicit continuity between heaven and earth.[144]

For, on the one hand, imperial rule on earth as regarded both the Tetrarchs according to their panegyrists, and Constantine according to Eusebius, was modelled on divine rule in heaven.[145] On the other hand—and this is peculiar to Eusebius and to certain late antique views of the Christian empire—Constantine in heaven with God exercised a continuing presidency over the empire of his sons, and in this way a connection and continuity was established not just between dead father and living son, but also between existence in heaven and existence on earth. In this way, the Tetrarchic view of imperial dominion on earth being related to or matching divine dominion in heaven was affirmed more strongly but in slightly different terms in the Christian empire, and these terms could ultimately become one of several means of differentiating the Christian from the pagan empire.[146]

4. THE RESOLUTION OF THE CONFLICTS ENTAILED IN IMPERIAL *CONSECRATIO* IN TERMS OF VISUAL ART IN THE FOURTH CENTURY

The pagan imagery of *consecratio*, like the literary exposition of it, could express, as has been seen, something of what the emperor's status after death meant for his successor and for his surviving subjects. In the fourth century, this pagan imagery disappeared almost entirely from imperial art. This is a significant pointer to the change in thinking about the emperor's afterlife which Christianity entailed.

It is well known that the church made use of the iconographical schemes of ancient art in general and of imperial art in particular to form its own language of images.[147] What is not as clearly realised is that when the church adopted images from imperial art, these same images ceased to be employed in imperial art. Aspects of this development have already been studied in the context of imperial *adventus*. In this way, imperial art ultimately became ecclesiastical art and ceased to have an existence of its own. We cannot say that images were dropped from the repertoire of imperial art because they were pagan; in themselves, images, like words, were neutral.[148] What mattered was that the meaning with which they were invested, and the meaning which two images of *consecratio* which will now be discussed came to convey in Christian art, made their continued application to the emperor impossible.

Eusebius describes these two images, both of which were applied to

Constantine after his death. One appears on the coinage, showing Constantine in a chariot pacing upwards and reaching out for the hand of God from a cloud.[149] This is one of the rare instances where an author of an eulogy makes explicit reference to a specific work of imperial art. The other image described by Eusebius was a painting or mosaic in Rome, which showed Constantine above the celestial spheres.[150] From surviving examples of this iconographical scheme we can infer roughly what this work looked like.

i. The Ascent to Heaven in a Chariot

In the posthumous coinage of Constantine, issued in bronze only after the division of the empire between Constans, Constantine and Constantius II in September 337, three months after Constantine's death,[151] an ephemeral attempt was made to translate pagan ideas of *consecratio* into terms compatible with Christianity. To illustrate more clearly the uncertainty which was felt at an official level at this time about images depicting *consecratio*, the whole posthumous coinage of Constantine, of which the chariot type formed one part, will be described.

The timing of these issues, which were produced after some of the disorders of the succession had been dealt with, indicates that a justification was sought for the arrangements after the event, by recalling the father of the present emperors. We have seen that Eusebius wrote with a similar aim in mind.

Two groups of reverses were produced, with a common obverse design, from the mints of Constantinople, Heraclea,[152] Antioch and Alexandria;[153] that is, in the East only, which is where the disputed succession was fought out. The obverse shows the veiled head of a youthful Constantine CONSTANTINUS P[A]T[ER] AUGG. Showing the consecrated emperor veiled was a regular feature of the coinage of the pagan empire and was here adopted to depict the special status of the departed emperor in the familiar visual idiom.[154]

One group of reverses read VN MR, or IUST VEN MEM, and shows a veiled figure who may be identified as Pietas, with her hands hidden in her robe. On the issue from Constantinople, Pietas faces towards a star, that old hint of divinisation, on her right.[155] Alternatively, this group of reverses has Aequitas, standing with scales in her right hand and her left hand hidden in her garment. Personifications constituted that part of Roman imperial iconography which survived longest in the Christian empire,[156] and here one of them appears in an unusually studied neutrality. Pietas had appeared earlier, sacrificing at an altar or with children, and in addition could usually be identified on the coinage by the legend.[157] The figure on Constantine's posthumous coinage, which has been interpreted as Pietas, is recognisable by none of these features. The star might be taken as a faint reminder of Constantine *sideribus receptus*. Aequitas is sufficiently identified by her scales,[158] and will have been familiar. Her appearance on these issues could be referred to the just division of the empire between Constantine's sons. The legend VN MR (*veneranda memoria*) or IUST VEN MEM links up with MEMORIA legends on Tetrarchic commemorative issues, but is so heavily abbreviated as to become almost insignificant.

The second group of reverses—that described by Eusebius—conveys a more positive message and ties up with earlier images showing the emperor rising to heaven in the chariot of Sol, like Trajan on the altar of Ephesus. According to Eusebius:

> Coins were also struck which bore the following design. On one side they displayed the blessed one with his head veiled, while the other side showed him as a charioteer on a four horse chariot, and on the right a hand stretched downward from above to receive him up to heaven.[159] (See plate 33.)

Iconographically, the reverse of this issue can be regarded as a mixture of Jewish and traditionally pagan motifs. The emperor in the chariot of Sol was a well-known image for conveying *consecratio* and immortality.[160] The hand of God was a device in Jewish art for depicting the presence and action of God, which conceivably found its way into imperial and thence into Christian art, where it became current in the later fourth century.[161] At the same time, however, we are here dealing with a quite distinct meaning of the image of the hand of God: that of bringing about the ascent of a human being to heaven. For this particular meaning, there was a pagan precedent in Roman art. On the Igel monument of the third century the apotheosis of Hercules in a chariot is shown, while Athena, her head and shoulders appearing above a cloud, is reaching down to assist his ascent.[162] (Plate 32) Without drawing on Jewish art, one could therefore interpret Constantine's coins as an abbreviated version of such a scheme. The hand of God, assisting an ascent to heaven, also existed in a pagan literary idiom, as we see from the panegyric which described Constantius' ascent to heaven:

> The temples of those who live above stood open for him and he was received among the dwellers in heaven, with Iuppiter himself holding out his right hand.[163]

Whatever its origin, the motif of the divine hand was absorbed into Christian art. An image relevant to our present context appears on the Munich ivory diptych of the late fourth or early fifth century, showing the women at Christ's tomb and His ascension. Here the hand of God from a cloud draws Christ into heaven.[164] (Plate 34) This manner of ascent is clearly related to the ascent shown on the Constantinian posthumous coinage which Eusebius describes. An image which we first saw in imperial art had become a Christian image, and had in this new context acquired a specifically Biblical frame of reference. This frame of reference removed the image from its imperial context: the emperor's journey to heaven, however personally and explicitly he might be summoned there by God, could not stand side by side with the ascension of Christ.

So much for the hand of God in Constantine's ascent. As for Constantine's ascent in a chariot, this image with its long pagan history also entered Christian art, but by a different route. For, while the hand of God assisting an ascending figure transferred itself directly from a pagan imperial into a Christian idiom, the figure of the rising charioteer entered Christian art by a more gradual process of assimilation of imperial images into Christian contexts. The Christian ascending charioteer was Elias, who appears on sarcophagi, from the late third century, rising in a *quadriga* and dropping his mantle to Elisha.[165]

The sarcophagus which is iconographically the simplest, and therefore, I think, among the earliest,[166] in the Vatican, shows Elias mounted in his *quadriga* above the waves of the Jordan (plate 30). The reins are tied around his waist in the manner of Roman charioteers; he drops his cloak to Elisha who stands behind the chariot, wearing a short tunic and raising his hand in acclamation and farewell. Above are three stars which may be understood as a hint at *consecratio*. Although the essentials of this composition come from Roman imperial art and its representations of the emperor's ascent, we must note that on the sarcophagus the Biblical narrative is followed as faithfully as the imperial prototype will allow.[167]

Another sarcophagus in the Vatican shows the next stage of the iconographical development which takes the viewer further away from the Biblical story. Elias is shown in his *quadriga*, below which is a sheep, perhaps adopted from Roman pastoral sarcophagi. The river Jordan is not shown. Behind the *quadriga* stands Elisha wearing a long tunic and receiving his master's cloak with veiled hands, a courtly gesture adopted from imperial art. In the background is a double arch, which probably represents the city gate of Jericho. City gates also figure in imperial art, that is, in depictions of *profectio* and *adventus*. Thus, the present city gate on the one hand contributes further to incorporating Christian into imperial iconography, and on the other, it places the ascent of Elias into a framework of ascent viewed as departure, such as we have encountered in the ascent of divinised emperors. This sarcophagus depicts a simple version of the iconography of later city-gate sarcophagi.[168] In general terms, however, it amplifies the rendering of Elias' ascent which we considered first, by adding features of imperial art.[169]

A group of city-gate sarcophagi of the later fourth century in Milan, Rome and Paris combines the ascent of Elias with a scene showing Moses receiving the law from the hand of God from a cloud. In the background is shown a most elaborate city gate.[170] The sarcophagus in Milan, in all likelihood made during Ambrose's episcopate, shows Elias in a *quadriga* dropping his mantle to Elisha who receives it with veiled hands. Below the *quadriga* are the waves of the river Jordan, and, on a smaller scale, Adam and Eve on either side of the tree, around which winds the serpent (see plate 31). Apart from Moses and the city gate, this sarcophagus adds to the earlier representation a piece of exegesis which is also found in a sermon of Ps. Augustine, where Elias is understood as a type for Christ:

> . . . and finally, just as the Lord after He had shown forth many virtues, and after He had suffered and was resurrected, ascended to heaven, so Elias also, after God had done wonderful things through him, was raised up to heaven in a fiery chariot.[171]

The sarcophagi in Paris and St. Peter's, Rome replace the figures of Adam and Eve with the reclining river-god of the Jordan, who raises his hand in acclamation. These two sarcophagi are to be dated in the late fourth century. They show a further elaboration of the original design, with a closer approximation of imperial iconography.[172] In the figure of Jordan is to be recognised the descendant of the reclining Campus Martius, Tellus or Oceanus on representations of imperial *consecratio* (see plates 28–29).

The Milan sarcophagus is slightly earlier than Ambrose's *Consolatio* for Theodosius, who speaks of an ascent. No surviving official work, however, shows the emperor ascending in a chariot, after Constantine's posthumous coinage, or ascending at all. Since the iconographical scheme survived, and was used at the very time and place when the imperial ascent was spoken about, this disappearance of the ascent from imperial art is to be regarded as the result of deliberate policy, for the ascent of the departed emperor by means of some vehicle came to be a characteristic of the pagan ascent to heaven. But at the same time, the pagan core of the image, the imperial ascent on Sol's *quadriga*, had been overlaid with new meanings and associations.

However similar these now Christian images of ascent were to their pagan imperial prototypes, to the extent even of associating components—such as the river-god and the ascending charioteer—in the same way as they had been associated in pagan art, the impact of the Christian images was different and new. The Elias sarcophagi which we have discussed draw our attention to the process by which this new impact was formulated. At first, a single reference to imperial art serves to illustrate the Biblical story of Elias' ascent. The story is then elaborated by further references to imperial art. These accretions, so far from making the story into a pagan one, dignify it, make it publicly viable. The images themselves were converted to Christianity, acquired a new sphere of relevance, and it is this which took them out of the imperial context. Generations of debate about the imperial afterlife in paganism and the gradual evolution of the imperial funerary ceremonial made it possible for pagans to visualise the emperor ascending like, or with, the sun god. But in Christianity, the emperor could not ascend like Elias. Christianity had not as yet come to formulate the parallels between emperors and Christian sacred figures which could have made viable such an ascent, with all the fine, if precarious, balance of metaphor and reality that the visual formulation of imperial ascent had required in paganism.

In other words, in using pagan motifs, Christian art had to disperse the pagan associations of these motifs. If we now return to Constantine's *consecratio* image of ascent in a chariot with the hand of God, we may observe how the combination of the two motifs of this image, neutral and non-specific though it looked to Eusebius, crystallised visually one version of the imperial ascent as formulated in paganism. In literature, this had been done most clearly and fully in the Tetrarchic panegyrics which we have studied and which drew on earlier imperial imagery and ceremonial. We may thus understand why the image which, according to Eusebius, could appropriately represent Constantine's ascent to God—even though one part of it was used in Christian art for Elias, and the other part of it for Christ—was, after all, not a viable one in Christian imperial art.

Furthermore, we now see more clearly why Eusebius as a Christian concentrated so heavily on the ceremonial aspects of imperial funerals: he thereby avoided commenting in any detail about what could not be formulated in Christianity, that is, the ritual of imperial ascent to heaven. This negative approach of Eusebius was to become positive in the hands of Gregory Nazianzen and Ambrose. There was not simply a funeral, but an *adventus* in heaven, with all the potential for extended and multiple meaning that this entailed. Once the ideology of such an *adventus* had been established within the old funerary ceremonial, any pagan speculation, philosophical or other, along with its imagery in visual art, of how the emperor attained the beyond could, in due course, be set aside.

ii. The Emperor Enthroned on the Globe

The history of the second image described by Eusebius is more clear-cut because in Christian art it was applied to Christ himself. It shows the emperor enthroned over the globe or the celestial sphere. Such an image, according to Eusebius, was painted in Rome after Constantine's death, showing him "abiding in a celestial dwelling place above the vault of heaven."[173] This image matches Eusebius' own concept of the departed emperor abiding with God in the vault of heaven.[174] Such configurations, although rare, did occur in earlier imperial art.

Dio described what was perhaps the earliest one and showed an εἰκών of Caesar above the οἰκουμένη.[175] Another instance of this iconographical scheme comes from the coinage of Domitian,[176] 81–83 A.D. On the reverse appears DIVUS CAESAR IMP DOMITIANI F, Domitian's little son, seated on a sphere, surrounded by seven stars, the planets. A medallion of Antoninus Pius[177] shows on the reverse TR POT COS III ITALIA, Italia seated on a sphere, which may be understood as being the *oikoumene*. A related issue appeared on the regular coinage of Antoninus Pius[178] showing on the reverse ITALIA, Italia towered, holding sceptre and cornucopia, and seated on a sphere.

This iconographical scheme enjoyed a measure of popularity in imperial art during the third century, when medallions of Alexander Severus[179] TEMPORUM FELICITAS (plate 41), Gordian II TEMPORUM FELICITAS, Tacitus AETERNITAS AUG[180] and Probus ROMAE AETERNAE[181] showed an elaboration of it.[182] The emperor appears seated on a starry sphere, the heavens. He is crowned from behind by Victory, holding a sceptre with his left hand and with his right the zodiac or circle of the year, from which emerge the Seasons. Behind the zodiac sometimes stands the personification of the Saeculum, indicating that imperial dominion operated not only in space, but also in time; that it was, in effect, a replica on earth of divine dominion.

Some fourth-century texts indicate how a supreme deity above the stars was actually visualised. For example, Lactantius, quoting from the text of the 'Edict of Milan,' says:

> We have decreed that we should give both to the Christians and to all others the unconditional faculty of following the religion that each one chooses; so that by this measure whatever divinity resides in the celestial throne may be well disposed and favourable to us and all who live under our governance.[183]

The panegyrics of 289 and 307 show how this notion could be applied to the emperor, and suggest the iconographical scheme of the emperor enthroned on the globe as lord of the *oikoumene* like Caesar, and holding the zodiac, as *fatorum arbiter*. The orator of 289 says of Maximian, after describing the terrestrial triumphal ornaments of the emperor:

> But how much greater are the services which you have bestowed [on us] as an act of your favour when the empire was granted to you: to admit into your soul the care for so great a commonwealth, to take upon yourself the destiny of the whole world, and, forgetting yourself, as it were, to live for the nations, and to stand upon such a high pinnacle of human affairs from which you may in some way look out, with your eyes and your mind acting in coordination, upon all land and sea, [to behold] where there exists secure calm, and where uncertain uproar, [to see] which judges emulate your justice and which generals serve the glory of your virtue, to receive from everywhere countless messengers, and to send out as many commands, to think upon so many cities, nations and provinces, and to spend all your nights and days in perpetual concern for the welfare of all. And since you have accepted all these [duties which were] laid upon you, together with your most excellent brother [Diocletian], you perform them with fortitude, he with wisdom.[184]

The emperors are here placed outside a strictly human context, they have no human peers, and they achieve this status at the time of becoming emperor by fulfilling their imperial function. This concept of imperial rule, formulated clearly under the Tetrarchs, outlasted the Tetrarchy of Diocletian. The roles of Augustus and Caesar and the exalted status this implied for both could be attributed to a new set of emperors. Thus, in 307, a panegyrist said to Maximian and Constantine:

> For you, Father, it is right that you should, from the very height of empire, look out upon the world which you share, that with your celestial assent you should decree the destinies of human affairs, should grant the auspices to wars which are to be fought and set down the laws when peace is to be made. For you, young emperor, it is right that you should indefatigably patrol the frontiers which set apart the Ro-

man Empire from the nations of the barbarians, that you should send many laurels of victories to your father-in-law, should request his commands and report to him when they have been performed.[185]

The perfect illustration of these passages appears on the arch of Galerius. Diocletian is enthroned over the sky as Iovius, and Maximian over the earth as Herculius.[186] (Plate 10) They, the two senior Augusti, are portrayed as stationary, inactive: "They stand upon such a high pinnacle of human affairs," or, in the words of the panegyrist of 307, "For you . . . it is right that you should, from the very height of Empire, look out upon the world." The two Caesars approach from left and right introducing subdued provinces.

In 289 the different roles of junior and senior emperors were summarised in the words, "These duties . . . you [(Maximian)] perform with fortitude, he [(Diocletian)] with wisdom." The words of the panegyrist of 307 are more directly applicable to the Caesars on the relief on the arch of Galerius: "For you, young emperor, it is right that you should indefatigably patrol the frontiers . . . should send many laurels of victories." The arch of Galerius thus shows a perfect image of the Tetrarchy, with the careful differentiation of roles and status within it, and this image could be expounded in the light of the Tetrarchic panegyrics and of earlier imperial art.

The Tetrarchs did not need to be received among the stars, as the earlier imperial coinage sometimes said of consecrated emperors,[187] because this status was already theirs from the accession. It was this idea which made the emperor's enthronement over the sky, as on the arch of Galerius, possible during his lifetime. The Tetrarchy thus saw a resolution of the old conflict between Roman political egalitarianism which expressed itself in the official Roman *consecratio* procedures on the one hand, and the Hellenistic tendency to divinise rulers and statesmen in their lifetimes on the other.

With the collapse of the Tetrarchic system the notion of imperial *consecratio*, of ascent to heaven, was revived, even though it was considerably changed; hence Constantine after his death was depicted on the Roman picture *sideribus receptus*. However, this rendering of the old iconography marked the end of an epoch,[188] for the image of the emperor enthroned on the globe had a history similar to that of the emperor ascending to heaven in a chariot. It also was absorbed by the art of the church, where it can be traced from the mid-fourth century and where it was applied to Christ.

One of the most interesting examples, and perhaps the earliest, occurs on the sarcophagus of Junius Bassus, dated by its inscription in the year 359 (plate 25). The sarcophagus shows scenes from the life of Christ in two superimposed registers, the central scene in the lower register being Christ's entry into Jerusalem. This was an event which occurred at a certain date and in a certain place where it could be re-enacted on that date in an annual liturgical ceremony. Like an imperial *adventus* of the mid-fourth century, Christ's *adventus* in Jerusalem was an historical event. But on the sarcophagus of Junius Bassus it has a further dimension, for in the central scene in the top register the teaching Christ between two apostles is enthroned over Coelus, like Diocletian on the arch of Galerius.[189] A slightly later column sarcophagus shows the *traditio legis* with Christ similarly enthroned over Coelus, and this is only one of many examples of this imperial iconography in a Christian context.[190]

But at the same time both the teaching Christ and Christ handing over the law were depicted on sarcophagi not enthroned over Coelus but enthroned or standing over the four streams of Paradise. The four streams of Paradise are to be understood as an image of Biblical origin to denote the universe which, in pagan imperial art, is rendered by Coelus or the globe on which the emperor is enthroned. The apse mosaic of San Vitale, where Christ handing a wreath to Vitalis is enthroned over the globe—which in turn is set over the four streams of Paradise—combines these two images into one.[191] (Plate 42) The imperial and the Biblical images had merged.[192]

If we return now to the sarcophagus of Junius Bassus and to Christian art of the mid-fourth century, we may observe that the motif of the emperor enthroned on the earth or the universe, like the motif of the emperor ascending to heaven in a chariot, disappeared from imperial art at the very same time that it emerged in Christian art. This was because, once this image of majesty had been applied to Christ, it was impossible to apply it again to the emperor. A direct μίμησις θεοῦ was possible in the pagan empire, even though it was restricted and defined, but not in the Christian empire. In heaven the emperor joined the crowd of other emperors, even of saints and angels, but God was on an entirely different level.

The sarcophagus of Junius Bassus thus allows us a glimpse into the changing views of the status of the emperor *vis-à-vis* the divine in the mid-fourth century. For Christ, it was possible to reapply, in Christian times, one part of the ancient imagery of divinisation, of transcending time, and of universal dominion, and to juxtapose all this to Christ's earthly dominion as represented by his entry into Jerusalem. Dominion over the cosmos, and specific, historical dominion over the empire both were imperial themes, had both been applicable to the pagan emperor and had both found various expressions in imperial art and iconography. On the sarcophagus of Junius Bassus, two imperial iconographies were applied to Christ in such a way as to show Christ in his divinity, his majesty, in heaven, and in his humanity on earth. The debate about the nature, whether human or divine, of the emperor, was at all its stages beset with difficulties. Its field of application was therefore limited, but, as we have seen, crucial. In the course of the fourth century, this debate was supplanted by the debate about the nature of Christ, the first stage of which was officially defined by the Council of Nicaea, and which was of universal application. The two scenes on the sarcophagus which concern us here may be understood, therefore, as a carefully deliberated theological statement.[193] This statement reflects also on the role of the emperor in the Christian empire. Interpretations of the order of the universe which, under the Tetrarchs, still could be validated and illustrated by reference to imperial dominion, in the Christian empire could no longer be validated and illustrated in this way. For, the order of the universe now focused on a new and different principle, the incarnation of Christ. As a result, the order of the universe could be described in terms of a hierarchy of God, emperor, and mankind; it could no longer be described, however tentatively and speculatively, as focusing on an imperial *kosmokrator*.

And so, there occurred a dividing line, a watershed, in late antique thought during the early decades of the Christian empire, which is here being approached from the point of view of the ceremony of *consecratio*. The existing ceremonial was reformulated in a fundamental way; it became more precise, narrower, less open to speculation, for areas of speculation had shifted and changed. In *consecratio*, a ceremonial of conflicts was shaped into a generally acceptable whole—the ceremonial of imperial funerals—and this was the first imperial ceremony to find a cogent Christian expression. Thus, by the mid-fourth century, Christian emperors could offer to their subjects a new, though at times confused, Christian ceremonial of imperial funerals to which any pagan ceremonial, insofar as it survived, was no longer a fully viable alternative.

Nonetheless, we will see that something of paganism did survive, even when, as in the sixth century, Christianity could be taken for granted. Next to radical discontinuity we will encounter again the tenacious continuity in habits of thought, and in habits of making assumptions, which was a characteristic of the classical world, and which allowed so much of the classical world to survive beyond its institutional transformation and collapse.

5. A CHRISTIAN VIEW OF FUNERARY CEREMONIAL: GREGORY NAZIANZEN ON THE FUNERALS OF CONSTANTIUS II AND JULIAN

In his second oration against Julian, Gregory Nazianzen treats the funerals of Constantius II and Julian. The narrative allows some insight into how far Christian views of the emperor's death, funeral and after-life had stabilised in the generation following Constantine. For, where the funeral of Constantine in the Church of the Apostles, described by Eusebius, had been a novelty and set a precedent, that of his son Constantius could be and was regarded by Gregory as continuing a tradition.[194] The honorable burial of an emperor in the right place could be understood as a retrospective token of his legitimacy and of the acceptability of his rule.

In the Tetrarchic panegyrics, what was discussed was not burial, but *consecratio*, the ascent of the emperor to heaven. However, the function of honourable burial in Gregory and *consecratio* in the Tetrarchic panegyrics was the same: both were a form of ratification of a reign after the emperor's death, the opposite of *damnatio memoriae*. The fact that burial could take on this function may be regarded as an important outcome of Eusebius' cautious, often ambivalent formulations of the emperor's status after death on the one hand, and his clear and decisive account of the funerary ceremonial on the other. This new development in the interpretation of the funerary ceremonial went hand in hand with the establishment of the imperial mausolea of Constantinople in the fourth and fifth centuries.[195]

Gregory describes the honours bestowed on Constantius after his death as a reward for his reign, and the dishonour bestowed on the dead Julian, as a punishment for his apostasy. Thus, the ceremonial form of the imperial burial, as understood by Gregory, provided the basis for a judgement of an emperor's reign. The ceremonial now enshrined the old contrast between *consecratio* and *damnatio memoriae* in a new form. Both Constantius and Julian died away from Constantinople, and Gregory recounts the two funeral processions thus:

> [The body of Constantius] was sent forth with universal acclamations and solemnity, with our religious observances, such as singing throughout the night and torchlight, which are the rites with which we Christians think it right to honour a holy death. Thus the carrying forth of

the corpse is an occasion for solemn rejoicing mingled with mourning. . . . And also this has been heard by many, that, when the body
passed the Taurus mountains, to be brought to its home city . . . there
was a voice from the mountain-tops which was heard, as of beings
singing and sending [Constantius] forth, the voice, I think, of angelic
powers, a reward for his piety, and an offering for his funeral.[196]

And then, when he approached the great and regal city, how may I
describe the torch-bearers from the entire army, and the armed men
[standing in] order, as though it were done for the living emperor, how
shall I describe the outpouring [of people] from the noble city, which
was the most notable of all, past or future?[197]

The army had been so devoted to Constantius, says Gregory, that
even Julian, though proudly arrayed in his new imperial purple, was
forced to pay honour to Constantius by taking off his diadem and es-
corting him to the tomb of his family in the Church of the Apostles.[198]
There follows the contrast with Julian's funeral:

His campaign was ignominious, and more so was his return, for he
was driven away by cities and nations, by common consent and deri-
sion, which is remembered even now by many. And what was his disgrace? Actors accompanied him with their mockeries, and he was
escorted by the indignities coming from the stage . . . and was re-
proached for his apostasy, his defeat and his death. What injuries did
he not suffer, what did he not hear of the outrages perpetrated by those
who practise outrage as their profession, until the city of Tarsus received him. And I know not how, or for what reason it was condemned
to suffer this disgrace. And there [Julian] has an ignoble precinct, an
impure grave, a sanctuary which is an abomination and not to be beheld by the eyes of the pious.[199]

These narratives contain no direct reference to afterlife or divinisation
other than the singing of the angelic powers for Constantius. The ceremonial, on the other hand, is very clear: the progress of the imperial
funerary cortege is described as an *adventus*, an *adventus* to the emperor's final resting-place. It was by means of the ceremonial that a verdict of approval or disapproval could be made on the departed emperor.
In this form the Roman and pagan antithesis of *consecratio* and *damnatio
memoriae* survived into the Christian Byzantine Empire. There are numerous subsequent examples of such judgements being made, that is,
on the one hand the honourable burial of recognised emperors and on
the other the scattering of the ashes or bones of one labelled as a tyrant
or usurper, like Phocas.[200]
In Gregory, it was the ceremony of the imperial funeral, conceived in
the very traditional terms of *adventus*, that formulated the status in life

and death of the emperor. The *adventus* was not yet what it was to become, as handled by Ambrose—an *adventus* in heaven—but a terrestrial *adventus*, such as had already been described by Suetonius in the context of imperial burials.[201] In Gregory, a judgement upon the emperor was no longer made by any constitutional mechanism such as a *senatus consultum*, but by a popular consensus, whereby one emperor was honoured, another not. Here again, Christianity helped to override and remove an ancient source of conflict; this removal of conflict was a process which for imperial *consecratio* began, as we have seen, under the Tetrarchy.

By means of articulating such a consensus the population of the empire, in particular the population of the imperial capitals, could relate itself to the emperor. From an administrative point of view the empire of the fourth century was rigid and highly stratified. But from a doctrinal, ideological point of view, we can see how, while some traditional forms of consensus which related emperor and subjects, such as the ceremony of *adventus*, had lost some of their old significance, new forms of consensus had developed on the basis of the now Christian empire.

6. THE LAST PAGANS

i. Pagan Ideas of Julian's Afterlife

While Christians of the fourth century came to use the ceremonial of imperial burial as one basis for their interpretation of the nature of the emperor's rule, pagans, in their considerations on the death of Julian, turned to more ancient concepts and images. Thus, Ammianus would have wished to see Julian buried in Rome, "the eternal city," amidst the monuments of the earlier divinised emperors, his tomb being washed by the waves of the Tiber. Thus would Julian's glory have been perpetuated. Just as for the living emperor, Rome was the home of empire and the virtues, *lar imperii virtutumque*, so it should be the resting-place of the good emperor after his death.[202] Honourable burial, according to these traditional ideas, was a reward for virtue.

Not all Julian's adherents, however, viewed his death in the impersonal frame of reference which was provided by the great Roman past. Libanius envisaged a more immediate presence of the dead Julian than the mere remembrance of his glory. Writing of Julian's immortality, Libanius mentions first a pragmatic view, namely that Julian will survive through his works, which will serve as an image of him. He then goes on to say:

And since I have made mention of images, many cities have set up images of [Julian] in the temples of the gods, and already, whoever has with prayer sought some blessing from him, has not failed to obtain it.[203]

Elsewhere, Libanius exhorted Theodosius, in a speech never published, to punish Julian's murderers, in return for which Julian would assist Theodosius in restoring the empire to a happier state:

Prove the truth of my suggestion by testing it, my Emperor, take hold of this support, and you will attain good fortune. It will show you Thrace being cultivated, it will show you Thermopylae opened up; exiles will return because of it, and the present defeat and rout will be transformed into their opposites. . . . Julian will assist in all this and will make everything easy, and although not seen by the eyes of the soldiers he will be known by his works.[204]

These two statements, while evoking ancient concepts of the ruler as θεὸς ἐπιφανής or *deus praesens*, as a figure present to aid and assist (such as it had been articulated in the cult of living rulers from the Hellenistic age), are nonetheless almost unparalleled in the history of the cult of rulers and the imperial cult, for rarely indeed were prayers addressed to the departed emperor; nor, more importantly, were they thought to be answered by him.[205] The novelty may be explained from two converging points of view.

Firstly, the prayers addressed to the dead Julian were quite simply a continuation of the hopes that were pinned on him while he was alive, when his deeds and personality guaranteed the fulfilment of these hopes.[206] While Libanius' statements were an expression of such hopes, they constituted at the same time a new formulation of an attitude, latent in paganism, toward the attainment of divinity by human beings. During the earlier empire, the attainment of divinity by the emperor had been defined and delimited by the *senatus consultum* of *consecratio*. This changed during the Tetrarchy, as we have seen, so that the divine status of Julian, as understood by Libanius, was foreshadowed in the post-Tetrarchic panegyrics where the emperor rose to the gods unaided by man. At the same time, Julian's status after death, as seen by Libanius, was a continuation of the veneration shown him during some of his ceremonial entries when he was alive.[207]

Secondly, however, Libanius' idea of prayers answered by Julian touched on the more widely-based phenomenon of miraculous or supernatural impingement on the natural order as understood in late antiquity. Christians were beginning to define such impingement with reference to the relics of martyrs. For pagans like Libanius, the impingement continued to operate in the framework of ancient cult-sites and rituals.[208] Christianity and paganism held each other in balance, even as late as the late fourth century, by fulfilling analogous religious needs which could at times focus on the emperor. Thus, Julian averted the anger of Poseidon by his prayers;[209] Theodosius by his prayers won the battle of the Frigidus.[210] Both pagans and Christians claimed for their side the rain miracle of Marcus Aurelius in the land of the Quadi, which is represented on his column. And characteristically, it was Themistius, the pagan advocate of the Christian empire, who fitted the miracle into a framework of imperial theory which was designed to suit both Christian and pagan Hellenes.[211]

A different aspect of Julian's divinisation was articulated in an oracle which he received and which was recorded by Eunapius:

> But when you have overpowered the Persians under your sceptre and have driven them in confusion with your sword as far as Seleucia, then a fiery chariot shrouded in storms and whirlwinds shall convey you to Olympus, freed from the burden of your mortal members. You will attain your ancestral halls of radiant light, from which you have fallen and come into a mortal body.[212]

According to this oracle, Julian was to be snatched up to return to heaven whence his soul had descended at birth. This return of the soul to the stars was a deep preoccupation which Neoplatonist philosophy had inherited from the pagan past, and we may thus place the oracle in this framework. At the same time, the imagery of the ascent, the fiery chariot with whirlwinds, came from the ancient Near East. It recalls in exact detail the ascent to heaven of Elias which was depicted on late antique Christian sarcophagi.[213] (Plates 30–31)

Thus, an ancient Eastern method of ascent to heaven was applied to Julian, an ascent, moreover, which had, by this time, found its way into Christian art, taking it out of the realm of images which could be applied to the Christian emperor, as we have seen. The oracle repeated by Eunapius therefore emerges as not just a reformulation of ancient ideas, but as a formulation with a specific contemporary context.

Imagery analogous to that of the oracle comes from another pagan text of the late fourth century, the *Historia Augusta*. In a dream which Septimius Severus had shortly before his death, he was snatched away in a chariot drawn by eagles:

> The omens of his death were as follows. He himself dreamt that he was snatched away to heaven by four eagles and a jewelled chariot, with I know not what kind of huge apparition in human form flying

ahead. And while he was snatched away, he counted as far as eighty-nine, and he did not live a single year longer than this. . . . And when he was placed on a huge circle of air he stood for a long time alone and bereft, but when he was afraid that he would fall down headlong, he heard himself being called by Iuppiter, and was placed among the Antonines.[214]

The *circulus ingens aereus* is perhaps to be identified with Eusebius' ἁψῖδες οὐράνιαι, which could be represented visually by showing the emperor enthroned on a globe (plate 10). However, the feature which places the *Historia Augusta* passage more directly into the present context of pagan imperial ascents is the eagles which draw the jewelled chariot. A cameo now in Berlin, which may represent Julian, shows a chariot supported by two eagles carrying wreaths, a bearded laureate emperor crowned by a city goddess. Between them stands a small armed statue of Athena (plate 27 with 26). The emperor holds a sceptre in his right hand and the city goddess one in her left hand. The design is almost symmetrical and foreshadows the heraldic representations of a later period. If the emperor is indeed Julian, the city goddess could be Constantinopolis, and the statue the Palladium, which was supposedly taken to Constantinople by Constantine.[215]

The chariot drawn by eagles points to the Near East for its place of origin. The eagle clutching a wreath appears in Syrian funerary art, whence it was adopted by Roman funerary art in the first century.[216] In the Near East, since Babylonian times, royal and divine thrones were visualised as supported by a chariot drawn by various creatures, which were often winged. Examples contemporary with Julian appear on Sassanian silver platters, showing the King of Kings seated on a throne-chariot supported by griffins.[217]

This is the type of vehicle to which Eunapius' oracle probably refers. The cameo with Julian's eagle chariot translates this image into the terminology of Roman imperial art, where, however, it was a short-lived phenomenon. But outside the confines of strictly official art, the motif of a winged chariot lived on in representations of the ascent of Alexander in a chariot drawn by griffins.[218] A related motif is the throne-chariot of Christ, supported by the apocalyptic beasts, and in one case, surrounded by huge wings, in apse paintings at Bawit.[219] In the Syrian Rabbula gospels (589 A.D.) a chariot with the winged apocalyptic beasts supports a mandorla in which stands the ascended Christ, the whole being surrounded by little tongues of fire.[220]

Neither the chariot of Christ, however, nor the chariot of Alexander ever entered the official repertoire of images in imperial and ecclesiastical Byzantine art. The griffin chariot of Alexander was not applied to the emperor, and Byzantine ecclesiastical art never represented any means whereby Christ, or even a human being, could have reached heaven. The official art forms of the late antique empire defined such graphic renderings of attaining the supernatural world as pagan.[221] For Christians to define how the beyond might be reached was in part, at this time, a process of excluding the various pagan methods. For pagans on the other hand, it was, still, a process of inclusion and of reapplying ancient imagery, whether visual or literary, to present circumstances.

ii. The End of Pagan *consecratio* in Rome

This pagan inclusiveness emerged particularly clearly in the late fourth and early fifth centuries in Rome and Italy.[222] Claudian, the panegyrist of a Christian court, retained a pagan view of *consecratio*. It is impossible to see anything in common between the Theodosius whom Claudian consigned to heaven and the Theodosius whose funerary *consolatio* was pronounced by Ambrose. However, Claudian's ideas were nonetheless determined by the circumstances of his time in that he had to reformulate paganism in such a way as to bypass, firstly, all acts of worship, pagan or Christian, and secondly, the pagan debate concerning the dichotomy between divine and human existence and the transcending of it.

Claudian, as was explained in the context of *adventus*, created a coherent framework of meanings on many levels which could, in Italy and Rome, exist in its own right, a framework in which the values of paganism acquired a certain universality and timelessness, and thereby could become non-controversial, at least to the extent of being acceptable at a Christian court. In his rendering of *adventus*, Claudian coordinated history with myth and set particular events into a wider context. The same applies to his approach to *consecratio*, where, however, the coordination was not between history and myth, but between different aspects of myth or, as I have called it elsewhere, pagan sacred story.

The presupposition of pagan *consecratio* was that the transposition of a human being from this world to another was possible. Claudian approached this question not so much from the point of view of *consecratio* as from the wider, and less controversial, point of view of the position of a subject *vis-à-vis* the emperor. To face the emperor amounted to a transposition from one realm of existence into another; it was a testing, for which Claudian, in the preface to his first panegyric on Honorius, used the simile of the young eagle outstaring the sun. An ordinary mortal could not support the emperor's presence. This idea was clarified and

refined in the preface to the panegyric on the sixth consulship of Honorius, when Claudian juxtaposed the court of heaven and the court of the
emperor. He saw himself in both and thereby underwent a kind of
divinisation.

> In the silent night, devotion to the Muses
> Urges me to follow my accustomed tasks.
> For I dreamt that I stood upon the vault of the starry heaven
> And laid my songs at the feet of Iuppiter on high . . .[223]
> I sang of Enceladus and of conquered Typhoeus,
> One buried beneath Inarime, the other beneath mighty Aetna.
> How glad was Iuppiter when heaven welcomed him, the war
>   completed,
> When he brought home the spoils of the field of Phlegra!
> The image has come true, and has not misled me;
> The deceptive ivory gate has not sent up an empty dream.
> Behold the Emperor, head of the world, who is equal to Olympus!
> Behold the gods, such as I dreamt of, worthy of reverence!
> A dream could not invent anything as great, and this exalted court
> Is for the singer an assembly rivalling that of heaven.[224]

The divinisation of the poet in heaven of which he dreams is made
real and tangible by his experience of the presence of the emperor,
through which he lives while awake. Two levels of experience are thus
made concurrent; they are made concurrent not only as regards Claudian, but also as regards the emperor, for Iuppiter is the dream-image of
Honorius. Moreover, the validity of the dream-image is asserted in real
life: "Behold the Emperor, head of the world, who is equal to Olympus!"

Here then is one example of a transposition of human beings from
this world to another. In a world of the imagination where this was possible, the emperor's divinisation, his ascent to heaven, became a cogent,
comprehensible event. In the panegyric on Honorius' third consulship,
Claudian describes the actual divinisation, the ascent, of Theodosius:

> As he was [in human form] he crossed the clouds on a trail of light,
> He entered the sphere of the moon and left the threshold
> Of the god of Arcady, and flew on to the wild breezes of Venus.
> From there he crossed the path of Phoebus, the dangerous fire of
>   Mars
> And peaceful Iuppiter; he stood on the highest vault
> Where is the frozen zone of Saturn.
> The fabric of heaven opens and of their own accord the radiant gates
> Stand wide. Boötes holds ready the northern region,
> While swordgirt Orion unlocks the gates of the South.
> They welcome the new star, uncertain each
> As to which part of the sky he would choose, what stars
> He wished to grace with his presence, or where he would abide.

You glory of heaven, once the glory of the earth,
Your own Oceanus, when you are wearied in your course, receives
    you
In its waters which wash the shores of your familiar Spain.
Blessed parent, when you first rise
You see Arcadius, and when you lower your course,
Honorius holds back your fire in the West.
And in whichever hemisphere you take your wandering course
You traverse the kingdoms of your sons who in serenity
And wise discretion rule neighbouring nations,
And who create again an age of nobler metal.[225]

The ascent of Theodosius, like that of Caesar, is visualised as the ascent of a star, and in picturing this ascent, Claudian describes the celestial landscape in the terminology of astrology.[226] With Theodosius residing in heaven, and his sons ruling on earth, the universe is understood in terms of the dominion of an imperial dynasty, is populated by emperors. This idea had also been expressed by Eusebius and had as crucial a political dimension in 395–396 when Claudian wrote as it had had in the years after 337. The existence of the emperor, whether living or dead, was in harmony with the universe, and everything in the ordering of this universe could be made comprehensible and explicable under this denominator. Claudian thus expounded an aspect of the old pagan view of the universe revolving around the figure of the emperor. But at the same time, it should be noted that Theodosius—unlike Julian in Eunapius' oracle and other pagan emperors—resided in heaven alone, without the company of the gods. This was one of the ways in which Claudian avoided any direct, and thereby political, reference to paganism.

In short, imagery was for Claudian an imagery of art, of culture, not, as for Julian, and, in different terms, for Christianity, an imagery of cult, of religious worship. Therefore Claudian's verse would have been pagan to those pagans and Christians who still refused to make a distinction between culture and worship. And it was very much part of the mood of his age that a cultivated Christian such as Prudentius could, for the first time, adumbrate such a distinction.[227]

In such a context, Claudian could link up the divinisation of Theodosius with the legitimate terrestrial dominion of his sons.[228] Thus, *consecratio* gave rise to the customary praises of the ruling emperor, Honorius, who equalled and outshone his great father,[229] and of the father, who rejoiced in the deeds of his son.[230]

Claudian thus gave a consistent view of imperial divinisation, a view in which the traditional and practical aspects of *consecratio* played their part, and which, on the other hand, was also theoretically satisfying. There were no conflicts in this cultured, literary and sophisticated variety of late antique paganism, and no latent unreconciled problems. Divinisation was a carefully articulated, overtly pagan process.

There were, as has been seen already, different types of paganism. One way of classifying them is to contrast Julian's cultic, and at the same time philosophical paganism, with Claudian's paganism, which was articulated in terms of a pagan courtly culture without direct reference to religious practice. It was this latter kind of paganism that could produce a view of divinisation, parts of which, as may be seen in Corippus, could be acceptable within Christianity, precisely because they did not depend on the performance of any pagan cult, like the incipient cult of Julian to which Libanius referred. Nor did they depend exclusively on any pagan imagery of the method of the imperial ascent, such as was revived for Julian. Claudian's was a paganism of erudition, and of art, the vehicle of his poetry. As such, it was fundamentally different from Julian's paganism.

Claudian's paganism, his explanation of the ascent of Theodosius, was an outcome of the new-found respectability of imperial Christianity as expressed, in the West, by Ambrose. We shall see that as handled by Ambrose, the ascent of the emperor had become a non-controversial matter; it was capable of a Christian explanation and elaboration, but not of controversy.[231] This attitude was reflected exactly in Claudian, who also took a non-controversial approach, but a pagan one. Insofar as there was no controversy, and no tension in Claudian's rendering of the imperial ascent, Christianity determined his approach, for tension, even if it was resolved tension, was fundamental to the pagan view of imperial afterlife.[232]

The old pagan tension between different concepts of divinisation was for a last time depicted on the *consecratio* diptych of c. 430 A.D. in the British Museum.[233] (Plate 36) At the same time, however, the diptych depicts the ascent of a divinised emperor within a structured universe, just as Claudian had done, and as, in a different idiom, Macrobius[234] did in his commentary on the *Dream of Scipio*. Furthermore, the diptych shows the imperial ascent in the framework of the old pagan Roman *consecratio* ceremonial.

In the lower part the statue of a bearded *divus*, perhaps Julian, in a toga of the Antonine period, is seated in an *aedicula*. The statue holds a long sceptre in its left hand and a branch in its right. The *aedicula* is on a cart which is drawn by four elephants. Each elephant has its rider, two of whom have goads, while the other two feed their elephants with loaves.

Behind the *quadriga* is a pyre with three tiers, from which escape two eagles; on top of it is a *quadriga* reined by a nude figure with a billowing cloak (cf. plate 35). In the upper part of the diptych, two wind-gods lift the togate *divus* up to heaven, where, on the left upper edge of the ivory, appear five divinities, two of whom extend their hands to the *divus*. At the right upper edge of the ivory is a section of the zodiac, behind which is the figure of Sol.

The image on the diptych thus consists of two parts. Below are depicted the pagan Roman funerary ceremonies for an emperor. On second-century *consecratio* coins, the elephant *quadriga* and *rogus* appear exactly as shown on the diptych,[235] which simply combines these two motifs. One may also recall the golden chariot of Pertinax on his pyre. The figure in the *quadriga* on the pyre accordingly is the *divus* about to depart for heaven, as is indicated by the billowing mantle.[236] We know from Dio and Herodian that when the pyre was lit eagles were released to symbolise the flight of the soul,[237] exactly as shown on the diptych.

This lower part of the diptych is therefore thoroughly in accord with a Roman and pagan provenance: it shows images which were characteristic of the Roman view of *consecratio* in the second and early third centuries. The diptych is the last extant work to show these images, which it revives after an interval of over a century. The images were specifically associated with Roman imperial *consecratio* and with the city of Rome, for which they had originally been created. The diptych was thus produced for a patron who was aware of this imagery and wished to refer to it. One can therefore see expressed in it the same Roman adherence to pagan past and pagan tradition as in the works of Servius and Macrobius.

The upper part of the diptych is not specifically Roman although it also refers to a pagan view of immortality and the ascent to heaven, but in broader and more widely applicable terms.[238] Unlike the lower part of the diptych, this upper part follows no iconographical schemes which can be traced elsewhere, but the elements of the representation do appear in other works. The heads of the wind-gods who were thought to carry the soul to heaven are often represented on the corners of lids of pagan sarcophagi. The zodiac also appears on pagan sarcophagi, framing the bust of the deceased, as a sign that he had attained the heavenly regions.[239] On the Igel monument the zodiac frames the ascent of Hercules, who is assisted by Minerva extending a hand to him (plate 32). Two of the divinities on the diptych make a similar gesture towards the *divus*. Although these parallels are not exact repetitions of the motifs of the upper part of the diptych, they do show that the concepts illustrated there had been generally familiar at an earlier period. The upper part of the diptych, like the lower, revives ideas which were current in the pagan past, but it does so in a new combination of images.

We have, then, in the diptych, a double representation of one single process: the ascent of a divinised emperor depicted in the framework of Roman imperial funeral and *consecratio* of the second and early third centuries on the one hand, and his ascent to the stars and welcome in heaven, which were not specifically Roman, on the other. If the emperor shown is indeed Julian, we may interpret the lower part of the diptych as depicting, if only as a fiction, a posthumous funeral for him such as was given to Pertinax and Septimius Severus, a funeral, furthermore, such as Julian's admirer Ammianus thought he should have had.

Consecratio and imperial divinisation were among the areas where there existed a crucial divergence between Byzantium, with its largely Greek roots, and the Latin West, with its Roman roots. The imperial funerary ceremonial as depicted, for a last time, on the British Museum diptych, was of Roman origin. This ceremonial had been a means of reconciling Roman reservations about divinised human beings with the spontaneous Greek divinisation of human beings as it was experienced in the early Roman Empire. This conflict of ideas had been operative up to the later third century. The advent of Christianity in the empire, and its official role within it, transformed the pagan debate over different concepts of being human within paganism into a debate between pagans and Christians on the same subject.

In this transformation the ground of the debate also shifted and changed. For Christian protagonists in this debate, the ceremonial of imperial funerals became of fundamental importance because it could serve as a direct expression of their views of the emperor's status, both of his posthumous status on earth and his status with God in heaven. For pagans this was not so. Whether directly, in a contemporary and political context, as in formulations of Julian's death and afterlife, or whether in a more theoretical framework, as in Macrobius, the afterlife of the statesman, of the man who in his lifetime had exercised the ancient pagan virtue of justice, had to be understood in a philosophical and religious context, toward which, as on the diptych, ceremony could be, but did not have to be, a vehicle. Claudian was, moreover, able to capture the dynastic significance of *consecratio* when speaking of Theodosius in heaven surveying his imperial sons on earth, and he did so in the pagan idiom which had had to discard the now Christian ceremonial of imperial funerals.

In short, by the late fourth century the funerary ceremonial of the Roman Empire had become Christian, even if Roman imperial ceremonial could still carry some pagan content. Since imperial ceremonial in late antiquity was a vehicle for *consensus* between ruler and subjects, the Christian meaning which the ceremonial of imperial funerals could now convey marked a clear stage in the Christianisation of the empire, the Roman body politic.

At the same time, however, we must note that while the shift from a debate among pagans to a debate between pagans and Christians reformulated the grounds of debate and raised new issues, it also perpetuated many old ones. We have already seen how Eusebius' view of Constantine's afterlife raised the emperor above the ranks of ordinary Christians and exempted him from the last judgement. Here, Claudian's version of the ascent of Theodosius, pagan though its imagery is, was not incompatible with Christian ideas on the emperor's afterlife, such as we encountered in Eusebius and will encounter again in later Christian authors. We have here a perpetuation of that old pagan divinisation of the statesman, which, whether in this life or the next, removed him from the common human lot.

PART · II

THE CHRISTIAN RESOLUTION

7. THE CHRISTIAN VIEW OF THE EMPEROR'S DEATH AND AFTERLIFE IN THE WEST: AMBROSE ON VALENTINIAN II AND THEODOSIUS

Ambrose of Milan delivered two orations, *Consolationes*,[240] on the deaths of Valentinian II and Theodosius. Here, as in Gregory, and to a degree in Eusebius, the funerary ceremonial appears in an unmistakably Christian interpretation, although the function of the ceremonial, which was, on the one hand, to express and maintain a certain continuity between one emperor and the next, and on the other, to consign the departed emperor to his place in heaven, remained stable. But unlike Eusebius and Gregory, Ambrose could call on a Christian tradition of imperial funerals, and he could achieve his *interpretatio christiana* on many different levels.

When speaking of the period which elapsed between the death of Theodosius and the funerary rites observed for him in Milan after forty days, he recalls the burial of Jacob by Joseph as a precedent for this space of time being allowed to elapse. The procession of the dead emperor to his final place of rest is rendered by Ambrose in triumphal imagery, recalling the existence of the triumphal imagery in the imperial funerary processions of the earlier empire.[241] The triumph which Ambrose describes, however, was a Christian and unearthly one; he addresses Honorius to assure him that his father's remains will be duly honoured, even though Honorius himself will not be able to accompany them back to Constantinople:

> And do not be afraid that the triumphal remains [of Theodosius] should appear to be without honour in whatever place they come to. Italy does not think thus, Italy who beheld his renowned triumphs and

who, twice freed from tyrants, rejoices with the author of her freedom; and Constantinople does not think thus, who sent out her emperor to victory for the second time, and, although she wished to keep him, could not. And for his return she expected triumphal celebrations and the titles of victories, she expected the emperor of the whole world escorted by the Gallic army and supported by the power of the whole world. But now Theodosius returns to her more powerful, now more glorious, for the host of the angels leads him on, and the crowd of the saints follows him. Clearly you are blessed, you who receive the inhabitant of paradise, you who shall hold, in the revered dwelling place of his body when it is buried, him who lives in that city which is above.[242]

Just as in Gregory Nazianzen, we here encounter the imagery of the victorious *adventus*, which is also evoked by Herodian in a similar context. Dio records that the funerary procession of Pertinax comprised images of subject nations wrought in bronze, and the presence of the city guilds in that procession[243] recalls the procession which welcomed Constantine to Autun.[244] The funerary processions of Pertinax and Severus, like some *adventus* processions, had military and senatorial escorts. These are replaced in Ambrose by the *angelorum caterva*, the *sanctorum turba*, and it is not the victorious emperor who is welcomed, but the *paradisi incola*, the *habitator supernae illius civitatis*.

Theodosius was escorted not, as his terrestrial city of Constantinople expected, by the Gallic army and the power of this earth as in a terrestrial *adventus*, but by angels and saints, so that the explicit imagery and ceremonial of *adventus* on earth were transformed into a new imagery of *adventus* in heaven, in that city which is above. Ambrose speaks elsewhere in the *Consolatio* of the heavenly Jerusalem, the emperor's lasting home,[245] and thus a link is established between heaven and earth, the city above, and the city on earth, in a much more substantial, direct form than that which Eusebius was able to formulate. Eusebius was still dependent on the pagan imagery of the death of the emperor, which he sought to reinterpret and enliven with a Christian meaning.

Ambrose, preceded by Gregory Nazianzen, created an entirely Christian imagery, by means of which, in the passage under discussion, Constantinople, home of the emperor's terrestrial remains, was linked to the heavenly Jerusalem, home of the emperor's soul. This was one of the processes of thought whereby Constantinople became a sacred city, the image, as it was later expressed, of the heavenly Jerusalem, image also of the Jerusalem on earth.[246]

The *adventus* of Theodosius, both in Constantinople and in heaven, was a victorious one. The imagery of death swallowed up in victory, although not the same in paganism and Christianity, yet existed in both spheres. In paganism, as has been seen, the emperor's *consecratio* could be an object-lesson showing that it was possible to overcome death. In Christianity the imagery of victory in death was differently formulated: it was an agonistic victory, the prototype of which was the death of the martyrs.[247]

Thus, there was in paganism and Christianity a convergence of approaches to the death of the emperor, although the method and imagery of the two approaches differed. This brought about a certain continuity of tradition in ideas of what the imperial funerary ceremonies conveyed. As in paganism, so in Christianity, these ideas assumed for the emperor a fate far more secure and tranquil than that envisaged for the average human being. For the average Christian of the late fourth century, death was no triumphant *adventus*; it was an anxious encounter with the demonic officers of the customs house of the other world.[248]

Just as Ambrose reformulated in Christian terms the old theme of overcoming death in his *Consolatio* for Theodosius, so he also gave a Christian interpretation to the theme of the continuity between the emperor in heaven and his successors, his sons, on earth. He thus validated the accession of the new emperors, and this had been one of the principal functions of imperial *consecratio* and funeral from the first century. In so doing, Ambrose redefined the meaning of *fides*: "What is faith but the substance of things hoped for?"[249]

The bond between Theodosius and his army was such, Ambrose asserts,[250] that the army would continue to serve his sons, and their service was given a Christian, religious meaning, to make it the more imperative. *Fides*—or the loyalty of the soldiers—was the substance of things hoped for, that is, the maturity of the emperors. Ambrose adds: "For the just live by faith." The examples of the just that he gives are Abraham, Isaac, and Jacob, and by means of a further example from the life of Elias, he states that perfidy would lead to defeat, "but, where there is faith, there is the army of the angels."[251] Finally he re-emphasises the continuity between father and sons when he says, "Perform for the sons what you owe to their father . . . for the sons of an emperor who was holy, compassionate, faithful."[252] The teaching of the church to the faithful is thus used to secure the continuance of peace and security in the empire.

After such a *tour de force*, an explanation of the emperor's existence in heaven was required. Ambrose supplied it. Unlike Eusebius, he presented a very specific view of the afterlife of the emperor. He had found a Christian version of *consecratio*. Even the actual ascent of the soul was translated into a Christian terminology. Of Valentinian II he says:

> When [Valentinian's] soul ascended, Gratian, his brother, met and
> embraced it. . . . 'Come,' he said, 'my brother, let us go out into the
> field, let us rest in the hills; at dawn let us go up into the vineyards.'
> That is, 'you have come to that place where the fruits of the different
> virtues are granted for the deserts of each, where the rewards for de-
> serts overflow.'[253]

Ambrose uses the pagan and philosophical image of the ascent of the
soul; yet he hardly mentions this image before turning it in a different
direction: Gratian addresses Valentinian in the words of the Song of
Songs. He describes heaven in the imagery of the New Testament and
says nothing of the emperor's reward for toils. Instead Ambrose uses
the Christian image of reaping in heaven what is sown on earth. Ambrose treats Valentinian as a Christian who has been saved. There is
nothing particularly imperial about this entry into heaven. Gratian welcomes Valentinian as a brother, not as emperor. This approach by Ambrose was, of course, conditioned by the circumstances.[254] In the *Consolatio* for Theodosius, Ambrose could be more explicit and described
what could be termed an imperial welcome in heaven, although in
Christian terms.

In the *Consolatio* of Theodosius, Ambrose defines the hereafter not in
philosophical terms, like Eusebius, but in terms of the contemporary
political and religious establishment. He creates a beyond to which Theodosius had attained, which his listeners could understand in terms of
what they already knew of the here and now. We meet, in this heaven,
the *principes Christiani* of the fourth century, that is, Constantine,
Helena and Gratian. Theodosius' entry into heaven is phrased as an entry into rest, into Jerusalem, but Jerusalem, unlike the bosom of the pa-
triarchs in Valentinian's *consolatio*, is a resort for kings, a place of glory:

> Into that rest Theodosius hastened to enter; he hastened to enter the
> city of Jerusalem, of which it is said, 'and the kings of the earth shall
> make their glory in it.' That is the true glory, which is taken up there,
> that is the most blessed kingdom that is owned there, to which the
> apostle also hastened. . . . Relieved, therefore, of the doubt of con-
> flicts, Theodosius of worshipful memory[255] now enjoys everlasting
> light[256] and eternal tranquillity, and for the deeds which he performed
> in this body, he is recompensed with the fruits of divine reward. And it
> is because Theodosius of worshipful memory loved the Lord his God,
> that he deserved the company of the saints.[257]

The specific and Christian terms in which Ambrose describes the imperial heaven distinguish his account from the looser and less precise
philosophical description of Eusebius. There is, however, a feature
which Ambrose and Eusebius have in common. In Eusebius, as in Am-

brose, the emperor's opponents come to an evil end. Ambrose explicitly juxtaposes Theodosius' blessedness and the fate of Maximus and Eugenius:

> Therefore Theodosius remains in the light and rejoices in the company of the saints. There he embraces Gratian who no longer grieves over his wounds because he has found an avenger. . . . About them it is well said: the day brings forth knowledge of the day. But on the other hand Maximus and Eugenius in hell are, as it were, like the night teaching knowledge of itself to the night, and they show by their wretched example what a hard thing it is to raise arms against the emperors. About them it is rightly said, 'I saw an empire exalted high and raised above the cedars of Lebanon, and I passed by, and behold, it was not.' For the holy [Emperor] has passed from the turmoil of this world into eternal light. . . . Now Theodosius of worshipful memory knows that he rules, when he is in the kingdom of the Lord Jesus.[258]

This theme highlights both change and continuity in the role of the Christian emperors as compared to that of the pagan ones. The emperor's *pietas erga deos*, resulting in general well-being, had always been one of the imperial virtues, and was especially emphasised during the Tetrarchy.[259] Hence Eusebius also was prepared to label as a tyrant, and moreover a persecutor,[260] any opponent of Constantine, and in the same way Ambrose consigns Maximus and Eugenius to hell. The result was a Christian variety of *damnatio memoriae*. In terms of ceremonial, this was very clearly expressed in Gregory Nazianzen's derisive account of Julian's funeral.

The propaganda of the Christian empire of the fourth century covered the same ground as imperial propaganda in earlier periods, because the tasks of government, the maintenance of peace and order, and the securing of a regular succession, remained the same. But the propaganda of the Christian empire covered this ground in a different idiom, because fundamental suppositions about the purpose of government changed. Even so, Christian propaganda took as its starting point the situation at the end of the Tetrarchy. For *consecratio* this starting point meant that the ascent of the emperor to the above remained, as it had been, unaffected by human intervention; it was a *fait accompli* at death. Also, *consecratio* remained relevant in the context of the succession: it confirmed the status both of the departed, 'consecrated' emperor, and of his successors, his sons. It helped to secure the continuance of a dynasty.

The initial changes brought about by the Christian empire in the context of *consecratio* emerge in Eusebius and are explicit in Ambrose. In Eusebius the cause of the legitimate emperor who protects the church is confirmed by success, which culminates in a good death and communion with God thereafter. By contrast, tyrants end in defeat. In Gregory Nazianzen and Ambrose the contrast emerges more clearly, because the fate of the legitimate and Christian emperor and that of his predecessors is quite explicitly contrasted with the fate of usurpers. The fate of usurpers in hell is made relevant to the *consecratio* and bliss in paradise of the Christian emperor, because in the Christian empire of the fourth century the enemy of religion and the enemy of the state were explicitly united as one.[261] Eusebius and Ambrose do not differentiate between the two. The attainment by the legitimate emperor of a state of bliss is a vindication of religion and the *respublica*, as well as of the dynasty. It was on this basis that Ambrose made his appeal to the soldiers.

Thus we see that *consecratio*, or rather, the ascent of the emperor into heaven, his entry into Jerusalem, was still regarded as relevant to the political issues of the day, although the method whereby *consecratio* was attained had changed in the late third century, and the meaning which it was given changed when Constantine became a Christian. It was possible for the Christian empire to express itself in such a way, *à propos* of the emperor's afterlife, that it could stand for stability of tradition and values while at the same time changing its exegesis of this tradition and these values. As a result Julian's paganism not only seemed innovatory and could be combated on this basis by Christians. In some respects Julian's paganism actually was innovatory. Hence, by the end of the fourth century, it was Christianity which could stand for security, continuity and imperial respectability.

8. THE CHRISTIAN EMPIRE AT WORK AS THE ESTABLISHED ORDER: CORIPPUS

Any account of the emergence of a Byzantine ceremony must do justice to the inherited conglomerate of frequently inconsistent ideas which men of the later phases of antiquity brought with them. Accordingly, before discussing the account of the imperial ascent in Corippus, it would be best to sum up some conclusions on the subject of *consecratio* as treated so far. There was a first stage, when *consecratio* could be defined as an official act, a method of keeping a check on the divinisation of the emperor in his lifetime. The fact that *consecratio* was an official act necessitated that, at least initially, it should have been achieved by some human agency, whether Senate or emperor. The character of the official act changed, in that the role of the Senate and then the role of the consecrating emperor, crucial at first, became increasingly peripheral.

When we come to the Tetrarchic panegyrics, *consecratio* can no longer be defined as an official act, for it was no longer achieved by any human agency. The emperor rose to the gods in his own right. Thereby the traditional safeguard against the emergence of a divine emperor had fallen away: emperors ascended to the gods and there was nothing any human being could do about it. Simultaneously, there emerged more explicitly than before the idea that the emperor was the chosen of the gods, ruling by divine authority, which is clearly expressed in the panegyrics of 289 and 291.

The divine status which *consecratio* conferred after death was therefore claimed by the Tetrarchs and some third-century predecessors during their lifetime. Under Constantine there occurred a return to the idea of *consecratio*, or divinisation, to be understood in terms of a description of the status of the emperor after death. The divinisation after death of Constantius was used as an argument to support Constantine's accession. At the same time the idea of the emperor's rule by divine authority was retained as a regular part of Byzantine imperial theory. The old aspect of *consecratio* or divinisation as a notion to support the accession recurred in the fourth century, and can still be traced in Corippus.

Christian authors were prepared to contemplate the blessed state of the emperor in heaven. We have seen how in Ambrose this state was translated into Christian terminology by means of Biblical language and allusion. Bliss in heaven had become the reward for the labours of the *princeps Christianus*. Our study of Julian's afterlife shows what elements of the old notions of *consecratio* had been discarded because they could be defined as pagan; these were concerned with pagan cult and the method of ascent. Once this pagan obstacle had been removed, the Christian emperor could ultimately rise to a heaven which no longer needed to be defined as Christian, because Christianity could be assumed to be the emperor's religion, and in heaven the emperor could rule with God. This would not yet have been possible in the fourth century.

However, Byzantium produced no pictorial renderings of the emperor's ascent to, or residence in, heaven. The traditional images could no longer be used. At the same time, in rendering the imperial ascent to heaven in language, Christian authors moved away from too close an interpretation of the emperor's otherworldly status towards an interpretation and description of the ceremony of the imperial funeral. Imperial ceremonial finally replaced imperial art and imperial panegyric.[262] Hence, my last example of the theme of divinisation is an account of a ceremony: this is Corippus's narrative of the events of Justinian's death and Justin's accession. We have here a particularly clear example of the interlocking of death and accession as formulated in ceremonial. The early Byzantine ceremonial of imperial funerals thus preserved one of the salient aspects of the late antique ceremonial; in other words, it served the same purpose—of orchestrating a smooth succession.

The succession had not been definitely settled when Justinian died in 565. However, Corippus describes the succession of Justin II as a foregone conclusion, and it did indeed take place peacefully. But one can see from his account that there was an element of danger.[263] Corippus concealed this with all the means that the old topics of *consecratio* and accession could provide. He used them to establish the accession of Justin in terms of his election by God, by the Senate and by Justinian himself. But a change is to be observed, if one compares Corippus' account with the earlier ones. The ceremonial emerges much more prominently, and it is by means of the ceremonial that death and accession are related to each other. Because ceremonial, as we have seen, provided a method of presenting the death and accession of succeeding emperors in an orderly manner, it could serve as the framework for dealing with a situation of potential disruption and chaos, of which Corippus was aware.

> Under higher auspices I sing of how the peak of Empire was attained, not snatched by force of arms or taken by ambition.[264]

Thus begins the panegyric of Justin II. The subject of the death of Justinian and accession of Justin is introduced by a dream of Justin in which the Virgin crowns him.[265] After the dream, but still at night, comes a delegation of the Senate led by the patrician Calinicus,[266] announcing the death of Justinian and offering the throne to Justin. He declines. There are two stages in the argument between Calinicus, who speaks for the Senate, and Justin. Calinicus points out that even during Justinian's lifetime Justin shared the empire with him,[267] *solo diademate dispar*,[268] but *dispositu Caesar eras*,[269] and Justinian died, according to Calinicus,

> making you his successor. Accept and be glad. Your uncle has bequeathed his world into your hands. The most holy Emperor did not consider you his kinsman merely, but his son. The Law calls you, the court upholds you.[270]

Here and elsewhere,[271] Justin is said to succeed as Justinian's son, a point which is intended to confirm the legitimacy of his title. When Justin rejects Calinicus's offer,

> The whole crowd lying prostrate at his feet begged him, 'take pity on your suppliants; for your own good, revered Lord, help us in our danger. Soon, when the day comes you will see that all will be lost if the

people find the court empty of an emperor. . . . [Justinian] himself
when he died with his own lips commanded you to rule.'[272]

The idea that the throne had been bequeathed by the old emperor to
his successor with his dying breath has already been encountered in the
context of Constantine's accession. Corippus' reference to the danger of
the situation was new in panegyric, and adds an air of realism and
urgency to the situation. To the repeated plea of the danger of an empire
without an emperor Justin accedes, and with the senators and his consort Sophia, proceeds to the palace:

> They passed through the peaceful city in the middle of the night. Their
> faces were sorrowful, although they set out to gain their dominion
> amidst the rejoicing of the Senate, and although everything seemed to
> be at peace.[273]

As a precaution, guards were stationed at the entrances of the palace:

> for who would dare to resist, when God's holy verdict had already be-
> stowed the empire on Justin and Sophia, and had surrounded the pal-
> ace with a strong wall and with the armour of heaven?[274]

Meanwhile, the body of Justinian, "embalmed for eternity," was laid out
in state in the palace, surrounded by mourners, but

> Justinian retained the great insignia
> Which he had held in life, he did not change colour at death
> But still had the colour of life. His noble death
> Showed clearly that he had conquered the world.
> To all the mourners, he alone seemed to rejoice
> By his holy appearance; he was adorned with the diadem
> And lying in his purple it was possible to believe
> That his body rested in sleep, and not in cruel death.[275]

This motif, the idea that the emperor was still alive, or sleeping, as it
may be put, has been encountered in the Roman Empire also. The departed emperor wears diadem and purple and is in full possession of his
earthly honours. At the same time he is mourned, which provides an
occasion for praising Justin's *pietas*,[276] a virtue which had long been
thought appropriate to this occasion: the successor should concern himself with the honours—formerly divinisation—of his predecessor.[277]

Justin's accession is now an accomplished fact; while he still mourns
for Justinian, he is already in command of the imperial armies,[278] and
next, amid general rejoicing, he is acclaimed in the Hippodrome,[279]
raised on the shield, and crowned.[280] That accomplished, the imperial
funeral takes place.

It is important to notice how the procedures of death and accession are woven into each other and interlock, so as to form a continuous whole. There is no distinct timespan between the predecessor's death and the successor's installation, no interim period. As the predecessor recedes stage by stage from the worldly scene—he dies, lies in state as though sleeping, is buried—his successor emerges, also stage by stage—he is chosen by God, his predecessor, the Senate, is acclaimed and crowned—and takes up the old emperor's place. Calinicus, when he first addresses Justin, actually avoids answering the question, *pater inclitus orbis, occidit an vivit?* [281] but goes straight to the subject of the accession. By the time we hear of Justinian's lying in state, Justin has in his dream been crowned by the Virgin, having already—so we are led to believe—been chosen as successor by Justinian; he has also been chosen by God and the Senate. Death and accession are recounted concurrently.

The funeral of the emperor was an occasion of triumph. Sophia arranged for the making of a funerary *vestis*, which depicted the triumphs of Justinian:

> Sophia brought the pall woven in precious purple
> Where the whole range of Justinian's labours
> Were depicted in pure gold and shining with gems.
> On one side stood the rows of barbarians bowing low,
> And with his fine needle the artist had formed
> Dead kings and rows of subject nations. . . . (Cf. plates 20–22.)
> And in the midst of his palace he depicted the victor himself
> Trampling on the proud neck of the Vandal tyrant,
> With Libya acclaiming him and offering fruits and the laurel.
> And he added the old Rome extending her arms
> Her dress showing the bared breasts of her who is
> The nourisher of Empire and parent of freedom.
> Living Wisdom commanded these things to be done
> So that his last hour should lead Justinian
> Adorned with his own triumphs to his imperial tomb. [282]

On the day of the funeral, the bier was adorned with the jewels which Roman might had captured in the past, treasures of the sea, of India and Egypt, [283] which vividly recall the jewelled cloak worn by Honorius in his consular processions, as described by Claudian. [284] The whole palace was submerged in light. Justin then entered and kissed Justinian a last farewell. His words, as reported by Corippus, contrasted the sorrow of the bereaved with the joy in heaven of the departed emperor. [285] Justin then commanded the funerary procession, *pompa*, to leave the palace. [286] In it walked Justin himself, the people and Senate. Participants in the pompa carried candles in gold and silver candleholders, [287] while others burnt incense and priests and nuns sang. [288] As in an *adventus* ceremony,

Men and women of all ages came out;[289]
Who could record the wonders of such a procession?[290]

As in *adventus*, people watched from windows and housetops. The only feature that distinguished *adventus* and *pompa funebris* was the mourning of the participants.[291] The body of Justinian was then laid in a gold sarcophagus in the Church of the Apostles.[292]

Imperial death, in early Byzantium, could still raise the two clear-cut issues of the succession and the emperor's afterlife. Corippus makes the connection between ascent and accession more regularly and consistently than earlier authors had done. Apart from this, in their function of supporting the accession of the succeeding emperor, the funerary ceremonial and concepts of the ascent of the departed emperor in Corippus run parallel to each other, but the ascent is not dependent on what is done in the ceremonial. This had already been the case in Eusebius, and more so in Ambrose, where the entry of the emperor's soul into heaven is used, instead, to interpret the ceremonial of the funeral. According to Eusebius, Constantine hoped to enter heaven as the servant of God, and Eusebius specifically stresses his Christianity as the operative factor in both his success on earth and in his ascent to heaven. Ambrose, describing the life of Theodosius, did the same. Thus, on the one hand, the Christian emperor, like his pagan predecessors, enters heaven by virtue of his office, which he has fulfilled worthily. But on the other he also enters heaven, the final place of rest of all Christians. *Ergo quia dilexit . . . Theodosius dominum deum suum, meruit sanctorum consortia.*[293]

We thus have an entry into heaven resulting both from the position of the emperor as emperor, and from his standing as a Christian. In Byzantium no further explanations about, and qualifications of, the emperor's ascent had to be made. The Christian religion was the religion of the empire, and those elements of the ascent which, in the fourth century, had been defined as pagan had been discarded; but so also were strenuous attempts at importing Christian language into the event. A great many verbal images of pagan origin were left intact. Corippus' account of Justinian's ascent to heaven is not incompatible with the expressions of pagan authors: there is no trace of Biblical language as in Ambrose, or of philosophic circumlocution, as in Eusebius. Yet this should not be understood to mean merely that the pagan ascent lived on unchanged. What Corippus says should be understood as a part of the historical development which we have outlined.

In Corippus' account of the funerary ceremonial we have been able to detect many of the elements which occurred at earlier times. He provides what amounts to a summary of the ceremonial procedures, part of which were taken over in Byzantium from pagan Rome. His account of the imperial ascent contains a similar summary. The Virgin addressing Justin in his dream says:

> Why do you shed tears? Why do you mourn over gladness?
> Cast aside your sadness, your father lives, he lives in heaven,
> and enjoys a greater day. You must succeed to his labours.[294]

At the funeral, Justin addresses Justinian for a last time:

> We are sad and weep. . . . You, most holy father, go away gladly amidst the angelic host and, having laid aside your body, already see God, and you enjoy a better day under a sunlight which is quenched by no night.[295]

Before his death, Justinian entrusted Calinicus with the task of persuading Justin to accept the empire:

> I am called, my friend, and my last day approaches; at the behest of my creator I am taken from this kingdom to the other. God has given all the Latin Empire to Justin. . . . When, leaving the flesh, my spirit, ascending, will have passed through the shining vault of heaven, go to the house of Justin with the senators. You must make him emperor, even if he refuses to accept.[296]

There is here the imagery of the ascent of the soul, the vault of heaven, of heaven as a place, and of endless day, which has been met with so frequently in paganism. Justinian, like earlier emperors,[297] knows that his death is approaching, and makes the appropriate arrangements. Death is a planned, dignified event, and is followed by the imperial entry into immortality.

Corippus documented an established ceremonial which would remain stable.[298] Yet we should not underestimate the slow change which late antique ceremonies underwent in the distinctive spiritual world of Byzantium. For, Constantine Porphyrogenitus reported a further element in the ceremony, as performed in his day, which added a new and personal note to it. Before the funerary procession left the palace, the master of ceremonies addressed the departed emperor three times with the words, "Depart, Emperor, the King of those who rule and the Lord of Lords calls you," which he repeated when the procession entered the Chalke. When the procession had entered the Church of the Apostles, the master of ceremonies said three times, "Enter, Emperor, the King of those who rule and the Lord of Lords calls you," and then he said, "Take the diadem from your head."[299] The diadem was removed from the emperor's head and replaced by a purple band, and the body placed in the sarcophagus. The emperor was here addressed personally, as though he were still living, and did not finally leave this world until the diadem was removed from his head, and until his successor ruled in his stead.

By means of the words with which the master of ceremonies addressed the emperor, a personal, immediate link was established between the dead emperor and God, which had not existed so explicitly in the earlier ceremonial. In other words, we have here, clearly formulated in the ceremonial language of a Christian imperial funeral, that continuity between heaven and earth which was touched on by Eusebius, and which earlier imperial theory had sought to bypass and avoid.[300]

When this link between emperor and God was incorporated into the Byzantine ceremonial of imperial funerals, the imperial ascent received its final definition in Christian terms, even though that particular definition also rested on pagan antecedents. The Byzantine, Christian definition in its turn was defined and qualified by the removal of the diadem from the emperor's head and its replacement by a purple band. In the pagan Roman Empire, it had been possible to bypass, to a certain extent, the question of the divinity of the emperor by means of *consecratio*. In *consecratio*, the emperor entered eternity, the abode of the gods, by virtue of having been emperor, by virtue of his terrestrial dominion, his status among humans.

In Christianity, the question of the posthumous status of the emperor could be resolved by other means, and more decisively, so that terrestrial dominion did not have to be the sole criterion of the emperor's status after death, for Christianity correlated terrestrial dominion with the dominion of God. When he died, the emperor indeed went *a regnis in regna*, to Jerusalem, the dwelling-place of kings. The diadem was not merely removed to be passed on to the successor; it was replaced by another token of kingship, the purple band.

A further issue was involved, however. Once the question of the divinity of the emperor had been resolved in different ways by the Tetrarchy and the Christian empire, the emperor's accession, the point in time when he entered on his career on earth, could safely be highlighted instead of the emperor's death, the point in time when his earthly career was completed.

What happened was this: the political theory of the classical world defined the ruler in relation to his fellow-humans; it was a horizontal definition which at times made it very difficult to avoid formulations such as the one which claimed that the ruler was "a god among men."[301] The ruler had to be marked out somehow, and it mattered little, ultimately, whether one calls this flattery or political theory.

But during the later part of the period I have here considered, beginning with the Tetrarchy, the ruler was defined not in relation to his fellow-humans, but in relation to the gods, or God. This was a vertical definition, and Christianity made it fully viable once Christian theological debate had established that divinity and humanity were joined in Christ, and in no one else. In this context, the classical dictum, "God needs nothing, and the king needs only God," [302] acquired a completely new meaning. Hence, Christ could be described very accurately with reference to imperial dominion as the "King of those who rule," [303] without any misrepresentation either of his divine status, or of the human status of the emperor and his subjects, or of the office which the emperor bore. In short, the Byzantine ceremonial of imperial funerals was a formalised expression of the resolution of the conflicts inherent in imperial dominion in the classical, pre-Christian empire.

Imperial funeral was one method of stating this resolution; the other was the ceremonial of accession as it came to be formulated in Christian Byzantium. To this we now turn.

III · ACCESSION

PART · I

ACCESSION IN A CLASSICAL FRAMEWORK: THE CONSENT OF GODS AND MEN, *VIRTUS* AND DYNASTIC RULE

1. THE ROMAN BACKGROUND

i. Conflicts in Theories of Imperial Accession

From the beginning of the Roman Empire, the accession of an emperor had been laden with conflicting ideas. In Rome itself the idea of an aristocratic form of government by the Senate, which, albeit in changing forms, survived into late antiquity, kept alive some institutions of the Roman republic. These presented a series of constant potential discords with the realities of empire, that is, government by one single individual.[1]

One of the most fundamental of these discords was that between military and civilian power. The institutions of the Roman republic had attempted to forestall this discord in that no military commander was permitted to cross the *pomerium*, the sacred boundaries of the city of Rome, with his troops except for the purpose of celebrating a triumph.[2] In other words, the bestowal and exercise of power was thought to rest upon a civilian base, that is, upon the votes of the Roman people and the decision of the Senate. This idea could at times correspond to reality. As a result, so the theory ran, if there were to be an emperor, he should be elected by the Senate, and he should be the best man, distinguished by his virtues.

This theory matched only partially the reality of how imperial power was passed on: not only was the emperor frequently chosen by the army, but also, in Tacitus' famous dictum,[3] the emperor could be chosen outside of Rome. This meant that the power of the Roman people as expressed in the actions of the Senate often had little to do with imperial elections. As a rabbi expressed it very aptly in the third century:

> The legions clothed a *dux* in the purple. What did he do? He remitted the tax-arrears,[4] burnt the records of them and led forth the legions. And this is what is known as the beginning of his reign.[5]

Nonetheless, when the emperor had been elected by the army, he had to come to terms with the civilians, people and aristocracy, of Rome and of the provinces. A consensus had to be formed. The ceremony of *adventus* was, as we have seen, one process of reaching a consensus. Accession was another, but it did not find empire-wide expression. Also, it did not reach any clear form until late antiquity.

Imperial art and panegyric offer evidence for the various attempts that were made of communicating the election of an emperor to different groups of people, in a form which could accommodate the discord and conflict between military and civilian power. Imperial art and panegyric interpreted political realities so as to make them acceptable. Both were principally civilian means of communication: panegyrists addressed urban audiences—it was only the emperor who, in his *adlocutiones*, addressed the army—and imperial works of art adorned buildings which were, for the most part, in cities. The main visual medium of communication with the army was the coinage, which, as we have seen, could at times convey the same messages as did panegyrics and urban monuments.

The aim of civilian propaganda was to reconcile the two poles of imperial power so that, as Claudian expressed it, Quirinus could go hand in hand with Mars.[6] How problematic this joining of Mars and Quirinus turned out to be, however, is demonstrated by the fact that a regular ceremonial of accession emerged only in late antiquity; it did so, characteristically, by means of emphasizing one concept which from the beginning had figured in imperial elections, namely, the election of the emperor by the gods. This concept was a useful one because it sidestepped the conflict between soldier and civilian altogether, by attributing imperial elections to a higher authority. The progressive articulation in ceremonial form of the divine election of the emperor finally laid to rest the old conflicts of the transition from republic to empire.[7]

We are not, however, dealing with a development that progressed in a straight line. Reservations on the part of the Senate about empire as a form of government—even if empire was accepted as a *fait accompli*—

ensured that no regular mode of succession emerged. Expedients vacillated between election of the best man, however this might be brought about, and a dynastic mode of succession which was epitomised by the imperial adoptions of the second century, and, in a different form, in the adoptions of the Tetrarchy and the late antique and Byzantine dynasties which followed.

All these issues were still very much alive in late antiquity and were manifested in different ways. Thus, the period from the Tetrarchy to Heraclius which is here discussed can be subdivided in different ways: chronologically, or according to whatever ideas were dominant in the various imperial elections which occurred during this time span. The subdivision here chosen is chronological; it will highlight themes which are already familiar. These are the gradual emergence of Christian ways of thought in the propaganda, the official self-expression, of the Roman Empire; the way in which the legality of the accession of one emperor was made to depend on that of his predecessor; and the way in which the emperor was elected by divine inspiration.[8]

The first part of this discussion, covering the period to Theodosius the Great, seeks to isolate and explain certain strands of thought and imagery regarding the succession. This in turn provides a context in which to view the missorium of Theodosius (plate 55), one of the most distinguished works of art of the fourth century. The missorium does not present every one of the ideas which will be touched upon here: it is significant both for what it does not, as well as for what it does show.

This first part covers a period of confusion, and any order one may discern merely provides fixed points against which to measure the surrounding uncertainty. Yet, those very elements which contributed to the confusion of ideas on accession in late antiquity came in Byzantium to group themselves in such a way that they could be enacted in a regular and coherent ceremonial. It is all the more important to establish what the picture was before this ceremonial became formalised.

We must begin with a divergence in literature and art. Many literary sources of late antiquity, as of an earlier period, place considerable emphasis on the processes whereby an emperor came to the throne, and on how the consensus needed to make an emperor was achieved. This emphasis is rarely reflected in art. Leaving aside the unique intaglio of Romulus of the early fifth century (plate 43), there was no representation in art referring exclusively to an emperor's accession.[9] Emperors might appear being crowned and receiving globes on the coinage, but such issues were not to be associated with accession itself, because they continued throughout the various reigns.

No fixed ceremonial of accession had as yet developed. This may be explained by the circumstances in which late Roman imperial elections, like those of an earlier period, took place. In the third century, some emperors were still proclaimed in Rome, so that the Senate could claim its traditional role in the proceedings, but others were proclaimed by the troops in different parts of the empire and the various circumstances obtaining at each election were not formulated into such patterns as could make up a regular ceremonial.

Nor were Roman imperial accessions governed by any regularly applied legal or constitutional rules. Rather, as the panegyrics amply demonstrate, theories were made to fit circumstances. On the other hand, circumstances, in panegyric accounts, were also made to fit theories. The aim of the present discussion is to isolate various nuances of late Roman theories regarding imperial accessions, and to show how they were applied to circumstances and also how new theories emerged.

The political concepts which underlay imperial accessions changed profoundly during the late third and fourth centuries, and it was these changes which conspired to make possible the formulation of a regular ceremonial of accession in Constantinople. After the mid-fifth century ceremonies of accession regularly took place in this city and a ceremonial framework—although not an immutable one—became established. It is perhaps not accidental that the first Byzantine accession described in the *Book of Ceremonies* is that of Leo I, successor to Marcian, in 457. There was no means, marriage or other, whereby Leo could be associated with the Theodosian dynasty, and a public validation of his accession, in the form of a ceremony, was, accordingly, more urgently required for him than for his immediate predecessors. In the second part of this discussion, we will therefore expound the accession ceremonial of early Byzantium as set down in the *Book of Ceremonies* and its context in East and West.

As has been said, two divergent strands may initially be distinguished in theories, as well as ceremonies, of accession. An emperor could come to rule by birthright, or he could come to rule because he was the most deserving candidate chosen by the gods or God. The method of election could be proclamation by the army, or co-option by the senior emperor. This latter was the dynastic viewpoint, for most often the senior emperor would co-opt a son or kinsman. When, in the absence of dynastic claims, a man was said to be the most worthy candidate elected by the gods or by God, he was generally said to have come to the throne by some form of consent, divine or human, which in practice was expressed by the proclamation of the soldiers. It must be emphasised, however, that these two strands, consent and co-option, constantly intermingled, with one or the other dominating at particular instances, and that both, in Byzantium at least, continued to be applied as necessity demanded.[10]

ii. The Imagery of the Imperial *vota*

Between the military and senatorial recognition of a Roman emperor and the early medieval coronation orders[11] lay the late antique ceremonial of accession. Although no continuous imagery, no coherent set of iconographies depicting late Roman accession was created in late antiquity, there did exist a constellation of images of varying fixity which could be associated with imperial accessions. What can be most clearly related to the accession ceremony is the late antique imagery of imperial majesty which shows the emperor enthroned, and the imagery of the felicity of the times, which appeared with particular frequency on the coinage.

From the Tetrarchy, a recurring image on the coinage to denote the emperor's status was the image of enthronement (e.g., plates 44, 47). Such issues, however, cannot be directly and definitely linked to any accession. The types in question simply show the emperors in majesty, sometimes together with Victoria spreading her wings over them, in a metaphorical image (plate 50). A parallel image, showing the emperors enthroned side by side, but without Victoria, can, however, be linked to a set of occasions, namely the imperial *vota*, that is, the rites which were performed on the various imperial anniversaries, in particular the anniversary of the emperor's accession.[12]

This image appears regularly in the fourth century after the quinquennalia of Valentinian and Valens in 367, VOTA PUBLICA, showing two nimbate emperors enthroned side by side, each holding a *mappa* and sceptre.[13] (Plate 48) The *mappa* points to the consular games which the emperors might give on the occasion of anniversaries when they took up the consulship, as did Valentinian and Valens in 368.[14] The emperors are also depicted with a triumphal aspect, for most of the issues in question show a pair of captives beside or underneath the throne.

The iconography of these coins is not unlike that of some consular diptychs, which show the giver of the games with the *mappa*, and beneath him the games in progress. But the emperors, unlike any private individual, were shown nimbate, the nimbus—or, in the words of the panegyric of 289, "that light surrounding your venerable head with a luminous sphere"[15]—being an imperial attribute which was depicted with increasing frequency from the fourth century.[16]

The *vota* coinages, unlike the enthronement coinages with Victoria, discriminated between emperors; the rank and seniority of emperors could be and was indicated by their differing size. Although these coins had a means of distinguishing between emperors by their rank, they did not, with one exception, cater for times when there was an imperial college of more than two.

Because of the stereotyped nature of the coinage in this period, however, exceptions are all the more revealing. The one here referred to is a set of solidi from Antioch of the period 367–375, with obverses for Valentinian, Valens and Gratian.[17] Two nimbate emperors, Valentinian and Valens, are enthroned frontally, wearing military dress. The emperor on the left holds globe and sceptre, the one on the right, sceptre and globe. The legend is SPES RP. Between the emperors stands a small togate figure holding a globe, and above his head is a shield inscribed VOT V MULT. This is the young Gratian.[18] (Plate 49) The image combines the concepts of enthronement and imperial majesty, and of the recurring celebration of the accession at the quinquennalia and decennalia. Gratian is shown as the young emperor on whom the empire will ultimately devolve, as stated by Symmachus in his panegyric on this emperor, in which he was looking forward to a golden age. The legend SPES RP is a particularly apt slogan to match Symmachus' hopeful outlook on the coming reign.

The age of felicity, at last being attained under the reigning emperor's dominion, is a recurring theme in panegyrics dealing with the celebration of accessions and anniversaries. Thus the panegyrist of 297 said of the day when Constantius became emperor:

> Let the beginning of my praises today be made with the divine accession of your majesty which was more exalted even than the happy augury of spring on which it shone; the day was bright and—we felt it while we were celebrating—a sun of summer shone more warmly than is usual for that time of year. It radiated on that day with a more august light than it did when it enlivened the birth of the world, when, so it is said, it moderated its vigour lest it do harm to the tender beginning of the universe. But now it seems that the sun must strive lest it be outshone by your majesty. Oh spring, glad and blessed with new fruits, you are blessed and worshipful not so much because of the grace of your flowers or the green colour of your crops, not so much for the sparkle of your vines, or for the very west wind and for your serene light; rather, you are blessed and worshipful because of the accession of the great Caesars.[19]

Similar thoughts are voiced by Claudian about the day when Honorius, the purple-born child, came into the world;[20] and the author of the *gratiarum actio* of Autun to Constantine in 312, for a remission of tax,[21] expressed himself in a related idiom about Constantine's quinquennalia:

You have remitted for us the arrears of five years! Oh *lustrum*, more blessed than all others! Oh *lustrum*, which fittingly corresponds to the duration of your rule! It is for us particularly that the immortal gods have made you emperor, because for each one of us felicity was born when you began to rule. The oration of Cato on the felicity of his *lustrum* is justly famous. Even in that republic of old it pertained to the worth of the censors if they completed a blessed *lustrum*, if the granary was full of corn, if there was an abundant vintage, and if the oil from the olive groves flowed richly. How then can we thank you for this *lustrum* of your kindness, a *lustrum* when, although the harvests failed, you brought it about that everything seemed to have been more abundant than it was? . . . Your generosity bestows on us the gifts of the Earth, mother of fruits, and of Iuppiter the ruler of the winds; whatever they gave only sparingly, has come to us as a gift from you.[22]

The day of the accession on which nature smiled could be re-enacted on subsequent anniversaries, when the subjects looked back on a period of prosperity and found the experience highlighted by the fact that the actual day of the anniversary was beautiful and sunny.

What for the panegyrist of 312 was a simple association of ideas—Constantine's accession, its fifth anniversary, and the felicity of the times—was built by Eusebius into a theory of the Constantinian succession in a much more far-flung imagery of solar symbolism, which made of imperial rule on earth an image of God's rule in heaven.[23] In the first Tricennial Oration, Eusebius said:

> And God . . . bestows on [Constantine] additional long periods of rule, . . . and He allows him to carry out every one of his celebrations with great relief from the burden of sole rule, having readied some one of his sons for partnership in the royal throne at each tenth anniversary, as if to prolong the bloom of a flourishing plant. . . . Thus surely has God Himself, the Ruler of All, who has given his bounty of years and offspring to the most God-beloved ruler, made his leadership of the peoples on earth to be young and blooming as if just now beginning to bear. . . . Thus, having yoked the four valiant Caesars like colts beneath the single yoke of the imperial chariot, he controls them with the reins of holy harmony and concord. Holding the reins high above them, he rides along, traversing all lands alike that the sun gazes upon, himself present everywhere and watching over everything.[24]
>
> Thus outfitted in the likeness of the kingdom of heaven, he pilots affairs below with an upward gaze, to steer by the archetypal form.[25] (Cf. plate 45.)

This symbolism echoes the cosmic images used by the panegyrist of Constantius I in 297, but it is here more explicitly associated with anniversaries—the occasion of the *vota*—and the imperial succession. Eusebius transforms the pagan imperial *vota* into a Christian festival; elsewhere he also links the *vota* to the dedication of the Church of the Holy Sepulchre.[26]

In the pagan celebration of the *vota*, prayers had been made to the gods to vouchsafe the safety of the emperors.[27] The official calendar of imperial Rome was littered with imperial anniversaries,[28] and allusions to them are not infrequent in panegyrics; indeed, they provided the occasion for panegyrics.[29] Official life took place in the setting of an ever-recurring cycle of imperial feast-days. In the course of the fifth century, the *vota* disappeared; the *votorum nuncupatio* of January 3rd still figured in fourth-century calendars, but lapsed thereafter, although it was still mentioned, together with somewhat esoteric beliefs supposedly associated with the occasion, by John Lydus.[30]

The calling upon divine protection on behalf of the emperor survived in the acclamation of the early Byzantine accession ceremonials as recorded in the *Book of Ceremonies*: "God has given you; God shall keep you."[31] The ceremonials of the *vota* of the *natalis* of the emperor's accession, and of the *vota* of January 3rd were ultimately assimilated into the ceremonial of accession. But during the fourth century, accession and the different *vota* still ran parallel to and interpenetrated each other, in such a way that in visual terms no distinct imagery of accession evolved.

The various sets of *vota* came to be assimilated and summed up in the one ceremony of accession because the perception of what constituted an imperial reign changed. The annual cycle of imperial feast-days, together with the pagan festivals—most of them related to the seasons of the year—made of time a perpetuity, something solid and recurringly continuous, of which very clear expressions still occurred under the Tetrarchs. But in a Christian era, time was doctrinally limited: it had a beginning and an end and was no longer a perpetuity.[32] With that, an imperial reign also lost the aspect of lastingness it had had in the pagan empire. It could be viewed, as by Ambrose in his *Consolatio* for Valentinian II, as a journey, whose outset was to be marked by the accession ceremony of which there need not and could not be any repetition.[33]

2. THE TETRARCHY

i. The Consent of the Gods and Imperial *virtus*

However an emperor may have come to the throne, remaining there necessitated a degree of consent by his subjects. In the earlier Roman Empire this consent was expressed in the proclamation of the emperor by the troops and the acknowledgement of him by the Senate. In itself this event was unique, but it was re-enacted periodically in a variety of ways. The most important of these were the *vota* which, throughout the empire, were taken for the emperor's safety on the *natalis* of his accession.

Another recurrent re-enactment of the consent which was achieved at an emperor's accession, was, as has been seen, *adventus*. During the first part of the period here covered, an imperial accession was not a moment in time past, but a moment which could be extended into the present and future. This extension was expressed by different types of consensus. Consensus itself was a variable quantity, and therein lay its usefulness as a political ideal in the Roman Empire. It was a notion which, before it was incorporated into the Byzantine accession ceremonial, was never defined but simply stated in various contexts; and from the context is to be explained the specific meaning which consent was intended to acquire on different occasions. Even a form of consensus such as could be expressed about dynastic rule was a variable quantity and the genealogies which could be claimed might be divine or human, and if the latter, true or false. Moreover, a dynasty's claim to rule was never stated in isolation, but was intermingled with claims of divine and human consent, merited by virtue, as the situation demanded.

The Tetrarchs offer one particular example of rule by consent, the consent of the gods being the dominant factor. Nothing whatever is said in any Tetrarchic panegyric of the consent of mankind, of Senate, people and army, which were aspects of consent that had been prominent in the earlier empire and were again to acquire importance in the fourth century. Rather, Diocletian became emperor as the chosen of Iuppiter, and himself chose Maximian, who was the chosen of Hercules.[34] It is not possible to extract from the panegyrics any constitutional precision of how this relationship between the emperors affected the empire; such precision was not the aim of panegyric. Instead, the Tetrarchic panegyrics provide a conceptual framework within which imperial rule was communicated.

The panegyric of 289 was held in Trier on the Parilia,[35] the anniversary of the foundation of Rome, "on the day on which the origin of the city, which is the undying mistress of the nations, is celebrated."[36] This occasion provided an opportunity for interrelating the visit to the site of Rome by Hercules in a mythical yet historical past, and the *restitutio* and new foundation of Rome by the present emperors, a project upon which they entered at their accession.[37] This accession is described in terms of the descent of the two emperors from Iuppiter and Hercules: Hercules was *princeps ille tui generis*,[38] and Diocletian, Maximian's *cognatus*,[39] was descended from Iuppiter. This sacred tale of divine descent, however,

did not exclude, or in any sense deny, the human descent of the two
emperors:

> For who may doubt . . . [that] Italy is the mistress of the nations by the
> antiquity of her glory, and Pannonia by her valour? And shall I now
> relate the divine origin of your family, to which you bear witness not
> only by your immortal deeds, but also by the name to which you
> succeeded?[40]

The relationship between the emperors and the gods must not be
viewed as mere propaganda, but as a genuine removal of the emperors
to a higher sphere, to which they attained by taking upon themselves
the *cura* of the empire.[41] The taking up of this *cura*, the imperial power,
by Diocletian and Maximian was described by the panegyrist Mamertinus in 289 both in the context of Roman history from its beginning,
and in the context of the contemporary situation. In the former context
Maximian was the successor of Hercules whose activities on the site of
Rome were an augury of this emperor's reign, so that the emperor could
take the place of Hercules as *praesens deus*. In terms of contemporary history on the other hand, Maximian was the right emperor because he
was *toto orbe victor* and because of his *virtus*, in which he was the emula-
tor of Hercules:

> Therefore if today all the magistrates of Rome, the pontiffs and priests,
> honour the temple of Hercules in the same manner in which they hon-
> our those of the parent deities of the city because Hercules in times past
> brought the booty of his victory [the herds of Geryon] to Tyrrhenian
> pastures from a Spanish river, and because he left on the Palatine Hill
> traces which pointed to your coming,[42] how much more becoming is it
> for us here [in Trier] to expend all we have of voice and breath in your
> praises, and, if we must, do even more than we are able? For we see
> you here, a present god, and victor over the whole earth, you who on
> this same Western shore did not merely suppress some monstrous
> three-headed herdsman, but you suppressed a horror much more
> frightful.[43]

The panegyric does not propound a constitutional theory, but political realities—the fact that Maximian was emperor. Ultimately, it was political realities, in particular victory, which made an emperor; the theory,
or, more properly, in this context, the sacred tale, came afterwards,
when by their deeds the emperors had proved that they were truly the
descendants of Iuppiter and Hercules, or rather, had been chosen by
these gods to be their descendants without denial of their human descent. The Roman antiquarian appeal of this panegyric is paralleled on
the Decennalia Base in the Forum Romanum where an emperor is seen

performing a specifically Roman and very ancient ceremony, the Suo-vetaurilia.[44] (Plate 8) Both panegyric and art could use the Roman past to expound contemporary events. The exegesis of imperial rule in the context of the deeds of Hercules and the origins of Rome in the panegyric is matched on the Decennalia Base by the celebration of the tenth anniversary of the Caesars and by the imperial performance of an ancient Roman agricultural rite.

In 289, Mamertinus referred to the accession of Maximian and Diocletian in terms of Hercules' foundation of Rome, and sought to explain imperial dominion by showing that the emperors imitated the virtues of the gods. These views were still held by him in 291, but were stated with greater assurance and firmness, and were associated explicitly with the accession of the emperors.[45] The ideas were more explicit in that they were now dissociated from the foundation legend of Rome. Iuppiter was stated to have been the *auctor*[46] of Diocletian, just as later the Christian God was *imperii nostri auctor*,[47] while for Maximian, Hercules was *Hercules tuus*.[48] The emperors were born of the gods, as was shown by their names and their virtues[49] and at the same time were worthy sons of Illyricum.[50] The accession of Diocletian, and of his *cognatus* Maximian, was thus the result of divine election, and this divine election was justified by the virtues of the two emperors.

According to the rhetor Menander,[51] it was acceptable for a panegyrist to claim divine descent for the subject of his oration if this was felt to be appropriate, and among the contingencies that this device was to cover was the possibility of inglorious lineage on the part of the subject of the eulogy. Neither Diocletian nor Maximian came from a distinguished family, and it was in accordance with Menander's rules that Mamertinus praised their home country and called them descendants of the gods. Divine descent in the case of the Tetrarchs was, however, more than a panegyric commonplace. It was, in itself, a sacred tale which, as may be seen from the panegyric of 297 on Constantius, gathered momentum in Gaul as the Tetrarchy became more firmly established.

Diocletian and Maximian, according to the terms of the sacred tale, had family ties with Iuppiter and Hercules and with each other, the latter, however, not only in the sacred tale, for they were also related by marriage. Similarly, the Caesars Galerius and Constantius were related by marriage to the Augusti, but were also related to them as Iovius and Herculius. The panegyric of 289 had set the link between the emperors and Iuppiter and Hercules into the context of the ancient history of Rome.

The panegyric of 297 went a step further. Not only were the four emperors linked by name and *res gestae* to Iuppiter and Hercules, but their number was symbolic of the order of the universe, the four seasons, the four elements, the four lights of the sky and the four coursers on the *quadriga* of Sol[52]—those coursers which, when later harnessed to the chariot of Christus Sol stood for the four evangelists,[53] and which were yet another ingredient of Christian literary and artistic metaphor that was derived from the imperial court.

> Setting aside the interests of the *respublica*, and your care for it, that majesty which is in Iuppiter and Hercules, demanded on behalf of the emperors Iovius and Herculius an approximation to the order of the world and the heavens. And hence everything that has greatness is adorned with and rejoices in that number four which is yours. There are four elements and as many seasons, there are four parts of the world divided by a twofold ocean, there is the *lustrum* which returns after four revolutions of the sky, there is the *quadriga* of Sol,[54] and to the two lights of heaven are joined Vesper and Lucifer. But not the sun himself nor all the stars look upon human affairs with as lasting a light as you look, who shine upon the world without setting night apart from day.[55]

The emperors had a natural, inborn kinship—based though this was on their *virtus*—with Iuppiter and Hercules, and with the universe as a whole. Thus the underlying theme of the panegyric of 297 is the order of the universe established by divine providence under the government of the Tetrarchs, who were themselves the descendants of gods. Accordingly, the day of the accession of Constantius could be viewed as itself a cosmic event:

> Oh for that season [of spring] when rightly, it is believed, all things were born in the past, since now, during this season we see all things established. Oh Kalends of March, as once you were the initiating omen for the ever-returning years, so now you are the initiating omen for the eternal emperors.[56]

The Tetrarchic panegyrists acquired an increasingly precise and specific grasp of their task of communicating the accession of the emperors to their listeners, a grasp which became more specific as imperial policy itself matured and was gradually realised. As has already been seen in different contexts, the foundation of the Tetrarchic claim to rule lay in the connection which, on the basis of their *virtus*, the emperors made between themselves and Iuppiter and Hercules. This claim could be illustrated in various ways by applying to the existing situation the ceremony of *adventus* and the familiar theories of rule thanks to virtus and to the link between emperor and Rome, where Rome, whether as concept or personification, could stand for the civilian population of the empire. The application of these theories to the situation in hand could become the means of understanding that situation, of creating a human consensus about it, based as this was on a divine consensus and the divine patronage claimed by the Tetrarchs.

ii. Images of Wreathgiving, *adventus* and Enthronement

What did the artists add to this picture? The complexities of the methods whereby claims to imperial dominion were asserted in the later third century and after are revealed in one of their several aspects in the imperial portraiture of the period, where one may distinguish, as has been seen, the portraits of the divinely inspired ruler, such as Gallienus on the one hand (plate 1), and on the other, those of the soldier emperors such as Claudius Gothicus, Probus and Aurelian. The portraiture shows that the Tetrarchic claim to rule, however new in itself, rested on this latter tradition, the tradition of the military emperors of the later third century (plates 2, 3, 44).

While the panegyrics begin by emphasising the uniqueness of Tetrarchic rule and by idealising it, the portraiture, especially that of the coinage, highlights a certain continuity between reigns, and a choice of milieu on the part of Diocletian which was deliberate, and which was discarded equally deliberately by Constantine, as is demonstrated by the latter's return to the flattering, youthful portraiture of the third century.[57] (Plates 4, 11)

In short, for the empire at large, divine election, as propagated by the Gallic panegyrists, was not enough. Rather, Diocletian and his colleagues fell back on an idiom which had been created by their predecessors, an idiom which the Gallic panegyrists incorporated into their orations by stressing imperial victories. If one translates the Tetrarchic panegyrics into practical language, it emerges that an imperial accession was validated by success, and success, even in the civilian milieu of panegyrists, was principally military.

A similar message is recorded on the Tetrarchic coinage, on coin types which can be related not as much to accession as to the wider question of the status of an emperor once he had reached and secured his position. There is very little that was absolutely new on the reverses of the Tetrarchic coinage; on the other hand, throughout the Tetrarchy, Iuppiter and Hercules were proclaimed as the protectors and *comites* of the emperors, and other gods, Mars, Minerva, and Sol appeared in the same role but to a lesser degree. The concept of a divine *comes* of the emperor was by no means new,[58] but in the Tetrarchy it was propagated more specifically and distinctly. Panegyrics, especially that of 289, explained how Iuppiter and Hercules were the models of the emperors, and a series of coins showing the works of Hercules matches this explanation.[59]

Some other images used to convey the idea of dominion may be divided into two groups: on the one hand, the emperor receives a globe, and on the other, he is crowned by another person, usually a deity, or by Victoria. The proclamation of Diocletian by the army was referred to by means of an issue from Siscia, FIDES MILITUM, where Diocletian is shown receiving a globe from a soldier.[60] Later, Diocletian was shown on reverses of Heraclea (291–292 A.D.) and Antioch (uncertain date) receiving a figure of Victoria from Iuppiter, CONCORDIA MILITUM.[61] Another version of the image of the emperor receiving a globe was made for Maximian: an undated issue from Cyzicus shows Diocletian handing a globe to Maximian, his junior colleague. The same image appeared in Cyzicus in 285–286 with the legend FIDES MILITUM and Maximian on the obverse.[62] Subsequently Maximian was also shown, more exaltedly, receiving a globe from Iuppiter,[63] and issues showing Iuppiter handing a globe to an emperor appeared for all four Tetrarchs with the legend CONCORDIAE AUGG, 294–397 A.D. in the West,[64] and with CONCORDIA MILITUM, 295–307 A.D. in the East.[65]

The wreath or crown in antiquity conveyed victory, as well as dominion,[66] and it was primarily in the former sense that the image of the crowning was used on the Tetrarchic coinage, as may be understood from the legends accompanying the image of the emperor crowned by Victoria. Such legends often referred to *virtus* and *Victoria*.[67]

It was at the time of victory that the emperor revealed one aspect, a military one, of himself, just as he could reveal his role as a civilian in *adventus*. Such a military revelation is depicted on a battle scene on the arch of Galerius.[68] Galerius is shown mounted, attacking his mounted Persian enemy, whose horse is about to topple over backwards under the onslaught of the emperor, while an eagle carrying a wreath in its claws is hovering over the head of Galerius (plate 10). This eagle image was used for almost the entire imperial period to convey the notion of *consecratio* and apotheosis after death, but here it is joined to the living emperor, who could now in life acquire those honours which formerly were only to be had after death. He acquired these honours through victory, the present realisation, not the past acquisition, of power, and he acquired honours not retrospectively for past achievements, as in *consecratio*; rather, honour and divine status came to the emperor in the fulfilment of his *cura* for the empire.

In these images of coronation and majesty the military appeal was predominant. Such an appeal on its own would cut little ice with the civilian population of the empire, and it was for this reason, we may presume, that the panegyrists were silent on the military aspect of the election for empire of the Tetrarchs, and instead spoke about their divine election on the one hand, and about the urban ceremony of *adventus* on the other.

But the military and civilian aspects of the emperor's life were not kept totally distinct, even on the coinage. Of the many issues showing the emperor crowned by Victoria, the PIETAS AUGG gold multiple of Constantius may be singled out for comment in this context (plate 9). It belongs to a series of gold multiples of which the Arras medallion is one.[69] The series celebrates, like the panegyric of 297, Constantius' conquest of Britain. Constantius is to be seen, crowned from behind by Victoria, raising the kneeling and suppliant personification of Britain. *Pietas* in the legend refers to the act of restoring Britain to the empire, after the role of a usurper; at the same time *pietas* is a primary imperial virtue.[70] One aspect of imperial *pietas* was victory: in visual terms this is here depicted by Victoria crowning the emperor.

The series to which this multiple belongs celebrates imperial triumph in terms of *adventus*. The iconography reproduces the traditional *adventus* imagery, where the arriving emperor might raise, 'restore,' his kneeling, downcast province. It was in such terms that the panegyrist of 297 conveyed the accession of Constantius I:

> You made your Gallic provinces your own by your mere coming. Indeed the very speed with which you anticipated all messengers of your accession and arrival enabled you to capture that tenacious . . . gathering of pirates at Gesoriacum.[71]

Constantius' accession and dominion over Gaul are here expressed by means of an arrival and a victory, exactly as the PIETAS AUGG multiple and its numerous parallels depict it visually.

Some *adventus* issues, particularly in the later fourth century, can be related to the beginning of reigns. In the Tetrarchy, however, *adventus* was an occurrence too frequently celebrated to allow any direct correlation between it and accession. *Adventus* was merely one of the many strands of imagery which could be used to convey accession, although it has already been seen, in Mamertinus' panegyric on Julian, and in Claudian, how persistent it could become. The coins here discussed therefore refer to accession only in general terms; even the scene of handing over the globe recurs too often throughout the Tetrarchy for it to be associated with accession only.

In short, the Tetrarchs, although propagating on the coinage the divine support of their dominion—not only on the issues here referred to, but in the very extensive IOVI CONSERVATORI issues and the coinages dedicated to Hercules under various titles—did not emphasise the moment of their accession. The overall import of the panegyrics is the same; only the panegyric of 297 on Constantius goes into any detail regarding the day of accession, and in passing links it to the dawn of an imperial *adventus*. But even in this panegyric the day of the accession is placed side by side with notions and images, such as the Seasons, Sol, and Luna, which convey a perpetuity, not a moment in time.

We come now to a Tetrarchic image of enthronement[72] which, because of its connection with later images, is of particular interest here. It appears on a gold multiple from the mint of Rome. The Augusti, Diocletian to the left, Maximian to the right, are seen enthroned frontally in military dress, the former crowned by Iuppiter, the latter by Hercules (plate 44).

The legend PERPETUA CONCORDIA AUGG[73] suggests once again that, insofar as the accession of the Tetrarchs was viewed at all as a unique moment in time, the aspect of it that mattered most was the outcome of accession, that is, a duration of time. This multiple is among the earliest coins to show the emperor enthroned frontally,[74] to set him face to face with the viewer, in majesty,[75] in the style of the Christian icons of a later period.

On the arch of Galerius, the imagery of wreath-giving and majesty is combined with that of imperial *pietas*, of raising a kneeling province, into an elaborate tableau of cosmic rule. Diocletian and Galerius, the two Augusti, in the centre, are enthroned over the sky—the realm of Iuppiter—and the earth—the realm of Hercules—precisely as envisioned by the panegyrists of 297 and 307 A.D.[76] They are flanked by the two Caesars, Maximian and Constantius, who each raise a kneeling province. The rest of the composition is filled with the protecting deities of the Tetrarchy and the whole is framed by personifications of earth and sea, while two victories crown the Augusti with wreaths (plate 10).

On this relief of the arch of Galerius we may see how, for all its apparent cultural and religious conservatism, the Tetrarchy was a period of change and innovation which became fundamental to the Christian empire. Tetrarchic change and innovation have been viewed, in the present context, from two angles: on the one hand, there has been the view of Tetrarchic dominion as propounded in the panegyrics, where we witnessed a growing certainty of touch in subordinating different themes relevant to accession under the main Tetrarchic theme of the dominion of Iuppiter and Hercules, as paralleled on earth by the dominion of Iovius and Herculius. On the other hand, we have examined Tetrarchic change and innovation from the visual angle and seen how old and new images were adapted and combined to express the concepts which underlay the rule of the Tetrarchs.

While the clearcut pagan imagery of Tetrarchic dominion had no future in the Christian empire, the concept of imperial rule as an earthly reflection of divine rule in heaven was to become definitive by the fifth century. Moreover, the Tetrarchic images of enthronement and majesty, where the chief visual characteristic was frontality, stand at the head of a long series of Byzantine and Western mediaeval renderings of the majesty of both Christ and terrestrial rulers. In the proliferation of iconographic themes relevant during much of the fourth century, this frontal imagery when stripped of its pagan ingredients can accordingly provide something of a guideline.

3. CONSTANTINE

i. The Establishment of a Divinely Appointed Dynasty and Early Formulations of a Ceremonial of Accession

The eulogistic accounts of the accession of Constantine in the *Panegyrici Latini* and Eusebius illustrate particularly well the point made above: how theory regarding imperial accession was made to fit the facts. The information for Constantine is much more precise and varied than it is for the Tetrarchs. The earliest source on Constantine's accession is the panegyric of 307 devoted to the marriage of Constantine and Fausta. This panegyric had a complicated task to perform, some aspects of which are reflected in the description of Constantine's accession. Firstly, Maximian's return to power had to be explained and, in accordance with the perspective of this panegyric, was viewed as a necessary correlative to Constantine's accession. The approach was simple and illogical: the orator praised Maximian's re-emergence as emperor without analysing his motivation. But some familiar features enter into the presentation. Maximian had originally become emperor as the chosen of Diocletian—a choice he justified by his deeds. Now, however, he continued to be emperor as the chosen of Roma, who commanded his return to power.[77] Two points need stressing here.

Firstly, Roma has subtly taken the place of Iuppiter and Hercules as the deity at whose behest the emperor acts, although Iuppiter and particularly Hercules are still emphasised.[78] Roma is one of the figures of the pagan empire, which, despite the profound attachment of pagans to their concept of Rome, survived into Christian imperial art. Indeed, because the other deities were dropped, Roma emerged all the more strongly, and one aspect of the idea of Rome, which as a result was developed particularly carefully in late antiquity, was the link between Rome and the emperor.[79] (Cf. plates 56–57.) In the fourth century, therefore, Roma, although for pagans still the recipient of a cult,[80] acquired another role: she could now figure as one of the electors to the empire, as she does in the panegyric of 307.

On the coinage this role had been anticipated in the third century,[81] in representations of Roma handing a globe or victory to the emperor. During Diocletian's Tetrarchy she was supplanted in this role by Iuppiter and Hercules,[82] but re-emerged handing a globe to Maxentius, and, after 312, to Constantine.[83] That image disappeared definitively from the coinage in the later reign of Constantine, but was replaced by a series of issues showing Roma and Constantinopolis, or each separately, enthroned frontally like the emperors.[84] Rome and Constantinople and their emperors were thus to be seen filling parallel roles. The panegyric of 307 marks a precise moment in the reopening of relations, so to speak, between Rome and the emperor.

Secondly, while emphasising the link between emperor and Rome, the panegyric of 307 also states the empire to be an inalienable and permanent charge, Maximian being one of the emperors who are *semper Herculii*:

> Just as the Ocean which provides all the waters of heaven and earth is complete, although it is always in motion, so you, Maximian, can give the empire, but you cannot not possess it.[85]

Maximian, like Sol after the universe had been endangered by Phaethon,[86] took up the reins of government again and was able to do so since "there was in [him] an innate majesty."[87] The imperial majesty is thus stated to be an office, a function, which marks the bearer for life. It was a significant moment in the evolution of Roman imperial thought, and casts a revealing sidelight on the meaning of those timeless and placeless images showing the emperor receiving a globe or wreath, which the Tetrarchs took over from earlier times, and those other images, showing the emperor frontally enthroned, which became so frequent in the fourth century.

As regards Constantine, he became emperor in 306, according to the panegyric, through his marriage to the daughter of Maximianus Herculius,[88] this being an occasion of particular rejoicing since the marriage promised an unending row of successors to Maximian and Constantine, in short a dynasty.[89] On the other hand, Constantine already was the son of Maximian *maiestatis ordine*,[90] that is, he was already emperor when he married, a statement which is more in agreement with the facts. Further, Constantine was left the empire by his consecrated father,[91] was acknowledged as Caesar by Galerius and destined to be Augustus by Maximian. Thus within the framework of the Tetrarchy, the orator produced every conceivable theoretical justification for arrangements which had been made in a very *ad hoc* fashion.

The panegyric of 307 in one sense provides an ideal basis for the formation of theories regarding the justification of imperial rule, for it shows how consent of the gods could not exist without *virtus*, how *virtus* was dependent on distinguished ancestry, and how a man became emperor because he was needed and because his rule promised lasting security. Nuances of these ingredients could be dispensed with or suppressed, but in some sense they were all present in most imperial elections; indeed, these reasons are the commonplaces around which, according to the textbooks, panegyrics were to be composed. Later on these commonplaces were repeated and enacted in the ceremonial of the Byzantine court.

The panegyric of 307 gives evidence of the existence of a stereotype which could be called upon in case of need, in a complex situation when the future was not certain. The panegyrist of 307 provided something for all contingencies. One of the various aspects of imperial accessions which he brought forward was bound to emerge as important in the coming reign, but which aspect it was to be, was as yet uncertain. The panegyrist simply related the repertoire of panegyric to the situation in hand, and did so with some skill. But the historian must not be misled into thinking that the repertoire, the stereotype, brought forward in this panegyric amounted to any kind of constitutional theory. All the stereotype did was to provide a facade until the position became clearer.

The aspect which did come to predominate for Constantine was the dynastic one, as may be seen from the panegyric of 310, held in Trier after the death of Maximian. At some point between 307 and 310 the story of Constantine's descent from Claudius Gothicus emerged in Trier and was reflected in the numismatic iconography of this period at the mint of Trier. In the panegyric of 310 it was told in a tone of mystery as known to those "who love you."[92]

Another aspect of a dynastic succession, utilised extensively for Constantine, was the emphasis placed on the similarity between father and son. The panegyrics of 307 and of 310 both began their eulogies of Constantine with eulogies of his father, in order to make the point that Constantine resembled his father in virtues and appearance.[93] The point was taken up again in the panegyric of 313.[94] In the art of the Constantian period it was elaborated with a somewhat different bias in the very noticeable emphasis on Constantine's appearance in portraiture, which can be followed in some detail on the coinage. Constantine's face is always handsome; as the panegyric of 310 expressed it: "You are . . . youthful and glad, and most beautiful, our Emperor."[95]

The dynastic element was emphasised in 310 by acknowledging but setting aside most other elements in the accession. The day on which Constantine was clothed in the *habitus* of empire, the chlamys,[96] and entered the *sacrum palatium*[97] might properly be celebrated as the *natalis* of his empire. But in truth the *imperii fortuna* was his from birth,[98] because he had "that ancient prerogative of an imperial family," a point which distinguished him from and exalted him over his co-emperors.[99]

However, accession by descent was not an accident of birth. Rather, it expressed the deliberate choice of Constantine by the gods, and ensured that the emperor should not be chosen by "some random consent of men," or "a sudden burst of popularity."[100] Rather the emperor should be chosen "without scheming and electioneering."[101] In the idiom of the coinage, this set of ideas was conveyed by the familiar image of a god—in this instance Sol—crowning the emperor, or handing victory on a globe to him.[102] The definitive nature of Constantine's claim to the empire was emphasised further by his descent from Claudius Gothicus and Constantius, who chose Constantine, his first-born son, as his successor, thereby acting in accord with the gods.[103]

It was only after these theoretical and doctrinal points had been settled that the panegyrist turned to the actual events of Constantine's accession. When Constantius had died,

> The whole army consented to your election, the minds and eyes of all pointed to you, and although you referred the question as to what should happen concerning the government of the commonwealth to the opinion of the senior emperors, your electors by their eagerness anticipated what the emperors shortly confirmed by their verdict. As soon as the soldiers could gain access to you, when you came out to them, they clothed you in the purple, serving thereby the interests of the common weal rather than your own desires, and you wept. But it was not right for the elected emperor to weep any more.[104]

In this scene the emperor who had, so to speak, already been chosen in heaven, was chosen against his own will[105] by the inspirational act of election by army and people. *Universi* and *omnes* are vague terms; whatever the context, they could only be vague, and herein lay their utility.[106]

The term *princeps consecratus* which is here used to describe the elected emperor points to an important semantic change in Latin, for *princeps consecratus* had formerly denoted the divinised emperor after his death. We have here a linguistic development which is paralleled by a development in art: that is, attributes of *consecratio*, such as the wreath-bearing eagle, were applied to the emperor during his lifetime, as on the combat relief on the arch of Galerius.[107] (See plate 10.) Late antique formulations of imperial accessions came increasingly to heighten the status achieved by the emperor at his accession; the use of the term *princeps consecratus* in the panegyric of 310 marks a distinct stage in this process.

The panegyric also points to an emerging ceremonial of accession, in that it mentions certain formal moments: Constantine's election by consent of army and people,[108] his clothing in the purple[109] by the soldiers[110] and his entry into the palace.[111] This does not yet amount to a descriptive narrative of the accession formalities. Such a narrative was, however, produced nearly a generation later by Eusebius, who in the *Life of Constantine* described the same scene as had the panegyric of 310.

Eusebius begins by treating the settlement of the succession to Constantine I as a family affair, for his preoccupations differed greatly from those of the Gallic panegyrists.[112] The latter were still, between 307 and 313, concerned with showing up some continuity between the rule of the Tetrarchs and that of Constantine, for, from the Gallic point of view, the Tetrarchy had been a period of stability and peace.[113] Eusebius, like Lactantius, on the other hand, was committed to portraying the Tetrarchs—with the exception of Constantius—as persecutors who had been struck down by the wrath of the Christian God.

The rise of Constantine and the succession of his sons seemed perfectly in order to Eusebius, and when explaining Constantine's accession in secular imperial terms, he simply and complacently referred to the law of nature.[114] This meant that Constantine, being Constantius' eldest son, succeeded to Constantius' part of the empire, and the succession was arranged while Constantius' sons and daughters crowded around the deathbed of their father.[115] When Constantius had died, Constantine, clothed in his father's purple, came forth from his father's palace. Next, after Constantius had been buried, Constantine, "showing himself forth to all as the coming to life again of the emperor his father," was acclaimed by the troops as Autokrator and Augustus.[116] In this way, says Eusebius, Constantine, the worthy son of his father, became ruler of practically the whole world,[117] and the fact that he was the chosen of God was displayed by his victory over the persecutors and his universal dominion.[118]

The account of Eusebius illustrates well the almost illogical coexistence of the different claims to rule that could be made by a Roman emperor, each of which claims would have been in itself sufficient to justify an accession. Less pronounced than the formal elements—the family arrangement, proclamation by the troops, election by God—but equally vital was the element which none of the late antique authors mentioned explicitly in connection with accession, but which confirmed legality: namely, victory. The victory which, in the case of Constantine, was particularly telling in the Latin panegyrics was that over Maxentius, and in Eusebius, the victories over Maxentius and Licinius. For these victories, as interpreted in the official literature, juxtaposed the rightly chosen emperor who cared for his subjects, and the tyrant, the enemy of his people and the enemy of God.[119]

The panegyrist of 313 gave an account of the victory of the preceding year mainly in narrative terms, but included a comparison of Maxentius and Constantine on grounds of virtues and ancestry in order to show that Constantine was bound to prevail. This passage was later taken up in a similar situation by Pacatus and applied to Maximus and Theodosius.[120] Eusebius' views are analogous: not only were Maxentius and Licinius oppressors, tyrants who had come to rule by unlawful means, but also, Constantine excelled them in virtues, and—herein lies the difference for Eusebius—*eusebeia*.[121] Eusebius constantly returned to the links between the emperor and God, which were exemplified by Constantine's attainment of victory through prayer and the use of the *labarum*.[122] Victory was the outward and continuing manifestation of a rightful accession.

As we have seen, many criteria were available for identifying the true emperor, but ultimately there was no way of reaching absolute certainty apart from success. Maximian, the colleague of Diocletian, whose rule in the West had, according to the panegyrics at least, been a success, could, by the prestige of his tenure of the imperial office, impart an aura of legitimacy to Constantine in 307. But in 310, when he had been defeated by Constantine and had perished, he was nothing but a miserable failure[123] remembered with a certain respect for past glories, but otherwise dismissed, because eclipsed by the rule of the newly dominant Constantine.

Like the Tetrarchy, the period of Constantine produced no surviving image which could be directly referred to the moment of accession, and to the ceremonial then enacted. However, the moment when the emperor appeared before his army to be honoured and acclaimed recurred many times in his career, when the imperial *vota* were taken and after each victory. These military acknowledgements of the emperor's rule and success were in certain ways parallels to the civilian *vota* and accession ceremonies then in existence.

Such a military acclamation is represented on a Ticinum silver multiple of 315 marking Constantine's decennalia.[124] (Plate 51) The obverse has the much-discussed portrait of the helmeted Constantine in three-quarter frontality with the Chi Rho monogramme.[125] But here we are interested in the reverse, SALUS REIPUBLICAE. Constantine holding a trophy stands on a platform being crowned by Victoria in the usual way. His right hand is raised in *adlocutio*. The platform is surrounded by nine soldiers, some with horses, and the figures are neatly fitted into the available circular space. This type is unique in the Constantinian coinage and the coinage of any period, in that it differs considerably from the *adlocutio* scenes of the third century and before, which consisted of a representation in profile, whereas the present scene features frontality, and at the same time shows the emperor crowned by Victoria. This coin type is the closest approximation in Constantinian official art to representing the moment when the victorious emperor was formally recognised by his troops.

It is a military image, where the emperor is related to his army. Civilian counterparts to it appear on the *largitio* and *adlocutio* panels of the arch of Constantine (plates 14–15), where the emperor is related to the citizens of Rome, the city which for Maximian had figured as the elector to empire. On the two panels we meet again the frontality which has been identified as a characteristic of Tetrarchic images displaying the majesty of the enthroned emperors, highlighted on the arch of Constantine by a rigorous symmetry whereby the emperor becomes the centre of the image, just as he was the centre of the accession ceremony as described by Eusebius. It is precisely the frontality and the symmetry on the arch which differentiate these reliefs from all earlier representations of *adlocutio* and *largitio*. These panels show the emperor in that position of undisputed and closely defined pre-eminence which the Constantinian panegyrics, and, to a much greater degree, Eusebius, attribute to him. We witness here a certain hardening of the boundary lines between emperor and subjects which was not yet visible in Constantinian *adventus*, but was visible in Constantinian *consecratio*.[126]

The accounts of Constantine's accession, both Greek and Latin, present many elements which are familiar from earlier times; what was new in them was the emphasis on a ceremonial of accession. This ceremonial emerged, as has been seen earlier, in correlation to the ceremonial of imperial funerals and changed ideas of imperial *consecratio*. Insofar as *consecratio*, of whatever kind, was a ratification of an emperor's rule and actions, it necessarily reflected on that emperor's successor, who was inevitably obliged to take up a position of approval or disapproval *vis-à-vis* his predecessor.

In the early fourth century, this reflection of two succeeding emperors upon each other was for the first time expressed in a set of ceremonial actions, in which funeral and accession came to be interrelated. With that a further avenue of claiming legitimacy became established, and this was a ceremonial of accession carried out according to rules which were in the course of becoming established at this period. Here it is noteworthy that Eusebius, according to whom, given his premises, the dynasty of Constantius I had an unquestionable right to rule, nonetheless reported the ceremonies of funeral and accession in meticulous detail.

Once these ceremonies had been performed, there came into existence a new kind of consensus, both human and divine, new in that it could now be registered and documented by precise ceremonial actions which had to be commonly agreed upon. Consensus could be said to have taken place at a particular place and time and in a particular form. Before Constantine, the consensus was said to have taken place, but could never be agreed upon as the factual occurrence it became once it was clothed in an increasingly carefully elaborated ceremony of accession. In Eusebius, this ceremony, linked as it was to the death and funeral of Constantius I, provided the foundation of Constantine's progressive claim to rule.

Both Eusebius and the Constantinian panegyrists introduced elements into imperial accession which had been alien to the Tetrarchy. But there was also an important strand of continuity between Constantine and the Tetrarchs, and, for that matter, the earlier Roman Empire: this was the acknowledgement that imperial victory was the tangible manifestation of a legitimate accession.

Hand in hand with the emergence of the ceremonial of accession went the emergence of the imperial insignia.[127] Eusebius says that Constantine was clothed in his father's purple and came forth from his father's imperial palace.[128] We may interpret this as meaning that the imperial insignia in themselves were acquiring a sacred significance and were no longer to be produced *ad hoc* for each accession. The passing on of the insignia from one emperor to the next accordingly had to be integrated into the accession ceremonial. By the late fifth century, this integration had taken place and its meaning was understood, for after dethroning Romulus Augustulus, Odovacar sent the imperial insignia to

Constantinople,[129] and at the accession of Justin, the actual insignia, τὸ σχῆμα τοῦ βασιλέως, were needed before the accession ceremonial could be carried out.[130] (Cf. plate 61.)

As for Constantine's accession, we have seen that it was justified and explained initially by linking it to the Tetrarchic *status quo*, then by dynastic arguments, and finally, in Eusebius, by dynastic arguments which were ratified in a public ceremonial, that is, the proclamation by the soldiers of Constantine clothed in his father's purple. As had been the case earlier, the validity of this accession was made explicit, according to both the panegyrist and Eusebius, by Constantine's victories.

4. THE DESCENDANTS OF CONSTANTINE

i. A Christian Dynasty

From the outset, Constantinian panegyrics emphasised the dynastic aspect of imperial rule. Constantine's own accession was explained and justified in panegyric at some length, and it has been seen that the resources of Roman imperial ideology were fully utilised for the task. The fact that Constantine's sons should succeed him, on the other hand, was taken for granted. The panegyrist of 313, celebrating Constantine's victory over Maxentius, recalls in his concluding passage the deeds of Constantius, which were excelled by Constantine. In a final supplication to the *summus rerum sator*, a phrase which sums up the uncertainties of 313 with the utmost conciseness, he prays that the present regime will last:

> Grant therefore that the high blessing which you have bestowed on mankind may remain for ever and that Constantine may abide on earth from one period of time to the next. For, unconquered Emperor, although your divine descendant has already come forth, according to the wishes of the commonwealth, and although more descendants are hoped for, posterity will be truly fortunate if, while you bring your children to the helm of the governments of the world, you yourself nonetheless remain the greatest emperor among them.[131]

The descendant, *suboles*, referred to here was Crispus, and we may think in this context of Vergil's *cara deum suboles* of the Fourth Eclogue, a poem which Constantine himself expounded in his address to the Holy Assembly.[132]

Nazarius in 321 could be more specific, if less evocative, about Constantine's descendants. His panegyric was held in Rome on the occasion of Constantine's quindecennalia and the quinquennalia of the Caesars Crispus and Constantine II.[133] It was possible to praise Crispus' deeds in war and, since both Crispus and Constantine had become Caesars, to visualise a secure and definite future, a time when, as the panegyrist of 313 said, Constantine, supported by his sons, would be *maximus imperator*.[134] This expression of the panegyrist is reflected in the titulature employed by Constantine on the coinage after 329, CONSTANTINUS MAX AUG (cf. plate 47).

Neither the orator of 313 nor Nazarius mentioned the actual moment when, or ceremony whereby, Constantine's sons became Caesars. Nazarius, however, referred to the commemoration of this occasion, the *vota*, in some detail.[135] Again, it was not the precise historical moment that was emphasised, but, as on the coinage, a perpetuity, a happy age, which would last indefinitely.[136] The *natalis* of the empire, the anniversary of the emperor's accession, when the *vota* for the future were taken up, was a regular fixture in the official calendars of the empire, observed universally from the first century A.D. But when the Romans came to consider the *natalis*, or the accession, they still preferred to think of a stretch of time, not a moment.

Nazarius pointed out how the Caesars benefited from their father's example and from being educated by him,[137] a point which was also made by Eusebius, Libanius, Julian and Themistius.[138] In short, Constantine succeeded, in the years after 312, in establishing a dynasty which was accepted throughout the empire and was propagated by means of a coherent body of ideas,[139] although in an idiom which differed widely from author to author.

Eusebius regarded the three sons of Constantine, who succeeded their father after the disorders of the succession were over, as a divinely granted reflection and continuation of his glory.[140] According to Eusebius, the sons had been chosen by their father to succeed him. In fact, the succession in 337 was not a smooth transition from father to sons, for it involved conflicts in which the greater part of Constantine's family perished. Eusebius had to take up some position *vis-à-vis* these events. He did so by saying that after Constantine's death the three sons of Constantine—Constantine II, Constantius II, and Constans—were elected by the army divinely inspired, ἐξ ἐπιπνοίας κρείττονος, simultaneously in all parts of the empire.[141]

In other words, Eusebius drew on one of the *topoi* of imperial elections, a *topos*, moreover, which in the Christian context was acquiring a new significance with regard to the divinely inspired election of bishops by popular acclamation.[142] Contemporaries, like subsequent historians of late antiquity, have found that such a divinely inspired election was hard to deny; hard to affirm also, but it served if and until a pattern could be established, and it could then become official history, as it did in the case of the events after 337, where, as in 306, the removal to heaven, formerly *consecratio*, of the preceding emperor played an important part.

One must not be cynical about these attempts to bring some order into ideas which bore on the government of the empire. It was vital for the continuance of peace and security that the attempts should be made and should succeed, and that they should be made at many different levels, in order to convince the different groups of the emperor's subjects, and to cover the varying contingencies which an accession could produce. Eusebius placed in the foreground of his narrative the dynastic elements in the succession of Constantine's sons, and added the motif of divinely inspired election, in order to cover up the disorders of 337.

Libanius, likewise, made dynastic claims for Constantine's sons in his oration of c. 348 A.D.,[143] by which time only Constantius II and Constans were ruling the empire. Complacently, Libanius looked back to three generations of emperors—ἐκ τριγονίας ἡ βασιλεία προσήκουσα[144]—and accepted this as the best possible validation of the rule of Constantine's sons. The authority of Constantine himself, who shared responsibilities with his sons during his lifetime, was used to give further weight to this argument, which starts with the premise that kingship, of all institutions, most needs a just beginning.

His subject did not appeal to Libanius, as one may gather when comparing this panegyric to his very different speeches on Julian. Its sheer length and comprehensiveness make the oration on Constantius II and Constans one of the least convincing of panegyrics. What is worth noting, however, is the availability—if only, as here, at the most banal level—of arguments to explain the establishment then obtaining. Imperial government after 337 had an official image, provided largely by Eusebius, on whom Libanius drew for this panegyric,[145] although he dispensed with Eusebius' concept of divinely inspired election.

The arguments about divinely inspired election were also omitted by Julian in his panegyric on Constantius in 356. Instead, Julian returned to the Gallic tradition of Constantine's descent from Claudius Gothicus, stating that Constantius I obtained the empire both by inheritance and by being chosen by Diocletian;[146] Constantine in his turn was chosen by Constantius and elected by the soldiers. Thereafter Julian, like Libanius, continued by elaborating how Constantine educated Constantius II to succeed him and exonerated the latter with regard to the disorders of the succession by emphasising his mildness to his enemies.[147]

Two years later, in a second panegyric on Constantius, Julian returned to the dynastic argument of descent from Claudius, but now placed it into a Homeric setting, which opened up vistas of Hellenistic theories of kingship such as Julian had not previously touched upon. The house and dominion of Constantine were likened to the house and sceptre of Agamemnon, the sceptre given by Zeus himself to Pelops and handed down by the latter in his family for three generations.[148]

While both Libanius and Julian left the question of the divinely inspired election of the sons of Constantine to one side, Themistius came closer to Eusebius' theoretical framework. Like Eusebius, Themistius was prepared to view the succession as an expression of some link between the emperor and the divine, for he justified Constantius' rule on the ground that like God, Constantius was φιλάνθρωπος,[149] this being the only quality which could make man truly godlike. This argument recurs throughout Themistius' work in varying contexts.

In the eyes of the imperial panegyrists of the time, Constantine's sons, unlike Constantine himself, succeeded their father without an explicit ceremony of accession being performed for them. The only ceremony that can be mentioned is the divinely inspired proclamation of the three emperors by the army, as recorded by Eusebius, a ceremony which rested on the long-standing practice of the pre-Christian empire, whereby the new emperor, or the emperor who had achieved a victory, was acclaimed by his troops. To this ancient ceremony Eusebius added a variety of divine inspiration which was Christian in origin, and which was to have a long and important history in the context of imperial accessions.

ii. Coronation by God, Enthronement and Majesty

While the literary exegesis of imperial accession remained in many senses incomplete during the period now under discussion, visual representations of the emperor, chosen by divine inspiration and predestined to rule by his descent, advanced beyond the traditional boundaries, even though the most significant of these advances had no notable subsequent history.

We have above considered a medallion showing Diocletian and Maximian enthroned frontally, crowned by Iuppiter and Hercules respectively (plate 44). Apart from a precursor under Carinus, this was a new motif on the coinage, and conveyed admirably one of the essential features of Tetrarchic rule. The coronation of the emperor by some divinity or by Victoria, as has been seen, can be interpreted broadly in two ways, either to mark victory or to mark the emperor's attaining his office. The former ingredient was generally more prominent, although in the present context the latter has been examined more closely. When the empire became Christian, substitutes had to be found for the pagan deities who had crowned the emperor, although the more neutral images of the emperor being crowned by Victoria were retained. At the same time frontality became an increasingly regular feature in coin design and in imperial art in general.

The most interesting and important piece in the series of coins which concern us here is a thirty-solidi gold multiple of Constantius II as Caesar of 330 from Constantinople.[150] (Plate 45) The obverse shows Constantius FL IUL CONSTANTIUS NOB CAES, bust laureate, draped, cuirassed, and holding shield and spear. On the shield is represented a triumphant *imperator* in battle, stretching out his right hand like the general on the Ludovisi battle sarcophagus.[151] The reverse, GAUDIUM RO-MANORUM, shows Constantine standing between Constantine II and Constantius II, taller than either, crowned with a circlet by the hand of God from a cloud.[152] Constantine II on the right is crowned by Victoria, and Constantius to the left by Virtus. Both sons turn their heads towards Constantine, but are otherwise represented frontally, and all are shown in military dress holding spears.

This image summarises much of what appears in panegyrics on Constantine and his sons. Constantine himself rules by the direct authority of God, a fact which is conveyed by his being crowned from a cloud, while his sons, in a subordinate position, rule by virtue of descent from him. They are crowned by the allegorical figures of Virtus and Victoria, who belong to the traditional repertoire of imperial art, but the gesture of coronation from a cloud is new. In view of the date of this multiple, this gesture clearly does not mark Constantine's accession, but his continuing contact with the godhead, which confirmed and established his dominion; not a moment but a perpetuity is represented. He is crowned with a circlet, not the traditional laurel wreath.

Constantinian obverses demonstrate that Constantine assumed the diadem for himself in 325, while the Caesars still wore laurel wreaths. At the same time, Eusebius shows that the diadem definitely became one of the imperial insignia under Constantine.[153] Thus, the hand of God is probably depositing a diadem on Constantine's head, while Constantine's sons are perhaps being crowned with laurel wreaths, such as they are shown wearing elsewhere. The differing rank of this imperial college is also conveyed by their height, Constantine being the tallest and Constantine II, the shortest of the three rulers. Constantine's central position in the functioning of the empire is conveyed by the central position he occupies in the picture. The methods used on this multiple to form the image—centralised, frontal composition and gradation of persons by size—are characteristic of late antique art. These were new modes of expression, used on the Arch of Constantine and numerous later imperial monuments, which were devised to express new ideas, or, in many cases, old ideas formulated in a fresh idiom.

A similar piece to the thirty-solidi multiple was struck on the occasion, probably, of Constans becoming Caesar in 333.[154] The obverse, FL CONSTANS NOB CAES shows the bust of Constans laureate, draped and cuirassed, raising his right hand. On the reverse, SECURITAS PERPETUA, Constantine, holding standard and parazonium, is shown between his three sons, two on the left and one on the right, each holding a shield and spear. Again Constantine is the tallest, and the sons are shown in decreasing height; all the figures are standing frontally, Constantine facing the beholder, his sons with their heads turned towards him.

What these two pieces have in common with the Tetrarchic medallion showing the enthroned emperors (plate 44), which we discussed above, is frontality and the symmetrical method of composition. Another group of gold multiples displays similar methods—frontality and symmetry—and, like the Tetrarchic piece, shows the emperor Constantine enthroned on a podium between his sons, who are standing. The earliest of this group is a Roman bronze multiple SALUS ET SPES REIPUBLICAE of 326 A.D.,[155] the date of Constantine's vicennalia and the decennalia of the Caesars. The obverse, CONSTANTINUS PF AUG, shows a laureate bust of Constantine, where traces of Tetrarchic portraiture are still discernible in the sharp profile and pointed nose. On the reverse, Constantine, nimbate, raising his right hand and holding a globe in his left, is enthroned between two sons. The composition is absolutely and rigidly symmetrical.

The reverse legend and composition of this issue were repeated in a more refined rendering at Constantinople in 330, with the obverse showing Constantine, CONSTANTINUS MAX AUG, diademed, with long curling hair, glancing upwards (plate 47), and in 335–336, with Constantius II on the obverse. Both these pieces are multiples of nine solidi and are to be associated with anniversaries of Constantine and his sons. A further variety, struck in multiples of nine solidi at Nicomedia in 335 A.D.,[156] for Constantine as CONSTANTINUS MAX AUG and Constantine II, shows on the reverse Constantine similarly enthroned between two sons, FELICITAS PERPETUA AUG ET CAESS NN. Iconographically related is the SECURITAS PERPETUA nine-solidi multiple from Constantinople for Constantius II of 335–336.[157] It shows Constantine, nimbate, enthroned frontally surrounded by four Caesars all in military dress. This is the image of the succession as intended by Constantine himself just before his death. The particulars of his arrangement were not realised, but the dynastic principle itself, as has been seen, survived.

As in Eusebius and the Latin panegyrics, so on these coins, Constantine is represented as the central figure in the empire, by his position, his attributes—in particular the nimbus—his height and his title. He is Maximus Augustus.[158] The legends emphasise, here as elsewhere, the lasting nature of the arrangements that were made, rather than the moment at which they were made. *Felicitas perpetua, securitas perpetua, salus et spes, gaudium* all convey durability. After Constantine's death, these slogans and iconographic ideas were taken up and adapted to the new circumstances.[159] We now see the imperial college of Constantine's three sons, shown without the dominating figure of their father.

One further coin design is relevant to our present context. It shows the college of emperors, all standing in military dress, their rank indicated by height, under an archway. One of the earliest versions appeared for Constantine II in Cyzicus in 325, FELICITAS ROMANORUM (plate 53). The type was also used for Constantius II, Gallus, Julian, Jovian, Valentinian I and Valens.[160] Thereafter emperors were shown in similar attitudes with similar legends, but without the archway.[161] The archway may be understood as an abbreviated and simplified rendering of the entrance to the palace, which is represented in greater detail on the missorium of Theodosius and the Palatium mosaic of S. Apollinare Nuovo.[162] (Plates 54–55) The emperor as *felicitas Romanorum* is displayed in the palace. It was at the time of his accession that, according to Eusebius and the Latin panegyrics, the emperor took possession of the palace. Thus, one of the ways in which the subjects could acknowledge their emperors was by beholding and greeting them in the imperial palace "as within the innermost sanctuary."[163] The coins here described allude to the emperor's dwelling in the palace and the ideas associated with it, as will be seen in greater detail in the discussion of the missorium of Theodosius.

Among this group of coins displaying the emperor standing or enthroned frontally, the most evocative is undoubtedly the thirty-solidi multiple showing Constantine crowned by the hand of God (plate 45). It replaces the large group of pre-Christian images which show the emperor crowned by some pagan deity. However, in the early fourth century the iconography of the hand of God in this context is unique and it was only taken up again, cursorily, as will be seen, in the late fourth and fifth centuries. The thirty-solidi multiple presents a bold image, a daring synthesis of Christian future and pagan past, the latter represented in the figures of Virtus and Victoria who crown the Caesars.

This image presents an integrated, well-balanced and artistically beautiful image of Christian empire, an empire which, although converted, preserved the traditions of the past. The image on the multiple summarises in particular the optimistic views of Eusebius. But the image was to remain a vision, as shown both by the course of events after 337, and by the methods of the propagandists after that date, who were more cautious and less definite in their approach than Eusebius. Their views were paralleled by the other images here considered, which show the emperors in formalised frontality, standing or seated, sometimes under an arch. These are images which were capable of a wide range of interpretations and they portray more faithfully than does the thirty-solidi multiple the fluid state of affairs obtaining when the empire became Christian.

On the other hand, the imagery here discussed had gained in precision, and it is more consistent than the earlier imagery of imperial majesty. Methods of portraying the emperor could still be original, but what had gone was the element of variation and experimentation, the mixture of old and new in most aspects of imperial art and panegyric which we met with during the Tetrarchy. This change has also been documented in the context of *adventus*.

iii. The Rejection of the Dynasty under Julian

An alternative idiom of accession and imperial majesty, however, was still available. It was possible, firstly, to render Julian's accession as Augustus as a triumphal *adventus*, the rising of a health-giving star under whose ascendance the empire and the world would be renewed. This idiom, as has been seen, had deep roots in paganism, and it set the tone for much of Julian's reign.

Secondly, it was still possible to dispense with a dynastic claim to rule in spite of the considerable and consistent propaganda that had been expended on establishing the dynasty of Constantius I and Claudius Gothicus. Moreover, in this area the accession of Julian re-established the old imperial Roman dichotomy of dynastic and non-dynastic rule. In the later Roman Empire and in Byzantium, attempts to the contrary notwithstanding, this option always remained open; there was never to be, as there was in Sassanian Persia, one single family which carried a charisma within it.[164] Rather, as will be seen, the *status quo* of the earlier empire, an often precarious coexistence of elective and hereditary monarchy, continued.

Julian was the last descendant of Constantine, and succeeded to the empire as Constantius' heir. This fact was recognised with the utmost brevity by his panegyrist Mamertinus[165] in 361, for the real validation of Julian's accession in this panegyric rested on non-dynastic grounds. This was in accord with Julian's own views, for, notwithstanding his descent, he dissociated himself from the policies of his family. Mamertinus, accordingly, while recognising Julian's descent, concentrated on his merits and founded his claim to rule on the fact that he was the best man to be emperor because of his deeds and virtues.[166] On this basis Mamertinus gave an explanation of Julian's accession to the Senate of Constantinople, but at the same time he managed to bypass the problems of the procedures of the accession altogether. He said nothing at all about Julian's creation as Caesar or about his proclamation as Augustus. Rather, he described quite truthfully, if one may take Ammianus as a relatively independent witness, Julian's journey to the East and arrival in Constantinople. In short, he phrased Julian's accession in the terms of a victorious *adventus*.

On the other hand, Libanius in Antioch in 362, when Julian's position had become clearer, could be more precise and positive. He stated that Julian's *aretai* necessitated his proclamation as Augustus by the soldiers. The act of election by the soldiers, according to Libanius in 362, was inspired by the gods. This is a point to which he returned with greater emphasis in the consular panegyric of 363:

> What really happened? A God inspired the soldiers who were planning nothing in particular, but their voices uttered the thought, and this came from God. Then came an exhortation akin to the first, which attributed to Julian, beside the chlamys of purple from the sea, the jewelled diadem, adorned with [pearls], likewise fruits of the sea. And Julian looked up to heaven, for both the giving and the receiving of empire happened by the will of the gods.[167]

This narrative of spontaneous election, with the ceremonial ingredients of clothing in the purple and coronation, recalls Eusebius' accounts both of the accession of Constantine and of the proclamation of Constantine's sons by the army, except that in Libanius, unlike Eusebius, dynastic reasons were altogether excluded. The act of election according to Libanius took place under the direct inspiration of the gods. Thus, although Julian's attaining the throne was, by implication, a confirmation of the success of Constantine's dynastic policy, Julian's

own policies and his panegyrists' procedure, together with Julian's refusal to appoint a successor, were a denial of it. The discontinuities of
Julian's reign were highlighted from the beginning by his panegyrists'
views of his accession.

On the other hand, however, Ammianus' narratives on the nomination of Julian as Caesar and his proclamation as Augustus indicate that,
together with this discontinuity, there existed a degree of continuity,
and also, that the ceremonial of accession as described by Eusebius developed and could be used as a vehicle to express legitimate rule in circumstances almost as disturbed as were the accessions of Constantine
and his sons.

Julian's nomination as Caesar[168] by Constantius II before the army
was a military event. The consensus which the ceremony aimed for was
the consensus of the army; the civilian consensus expressed in Julian's
arrivals was a different matter. However, as in Julian's arrivals, the consensus of the army, of human beings, was not all that was at stake. During Constantius' oration proposing Julian's nomination,

> the assembly [of the soldiers] interrupted and gently prevented him
> from saying more, and thereby declared with a certain foreknowledge
> of the future that the decision was the decree of the highest deity rather
> than being of human devising.[169]

In other words, human consensus is here seen as a means of expressing the divine election of the emperor. There follow the regular ceremonial actions of an accession: Julian's clothing in his ancestral purple
(avita purpura), as was fitting for a dynastic succession, Constantius' address to Julian as Caesar, Julian's entry into the imperial palace, and his
marriage to Constantius' sister, Helena. These events, formed and defined by a regular and planned ceremonial, now served to mark the accession as a particular moment in time.

When Julian was proclaimed Augustus, the milieu was again military,
but both the dynastic aspect of the ceremonial and the official planning
of it were absent.[170] It was therefore the ceremonial itself on which the
full weight of the question—legitimate emperor or usurper—had to
rest. Julian, according to Ammianus, was raised on the shield by his soldiers and crowned with a torque. The shield-raising was a non-Roman
ceremony performed by Julian's German soldiers; the coronation with
the torque was clearly intended to serve as a substitute for coronation
with the Roman imperial diadem.[171] Under Constantine the diadem became one of the regular imperial insignia. What was not then clear, but
became clear with Julian, was how the emperor should be endowed

with it. Coronation for various kinds of victory was a familiar event in antiquity, but coronation for accession was new. It is significant that Libanius, in an oration delivered less than a year after Julian's proclamation, joined the two, and made the latter explicable in terms of the former: "Blessed are those soldiers who saw you crowned with trophies and could not refrain from placing on your head the crown of precious stones."[172]

The coronation of Julian marks a decisive turning point in the formulation of the ceremonial of accession. The diadem was no longer, as it had been in Eusebius, a merely tacit means of distinguishing the emperor from his subjects. For Julian, the distinction was overtly performed in the military ceremony in which he was crowned and which made him Augustus. With that, the significance of the diadem, στέφανος, changed. For Constantine, it could still be a simple token of his victoriousness, and Libanius saw the crown in this light. But he also differentiated between Julian crowned with trophies and Julian crowned with a crown of precious stones. That such a differentiation was now possible became crucial for the future.

At the time, however, this differentiation was assumed by Libanius without further comment. What was discussed instead was the old problem of the consent of the gods, which, according to Ammianus and Julian's panegyrists, was the foundation of his claim to the title Augustus. Herein these authors agreed with Julian himself, who in the *Letter to the Athenians*[173] considered the consent of the gods, or, more precisely, their urging him to be Augustus as the foundation of his imperial title, while the exact circumstances of his election were subsidiary. The circumstances produced within him an inner struggle, which was resolved by divine intervention, at a time when human intervention, the desires of the soldiers, so far as Julian was concerned, remained indecisive. In such a framework, the traditional supports of imperial rule, dynastic claims and human consensus, were incidental. Julian did not see the ceremonial actions which made him Augustus as related to the divine consent. Rather, the divine consent authorised him to participate in the ceremony.

On this point, Ammianus' view of Julian's proclamation agrees exactly with Julian's:

> On the night before he was acclaimed Augustus, the emperor told his more intimate friends that in the stillness he saw a figure in the appearance in which the Genius Publicus is usually depicted, who, exhorting him, said: 'Julian, for a long time have I secretly watched the access to your house thinking to increase your dignity, and many times,

as though rebuked, I have gone away. If I am not received even now, when the opinion of many men is in agreement, I shall go away, downcast and forlorn. And keep this in your inmost heart, that I shall no longer dwell with you.'[174]

Before Julian would present himself to the soldiers, he was convinced by the higher powers; divine consent preceded human consent and conditioned it. In the face of this divine consent, the individual on whom it rested stood isolated and alone. The shouts of the multitude, necessary though they were to make accession effective, could not in themselves convince.

What remains to be seen is how gradually divine consent and human action, or more precisely, divine consent and the ceremonial of accession, came to form a coherent whole, a whole which was anticipated by Eusebius and by Libanius in his account of Julian's election. For here, on the particular occasion of accession, divine inspiration came not so much to the emperor who was to be elected, as to the army who was to elect him.

What made Julian, the pagan emperor, different from his Christian predecessors and successors was that he was prepared to be the bearer of divine inspiration in his own person. Contrary to the doctrine of Themistius, Julian considered that the emperor's nature was not related specifically to the nature of the gods; yet, the emperor could be divinely inspired, although, for Julian and his Neoplatonist teachers, this was as true of any human being as of the emperor.[175] This is what becomes explicit from Julian's view of his accession. Hints of the two-edged aspect of Julian's position *vis-à-vis* the divine as he saw it—limited and human on the one hand, capable of inspiration and extension on the other— appeared also in the oracle given to Julian about his ascent to the heavenly halls of his divine parent, and in Julian's ceremonial arrivals.

5. THE HOUSE OF VALENTINIAN

i. Themistius, Symmachus and Ammianus: Dynastic Rule and the Emergence of a Military Ceremonial of Accession

The house of Constantine came to an end with Julian. It might be thought that this could have produced, in the panegyrics, a clear and exclusive emphasis on the principle of election, the election of the best man. But this was not the case; indirectly, perhaps, the dynastic policy of Constantine was still at work.

This is made plain in Themistius' consular panegyric on Jovian which, although it is an exhortation for religious tolerance, also treats

Jovian's accession.[176] Jovian had been elected by the army, which, as we have seen, had become one of the acceptable procedures for choosing an emperor. The circumstances of the election, however, were far from ideal, since Julian had been killed in mid-campaign, beyond the imperial frontiers. Moreover, the election of Jovian, a Christian emperor, was bound to call in question many of Julian's policies. Themistius therefore kept his options open by touching on many nuances and shades of meaning which had been employed earlier to justify and explain a difficult accession. The complexity of what he had to say was heightened still further by his definition of the nature of rulers at the beginning of the speech, a definition which, he says, was the special gift of philosophy to kingship:

> But do you desire to know the contribution of philosophy? She says that the king is the living law, a divine law which has come down into time from above, from the eternally good. The king is an outflowing of the nature of the eternally good, he is providence, abiding near the earth. He always looks to God, in short he is born of and nourished by God, as is also said by Homer. The king shares with God the other epithets also, for he is called he who welcomes strangers, he who receives supplications and guards friendship, he who makes fruits grow and brings the winds, administers justice, and is the steward of well-being, and giver of blessedness. Such offerings are brought to kings by those philosophers who tell no lies.[177]

If kings were διογενής and διοτρεφής,[178] if they were νόμος ἔμψυχος, no further justifications of their rule should have been necessary, but in practical terms, this did not follow. Being divinely inspired, like being born of God, nourished by God and being the living law, could only be proved in the outcome; and in that outcome, election,[179] descent,[180] virtue[181]—whichever might be most prominent—played an important role, which, however, depended ultimately on the emperor's ability to keep himself on the throne. It was this practicality and openness of Roman propagandists which contributed to preventing in the Roman Empire the rise of one family, actual or fictitious, which alone bore the charisma of kingship.

This practicality is evident in Themistius' speech on Valentinian and Valens, addressed to the latter in 364. Like the speech to Jovian, it contains, on the topic of the accession, a combination of exalted philosophical theory and of common sense.

By comparing the brotherly sharing of the empire between Valentinian I and Valens and their joint rule to the discords of earlier periods, Themistius arrives at the conclusion that theirs was the kingdom which was the model of all kingdoms,[182] and the proof that Valentinian I was

elected from above lay in the fact that his mind was turned towards God
and that he ruled justly. Thus there is always in Themistius an outward
and visible sign of divine kingship; there are criteria whereby it can be
distinguished, and judged. In this sense, imperial rule never became
absolute, as may also be seen from the very great liberties Themistius
took in advising emperors, even when his advice was in open conflict
with declared policy. Nonetheless, Themistius did have a most exalted
view of the position of the emperor, and one of the passages where this
was expressed most clearly is his exposition of the election of Valentinian I, which was strangely anticipatory of the mediaeval maxim *vox populi vox Dei*.[183]

> You must not think, noble Emperors, that the soldiers are the masters
> of such an election, but the very vote descends from above, and the
> acclamation is performed from above—for this, as Homer says, is the
> counsel of Zeus—by means of the ministration of men. Therefore it is
> your task to show that the soldiers were the ministers of God. Thus, if
> you trust your might alone, it will appear as though you acquired
> power by force of arms. But if you trust in excelling by virtue, you will
> appear as though having descended from heaven. For, the sign of your
> election from heaven is not a golden eagle, nor documents of honour,
> nor any other outward sign, but a mind directed towards heaven and
> striving to imitate heaven. . . . Whether, then, dignity is bestowed by
> the acclamation of the multitude or by God, the two have been con-
> joined in you.[184]

Here, then, the army, inspired by God, elected Valentinian and Valens.
At the same time, however, other options for expounding an imperial
accession remained open. In his address to Valentinian II, Themistius
not only referred to the merits of this emperor's father,[185] but also explored other aspects of the dynastic idiom by drawing on every *topos* of
the purple-born infant, nurtured by Zeus and the Muses, and born to
honours which others could only achieve by sweat and labour.[186] Moreover, Themistius here produced, albeit couched in his theoretical framework, a panegyric narrative of the ceremony of accession, such as had
been found earlier only in Eusebius. In doing so, he showed a clear
grasp of the importance of a particular historical moment as expressed
in ceremonial.

A similar phenomenon may be observed in the West in the panegyrics of Symmachus on Valentinian and Gratian. Symmachus, in 369,
in accord with the cautious tone of his first panegyric on Valentinian I,
drew upon all the relevant *topoi* to justify the accession. He begins with
Valentinian's home country, upbringing and descent, all of which, he
says, pointed to his future dignity.[187] He then goes on to narrate the elec-

tion in the historical manner, emphasising the order and leisure of the proceedings. This is an interesting counterpart to Themistius' account of the election of Jovian, where the opposite circumstances had been used to explain and justify the election. Symmachus also praised Valentinian's reluctance to accept his nomination; this was a *topos* of panegyric, which served to describe the good emperor who would not seize power for his own advantage. Next, Valentinian's choice of his brother as co-emperor is praised.[188] The ground for this had been prepared in the preceding narrative, where Symmachus praised Valentinian's descent. Like Themistius, Symmachus extolled the brotherly love and harmony existing between the two emperors, and their selfless care for the state. Side by side with this relatively sober narrative, however, Symmachus also produced a short description of the emergence of the empire of Valentinian, which might be paralleled by a baroque sunburst, or, more appropriately for late antiquity, the coin slogan of *oriens* or *oriens Augustus*,[189] which, however, was no longer in use in Valentinian's time.

> I am urged forward, venerable Augustus, so that after your private origins you should be brought forth in my speech clothed in purple, like some light of the stars. I feel the impact of divine light, as happens when a beam of light shines forth and the splendour of the world is opened up, or when the purple dawn leads out her red at sunrise. When at last you were asked for, you rose like a new star, which the ocean brings forth, washed in its sacred waves, as a renewed homage to the break of day. Let the candidate for empire come forward, distinguished by his armour which even earlier served the public interest, for he who alone met with the approval of all has always been of outstanding worth. Let the helmet be exchanged for a diadem, the lance for a sceptre. You have earned the reward of gold with the labour of the sword. But this is the only reward which your electors could achieve for you, for, as regards your conduct of life, your high fortune brought you only this, an increase in cares.[190]

This passage is a good indicator of the linguistic and artistic profusion of imagery and terminology of the later fourth century. The *oriens Augustus, sidus novus* was now out of date, while the image of the bejewelled and stiffly majestic emperor, which the passage also evokes, had not yet found a fully validated official expression.[191]

Gratian, like the sons of Constantine, could have succeeded on the dynastic principle which operated once a family had been established on the throne; not so, however, according to Symmachus. Of all the scenes painted by panegyrists, that which Symmachus painted of the election of Gratian is among those which can be visualised most clearly:

If some Zeuxis with wax of different colours were now to paint for me
these *comitia* to be looked at, if some follower of Apelles were to ani-
mate that celestial verdict with the inspiration of art which gives substance to things, posterity would behold miracles which can hardly be
believed. On one side is the Augustus, on the other the legions and in
the midst of these is the young candidate of empire. There was a pro-
longed and twofold contest on both sides as everyone eagerly acclaimed the father who only slowly gave in. The squadrons beseeching
the emperor, the divisions canvassing support—this is a scene worthy
of the ages, an image worthy of times to come, when emperors deserve
to be elected, rather than seeking to be elected.[192]

Yet, no work of art survives from the fourth century that could in
any sense provide an illustration. The closest approximation is the silver multiple of Constantine, which has been discussed above, and
which shows the emperor on a platform surrounded by soldiers, being
crowned by Victoria (plate 51). The vision of the young emperor-to-be
and of his father standing on a podium before the legions is so close to
many *adlocutio* scenes on Roman triumphal monuments, and on the
coinage of the second century, that one must wonder whether Symmachus' image originated there. That Roman monuments were actually
studied and admired in late antiquity may be gathered from Ammianus'
account of the visit of Constantius II to Rome, and more specifically
from a passage in Themistius, where the rain miracle of Marcus Aurelius as depicted on his column is commented upon.[193]

While pictorially describing the election of Gratian in this way, Symmachus did not, however, overlook the dynastic aspect. As Themistius
did for Valentinian II, so Symmachus did for Gratian: blessed was Gratian for being born a *candidatus* for empire, and for being a consul in his
early youth (cf. plate 49). At the same time, Symmachus brought up the
theme of the golden age, as rendered in Vergil's Fourth Eclogue, with
the associated ideas of the child born to bring happiness to the world.
Like Themistius, Symmachus thus joined a narrative of the accession to
more general ideas that accompanied this event.

The accession narratives of Themistius and Symmachus should be associated with those of Ammianus, for it will then become evident that
what Themistius and Symmachus—despite the entirely different traditions in which the two authors wrote—do have in common rests on a
ceremonial of accession, which was being created in and by the army.
Both Symmachus and Themistius stressed the role of the army in imperial elections and in so doing, they pointed to an historical development
of their own time.

The ceremonial whereby Julian was made Caesar was already precise and deliberate. This emerges more emphatically when Julian's nomination as Caesar is compared to Gratian's accession, which was also presided over by a senior emperor. Gratian's election was proposed to the army at Vienne in an oration delivered by Valentinian while he held Gratian's right hand, just as Constantius, while addressing the soldiers, had held the right hand of Julian. We see here at work that *concordia imperatorum* which is portrayed in the Venice Tetrarchs (see plate 3), and, in a different idiom, on the coinage, where the emperors are shown enthroned side by side (see plates 44, 48). The consensus of the army and the investment of Gratian with the imperial insignia follow:

> [Valentinian] had not yet finished his oration when his words were greeted with a happy consent . . . and the soldiers, as participants in prosperity and rejoicing, acclaimed Gratian as Augustus. . . . Seeing this, Valentinian, glad and more confident, adorned his son with the crown and the robes of the highest dignity and kissed him.[194]

Then Valentinian addressed an exhortatory speech to his son, just as Constantius had done with Julian. This procedure may be supplemented with the more concise account of the election of Valens by Valentinian.[195] In the Hebdomon, where later the emperors of early Byzantium were elected, Valentinian, "with the assent of all—for nobody dared to oppose—pronounced [Valens] Augustus, adorned him with the robe of empire, placed a diadem on his head, and brought him back in his own carriage." Julian had also returned to the palace in the same carriage as Constantius.[196]

Such was the ceremonial of electing a co-emperor.[197] When the throne was vacant, the consensus on which the enactment of the ceremonial was based could not be initiated by a senior Augustus, and therefore had to come about by other means. This is the point where divine inspiration became a crucial factor. In the case of Jovian, Themistius, as has been seen, all but bypassed this difficult question, and in so doing agreed with Ammianus. This is a good indication that much of the rhetoric of panegyric was rooted in concrete fact. However, Ammianus as a historian, writing long after the event, was able to face the difficulty of Jovian's accession more forthrightly. There was no divine election and no divine inspiration of the soldiers:

> But if any serious searcher after justice should rashly object that [the election] was made at a moment of desperation, such a person would more rightly blame the sailors who, having lost an experienced pilot, amidst the roaring of the storm and sea, have committed the guidance of the ship to some companion in danger. These matters [were] transacted by some blind decree of fortune.[198]

Such could be, if it had to be, the election of a legitimate emperor: a disorderly ceremonial, and no divine inspiration. The soldiers, Ammianus one of them, were pragmatists, with Themistius not far behind. But it is important to realise that a line could be drawn between an accession such as Jovian's—justified as it was by the outcome—and a usurpation, such as that of Procopius, where Ammianus described the attempt that was made at observing the military ceremonial of accession as a perversion and parody, so that the failure in ceremonial correctness as described by Ammianus led directly to his account of the outcome of this usurpation.[199] The ceremonial, accordingly, had become the means of validating an imperial accession.

A rightly performed election, slow, carefully deliberated and divinely inspired, was that of Valentinian. Again, Ammianus and Themistius are fundamentally in accord here:

> Valentinian, being suited to the requirements . . . was elected with the inspiration of the power of heaven, and with not one dissenting voice.[200]

He subsequently appeared on a tribunal before the army, was acclaimed as emperor, clothed in purple and diadem, and addressed the soldiers, after which he was conducted to the palace.[201] This particular ceremonial was initiated by the divine inspiration which preceded it, as it preceded the election of Julian as Augustus. But whereas we have seen Julian himself as the recipient of the inspiration, both according to Ammianus, and more clearly in his own account of the event, in the case of Valentinian, the inspiration rested on the electors, the group, rather than the individual. The ceremonial had become a publicly enacted expression of inspiration: *vox populi vox Dei*.

ii. Imagery of Majesty

The visual evidence for the ideas discussed above comes largely from the coinage. An attempt has been made above to highlight a certain development in ideas relating to accession: the emergence of an awareness of the historical moment of accession and, running concurrently with this, the emergence of a ceremonial framework in which the imperial insignia, especially the diadem and the purple, became more important. The evidence of the coinage, however, gives only very partial support to these ideas and provides yet another warning of the state of flux of imperial ideology after Constantine. The Constantinian thirty-solidi multiple showing Constantine crowned by the hand of God (plate 45) is a perfect illustration of Themistius' ideas of the emperor διογενής and διοτρεφής and of Ammianus' account of Valentinian's election, yet no repeat of it is known.

On the other hand, Jovian, Valentinian I and Valens were shown, like their predecessors, standing under the archway of the palace (cf. plate 53), and the imagery of majesty, of the emperor enthroned frontally, was further developed under Valentinian I and his successors.

A gold multiple issued at Rome for Valens at the outset of his reign shows a beautiful and refined version of the enthronement picture, now with the legend GLORIA ROMANORUM. The image, with different legends, had been used with some regularity in the later years of Constantine, showing Constantine enthroned between his standing sons.[202] The multiple of Valens shows on the obverse his draped and cuirassed bust with a pearl diadem, and a large jewel set over the forehead, DN VALENS PF AUG. On the reverse the two Augusti, nimbate, are seated in ceremonial dress on a double throne with footstools, each holding a globe and raising his right hand. The composition is severely symmetrical and the Augusti are shown as absolute equals, as portrayed by Themistius and Symmachus (cf. plates 48–49). Another version of this image from Trier[203] shows the two Augusti enthroned frontally, one on a slightly lower throne than the other. They hold the globe jointly, and are crowned by a Victoria flying above, holding a wreath in each hand. The legend is VICTORES AUGUSTI so that one may conclude that the emperors were crowned for victory.

This image, in a slightly adapted form, appeared frequently on the coinage of the later fourth and fifth centuries. The adaptation made the image symmetrical: Victoria flying from right to left, crowning the two emperors, is shown instead spreading her wings over two enthroned emperors who hold a globe between them.[204] Such issues appeared for Valentinian I, Valens, Gratian, Valentinian II, Theodosius (plate 50) and Arcadius. The legend is invariably VICTORIA AUGG and both legend and image ignore the third colleague where he existed.

On one exceptional set of coins of 378–383, GLORIA REIPUB or VICTORIA AUGG[205] Victoria hovering stationary above the throne crowns both emperors. On one of the latter types, issued at the mint of Thessalonica, perhaps while Valentinian II was there in 387,[206] the legend admits the existence of the third colleague Valentinian II, who, although senior to Theodosius, played a subordinate role.

Like the other images we have discussed, that of two emperors enthroned beneath the outspread wings of Victoria cannot be directly linked with any accession; it simply shows the emperors in majesty. However, some further light can be shed on the question. Just as Carausius, in his EXPECTATE VENI coinage, summarised a particular mood of his period more poignantly than the legitimate emperors did in most of their issues, so the usurper Maximus issued for his son Victor a set of coins with the image here under discussion: two emperors are enthroned under the wings of Victoria, and the legend reads BONO REIPUBLICAE NATI.[207]

The panegyric of 307 had already raised the idea that the empire was a sacred office which could not be relinquished once it had been assumed. Themistius, and, less emphatically, Symmachus, praised the purple-born child. It is here that Victor's coins fit in. His father claimed for him the divine right—if one may thus express a concept which, as is here being shown, the Romans consistently refrained from putting into words in any clear-cut manner—of the child born in the purple, whose birth was in a sense an accession. This latter idea was to recur in Claudian.[208]

Moreover, as these coins proclaim, the child was born for the good of the state. There is again the hint of the birth of that child, referred to by Symmachus in his panegyric on Gratian, whom Vergil greeted in the Fourth Eclogue. The coins, however, are at the same time strictly practical. The obverses are indeed devoted to Victor, but the reverses show two emperors enthroned: father and son, and it was the father who ruled.

Both Themistius and Symmachus, but particularly the former, placed considerable emphasis on the emperor's being elected by the army, and Themistius elaborated the concept that the vote of the army expressed the will of God. This aspect of the imperial dignity is not illustrated on the coinage of the later fourth century. There are merely the customary issues of VIRTUS EXERCITUS, now becoming less prominent than they had been earlier in the century. The *largitio* bowl commonly attributed to Valentinian I,[209] however, does capture something of the aura spread by Themistius (plate 52). The emperor is armed, standing on a low podium, holding in his left hand a standard, and in his outstretched right a large globe on which is poised a graceful Victoria, who in her right hand holds out a wreath with which to crown the emperor.

This part of the image is a very gracious rendering of a common theme which has already been encountered. The emperor's head is encircled by a nimbus in which is set the monogramme of Christ. Behind the emperor stand, in wedge formation, six soldiers, three on either side, holding shields. In practical terms they might be described as bodyguards, but in the present context this is hardly an appropriate description. The emperor, displaying himself to his subjects' gaze in that graceful yet firm stance, at the ceremonious moment of being crowned by Victoria, with his head encircled by the nimbus, is not in need of bodyguards.[210] The soldiers are the representatives of the army which elected him, the army by whose vote he is now nimbate and crowned by Victoria. They stand behind him, their leader, and support him.

It was again a continuity being shown in visual art, not the moment of election; the election was assumed. Beneath the podium are to be seen a shield, a baton and a helmet, tokens of the conquered enemy. In this way the ceremonious display of the emperor's majesty when surrounded by his army was also a display of the triumph, the victory, which was required to sustain imperial dominion. The victory was general, non-specific, and the serenity of the composition not disturbed by anything so crude as the presence of a fallen enemy in person. The bowl is inscribed LARGITAS DN VALENTINIANI AUGUSTI. Although it is badly worn, the style of the work can still be gathered from the graceful outlines and the carefully balanced composition of the figures within the round. The bowl is related to the sensitive and refined works of the Theodosian renaissance, and is in some respects a military counterpart to the civilian composition on the missorium of Theodosius.

6. THEODOSIUS AND HONORIUS

i. A New Dynasty

The circumstances under which Gratian elected Theodosius as his co-emperor and the obscure circumstances under which Theodosius the elder died, make panegyric accounts of the accession of the emperor Theodosius more ambivalent than others. The note which predominates is neatly summarised by Claudian: *digna legi virtus*.[211] Pacatus, ten years after the event, did engage in praise of Theodosius the elder,[212] but even then with a certain caution and anonymity, in that what he said of Theodosius the elder might have applied to any distinguished general. The praises of Constantius I in the panegyrics of 307 and 310 are much more personal and intimate. Pacatus sums up his eulogy of Theodosius the elder with a phrase which tells all: *patrem imperator tuum de te aestimemus*.[213]

These somewhat unusual circumstances made it possible for the theory of accession arguing from personal merit to emerge with uncommon force in the case of Theodosius. The earliest panegyric treating the topic is the *Presbeutikos* addressed by Themistius to Theodosius in Macedonia

in 379, shortly after the latter's accession. Both this speech and the one
of three years later emphasise the rightness of Gratian's choice on the
ground that Theodosius was the most deserving candidate:

> You attained the purple not thanks to kinship ties, but thanks to excel-
> lence in virtue; not thanks to an imminent emergency, but thanks to
> showing forth strength and virtue. And Gratian acted wisely, and in a
> manner befitting old age rather than youth, in that he chose not his
> closest kinsman as the man who is best, but rather, he chose the best
> man as being his closest kin. And he cast the vote in a manner worthy
> of himself, that vote which, in anticipation, had already been cast by
> the present situation.[214]

The atmosphere of emergency after the defeat of Adrianople is conveyed very distinctly in Themistius' speech of 379, and he emphasises
the hopes of renewal and victory which centred on Theodosius.[215]
Themistius was very specific about the details of Theodosius' accession
in attributing the initiative to Gratian, an initiative which on behalf of
Constantinople he confirmed and accepted.[216] It is interesting to note
how he attempted to bring Constantinople into the scene of the election, in which that city clearly played no part. There was a practical reason for this: Themistius wished Theodosius to bestow privileges on the
Senate of Constantinople, as the remainder of the speech of 379 disclosed. At the same time, Constantinople here played a role parallel to
that played by Roma in the return to power of Maximian: the emperor
ruled at the behest of the capital,[217] and during the fourth century, Constantinople emerged as a metropolis in its own right, with a culture and
atmosphere peculiar to itself, of which Themistius was one of the most
prominent spokesmen.

Three years after the accession of Theodosius, when the shock of the
battle of Adrianople had somewhat receded into the background, Themistius, although still emphasising that Theodosius had been elected by
Gratian for his ability and success in war,[218] returned to his own favour-
ite theme of imperial *philanthropia*, of the emperor akin to God, of kingship descended from heaven, and, thereafter,[219] the emperor as the living law. For Theodosius, Themistius approached the theme of the
relationship between God and emperor from two angles. In 381 he
spoke of it in terms of an approximation to God on the part of the emperor who performed godlike acts and possessed godlike virtues. This
was a ὁμοίωσις πρὸς τὸν θεόν on the part of a human being:[220]

> Gratian greeted you with the wreath of kingship as a leader and gen-
> eral of the Empire. But mark well, exalted Emperor, that neither beauty

nor stature, neither speed nor prowess make a good ruler, if he does not bear in his soul some form of being like God. Therefore let us enquire ourselves and call upon the poet [Homer] to teach us how a being walking on the earth and clothed in flesh can be thought to have the form of him who is enthroned above the highest vault of heaven and above everything that exists. Let us listen to him, for he does not call on us to listen long as to how he thinks a godlike ruler may be recognised:

> Like the fame of some noble godlike king
> Who holds up justice, and the black earth
> Brings forth both wheat and barley, the trees are laden with fruit,
> The beasts have their young and the sea brings forth fish,
> All rewards of good rule, and the people live well in his care.[221]

Justice and good rule are the works of this art [of government] and thence come the names divine and godlike. And it seems that the divine Plato has learnt this very thing from Homer. For he says that justice with prudence are an approximation to God.[222]

The ruler who rules with εὐδικία will be sufficient unto himself,[223] and is in no need of body guards, so that one may truly ask, as the Pythia did about Lycurgus, "whether you are god or man."[224]

In his nineteenth oration, Themistius begins with a full quotation of this oracle to Lycurgus:

> You have come, Lycurgus, to my glorious shrine
> A friend of Zeus and all who live on Olympus.
> I am in doubt whether to call you a god or a man,
> But yet I think to call you a god, O Lycurgus.[225]

Here, Themistius views the question of God-inspired rule from the opposite angle—the ὁμοίωσις πρὸς τὸν θεόν is possible for the ruler because he comes from God:

> Will you doubt and enquire whether a god or a man has entered into the temple, and will not this seem more bold than to ask how much sand there is on the earth? To query the fact that to this emperor rightly belongs the proclamation from above? . . . For he himself is the living law which does not exist in unchangeable and rigid letters. For this reason, it appears, God sent kingship from heaven down to earth, that man might have a refuge from the unmovable law to the law that is inspired and lives.[226]

The exercise of justice was one of the several object lessons which Themistius used to explain the divinely inspired nature of imperial rule and divine election. In the present instance, where Themistius argued that imperial justice was a means of setting free, and giving life to those who had been condemned by the law,[227] he was able to incorporate into

his own pagan-based theory of the empire the Christian empire of the
fourth century:

> The emperor rightly believes in the Assyrian saying, according to
> which the heart of the king is guarded in the hand of God,[228] and it is
> impossible that the hand of God should contain letters of death.
> Rather, it must needs be that he who writes such letters quickly slips
> from the hand which always bestows life. The state has attributed to
> you, Oh Emperor, the name of divinity by inspiration from above . . .
> because to give life is in the power of God and the emperor alone.[229]

Themistius discussed the accession of Theodosius in terms of the circumstances in which it occurred, pragmatically, but this in no way
restricted his ability to unfold, in the context of these particular circumstances, his own wider theme of divinely inspired election and
dominion.

Themistius' specific and generally accurate details regarding Theodosius' election were diluted somewhat in the panegyric which Pacatus delivered in 389. This speech, like the panegyric of 307, is another
instance of a panegyric which sets down a large part of the theoretical
paraphernalia of accession. But, as in the earlier example, this must not
be taken straightforwardly as a variety of a mirror of princes, but as an
expedient to cover a certain situation. Themistius, an experienced exponent of imperial policies, had the independence to state matters in his
own particular idiom; Pacatus, probably newly arrived in Rome from
Bordeaux, did not.

> Let a good augury for this my oration come from the day which initi-
> ated our general felicity, the day which was the first of your empire. For
> just as, when we are engaged in a religious observance, we turn to that
> part of the sky from whence light comes, so I, now that I am about to
> perform the vow of speaking to you, which I made in the past, shall
> look in my oration towards the time when the Roman light arose.[230]

He then refers to the precarious state of the empire at Theodosius'
accession:

> Let us suppose that the whole question is in the balance and let us, in
> an electoral assembly of the whole earth, as it were, ask who should be
> the man who is to support such a great weight and to sustain the
> changeable destiny of Rome. Would not the vote of all, tribe by tribe,
> and centuria by centuria, elect him who has a blessed homeland, and is
> of distinguished family, whose aspect is god-like, whose youth is unim-
> paired, and who has experience of civil and military affairs?[231]

In the sequel he goes through the topics raised in this passage in order
to point out with each that Theodosius was the proper candidate.[232]

That is the theoretical angle, familiar under a different guise from the panegyric of 307. Pacatus then turns to the practicalities, Gratian's act of election, but Gratian, being now dead, is only mentioned anonymously as the *princeps*.

> The proof [of Theodosius' disinterestedness in becoming emperor] may be gained from that day which initiated the common welfare, when you, being called upon to take the commonwealth into your care, refused the empire which was offered to you. And you did not do this for the sake of mere appearance, so that you would seem to be constrained to becoming emperor, but you held out tenaciously and long, like one who intends to gain his point. Indeed, there was no cause for making a pretence of your unwillingness. The emperor did not approach you alone and in private and, as it were, to test you; rather he did it in public, in an electoral assembly, leaving himself no other choice, so that you could have accepted the empire even if your refusal had not been genuine.[233]

Theodosius refused to take up the charge—a further token of the legitimate emperor, who, unlike the tyrant, does not seize power but has it bestowed on him by some form of consent. Pacatus, like other panegyrists, including the one of 307, emphasises consent so that there is not merely, as in Themistius, the metropolis confirming the election, but the entire *respublica* in personification is conjured up to plead with Theodosius.[234] Thus,[235] Theodosius, according to Pacatus, was the only emperor among all his predecessors who did not corrupt the legions, succeed by inheritance, or come to the throne by force of necessity when there was no ruling emperor.

Just how relative to the specific situation all this was, however, is demonstrated by Pacatus himself, as well as by Claudian, when they refer to the sons of Theodosius as his heirs.[236] To this is to be added the fact that Claudian and other authors of the period claimed for the Spanish emperor Theodosius descent from Trajan,[237] so that ultimately, like Constantine, Theodosius could claim the throne on several scores, of which each could in a sense stand independently.[238]

Yet a further note is struck in Claudian's poem on the sixth consulship of Honorius, which has been discussed in the context of *adventus*. Here, Roma appears not so much to give her assent to Honorius' accession, as to plead for his presence in Rome[239] during his triumphal celebrations over Alaric. Claudian then describes Honorius' *adventus* in Rome, with the goddess herself, radiant, coming from her temple[240] to welcome the emperor. This passage contains on the one hand the terminology of the victorious *adventus*, and on the other it emphasises the personal link between Roma personified and the emperor. This personal link between the emperor and his capital was no mere cliché in late antiquity. In Claudian the enthusiasm not only of the population of Rome over Honorius' arrival is described but also the enthusiasm of Roma herself, and one might indeed substitute the personification of the city for its inhabitants.

The cities Roma and Constantinopolis, seen so frequently enthroned together or separately on the fourth-century coinage, conveyed a meaning in themselves as entities, in short as personifications. This is illustrated in a moving scene on the consular diptych depicting Constantius III before he became emperor (see plate 56). In the top section of the diptych Honorius and Theodosius II are enthroned between Roma and Constantinopolis, who are both nimbate; Constantinopolis, who sits next to Theodosius, places her hand on the shoulder of her young emperor in an affectionate and protective gesture.[241] This gesture conveys, more convincingly than the many representations of the two personified cities in late antique art[242] (e.g., plate 57), what could at this time be felt about Roma and Constantinopolis. It also conveys the mixture of personification, person and concept, as expressed for instance in Rutilius' prayer to Roma.[243] It was on this foundation that the idea of *Roma et Augustus* was revived in the fourth century, and was expressed so eloquently, yet elusively, by Claudian.

Whatever the precise mixture of claims to rule might be, the general setting of the praises of the emperor who had recently come to the throne, in Themistius, Claudian and other panegyrists, was the resulting felicity of the present and future. Thus, Themistius said in 382:

> Look, look, what great benefits Kalliope says will follow: the crops will prosper for the good king, and so will the trees and vines, many animals will be born, and many men, and everything will be full of movement and life. The earth will offer her fruits and the sea her fish. Behold, how great is the power of just rule, the rewards of which extend not only to palaces and law courts, but to living beings and plants, and even to seeds and children yet in the womb.[244]

At such a time, Justice returns to the earth, where she had lived in the golden age.[245] Claudian also mentions Justice returned to her rightful place when Theodosius had ousted the tyrants:

> Those triumphs established justice and taught us that the gods are present.[246]

He describes the birth of Honorius in almost apocalyptic imagery[247] as noted by Chaldean seers and the Sibyl of Cumae. On the day when Honorius was raised on the shield, nature itself noted the magnitude of the event:

Black winter had covered the light in darkness and the south wind gathered heavy rain. But soon, when the soldiers raised you with their accustomed shout, Phoebus scattered the clouds and the same moment bestowed the sceptre on you and light on the world. Free from clouds, the Bosphorus permits the sight of Chalcedon, lying opposite. But it was not only the area close at hand that shone with light; the clouds are driven back and all Thrace is revealed, Pangaeus is seen in the distance and lake Maeotis reflects those unaccustomed rays. The north wind did not put the mists to flight, nor did the sun shine brighter: this was the light of empire, a radiance of good omen covered all, and with your brightness nature smiled.[248]

Under Honorius' rule enemies submitted without warfare, and his consulships were a sure augury of victory.

Claudian's terminology is different from that of Themistius. The unusual brightness of the day of Honorius' accession is reminiscent of a similar phenomenon on the day of the accession of Constantius. The details of Claudian's present blessedness are more practical—or perhaps more imperial—than Themistius' details. Claudian visualises victory abroad, and order and liberty at home, whereas Themistius has a vision of a Saturnian golden age, the imagery of which also appears in Vergil's Fourth Eclogue.

As regards the ceremonial of accession, the group of panegyrics here considered confirms some details and reveals some new features. From Themistius' terminology it is quite clear that the act of coronation was now a part of the ceremonial of accession, and old imagery went hand in hand with what was new. The old imagery is predominant in the panegyric of 379, where Themistius speaks of two wreaths offered to Theodosius by his capital, one of gold and the other of *eunoia*. This old imagery is represented countless times on the coinage. In another beautiful and suggestive image, Themistius expounds how earth and sea acknowledge the imperial election of Theodosius, whose dominion thus extends not over the Roman empire only, but over the whole world. Such world-wide dominion had already been ascribed to Diocletian, crowned by Jupiter lord of the universe and enthroned over the sky.[249] (Plates 10, 44)

Themistius elaborated a further meaning in the act of coronation when he said that Gratian wreathed Theodosius and that his own dignity was not thereby lessened: "The emperor wreathes the other emperor; he is not diminished thereby, but, rather, gains an advantage."[250] The latter part of this statement has its exact parallel in the panegyric of 307, where it is said that Maximian could bestow the empire on Constantine, but could not thereby relinquish his own dignity. With respect to the crowning, Themistius was more specific in the panegyric of 382: "Gratian greeted the leader and general of the empire with the wreath of kingship."[251] This does imply that Theodosius was actually crowned, but Themistius does not mention the clothing in the purple, which must also have taken place, and became a regular part of the Byzantine ceremonial.[252]

Themistius visualised the accession of Theodosius in part as a coronation of the junior emperor by the senior and herein he isolated what was to become a regular feature of the later Byzantine ceremonial, met with also in Ammianus; not so in Claudian. The only distinct reference he made to Honorius' accession is the description of the brightness of the day when Honorius was raised on the shield. The beginning of Honorius' reign and the re-enactment of that beginning in his consulships is seen rather as a series of victorious arrivals. When Honorius travels to the West so that "[Theodosius] might hand over to you in your presence the world now at peace,"[253] Claudian does not describe any ceremony whereby the empire was handed over, but a victorious *adventus*.[254] Similarly, the fourth and sixth consulships are described as ceremonies of arrival.[255] These accounts of Claudian's are the last full descriptions of imperial *adventus* in the West. They are, as we have seen, the summary of a tradition, which is relevant to our present theme, because *adventus* could form an element in accession, as it had done in the case of Constantius I. Similarly, the panegyrist of 307 said of Constantine's *adventus* in Britain, shortly before his accession:

> You were called to save the commonwealth by the verdict of heaven even at that time . . . when your sudden arrival lit upon us and it seemed that you had come, not on the public post, but by some vehicle of the gods.[256]

Mamertinus, speaking about Julian, used the *adventus* terminology to bypass the question of the accession altogether. The reason for this procedure in 361 was obvious. But Claudian had no such reason. He used the *adventus* terminology for accession because it could still be a suitable vehicle to convey the idea, and in his account some concepts which had been important in the past but had since lapsed, like the image of the emperor as *sol oriens*, so prevalent on the third century coinage,[257] appeared once more. Claudian's procedure seems out of date when it is compared to the emerging accession ceremonial, which may be observed in other authors, in particular Ammianus; yet it sheds a revealing sidelight on some aspects of the Theodosian renaissance.

This renaissance, to judge by the bulk of the surviving evidence, both literary and visual, was in part a Western phenomenon.[258] A clear distinction between East and West can now also be made in panegyric. From the East, there comes through Eusebius and Themistius, as well as, in a different idiom, Libanius, a consistent body of thought about the divine election of the emperor, thought which could be adjusted to widely divergent circumstances, and which is supported in Ammianus.

In the Western panegyrics, on the other hand, apart from the Tetrarchic ones, this strand of thinking about imperial accessions is largely absent. The discourse between Theodosius and Honorius in Claudian's poem about the fourth consulship of Honorius[259] expresses this state of affairs in the traditional Latin and Roman idiom and in terms of *topoi* contrasting the freedom-loving Romans of the West with the servile Greeks of the East, who could prosper under a rigidly monarchical government. In more factual terms, Greek-speaking people appear to have been readier to articulate god-inspired imperial dominion.

It has been seen how the ideas of election for merit both in Greek and Latin were reiterated to explain the election of an emperor who had no previous connection with the ruling house of Valentinian. In numismatic iconography also, a minor break can be observed, in that the image of the two emperors enthroned frontally overshadowed by the outspread wings of Victoria, disappeared from the coinage,[260] with a few exceptions. A more usual image to replace this dynastic one came to be that of the personification of one or both capitals enthroned frontally. An example is a series of coins of Theodosius from Constantinople, CONCORDIA AUGGG, where Constantinopolis holds either a globe, or a shield inscribed VOT V MULT X.[261] Two gold multiples for Honorius, GLORIA ROMANORUM, show Roma enthroned,[262] an echo, though remote, of Claudian's elaborate imagery of the connection between Roma and her emperor.

As for the classical *adventus* imagery of the mounted emperor, which could be connected with accession, it survived after the fourth century only in a fragmentary fashion and not in the mainstream of imperial art, despite the prominence which this theme still enjoyed in Claudian. The ceremony of *adventus* was a ceremony of movement, and accordingly was generally shown in profile as the theme required, so that the participants could actually be seen moving. The three-quarter frontality of the mounted emperor both on the *largitio* bowl of Constantius II and the gold multiple of Justinian (plates 16, 23) shows the dissolution of this imagery of movement, in that the emperor here does not progress as he did on earlier *adventus* issues of the coinage and on monumental representations of the theme in the early fourth century.

The imagery of imperial dominion, like late antique art as a whole, tended increasingly towards the stationary and immobile image, an important aspect of which was the frontality which we have seen emerging both in renderings of *adventus* and in the imagery of enthronement. Thus, although the *adventus* coinage of the later fourth century could mark the time of accession, it was less appropriate to the artistic idiom of the time and the ideas which that idiom conveyed than the enthronement images of the emperor, Roma, and Constantinopolis.

The same timelessness is also apparent in many late antique imperial portraits. We noted the multifarious changes on Constantinian portraiture and the emergence of Constantine's late portrait on the coinage, diademed, with long hair and features which were often idealised. This portrait became standard for all emperors during the fourth century. Constantine's sons were simply shown as youthful counterparts to their father, with few personal features to differentiate them from the latter. For later emperors also personal features were subordinated to the imperial stereotype.

On the other hand, the two strands of portraiture distinguished above—the military, naturalistic and unflattering portrait in contrast to the idealised, beautiful one—can still be traced after Constantine. The Barletta statue (plate 7) is an example of the former type, and an attribution to Valentinian I is plausible, although, for similar reasons, Marcian, the emperor who has also been suggested, is another possibility.[263] During the Theodosian age, however, the non-military tradition in portraiture prevailed. A good example is the portrait head of the young Arcadius from Constantinople, showing a dreamy face with gentle, slightly uplifted eyes and soft outlines, the face surmounted by a heavy, stylised crown of hair, and by the wide heavy diadem (plate 5). The portraits of the missorium of Theodosius are of this same type.

ii. The Missorium of Theodosius

The missorium of Theodosius (plate 55), among the surviving works of imperial art of late antiquity, marks a significant moment in imperial art. On the one hand, it represents, for a last time, certain aspects of the imperial iconography of the past, and on the other, it points forward to the art of the Byzantine Empire and Byzantine artistic sensibilities. The emperor is to be seen, enthroned in his palace, between Valentinian II and Arcadius, on the occasion of his Decennalia, handing the *codicilli* of office to a dignitary. Below the palace, as if in the exergue of a coin, is to be seen the reclining figure of Tellus with the seasons, a symbol, as the coins of the past had proclaimed, of the felicity of the times and of earth established under the protection of imperial dominion.[264] In the silver sky has not yet appeared the figure of Christ the ruler of all, but rather two winged and wreath-bearing children are to be seen in the pediment of the palace.

Not only the iconography, but also the style of this accomplished and refined work of art evokes the Hellenism and the art of the mid-third century and of the Hadrianic age, where also are to be found some of the iconographic prototypes. The proportions of the work and the distribution of the different parts of the representation on that circular space recall the layout of many imperial coins, both those of the past and those contemporary with the missorium.

The missorium utilises a form long chiselled and perfected in respect to every detail of content and proportion. The perfectly drawn arch of the palace, the incline of the roof, the positioning of the segment which divides the representation of the emperors from that of Tellus, and the delicate interplay of symmetry and the interruption of symmetry in the image as a whole foreshadow the long-drawn out processes whereby Byzantine artists over the centuries were to vary the nuances of their iconographies, of those iconographies which provided the framework of much of the Christian art of the East, so as to arrive at a perfect reality in the image.

Although the spacing of the missorium, and the distribution of its figures, follow classical norms, there are some aspects which differentiate it from the art of the second century and even from contemporary ivory diptychs of the Symmachi and the Nicomachi. Although the representation is realistic, and the proportions of the human body are faithfully portrayed, the figures have an incorporeality which is late antique. They do not stand on firm ground, but are suspended weightlessly in space, their feet barely touching the ground. The image is three-dimensional: it can be seen clearly that the thrones of Valentinian and Arcadius are somewhat recessed behind that of Theodosius.

Yet in other respects the third dimension is ignored, as for instance in the positioning of the guardsman next to Arcadius, who is partly in front of and partly behind a column. Indeed, the content of the image, as will be seen, precludes an entirely realistic and naturalistic approach to the dimensions on the part of the artist for, what the image shows is a metaphor, an exposition of imperial majesty, which cannot be expressed in realistic terms only.

This exalted nature of the subject of the representation is further emphasised by the choice of material, the combination of silver and gold, the use of the "silver page," as Sidonius had it.[265] The "silver page" forecast the predilection of Byzantine artists for precious materials, for their refinement of execution and taste, and for the pointing out of hidden meanings which the use of such materials would encourage.[266] As Philo said, "Gold belongs to incorporeal and intelligible things, while silver belongs to the sense-perceptible heaven."[267]

The import of the image on the missorium of Theodosius may be gathered by considering its several iconographic ingredients, which in turn may be expounded from imperial panegyric. The missorium shows an ageless image, because it sets the individual moment—the handing over of the *codicilli*—into a permanent and enduring context, the context of the everlastingly recurring imperial *vota*—DN THEODOSIUS PERPET AUG OB DIEM FELICISSIMUM X, the inscription reads—and of worldwide and eternal imperial dominion.

The agelessness of the image is demonstrated initially by the portraiture of the three emperors. The face of Theodosius, the oldest of the three, shows no sign of age, and all three emperors are portrayed in the soft, idealised lines of that distant and impersonal beauty which also appears on some fourth-century numismatic portraits, portraits which descended from the later portraiture of Constantine. All three emperors are crowned with a heavy, carefully worked pearl diadem, and Theodosius himself is nimbate, the nimbus framed and emphasised by the semicircles of the arch under which he is enthroned.

We have seen that the *vota* coinage made some attempt at differentiating between emperors according to rank. On the missorium, Theodosius is obviously the chief emperor, although, in fact, Valentinian II, shown enthroned on Theodosius' right, on a lower throne and of smaller stature, was senior to Theodosius. Arcadius, Theodosius' elder son, is shown on his father's left, smaller still than Valentinian, for he was the most junior member of the imperial college. The missorium, then, does not observe a ceremonial correctness, but portrays a *de facto* state of affairs: Theodosius on his Decennalia in 388—the year before Pacatus delivered his panegyric—conferring office on a dignitary who is about to kneel to the right of his throne, attended by his two imperial colleagues.[268] Theodosius calmly hands down the *codicilli* to, one might almost say, his suppliant, while he himself looks directly out of the image at the beholder. The bestowal of the *codicilli* is incidental to the main scene, which shows the emperors enthroned in the palace, the palace of which, as is inferred in some panegyrics, they had become the rightful possessors at their various accessions.[269]

The missorium is one of the official works of the later fourth century—two further examples being the *largitio* bowl of Constantius II

and the obelisk base of Theodosius—which show long-haired barbarians attending the emperor. During this period, barbarians became in
some senses respectable; they were no longer merely the anonymous
enemy brutally conquered and annihilated,[270] but also a recognised and
important constituent in the army and therefore at court, able for a time
to exercise a certain influence on the imperial ceremonial of accession,
in that the ceremony of raising the emperor on the shield was a Germanic one.

The presence of the barbarian soldiers on the missorium may be paralleled by Themistius' address to Theodosius,[271] which argues that the
good emperor is not merely a lover of Romans but also of barbarians,
that, like Zeus, he is a lover of all men, *philanthropos*. The depiction of
the barbarians on the missorium represents an iconographic advance,
and also, in the realm of ideas, an advance on the design of *vota* coins
which show the emperors enthroned between crouching barbarians
(plate 48). On the missorium, the serenity of the imperial majesty, *se-
renitas nostra, tranquillitas nostra*, as is so often said in the Codes, may not
be disturbed and impaired by the affliction of a conquered enemy.[272]

On the other hand, the pediment of the palace displays a playful version of the iconography of victory, a version of the kind that was compatible with the golden age, which is being alluded to in the exergue of
the missorium. To the left and right of the arch under which Theodosius
sits enthroned fly two winged boys, each carrying a wreath of leaves
and flowers on veiled hands. The corresponding space on triumphal
arches is usually occupied by flying victories holding wreaths in their
outstretched hands, wreaths which on the coinage are to be deposited
on the emperor's head. That idea is somewhat remote on the missorium, but, on the other hand, the two winged little boys are reminiscent
of those winged boys carrying garlands on the *vota* coinage of the sons
of Constantine when Caesars.[273] On the missorium also they appear in
the context of the *vota ob diem felicissimum* X. Their location suggests the
iconography of victory on public monuments, and their appearance
suggests the felicity of the times.

The commonplace image to mark the *vota* at this time and earlier was
Victoria inscribing the *vota* on a shield, or simply, the *vota* inscribed in a
wreath. In 330, however, to mark the *vota* for the decennalia of Constantine II, the mint of Thessalonica issued gold multiples showing
Constantine on the obverse, and on the reverse VOTIS DECENN DN CON-
STANTI CAES, with two winged genii holding a garland.[274] This same design was used again in connection with the dedication of Constantinople and an imperial anniversary,[275] and simultaneously with the coin

types issued to propagate the Constantinian dynasty,[276] although the legend, GAUDIUM AUGUSTI NOSTRI, while announcing a time of joy, leaves the precise context vague. These genii were virtually a Constantinian numismatic innovation; they had previously appeared on the coinage only once, and did not do so again. The Constantinian pieces in themselves are rare, but this very rarity, the restriction of these coins to a set of identifiable occasions, makes it possible to associate in the image, as in corresponding panegyrics, the ideas of felicity and anniversaries. On the coinage the genii appear only in those two contexts, which are also the contexts of the missorium.

Although the genii design is almost unique to the coinage, similar imagery did appear on the porphyry sarcophagus of Constantina and in her mausoleum, a product of official art. Here the genii, or cherubs, are seen harvesting, in one of the attitudes, that is, of the seasons. The seasons as cherubs appeared frequently on second-century multiples and subsequently on the regular coinage as a sign of TEMPORUM FELICITAS,[277] and they were one of those many Constantinian rediscoveries of the second- and third-century idiom, which were made before Christianity became a firm feature in Constantinian policies. Solidi of 316 from Ticinum for Constantine FELICIA TEMPORA[278] show the four seasons as cherubs, exact replicas of those of the second century. The image was repeated in 319 at Aquileia for the consulship of Licinius II, this being the last time that the seasons appeared on the coinage.[279] Legend and image were both a revival, and the image had a decidedly pagan flavour; it did, however, carry a message which did not need to be restricted to paganism, nor was it, for, like the image of the winged genii, that of the seasons as cherubs was revived on the missorium, where cherubs are shown with Tellus in the exergue.

The felicity of the times, as has been seen, was conveyed in panegyric by various means. Panegyrists might emphasise the emperor's beneficial influence on the course of nature by describing the day of accession or arrival as unusually bright and serene (as did the panegyrist of 297 and Claudian); or he might refer, like the panegyrist of 312, to the emperor's bounty, which rivalled and supplemented the bounty bestowed by Terra *mater frugum* and Iuppiter *moderator aurarum*.[280] Or, like Claudian, the panegyrist could emphasise the peace and order of the present by expounding Roman external and internal politics. Finally, as in Symmachus and Themistius, present felicity could be described in the terminology of the *Saturnia regna*, when the crops grew freely and without toil, when animals had many young and the trees brought forth much fruit.[281] These, according to Themistius, were the results of just dominion.

Thus also do we see the dominion of Theodosius represented on the missorium. Beneath the palace reclines the figure of Tellus holding a cornucopiae, and surrounded by ears of corn. Like the seasons imagery on the Constantinian coinage, this motif goes back to a Hadrianic coin type, Tellus reclining, leaning on a basket of fruit, and holding a globe or vine branch, TELLUS STABIL.[282] A similar type, where Tellus holds a cornucopiae and is surrounded by the four seasons, was struck for Antoninus Pius.[283] On the missorium we have a version of this last image. There is Tellus with her cornucopiae and ears of corn, reclining, and surrounded by three seasons, not four. It is the golden age, and the winter season, usually shown clothed, has been omitted.[284] There remain the other three seasons, all nude, flying up to make their offerings to the emperor with veiled hands.

Tellus is the earth personified. She reclines under the palace, not only to convey the felicity of the times, but also to convey the idea of the emperor's dominion over the whole earth, acquired at his accession, as frequently stated in the panegyrics. Pre-Christian imperial art had an image to convey the idea of universal dominion and at the same time of divinisation and *consecratio*: this was the emperor enthroned on the globe or the vault of the sky. In the fourth century this iconography was transferred to Christ and therefore could no longer be used for the emperor (plates 10, 41, 25, 42). But on the missorium, the reclining figure of Tellus acts as a substitute for the older image of universal dominion. Reclining river gods and personifications figured largely in earlier imperial art[285] to define a locality and set a scene, but the use of Tellus to convey the idea of lordship was a fourth-century invention.

In earlier numismatic design, Tellus is found alone to convey the concept of the felicity of the times; but by setting her below the representation of the emperors on the missorium of Theodosius, in the position occupied by conquered barbarians on other imperial works of art (such as the Grand Camée de France, and numerous representations of the fourth century), Tellus *mater frugum* not only conveyed the idea of the felicity of the times, but also that of imperial dominion. Both ideas are still present on the Barberini diptych (plate 22), where Tellus half-sitting, half-reclining, with some fruits in her lap, supports the foot of the mounted emperor.[286]

Tellus betokens both imperial dominion and the felicity of the times. The image of the emperors enthroned over Tellus unites the vision of

the golden age as expressed by Themistius—a time when nature flour-
ishes and blooms—and as expressed by Claudian—a time when the
emperor enjoys the fruits of victory, that is, universal dominion.

The emperors on the missorium wear the chlamys, not armour. The
image is a civilian one of peace and prosperity, a counterpart, as has
been said, of the military image on the *largitio* bowl of Valentinian I.
Both images observe a certain symmetry which is broken by the representations in the exergue: Tellus in one, and captured armour in the
other. Herein the two silver plates correspond with much of the numismatic iconography of the fourth century. The symmetry has been noted
particularly in the enthronement images of the coinage, but is evident
also in fourth-century and later imperial art treating topics other than
accession.

The emergence of symmetry in imperial art meant that representations of movement, of *adventus*, for instance, generally had to disappear
or be radically altered. Symmetrical art treated less a historical than a
ceremonial moment. This is one of the reasons why in late antiquity,
panegyric and artistic accounts of accession diverged, or rather, as we
see now, appeared to diverge. Both treated a ceremonial moment, but in
different terms. In panegyric the treatment of accession developed, as
will be seen more clearly in the sequel, into the description of a ceremony, while in art the culmination and result of that ceremony was
represented. The result of accession was the lasting majesty of the emperor, a perpetuity, and this was expressed visually in the imagery of
enthronement.

The missorium of Theodosius is the most perfect expression of the
concept of enthronement in the fourth century, the concept in which the
historical, and at the same time symbolic, moment as the panegyrists
grasped it, the moment when the emperor acquired tenure of the palace
in which he was now enthroned, was transformed into a universal,
timeless and ageless image. The missorium sums up what has survived
of the pagan imperial imagery of the past into the later fourth century,
while not infringing on the Christian preoccupations of the reign of
Theodosius. At the same time, there is nothing superficially Christian
in the missorium. In that sense it looks to the past; but it is also a foretaste of Byzantine aesthetics. It represents a moment of poise and balance, before the traditions which it united into one image diverged into
the separate streams of Byzantine minor arts and secular poetry on the
one hand, and Byzantine imperial art and propaganda in Christian
terms on the other.

A foretaste of the literary characteristics of this Byzantine propaganda appears, as we have seen, in Eusebius. In art, the diptych of Probus points the way to future representations of *maiestas*, and also demonstrates how greatly impoverished imperial art became when pagan and traditional imagery were discarded.

This diptych,[287] made for the consulship of Anicius Petronius Probus in 406 (plate 6), shows on both its wings the emperor Honorius armed, diademed, and nimbate, standing under an archway. Over the nimbus is the inscription DN HONORIO SEMP AUG. Iconographic parallels of the archway are to be found on the dynastic coinages discussed above (e.g., plate 53), and also on the missorium of Theodosius. The diptych, like the coinage, as here interpreted, shows the entrance to the palace in an abbreviated fashion.

On the front plate, Honorius holds a standard, which is surmounted by a small Chi Rho, and which is inscribed IN NOMINE XPI VINCAS SEMPER, in his right hand, and in his left he has a globe surmounted by Victoria, who extends a wreath to him. On the right wing of the diptych Honorius holds a shield in his right hand and a long sceptre in his left, so that the two wings in relation to each other are symmetrical (standard and sceptre are on the outer edges of their respective wings). The image of either wing taken in itself also has a certain symmetry and overall balance, which is, however, not so rigid as to make the presentation dull and arid. The emperor is depicted as being victorious, and, because of his victoriousness, is in majesty, but he has neither the pagan nor the Christian attributes and settings which could make that majesty rich and colourful. Artistically refined, the image has little content.

The imagery of Claudian, which in a more moderate version appears also on Theodosius' missorium, had been discarded, and little had as yet taken its place. Four years before the sack of Rome, as is to be seen from this diptych, there was little to be communicated about the emperor, withdrawn as he was behind the safety of the marshes and walls of Ravenna.

On the other hand, however, this moment of hiatus, when the shackles of past imagery had been shed and discarded, also pointed towards a richer and more colourful Byzantine future, when the basic iconographic scheme reproduced on the diptych of Probus, among other works, was filled with new content, as it was, for instance, on the diptychs attributed to the empress Ariadne (plate 61).

PART · II

THE PARTING OF THE WAYS BETWEEN EAST AND WEST AND THE FORMULATION OF A BYZANTINE CEREMONIAL OF ACCESSION

7. THE FIFTH CENTURY IN THE WEST

The fall of Rome in 410 provoked a passionate outburst of loyalty for the "eternal city." In numismatic design, this loyalty was expressed on some silver medallions of Attalus, the senatorial emperor installed by Alaric. In view of the contemporary circumstances, these multiples constitute one of those paradoxes familiar from Roman imperial propaganda. Within a year after the capture of the city, Roma could be seen on medallions, enthroned frontally on a throne with lionheads, leaning on a sceptre, holding a globe surmounted by Victoria, and holding her customary helmet: INVICTA ROMA AETERNA.[288] While the legend was new, the image of Rome enthroned had occurred on the coinage in the fourth century and before, but never with such prominence, and with its import so pointedly stated in words. It was a pagan, hitherworldly image and message, which matched Rutilius in his realistic yet hopeful lines:

> What seals the destiny of other kingdoms for you means renewal: there
> is a way of being born again, an ability to grow out of ill.[289]

Roma as a figure in her panoply (see plate 57) emerges prominently in the very Western panegyrics of Sidonius. These verse panegyrics on Avitus, Majorian and Anthemius, although they attempt to see the fifth century in the context of the rest of Roman history, make it clear just how much the Western Empire had changed in the years between Claudian and Sidonius.

In 456, Avitus' panegyrist had to explain that emperor's accession and his election by a Visigothic king to the nobility of Rome in terms acceptable to the latter—a difficult task, which Sidonius performed with some vigour and more imagination than he has been credited with. He brings before his audience the figure of Roma weary, yet still majestic in her defeat, appearing before the throne of Iuppiter pleading for help. Iuppiter[290] tells her of the homeland, birth, upbringing, deeds and finally the proclamation of Avitus as Augustus.

In short, Sidonius set the proclamation into a familiar and time-honoured setting of mythological and allegorical figures which were known to his educated contemporaries. He also used, for the purpose of justifying the choice of Avitus, the traditional *topoi* of the emperor's birth, upbringing and virtues. Within the narrative of the accession itself there is a remarkable mixture of fact and fiction. Theodoric, king of the Visigoths, offered his services to Rome as an expiation for the crimes of Alaric his ancestor, provided that Avitus became emperor.[291]

> I swear to you Rome, by your name which we revere, and by our common descent from Mars—for among everything that has existed from the beginning of time, the world contains nothing greater than yourself, nothing greater than the Senate—that I will keep the peace with you and desire to make amends for the offences of my ancestor, who is stained by this one fault, that he captured you, oh Rome. But if the gods favour my desires, my vengeance on your present fate will purge the crime of that other, if only you, noble leader [Avitus], will accept the name of Augustus. Why do you avert your eyes? It becomes you more to be unwilling.[292]

This most unconventional setting was yet made respectable by the appearance in it of Roma, and of the familiar *topos* of the emperor unwilling to rule. Sidonius went on to tell of the assembly of the Gallic nobles who also desired Avitus as emperor, since he would restore the fortunes of Rome, ruined as they were by the misrule of incompetent members of the imperial dynasty.[293] And he pointed out that Avitus' accession was not a usurpation, since the throne was vacant. These were the preliminaries to a scene of election in which the theoretical components were assembled in their entirety:

> The nobles met together, and accompanied by the army placed [Avitus] on a mound, crowned him with a torque and gave him, although he sorrowed, the insignia of kingship. For before that he had only been invested with an emperor's cares.[294]

The only constituent which could not be mentioned was the Roman Senate. Apart from this, if we are to believe Sidonius, the election could not have been more correct. It is this very correctness which raises suspicions. The case made out is too perfect, too orderly. Sidonius as a propagandist—unlike, for instance, Themistius or Jovian—could not admit any disorders, any spontaneity, at the election of Avitus, because, as the outcome was to show, the emperor's position was too precarious. Taking into account the role of the Visigoths in the election, the panegyric discloses that Roman imperial propaganda could no longer fall back on the support of an ordered state. Avitus' victory over the Vandals was prophesied by Sidonius; it could not be praised as a fact.[295]

It was not possible for Sidonius as a propagandist to develop a consistent, coherent line of approach, because events were changing too rapidly. There had been changes in the fourth century also. But in the *Twelve Panegyrici* and in the panegyrics of Themistius, it is possible to pursue continuously and coherently evolving theories, which could be applied to different circumstances. Sidonius, by contrast, although aware of what the main points in an election ought to have been, could not produce any coherent line of thought, but had to juggle with the facts as best he could.

This he did with remarkable aplomb. Late in 458, he composed a panegyric to welcome to Lyon Majorian, who had displaced Avitus. Roma had now regained her composure, and is described enthroned on her porphyry throne, warlike and beautiful, receiving the submission of the provinces, like the emperors on the column base of Arcadius.[296] (Plate 20) It was now a dishevelled Africa, who, seeking liberation from the Vandals, commended the deeds and virtues of Majorian.[297] As in the case of Avitus, no dynastic case could be made, and Sidonius had to concentrate on the election, which he did very briefly, inserting it between accounts of a victory in the Alps in 457 and one over the Vandals in 458, "After the throne was bestowed on you in due order by all orders, the people, the Senate, the army, and your colleague."[298]

This account again suggests an orderliness which did not in fact exist,[299] even though Leo in due course recognised Majorian as Augustus. The phrase *plebs, curia, miles* describes the people, Senate and army, who in theory, but never in fact, elected the emperor. The theory had been current since Augustus, but was not realised in an actual constitutional mechanism, although, in Byzantium, it was realised in a ceremony. However, as has been seen, the assent of the imperial colleague was real and often vital; the Byzantine ceremony was to allow for this factor.

Sidonius on the one hand elucidated the election of Majorian, although briefly, and on the other began his panegyric with a description of him in the insignia of power which is reflected in several late antique works of art, where the imperial insignia, the increasing importance of which we have had occasion to note, are very accurately rendered:

> Remember in your mind, people of Rome, your past triumphs: now a consul holds the empire, who is clothed both in the purple and in armour; the diadem encircles his head not by empty show but by law, and to him, as a reward of his labours, comes the consular toga after the palms of victory. The *fasces* crown all the splendour of royalty, and the emperor's dignity is enhanced by his consulship.[300]

In the panegyric of Anthemius of 467, Sidonius praised another accession. Again, Roma, in search of an emperor, figures prominently. Sidonius' panegyrics mark a last stage of the imperial concept of *Roma et Augustus*, which has been touched upon above, a concept now mythologised and to a certain extent fossilised, but still usable to explain imperial policies. The panegyric on Anthemius, like the two earlier ones, is more realistic than the mythological stage-works would lead one to suppose. Here the predominant position of Constantinople is acknowledged: "Greeting to you, pinnacle of Empire, Queen of the East, and Rome of your world."[301]

The emergence of Constantinopolis can be documented on the coinage, where, after 330, she acquired a position parallel to that of Rome. It can also be documented in the work of Themistius. In 354, in his panegyric on Constantius, he still regarded Rome as the capital of the world, with Constantinople in second place. This emphasis shifted, and in his later panegyrics on Theodosius, Themistius acted solely as the spokesman of Constantinople, which he regarded as existing in its own right.[302]

Finally, Constantinople overshadowed Rome in political importance, a fact which Sidonius states by implication when he presents Roma begging for an emperor as a suppliant before Aurora-Constantinopolis. In this framework, the descent, virtues and deeds of Anthemius were elaborated, and Sidonius, able on behalf of the subject of his panegyric to make a double claim, does so. His descent entitled Anthemius to the empire by inheritance, but to his greater credit he was also elected by his colleague, Leo.[303] Not only this, but the familiar *universi*, enumerated in specific detail, sought Anthemius' dominion. But he, as befitted him, was reluctant to accept.

> Here is the man, Senators, who was sought out by Roman virtue and by your affection. To him the republic, overcome by storms and lacking

a pilot, entrusted her broken frame, so that, guided better by a worthy
steerman, she might no longer fear either storm or pirate. The farmer
sought you with his prayers, our allies consented, you were welcomed
by the trumpet of the camp, and your colleague sent you to us, sent
you to dominion. As many votes as the world can provide are cast in
your favour.[304]

The description of Anthemius' election by the whole world is preceded by a description of him adorned with the imperial insignia.
Sidonius here used the same procedure as in the panegyric on Majorian:

Raise up your second *fasces*, seconded by fortune, and shining with
heavy gold upon your consular robe, open the new year, yourself a
consul of earlier standing, and think it no disgrace to grace the *fasti*
twice with your name. Although you came forward with a diadem
crowning your hair, and a purple chlamys covers your shoulders after
the custom of the ancients, the purple of the consular toga graces you
yet more, because repeated consulships have always been rare.[305]

This passage again is notable for its official correctness, a correctness which was absent in earlier panegyrics, because there were other
more complex and important issues to discuss. From the first century,
emperors at their accession regularly took up the consulship. But it
was only among the late panegyrists, Claudian and particularly Sidonius, that an issue was made of this, in itself, merely formal part of
accession.[306]

Sidonius, like Claudian, still incorporated the praises of the emperors
in his panegyrics into a mythological framework. This was a procedure
which was reflected in the official art of the period, but only to a very
limited extent. And by the time that Priscian, also a Westerner, composed his verse panegyric on Anastasius, the mythological framework
had disappeared for good. Sidonius wrote at a time of political uncertainty and he used an ancient method of creating some order within that
chaos. In other words, he used the trained perception of a late antique
man of letters for whom classical mythology and history, and in particular the mythology and history of Rome, were still to be taken for
granted. Within such a framework, the accession of a new emperor
could be understood as a regular, recurring event, however chaotic the
particular circumstances. In a different context, it has been seen how the
interpretation of the ceremony of *adventus* depended on a trained and
carefully formulated method of perception on the part of those who described it.

In accession, the position was slightly different, for the mythological and historical framework played a very particular role. It was in a sense external to late antique accession, for unlike in *adventus*, it did not provide some fundamental concepts for the articulation of the ceremony. Whereas *adventus* could be described in mythological terms, in terms of pagan sacred story, to make it more pervasive and important, the importance of accession was heightened by expanding it in philosophical terms, as was done by Themistius. Nonetheless, pagan sacred story could not only give an appearance of order to chaotic events but also it placed these events firmly on earth, at a time when according to Eusebius, Libanius and Themistius, such events could become the focal points of God's intervention on earth, could be the demonstration of the theory that the emperor was divinely elected.

This theory was not articulated either in Claudian or in Sidonius. Nobody believed that the gods actually conversed with each other as they do in Sidonius. Such conversations were, as Servius puts it, *conficta*, to be contrasted, as Servius likewise does, with what actually happened on earth.[307] Therefore, a scene like Iuppiter's appointment of Avitus as the emperor for his suppliant Roma is in no way an equivalent to the divine election of the emperor as articulated by Themistius, a divine election which found lasting expression in the Byzantine Empire. Sidonius was true to the tradition of earlier panegyrists who preferred to explain accession in terms other than of divine election. For Sidonius, as for Claudian, the means of doing this was precisely pagan myth and history.

In art, this terrestrial outlook of Sidonius may be matched by the familiar imagery of the two capitals and of imperial enthronement. The divine found no direct expression in the context of accession. Rome and Constantinople enthroned together or separately were, on the coinage, an iconographical parallel to the emperor or emperors enthroned. Moreover, there existed certain connections between the emperor and his capital, which emerged, among other authors, in Sidonius, where Roma and Constantinople are elaborately described as personifications who act in imperial accessions. As such they appear with some frequency in official works of art of the fifth century.

The consular diptych of Constantius (plate 56) and Attalus' INVICTA ROMA AETERNA issues have already been referred to. Another consular diptych of the fifth century from the West, which possibly was carved under Anthemius[308] (plate 57) shows the two cities personified, each standing in an *aedicula*, the stance of one balancing that of the other, so that the two wings of the diptych form a symmetric whole. Roma wears her customary helmet, leans on a long sceptre, and in her right hand holds a starry globe, surmounted by Victoria holding a wreath. Certain details of her attire, the helmet and the clasp of the dress, recur in Sidonius' panegyric on Majorian, where, however, she holds a shield and is seated.[309] Constantinople on the diptych wears a mural crown and holds a cornucopiae, and like Sidonius' Aurora, a torch.[310]

On the coinage, the legends set the figure of Roma into a context which relates her more directly to the literary evidence. We have already met *invicta Roma* on the coinage; and the idea of Rome's growth out of setbacks was also voiced by Sidonius. Other legends,[311] showing Roma enthroned, connect her with imperial occasions. Valentinian III's URBS ROMA is a specifically Roman issue and shows Roma seated on a cuirass holding a figure of Victoria.[312] Under Avitus there was URBIS ROMAE, Rome enthroned, holding a spear and Victoria on a globe,[313] and a similar issue, SALUS REIPUBLICAE, was issued for Anthemius.[314]

A last revival of the imagery of Rome on the coinage occurred on the autonomous senatorial issues under Odovacar and the Ostrogoths.[315] At the same time, however, the classical notion of the personification of cities and of concepts finally disappeared from the mental furniture of the inhabitants of the Roman Empire. When the emperor Justin II issued coins with Constantinopolis on the reverse, the population of the capital rioted, in the belief that this figure was Aphrodite.[316] The link between Roma and the Augustus which sometimes was so very abstract, but sometimes quite intimate and concrete, thus came to an end. The will of the population of the capital as made tangible in a personification no longer played a role in imperial accessions, or, as they were to be in the West, royal accessions.

The image of imperial enthronement or majesty, however, which became increasingly prominent from the time of the Tetrarchy, was among the few late antique coin types to survive the fifth century. A fine example is a gold multiple of Galla Placidia from Ravenna, showing the nimbate and diademed empress enthroned on an elaborate throne, SALUS REI-PUBLICAE RV COMOB (plate 60). The portrait on the obverse shows in detail the empress' diadem, jewels and attire, including a Chi Rho monogramme on her sleeve.[317] This, like other imperial portraits of late antiquity with their formalised faces but carefully rendered insignia, matches Sidonius' two descriptions of the emperor in his regalia.

On the one hand, visual art remained out of step with the panegyric evidence on accession as a whole, in that the images that have been discussed do not reflect the moment which the panegyrists came to focus on. But on the other hand, from the age of Constantine, the insignia and attributes of emperors, and their ceremonial role were depicted in imperial art with increasing accuracy. Imperial art thus points to the growing importance of court ceremonies, of which accession came to be one, and to the order and harmony which these ceremonies were intended to convey.

The early fifth century produced one work of art representing an accession which is inconsistent in that it does not represent imperial power and majesty and a ceremonial setting in general, but the specific moment of accession, or rather, investiture, the moment when, as several fourth-century panegyrics state, the emperor was clothed in the chlamys and crowned with a diadem.

The work in question is the sardonyx of the engraver Romulus, who inscribed his name on it, FL ROMUL VEST FECIT (plate 43). This was not necessarily an official or imperial work, but its theme suggests a courtly milieu. We see in the centre a boy standing on a podium between two older men, of whom the one on the left is wearing a diadem and therefore is an emperor. Both men are being crowned with a wreath by winged creatures in short tunics. The emperor is in the act of clothing the boy in a chlamys, while the man on the right is about to lay a laurel wreath on his head. Above the boy's head is the Chi Rho between A and Ω. This is a highly unusual work in that, like the thirty-solidi multiple of Constantius II, it has no contemporary parallels at all.

The persons on the stone have been identified as Valentinian III being invested as Nobilissimus by Honorius and Constantius III before the latter became emperor.[318] However, the wreath over the boy's head may define the scene as an imperial investiture, even though one would expect a diadem.[319] Investiture of a junior by a senior emperor was a common procedure in Byzantium. Here then we have a unique work, which may show an emperor at the specific moment of his accession. There are no earlier and few later parallels. This gem stands on its own, thus demonstrating that the mainstream of imperial art on the subject of accession was moving in a different direction.

8. THE OSTROGOTHS

i. Cassiodorus and Ennodius

The true nature of Ostrogothic kingship has been obscured, on the one hand, by vigorous Italian propaganda, and on the other, by Germanic legends.[320] The propaganda for the Ostrogothic kingdom provides both an epilogue to the Roman traditions of accession in the West, and an outlook on Byzantium. For, the propaganda discloses both the Roman double-mindedness, the many-layered irrational message, on which I have sought to elaborate, and the rudiments of a popular ceremonial of accession, as developed under different circumstances in Byzantium.

If one looks at technical vocabulary, the panegyric of Ennodius draws a distinction between the emperors of the past and of Byzantium on the one hand, and Theodoric on the other, in that the latter is called *dominus*,[321] *ductor*, *rector*, and *rex*,[322] but never *imperator* and Augustus. The crucial word Augustus only appears in one inscription.[323] This impression, derived from Ennodius' terminology, is deceptive, however. Theodoric, according to Ennodius, did all that a legitimate emperor would do, and this is the crux. Ennodius' panegyric is a chaotic performance, and the message he conveys is accordingly also somewhat chaotic. But this, as has been seen in the context of accession, was no novelty, and one might even say that the lack of organisation in Ennodius' panegyric, although not deliberate, reinforces what he has to say on accession.

Taking the points Ennodius made in order, the first one is this:

> You, noble lord, have as your own the distinction of one who both bestowed and defended the diadem. If the master of those lands did not love you, then he stood at the head of the commonwealth as an exile. If he did love you, it was as an expression of obligation. In your actions, you trusted your deserts, and the emperor is your witness.[324]

Theodoric gave and defended the imperial diadem, and it is implied that but for Theodoric, Zeno would not have been emperor at all. This was a large claim, and in the Byzantine context, unheard of for, in terms of the Byzantine ceremonial, which was at this time becoming established, and also in terms of the imperial accessions of the fourth century, Theodoric here assumed the role of the senior emperor who performed the elections of his junior colleague. This is perhaps the crucial point of Ennodius' message on accession. As a result, Theodoric's dominion in Italy could be taken for granted. This is stated by implication, rather than directly, and is stated in terms of deeds and descent. No process of election is described.

Theodoric was born in Greece, the mother of the arts,[325] of a father distinguished in all warlike virtues.[326] Ennodius simply applied the *topoi* of panegyric to a barbarian king. Theodoric's descent was an important argument in Italian propaganda for the Ostrogoths, and was developed at length in the history of the Goths by Cassiodorus. It mattered even in the last tragic days of the Ostrogothic kingdom, when Cassiodorus pinned his hopes on the marriage between Germanus, the nephew of Justinian, and Matasuntha,[327] which was a dynastic marriage of crucial, if perhaps ephemeral, importance.

Both Ennodius and Cassiodorus underpinned their praises of Ostrogothic kingship with an unusual abundance of examples. Achilles, Cyrus, Semiramis, Alexander—the legendary figures of the classical past[328]—as well as the less legendary figures of the Roman republic— the Decii, Fabricii, and Catones—all figure. Urban Roman sentiment was centred on the latter group, and it was the urban nobility, who needed most convincing, whom Cassiodorus addressed in his refined and sometimes exquisite panegyrics. Against the example of the re- public and of the city of Rome,[329] the Ostrogothic panegyrics pitched the solid, late antique theme of a dynasty of rulers, a dynasty which needed and had acquired an heir.[330] The premature death of that heir, seen in the light of this propaganda, shows up a flaw in the Ostrogothic state as acutely as do the six books of Procopius' *Gothic War*. This is one of the spotlights which late antique propaganda provides to sensitive listeners.

Another theme in the Ostrogothic panegyrics is the Christian faith of Theodoric. Theodoric's Christianity could serve as a way of setting aside the Roman urban example as outdated and devoid of any contemporary relevance. But at the same time, Ennodius, unlike Eusebius, did not use the ruler's Christianity as a lever whereby to argue that the ruler was divinely elected; as was usual for the West, Ennodius did not touch on this theme of accession. Nonetheless, Ostrogothic propaganda was sen- sitive to current strands of thought. Thus, Ennodius said:

> Your conduct is such that you will be rewarded with prosperity, yet, having attained it, you ascribe everything to your creator. By your strength, vigilance, success, you appear as a king, by your kindliness as a priest.[331]

This is the theme which in different ways was to occupy Western and Byzantine theories of kingship for centuries. Although the increasingly important role of the patriarch in the Byzantine state may be stressed, and although functionally, it is true that the patriarch crowned the em- peror, imaginatively and in theory, this did not matter. In official art, the emperor came to be crowned by Christ or the Virgin. The emperor was divinely appointed to care for all aspects of his subjects' welfare, as is clearly expressed in Byzantine legislation.[332] Byzantine theorists drew on the parallel roles of Moses and Aaron to express the relation between the emperor, the new Moses, and the patriarch. But Aaron was only Moses' delegate, and it was Moses who received the tablets of the law.[333]

There is thus not so much a split between the roles of patriarch and emperor as a coordination, or rather, subordination of one to the other, expressed by the pre-eminence of the emperor, who assimilated both functions in himself and delegated one of them. Ennodius, reflecting developments in contemporary Byzantium, used a catch phrase, *princeps et sacerdos*, to express this state of affairs.

We have examined the new departures and failures of Ostrogothic propaganda. Apart from these, however, there was an important body of ideas, which linked up with earlier lines of thought, and set up the Ostrogothic kings as successors to the Roman emperors. Both Ennodius and Cassiodorus carefully avoid mentioning the terms *imperator* and *Augustus*, but do discuss the functions which these titles conveyed. In their political vocabulary both panegyrists thought in imperial terms, and asserted that Theodoric had restored the imperial boundaries to their old extent. Like the earlier emperors, Theodoric received embassies from submissive neighbours and enemies. The point about the frontiers, although untrue, betrays a way of thought characteristic of Ostrogothic propaganda. It went hand in hand with the idea of a personified Roma, gratified by royal victories, and the idea of renewal and rebirth.

For his account of the battle of Verona, Ennodius conjures up the venerable figure of aged Roma, who, approaching with tottering steps, is to be rejuvenated by the victory[334]—an image very much in the style of Sidonius. Theodoric's panegyrists viewed Rome as foremost among the cities to be revived by his beneficence.[335] At the same time, according to Cassiodorus, Theodoric reformed Rome's outdated *mores*, that is, he abolished ancient superstitious practices at consular elections. This *topos* of panegyric, which had also been reiterated by Mamertinus in 362 and by Ausonius,[336] served to place achievements of the present over those of the past.

The Western Roman method of conveying accession thus put into the hands of the Ostrogothic panegyrists the tools which they needed to overcome a problematic takeover of power. Everything could be presented with perfect respectability and in the context of a continuous tradition. It was Sidonius, with his legalistic emphasis on the constitutional process of election, who was exceptional, rather than Ennodius and Cassiodorus. For, unlike Sidonius, Cassiodorus and Ennodius had the advantage of being able to base their works on a long reign which was, in many respects, very successful. Of the stresses and strains that seethed underneath that placid surface, however, the legends of Dietrich of Bern give some inkling.

The Ostrogothic panegyrics also contribute to our knowledge of the ceremonial of accession, and give further indication of the growing importance of the insignia of dominion. As regards the ceremonial, the fragmentary panegyric of Cassiodorus, which may be attributed to the occasion of the accession of Vitigis and his marriage to Matasuntha,[337] provides some evidence which is unique for this date in the West. Having gone some way in his praise of the war-like virtues of Vitigis, Cassiodorus stopped to allow the army to make their acclamation of the newly elected king and to confirm his oration.[338] In other words, Cassiodorus visualised the accession not only in terms of a dynastic marriage, but also in terms of a military election, such as was described for emperors of the fourth century by Ammianus.

Acclamation by the army formed a fundamental part of late antique imperial elections, and here, as elsewhere, the Ostrogothic kingdom preserved Roman mechanisms. Moreover, seeing that panegyrics were a fundamentally civilian means of communication, Cassiodorus, by making room in his panegyric for the acclamations of the army, integrated the civilian with the military aspect of accession. He thus overcame one of the main sources of conflict in the theory and practice of Roman imperial accessions, the conflict between Mars and Quirinus, soldier and civilian, which was particularly acute in Ostrogothic Italy, since the soldiers were Goths, and the civilians were Romans. In this way, Cassiodorus as panegyrist was truly able to speak on behalf of all, and to make the accession ceremonial into an image of the smooth functioning of a whole society, even though the circumstances of the time prevented this image from acquiring any lasting practical validity. As we shall see, the Byzantine ceremonial of accession overcame this same conflict between soldier and civilian, but by a different method.

As for the insignia of dominion, we have a fine exegesis of their importance at this time in Ennodius' closing passage, which describes Theodoric clothed in his jewelled imperial purple, his head adorned with the long hair of Germanic kings:

> Deserts and innate virtue make up your personality, while your actions are the result of your highmindedness. Your birth made you lord, and your virtue is commensurate. Your exalted origin granted you the sceptre, but if your origin had lacked distinction, your disposition would bring about your election as our ruler. Nor is the nobility of your appearance to be numbered among the least of your assets, when the bloom of your royal countenance shines upon the purple of your royal station. You men of China, bring out your garments which you colour with precious purple dye, and do not with a lesser material debase the vestments which, with the dye, imbibe royalty. Let the cloth be woven with precious stones of different colours, and bring forth the stone which is guarded by a powerful serpent. Whatever ornaments are sent to you by your subject world, they will shine the more when they are adorned by the breath of your majestic frame. Your stature is such that by its height it announces a king; the whiteness of your cheeks is in

harmony with the red. Your eyes bloom with a lasting serenity. How
becoming are the hands which allot to rebels death, but to the conquered honour. Let no one boast inappropriately, for what other rulers
gain from the diadem is achieved for my king by god-given nature.
Those others are made conspicuous by the support of their great
wealth, while Theodoric is outstanding by his natural and unchange-
able stature. Indeed, let them labour in vain who wish to acquire a
beauty that is not their own.[339]

Here again are described the results of accession, rather than accession itself. Theodoric's accession, according to Ennodius, took place by
implication during his victorious onslaught on Odovacar, who is of
course called a tyrant. It was the old conflict of the legitimate ruler
against the usurper, which the earlier panegyrics had also explored. We
have noted Ammianus' insistence on order and dignity in legitimate accessions. Ennodius' description of Theodoric is a counterpart to Ammianus, for Ennodius describes the legitimate ruler in his panoply, exercising the functions of kingship. Ennodius accomplishes an interesting
fusion of Roman and Germanic ideas of kingship: the purple was an indispensable Roman attribute of empire, which Claudian and Sidonius
had also described, but equally indispensable at this time was the diadem, which Theodoric never wore. This was replaced, as on Theodoric's gold medallion,[340] by his long hair, which was also a distinguishing mark of the Frankish kings.

How appropriate a description of the king in his glory could be to the
theme of accession is demonstrated by Cassiodorus' panegyric on the
accession of Vitigis and Matasuntha. Here the queen, laden with jewels,
which, however, were outshone by her own beauty,[341] is described coming forth from her palace which radiates with marbles and mosaics. The
conception is Byzantine, a perfect match to the ivory diptych attributed
to the empress Ariadne (plate 61). As regards the imagery of majesty
and the description of the insignia and glory of the ruler, the Ostrogothic panegyric, as well as Sidonius, foreshadow and reflect Byzantine views of the emperor, the meticulous rendering of the imperial insignia in art, and the careful definitions of the exalted position of the
ruler among his subjects, which as yet was a terrestrial position.

From another point of view, however, Sidonius and the panegyrists
of Ostrogothic Italy were thoroughly Western. The topic of the divine
election of the ruler was either omitted altogether or merely touched
upon by an incidental phrase; it did not form one of the strands of argument whereby accession was to be explained and justified. In Western
panegyrics, accession was explained, after the Tetrarchy, in terrestrial

terms and could be articulated by means of the imagery of the ruler and his city, which was employed once more in Ostrogothic Italy.

ii. Images of the Ruler and His City

In his panegyric Ennodius evoked the personification of Rome, so as to dignify Theodoric's victory of Verona. In the constantly decreasing iconographic repertoire of the late Roman coinage, Roma was one of the few figures who survived in the West. The legend INVICTA ROMA with motifs such as Victoria, or the monogramme of Theodoric, or a star,[342] appears on the reverses of the Roman senatorial coinage under Theodoric, while the obverse shows the legend and bust of the emperor. Under Athalarich, at Ravenna, INVICTA ROMA was moved to the obverse, while the legend DN ATHALARICUS REX occupied the reverse,[343] showing, in some cases,[344] Athalarich standing armed. A similar combination was repeated for Theodahad[345] and Vitigis.[346] Roma, however, also led an existence in her own right on the quasi-autonomous coinage of Rome as INVICTA ROMA, with the image of her helmeted, draped bust on the obverse,[347] sometimes associated on the reverse with scenes from the urban past, the fig tree, and the wolf and twins.[348]

The imagery of ruler and capital in Ostrogothic Italy was perhaps more than a pious revival, in that in this field, Ostrogothic artists actually made an addition to the repertoire of official images in the person of FELIX RAVENNA, draped bust with mural crown.[349] This image was conceived in the old idiom of the city goddess, who could be identified by her mural crown. Furthermore, a mosaic in one of the Ostrogothic churches showed a more distinctive personification of Ravenna: the city with her mural crown was to be seen standing with one foot on the dry land and with one foot on the sea[350]—an apt illustration of the harbour and city of Ravenna, which are more literally depicted in the surviving mosaic in S. Apollinare Nuovo, balancing Theodoric's palace (plate 54).

The positioning of these latter two mosaics, opposite each other at the end of the nave, is important, for this positioning, as well as the content, shows how city and palace, subjects and ruler, supplement each other. The mosaics depict, in the subtle and often indirect language of late antique iconography, a similar kind of interplay between ruler and subjects as is evoked by Cassiodorus' panegyric on Vitigis and Matasuntha, when he paused for the acclamation of the army. In the Ostrogothic personification of Ravenna, we see visual art once more stepping ahead of panegyric, in that art created an image in the traditional idiom which yet had a precise contemporary relevance.

The partnership on the coinage between Rome or Ravenna and the

Ostrogothic kings ran parallel to another partnership, that between the Byzantine emperor and the Ostrogothic king. Ennodius unhesitatingly made the two equals, although Cassiodorus, in the surviving fragments of the panegyric, does not touch on the topic. The coinage again is illuminating. Theodoric started with a constitutionally correct version,[351] showing on obverses Anastasius and Justin I,[352] and on reverses mostly Victoria, with the legend VICTORIA AUGG (or AUGUSTORUM).

Elsewhere on the Ostrogothic coinage, however, a gradual edging forward into an imperial position may be observed: a set of coins shows on the obverse the legend and image of the Byzantine emperor, and on the reverse the monogramme or legend without image of the Ostrogothic king.[353] The next step, taken under Theodahad, was that the Gothic king should move to the obverse; the reverse, VICTORIA PRINCIPUM SC, showing Victoria on a ship's prow, embraces king and emperor in one phrase.[354]

Totila went one stage further by having his image and legend on the obverse, and his legend or monogramme in a wreath on the reverse of the same issue.[355] A Roman issue of Totila showing on the obverse his bust and legend, and on the reverse the king standing with a miscut legend to the effect *floreas semper* rings a curiously antiquarian note, reminiscent of the contorniates.[356] The later Ostrogothic issues, produced during the Gothic wars, thus show how Ostrogothic propaganda became increasingly independent of Byzantium, this being a development which is foreshadowed in the panegyric of Ennodius.

It was Theodoric himself who had, so far as the coinage is concerned, taken the crucial step. His triple solidus from Rome shows on the obverse REX THEODERICUS PIUS PRINCIS, the draped and cuirassed bust of the king, and on the reverse REX THEODERICUS VICTOR GENTIUM COMOB, Victoria with palm branch. Theodoric issued this multiple in his own right. Here and elsewhere[357] the Ostrogothic kings are shown undiademed, with long hair, just as Ennodius describes Theodoric. In view of the Ostrogothic panegyrists' avoidance of the title Augustus, which was the one title that distinguished the emperor from all other dignitaries, one may suggest that the diadem was now the crucial imperial insignia, which therefore the Ostrogothic kings avoided using, although they did use the purple. If this suggestion is correct, the Ostrogothic kings did, their claims notwithstanding, preserve a certain reserve *vis-à-vis* the imperial dignity, which is expressed in panegyric and art.

Cassiodorus and Ennodius, the panegyrists of the Ostrogothic kingdom whose work survives, were both learned antiquarians, eager to apply their scholarship to a contemporary situation. For this reason one

aspect of what can be learnt about Ostrogothic Italy has a strong classicising note, the tone of yet another *renovatio*. A similar note is struck in
the Palatium mosaic of Theodoric in S. Apollinare Nuovo (plate 54). We
see the arcaded facade of Theodoric's palace.[358] In the original version of
the mosaic, a figure stood under each arch, while in the central arch was
probably to be seen Theodoric himself,[359] appearing to his subjects surrounded by the splendours of his palace and by his court dignitaries
who performed the courtly ceremonial around their king.[360] After the
Byzantine conquest of Ravenna, this mosaic was reset and the dignitaries standing in the arcades, together with Theodoric himself, were
erased to be replaced by a blue and gold background. A similar revision
was made on the opposite mosaic showing Classe, where the figures
walking outside the city walls were replaced by plain masonry.

The iconography of the Palatium mosaic is closely related to that of
the missorium of Theodosius (plate 55). Both works show the lasting
result of rightful accession, rather than the moment when the accession
took place, and are in accord with the enthronement imagery of the
coinage. The paganising, classicising imagery of the missorium, however, was left out in the mosaic. In the pediment of the palace, there was
probably the equestrian statue of Theodoric while in the city gate next to
the palace stood the Tyche of Ravenna.[361] It has been seen how in comparison to the missorium, the imagery of the consular diptych showing
Honorius is somewhat colourless, bereft as it is of many of the nuances
which imperial art in the older idiom could convey. The gap in communication, which had been left by the conversion of the imperial images to Christianity, was now filled by depicting ceremonious occasions
without pagan points of reference.

The Ostrogothic version of the Palatium mosaic showed the ruler in
his majesty. The association to be made between literary accounts of accession and the imagery of enthronement and majesty in imperial art,
which has been a guideline among the diverse strands of late antique
thought on imperial accessions, which we have traced, is not merely a
conjecture. Sidonius in his panegyrics on the imperial consulships marking the various accessions, described each emperor in his majesty,[362]
while also outlining the processes of election. Whether Cassiodorus, in
a lost section of his panegyric on Vitigis and Matasuntha, also described
the process of election, is uncertain. What he did was to celebrate the
accession of Vitigis and Matasuntha in terms of the queen's appearance
in the palace.

We have seen that the act of taking possession of the palace was a
part of the accession ritual,[363] while enthronement in the palace was a

timeless visual expression of that ritual. For Cassiodorus, the palace expresses the ruler's majesty.

> [The beauties of the palace] are the delight of our might, the becoming
> countenance of empire, the exalted testimony of kingdoms: [the palace]
> is displayed before the admiring eyes of emissaries and on first impact
> the lord is considered to be such as his dwelling place is perceived to
> be.[364]

Queen, throne and palace are the themes of Cassiodorus' *laudes* of
Matasuntha. Cassiodorus' style and vocabulary, never simple, are here
at their most ornate and complex. The queen in her glory is described in
one long sweep of highly coloured rhetoric, which sets aside any rule
ever written in rhetorical textbooks regarding moderation and sobriety,
giving the impression that the theme was indeed, as was so often said in
panegyric, too great to be rendered justice to. In some ways the theme
was too great. Cassiodorus' hyperboles and allusions defy description,
and any interpretation of works of art must ultimately remain tentative.

The Byzantine ceremonial of accession expressed in a different medium some of the meanings which have been explored, and it was, I
would suggest, in the light of the doctrine of Byzantine ceremonial and of
Byzantine rule in Ravenna that the mosaics of S. Apollinare Nuovo, formerly dedicated to St. Martin, were altered under Bishop Agnellus.[365]
This alteration of the mosaics left the palace empty. The arcades are filled
merely with curtains drawn aside to disclose an empty background.

Can we ascribe to this imagery any message other than one of con-
venience, imposed by the necessity of eradicating any trace of the Ostrogothic figures who stood in these archways? I think we can. In Ravenna, the imagery of the empty throne, the throne made ready for the
lord[366] was frequently used. S. Apollinare shows not an empty throne
but an empty palace, a palace made ready for the advent of the emperor
or his delegate,[367] which would draw the minds of the beholders into a
state of expectancy and awareness of their absent ruler. One may note in
this context that the central archway, reserved for the ruler, has a golden
background, whereas the space in the arcades at either side is blue. The
history of the Palatium mosaic is a perfect illustration of the changing
status of Ravenna under Ostrogothic and Byzantine rule.

Moreover, both in the composition as completed under Agnellus,
and in the Ostrogothic prototype, the palace, at the west end of the
nave, is balanced at the east end by Christ shown enthroned on a starry
cushion between a guard of angels, the ruler of heaven counterpoised
against the ruler on earth, the two joined up by the procession of mar-

tyrs and saints. While the palace is juxtaposed with Christ, the city at the west end of the nave, by contrast, is juxtaposed at the east end by the enthroned Virgin.[368] Ravenna was not the only city to be placed in relation to the Virgin. In the prologue to the Akathistos hymn, Constantinople addresses the Virgin, the Protostrategos, bringing her the offerings for victory as "I your city."[369] At the same time, the emperor in Byzantium was "protected by Christ."[370]

The juxtaposition of heaven and earth fills the terrestrial, imperial—and, formerly, royal—imagery of Ravenna with a new content, replacing the paganising, classicising content of imperial art at an earlier period. The Palatium mosaic, so similar to the missorium iconographically, yet has an entirely different message. In the first place it is no longer a self-contained image, for it is balanced at the other end of the church by the figure of Christ enthroned. In the second place, the distance to be covered by the beholder, as he sees first the Palatium, then Christ, makes this composition an image of movement, of procession, and no longer a still stationary image like the missorium. The mosaic thus has a more explicitly ceremonial content, a content which renders ceremony as action.

This element of movement and action was present even more clearly in the Ostrogothic version of the composition, for the outline of the erased figures which can be traced on the Classe and Palatium mosaics show that these figures were moving in procession towards the east end, the sanctuary of the church. We have here a representation of part of the royal liturgy which was later transformed into an imperial liturgy. Processions of arrival and triumph in sixth-century Byzantium, like their Roman predecessors, enacted in the present a past event, such as victory, or a state of affairs, such as the results of accession.

These themes were sensitively and skilfully taken up by the artists of Ostrogothic Ravenna, and by their Byzantine successors. In this context emerges once again the movement which had been such an important characteristic of *adventus* in the earlier fourth century, *adventus* itself having been one of the ways in which accession at that time could be rendered. But in S. Apollinare Nuovo there is only a very distant echo of this kind of *adventus*:[371] it is the dignitaries of the court, be it the Ostrogothic dignitaries of Theodoric, or the saints, the dignitaries of the court of heaven, who are seen moving. Christ and his mother, like the emperor in many of the images here considered, and probably like Theodoric in his palace, are seated in frontality, in repose.

We have expounded a world of the imagination which, while able to account for the individual moment in historical writing and panegyric, was at the same time able to transcend that moment in the same media, but particularly in art. The ability to transcend made the message more significant, more pervasive, but at the same time more elusive. The eyes of the people shown in late antique portraiture search and yearn for the beyond, and express an awareness of the possibility of seeing an inner meaning in events. Imperial art was created for such eyes, and imperial panegyric provided the framework which could set the imagination of the beholder on the right track.

Late antique art and panegyric, meeting, as they often did, in the portrayal of a ceremony, were means of making ideals and concepts tangible, insofar as this was possible. One of the processes which is being observed here in the context of accession is that by which the ceremony itself not only took over from art and panegyric, but also commanded and changed their content. A specific instance of this process occurred in the panegyric of Cassiodorus on Vitigis and Matasuntha, when the orator, as we have seen, interrupted himself to let the army acclaim their new ruler. In this way, the civilian panegyric was fused with the military acclamations, so that this particular accession ceremony included all members of society. The downfall of the Ostrogothic state soon after this ceremony took place belied a large part of the ceremony's message, for the message could find no practical expression. This notwithstanding, the performance of the ceremony of accession in this particular form demonstrates that in Ostrogothic Ravenna the imagery, whether literary or visual, of the ruler and his city had a much more broadly based foundation in the structure of society as envisaged in ceremonial, than did its fourth and fifth-century ancestry. As for the integration of civilians with soldiers in the framework of ceremonial, this theme will also emerge in early Byzantine coronation ceremonies.

9. EARLY BYZANTIUM

i. The Ceremony of Coronation

The literary descriptions of imperial accessions which have concerned us so far have all come from panegyrics and works of history. In either of these two contexts, an accession narrative could be relevant to the purpose of the author. For Byzantine accessions of the fifth and sixth centuries, however, we have a new type of document, the accession narratives, which were probably written by Peter the Patrician. They have come down to us as part of Constantine Porphyrogenitus' *De Ceremoniis*.[372]

Here the ceremonial of accession is recorded in its own right, and we find that, as in the other accounts we have considered, two different types of accession are recorded and differentiated. On the one hand, there are the accessions of Leo II and Justinian, who were crowned by Leo I and Justin I respectively. These accessions are analogous to earlier nominations of emperors by their senior colleagues.[373] On the other hand, there are the accessions of Leo I, Anastasius and Justin, when there was no senior emperor, although, in the case of the election of Anastasius, Ariadne, Zeno's widow, was central to the course of events.[374] This latter group of accessions also has late antique antecedents, principally the proclamation of Julian as Augustus in 361, when he was raised on a shield and crowned with a torque by the *hastatus* Maurus.[375]

This and the other accessions of emperors we have so far considered all occurred in a military setting. The election of the emperor was made by the army, or, in the case of a junior emperor being proposed, the army gave its consent, and then performed the ceremonial actions which officially and publicly validated the election. Shield-raising and crowning with a torque were military ceremonies, which continued to be performed in the city of Constantinople. While Leo was crowned with a torque, Anastasius, Justin, as well as later, Justin II, were not only crowned with a torque by a representative of the army, but were also raised on the shield. Justin II was the last to be thus crowned, while shield-raising continued for some time thereafter in military usurpations, but not in the context of the urban accession ceremonial of Constantinople.[376]

Ammianus' account of Julian's proclamation as Augustus makes it clear that the torque was a substitute for a diadem, which was not available. Despite this *ad hoc* choice of the torque, Julian's coronation with it does seem to have set a precedent, and the question is, why was this precedent observed for two hundred years? Here the role of the army as an elector of the emperor is worth bearing in mind.

It has been suggested that the torque, an ornament of the barbarian soldiers of the emperor as well as of certain Germanic deities, had a sacred significance which made its continuing use as a substitute for the diadem appropriate.[377] At the same time, however, the distinguishing mark of the emperor in imperial art from the fourth century was never a torque, but always the diadem, which the emperor actually wore.[378] It was principally the civilian population of the empire, to whom imperial monuments were addressed, who expected to see their emperor crowned with the diadem, and on this basis we may explain why, in

Constantinople, from the fifth century, coronation with a diadem followed the military coronation with a torque, thus making two coronations, one after the other.

Residence in Constantinople, rather than residence in the various frontier capitals of the empire, changed imperial ideology from a predominantly military to a more civilian and urban ideology, a process which Synesius in his *De Regno* observed and which he hoped to see reversed. The emperor's personal presence at victory in battle, as advertised in the panegyrics of the fourth century, was to an extent replaced by the emperor's personal presence at the recurring victories of the Hippodrome, which came to stand for imperial victory.[379]

As part of this change, coronation with the torque, a military insignia, was from the later sixth century displaced by coronation with the diadem, and coronation with the diadem was in due course performed by the patriarch in a church. Accordingly, it has been asked whether coronation with the torque was secular, while coronation with the diadem was ecclesiastical?[380] Also, it has been asked, which of these two acts had constitutional validity? The answer has been that in early Byzantium, coronation by the patriarch was a voluntary addition to the election and designation of the emperor by army and people, but that it became more important later.[381] Because it attributes marginal significance to a major ceremonial innovation which took place in an age when people were highly sensitive to ceremonial actions, this interpretation is unsatisfactory.[382] Also, it is misleading to distinguish between the secular and the ecclesiastical spheres in early Byzantium, for the distinction cannot be firmly anchored in the evidence.[383] Eusebius portrayed Constantine as involved in the church by virtue of his imperial position. Marcian was acclaimed at the council of Chalcedon as filling a priestly as well as an imperial role; Procopius praised Anastasius as priest and emperor,[384] and Ennodius attributed a similar status to Theodoric. In more general terms, the deacon Agapetus wrote for Justinian:

> Since you occupy a position more exalted than any other, honour above all God who has thus exalted you, for He gave you the sceptre of earthly rule in imitation of the kingship of heaven. . . .

> Above all other honours belonging to kingship does the crown of piety adorn the king. For riches go away and glory passes, but the fame of a divinely inspired government extends throughout all time and removes those who conduct it beyond the reach of forgetfulness.[385]

If we cannot, thus, distinguish absolutely between church and state in early Byzantium, we can, together with late Romans and early Byzantines, distinguish between the civil and military functions of the emperor,[386] and here, I think, lies the answer to double coronation. Coronation with torque or *corona* in the camp, as described by Ammianus, was a viable ceremonial as long as the imperial elections took place in a military milieu, but was no longer fully valid in an urban environment. Hence the double coronation, reported in the *Book of Ceremonies*.

The first of these is that of Leo I, and it is possible to distinguish a military and a civilian aspect to the ceremony. After Leo was crowned with a torque, the military standards were raised from the ground, and Leo was acclaimed. Next, behind a wall of shields, he was clothed in purple and diadem, and was given lance and shield, "and, appearing before the people in this way, he received the *proscynesis* of all the Senators, in order of their rank." [387]

The procedure for Anastasius was parallel. While the standards lay on the ground, he was crowned with a torque, the standards were raised, and the emperor was acclaimed by army and people. Then, in the triclinium, the patriarch crowned him with the diadem and clothed him in the purple, after which army and people acclaimed him once again. Possibly one may see a development in the ceremony between Leo and Anastasius in that under Leo the first set of acclamations have a military theme, while the second set were to the effect that Leo might rule many years, which may be called a civilian theme.

For Anastasius and successors the acclamations are not reported, and for them, unlike for Leo, there is no distinction made between the emperor's appearance before the army and his appearance before the people and the Senate. Thus, it seems that after Leo, the civilian and the military parts of the ceremony were more closely assimilated to each other. For Justin I, the procedure was the same as for Anastasius, but we are given the additional information that the imperial insignia were obtained before the coronation ceremony started.[388]

Thus, the civilian ceremony was added to the already existing military one; torque and diadem were the means of keeping the two distinct. There was need of a civilian ceremony as soon as the imperial election regularly took place in Constantinople, where the people were able to take up the role which that quasi-fiction of imperial elections, the theory of the *consensus universorum*,[389] had always attributed to them. They could now take an active part in imperial elections, and this active part was expressed in the ceremonial. As for the coronation, the senior emperor always retained the right to crown his colleague, while the patriarch filled this role when there was no senior emperor. The first instance is the coronation of Anastasius[390] when, according to the *Book of*

Ceremonies, Ariadne the Augusta, although deferred to in the election procedures and acclaimed as victorious, did not perform the coronation.

The emergence of the civil aspect of the ceremony of accession and of the participation of the people is perhaps best illustrated by the usurpation of Hypatius in the Nika riot.[391] It took place in Constantinople and had the support of the people, rather than the army, which is not mentioned in this context at all. As a civilian usurpation, this one is almost unique in late Roman history.

Once the civilian aspect of the accession ceremony had been developed in Constantinople, it was possible for this, like other Byzantine institutions, to be absorbed into the ritual of the church. At the same time, the strictly military aspects of the ceremony—coronation with the torque and elevation on the shield—were dropped. The ritual of accession was absorbed into the ritual of the church in that the patriarch crowned the emperor, initially in the hippodrome, and ultimately in S. Sophia.

But this cannot serve as a basis for the historian to distinguish between state and church in Byzantium in the Western fashion. How church and state interlocked[392] is illustrated by the acclamations with which the newly elected emperor was greeted. The terms in which Ammianus recorded accessions suggest that they were of a eulogistic character. But even in Ammianus, and more particularly in the Greek panegyrics that have been studied, the intervention of the godhead in imperial elections is regularly referred to. In the *De Ceremoniis* this divine intervention is voiced and highlighted in now Christian terms in the acclamations which were addressed to the newly elected emperor. At the election of Leo, "all began to shout":

> Give ear, oh God, we call on you. Hear us, oh God. To Leo, life. Give ear, oh God. Leo shall rule. Oh God, who loves mankind,[393] the commonalty asks for Leo as emperor; the army asks for Leo as emperor; the laws are ready to receive Leo; the palace is ready to receive Leo.[394] These are the prayers of the palace; these are the desires of the army; these are the prayers of the Senate; these are the prayers of the people. The world expects Leo. The army receives Leo. Let Leo come, he, the ornament of all. Leo shall rule, he, the good of all. Give ear, oh Lord, we call on you.[395]

After the coronation with the torque, the people again shout:

> Leo Augustus, you conquer, you are pious, you are worshipful. God has given you, God shall keep you. Worshipping Christ, you conquer always. Leo shall rule for many years. God will protect the Christian Empire.[396]

Having been adorned with purple and diadem, and having received the *proscynesis* of the Senate, together with further acclamations, Leo in his own address to the people himself acknowledged the divine and human *consensus* which made him emperor:

> [I] Emperor, Caesar, Leo, Victor, and always worshipful, [say]: God almighty, and your judgement, most powerful fellow-soldiers, have felicitously made me emperor of the Roman commonwealth. From all came the shout: Leo Augustus, you conquer; he who has chosen you will preserve you. God will guard his own elect. God will keep a holy empire. [He is] holy and mighty.[397]

The acclamations which were made to Anastasius after he had received the insignia ran:

> Lord have mercy; Son of God, have mercy on him; Anastasius Augustus, you conquer; God will keep a holy emperor; God has given you, God will keep you.[398]

And when Justin was elected, the people shouted, after his investiture with the imperial insignia:

> Well-being to the world. As you have lived, so rule. Well-being to the Commonwealth. King of Heaven, preserve the King on earth. Justin Augustus, you conquer. Many years for the new Constantine. We are the slaves of the emperor.[399]

Here a hierarchy is established between God, the King of Heaven, and the emperor, and thence, indirectly, between the emperor and his subjects, his slaves. In this hierarchy there was no room for a distinction such as the Western one of the two swords.

The theme of the emperor's election by God is also expressed in the personal accounts by emperors of their own election.[400] The definitive ceremonial expression of divine intervention in imperial accession appears in the acclamations addressed to the newly elected Nikephorus Phocas. In these acclamations the image on the gold multiple of 330, showing Constantine crowned by the hand of God with a circlet (plate 45), was translated into words, for the people shouted, "Receive Nikephorus, crowned by God."[401]

The stages in imperial coronation that have been traced are: first, Julian's military coronation with a torque, which has fourth-century parallels; second, the double coronation with torque and diadem which took place in Constantinople in the fifth and sixth centuries, and which we have interpreted as being, initially, two separate ceremonies, military and civilian, which were then fused into one; and third, the civilian ceremony of coronation with the diadem by the senior Augustus or the patriarch.

The elections of the fourth century, because they were made by or in the presence of the army, could only register, *de facto*, the support of the soldiers, although the claim of universal consent, implying citizens, was nonetheless made and could, in the fourth century, be articulated in *adventus*. In the urban community of Constantinople it was possible for this theory of the consent of all, soldiers and citizens, to find some practical application. Even if the people took no active part in the election, they were present in the hippodrome to express their consent once the candidate was proposed, by acclaiming him.

These acclamations of consent are interesting in that they enumerate the factors involved. For Leo, the people shouted that he was desired by τὸ πρᾶγμα τὸ δημόσιον, the army, the laws, the palace, the Senate and the world, κόσμος. Anastasius was welcomed as emperor by κοιναὶ εὐχαὶ and the οἰκουμένη; Justin by the army, and the world,[402] while the acclamations welcoming Nikephorus were almost identical to those addressed to Leo I. It should perhaps be pointed out that the church was never mentioned in the acclamations, showing once more that church and state were not conceived of as distinct from each other. The church and the state were composed of the same people, and their wishes were expressed in the same set of acclamations.

There is one further point to be noted in the ceremonial of accession as disclosed in Eusebius, Ammianus and the *De Ceremoniis*. According to Eusebius, the ceremonies of Constantine's accession took place, stage by stage, alongside those of Constantius' burial, so that Constantine, when he finally stood before the army as Augustus, could be called the ἀναβίωσις of his father, who had just been buried. In Ammianus similarly, in the three cases where the death of an emperor leads to the election of a successor, the rites to be performed over the dead emperor are recounted alongside those whereby the successor was appointed. The beginnings of the funerary rites for Julian, Jovian and Valentinian I open the procedures for the election of the successor, so that, as in Eusebius, the performance of the state funeral of his predecessor was among the new emperor's first official actions.

As has been seen in the discussion of *consecratio*, the parallel enactment of the two ceremonies—the funeral of the old and the election of the new emperor—preserved a certain continuity in imperial dominion and was also the last vestige of the rite of *consecratio*, which in former days the succeeding emperor bestowed on his predecessor. The *De Ceremoniis* relates the accession of Anastasius after Zeno's death, which is explicitly mentioned. Ariadne appointed Anastasius as Zeno's successor, Zeno's funeral was prepared,[403] and only then was Anastasius crowned with the torque and raised on the shield. At the election of Justin I, Justin, "he who was divinely elected[404] but then count of the excubitors," addressed the palace troops:

> Our Lord, being a man, has died. Therefore we must all take council together and elect him who is pleasing to God and a support to the commonwealth.[405]

Corippus relates this same procedure of the death of one emperor and the succession of the next in greater detail, as we shall now go on to see.

ii. Divine Election as a Regular Theme in and Definition of Accession

It remains to be seen how far panegyric and imperial art reflect the framework provided by the De Ceremoniis. There are two panegyrics on Anastasius, one in Latin by the grammarian Priscian, and one in Greek, by the rhetor Procopius of Gaza. These two panegyrics, roughly contemporary with each other, differ, as might be expected, as regards their cultural background, but they do not differ so much in content. Priscian praises first of all Anastasius' descent, attributing to him Pompey the Great as an ancestor, then his personal virtues and compares him to the Roman emperors of that golden age of Romans, the second century. Procopius proceeds in similar fashion but in more detail. He praises Anastasius' home Epidamnus, and, less specifically, his family, and next his personal virtues. Procopius observes the rules of writing panegyrics to the letter: the scheme praising home country, family and the individual himself is exactly Menander's sequence. Priscian, who knew this sequence,[406] also observed it, but less obviously so.

In short, both panegyrists establish, in compliance with the rules of their literary genre, the emperor's claim to dominion. Part of this claim consists of an enumeration of the emperor's personal virtues. A reflection of this convention may be found in the acclamations addressed to Anastasius and Justin I at their accession, exhorting them to rule as they lived.[407] Both panegyrists also emphasise the change for the better which set in with the beginning of Anastasius' reign.[408] These are all themes familiar from earlier panegyrics.

Like the earlier panegyrists, Priscian and Procopius also make a double claim for Anastasius' right to succeed, when a single one might have been sufficient. Priscian begins his panegyric with the highly significant lines:

Receive my Latin poem with kindly heart, receive what I am accustomed to offer to the celestial king for his gift of life and the lovely light
of the sun. You will understand, most just Emperor of right mind, that
in my poem God whom you follow is made propitious, God who gave
you your dominion, to whom alone you owe all your fortune, and
whatever you achieved in peace or in war.[409]

The complicated and lengthy process of election described in *De Ceremoniis* is here summarised by the one element which became increasingly important in Byzantine imperial propaganda: *Deus qui tibi regna
dedit.*

Procopius is brief in his description of the election of Anastasius, but
it contains most of the features which, as has been seen, were of importance in the ceremonial:

In truth, some divine decree directed the vote in your favour, and the
people all together cried out as though one thought moved them all.
The great Senate supported them and the empress agreed. The vote
was carried.[410]

Dominion by divine gift heads this enumeration, but it is followed at
once by the inspirational election of Anastasius by the people, to which
is added the voice of the Senate and Ariadne. The panegyric *topos* of the
consensus omnium had come to coincide with a certain part of the ceremony of election, that is, with the acclamations which were addressed
to the emperor. However, Procopius leaves out the crowning moment of
the ceremony, the coronation of the emperor, and in so doing, he also
omits all mention of the army, for their contribution in the accession of
Anastasius did not consist in actually electing him (this was done by
Ariadne with the advice of the Senate, as Procopius and the *Book of Ceremonies* state) but in crowning him with the torque and raising him on the
shield.

The military coronation was the most conservative element in imperial accession in late fifth-century Byzantium. It continued to find expression in the ceremony of accession, but the soldiers were not the
electors of the emperor in the same overriding sense as they had been in
the fourth century. This becomes clear as soon as one compares Procopius' account to any panegyric of the fourth century describing an accession. In the latter, the military aspect together with divine election,
sometimes supplemented by dynastic considerations and personal
merit, predominate, whatever the exact circumstances; whereas Procopius had in mind the civic imperial election which took place in Constantinople. In this civic election, the people of Constantinople had
largely usurped the role formerly played by the army.

Victory had become more metaphorical in this urban context, and Ariadne, who would not lead an army in war, could thus nonetheless, like the emperor, be acclaimed *tu vincas*. The hippodrome had become the scene of victory as it had become the scene of elections; the hippodrome supplanted the military camp, as the people supplanted the soldiers. This was one expression of those manifold meanings so cherished by Byzantines. The ceremony of accession came to embrace, as was explicitly stated in the acclamations, the ceremony of triumph.

Procopius of Gaza and Priscian say little about ceremonies of accession, although Procopius does make clear the changes in meaning which had taken place. It needed the transformation of panegyric, an analytical composition, into epic, or, more broadly, narrative and description,[411] to take due account of the development of the actual ceremonial of accession. Our example here is Corippus' *Laus Justini*, which is a detailed account of Justin II's accession.

Just as Procopius' opening concept on the accession had been Anastasius' choice by God, so in Corippus: Justin has a dream in which the Virgin tells him of Justinian's death and enumerates his claims to the throne. God and Justinian, in that order, chose him.[412] Next the Senators, headed by Calinius, come to him and offer him the empire, because Justinian had already chosen him.[413] There is also the sentence, echoing the *De Ceremoniis*: "The Laws call you, the court welcomes you."[414]

Justin, in accord with the panegyric *topos*, but no longer with the ceremonial, refuses to rule but is finally convinced and enters the palace,[415] thereby making the traditional gesture of taking possession of the empire. Then, in the palace, the funerary rites for Justinian begin,[416] and when the day dawns, the people assemble in the hippodrome, which, Corippus explains, is a symbol for the world, and acclaim Justin as the new phoenix risen from the ashes of the old:

> All people, boys, young and old men, all with one voice and one mind acclaim him: the one name pleases all. Just as when the phoenix renews its burnt-out vigour when rising from its pyre . . . so the glory of the empire, so the sacred letter I has risen again from his end, and in the emperor Justin of the upright name lives again Justinian his author. The people, moved by love for their lord, ran together from all sides. . . . 'May you conquer, Justin' they sing; the huge uproar grows, and mourning departed from the palace when new joy came. The sound arouses everyone. All the elements support Justin, everything rejoices with him. Called forth by the clamour, all the Senators approach. Light fills the sacred palace, . . . God Himself gave clear signs and confirmed the election, to place on Justin's head the glorious crown of empire.[417]

At this point Justin and Sophia were not present in the hippodrome, but were praying in the palace.[418] These acclamations correspond to those which, as recorded in the *De Ceremoniis*, were made before the chosen emperor actually appeared.[419]

Corippus' comparison between the hippodrome and the world is important in this context, as it is also in the context of Byzantine triumphs. The emperor is lord of the city and the world, *urbis et orbis*,[420] for this expression as applied to emperors of Rome was transferred to the Byzantine emperor. The acclamation "the city desires you, the *oikoumene* desires you," when sung in the hippodrome of Constantinople, which stood for the world, acquired a more realistic meaning because of this symbolism. Constantinople had now supplanted Rome.

As I have attempted to show, the formation of a ceremony in late antique Rome and in Byzantium points to the formation of a viewpoint, even a theory. The Constantinopolitan ceremonial of accession showed the city and the empire in theory at one. This is an important development, even if it remained, largely, a theory expressed, for instance, in the analogy between the hippodrome and the world. What was less theoretical, as has been said above, was the involvement of the people of Constantinople in imperial accessions.

In the *De Ceremoniis* and Corippus the *consensus omnium* of earlier panegyrics is factually expressed in the acclamations which were made by all, as in the passage cited above, and again when Justin was crowned by the patriarch.[421] The worldwide significance of imperial accession is repeatedly expressed by Corippus, who emphasises the participation of the elements in it,[422] a point which, as has been seen, was also made in earlier panegyrics.

While the people acclaimed them, Justin and Sophia prayed in the palace, and, as also stated in the *De Ceremoniis* account of the accession of Justin I, the insignia were made ready.[423] Justin's investiture with the insignia, as described by Corippus, progressed exactly as stated in the *De Ceremoniis*, except for the first episode, since Justin was invested initially with the imperial purple shoes:

> And he shod his royal feet in purple shoes (of) Parthian leather . . .
> which had been chosen to adorn the imperial feet—those feet with
> which the conqueror is wont to trample subject tyrants underfoot and
> to tame barbarian necks. Only emperors may accept such noble attire,
> for under their feet is the blood of kings.[424]

Next, Justin was clothed in the chlamys:

> The chlamys covering the emperor's shoulders surrounds him with
> shining purple, and, adorned with reddish gold outshines the sun

when the emperor stretches forth his right hand. A hooked golden
fibula held the chlamys together, and the jewel pendants which hung
down from it on chains shed their light (cf. plate 61)—those jewels, the
fruits of the blessed victory in the Gothic war, which Ravenna, obeying
her lords, returned, and those other jewels which Belisarius brought
from the Vandal court. Blessed Justinian, those tokens of your triumphs will endure while Justin rules the world in safety.[425]

The chlamys thus was a token of victory and triumph. Justin now had
the torque placed round his neck:

> The sacred circlet of gold, placed round Justin's neck by the hand of Ar-
> matus, bestowed on him the exalted empire. Armatus offered it three
> times, three times extending his right hand with his offering, he said,
> 'Justin Augustus, I bestow on you your office.' And the emperor said,
> 'And I command that you shall be made a tribune.' Blessed is Armatus,
> who was the first to hear the words spoken, and was the first to receive
> a solemn gift from the emperor.[426]

Then Justin was raised on the shield by four young men:

> Now the greatest benefactor of the entire world is present. Before him
> lie low the necks of subject kings who tremble at his name and adore
> his sacred person. On that shield stands the most mighty emperor,
> looking like the sun; another light shines from the city. One single
> blessed day is amazed that two suns rise together. Or has my song now
> transgressed due measure? You may perhaps marvel that I said that
> twin suns rise together. But, if you ponder it, you must not think that
> this my utterance has passed my lips as empty words or pointless meta-
> phor: the mind of a just man shines more brightly than the sun. It is not
> submerged in the waves, does not give way to darkness, and is not cov-
> ered by dusky shadow. The light of good deeds shines with the eternal
> splendour.[427]

This again is an expression of triumph and victory, more abstractly so
than the donning of the shoes and the chlamys. Merged into the triumph is the old imagery of the Augustus as *sol oriens*, the rising sun,
which had, in the third-century iconography of the coinage, been an image for the coming of the emperor.[428]

Finally the patriarch crowned Justin amid the acclamations of the
Senate and people, who wished perpetual dominion for Justin and
Sophia: *regnate pares in saecula*.[429] Then, seated on his throne—evoking
the numismatic image of the enthroned emperor—Justin addressed the
Senate and was acclaimed. Accompanied by the Senate, he addressed
the people in the hippodrome, where he was also acclaimed, this time
by alternate groups. Justin's first official act was the reception of Avar
ambassadors to whom he refused to pay the subsidy which Justinian
had paid. Here also the element of triumph and victory is emphasised.

Corippus' account ends with Justin taking up the consulship, which could form part of the procedures of imperial accession.[430]

Several points should be noted about this account. First, the investiture with the chlamys, formerly the operative act of accession, is only one element in the proceedings; unlike the other parts of the ceremony, it is not followed by acclamations, and therefore is probably of lesser importance. This is a change from the accession ceremonies described in the De Ceremoniis, which, apart from the accession of Nikephorus Phocas, are all earlier. Here, investiture with the chlamys had been part of the main ceremonial of accession. By contrast, the positioning of investiture with the chlamys among the preliminaries of the ceremony of accession in Corippus highlights the investiture with the torque and the shield-raising, which formed the military constituent of the ceremony, while the subsequent coronation with the diadem by the patriarch formed the civilian constituent.

Second, Corippus' account of Justin's accession throughout has a triumphal character, beginning with the speech by the Virgin in Justin's dream.[431] The actual accession ceremony, when Justin put on the imperial shoes, is an occasion to bring to mind the calcatio colli of fallen kings, and the fibula holding the emperor's purple sparkles with jewels captured from Goths and Vandals. The shield-raising also is made an act of triumph,[432] and when Justin meets the embassy of the Avars, he asserts Roman victoriousness, although he has not fought a single battle against them. Here, as well as elsewhere, the accession ceremonial proclaims not only accession itself, but the result of accession, victory. In this, as we have seen, ceremonial and imperial art worked hand in hand.

Finally, Corippus' account still discloses the multiple claims which were made on behalf of the emperor. On the one hand, he dreams that he is crowned by the Virgin, and in the coronation ceremonial he is said to be crowned by God, and chosen by God. But on the other hand, he has also been chosen by his predecessor, the Senate and the people, whose consent was expressed in the acclamations. The multiple claims are, however, weighted towards one side which was to become more important in the future: namely, election by God. Parallel to what is said in the Book of Ceremonies, Justin, in his address to the Senate, stated this in unequivocal terms, his election by Justinian and the Senate notwithstanding:

> God who rules over all kingdoms has bestowed on us our ancestral dominion and granted us our father's diadem, and the creator of all things has imposed on us the cares of ruling which he himself has caused to exist. We praise the work of our creator and look up to the awesome King of all. We render thanks and acknowledge our gratitude. What-

ever we are, we declare it truly, comes from him. . . . One living crea-
ture is composed of several members, but it is the head that rules the
members. And thus God the creator, making man, [commanded] that
the head should rule over all the limbs.[433]

He then launches into an exposition of the ancient simile which likens
the state to the human body, the emperor, under God, being the head.
This simile is further elaborated in Justin's address to the people. As the
acclamations for Nikephorus Phocas still show, however, the element of
the emperor's election by the people was never dropped altogether. In
that sense the Byzantine ceremonial of accession always portrayed a reality as much as a theory. Hence also, it was never absolutely fixed and
static.[434] Details could be changed from one occasion to the next, and no
two accounts of accession are exactly alike. The notion of election by
God did, however, acquire increasing importance at the time when the
idea of the emperor as the agent of God was also worked out in the Byzantine context, above all by the deacon Agapetus.

It is in this context that the nomination of Tiberius as Caesar should
be considered.[435] The framework is familiar from Ammianus and the *De
Ceremoniis* for the election of a co-emperor, and was re-enacted at the
accession of Maurice.[436] Justin addressed a short speech to Tiberius, and
the rites customary for an imperial accession were performed. We have
here the constituents of a *consensus omnium*, but Justin's choice and his
address to Tiberius form the operative element in the accession. In his
address, Justin pointed away from himself and to God as the elector of
the emperor.[437] This was followed by a series of counsels for Tiberius'
conduct as emperor. As regarded himself, Justin said:

> Do not imitate me in making enmities. For I, being a man, have been
> repaid because I have erred and have received according to my sins.
> But I shall plead my case against those who also have done this to me
> before the judgement seat of Christ. Do not let this imperial garb elate
> you, as I let it happen. Care for everyone as you would for yourself.
> Think what you were and what you are now. Do not be overbearing,
> and do not sin. You know who I was, who I became, and who I am. All
> these are your children and your slaves.[438]

And finally, when the patriarch had prayed, and Tiberius had fallen at
Justin's feet, Justin said:

> If you so wish it, I am; if you so wish it, I am not. God who has made
> heaven and earth and all creation, will himself put into your heart what
> I have forgotten to tell you.[439]

This is the other aspect of the emperor's election by God. There are
extremes at both ends: on the one hand, the emperor is raised above all

his subjects; they are his slaves, his children, just as they are the slaves and the children of God. On the other hand, precisely because of his exalted position, the emperor can be abased more than any of his subjects when he falls from his station: "If you will it, I am; if you will it, I am not." The empress Theodora, when placed face to face with this possibility during the Nika riot, had still rejected it out of hand: "The empire makes a good shroud." That proud statement summarises the attitude to empire of the age of Justinian, which was still voiced in the panegyric of Corippus, and which found a distant echo in the early seventh century in the words of a Lakhmid queen faced with exile.[440]

Theodora considered the imperial dignity inalienable. The station of the emperor had explicitly become one which marked its bearer for life, a view which had already been expressed by the panegyric of 307. The Christian concept of empire added one crucial qualification to this view: on the one hand, it idealised the Christian emperor, and on the other, the grounds for criticism of him became that much more fundamental. It was not only inefficient government or military defeat that were thought to disqualify an emperor from filling his station, but also sin. *Consecratio* after death, despite the accompanying hazard of *damnatio memoriae*, had been a less precarious way of exalting the emperor. The results of failure were less calamitous.

The overall development of the theme of accession can be summarised as follows. At no time in the period treated had there been a definite, hard and fast rule about how an emperor should be elected, and who should be elected. Certain strands have been identified, however, some of which are regularly present in imperial accession: the dynastic claim, the consent of all, election as a reward for personal virtues, and, most important perhaps, because most flexible, divine election. The link between the emperor and his capital, which was transformed into a link between the emperor and the people of the capital, plays a role; the moment of the emperor's first entrance into his palace can be highlighted.

In art, and to a certain extent in panegyric, even in Corippus, accession was described and understood not so much in terms of the actual moment, but in terms of long-term results: a golden age would begin; the new emperor would be victorious. Hence we have the imagery of the enthroned emperor and the emperor with his soldiers, as on the *largitio* dish of Valentinian I. This latter image applies as much to Valentinian I as it does to the military aspect of the accession ceremonial in the *De Ceremoniis*.

In Byzantium, first documented in the mid-fifth century, the somewhat diverse body of ideas concerned with accession was formed into regular, coherent ceremonial which was adaptable for particular cases but had some uniformity and consistency. We have traced how the more or less random and abstract ideas on imperial accession acquired a definite and specific form in the ceremonial, and a less definite and specific but nonetheless consistent form in art. Ceremonial made theories concrete. Thus, the general action of the emperor being crowned and acclaimed on a variety of occasions for victory became concentrated on the accession. Once the accession ceremonial had been shaped, it was possible to form theories on the basis of it. This happens already to a degree in Corippus, where Justin's addresses to the Senate and the people, which are incorporated into the panegyric account of the accession, express a theory of the position of the emperor which is enacted in the emperor's coronation; and the theory is supported by descriptions of ceremonial actions.

George of Pisidia also wrote an account of an accession, that of the emperor Heraclius in 610.[441] Here, by contrast to Corippus, nothing at all is said about the ceremony of accession. Rather, Heraclius' accession, his liberation of Constantinople from the tyrant Phocas, is described in terms of the theory of divine election. There is no *consensus omnium*, no mention of the Senate, the people, the army or the city, and no mention of coronation, although Heraclius was in fact crowned by the patriarch Sergius.[442] An earlier panegyrist would have felt obliged to clothe Heraclius' accession in an elaborate framework of the ancient multiple claims; not so George of Pisidia. Heraclius' accession is described entirely in terms of his relationship with God and of his war against evil as personified in the tyrant Phocas, and against external enemies.

This poem shows that it was still possible for a Byzantine of the early seventh century to think of the accession of the Byzantine emperor in the abstractions of Hellenistic theories of kingship. The concepts which are used—the kinship between Heraclius' soul and the *logos* of God, the consideration of his ψυχικὰ κινήματα and λογισμός, his ἔρως for God and his ψυχικὸν κάλλος which he imprints on others, the designation of Heraclius as χορηγὸς τῶν καλῶν χαρισμάτων as well as the allusion to the simile of the 'ship of state'[443]—are reminiscent of the panegyrics of Themistius. But unlike Themistius, George of Pisidia could create his topic out of the now fixed ceremonial of accession, which expressed concretely and in Christian terms the ideas Themistius voiced in the abstract.

Here, at the end of our survey of late Roman and Byzantine accessions, we may observe how ancient pagan terms survived in Christian contexts. In late antique panegyric and art, and later in Byzantium there were always the two strands, constantly interacting, but ever since Eusebius not in inevitable open conflict: the classical, formerly pagan, and the Christian. However, the account we have examined of the accession of Tiberius discloses an aspect of the Christian view of empire which could not have grown out of pagan philosophy alone. In Justin's speech of advice to his successor the age-old counsels to kings are once more repeated but in a context which discloses a view of personal tragedy conceived in terms of sin, such as paganism could never have produced.

iii. The Accompanying Imagery

We have studied the evolution of the ceremonial of coronation in the *De Ceremoniis*, the description of that ceremonial in Corippus' *Laus Justini* and the more abstract treatment of Heraclius' accession by George of Pisidia. It remains to be seen how this ceremony was reflected in art.

In the accessions of the *De Ceremoniis* the emperor is acclaimed with the words, "God has given you, God will preserve you." Justin II dreamt that he was crowned by the Theotokos, and metaphorically was said to be crowned by God, and Nikephoros was acclaimed as crowned by God. Justin, in his dream, is crowned with the diadem, not the torque, showing that the diadem was now the operative insignia. In this context we may mention a series of coins of the early fifth century, stretching from Honorius and Arcadius to Zenonis, the empress of Basiliscus, where on the obverse the imperial head is crowned by the hand of God with a diadem.[444] (Plates 46, 59) Another set of coins, issued for Honorius, Valentinian III and Leo, shows on the reverse the emperor, crowned by the hand of God and treading on a human-faced serpent, embodiment of the Arian Vandals.[445] Since Valentinian is crowned by the hand of God, but not the senior emperor, Theodosius, one may relate these solidi to the accession of Valentinian III.

The iconography of the divine hand is reminiscent of the multiple of Constantius II showing Constantine thus crowned (plate 45). The human-faced serpent series showing the emperor crowned by the hand of God on the reverse continued until Leo I, who in the *De Ceremoniis* is said to have been acclaimed as the chosen by God, but the issues which show crowning by the hand of God on the obverse were produced for Arcadius and Honorius and thereafter only for empresses. In the fifth century the iconography of the hand of God crowning the emperor was perhaps still felt to be too explicit and direct a statement of the link between emperor and God.

There is another object which may be mentioned in this context. This is a gold amulet showing on one side an emperor standing facing, hold-

ing globe and cross.[446] He is approached from either side by the personified sun and moon and in the centre, above the emperor's head, is a
hand holding a wreath between the symbols of the sun and moon. The
iconography of this amulet should not be over-stressed because, unlike
the coinage, it is not strictly speaking official. However, it does illustrate
admirably the divine choice of the emperor in a Christian context, with
the symbolism of cosmic rule, which the pagan empire had also used,
applied to an imperial crowning as is done in the shield-raising scene by
Corippus.[447]

The iconography of the emperor crowned by the hand of God was
not further elaborated or even continued in early Byzantium. This line
of thought in art was brought to its conclusion on a set of ivories of the
late ninth and early tenth centuries which show the emperor crowned
by the Virgin or Christ; divinity here is no longer represented by a symbol but is present in person. Similar iconographies appeared at the same
time on the coinage.[448] In early Byzantium, however, although the emperor was said to have been given by God, artists were still reluctant
to show divinity and the emperor in the same picture and in the same
framework. On the rare occasions when the emperor was shown crowned
by God, he was crowned by the impersonal hand of God, not by God or
Christ himself.

Earlier we interpreted the image of the emperor enthroned as a representation of the results of accession. In early Byzantium this image was
not used nearly as frequently as in late antique Rome. However, a set of
coins shows Justin and Justinian enthroned side by side, and when Justinian became sole ruler, he was to be seen enthroned alone.[449] Justin II
and Sophia were shown enthroned side by side[450] (plate 58), and Maurice had himself depicted on the coinage in similar fashion, enthroned
side by side with Constantina.[451] In some cases his designated successor
Theodosius was shown on the reverse of such issues,[452] so that a dynastic policy was declared. Following the model of his predecessor and of
Justin II, Phocas had himself represented standing with Leontina.[453] A
panegyric precedent for this concept of the emperor and empress ruling
jointly was set by Corippus.

We discussed above the consular diptych of Probus, showing the emperor Honorius (plate 6), and commented on the lack of imagination
and content of that diptych. The pagan imagery of the past had disappeared and had not yet been replaced by any Christian imagery. This
gap was filled during the following generation, and involved a complex
reorientation in imperial art. Two diptychs, generally attributed to the
empress Ariadne and dated c. 500 A.D. are relevant here.[454] (Plate 61)

Both show the empress inside a vaulted *aedicula*, with curtains drawn aside. Two eagles perch on the *aedicula*, one on either side, which on one diptych hold a garland between them—remnants of imperial pagan Rome. On the latter diptych, the empress is shown standing. She holds a sceptre and globe with cross, wears a jewelled chlamys and necklace and a diadem with long strings of pearls. The segment of her chlamys shows the bust of an emperor raising the consular mappa.

The other diptych shows the empress seated on a throne, holding a globe with cross in her left, and stretching out her right hand in a gesture of *adlocutio*. She is dressed and jewelled as in the first diptych. The throne is slightly recessed into the *aedicula*, so that this diptych in particular gives an impression of depth, of the third dimension, showing how the empress is enthroned within her palace and looking out. Although this diptych is Eastern, the closest literary parallel is the panegyric of Cassiodorus where he describes the beauty of Matasuntha in her palace, adorned in her jewels. The diptych, unlike the panegyric, cannot be directly associated with an accession, but shows a more general aspect of majesty and empire.

When the Ariadne diptychs are compared to the consular diptych of Probus, the contrast could not be more complete. The elaborate *aedicula*, the finely stylised and three-dimensional acanthus of the column capitals, the eagles, the jewelled empress herself, and the colourful character of the image, all point to a fertile imagination which had at its disposal a variegated repertoire of images. Unlike Honorius, the empress is shown in a civilian context, and could not be shown in any other way; nonetheless, the aptness of this civilian imagery and its wide scope are revealing. Just as the empress Ariadne was acclaimed in the hippodrome "you conquer," so the empress on the diptych stands in an *aedicula* surmounted by triumphal eagles which in one case hold a laurel garland of victory in their beaks. She wears the chlamys which, originally a military garment, had now become court attire.

If we were to use the vocabulary of Corippus and Claudian, we would say that the chlamys was adorned with the jewels of conquered barbarians, of Italy and Africa. Both in Claudian, and in the context of accession in Corippus, the imperial jewels have a triumphal connotation, and in images depicting victory or triumph jewels are offered to the emperor.[455] The seated empress makes the gesture of *adlocutio*. There were many occasions on which a ruler could address his subjects. Among them were the military *adlocutio* and the speech from the throne at the accession, as reported by Corippus. Justin II first addressed the Senate in the palace and then the people in the hippodrome. It is an address from the palace that the diptych represents, such as Corippus describes.

By contrast to the diptych of Honorius, the triumphal and military imagery on the diptychs of Ariadne is conveyed in an idiom of urban, metropolitan luxury. The diptych of Honorius is austere, simple, and somewhat empty. It has neither the intense vigour of the Barletta statue (plate 7), nor the richness of imagery of the Ariadne diptychs. A comparison of the Ariadne diptychs with that of Honorius reveals the same as a comparison of panegyrics from the fourth and the later fifth and sixth centuries: the transition from an emperor oriented towards the army to an emperor oriented towards a city, Constantinople.

The two ivories of the empress in her *aedicula*, holding her cross-bearing globe and her sceptre in one hand, and holding the globe or making the gesture of *adlocutio* with the other, are generalised, non-specific images, which relate to no particular point in time. Yet, as has been seen, they can be interpreted in terms of a specific context, for the various imperial gestures and attributes bring to mind particular aspects of majesty. These images, although created for a certain occasion, perhaps an imperial consulship, are deliberately not formed to apply to that occasion alone. Their intention and meaning are non-historical, non-specific; they translate and transfer the urban ceremonial of Constantinople into a chronologically and geographically wider setting.

iv. San Vitale

The imperial mosaics in S. Vitale have a similar intention and meaning. The building of this church, although it had been planned before the Byzantine reconquest of Ravenna, was probably only begun after the reconquest in 540, while the mosaics were set under Bishop Maximian, who appears in one of them. The date of dedication fell in the year 547 A.D.[456] (Plates 62–63)

The mosaics of San Vitale are the last major work of imperial art to survive before Iconoclasm. After Iconoclasm, as is shown by the ninth- and tenth-century ivory reliefs already referred to, concepts of the majesty and coronation of the emperor had settled into another form. We can see that these ivories were related to the world of late antiquity, in that words were written in late antiquity which can be used to expound them. Nonetheless, they belong to a different world. They are, in their message, straightforward, they communicate one single idea. But in late antique imperial art nothing was ever straightforward in this way. The images that have been examined—other than a number of the abbreviations on the coinage—always have many strands, not only as regards the political concept they convey, but also as regards their cultural and theological background.

The procedures of imperial accession were crystallised into a ceremony in the fifth century, which allowed most of the nuances and innuendos of an earlier period to be played upon. Yet in itself, the ceremony followed a basic pattern. Like the imperial mosaics in San Vitale it was in fact deceptively simple, and like those mosaics, carried meaning on many levels. The ceremony allowed the people of Constantinople to participate. Similarly, on the mosaics, the imperial couple make an offering which may be seen as parallel to the offering made by their subjects at the offertory of the liturgy.

Yet the imperial insignia and the positioning of the mosaics in the church remove Justinian and Theodora from any everyday context. Moreover, the couple are differentiated from each other by the company and the spatial environment in which they appear. Company and environment highlight the complex network of concepts which made up the status of the emperor elected and crowned by God, yet also chosen by his people and desired by the laws, the palace, the city and the world, the emperor who, according to Agapetus, needed only God and who, according to George of Pisidia, was enthroned with Justice, or, according to Corippus, with Wisdom, Sophia, who was at the same time his consort.

Like other works of imperial art, the mosaics of San Vitale were produced at a certain time for a certain occasion, but they were intended to retain their significance independently of that occasion, once it was past and forgotten. For that reason, their significance had to be wider than that of the occasion which led to their production. The mosaics show Justinian and Theodora each carrying an offering, making an imperial gesture in the framework of the Christian liturgy. The *De Ceremoniis* notes the offering to the Church made by emperors on their accession. Nonetheless, it is, of course, not Justinian's offering at his accession that is referred to in the mosaic. The gesture of making the offering, however, was the same whatever the occasion, and thereby it acquired the timelessness which is here being discussed.[457] Majesty was lasting. At the accession, as Corippus and other panegyrists say, echoed by the *De Ceremoniis*, the subjects looked forward to a new period of happiness, a lasting state. It was this lasting state, which on numerous occasions the emperors impressed on their subjects. With this intention, Justinian legislated that documents be headed not only with the consular date and the indiction, but first of all with the regnal year of the emperor.[458]

Thus, Justinian attended by two courtiers, by another dignitary who is shown behind him on his left, by Maximian the bishop with two clerics, and by his barbarian soldiers, the supporters of his dominion, and Theodora, attended by her ladies and courtiers, make their offerings. They wear the imperial jewels reminiscent of triumph—particularly appropriate in recently conquered Ravenna—the purple chlamys and, in Justinian's case, the purple imperial shoes beneath which are to be imagined, according to Corippus, fallen kings. The two mosaics will be considered first of all each by itself, then as related to each other, and finally as related to the decoration of the apse as a whole.

In the Justinian mosaic, the emperor's whereabouts are not specified, and I think this is deliberate. In that *kosmos* of the imperial ἔνθεος φρόνησις[459] which is depicted, the emperor is the centre. Next to the emperor, who is identified by his insignia, chlamys, diadem and purple shoes, walks Maximian the archbishop of Ravenna, also identified by his insignia of office, the priestly garments and the jewelled cross, which he holds in his right hand. The emperor is slightly off-centre in the composition as a whole, while the archbishop is set to one side. Justinian is followed by his dignitaries, civil and military, just as Maximian is followed by his clerics. The picture thus has a certain internal balance. It is not to be mentally cut in half, however. We cannot say that the emperor has precedence because he occupies the centre of the picture and has more followers, who occupy more space than the followers of Maximian. The composition is more subtle than this.

What is shown, if one studies how the feet of the figures are arranged and cut across each other, is three rows of people. In the first, nearest the altar, is Maximian with his two priests. The second row consists of the emperor with his attendants. Justinian walks slightly ahead of his three courtiers, as may be seen from the position of his feet. The last row is made up of the barbarian body guards, one of whom carries a great green shield inscribed with the Chi Rho. Thus, those who are furthest away from the altar are marked with the sign of the church even more prominently than the bishop himself.

The mosaic was not intended to be looked at once and to be comprehended in one single linear mental process; rather, it was intended to be contemplated. The onlooker was to weave his thoughts as the panegyrist Corippus wove his verses, around each person in turn. When thus considered, the emperor does not have any absolute priority over the other figures, and this impression is heightened when one considers the colours and the outlines of the mosaic. By ignoring the rules of linear, single-focused perspective, the artist has placed Justinian both in front of and behind his archbishop, and integrated him into the surrounding group. The colours of Justinian's chlamys match the segments in the chlamys of his courtiers, while the gold segment in the imperial chlamys matches in colour the chasuble of the bishop. This mosaic presents the groups within Byzantine society as a structured unity, in the same way that the coronation ceremonial presented them as a unity.

Whereas the emperor approaches the altar in a group linked together by a series of interweaving complex ties, but in a neutral environment, his consort advances to the altar in a defined environment but without the interweaving human ties. She is positioned under a vaulted niche, resembling the *aedicula* of the empress in the consular diptych (plate 61). She also is adorned with the jewels of triumph and the imperial chlamys. Her location within the niche is central, but in the mosaic as a whole it is off-centre, closer to the altar in the apse. Again like the empress in the diptych, Theodora is revealed between two veils which are drawn aside. Although off-centre in the composition as a whole, Theodora in fact forms the sole focal point in it, for the group of four which forms her immediate following goes forward in wedge formation, with her at the head. On the empress' left, there are another five ladies who do not form part of the central composition.

The unity of this central composition is emphasized both by the figure of Theodora herself, and by the niche in the background, which draws together the five leading figures. The image has something playful about it: Theodora's niche, with its strings of pearls, the fountain, the gaily patterned curtains and garments, even the elaborately embroidered imperial chlamys.

Yet, all this merely serves to emphasize the intense solemnity of the image, in which the eyes of the beholder are immediately drawn towards the majestic and sad, not to say mourning, countenance of Theodora. Theodora is the leading figure in this mosaic, in a way in which Justinian is not in the mosaic opposite. Neither for position within the image nor for majesty is there any figure to rival her, for she carries her own dignity within herself. Moreover, on the edge of the chlamys of the empress who is taking her gift to the altar are shown the three Magi who are also bringing gifts. The royalty of Theodora is thus placed side by side with the royalty of the Eastern kings who came to Bethlehem.[460] The metaphor carries within it both grandeur and profound humility: the grandeur of the first among the Gentiles, the wise, to whom Christ was revealed, and the humility of those who lay their gift upon the altar.[461] Thus is Theodora distinguished from among those accompanying her. She is also distinguished from them in stature, for unlike Justinian,

she is noticeably taller than any of her entourage. Where, on the Justinian mosaic, the beholder meets a row of faces on the same level, the face
of Theodora stands out from the rest, not only because of her height,
but also because of her expression.

We have here two different methods of viewing the imperial majesty:
Justinian is surrounded by personages whose presence spells out his actual, vested power in this world. The companions of Theodora, and the
setting in which she appears, on the other hand, barely hint at such
power. Unlike Justinian, Theodora is portrayed in an architectural setting, and it is through this that we may elucidate the meaning of her role
in the image. What is depicted is not some geographical locale in S.
Sophia or San Vitale. We can see from other mosaics in Ravenna itself
what the rendering of such a specific place could look like: The Palatium
and Classis mosaics of S. Apollinare Nuovo (plate 54), and even Bethlehem and Jerusalem with their gates and houses within, in San Vitale
itself. The architecture on the Theodora mosaic is not of this nature, but
the niche under which she stands does have parallels, especially in Ravenna but also elsewhere. In Ravenna, there are the niches under which
stand the prophets in S. Apollinare Nuovo, and more particularly the
niches surmounting the portraits of earlier bishops of this see in S. Apollinare in Classe. In Ravenna, such niches were a way of highlighting the
position of persons of special importance or sanctity, persons, furthermore, who had died.[462] It is chronologically possible that the S. Vitale
mosaic of Theodora was completed after her death.[463] She would then be
shown in her glory of this world, in purple and diadem, surrounded by
her court, but at the same time she passes through the glory of this
world into the glory of the next.

In this way we can interpret the significance of the doorway at the left
of the mosaic toward which Theodora moves with her offering: as she is
about to step through it, a courtier holds aside the veil—the veil, that is,
between this life and the next.[464] As befits the non-specific, metaphorical
architectural setting in which Theodora is portrayed, the fountain in
front of the doorway through which she is about to pass is to be understood as a fountain of living water, analogous to the fountains in the
Mausoleum of Galla Placidia.[465] The mosaic thus correlates the imagery
of imperial glory with the imagery of the glory of the life to come.

Theodora is portrayed in a way which leaves her position, however
exalted, ultimately undefined and open-ended. A canon of virtues and
deeds for emperors had been laid down during centuries of Roman politics and public life. In late antiquity, it became possible for empresses to
be represented in art in the light of this canon, as was Galla Placidia

(plates 59–60; cf. 61), but this defined their role only very partially. For, while the figure of the emperor remained caught in debates as to the nature of the imperial power which carried over from the pagan into the Christian empire, it was possible to catalogue and expound the virtues of a Christian empress independently of this legacy of the past.[466] In this new context, the virtues and deeds of an empress were directed not merely toward the manifold contingencies of this life, but toward the ultimate goal of the life to come. In this sense, in the Christian empire, the virtues of the empress supplemented, even clarified and exalted the virtues of the emperor. This is one of the themes which Corippus expounds in his panegyric of Justin II, the emperor who ruled with his consort Sophia.[467]

The partnership between emperor and empress, as articulated by Corippus, was relatively new in the sixth century. Before that, the main ways in which imperial consorts could achieve prominence was through their marriages—as did Fausta when she married Constantine, her beauty duly praised by the panegyrist of 307—and at the time of the birth of an heir, as advertised, for instance, on the coinage of the Antonines. But Corippus refers not merely to Sophia, the consort of Justin, but, playing on Sophia's name, to Wisdom, who, according to an idea which had a long history in antiquity and late antiquity, could be *synthronos* with the emperor.[468] Now, in Byzantium, it was possible for an ideal which had formerly been purely conceptual, to be made real and tangible, through the person of the empress, Sophia for Justin, and, for Justinian, as depicted in San Vitale, Theodora.

The distribution of functions between the imperial couple is illustrated in the overall layout of images in the apse of San Vitale, where the images of the emperor and his consort are juxtaposed with two sets of Old Testament images and the images of the four evangelists. The panel with the emperor, the law-giver, is set next to the mosaic showing Moses receiving the law on Mount Sinai, with the assembled Israelites, the people of God, waiting below, while the Theodora panel is next to the mosaic of Moses as a shepherd and Moses with the burning bush, which is pointed to by the hand of God in heaven: Moses seeing God. Thus, giving, making law, a this-worldly aspect of imperial activity, vested in the daily running of the empire, is in the person of Moses juxtaposed with an other-worldly activity, that of seeing God, which could not be vested in actual power in the same explicit way.

Beholding God, and giving, articulating the law were necessary imperial functions which supplemented each other and were exercised by the emperors on behalf of their subjects. In panegyric these ideas had been articulated by Themistius in his exposition of the emperor as the living law, while the emperor's beholding and comprehension of divine activity by means of re-enacting it in his own activity was one of the main themes of George of Pisidia.[469]

In the lunettes are, on the emperor's side, Abraham about to sacrifice Isaac, prototype of Christ, and Abraham giving hospitality to the three angels, the figures of the Trinity, while on Theodora's side, Abel and Melchisedech offer their gifts, figures of the Eucharist, which are received by the hand of God coming down from above. Both sets of images, while depicting both the vision of God and sacrifice to him in the Old Testament, also refer to the New Testament mysteries. These images are paralleled and made tangible in the here and now in the imperial panels by the offerings of the imperial couple.

For, what is depicted is not only a set of events with a meaning deeper and more far-reaching than the literal one from the Old Testament, but also the course of history, leading from the Old Testament Judaic kingdoms to the Christian kingdom of Byzantium, for which the people called on God's protection at imperial accessions. In this now Christian course of history, the emperors stand, in a well-defined position, at the head of the people of God. We have seen how this position was defined in panegyric, ceremonial, and now in art.

In San Vitale, the position of the imperial couple is defined not only from the point of view of past history, brought forward by the intervention and vision of God, as when God intervenes in history at an imperial election, but also from the point of view of the culmination and end of history, the *parousia* of Christ and the reward of the saints. For, in the apse we see Christ enthroned on the globe of *consecratio* above the four streams of Paradise, which flow amidst flowers and shrubs (plate 42)— images of the bliss that was paradise and the bliss that is to be: that ultimate golden age, no longer merely hoped for in the reign of the present emperor but positively asserted as to come under the kingship of Christ.

Whereas what is depicted in the sanctuary is what occurs within history and time, time now securely defined, when kings and emperors rule, what is depicted in the conch of the apse is what happens beyond time, when Christ rules, so that here, in visual terms, the position of the imperial couple is defined from above. The emperors exist within a now defined universe, a defined order of being. Imperial splendour may be, as Chrysostom said, a reflection, though a pale one, of the splendour of Christ.[470] That comparison, like the imagery of San Vitale, while on the one hand exalting the emperor, on the other allots a place to him, a place in history, a place among humanity, differentiated in terms more absolute than was ever possible in the pagan empire, from the place of God.

We have observed the emergence of a concept of imperial dominion which had its roots in the classical world, but it would have been impossible to state it there without ambivalence and in the simplicity that was found in Byzantium:

> God has given you. God will keep you.[471]

> King of Heaven, preserve the King on earth.[472]

EPILOGUE

Über Ströme hast du gesetzt und Meere durchschwommen
Über der Alpen Gebirg trug dich der schwindlichte Steg,
Mich in der Nähe zu schauen und meine Schönheit zu preisen
Die der begeisterte Ruf rühmt durch die staunende Welt;
Und nun stehst du vor mir, du darfst mich Heil'ge berühren,
Aber bist du mir jetzt näher, und bin ich es dir?

These lines of Schiller may serve to indicate the difficulty of formulating an historical enquiry such as the present one without overriding the categories of the past with categories of the present. What we can know about the past and a culture which are not our own is inevitably conditioned by what we know of our own time and our own culture. Accordingly, the content of what is written about history changes from one generation to the next. Questions which can now be asked, and answered, about the meaning of ceremonial actions, would have been inconceivable before Weber and Durkheim, among others, posited society, rather than simply the institutions of society, as a possible subject of enquiry;[1] that is, before the many anonymous participants in the late antique imperial ceremonies which we have studied could be viewed as agents, rather than merely as passive onlookers.

However, societies are fixed entities as little as are their institutions, and even in the comparatively articulate milieu of late antique panegyrists, definitions, fixed points to which hard and fast questions can be addressed, are impossible to find. Panegyrist and emperor, emperor and people, people and panegyrist related to each other and to their environments in such diverse ways that it has not been possible to pursue our enquiry through one single focal point, for such a focal point can only be imposed on the evidence we have artificially and from the outside; it can never arise from within it.

Themistius, among others, was aware of this state of affairs in his *Erotikos* to Gratian,[2] in which he described his search for the ideal ruler as defined by Plato, without, however, putting the question directly. For, being the late antique theorist that he was, Themistius would not and could not outrightly define this search. For one thing, his own experience as panegyrist to more than one emperor ruled out such a definition from the practical point of view: panegyrists were not, as we have seen, professional liars. But more was at issue.

Panegyrics, while explaining circumstances obtaining at any particular point in time, also gave expression to an ideal, to something lasting, and the language they employed, with its constant heightened effects, its complexity and the profusion of colouring, helps to point to this fact. The difficulty which beset the orators, and which accordingly besets anyone studying them, is that of finding in the often far from ideal circumstances of the later Roman Empire a trace of the perfection and idealisation of the empire which men carried about with them in their minds and which it was a panegyrist's task to express in terms of the present. It was not often that the present very readily lent itself to direct and explicit idealisation. Moreover, it lies in the very nature of an ideal, as of any explanatory system, that it should reach beyond immediate circumstances and validate them in a wider context.

The ideal of political life which the panegyrists were concerned with was therefore usually articulated in relation to a set of fixed points which were in some way external to and apart from the present, whether these fixed points were good events in the past, or observations about the nature of the gods or of God. In other words, late antique men sought to express and explain the discontinuities and changes to which they were exposed as far as possible in terms of continuity and tradition, for in late antiquity, continuity and tradition stood for all that was desirable in public life. As a result, there existed a constant tension between ideal and reality. The purpose of panegyric and imperial art was to suspend, or at least to lessen, this tension.

Accordingly, the ideal which was aspired to could never be static or definable. It was on the one hand present, but on the other encumbered by reality. Reality acted as a disguise. It was for this reason that some of the most definite statements of the eternity of Rome date from after Rome's fall, when the reality was so remote from the ideal that it could no longer encumber. Roma could become more abstract and therefore more perfect.[3] As regarded the idealisation of the emperor, on the other hand, the chief obstacle always remained the emperor himself; the obstacle was an ever present reality. For this reason, it was both safer and more practical to leave the ideal emperor ultimately undefined, and to let him be an image which might be glimpsed as in a mirror[4] or beheld "as in the innermost sanctuary."[5]

In attempting to understand late antique literature and art, we not only face many ways of expression which are deeply rooted in the culture of that time and are therefore alien to us; we also face the classical literary forms, the differences, for instance, which were thought to exist between methods of writing history and methods of writing panegyric. Antique literary form is not the same thing as stereotype or repetition, but these two categories look deceptively similar until it is understood that in antiquity, literary form, the deliberate use of language according to certain rules depending on what one wanted to say, was to a large extent considered to be the means which made expression possible in the first place.

However, when the empire became Christian, the content of language, of literary form, became a potential, and at times an actual, source of controversy. For, the creation and definition of the literary genres in Greek and Latin had taken place at periods when harmony between religion, culture and language could be assumed to exist and did exist. This harmony was disrupted, and in some instances shattered, by Christianity. The classical literary forms were, however, very tenacious and were capable of remaining stable at times when much else changed radically. With that, the content and form of many panegyrics also remained continuous with the pagan past for some time after the empire had become Christian. During the earlier decades of the Christian empire, the ideal as stated in panegyric could thus be at considerable variance with reality.

Hence, while allowing for the fundamental importance of literary form and *topos* in the present enquiry, I have nonetheless also examined the evidence independently of these criteria by raising questions which are not discussed in the analysis of literary form in rhetorical textbooks: this is what has led us to the topics of *adventus*, *consecratio* and accession. Here it is possible to a greater degree than elsewhere to watch the debate, whether explicit or implicit, between paganism and Christianity, without constantly having to take issue with stances taken up by either side with particular reference to this debate.

One can thus interpret panegyrics as indicators of political, cultural and religious climate at particular points in time and in particular places, even though much of what is said in many of them was rooted in the past. The exception is the Tetrarchy, a period when panegyrists achieved an almost unique balance between interpretations and realities, when, in other words, the tension between ideal and reality in public language was reduced to a minimum. This same reduction, even suspension, of tension, is also observable in imperial art during the Tetrarchy. Long-standing impasses regarding the representation of the emperors in relation to the gods and the supernatural were quite simply ignored and thus superseded.

Our study of imperial art has made much of what is said in panegyric more concrete. The initial reason for this is twofold. First, the scenes represented in imperial art and the way in which they are subdivided, as well as the captions, or legends, with which these scenes or abbreviations of them are labelled on the coinage, have enabled us to visualise pictorially what in panegyric was said in words, in exactly the way in which a person of the period might have visualised the meaning of these same words. In the third and early fourth centuries, but also later, certain themes in art and panegyric coincide, and we have explored these coincidences.

Second, however, our enquiry into imperial art has not been determined only by these coincidences, and by what panegyrics and art happen to say or not to say. In panegyric, we have followed up certain types of statements, *topoi*, which recur regularly. In the same way, we have followed up iconographic schemes, and in this way we have come to see that late antique art is, as Grabar has so well put it, a language of images. For iconography in late antiquity played the same role in the visual arts as *topos* and literary form did in language: iconography was what made visual communication possible, for it built on and elaborated certain widely understood visual forms.

We have found, accordingly, that texts and images ran parallel to each other in late antiquity. But did they ever fuse into one single whole? We found that they did so in the numerous passages when a panegyrist or historian described an event or a ceremony in such a way as to evoke a visual experience, when, in other words, panegyric and history used *ekphrasis*, description, as a means of communication. This is an important element in our enquiry, for it shows that in late antiquity images existed not just pictorially, but existed in language as well. Once this has been understood, it is possible to work not merely on the pragmatic basis that art and literature sometimes do run parallel, as they do in imperial art and panegyric. But one may work on the basis that literature and art in some of their aspects interpenetrate each other, and that Horace's dictum *ut pictura poiesis*[6] was not only the statement of a theory or a programme, but had, in late antiquity, become a reality.

Furthermore, art and panegyric are linked to each other by the court ceremonial to which they both relate. The three themes which we have discussed all refer to historical events as much as to ceremonies. Imperial art and panegyric often treat these themes in such a way as to fuse historical event and ceremony, narrative and *ekphrasis*—even ideal and reality—into one coherent whole. Our study has shown, not merely that this process occurred, but also how it occurred, and herein lies one of its principal contributions, as well as its complexity.

We have followed a multiple and complex line of enquiry, for we have examined the evidence from the inside, from within the courtly milieu of late antique Rome and early Byzantium. Court ceremonial linked art and panegyric factually, for works of art and panegyrics were produced for the same ceremonial occasions. Furthermore, court ceremonial also linked art and panegyric more theoretically, for like art and panegyric, it sought to relate reality and ideal, to express the ideal in the guise of reality. In a sense, ceremonial went further than either art or panegyric, for it enacted the ideal before the eyes. Thus, the spectacle which the orator would describe and the artist represent actually happened: here, late Roman art and panegyric were steps towards Byzantine court ceremonial. A victory, for instance, as described by a panegyrist, was not the same as a victory described by an historian. It was already on the way to becoming a spectacle, a ceremony of triumph, and the panegyric was the *ekphrasis* of that ceremony as it actually happened or was depicted in art. Similarly, imperial art came to represent less an historical event than the ceremony which would arise from it.

This unity between panegyric and art has affected our enquiry decisively. For as long as one can only set side by side certain works of art and certain parts of panegyrics—which should preferably be contemporary or near contemporary to each other—one is absolutely dependent on the accidents of survival of literature and art. Where two matching pieces do not survive, no conclusions can be drawn. Even where they do survive, the conclusions may be rather limited. Once it is realised, however, that a deliberate connection between visual and verbal expression was made in late antiquity, and moreover, that there did at certain points exist an organic harmony between visual and verbal expression, a greater freedom and a greater validity have been acquired for an exegesis which seeks to expound literature and art, one by reference to the other.

It is not possible to carry out an enquiry on such a basis without postulating that the explanations with which men at different times in history came to terms with the realities of their lives are as important as those realities, if not more so. Moreover, for the historian of the long distant past, these explanations, be they visual or literary, are fundamental, for they provide the only access there is to how people of a certain period understood themselves and their world.

The focal point, or rather series of focal points, of my enquiry has been the position of the emperor in society as articulated by a cultural minority whose views as to what actually was and what was ideally were expressed by panegyrists on the one hand, and by the creators of imperial art on the other. In that these individuals constituted a tiny minority in the Roman Empire, the results of an enquiry into their views are of necessity of limited import.

But this statement needs qualification. For what the enquiry has shown is that the Roman Empire did, as the Romans themselves thought, form a certain unity. It consisted of people associated together by acts of consensus, as Cicero expressed it,[7] acts of consensus which could be articulated by means of, among other ways, the ceremonies here studied. Thus, the range of the import of imperial art, panegyric and ceremonial was not as limited as might initially be thought. This is not to say that the Roman Empire did not also contain unwilling subjects, who were not integrated into it by any acts of consensus. These subjects of the empire have not, however, entered into the present study, which is concerned with propaganda addressed to those whom it was, potentially at least, possible to persuade.

The ceremonies of *adventus, consecratio* and accession have been studied from two points of view: firstly, from the point of view of their function and significance, and the changes which they underwent in these respects. Secondly, these ceremonies have been studied with regard to modes of expression used with reference to them, and changes in these modes of expression. We will look at these two points in turn.

First, then, we will look at the three ceremonies from the point of view of their function and significance and changes in this context. The ceremony of *adventus* demonstrates that during the earlier part of the period studied, society within the empire cohered not merely by the ability of a minority to form a consensus, that is, to articulate visually and in language a frequently repeated ceremony, but also by the ability of Roman subjects at large to enact this ceremony in a meaningful, often very sophisticated, manner. The empire cohered, in other words, by the ability of a large section of its subjects to form a particular kind of consensus.

In studying *adventus* up to the earlier part of the fifth century, therefore, the historian encounters through different modes of expression and at various removes the official opinions of a large variety of people from different parts of the empire. There existed the opportunity of articulating a consensus which was significant numerically, and significant also culturally and in religion, in that the ceremony of *adventus* could be a vehicle for expressing some of the most enduring and deeply felt aspirations of the ancient world.

During the later part of the period studied, it may be observed how the scope of consensus, so far as *adventus* was concerned, was reduced, not merely in numerical but also in cultural and religious terms. Therefore, if one is to use Cicero's definition of the *respublica*, it becomes less applicable to the Roman Empire, in that on the one hand there was less opportunity for expressing a consensus, and on the other, the need to express it was not felt so acutely.

This is, in a sense, a subjective judgement. But it is supported in less subjective terms by the evidence that came to light in studying *consecratio*. In the early empire, the *consecratio* of an emperor was decided upon by a human verdict, a human consensus, that of the Senate. In the early fourth century, this was no longer the case: *consecratio* was not subject to any human verdict. We therefore see that outside *adventus*, the scope for the various kinds of consensus of Roman subjects was in the process of being reduced even at the beginning of the period here studied.

At the same time, however, a different type of consensus, which one may perhaps call non-classical, came into existence, and came to be expressed, so far as the present study goes, in the ceremony of imperial accession. We find it more or less fully formed by the mid-fifth century, at the time when classical *adventus* with its pagan roots had disintegrated, and when the consensus whereby the emperor was consecrated had been reformulated into the ceremony of imperial funerals.

In other words, in what survived of the Roman Empire in administrative terms, the subjects were held together by a different kind of consensus, a consensus in which a new element—the divine inspiration whereby the emperor was elected—became fundamental. Divine inspiration expressing itself in public life was not a new topic in the fourth century, but its systematic, regular applicability and relevance in imperial elections, expressed formally in ceremonial from the mid-fifth century, was new.

Divine inspiration now contributed to and determined the nature of human consensus, and with that the classical, Ciceronian definition of the *respublica* has been substantially modified. We witness here a fundamental change in thinking about terrestrial existence and about the relevance of the divine to terrestrial existence. Two of the fundamental questions of classical philosophy, 'Do the gods exist, and if so, do they care?' could no longer, needed no longer to be asked.

There existed a certain kind of interchange, a dialogue between the ceremonies that have been studied. Thus one could say that *adventus* was a crucial and fundamental part of imperial politics as long as there was no one exclusive way of defining the status of the living emperor in relation to the divine and in relation to the human world; in other words, as long as this definition was not made in a regular ceremonial of accession. Accordingly, *consecratio*, the divinisation of the emperor, played an essential role in the definition of who and what the emperor was, even though it did so only retrospectively; that is, once the emperor had died. Accession, that essentially non-classical ceremony, in turn became viable once a clear differentiation between divinity and humanity had been made, and once the emperor could, without compromising his majesty, be placed within the latter category. In this process of differentiation and definition, Christianity played a vital part.

We now come to the second aspect of change which has been treated, and that is change which is to be assessed in terms of changing modes of expression in art and panegyric. *Adventus* was the primary example of a definite harmony, a coordination of expression between art and panegyric; *consecratio* showed up a certain harmony between these two media, but it was not nearly as extensive, the reason being that *consecratio* was not essentially a harmonious process, nor was it at any time the subject of a really widely articulated consensus, even though it was a feature in widely held religious feeling.

If one takes *adventus* in its earlier stages, which have been studied here, as a criterion of harmony of expression between art and panegyric, then little harmony of expression will be found to exist on the subject of accession. For, although in art images which evoked the imperial majesty were created during our period, the ceremony of accession in itself was not depicted in pictorial narratives such as we have for *adventus* in the earlier part of our period. The ceremony of accession, although a product, ultimately, of classical ideas, was itself not classical and outlasted the classical world in East and West because it was adaptable to non-classical circumstances. In this respect, it has a great deal in common with that outcome of *consecratio*, the ceremony of imperial funerals, which also, in its final stages, can be called non-classical. Here again we touch upon the dialogue and interchange between ceremonies here studied, but from a different angle, the angle, that is, of changing modes of expression, changing ceremonial forms.

Accession and imperial funerals were related and interdependent, not only as regarded their form, but also their content. Firstly, the ceremony of accession provided the definition of the emperor's status *vis-à-*

vis his subjects and the divine which formerly had been provided by *consecratio*, and, in different terms, by *adventus*. Secondly, by means of the interdependence of imperial funerals and accessions a crucial continuity and stability of government from one emperor to the next received visible expression.

This expression was, however, very limited so far as the number of those who could participate in it and could form a consensus was concerned. The consensus to be formed in *adventus* was, potentially at least, empire-wide, while the consensus of accession was expressed only by the citizens of Constantinople. From a factual, military point of view, the empire was much reduced in size during the sixth and early seventh centuries. This reduction was anticipated, in the realm of ideas, from at least the mid-fifth century.

The changes in ideas and their expression which have been studied lead from a pagan and classical to a Christian and post-classical, ultimately mediaeval, world. They also lead from pagan and classical to Christian and post-classical, mediaeval forms of literary and visual expression. What has been witnessed is, in literature, the transformation of panegyric, dependent as it was on the analysis of deeds and character, to forms of epic narrative and description. In art, we have watched the transition from Roman imperial art, the chief modes of expression of which were visual narrative and allegory, the interrelation of gods and emperors, and of supernatural and natural historical themes, to late classical and Byzantine art. Here God and emperor, the supernatural and the natural, are not interrelated but are juxtaposed, so that visual art no longer narrates events, but represents states of affairs which may be considered to exist regardless of events.

The breach of harmony in modes of expression in art and panegyric as it applied to *adventus* in particular, but also to *consecratio* and accession, can be attributed not only to changes in ceremonial but also to changes within imperial art and panegyric themselves, for the dictum *ut pictura poiesis* no longer has any direct practical application in relation to them. With this fragmentation of expressions, and therefore of perceptions, both of which had formerly been capable of a spontaneous unity, and harmony, we have passed over the watershed which separates the classical from the early mediaeval world.

NOTES

THE WORLD OF THE PANEGYRISTS

1. Augustine *Confessions*, 6, 6, 9.

2. On *laetitia*, see S. Mazzarino, "'Annunci' e 'publica laetitia': l'iscrizione romana di Fausto e altri testi," *Antico, tardoantico ed erà constantiniana* (1974) 229–250. Inscriptions to Maximian and Constantius I as *laetitiae publicae/caeremoniarumque omnium autori*, from Cyprus, 293–305 A.D., *Année épigraphique* (1971) 466 and (1972) 666. Public rejoicings were part and parcel of the workings of the Roman Empire. Note Salvian, *De gub. Dei* 6, 89:

> Ludicra ergo publica, Trever petis? . . . Iacent reliquiae infelicissimae plebis super tumulos defunctorum suorum, et tu circenses rogas! nigra est incendio civitas, et tu vultum festivitatis usurpas! Lugent cuncta, tu laetus es!

3. An example of a text which has been overlooked in this way is Vegetius *De re militari*; see W. Goffart, "The Date and Purpose of Vegetius' 'De re militari'," *Traditio* 33 (1977) 65–100, esp. 75ff and 92ff.

4. E.g., L. K. Born, "The Perfect Prince According to the Latin Panegyrists," *American Journal of Philology* 55 (1934) 20ff; F. Burdeau, "L'empereur d'après les panégyriques latins," in *Aspects de l'empire romain* (1964) 1–60.

5. E.g., Alan Cameron, *Claudian, Poetry and Propaganda at the Court of Honorius* (1970). For a balanced view of the effects of propaganda see K. Hopkins, *Conquerors and Slaves* (1978) esp. 197ff, where the integrating role of imperial rhetoric, art and ceremonial over widely diverging tracts of society is stressed. See also M. P. Charlesworth, "The Virtues of a Roman Emperor," *PBA* (1937) 105–133. On the Latin Panegyrics, R. Pichon, *Les derniers écrivains profanes* (1906) is an excellent study, still worth consulting; see esp. 86ff.

6. The literature is vast. For some of its stages see A. Riegl, *Spätrömische Kunstindustrie* (1927; 1964); G. Rodenwaldt, "Zur Begrenzung und Gliederung der Spätantike," *Jahrbuch des deutschen archäologischen Instituts* 59–60 (1944–1945) 81–87; A. Rumpf, *Stilphasen der spätantiken Kunst*, Arbeitsgemeinschaft für Forschung des Landes Nordrhein-Westfalen, Geisteswissenschaften, Abh. 44 (1957); E. Kitzinger, *The Art of Byzantium and the Medieval West, Selected Studies*

(1976); K. Weitzmann, *Greek Mythology in Byzantine Art*, Studies in Manuscript Illumination, 4 (1951) (iconography); and V. Lazarev, *Storia della pittura bizantina* (1967). G. Mathew, *Byzantine Aesthetics* (1963) is outstanding.

7. A. Marrou, *Saint Augustin et la fin de la culture antique* (1938 and 1949; 4th ed., 1958) is a landmark; see also Peter Brown, *Religion and Society in the Age of St. Augustine* (1972) esp. 9–21, and his *The Making of Late Antiquity* (1978).

8. This was only one of the outcomes of the 'restoration' undertaken by the Tetrarchs. See Géza Alföldy, "The Crisis of the Third Century as Seen by Contemporaries," *Greek, Roman and Byzantine Studies* 15 (1974) 89–111.

9. *Theodosian Code* 14, 1, 1.

10. On the Gallic schools, see R. Pichon, *Les derniers écrivains profanes* (1906) 36ff. The Latin panegyrics will here be cited after the edition by E. Galletier, *Panégyriques latins*, 3 vols. (1949–1955) (hereafter *Pan. Lat.*) with a general introduction and *mise-en-scène* for each panegyric. The edition of Sir R. Mynors, *XII Panegyrici Latini* (1964) may also be consulted. See also S. MacCormack, "Latin Prose Panegyrics: Tradition and Discontinuity in the Later Roman Empire," *Revue des études augustiniennes* 22 (1976) 29–77.

11. Clement *Recognitiones*, I, 25, 2.

12. On Menander, see most recently J. Soffel, *Die Regeln Menanders für die Leichenrede in ihrer Tradition dargestellt, herausgegeben, übersetzt und kommentiert*, Beitr. zur klass. Philologie, 57 (1974) 90–105.

13. H. P. Bütler, *Die geistige Welt des jüngeren Plinius. Studien zur Thematik seiner Briefe* (1970).

14. See *Pan. Lat.*, 12, 47, 6.

15. On the fusion between panegyric and epic in late antiquity, see Nissen, "Historisches Epos und Panegyrikos in der Spätantike," *Hermes* 75 (1940) 302–325; Alan Cameron, "Wandering Poets, a Literary Movement in Byzantine Egypt," *Historia* 14 (1965) 470–509, at 479ff, and his *Claudian, Poetry and Propaganda at the Court of Honorius* (1970) 260ff. The phenomenon also occurs in Sidonius, and in carmen I and II of Merobaudes. See F. M. Clover, "Flavius Merobaudes, a Translation and Historical Commentary," *Transactions of the American Philosophical Society*, n.s. 61, part 1 (1971) 11, 16–19, 27–28.

16. Cassiodorus, ed. L. Traube, 480f, in T. Mommsen, ed., *Cassiodori Senatoris Variae*, MGH AA (1894, 1961).

17. Aristotle *Rhetoric to Alexander*, 1422a; 1425b f; Aristotle *Rhetoric*, 1367b–1368a, cf. 1416b; [Cicero] *Ad Herennium*, III, 6, 7, 8; and Menander (ed. Spengel), 371f.

18. E.g., C. Halm, *Rhetores Latini Minores* (1863) 155–156, 218f, 300–304, 508, 548f, 567ff.

19. Below, pp. 132ff and 145ff.

20. See on this J. B. Bury, "The Ceremonial Book of Constantine Porphyrogenetos," *EHR* 22 (1907) 209–227 at 211–213.

21. Gibbon, *The History of the Decline and Fall of the Roman Empire*, ed. J. B. Bury, vol. 2, chapter XVII, 170.

22. *Decline and Fall*, ed. Bury, vol. 1 (1896) chapter XIII, 383; and see A. U. Stylow, *Libertas und Liberalitas, Untersuchungen zur innenpolitischen Propaganda der Römer* (1972). The latter is an unusual and excellent book because, rather than juxtaposing and contrasting one set of ideas with another, the author demon-

strates how the republican ideal of *libertas* was transformed from the inside, without positing a series of external, and therefore inevitably artificial, factors.

23. For the third century, see Louis J. Swift, "The Anonymous Encomium of Philip the Arab," *Greek, Roman and Byzantine Studies* 7 (1966) 267–289. The panegyric was edited by B. Keil, *Aelii Aristidi quae supersunt* (1898) 253–264. S. A. Stertz, "Pseudo Aristides ΕΙΣ ΒΑΣΙΛΕΑ," *Classical Quarterly* n.s. 29 (1979) 172–197, views this panegyric as a rhetorical exercise, not addressed to any specific emperor. Treatise XVIII of the *Corpus Hermeticum* is fragments of a panegyric, probably on the Tetrarchs. See W. Scott, *Hermetica* (1925) 2:461–482, and the text in A. D. Nock and A. J. Festugière, *Corpus Hermeticum* (1945) 2:244–255. For the later period, see A. Cameron, "Wandering Poets, a Literary Movement in Byzantine Egypt," *Historia* 14 (1965) 470–509; G. M. Browne, "A Panegyrist from Panopolis," *Proc. of the XIV Int. Congr. of Papyrologists* (1974 and 1975) 29–33; R. C. McCail, "P. Gr. Vindob. 2 9788C," *JHS* 98 (1978) 38–63; and S. MacCormack, "Latin Prose Panegyrics: Tradition and Discontinuity in the Later Roman Empire," *Rev. des ét. augustiniennes* 22 (1976) 29–77. See 41ff and n. 59 for the ceremonial occasions of panegyrics. In principle these coincide with the occasions listed by H. Mattingly, "The Imperial Vota," *PBA* 36 (1950) 155–195 and 37 (1951) 219–268. To these occasions should be added the most frequent one of all—at any rate in the late third and earlier fourth centuries—that is, *adventus*. For Byzantine panegyrics, see L. Previale, "Teoria e prassi del panegirico bizantino," *Emerita* 17 (1949) 72–105 and 18 (1950) 340–366, and in general H. G. Beck, "Antike Beredsamkeit und byzantinische Kallilogia," *Antike und Abendland* 15 (1969) 91–101. For the origins of panegyric as a political institution, see G. Williams, *Change and Decline: Roman Literature in the Early Empire* (1978) esp. 52–101.

24. A. Baumstark, "Bild und Lied des christlichen Ostens," *Festschrift Paul Clemen* (1926) 168–180. Some Byzantine sermons have a very clear visual dimension—see G. La Piana, *Le rappresentazione sacre nella letteratura bizantina* (1912; 1971)—which was later reflected in Byzantine church decoration.

25. E.g., P. Petit, *Libanius et la vie municipale à Antioche au IVe siècle après J.-C.* (1955); E. M. Wightman, *Roman Trier and the Treveri* (1970); G. Dagron, *Naissance d'une capitale, Constantinople et ses institutions de 330 à 451* (1974); R. Krautheimer, *Early Christian and Byzantine Architecture* (1965) esp. 17–65; and H. Stern, *Le Calendrier de 354, étude sur son texte et ses illustrations* (1953).

26. Cf. above, p. 6f. For early examples of *ekphrasis* in panegyric, see *Pan. Lat.*, V, 20–21, map in the school of Autun; *Pan. Lat.*, VI, 6, description of a painting in Aquileia showing Fausta giving a helmet to Constantine; *Pan. Lat.* VII, 22, 4–6, description of Trier. See also below, "*Accession*" at n. 192, Symmachus' *ekphrasis* of Gratian's election; P. Friedländer, *Johannes von Gaza, Paulus Silentiarius und Prokopius von Gaza, Kunstbeschreibungen von justinianischer Zeit* (1912; 1939; 1969); G. Downey in *R.A.C.*, IV (1959) s.v. *Ekphrasis*; and cf. H. Maguire, "Truth and Convention in Byzantine Descriptions of Works of Art," *DOP* 28 (1974) 113–140. On Corippus' *ekphrasis* of ceremonies, see Averil Cameron, "Images of Authority: Elites and Icons in Late Sixth-Century Byzantium," *Past and Present* 84 (1979) 3–35, at 10–15.

27. Eunapius fr. 78: see Lellia Cracco Ruggini, *Simboli di battaglia ideologica nel tardo ellenismo* (1972) 101–103.

28. On the coinage as a means of communication, see C. H. V. Sutherland, "The Intelligibility of Roman Imperial Coin Types," *JRS* 49 (1959) 46–55, being a reply to A. H. M. Jones, "Numismatics and History," *Essays in Roman Coinage presented to Harold Mattingly*, ed. R. A. G. Carson and C. H. V. Sutherland (1956) 13–33.

I. ADVENTUS

1. See T. C. Skeat, *Papyri from Panopolis*, Chester Beatty Monographs, 10 (1964) Papyrus, 1, 7 (cf. XII on the date), on preparations for the arrival of Diocletian. An occasion of this type, but more elaborate, was represented in the Tetrarchic camp at Luxor: J. G. Deckers, "Die Wandmalerei des tetrarchischen Lager-heiligtums im Ammon-Tempel von Luxor," *Römische Quartalschrift* 68 (1973) 1–34 and, without the drawings by Josef Sauer, Ioli Kalavrezou-Maxeiner, "The Imperial Chamber at Luxor," *DOP* 29 (1975) 227–251. See also, Santo Mazzarino, "*L'adventus* di Constanzo II a Roma e la carriera di Pancharius," *Antico, tardoan-tico ed erà constantiniana* (1974) 197–213, and F. Millar, *The Emperor in the Roman World* (1977) 28ff.

2. G. Deschamps and G. Cousin, "Inscriptions du Temple de Zeus Pan-amaros," *Bulletin de correspondance hellénique* 12 (1888) 82–104, at 101–103. A similar occasion in Trier in 287 A.D.: *Pan. Lat.* 2, 6, 1ff.

3. Athanasius *De Incarnatione* 9, ed. and tr. R. W. Thomson (1971).

4. Ammianus, 26, 5, 12, tr. J. C. Rolfe.

5. *Homeric Hymn to Apollo*, 440ff:

> ἔνθ' ἐκ νηὸς ὄρουσεν ἄναξ ἑκάεργος Ἀπόλλων
> ἀστέρι εἰδόμενος μέσῳ ἤματι· τοῦ δ'ἀπὸ πολλαὶ
> σπινθαρίδες πωτῶντο, σέλας δ' εἰς οὐρανὸν ἷκεν.
> ἐς δ' ἄδυτον κατέδυσε.

For the cult of Dionysus at Athens, see L. Deubner, *Attische Feste* (1932; 1966) 100–111; for accounts of divine revelations in Pausanias, M. Nilsson, *Griechische Feste von religiöser Bedeutung* (1906) 103f, 150ff passim, 258f, 267ff, 280ff passim, on Apollo and Dionysus.

6. On the architectural setting see R. Krautheimer, "The Beginning of Early Christian Architecture," *Review of Religion*, 3 (1939) 127–148, reprinted in his *Studies in Early Christian, Medieval and Renaissance Art* (1969) 1–19; note the post-script, 19–20. See also P. Beskow, *Rex Gloriae, The Kingship of Christ in the Early Church* (1962) 15ff; cf. 157ff.

7. Spengel, *Rhet. Gr.* (1856) 3:334–336.

8. M. Nilsson, "Die Prozessionstypen im griechischen Kult," *Jahrbuch d. Kai-serlich deutschen archeologischen Instituts* 31 (1916) 309–339, esp. 315f, *Epipha-nienzug*. We have evidence that Menander's treatise was used: Herwig Maehler, "Menander Rhetor and Alexander Claudius in a Papyrus Letter," *Greek, Roman and Byz. Studies* 15 (1974) 305–312. On panegyrists of the later fourth and fifth centuries, see Alan Cameron, "Wandering Poets, a Literary Movement in Byzan-tine Egypt," *Historia* 14 (1965) 470–509. The classical authors whom Menander mentions formed part of the regular reading of the urban public who would also hear panegyrics: W. H. Willis, "Greek Literary Papyri and the Classical Canon," *Harvard Library Bulletin* 12 (1958) 5–34.

9. *Agamemnon*, 905ff.
10. *Agamemnon*, 906–907:

> μὴ χαμαὶ τιθεὶς
> τὸν σὸν πόδ' ὦναξ, Ἰλίου πορθήτορα.

11. *Agamemnon*, 919–920.
12. *Agamemnon*, 921–930.
13. This is one of the themes treated by A. Alföldi in the fundamental article, "Die Ausgestaltung des monarchischen Zeremoniells am römischen Kaiserhofe," *Röm. Mitt.* 49 (1934) 3–118, reprinted in A. Alföldi, *Die monarchische Repräsentation im römischen Kaiserreiche* (1970).
14. See particularly *Agamemnon*, lines 914ff. A ceremonial formulated in a less serious tone occurs in Aristophanes, *Birds*, lines 1707ff:

> ὦ τρισμακάριον πτηνὸν ὀρνίθων γένος,
> δέχεσθε τὸν τύραννον ὀλβίοις δόμοις.
> προσέρχεται γὰρ οἷος οὔτε παμφαὴς
> ἀστὴρ ἰδεῖν ἔλαμψε χρυσαυγεῖ δόμῳ,
> οὔθ' ἡλίου τηλαυγὲς ἀκτίνων σέλας
> τοιοῦτον ἐξέλαμψεν, οἷον ἔρχεται,
> ἔχων γυναικὸς κάλλος οὐ φατὸν λέγειν,
> πάλλων κεραυνόν πτεροφόρον Διὸς βέλος.

This is quoted and discussed by Alföldi, *Die monarchische Repräsentation*, 88f. For the arrival of Demetrius Poliorcetes in Athens, see Athenaeus, VI, 253 c–d:

> οἱ Ἀθηναῖοι ἐδέχοντο οὐ μόνον θυμιῶντες καὶ στεφανοῦντες καὶ οἰνοχοοῦντες, ἀλλὰ καὶ προσοδιακοὶ χοροὶ . . . . ἀπήντων αὐτῷ . . . καὶ ἐπάδοντες ὡς εἴη μόνος θεὸς ἀληθινός, οἱ δ' ἄλλοι καθεύδουσιν ἢ ἀποδημοῦσιν ἢ οὐκ εἰσίν, γεγονὼς δ' εἴη ἐκ Ποσειδῶνος καὶ Ἀφροδίτης . . . . καὶ προσηύχοντο.

Part of the paean sung by the Athenians on this occasion ran (Athenaeus, VI, 253 d–f):

> ὁ δ' ἱλαρός, ὥσπερ τὸν θεὸν δεῖ, καὶ καλὸς
> καὶ γελῶν πάρεστι.
> σεμνόν τι φαίνεθ', οἱ φίλοι πάντες κύκλῳ,
> ἐν μέσοισι δ' αὐτός,
> ὅμοιον ὥσπερ οἱ φίλοι μὲν ἀστέρες,
> ἥλιος δ' ἐκεῖνος.
> ὦ τοῦ κρατίστου παῖ Ποσειδῶνος θεοῦ,
> χαῖρε κἀφροδίτης.
> ἄλλοι μὲν ἢ μακρὰν γὰρ ἀπέχουσιν θεοὶ
> ἢ οὐκ ἔχουσιν ὦτα . . .

On these two passages see C. Habicht, *Gottmenschtum und griechische Städte*, Zetemata, 14 (1956) 232–233 and, for the context, 48–55, 213–216. Much of this paean—the beauty of the person arriving, the image of the sun and stars and the emphasis on present divinity (*deus praesens*)—foreshadows late antique *adventus* ceremonies. See below, at nn. 50, 52, 112, 156. See also V. Ehrenberg, "Athenian Hymn to Demetrius Poliorcetes," in his *Aspects of the Ancient World* (1946) 179–198.
15. Ps. Dionysius of Halicarnassus, *Opuscula*, ed. Usener and Radermacher, vol. 2, 1: 272:

Ἰσοκράτης μὲν . . . . φησὶ χρῆναι προσεῖναι τοῖς σπουδαίοις ἀνθρώποις . . . . καὶ τὴν φιλοπροσηγορίαν. ὅ πέρ ἐστι τὸ προσφωνεῖν τοὺς ἀπαντῶντας, ὡς αὐτός φησιν. . . . . πολλῷ δή που ἀναγκαιότερον τὸ πρᾶγμα καὶ ὁ τοιοῦτος τρόπος τῆς προσφωνήσεως, εἰ πρὸς τοὺς ἐν τέλει καὶ ἐν ἀρχαῖς γεγονότας ὑφ' ἡμῶν γίγνοιτο καὶ μαλιστά γε δὴ τοὺς ἑκάστοτε ἐκ βασιλέων εἰς τὰ ἔθνη καὶ τὰς πόλεις τὰς ἡμετέρας παραγιγνομένους, ὅπως καὶ αὐτοὺς διὰ τοιούτου τρόπου καὶ πρὸς ἡμᾶς . . . . οἰκειοτέρους διακεῖσθαι παρασκευάσαιμεν. ἀμέλει γέ τοι καὶ τὸ πρᾶγμα ἤδη ἐπιχωριάζει ἐπὶ πᾶσι, καὶ καθάπερ τις οὗτος νόμος καὶ θεσμὸς δι-ελήλυθεν διὰ πάντων, ὡς εὐθὺς ἄμα τε τῇ πρώτῃ τῶν πυλῶν, ὡς ἄν εἴποι τις, εἰσόδῳ προσφωνεῖν τούτους δημοσίᾳ τὰς πόλεις ὑφ' ἑνὸς ὅτου οὖν τῶν ἀρίστων κατὰ τὴν παιδείαν ὥσπερ δημοσίᾳ τινὶ φωνῇ καὶ κοινῷ προσαγορεύματι προσαγορεύοντος.

We have no corpus of panegyrics for the second or third century such as the one that survives in the XII Panegyrici Latini for the late third and fourth. The statement that the rhetor speaks for the community, however, should be linked to the second-century network of sophists addressing emperors on behalf of their cities. See G. W. Bowersock, *Greek Sophists in the Roman Empire* (1969) 43ff.

16. This is to be done by following through, depending on their aptness for the occasion, the usual topics of panegyrics: the orator was to praise the home country, family, deeds and virtues of his subject, and to add the customary comparisons to the great figures of myth and history. It was precisely the stereotyped nature of this procedure, which everyone could know about, that facilitated the integrating function of panegyric and *adventus* ceremonial: Menander, 376, 381, 382.

17. Menander, 378f.

18. Menander, 381, 12. On the authorship of the two treatises attributed to Menander, see J. Soffel, *Die Regeln Menanders für die Leichenrede in ihrer Tradition dargestellt, herausgegeben, übersetzt und kommentiert*, Beitr. zur klass. Philologie, 57 (1974) 100–104. For a discussion of Menander's life and lost works, see 90ff.

19. Menander, 378, 10f.

20. See above, nn. 5 and 14.

21. Menander, 378, 16–23:

> εἶτα μετὰ τὸ προοίμιον τοῦτο ἥξεις εἰς τὸν περὶ τῶν ὑπηκόων λόγον. διπλοῦς δ' οὗτος · ἢ γὰρ κακῶς πεπονθότων αὐτῶν παρὰ τοῦ μικρῷ πρόσθεν ἄρχοντος δια-τυπώσεις καὶ ἀνξήσεις τὰ δυσχερῆ, μηδὲν βλασφημῶν τὸν παυσάμενον, ἀλλὰ ἁπλῶς τὴν δυστυχίαν τῶν ὑπηκόων λέγων, εἶτα ἐπάξεις, ὅτι ὥσπερ νυκτὸς καὶ ζόφου τὰ πάντα κατειληφότος αὐτὸς καθάπερ ἥλιος ὀφθεὶς πάντα ἀθρόως τὰ δυσ-χερῆ διέλυσας.

The image of a ruler arriving like the sun was an ancient one even in Menander's day and was to have a long history: see below at nn. 113ff and 261. For the Byzantine period, cf. M. Jeffreys, "The Nature and Origin of Political Verse," *DOP* 28 (1974) 143–195 at 178.

22. Menander, 381:

> προσαπηντήκαμεν δέ σοι ἅπαντες ὁλοκλήροις τοῖς γένεσι, παῖδες, πρεσβῦται, ἄνδρες, ἱερέων γένη, πολιτευομένων συστήματα, δῆμος περιχαρῶς δεξιούμενοι, πάντες φιλοφρονούμενοι ταῖς εὐφημίαις, σωτῆρα καὶ τεῖχος, ἀστέρα φανώτατον ὀνομάζοντες, οἱ δὲ παῖδες τροφέα μὲν ἑαυτῶν, σωτῆρα δὲ τῶν πατέρων· εἰ δὲ δυ-νατὸν ἦν καὶ ταῖς πόλεσιν ἀφεῖναι φωνὴν καὶ σχήματα λαβεῖν γυναικῶν ὥσπερ

ἐν δράμασι, εἶπον ἄν· ὦ μεγίστης ἀρχ ῆς, ἡδίστης δὲ ἡμέρας, καθ' ἣν ἐπέστη νῦν ἡλίου φῶς φαιδρότερον. νῦν ὥσπερ ἔκ τινος ζόφου προσβλέπειν δοκοῦμεν λευκὴν ἡμέραν. μετὰ μικρὸν ἀναθήσομεν εἰκόνας, μετὰ μικρὸν ποιηταὶ καὶ λογοποιοὶ καὶ ῥήτορες ᾄσουσι τὰς ἀρετὰς καὶ διαδώσουσιν εἰς γένη πάντων ἀνθρώπων· ἀνοιγέσθω θέατρα, πανηγύρεις ἄγωμεν.

23. E.g., in the *adventus* of Camillus (followed by his triumph), Livy, 5, 23, 2:

Immensum gaudium fuit, et priusquam senatus decerneret, plena omnia templa Romanorum matrum grates dis agentium erant. Senatus in quadriduum, quot dierum nullo ante bello, supplicationes decernit. Adventus quoque dictatoris *omnibus ordinibus* obviam effusis celebratior quam ullius umquam antea fuit.

On the late republican and religious significance of this occasion, see S. Weinstock, *Divus Julius* (1971) 71ff.; also H. S. Versnel, *Triumphus, An Enquiry into the Origin, Development and Meaning of the Roman Triumph* (1970) 67ff. For late antiquity, e.g., Julian at Vienne, Amm., 15, 8, 21, *omnis aetas et dignitas* came to meet him; *Pan. Lat.*, 12, 37, 3, Theodosius welcomed at Haemona by *nobilitas, senatores, flamines, sacerdotes*. For enumerations of classes of people at the arrival of relics, see K. G. Holum and G. Vikan, "The Trier Ivory, *Adventus* Ceremonial and the Relics of Saint Stephen," *DOP*, 33 (1979): 113–133.

24. See H. U. Instinsky, "*Consensus universorum*," *Hermes* 75 (1940) 265–278; and K. Oehler, "Der *consensus omnium* als Kriterium der Wahrheit in der antiken Philosophie und der Patristik," *Antike und Abendland* 10 (1961) 103–129.

25. E.g., Procopius of Gaza, *Panegyricus* 1, ed. C. Kemper, Diss. Bonn (1918): κοινῇ πάντες ψήφῳ τῇ τοῦ ῥήτορος ἀρκοῦνται φωνῇ. See below at n. 273.

26. See below at n. 258. Cf. Ps. Dionysius, 272; Menander, 381, 7–8; S. MacCormack, *Historia* 21 (1972) 721, n. 1, 724–725; K. G. Holum and G. Vikan, "The Trier Ivory, *Adventus* Ceremonial and the Relics of Saint Stephen," *DOP*.

27. Menander, ed. Spengel, 382; cf. 377–380. The *prosphonetikos* is a form of general panegyric, 414–418; cf. Nikolaos, *ibid.* 477. See also T. Viljamaa, *Studies in Greek Encomiastic Poetry of the Early Byzantine Period*, Commentationes Humanarum Litterarum Societatis Scientiarum Fennicae, 48, 4 (1968) 20.

28. *Pan. Lat.*, 8, 7–11 (The Latin Panegyrics will always be cited according to the chronological numbering of E. Galletier's Budé edition); see also below at nn. 56ff.

29. P. K. Hitti, *The Origins of the Islamic State* (1916), (being a translation of al-Balâdhuri), 214–215. Similar ceremonies for welcoming the conquerors and ratifying contracts that had been made took place elsewhere: 201–202 Hamâh, Shaizar, Ma'-arrat Hims and Fâmiyah.

30. *Ibid.*, 211. *Adventus* ceremonies of this type, where a contractual element was very clearly expressed, have earlier precedents: Ammianus, 24, 2, 21, the people of Pirisabora welcome Julian as *salutarem genium* after the completion of negotiations; similarly, Khusro I was welcomed in Apamea to ratify an agreement, Procopius *Wars*, 2, 11, 14ff., which Khusro later broke, *Wars*, 2, 11, 24. Cf. John of Ephesus *H.E.*, 6, 6, tr. E. W. Brooks (1936, 1952), for the sack of Apamea by Khusro, an outcome the citizens clearly had not expected.

31. Acclamations, a late antique method of expressing consent: for the Senate, see O. Hirschfeld, "Die römische Staatszeitung und die Akklamationen im Senat," *SB der Berliner Akademie* (1905) 930–948, reprinted in his *Kleine Schriften*

(1913, 1975) 682–702. For Byzantium, P. Maas, "Metrische Akklamationen der Byzantiner," *BZ* 21 (1912) 28–51, and M. Jeffreys, "The Nature and Origin of Political Verse," *DOP* 28 (1974) 143–195.

32. *Pan. Lat.*, 2, 4, 2: Iuppiter and Hercules in battle against the giants to expound the activity of the emperors. The simile is still in Claudian, *VI Consulship of Honorius, Praefatio*. But contrast the diffident question: Would Iuppiter choose primal chaos or Roman order for the world? Cf. Claudian, *VI. Cons.*, 149–151.

33. The literature on this subject is immense. For present purposes see A. Alföldi, *Die monarchische Repräsentation im römischen Kaiserreiche*, being a new edition of his "Die Ausgestaltung des monarchischen Zeremoniells am römischen Kaiserhofe," *Röm. Mitt.* 49 (1934) 3–118, and his "Insignien und Tracht der römischen Kaiser," *Röm. Mitt.* 50 (1935) 3–158; L. Cerfaux and J. Tondriau, *Un concurrent du christianisme: le culte des souverains dans la civilisation gréco-romaine* (1957) 269ff; and for late antiquity, M. Wes, *Das Ende des Kaisertums im Westen des röm. Reiches* (1967) 25ff. S. Weinstock, *Divus Julius* (1971), one of the best accounts ever written of the workings and tensions of Roman religion and politics, applies not only to Caesar's period.

34. The impact of this religious imagery was founded on the tangible political and military achievements of the Tetrarchs: Camille Jullian, *Histoire de la Gaule*, vol. 7 (1926) 3–98; and W. Seston, *Dioclétien et la Tétrarchie*, Bibl. des éc. fr. d'Athènes et de Rome, 162 (1946) 56–114. The evidence used in these studies applies largely to the Eastern parts of Gaul, which are also represented in the *XII Panegyrici Latini*. Elsewhere the Tetrarchic period was less clearly marked. See, e.g., M. Labrousse, *Toulouse antique, des origines à l'établissement des Wisigoths*, Bibl. des éc. fr. d'Athènes et de Rome, 212 (1968) 567–572. Where evidence is available, however, a picture consistent with that given in the *Panegyrici Latini* emerges. Thus for Egypt, J. G. Deckers, "Die Wandmalereien," *RQ* 68 (1973) 1–34.

35. For Demetrius, see above, n. 14; for Caesar, S. Weinstock, *Divus Julius* (1971) 296f.; and for the Tetrarchs in 296–297 A.D., *Année épigraphique* (1968), 514–517: ὑπὲρ σωτερίας καὶ νίκης τῶν κυρίων ἡμῶν . . . τῶν ἐπιφανεστάτων καισάρων ἀνεστάθησαν ὅροι κώμης καπροκηνῶν; similarly, *Année épigraphique* (1966), 383, for Constantius I.

36. For this, see Seston, "Jovius et Herculius ou l'épiphanie des Tétrarches," *Historia* 1 (1950) 257–266, with the important, and in my view decisive, critique by E. Wistrand, *Opera Selecta* (1972) 427–441. On the textual foundation of this debate over the question of whether this panegyric marks the 'epiphany' of the Tetrarchs (Seston) or the *natalis* of Maximian (Wistrand), see Mynors, ed., *Pan. Lat.*, XI, 19, 1; 3 where the Harleianus has *genuinus* (i.e., personal) *natalis*, but also 1, 1 and 7, 7 where the MS tradition agrees on *geminus* (i.e., a joint birthday of the Tetrarchs, referring, according to Seston, to their joint *dies imperii* and therefore to their epiphany as *Iovius* and *Herculius*).

37. In this description of *adventus*, the countryside and the control by the emperors over natural phenomena play an important role. See *Pan. Lat.* 3, 9–10. The theme is still in Claudian, e.g., *Cons. VI*, 25–28.

38. See E. Galletier, ed., *Panégyriques latins*, vol. 1, 42.

39. See S. MacCormack, "Roma, Constantinopolis, the Emperor, and His Genius," *CQ* 25 (1975) 131–150.

40. *Pan. Lat.*, 3, 19, 2:

> Etenim ceterae virtutes et bona cetera processu aetatis eveniunt, fortitudo annis accedentibus roboratur, continentia disciplinae praeceptis traditur, iustitia cognitione iuris addiscitur, ipsa denique illa quae videtur rerum omnium domina esse sapientia perspectis hominum moribus et exploratis rerum docetur eventis: solae cum nascentibus pariter oriuntur pietas atque felicitas; naturalia sunt enim animorum bona et praemia fatorum.

41. *Pan. Lat.*, 3, 8, 1:

> Inde igitur proxime illa impatientia vestrae pietatis erupit quod vos nulla regionum longinquitas, nulla iniquitas locorum, nulla tempestatis asperitas retinere aut morari potuit quominus ad conspectum vestri provolaretis.

42. *Pan. Lat.*, 3, 8, 3–4:

> Divinus quidam impetus fuit, quo repente in eumdem locum ab utroque solis adverso fine venistis; . . . ut . . . ceteri homines fortasse crediderint, quod dignum est maiestate vestra, diurna vobis et nocturna curricula utraque mundi lumina commodasse. Sed removeamus istinc fabulas imperitorum, verum loquamur: vestra vobis pietas, sacratissime imperator, volucres dedit cursus.

43. On the visual quality of significant experience, see A. J. Festugière, "L'expérience religieuse du médecin Thessalos," *Rev. bibl.* 48 (1939) 45–77, reprinted in his *Hermétisme et mystique païenne* (1967) 141f; cf. *Pan. Lat.*, 2, 6, 3f. stressing the experience of seeing (*vidimus te*), and cf. n. 52 below.

44. *Pan. Lat.*, 3, 8, 3–4.

45. *Pan. Lat.*, 3, 9, 2:

> Adeo ut res est, adversus inclementiam locorum ac siderum vestrae vos maiestatis potentia tuebatur et ceteris hominibus atque regionibus vi frigorum adstrictis et oppressis vos solos aurae lenes vernique flatus et diductis nubibus ad itinera vestra derecti solis radii sequebantur.

46. Lactantius, *Mort. Pers.* 17, 3 with notes by J. Moreau, *De la mort des persécuteurs, Sources Chrétiennes* 39, 2 (1954) 305; cf. below, n. 142. On the triumphal monument which was erected for this visit of Diocletian to Rome, see H. P. L'Orange, "Ein tetrarchisches Ehrendenkmal auf dem Forum Romanum," *Mitteilungen des deutschen archäologischen Instituts, Römische Abt.* 53 (1938) 1–34, reprinted in his *Likeness and Icon* (1973) 131–157, and H. Kähler, *Das Fünfsäulendenkmal für die Tetrarchen auf dem Forum Romanum* (1964).

47. *Pan. Lat.*, 3, 9, 5; cf. *Pan. Lat.*, 2, 1.

48. *Pan. Lat.*, 3, 9, 4–10, 3.

49. *Orirentur*: cf. E. Kantorowicz, "*Puer exoriens*: On the Hypapante in the Mosaics of S. Maria Maggiore," in his *Collected Studies* (1965) 25–36.

50. *Pan. Lat.*, 3, 10, 4–5:

> Nunc autem, ut primum ex utrisque Alpium iugis vestrum numen effulsit, tota Italia clarior lux diffusa, omnibus qui suspexerant aeque admiratio atque dubitatio iniecta est quinam dei illis montium verticibus orirentur, an his gradibus in terras caelo descenderent. Ut vero propius propiusque coepti estis agnosci, omnes agri oppleti non hominibus modo ad visendum procurrentibus sed etiam pecudum gregibus remota pascua et nemora linquentibus, concursare inter se agricolae, nuntiare totis vicis visa, arae incendi, tura poni, vina libari, victimae

caedi, cuncta gaudio calere, cuncta plausibus tripudiare, dis immortalibus laudes gratesque cantari, non opinione traditus, sed conspicuus et praesens Iuppiter cominus invocari, non advena sed imperator Hercules adorari.

51. The palace as a holy place: cf. Eusebius, *L.C.*, prologue, 3–5.

52. *Pan. Lat.*, 3, 11, 1–5:

> Quale pietas vestra spectaculum dedit, cum in Mediolanensi palatio admissis qui sacros vultus adoraturi erant conspecti estis ambo et consuetudinem simplicis venerationis geminato numine repente turbastis! . . . Atque haec quidem velut interioribus sacrariis operta veneratio eorum modo animos obstupefecerat quibus aditum vestri dabant ordines dignitatis. Ut vero limine egressi per mediam urbem simul vehebamini, tecta ipsa se, ut audio, paene commoverunt, omnibus viris feminis, parvulis senibus aut per fores in publicum proruentibus aut per superiora aedium lumina imminentibus. Clamare omnes prae gaudio, iam sine metu vestri et palam manu demonstrare: 'Vides Diocletianum? Maximianum vides? Ambo sunt, pariter sunt! Quam iunctim sedent! Quam concorditer colloquuntur! Quam cito transeunt!' Nemo studio suo par fuit oculis ad intuendum, . . . neutrum satis videre potuerunt.

Note the emphasis on seeing, beholding, in this passage.

53. Menander, ed. Spengel, 372, 25ff.

54. *Pan. Lat.*, 4, 19:

> Merito igitur statim atque ad litus illud exoptatus olim vindex et liberator appuleras, obvius sese maiestati tuae triumphus effudit exsultantesque gaudio Britanni cum coniugibus ac liberis obtulerunt, non te ipsum modo, quem ut caelo delapsum intuebantur, sed etiam navis illius quae tuum numen advexerat, vela remigiaque venerantes, paratique te ingredientem stratis sentire corporibus. Nec mirum si tanto gaudio ferebantur post tot annorum miserrimam captivitatem. . . . tandem liberi tandemque Romani, tandem vera imperii luce recreati. Siquidem praeter illam clementiae vestrae pietatisque famam, quae communi gentium voce celebratur, in ipso, Caesar, tuo vultu videbant omnium signa virtutum.

55. *Pan. Lat.*, 7, 7, 5:

> Iam tunc enim caelestibus suffragiis ad salutem rei publicae vocabaris, cum ad tempus ipsum quo pater in Britanniam transfretabat classi iam vela facienti repentinus tuus adventus inluxit, ut non advectus cursu publico, sed divino quodam advolasse curriculo videreris.

On the actual circumstances of this journey see Zosimus, II, 8, and Lactantius, *De mortibus persecutorum*, XXIV, 6–8. Constantine was said to have destroyed the horses in the *mansiones* to avoid pursuit.

56. *Pan. Lat.*, 8, 5–7. On the panegyrist and the occasion of this oration see E. Galletier, *Panégyriques latins*, vol. 2 (1952) 77–83. On second-century precedents of a sophist or rhetor advocating the cause of his home town before the emperor, see G. W. Bowersock, *Greek Sophists in the Roman Empire* (1969) 43ff; cf. 17ff. Eumenius, author of *P.L.* 5, of 298 A.D., was another local patriot and university teacher from Autun.

57. *Pan. Lat.*, 8, 7, 4–6:

> Et urbem illam sola opis tuae exspectatione viventem inlustrare dignatus es. . . . Di immortales, quisnam ille tum nobis illuxit dies. . . . cum tu, quod

primum nobis signum salutis fuit, portas istius urbis intrasti, quae te habitu illo in sinum reducto et procurrentibus utrimque turribus amplexu quodam videbantur accipere.

58. *Pan. Lat.*, 8, 8, 4:

Exornavimus vias quibus in palatium pervenitur paupere quidem supellectili, sed omnium signa collegiorum, omnium deorum nostrorum simulacra, paucissima clarorum instrumenta modulorum per compendia saepius tibi occursura protulimus.

59. *Pan. Lat.*, 8, 9.
60. *Pan. Lat.*, 8, 9, 5–6:

Vidimus misericordiam tuam umentibus oculis eminentem. Ibant per haec ora lacrimae nobis salutares . . . et nos invicem iam dolore discusso flebamus gaudio. Nam sicut agros diuturno ardore sitientes expetitus votis imber ubertat, ita lacrimae tuae pectora nostra gaudiis irrigabant, ut, quamvis nefas esset te flente laetari, vinceret tamen gratulatio religionem, cum lacrimae illae pietatis essent indices, non doloris.

61. J. M. C. Toynbee, *Roman Medallions* (1944) 182–183, 195 and pl. VIII, 4. On the panegyric of 297, the Arras medallion and the related PIETAS AUGG multiples, referred to below, see M. Christol, "La *pietas* de Constance Chlore: l'empereur et les provinciaux à la fin du IIIᵉ siècle," *Bulletin de la société française de numismatique* 30, 10 (1975) 858–861. The Arras hoard has now been published: P. Bastien and C. Metzger, *Le trésor de Beaurains (dit d'Arras)*, Numismatique romaine, 10 (1977).

62. See above, at n. 22.

63. For an example of spontaneous personification, see Demosthenes, *Olynth.* I, 2: ὁ μὲν οὖν παρὼν καιρός . . . μόνον οὐχὶ λέγει φωνὴν ἀφιείς.

64. Athens National Museum, no. 1467; K. Schefold, *Die Griechen und ihre Nachbarn* (1967) pl. 94b; cf. R. Binneboessel, "Studien zu den attischen Urkundenreliefs d. 5. und 4. Jhdts." (1932). Note esp. reliefs of treaties enumerated on 20.

65. See J. M. C. Toynbee, *The Hadrianic School* (1934) 7ff. For the *Tyche* of Antioch, see Tobias Dohrn, *Die Tyche von Antiocheia* (1960).

66. *Pan. Lat.*, 6, 8, 6.

67. H. Mattingly, E. A. Sydenham and others, *The Roman Imperial Coinage* (to be quoted hereafter as *RIC*), VI, 411ff.

68. 296–298 A.D., *RIC*, VI, 422f; the legends vary slightly. The fact that the issues are for all four Tetrarchs illustrates well how the emperors could impersonate each other, for only Maximian, and possibly Diocletian, were in Africa.

69. *RIC*, VI, 426, nos. 23–30 etc., 43, 50–51.

70. Toynbee, *Roman Medallions*, pl. 8, 5–6.

71. *RIC*, V² 439, 483, 510 with pl. 16, 6; 515, 528, an exception to this legend and image: 464 with pl. 16, 14, ADVENTUS AUG, mounted emperor.

72. See A. Alföldi, "Insignien und Tracht der römischen Kaiser," *Röm. Mitt.* (1935), reprinted in A. Alföldi, *Die monarchische Repräsentation im röm. Kaiserreiche* (1970) 161f.

73. *RIC*, I, 89, with pl. 3, 45, Gaius; pl. 7, 118, Nero and Drusus.

74. *RIC*, I, pl. 9, 172, 173. The theme was also treated in monumental art on the column base of Antoninus Pius in the Vatican but the context here is fune-

real. See below "*Consecratio*," n. 29; and, in a triumphal context, on the porphyry sarcophagus thought to have been intended for Helena in the Vatican, R. Delbrueck, *Antike Porphyrwerke* (1932) 215f, pl. 100f.

75. F. Gnecchi, *I Medaglioni Romani* (1912) (quoted hereafter as Gnecchi), I, 21, 6; II, 38, 1.

76. Cf. E. Kantorowicz, "The 'King's Advent' and the Enigmatic Panels in the Doors of Santa Sabina," *Art Bulletin* 26 (1944) 207–231, reprinted in his *Selected Studies* (1965) at 45f; Diocletian mounted, ADVENTUS AUG, e.g., *RIC* V² 241.

77. Dated 291 A.D. by Bastien and Metzger, *Le trésor de Beaurains*, Numismatique romaine, 10 (1977).

78. *RIC*, IV³ 28, 132; 50, 323 with pl. 11. J. Keil, "Ephesos und der Etappendienst zwischen der Nord- und Ostfront des Imperium Romanum," *Anzeiger der österr. Akad. d. Wiss. Phil. hist. Kl.* 12 (1955), 159–170, at 163–164.

79. *Pan. Lat.*, 8, 7, 6; *RIC* VII, 144, 162; and E. M. Wightman, *Roman Trier and the Treveri* (1970) 59 and pl. 2.

80. Gnecchi II, 59, 5. City gates also figure in imperial departure, *profectio*; see below at n. 90 and plate 10. For the ascent, i.e. *profectio* of Elias, represented with the city gate which was taken from imperial art, see plate 31.

81. See P. G. Hamberg, *Studies in Roman Imperial Art with Special Reference to the State Reliefs of the Second Century* (1945) chapter II; and I. Scott Ryberg, *Rites of the State Religion in Roman Art*, Memoirs of the American Academy in Rome, 22 (1955) 203ff.

82. *RIC* VI, index II; and cf. *RIC* V², index V.

83. See also *Pan. Lat.*, 2, 6, 3:

> Vidimus te, Caesar, eodem die et in clarissimo pacis habitu et in pulcherrimo virtutis ornatu.

The idea that the face expresses virtues is not restricted to panegyric: see, e.g., Marinus *Vita Procli*, ed. J. F. Boissonade (1814) 51.

84. H. P. L'Orange, *Apotheosis in Ancient Portraiture* (1947) 19. See also G. Mathew, "The Character of the Gallienic Renaissance," *JRS* (1943) 65–70. K. Weitzmann ed., *Age of Spirituality. Late Antique and Early Christian Art, Third to Seventh Century* (1979) 9–10.

85. Gnecchi, 124, 1.

86. Gnecchi, 5, 7. The reverses of this issue and Gnecchi 124, 1 are identical.

87. R. Delbrueck, *Antike Porphyrwerke*, 24f, 84f, pl. 31ff. This group is one of a series of Tetrarchic porphyry portraits of emperors. See D. E. L. Haynes, "A Late Antique Portrait Head in Porphyry," *Burlington Magazine* 118, 829 (June 1976) 350–357, and Kurt Weitzmann, ed., *Age of Spirituality. Late Antique and Early Christian Art, Third to Seventh Century* (1979) 14, on the British Museum Tetrarch. To describe the style of Tetrarchic portraiture, Haynes contrasts classical idealism combined with individualisation and "the rejection of organic structure" as exemplified in Plotinus' ecstasy (356–357). The latter criterion is applied to the Tetrarchic B.M. head. This analysis of methods in portraiture is, notwithstanding the more controversial analysis of late antique social ills which accompanies it, a helpful one. The style was not universal during the Tetrarchy, however: R. Miescher, "A Late Roman Portrait Head," *JRS* 43 (1953) 101–103. The Venice Tetrarchs came from Constantinople. See W. Müller-Wiener, *Bildlexikon zur Topographie Istanbuls* (1977) 267, *Philadelphion*.

88. *Pan. Lat.*, 3, 19, 2 quoted above at n. 40.

89. As in the Vatican Tetrarchs (R. Delbrueck, *Antike Porphyrwerke* (1932) 91f) and on the coinage.

90. South-west pilaster, north-east face, top: Hans Peter Laubscher, *Der Reliefschmuck des Galeriusbogens in Thessaloniki*, 61–64, pl. 45–50; on the badly damaged relief of *adventus* in Nisibis, 36–38, pl. 22–23. See also M. S. Pond Rothman, "The Thematic Organisation of the Panel Reliefs on the Arch of Galerius," *American Journal of Archaeology* 81 (1977) 442, 452–453. For earlier *adventus* scenes in monumental art, see I. Scott Ryberg, *Rites of the State Religion in Roman Art* (1955) 120ff.

91. Third from the top: Laubscher, *Der Reliefschmuck*, 69–78, pl. 45, 51, 58–60.

92. See below, "*Consecratio*" at nn. 173ff, for a detailed interpretation of this relief.

93. This change is analysed by W. Ensslin, "Gottkaiser und Kaiser von Gottes Gnaden," *SB der bayerischen Akad. d. Wiss. Phil.-hist. Kl.* (1943) 6. From a different standpoint, see D. A. Miller, "Royauté et ambiguïté sexuelle," *Annales* 26 (1971) 639–652.

94. Themistius, 42b.

95. *Pan. Lat.*, 6, 8, 6–9.

> Tu ferocissimos Mauritaniae populos inaccessis montium iugis et naturali munitione fidentes expugnasti, recepisti, transtulisti. Te primo ingressu tuo tanta laetitia, tanta frequentia populus Romanus excepit ut cum te ad Capitolini Iovis gremium vel oculis ferre gestiret, stipatione sui vix ad portas urbis admitteret. Te rursus vicesimo anno imperatorem, octavum consulem, ita ipsa amplexu quodam suo Roma voluit detinere.

Here the orator takes up a reference to Cicero's return from exile, cf. *Pan. Lat.*, 9, 19, 4. This passage at the same time deliberately recalls the panegyric on Maximian—*Pan. Lat.*, 6, 8, 7: *oculis ferre gestiret*; *Pan. Lat.*, 9, 19, 5: *oculis ferre gestivit*—an interesting sidelight on the techniques and schooling of the Gallic panegyrists.

96. On the retirement of Diocletian and Maximian, see G. S. R. Thomas, "L'abdication de Dioclétien," *Byzantion* 43 (1973) 229–247, proving that the event had not been planned in advance but was the result of pressure exercised by Galerius.

97. J. Straub, "Konstantins Verzicht auf den Gang zum Kapitol," *Historia* 4 (1955) 297–313, reprinted in his *Regeneratio Imperii* (1972) 100–118, which dates the refusal to sacrifice to 312. But see also F. Paschoud, "Zosime 2, 29 et la version païenne de la conversion de Constantin," *Historia* 20 (1971) 334–353, where the pagan evidence is discussed, and Constantine's refusal to sacrifice on the Capitol is dated to his Decennalia in 315. For the general background, see A. Alföldi, *The Conversion of Constantine and Pagan Rome* (1969); N. H. Baynes, *Constantine the Great and the Christian Church*, ed. H. Chadwick, (1972); and for depictions of triumph in earlier imperial art, I. Scott Ryberg, *Rites of the State Religion in Roman Art*, American Academy in Rome, Memoirs 22 (1955) 141ff.

98. *Pan. Lat.*, 9, 16, 3ff. On Maxentius, see D. de Decker, "La politique religieuse de Maxence," *Byzantion* 38 (1968) 472–562.

99. *Pan. Lat.*, 9, 16, 1f. The same method was followed in 321 by Nazarius, who reiterated before the Roman Senate the importance of the victory and entry into Rome in 312, and even used the term *triumphus*: *Pan. Lat.*, 10, 30, 5; 32, 1.

100. Note *Pan. Lat.*, 9, 20, 2:

> Quamlibet verba tua in senatu habita *nobis ignota sint*, tamen qualia fuerint clementiae tuae gloria nuntiavit.

101. *Pan. Lat.*, 9, 19, 1ff; 10, 1ff; *Pan. Lat.*, 10, 30, 4ff, 33–36.

102. Thus *Pan. Lat.*, 10, 32, 6 in its context should be taken as the *topos* which it is, and no more, for, unlike the *topoi* of the Tetrarchic panegyrics, it is not properly expounded.

103. See below, *"Consecratio"* at nn. 66ff, 145 f.

104. H. P. L'Orange and A. von Gerkan, *Der spätantike Bildschmuck des Konstantinsbogens* (1939) gives a comprehensive, still fundamental, interpretation of the arch. For the Sol tondo, see 162–164.

105. See *RIC*, V¹, Index V s.v. SOL AUG etc. On the Ticinum medallion and its numismatic context, see M. R. Alföldi, *Die konstantinische Goldprägung Untersuchungen zu ihrer Bedeutung für Kaiserpolitik und Hofkunst* (1963) 49ff.

106. Cf. E. Kantorowicz, "Oriens Augusti—Lever du Roi," *DOP* 17 (1963) 119–135.

107. See G. Mathew, "The Character of the Gallienic Renaissance," *JRS* 33 (1943) 65–70; also B. Haarløv, "A Contribution to the Iconography of the Emperor Gallienus," *Stud. Romana in honorem Petri Krarup* (1976) 113–121. The stages of Constantinian portraiture on the coins and in sculpture are traced by M. R. Alföldi, *Die konstantinische Goldprägung* (1963) 57–69 and 82f (Trajanic precedents); 93–94, 96ff, 115ff (diadem and upward glance); 122–138. Cf. P. Bruun, "Constantine's *Dies Imperii* and *Quinquennalia* in the Light of the Early Solidi of Trier," *Numismatic Chronicle* 7, 9 (1969) 177–205, at 192 and 196f, on early versions of portraits with flowing hair.

108. Already in 307 A.D.: *Pan. Lat.*, 6, 3, 3–6; then *Pan. Lat.*, 7, 17; 21; cf. *Pan. Lat.*, 9, 19, 6 and 10, 34 in the context of *adventus*.

109. *Pan. Lat.*, 7, 22.

110. Cf. MacCormack, *Historia* 21 (1972) 731–732 and n. 65.

111. Cf. the Athenian paean on Demetrius Poliorcetes in Athenaeus, above at n. 14.

112. *Pan. Lat.*, 7, 21, 4f:

> Vidisti enim, credo, Constantine, Apollinem tuum comitante Victoria coronas tibi laureas offerentem, quae tricenum singulae ferunt omen annorum. Hic est enim humanarum numerus aetatum, quae tibi utique debentur ultra Pyliam senectutem. Et immo quid dico 'credo'? Vidisti teque in illius specie recognovisti, cui totius mundi regna deberi vatum carmina divina cecinerunt. Quod ego nunc demum arbitror contigisse, cum tu sis, ut ille, iuvenis et laetus et salutifer et pulcherrimus, imperator.

On Victoria and the emperor, cf. Optatianus Porphyrius VII, intexti versus on the (Rho) of the Chi Rho: *sit Victoria comes Augusti et nati eius*; cf. I. Polara's commentary in his edition *Publii Optiani Porfyrii Carmina* II (1973) 60, 65. The poem was written within c. ten years of *Pan. Lat.*, 7, showing how smoothly the transition from paganism to Christianity could be made on some levels.

113. For a related version of this obverse see *RIC*, VII, pl. 10, 53; and on Constantine and Sol, M. R. Alföldi, "Die Sol *comes* Münze vom J. 325," in *Mullus, Festschrift T. Klauser* (1964) 10–16.

114. Referring to Licinius and Constantine in Milan 313, J. M. C. Toynbee, *Roman Medallions*, 109.

115. H. P. L'Orange and A. von Gerkan, *Der spätantike Bildschmuck des Konstantinsbogens* (1939) 72–80.

116. F. N. Versnel, *Triumphus* (1970) esp. 56–93.

117. L'Orange and von Gerkan, *Bildschmuck*, 52ff, 164–165.

118. On Iuppiter and Hercules, see H. Bloch, "The Pagan Revival in the West at the End of the Fourth Century," in A. Momigliano, ed., *The Conflict between Paganism and Christianity* (1964) 193–218. As regards the Christian potential of Constantine's sol imagery, see on the logos as light and sun in Philo, A. Wlosok, *Laktanz und die philosophische Gnosis* Abh. d. Heidelberger Akad d. Wiss. phil. hist. Kl., 2 (1960) 86ff. On the Parabiago plate, G. Mathew, *Byzantine Aesthetics* (1963) 17; K. Weitzmann, ed., *Age of Spirituality. Late Antique and Early Christian Art* (1979) 185.

119. Claudian, *IV Cons.*, 9; cf. *VI Cons.*, 5–10.

120. L'Orange and von Gerkan, *Bildschmuck*, 93ff. On the concepts underlying imperial largesse to civilians, see A. U. Stylow, *Libertas und Liberalitas, Untersuchungen zur innenpolitischen Propaganda der Römer* (1972) 58–87, esp. 81, on the arch of Constantine.

121. *Exodus* 15, 1–2; 11, and Eusebius, *Historia Ecclesiastica* (henceforth *H.E.*) 9, 9, 8. The actual entry is described with the customary enumeration of groups of people (all came to meet him, children and wives, Senate and other dignitaries): *H.E.* 9, 9, 9. Cf. Eusebius *Vita Constantini* (henceforth *V.C.*) 1, 39.

122. The battle of the Milvian Bridge: *Pan. Lat.*, 9, 17; the battle relief on the arch: L'Orange and von Gerkan, *Bildschmuck*, 65–71. F. Benoît, *Sarcophages paléochrétiens d'Arles et de Marseille*, Supplement à *Gallia* 5 (1954) catalogue numbers 44, 62, 64 and p. 22, n. 10 linking these sarcophagi with the arch of Constantine. J. Doignon, "Le Monogramme cruciforme du sarcophage paléocrétien de Metz représentant le passage de la mer rouge: un symbole de triomphe sur la mort dans le cadre d'une iconographie aulique d'inspiration constantinienne," *Cahiers Archéologiques* 12 (1962) 65–87. See also M. Lawrence, "Columnar Sarcophagi," *Art Bulletin* 14 (1932) 121–122, figs. 23 (Arles), 25 (Aix), 27 (Lateran); and A. Grabar, *L'empereur dans l'art byzantin* (1936; 1971) 95–96.

123. Eusebius, *V.C.*, IV, 15:

Ὅση δ' αὐτοῦ τῇ ψυχῇ πίστεως ἐνθέου ὑπεστήρικτο δύναμις, μάθοι ἄν τις καὶ ἐκ τοῦδε λογιζόμενος, ὡς ἐν τοῖς χρυσοῖς νομίσμασι τὴν αὐτὸς αὐτοῦ εἰκόνα ὧδε γράφεσθαι διετύπου, ὡς ἄνω βλέπειν δοκεῖν ἀνατεταμένως πρὸς θεὸν τρόπον εὐχομένου . . . ἐν αὐτοῖς δὲ βασιλείοις κατά τινας πόλεις ἐν ταῖς εἰς τὸ μετέωρον τῶν προπύλων ἀνακειμέναις εἰκόσιν ἑστὼς ὄρθιος ἐγράφετο, ἄνω μὲν εἰς οὐρανὸν ἐμβλέπων, τὼ χεῖρε δ' ἐκτεταμένος εὐχομένου σχήματι.

124. Cf. below at n. 352.

125. G. Dagron, "L'empire romain d'orient au IVᵉ siècle et les traditions politiques de l'Hellénisme, le témoignage de Thémistios," *Travaux et mémoires* 3 (1968) 88f, 125f, 135ff, 199f.

126. Claudian *VI Cons.*, 1–5.

> Aurea Fortunae Reduci templa priores
> ob reditum vovere ducum, non dignius umquam

haec dea pro meritis amplas sibi posceret aedes,
quam sua cum pariter trabeis reparatur et urbi
maiestas.

127. A. Alföldi, *The Conversion of Constantine and Pagan Rome* (1969) 91ff, and G. Dagron, *Naissance d'une capitale, Constantinople et ses institutions de 330 à 451* (1974) 19ff.

128. Dagron, *Naissance*, 49ff, 52–54, on Themistius; cf. F. Paschoud, *Roma Aeterna, étude sur le patriotisme romain dans l'Occident latin à l'époque des grandes invasions*, Bibliotheca Helvetica Romana, 7 (1967).

129. Cf. M. Wes, *Das Ende des Kaisertums* (1967) 14f.

130. Themistius, *Or.* III. On the circumstances, see G. Dagron, "L'empire romain d'orient," *Travaux et mémoires* 3 (1968) 205–212.

131. See, e.g., Themistius, 42c–44d.

132. Themistius, 41a: αὐτὴ γάρ ἐστιν ὅλη σὸς στέφανος καὶ ἀνάθημα.

133. Themistius, 41cd:

αλλ' ἐν τῇ βασιλευούσῃ τῶν πόλεων ἀναδεῖ τὸν βασιλεύοντα τῶν ἀνθρώπων ἡ
τὰ δεύτερα δι' ὑμᾶς βασιλεύουσα, καὶ ταύτην ἄρα τὴν πόλιν ποιεῖται μάρτυρα
τῆς τιμῆς, ἢ μόνη σεμνοτέρα τῆς τιμώσης ἐστίν.

Themistius' claims for Constantinople in an imperial context were paralleled in an ecclesiastical one: see T. O. Martin, "The Twentyeighth Canon of Chalcedon, A Background Note," in A. Grillmeier, S.J. and H. Bacht, S.J., *Das Konzil von Chalkedon, Geschichte und Gegenwart*, vol. 2 (1959) 433–458.

134. Themistius, 42c–43c.

135. J. M. C. Toynbee, "Roma and Constantinopolis in Late Antique Art from 312–365," *JRS* 37 (1947) 135–144, and "Roma and Constantinopolis in Late Antique Art from 365—Justin II," in *Studies Presented to D. M. Robinson*, vol. 2 (1953) 261–277.

136. Themistius, 44c.

137. Amm., 16, 10. Cf. Soz., *H.E.*, 48, who calls the entry ἐπινίκιον πομπήν. On the splendour of the occasion, see R. MacMullen, "Some Pictures in Ammianus Marcellinus," *Art Bulletin* 46 (1964) 438ff. R. O. Edbrooke, "The Visit of Constantius II to Rome in 357 and Its Effect on the Pagan Roman Senatorial Aristocracy," *American Journal of Philology* 97 (1976) 40–61, stresses that the practical importance of this visit regarding relations between the emperor and the pagans of Rome should not be overestimated and that the ecclesiastical politics of the period were of greater concern to the emperor (on which, cf. M. Meslin, *Les Ariens d'Occident 335–430*, Patristica Sorbonensia, 8 (1967) 29–44). In our present context, the time-honoured symbolism of *adventus* in Rome as described by Ammianus, largely pagan as Rome still was, can therefore be understood to speak with the *Tendenz* which Ammianus appears to have intended. See on this J. Straub, *Vom Herrscherideal in der Spätantike* (1964) 175–204.

138. See J. Gagé, "La théologie de la victoire impériale," *Revue historique* (1933) 1–43 and "Σταυρὸς νικοποιός, la victoire impériale dans l'empire chrétien," *Rev. d'hist. et de philos. religieuses* (1933) 370ff. See also G. C. Picard, *Les trophées romains, contribution à l'histoire de la religion et de l'art triomphal de Rome*, Bibl. des éc. fr. d'Athènes et de Rome, 187 (1957) 463ff.

139. Themistius, 45b; cf. G. Downey, "Philanthropia and Statecraft in the

Fourth Century after Christ," *Historia* 4 (1955) 199–208. At the same time, it should be noted that imperial ideology and ceremonial at this time sought to convey their message less by the differentiation than by the conflation of concepts. The fictions of the *Historia Augusta* illustrate this phenomenon. See E. Merten, *Zwei Herrscherfeste in der Historia Augusta, Antiquitas*, Reihe 4, Beitr. zur H.-A.-Forschung, 5 (1968).

140. *Sedebat aureo solus ipse carpento*: Amm., 16, 10, 7.

141. Amm., 16, 10, 8.

142. Amm., 16, 10, 13f, and contrast Lactantius *Mort. Pers.* 17, 2: Diocletian on the occasion of his Vicennalia, *cum libertatem populi Romani ferre non poterat, impatiens . . . prorupit ex urbe*. This comment is an expression of Lactantius' anti-Tetrarchic stance; cf. above n. 46. On liberties taken by the people of Rome when facing their emperor during circus games, see Alan Cameron, *Circus Factions. Blues and Greens at Rome and Byzantium* (1976) 157–180. See also P. Veyne, *Le pain et le cirque* (1976) 704–717, and F. Millar, *The Emperor in the Roman World*, 368f. Theodoret, *H.E.*, 1, 17 (GCS 44, 177) reports a particularly revealing instance of liberties taken by the people of Rome once the emperor had arrived. Constantius II had exiled Pope Liberius and installed Felix in his place. Upon popular petition, Constantius recalled Liberius, but would not remove Felix. Next, the people in the hippodrome declared the imperial ordinance to be just, since each of the two factions could now have its own bishop: οὕτω κωμῳδήσαντες τοῦ βασιλέως τὰ γράμματα κοινὴν ἀφῆκαν φωνήν· « εἷς Θεός, εἷς Χριστός, εἷς ἐπίσκοπος » whereupon Felix was sent elsewhere. For the acclamation cf. E. Peterson, Εἷς Θεός (1926) 181, 255.

143. Cf. below at n. 178 for Theodosius.

144. Eusebius *V.C.*, 3, 10f. The usual panegyrics graced the occasion: Eusebius *V.C.* 3, 11; Sozomen *H.E.*, 1, 19, panegyric by Eusebius himself; and Theodoret *H.E.*, 1, 16, another panegyric by Eustathius of Antioch. On Constantine's role vis-à-vis the church, cf. below "*Accession*," n. 384.

145. R. Delbrueck, *Spätantike Kaiserporträts* (1933) 47ff (pl. 57) dates it after 343; Grabar, *L'empereur dans l'art byzantin* (1936) 48, to the mid-fourth century. See also J. P. C. Kent and K. S. Painter, *Wealth of the Roman World* (1977) 25. The *adventus* coinage of Constantius II (e.g., Gnecchi 10, 10; 11, 2; 11, 4; cf. 10, 9) is not sufficiently specific in its imagery to allow definite connections to be made with particular arrivals. The emperor is shown in the usual idiom, mounted and raising a hand in greeting, FELIX ADVENTUS AUG N.

146. Also employed on the Barberini diptych and the medallion of Justinian, below at nn. 282ff and nn. 307f.

147. Delbrueck, *Kaiserporträts*, 147.

148. Early icons exhibiting these features: e.g., Virgin and Child between SS. Theodore and George, Mount Sinai, Monastery of S. Catherine, K. Weitzmann, *The Monastery of Saint Catherine at Mount Sinai. The Icons*, vol. 1 (1976) 18–21 and pl. 3; Virgin and Child between two angels, Santa Maria in Trastevere, Rome, illustrated in J. Beckwith, *Early Christian and Byzantine Art* (1970) pl. 77. Similar conventions are to be observed on almost any Christian image of late antiquity, and also characterized early Byzantine representations of the emperor. On a portrait of Heraclius and his family as Job and his family, see K. Weitzmann, ed., *Age of Spirituality* (1979) 35–36.

149. Vergil *Aen.*, 2, 681–700. Cf. Servius *Ad Aen.* 1, 382: the star of Venus guides Aeneas from Troy to Italy.

150. Suetonius *Caligula*, 13:

> Sic imperium adeptus, populum Romanum, vel dicam hominum genus, voti compotem fecit, exoptatissimus princeps maximae parti provincialium ac militum . . . sed et universae plebi urbanae . . . Itaque ut a Miseno movit quamvis lugentis habitu et funus Tiberi prosequens, tamen inter altaria et victimas ardentisque taedas densissimo et laetissimo obviorum agmine incessit, super fausta nomina 'sidus' et 'pullum' et 'pupum' et 'alumnum' appellantium.

Cf. S. Eitrem, "Zur Apotheose," *Symbolae Osloenses* 11 (1932) at 19.

151. Cf. *V.C.*, 1, 20f. and "*Accession*," at nn. 104f.

152. *Repentinus tuus adventus inluxit, Pan. Lat.*, 7, 7, 5.

153. Amm., 15, 9, 8.

154. H. Gärtner, "Einige Überlegungen zur kaiserzeitlichen Panegyrik und zu Ammians Charakteristik d. Kaisers Julian," *Akad. d. Wiss. u. Lit. Mainz Abh. Geistes u. Sozialwiss. Kl.* 10 (1968).

155. Amm., 15, 8, 17–20.

156. Amm., 15, 8, 21–22:

> Cumque Viennam venisset, ingredientem optatum quidem et impetrabilem honorifice suscepta omnis aetas concurrebat et dignitas, proculque visum plebs universa, cum vicinitate finitima, imperatorem clementem appellans et faustum, praevia consonis laudibus celebrabat, avidius pompam regiam in principe legitimo cernens: communiumque remedium aerumnarum in eius locabat adventu, salutarem quendam genium affulsisse conclamatis negotiis arbitrata. Tunc anus quaedam orba luminibus, cum percontando quinam esset ingressus, Iulianum Caesarem comperisset, exclamavit hunc deorum templa reparaturum.

See, on this episode, J. Fontaine, "Vienne carrefour du paganisme et du christianisme dans la Gaule du IVe siècle,"*Bulletin de la société des amis de Vienne* 67 (1971) at 23ff.

157. Amm. 21, 10, 1–2:

> Citis passibus incedebat, eumque suburbanis propinquantem amplis nimiumque protentis, militaris et omnis generis turba, cum lumine multo et floribus, votisque faustis, Augustum appellans et dominum, duxit in regiam. Ubi eventu laetus et omine, firmata spe venturorum, quod ad exemplum urbium matris populosae et celebris, per alias quoque civitates ut sidus salutare susciperetur, edito postridie curuli certamine . . .

Holding races was an act of claiming sovereignty: see Alan Cameron, *Circus Factions* (1976) 182f. For the Tetrarchic hippodrome of Sirmium, which was next to the palace, see V. Popović and E. L. Ochsenschlager, "Der spätkaiserliche Hippodrom in Sirmium," *Germania* 54 (1976) 156–181. The hippodrome of Thessalonica was similarly positioned: M. Vickers, "The Hippodrome at Thessaloniki," *JRS* 62 (1972) 25–32, with further literature. See also M. Frazer, "Maxentius' Buildings in Via Appia," *Art Bulletin* 48 (1966) 386f and n. 17.

158. A. H. M. Jones, J. R. Martindale, and J. Morris, *Prosopography of the Later Roman Empire*, vol. 1 (1971) 868. See also, Socrates *H.E.*, 5, 4. Theophilus, Patriarch of Alexandria, was more cautious: Socrates *H.E.*, 6, 2. Before the war between Maximus and Theodosius began, he sent one Isidore to Rome with letters

and gifts to be presented to whomever was victorious. The plan misfired, however, since the contents of the letters were divulged.

159. Compare Amm., 16, 10, 4: [Constantius] *stipatusque agminibus formidandis, tamquam acie ducebatur instructa* with 22, 2, 4 [Julian] *velut acie ducebatur instructa*; and 16, 10, 4: *omnium oculis in eum* [Constantium] *contuitu pertinaci intentis* with 22, 2, 4 *omnium oculis in eum* [Julianum] *non modo contuitu destinato*. The verbal parallels indicate that the mode of perception that has been discussed operated even in historiography.

160. Amm., 22, 2, 3–5:

> Properabat exinde sublimior, uti quodam Triptolemi curru, quem ob rapidos circumgressus, aeriis serpentibus et pinnigeris fabulosa vetustas imponit: perque terras et maria formidatus, nullis obstantibus moris, Heracleam ingressus est. . . . Quo apud Constantinopolim mox comperto, effundebatur aetas omnis et sexus, tamquam demissum aliquem visura de caelo. Exceptus igitur . . . verecundis senatus officiis, et popularium consonis plausibus, stipatusque armatorum et togatorum agminibus, velut acie ducebatur instructa, omnium oculis in eum non modo contuitu destinato, sed cum admiratione magna defixis. Somnio enim propius videbatur adultum adhuc iuvenem, exiguo corpore, factis praestantem ingentibus, post cruentos exitus regum et gentium, ab urbe in urbem inopina velocitate transgressum, quaqua incederet accessione opum et virium, famae instar cuncta facilius occupasse, principatum denique deferente nutu caelesti . . . suscepisse iactura.

161. Libanius *Or.* 13, 41:

> εἰ πάντες ἄνθρωποι νοσήματι κοινῷ τῶν ὀφθαλμῶν ἐστερημένοι θεοῦ τινος ἐξαίφνης εὐνοίᾳ τὰς ὄψεις ἀπέλαβον, οὐκ ἂν μείζονος ἐχόρευσαν. οὐ γὰρ φόβος ἠνάγκαζε πλάττεσθαι τὴν χαράν, ἀλλ' ἐπὶ τῆς ἑκάστου ψυχῆς ἡ πανήγυρις ἤνθει . . . βοὴ δὲ ἐκ παντὸς χωρίου πρὸς οὐρανὸν γεγηθότων ἤρχετο τοῦτο μὲν ἐξ ἄστεων, τοῦτο δὲ ἐξ ἀγρῶν, καὶ οἰκιῶν καὶ θεάτρων, καὶ ὀρῶν καὶ πεδίων, φαίην δ' ἂν ὅτι καὶ παρὰ τῶν πλεόντων ἔκ ποταμῶν τε καὶ λιμνῶν καὶ θαλάττης μέσης.

162. Julian *Letter to the Athenians*, 284b f; cf. "*Accession*," at n. 173.

163. Cf. "*Accession*," at nn. 5ff.

164. *Lapsum caelo . . . Palladium.* Cf. Amm., 22, 2, 4: Julian was seen *tamquam demissum aliquem de caelo*.

165. *Pan. Lat.*, 11, 6, 2–5:

> Itaque cum in ipso molimine opressisset Alamanniam rebellantem, qui paulo ante inaudita regionum, fluviorum, montium nomina exercitu victore peragraverat, per ultima ferarum gentium regna, calcata regum capita supervolans, in medio Illyrici sinu improvisus apparuit. Vidimus, felices illius viae comites, stupentes urbium populos dubitasse credere quae videbant. Non aliter consternatas arbitror gentes quae primae lapsum caelo excepere Palladium. Virgines, pueri, feminae, tremulae anus, titubantes senes non sine magno attoniti horrore cernebant imperatorem. . . . Voces gaudentium oppresserat miraculi magnitudo.

Here and below, cf. the commentary of H. Gutzwiller, *Die Neujahrsrede des Konsuls Claudius Mamertinus vor dem Kaiser Julian*, Basler Beitr. zur Geschichtswiss., 10 (1942). In general, see Hans Gärtner, "Einige Überlegungen zur kaiserzeitlichen Panegyrik und zu Ammians Charakteristik des Kaisers Julian," *Abh.*

Mainz Geistes u Sozialwiss. Kl., 10 (1968) with critique by J. Fontaine, *Latomus* (1973) 240. See also R. C. Blockley, "The Panegyric of Claudius Mamertinus on the Emperor Julian," *American Journal of Philology* 43 (1972) 437–450.

166. *Pan. Lat.*, 11, 7, 2:

> Quae navigationis illius fuit pompa, cum dexteriorem incliti fluminis ripam utriusque sexus, omnium ordinum, armatorum atque inermium perpetuus ordo praetexeret, despiceretur ad laevam in miserabiles preces genu nixa barbaria.

167. *Pan. Lat.*, 7, 3–10, 3. Cf. *Année épigraphique* (1969–1970), 631, *Romani orbis liberatori, templorum restauratori, curiarum et reipublicae recreatori, barbarorum extinctori d.n. Iouliano* . . . , from the Jordan valley. Similarly, Theodosius was praised as renewer of Corinth. See M. Guarducci, "Teodosio 'rinovatore' di Corinto in una epigrafe greca di Kenchreai," *Hommages Claire Préaux* (1975) 527–534.

168. Amm., 22, 2, 3.

169. Cf. Amm., 22, 9, 4: Julian's arrival at Nicomedia.

170. *Pan. Lat.*, 11, 2, 3:

> Haec tibi nominis novi, sed antiquissimae nobilitatis civitas patria est: hic primum editus, hic quasi quoddam salutare humano generi sidus exortus es.

171. Libanius *Or.* 13, 30 f.

172. Libanius *Or.* 13, 42:

> ὅπερ γὰρ 'Ασκληπιὸν φασιν 'Ιππολύτῳ γενέσθαι, τοῦτ' αὐτὸς ἐγένου τῷ τῆς οἰκουμένης σώματι. τεθνεῶτάς τε ἀνέστησας καὶ βασιλείας ὄνομα νῦν, εἴπερ ποτέ, προσέλαβεν ἔργον.

173. Note the graphic image.

174. Amm., 22, 9, 14:

> Urbique propinquans, in speciem alicuius numinis votis excipitur publicis, miratus voces multitudinis magnae, salutare sidus illuxisse eois partibus acclamantis.

See also E. Peterson, Εἷς Θεός (1926) 270–273, on acclamations to Julian recorded on milestones, which, like the acclamations of the Antiochenes, are to be understood not in the light of any specifically pagan or Christian *Tendenz*, but in the light of time-honoured love of custom, which was, of course, rooted in paganism, as well as, in Antioch, Judaism. See Eusebius *HE* 4,6,2 ἐστρατήγει δὲ τότε 'Ιομδαίων Βαρχωχεβας ὄνομα, ὃ δὴ ἀστέρα δηλοῖ . . . ἐπὶ δὲ τῇ προσηγορίᾳ, . . . ὡς δὴ ἐξ οὐρανοῦ φωστὴρ αὐτοῖς κατεληλυθὼς κακουμένοιςτε ιε ἐπιλάμψαι τερατευόμενος, with Num. 24,17, on the Star of Jacob.

175. Cf. below *"Consecratio,"* at 203ff and *"Accession,"* at 165ff.

176. Julian *fragt.*, 176, vol. I², 217 (Bidez-Cumont):

> Εἰ μὲν εἰς τὸ θέατρον λαθιὸν εἰσῆλθον, εὐφημεῖτε· εἰ δὲ εἰς τὰ ἱερά, τὴν ἡσυχίαν ἄγετε, καὶ μετενέγκατε ὑμῶν τὰς εὐφημίας εἰς τοὺς θεούς· μᾶλλον δὲ οἱ θεοὶ τῶν εὐφημιῶν οὐ χρῄζουσιν.

177. *Pan. Lat.*, 12, 37, 3:

> Ferebant se obviae tripudiantium catervae. Cuncta cantu et crotalis personabant. Hic ubi triumphum chorus, ille contra tyranno . . . carmen exequiale dicebat. Hic perpetuum victis abitum, ille victoribus crebrum optabat adventum. . . . Nullus cuiquam sui tuine respectus: blandam tibi faciebat iniuriam

contumacia gaudiorum. Quid ego referam pro moenibus suis festum liberae no-
bilitatis occursum, conspicuos veste nivea senatores, reverendos municipali purpura flamines, insignes apicibus sacerdotes? Quid portas virentibus sertis coro-
natas? . . . Nondum omne confeceras bellum, iam agebas triumphum.

See, on this panegyric, A. Lippold, "Herrscherideal und Traditionsverbundenheit im Panegyricus des Pacatus," *Historia* 17 (1968) 228–250; cf. Y.-M. Duval,
"L'éloge de Théodose dans la *Cité de Dieu* (V, 26, 1). Sa place, son sens, et ses
sources," *Recherches augustiniennes* 4 (1966) 135–179. On Pacatus, see J. F. Matthews, "Gallic Supporters of Theodosius," *Latomus* 30 (1971) 1078ff.

178. *Pan. Lat.*, 12, 47, 3–4:

> Ea vero quae Romae gesta sunt, qualem te urbi dies primus invexerit; quis in
> curia fueris, quis in rostris; ut pompam praeeuntium ferculorum curru modo,
> modo pedibus subsecutus alterno clarus incessu nunc de bellis, nunc de su-
> perbia triumpharis; ut te omnibus principem, singulis exhibueris senatorem; ut
> . . . remota custodia militari tutior publici amoris excubiis: hcrum haec linguis,
> horum, inquam, voce laudentur qui de communibus gaudiis et dignius utique
> quae maxima et iustius poterunt praedicare quae propria sunt.

179. *Pan. Lat.*, 12, 47, 5:

> O mea felix peregrinatio! . . . quam multo circumdabor auditore, cum dixero:
> 'Romam vidi, Theodosium vidi, et utrumque simul vidi; vidi illum principis pa-
> trem, vidi illum principis vindicem, vidi illum principis restitutorem.'

Cf. Themistius *Or.* XIV, to Theodosius, a short address on his accession, where
the orator stresses the intimate link between emperors and capitals: Constantinople desires to welcome Theodosius before the other cities of the East—προα-
παντῆσαι—for she excels the other cities as the emperor excels other men, thus
making a special relationship between emperor and capital: Themistius 183 ab.

180. For Claudian's poetic techniques, see Alan Cameron, *Claudian, Poetry
and Propaganda at the Court of Honorius* (1970) and, for a different approach, C.
Gnilka, "Dichtung und Geschichte im Werke Claudians," *Frühmittelalterliche Studien* 10 (1976) 96–104; cf. also C. Gnilka, "Götter und Dämonen in den Gedichten
Claudians," *Antike und Abendland* 18 (1973) 144–160.

181. Claudian *De Raptu Pros.* I, 5–9:

> Iam furor humanos nostro de pectore sensus
> expulit et totum spirant praecordia Phoebum;
> iam mihi cernuntur trepidis delubra moveri
> sedibus et claram dispergere limina lucem
> adventum testata dei.

182. It was only in Christian eyes that Claudian, whether baptised or not,
could be described as *a Christi nomine alienus* (Augustine *De civ. Dei* 5, 26), for
only in Christianity could a dichotomy of religion and classical culture arise,
with the consequent need for both pagans and Christians to define their position with regard to religion and classical culture.

183. Claudian *III. cons.*, 122ff; *IV cons.*, 365ff.

184. See, e.g., the speech of Roma in Claudian *VI cons.*, 361–425.

185. Claudian *VI cons.*, 374; cf. 383–385; 494ff.

186. E.g., Claudian, *VI cons.*, 640–660; cf. A. Alföldi, *Die monarchische Repräsentation im röm. Kaiserreiche* (1970) 94–98.

187. Claudian *VI cons.*, 146–147.

188. Claudian *VI cons.*, 361–425.
189. Claudian *VI cons.*, 178–192.
190. Claudian *VI cons.*, 361–493.
191. Claudian *VI cons.*, 1–52.
192. Claudian *VI cons.*, 22–23. There is double meaning here: Honorius is also *Latiae sublimis signifer aulae.*
193. On the whole passage, Claudian *VI cons.*, 18–25, especially on *caelicolae cum celsa tenant summoque feruntur cardine* = μεσουρανεῖν, cf. E. Peterson, Εἷς Θεός (1926) 263f.
194. Claudian *VI cons.*, 35–38:

> Ecce Palatino crevit reverentia monti
> exultatque habitante deo potioraque Delphis
> supplicibus late populis oracula pandit
> atque suas ad signa iubet revirescere laurus.

195. Claudian *VI cons.*, 579–610.
196. Claudian *VI cons.*, 494–522.
197. Claudian *VI cons.*, 523–528.
198. Claudian *VI cons.*, 543–559.
199. Claudian *VI cons.*, 560–577.
200. Claudian *VI cons.*, 603.
201. Claudian *VI cons.*, 611–639.
202. Claudian *VI cons.*, 640–660. The use of the *toga* and *arma 'topos'* in this passage serves to heighten the Roman, urban orientation of the panegyric, cf. below at nn. 222ff.
203. Claudian *VI cons.*, 611–613:

> O quantum populo secreti numinis addit
> imperii praesens genius! quantamque rependit
> maiestas alterna vicem. . . .

204. Claudian *III cons.*, 109ff; note 121–122: *oppida adventu sacrata tuo.*
205. Claudian *III cons.*, 126ff.
206. Claudian *IV cons.*, 565ff.
207. Claudian *IV cons.*, 584ff.
208. Claudian *IV cons.*, 565–572:

> Nunc quoque quos habitus, quantae miracula pompae
> vidimus, Ausonio cum iam succinctus amictu
> per Ligurum populos solito conspectior ires
> atque inter niveas alte veherere cohortes,
> obnixisque simul pubes electa lacertis
> sidereum gestaret onus. sic numina Memphis
> in vulgus proferre solet; penetralibus exit
> effigies.

On the pagan context of this passage, see A. Alföldi, *A Festival of Isis in Rome under the Christian Emperors of the IVth Century* (1937) 42–44; R. Hari, "Une image du culte égyptien à Rome en 354," *Museum Helveticum* 33 (1976) 114–121. For a living pagan cult in Claudian's lifetime, see J. Collins-Clinton, *A Late Antique Shrine of Liber Pater at Cosa* (1977).

209. A. Grabar, *L'empéreur dans l'art byzantin*, 125–162, esp. 159.
210. *Pan. Lat.*, 3, 14.
211. Cf. "*Accession*," at nn. 11ff.
212. *Pan. Lat.*, 9, 19, 6; Claudian *VI cons.*, 613f; cf. Amm., 16, 10, 13–14.
213. Difficilis quondam, dominis parere serenis
iussus et extinctis palmam portare tyrannis.
omnia Theodosio cedunt, subolique perenni
ter denis sic victus ego domitusque diebus
iudice sub Proclo superas elatus ad auras.

See G. Bruns, *Der Obelisk und seine Basis auf dem Hippodrom zu Konstantinopel*, Istanbuler Forschungen, 7 (1935) 30. H. Wrede, "Zur Errichtung des Theodosiusobelisken in Istanbul," *Istanbuler Mitteilungen* 16 (1966) 178–198, 182f, discusses competition between Constantinople and Rome in the late fourth century, as expressed in imperial building programmes, for which, see also R. Naumann, "Theodosiusbogen und Forum Tauri in Istanbul," *Istanbuler Mitteilungen* 26 (1976) 117–142. On the obelisk base in the context of the hippodrome, see G. Dagron, *Naissance d'une capitale, Constantinople et ses institutions de 330 à 451* (1974) 311ff, and Alan Cameron, *Porphyrius the Charioteer* (1973) 49–64. On the artistic style of the base and its late antique characteristics see H. Kähler, "Der Sockel des Theodosiusobelisken in Konstantinopel," *Acta ad archaeologiam et artium historiam pertinentia* 6 (1975) 45–55. On the inscription, cf. Alan Cameron, "Some Prefects Called Julian," *Byzantion* 47 (1977) 42–64, at 60–62. The imagery of the hippodrome lived on in Constantinople and elsewhere: E. Ville-Patlagean, "Une image de Salomon en basileus byzantin," *Revue des études juives, Historica Judaica*, 4th series, 1 (121) (1962) 9–33.
214. Bruns, *Der Obelisk*, 32ff, 36ff.
215. Claudian *VI cons.*, 70–72.
216. H. P. Laubscher, *Der Reliefschmuck des Galeriusbogens* (1975) 48–52. For the "stereotype of imperial ideology," cf. submission scenes on Dionysiac sarcophagi, themselves derived from Roman triumphal art, in F. Matz, *Die dionysischen Sarkophage* 3 (1969) 425–426 with numbers 243, 244, 245. However, here, the god (like, in imperial art of the second century, the emperor, cf. R. Brilliant, *Gesture and Rank in Roman Art* (1963) 75, 109, 122f, 189ff) by his gesture indicates that he accepts gifts and submission. No such gesture disrupts the imperial tranquillity in late antique art.
217. Claudian *VI cons.*, 71–72.
Positoque tiaram
summisere genu. . . .
218. See also below, section 6 (ii).
219. Wrede, "Zur Errichtung," 196–197. A clay copy in Vienna of a Tetrarchic silver missorium shows the emperors enthroned, as on the obelisk base, presiding at games. See H. Fuhrmann, "Die Konsulardiptychen und verwandte Denkmäler, II, tönerne Missoria aus der Zeit der Tetrarchie," *Röm. Mitt.* 55 (1940) 92–99.
220. These three figures have proved difficult to identify. For a list of views, see Wrede, "Zur Errichtung," 194. The interpretation of the south-east side, where the emperor (Arcadius) holds a wreath, is disputed: is he giving or receiv-

ing the wreath? See Alan Cameron, *Porphyrius the Charioteer* (1973) 50–51, arguing that he receives it; *contra*, most recently, H. Kähler, "Der Sockel des Theodosiusobelisken in Konstantinopel," *Acta ad archaeologiam et artium historiam pertinentia* 6, (1975) 45–55, at 52. The contrast between the two historical and the two non-historical reliefs on the obelisk base is made by Wrede, "Zur Errichtung," 194–197; Cameron, *Porphyrius*, 50, prefers to see artistic variation, without significant differences in content.

221. These two panels depict the emperor's presence in Rome, as distinct from his arrival, and they do so by means of frontality and symmetry: cf. above at no. 144. A systematic interpretation of these aspects of late antique art is H. P. L'Orange, *Art Forms and Civic Life* (1965) 89f, on the arch of Constantine.

222. The column base itself does not survive, but can be studied from the Freshfield drawings in Trinity College, Cambridge: E. H. Freshfield, "Notes," *Archaeologia* 72 (1921–1922) 87–104, and J. Kollwitz, *Oströmische Plastik der theodosianischen Zeit* (1941) Beilage 5f. Grabar, *L'empéreur dans l'art byzantin* (1936) 75, relates the relief to Theodosius-Arcadius and interprets it differently.

223. Kollwitz, *Oströmische Plastik*, 19–33, and G. Becatti, *La colonna coclide istoriata* (1960) 151–264.

224. Kollwitz, *Oströmische Plastik*, 50–51.

225. Grabar, *L'empéreur*, 76, designates these as *togati* and relates the gift of a crown to the custom of the ninth century of giving the emperor a crown after a triumphal return. More directly relevant is the interpretation by Kollwitz, who refers to the *aurum coronarium* of late antiquity: Kollwitz, *Oströmische Plastik*, 51f. See also F. Millar, *The Emperor in the Roman World* (1977) 140ff, and T. Klauser, "Aurum Coronarium," in *Gesammelte Arbeiten zur Liturgiegeschichte, Kirchengeschichte und christlichen Archaeologie*, Jahrbuch für Antike und Christentum Ergänzungsband, 3 (1974) 292–309.

226. Synesius *De regno*, 2; cf. Symmachus *Or.*, 1; cf. O. Seeck's edition 1883, 210. Cf. Gregory Naz. *Contra Iul.* I, 80, describing imperial images showing cities bringing gifts to the emperors, and barbarians trampled underfoot, indicating that the representations on the column base were not at all unusual.

227. Claudian *III cons.*, 1ff; *IV cons.*, 5f; *VI cons.*, 8–10; and 595f. On the traditional celebrations of January 1st, see M. Meslin, *La fête des Kalendes de Janvier dans l'empire romain*, Coll. Latomus, 115 (1970).

228. Grabar, *L'empéreur*, 32–39, 239–243.

229. Corippus *In laudem Iustini*, IV, 90ff. See Averil Cameron, *Corippus*, commentary on IV, 198f, 219, 264ff.

230. But the specific point of this symbolism as shown on the arch (also on the Parabiago platter) has been altered. On both these works the sun rises while the moon sets, thus attributing a particular time to the occurrences depicted, i.e., dawn. On the column base (as on other late antique works, e.g., the Ascension miniature in the Rabbula Gospels, below, "*Consecratio*," n. 220), on the other hand, sun and moon both rise or are not shown as personifications. Thus no point in time is referred to. We have rather a cosmic setting *tout court*.

231. According to C. O. Nordström, *Ravennastudien* (1953) 45, a parallel to this method of representation in registers occurs in the Baptistery of the Orthodox in Ravenna. The centre, showing the Baptism of Christ, with the surrounding Apostles bearing wreaths—an *aurum coronarium*—is related to the pairs of

registers showing the emperors and various forms of homage: the homage of the Senate, the provinces and the enemies of the empire. The altars and thrones in the Baptistery correspond to the panels of captured armour on the obelisk base. The parallel illustrates how, in the fifth century, art for ecclesiastical purposes and imperial art used a common idiom. See also K. Baus, *Der Kranz in Antike und Christentum*, Theophaneia, 2 (1940) 201–230, on Roman triumphal imagery in Christian art.

232. Synesius, *On Kingship* 15, ed. Terzaghi (1944): Θαλαμεύεσθε καθάπερ αἱ σαῦραι μόλις εἴ πῃ, πρὸς τὴν εἴλην ἐκκύπτουσαι, μὴ φωραθείητε ὑπὸ τῶν ἀνθρώπων ὄντες ἄνθρωποι; tr. A. FitzGerald, *The Essays and Hymns of Synesius of Cyrene*, vol. 1 (1930) 127; cf. *On Kingship* 13, 25, 21 (FitzGerald 9, 19, 21). A similar criticism was voiced by Sidonius: K. F. Stroheker, *Der senatorische Adel im spätantiken Gallien* (1948) 43f, on *principes clausi*; and, in more practical terms, by Vegetius. See W. Goffart, "The Date and Purpose of Vegetius' 'De re militari'," *Traditio* 33 (1977) 65–100, esp. 79f. The lines in question (DRM 3, 26) "can only fit a youthful emperor—not necessarily youthful in years but having the sort of perennial youth one associates with the tranquillity of the imperial palace." On the occasion of Synesius' speech, see Klauser, "*Aurum Coroniarum*" (above, n. 225), 301.

233. Cf. J. Kollwitz, *Oströmische Plastik*, 61f.

234. E. Demougeot, *De l'unité à la division de l'empire romain* (1951) 395–410.

235. Compare the Tetrarchic panegyric on universal imperial presence: *Pan. Lat.* III, 14, 2–3:

> Iovis omnia plena . . . id nunc ego de utroque vestrum audeo praedicare: ubicumque sitis, in unum licet palatium concesseritis, divinitatem vestram ubique versari, omnes terras omniaque maria plena esse vestri.

But here the point was used to praise a particular imperial *adventus*.

236. Vergil *Aen.*, I, 278–279; cf. expressions in the law codes such as *Cod. Theod.*, 10, 22, 3: *adoraturus aeternitatem nostram*.

237. On this tradition in late antique Byzantium, see T. Viljamaa, *Studies in Greek Encomiastic Poetry of the Early Byzantine Period* (1968); cf. E. Heitsch, "Die griechischen Dichterfragmente der römischen Kaiserzeit," I and II, *Abh. d. Akad. d. Wiss. in Göttingen Phil.-Hist. Kl.* 49 (1961) and 58 (1964) containing various panegyrics; I, 127f, on the arrival of an image of Justin II. On the West, see MacCormack, "Latin Prose Panegyrics, Tradition and Discontinuity in the Later Roman Empire," *Revue des études augustiniennes* 22 (1976) 29–77.

238. For the occasions of these three panegyrics, see A. Loyen, *Recherches sur les panégyriques de Sidoine Apollinaire*, Bibl. de l'École des Hautes Études, 285 (1942) 35f, 59ff, 85f.

239. *Pan. Lat.*, 7, 22, 310 A.D.

240. Loyen, *Recherches historiques sur les panégyriques de Sidoine Apollinaire* (Paris, 1942), pp. 79–82 and his Budé edition of Sidonius, *Poèmes*, 14–15.

241. Sidonius *Carm.* V, 574–603.

242. Sidonius *Carm.* V, 564–573.

243. Loyen, ed , Sidonius, *Poèmes* XV.

244. Sidonius *Carm.* V, 574.

245. Sidonius *Carm.* V, 576.

246. Ennodius was familiar with the panegyrics of Symmachus and quoted them: compare Ennodius, *Panegyricus* 9 with Symmachus, *In Val.* I, 1; *Panegyricus* 13 with *In Val.* II, 24; *Panegyricus* 29 with *In Val.* II, 9; *Panegyricus* 73 with *In Val.* II, 30; *Panegyricus* 76 with *In Val.* II, 29; *Panegyricus* 78 with *In Val.* II, 26: parallels identified by the Monumenta editor, F. Vogel. On the state of education in the late fifth and early sixth centuries see P. Riché, *Éducation et culture dans l'occident barbare VIᵉ–VIIIᵉ siècles* (3rd ed., 1972) 62ff: 69, "Rome a donc encore, au début du VIᵉ siècle, des écoles, mais la vie universitaire tend à se désorganiser." Cf. J. Préaux, "Securus Melior Felix, l'ultime *Orator Urbis Romae*," *Corona Gratiarum, Miscellanea Patristica, Historica et Liturgica Eligio Dekkers O.S.B. XII Lustra completenti oblata*, vol. 2 (1975) 101–121. A similar situation obtained in the Rhône valley: Riché, 71, "de petites groupes de lettrés et peu de professeurs." For some historical details in Ennodius' panegyric, see A. Lumpe, "Ennodiana," *Byzantinische Forschungen* 1 (*Polychordia, Festschrift Franz Dölger*) (1966) 200–210, at 207–210.

247. See for this T. Nissen, "Historisches Epos und Panegyrikos in der Spätantike," *Hermes* 75 (1940) 298–325.

248. Agnellus, ed. Holder-Egger, *MGH Script. Rer. Lang.* 303, and W. Ensslin, *Theodorich der Grosse* (1947) 76.

249. E.g., Gregory of Tours *H.F.*, 2, 28 (38), the consulship of Clovis, and *H.F.*, 8, 1, the *adventus* of Guntram in Orleans in 585 A.D., arranged to fall on the feast day of St. Martin with acclamations by Jews, Gallo-Romans (i.e., Latin speakers) and Syrians. Guntram accepted hospitality from individual citizens and received gifts; the first and second stages of *adventus* are still recognisable. For a possible representation of the latter, on the so-called helmet of Agilulf (591–616), see D. Bullough, "*Imagines Regum* and Their Significance in the Early Medieval West," *Studies in Memory of David Talbot Rice*, ed. G. Robertson and G. Henderson (1975) 223–276, 235 and fig. 93a: "Does this scene represent or commemorate a ceremony that actually took place in Agilulf's time? and if so, what?" Bullough suggests the reception of the *aurum coronarium* (as on the column base of Arcadius, above at n. 225) as a possible iconographic ancestor. For a discussion of the "helmet of Agilulf" in a Ravennate context, see A. Guillou, "Demography and Culture in the Exarchate of Ravenna" in his *Studies on Byzantine Italy*, 1970, 210–213. For Visigothic royal *profectio* and *adventus* ceremonies, see D. M. Férotin, *Le Liber Ordinum en usage dans l'église wisigothique et mozarabe d'Espagne*, Monumenta Ecclesiae Liturgica, 5 (1904) 150–155.

250. Egeria's account is printed in the Corpus Christianorum 175, *Itinera*, 76–77; cf. A. Baumstark, "Orientalisches in den Texten der abendländischen Palmenfeier," *Jahrbuch für Liturgiewissenschaft* 7 (1927) 148–153. Christ's entry into Jerusalem is the subject of one of Romanos' finest *kontakia*: E. Catafygiotu Topping, "Romanos, on the Entry into Jerusalem, a *Basilikos Logos*," *Byzantion* 47 (1977) 65–91.

251. *P.G.*, 35, 1117; cf. MacCormack, *Historia* (1972) 747 and n. 149.

252. John Chrysostom, "Homiliae II and III," *P.G.* 63, 467–472; 473–478; P. C. Baur, O.S.B., *Johannes Chrysostomus und seine Zeit*, Vol. 2 (1930) 34–37. The episode is discussed in detail in K. G. Holum's forthcoming book, *Theodosian Empresses: Women and Imperial Dominion in Late Antiquity*.

253. K. G. Holum and G. Vikan, "The Trier Ivory, *Adventus* Ceremonial and

the Relics of S. Stephen," *DOP* 33 (1979) 113–133. On the ceremonial of the arrival of relics, see also S. MacCormack, "Change and Continuity in Late Antiquity, the Ceremony of *Adventus*," *Historia* 21 (1972) 722–752 at 748.

254. E.g., Sidonius, ep. 7, 1, 7, the translation of the body of Ferreolus and the head of Julianus to protect the city of Vienne in very troubled times, as the letter discloses. For the earlier period, see N. Gussone, "Adventus Zeremoniell und Translation von Reliquien. Victricius von Rouen, de laude Sanctorum," *Frühmittelalterliche Studien* 10 (1976) 125–133; for Sidonius, see P. Rousseau, "In Search of Sidonius the Bishop," *Historia* 25 (1976) 356–377, at 362ff; and for the time of Gregory of Tours, P. R. L. Brown, *Relics and Social Status in the Age of Gregory of Tours*, The Stenton Lecture 1976, University of Reading (1977), esp. 20. On continuities in late antique Gaul in general, see also M. Heinzelmann, *Bischofsherrschaft in Gallien, zur Kontinuität römischer Führungsschichten vom 4. bis 7. Jahrhundert. Soziale, prosopographische und bildungsgeschichtliche Aspekte*, Beihefte der Francia, 5 (1976) and the beautifully differentiated article by J. Fontaine, "Vienne carrefour du paganisme dans la Gaule du IVᵉ siècle," *Bulletin de la société des amis de Vienne* 67 (1971) 17–36; see especially p. 31, a relief from Vienne depicting an *adventus* of relics.

255. For this topic, see E. Dinkler, *Der Einzug in Jerusalem, Ikonografische Untersuchungen im Anschluss an ein bisher unbekanntes Sarkofagfragment*, Arbeitsgemeinschaft für Forschung des Landes Nordrhein-Westfalen, Geisteswissenschaften, Heft 167 (1970); an early painted version of the entry into Jerusalem: J. M. C. Toynbee, "Christian Paintings in S. Maria in Stelle near Verona," *Kyriakon, Festschrift J. Quasten* 2 (1970) 651f and fig. 5.

256. F. W. Deichmann, *Repertorium der christlich-antiken Sarkofage*, Vol. 1 (1967) no. 14.

257. Sarcophagi: Deichmann, *Repertorium*, nos. 21, 26, 28, 40, 41, 63, 772, 841; iconographic changes leading to the Etschmiadzin Gospels: E. Kantorowicz, "The 'King's Advent' and the Enigmatic Panels in the Doors of Santa Sabina," *Art Bulletin* 26 (1944) 207–231, reprinted in his *Selected Studies* (1965) 37–64 at 50.

258. I Thess. 4, 17; see also Cyril of Jerusalem, *Catech.* 15, *P.G.* 33, 869ff. Elsewhere the New Testament uses ὑπάντησις as the technical term for welcoming: Matthew 8, 34, the city of Gadara comes out to meet Jesus; Matthew 25, 1, the virgins meeting the bridegroom in the parable of the wise and foolish virgins; John 12, 13, Jesus' entry into Jerusalem. I would like to thank Richard Cilley for these references. See also Kantorowicz, "King's Advent," 52–58; S. MacCormack, *Historia* 21 (1972) 724, 744f, with E. Peterson, "Die Einholung des Kyrios," *Zeitschrift für systematische Theologie* 7 (1930) 682–702.

259. Deichmann, *Repertorium*, no. 680; K. Weitzmann, ed., *Age of Spirituality* (1979) 427–429.

260. See further, "*Consecratio*," at nn. 189ff, below.

261. E. Kantorowicz, "Oriens Augusti—Lever du Roi," *DOP* 17 (1963) 135–149; cf. his "*Puer exoriens*: On the Hypapante in the Mosaics of S. Maria Maggiore," in his *Collected Studies*, 25–36, at 30ff. On the equestrian statue of Theodosius I in Constantinople, the inscription of which still addressed him as a second rising sun, see J. Kollwitz, *Oströmische Plastik der theodosianischen Zeit* (1941) 8–11.

262. F. Cumont, "L'Adoration des mages et l'art triomphal de Rome," *Atti*

della Pontificia Accademia Romana di Archeologia, Serie 3, Memorie 3 (1932–33) 81–105; cf. G. de Jerphanion, "L'Ambon de Salonique, l'arc de Galère et l'ambon de Thèbes," *ibid.*, 107–132.

263. Deichmann, *Repertorium,* 16, 33, 96, 135, 145, 147, 241, 350, 526, 618, 648, 735, 745, 792, 799, 803, 835. The imperial origin of the image is especially pronounced in 43 and 949, also on the small sarcophagus in the archi-episcopal museum in Ravenna. See also M. Loli, *Il sarcofago paleocristiano di Catervio nel duomo di Tolentino* (1971) 17a.

264. The three Magi approaching the Theotokos and Child are part of the Justinianic change in S. Apollinare Nuovo: F. W. Deichmann, *Ravenna, Hauptstadt des spätantiken Abendlandes,* vol. 1: *Geschichte und Monumente* (1969) 199 and plan at 258; *Kommentar,* I (1974) 150.

265. See E. Kitzinger, "The Cult of Images in the Age before Iconoclasm," *DOP* 8 (1954) 83–149, reprinted in his *The Art of Byzantium and the Medieval West, Selected Studies* (1976) 90–156.

266. H. Kruse, *Studien zur offiziellen Geltung des Kaiserbildes im römischen Reiche,* Studien zur Geschichte und Kultur des Altertums 19, 3 (1934) 12–18. Overthrowing imperial images amounted to rebellion: see R. Browning, "The Riot of A.D. 387 in Antioch. The Role of the Theatrical Claques in the Later Roman Empire," *JRS* 42 (1952) 13–20, reprinted in his *Studies in Byzantine History, Literature and Education* (1977). Defacing the coinage which bore the image of the emperor, or forging it, was an act of *lèse majesté: Cod. Theod.*, 9, 21, 9. At the same time, issuing coinage could be an expression of sovereignty. For the successor states to the Roman Empire, see S. Dill, *Roman Society in Gaul in the Merovingian Age* (1926) 164; Procopius, *Wars* 7, 33, 5–6; and P. Grierson, "The Monetary Reforms of Abd-al-Malik," *Journal of the Economic and Social History of the Orient* 3 (1960) 241–264.

267. Kruse, *Studien,* 12ff, 23ff; on the pagan significance of imperial images, cf. S. Eitrem, "Zur Apotheose," *Symbolae Osloenses* 15–16 (1936) 111–128; for late antiquity, R. Brilliant, *Gesture and Rank* (1963) 195ff.

268. Zosimus, ed. Mendelssohn, 4, 37:

> Θεοδόσιος δὲ ὁ βασιλεὺς ἐδέχετό τε βασιλέα Μάξιμον εἶναι, καὶ εἰκόνων αὐτῷ κοινωνεῖν καὶ βασιλέως προσηγορίας ἠξίου . . . ὥστε καὶ Κυνηγίῳ τῷ τῆς αὐλῆς ὑπάρχῳ πεμπομένῳ κατὰ τὴν Αἴγυπτον, προστεταγμένῳ τε πᾶσι τὴν εἰς τὰ θεῖα θρησκείαν ἀπαγορεῦσαι καὶ κλεῖθρα τοῖς τεμένεσιν ἐπιθεῖναι, τὴν εἰκόνα Μαξίμου δεῖξαι τοῖς Ἀλεξανδρεῦσιν ἐπέταξεν, ἀναθεῖναί τε δημοσίᾳ ταύτην, καὶ ὅτι συμβασιλεύσειν ἔλαχεν αὐτῷ προφωνῆσαι τῷ δήμῳ.

On the political context of these events see D. Vera, "I rapporti fra Magno Massimo, Teodosio e Valentiniano II nel 383–384," *Athenaeum* 53 (1975) 267–301 (present passage discussed 278f).

269. On the sacred qualities of imperial statues, see H. G. Niemeyer, *Studien zur statuarischen Darstellung der röm. Kaiser,* Monumenta Artis Romanae, 7 (1968) esp. 18–27.

270. W. H. Worrell, *The Coptic Manuscripts in the Freer Collection* (1923) 375.

271. *De Cer.*, 1, 87 (Bonn); cf. Reiske's commentary 381ff of the Bonn edition, vol. 2. On this passage and numismatic portraits see P. Bruun, "Notes on the Transmission of Imperial Images in Late Antiquity," *Studia Romana in honorem Petri Krarup* (1976) 121–131. A panegyric for the arrival of the portrait of Justin II

in Egypt: E. Heitsch, *Die griechischen Dichter-fragmente der röm. Kaiserzeit*, Abh. Göttingen, 49 (1961) 127–129.

272. Procopius of Gaza, *Panegyricus* § 1, ed. C. Kempen, *Procopii Gazaei . . . Panegyricus*, Diss. Bonn, 1918; also ed. Niebuhr and Bekker, Bonn, 1829; see also, Kilian Seitz, *Die Schule von Gaza, eine litteraturgeschichtliche Untersuchung*, Diss. Heidelberg, 1892, 9ff, and G. Downey, "The Christian Schools of Palestine, a Chapter in Literary History," *Harvard Library Bulletin* 12 (1958) 297–319. On teaching methods, see also M. Richard, "ΑΡΟ ΦΩΝΗΣ," *Byzantion* 20 (1950) 191–222, reprinted in his *Opera Minora*, vol. 3 (1977) no. 60.

273. Procopius of Gaza, ed. C. Kempen, *Procopii Gazaei . . . Panegyricus* (1918), 1 (cf. Kempen's commentary on this passage).

Ἤδη μὲν, ὦ κράτιστε βασιλεῦ, πᾶσα πόλις ἐπὶ σοὶ φρονοῦσα, καὶ τοῖς σοῖς τροπαίοις ἀβρυνομένη, καὶ τὴν εὐδειμονίαν ὄντως ἥτις ἐστὶ μαθοῦσα τῇ πείρᾳ, πάντα τρόπον μηχανωμένη μὴ κατόπιν ὀφθῆναι τῶν δωρεῶν, ἀμοιβῆς ἀπορεῖ τοῖς ἔργοις ἁμιλλωμένης· καὶ τὸν εὐεργέτην ἐντεῦθεν μᾶλλον θαυμάζει δι' ὧν εὖ ποιεῖ, τῶν εὖ παθόντων νικῶντα τὰς ἀμοιβάς. πρέπων γὰρ οὗτος βασιλεῖ κόσμος, μετὰ τῶν πολεμίων καὶ τοὺς ὑπηκόους νικᾶν, τοὺς μὲν τοῖς ὅπλοις, τοὺς δὲ τῷ πλήθει τῶν ὑπαρχόντων ἀγαθῶν, ἀμφοτέρους δὲ ταῖς ἀρεταῖς. ἡ δὲ ἡμετέρα πόλις, διὰ τῆς εἰκόνος αὐτὸν ἀπολαβοῦσα τὸν εὐεργέτην, ὥσπερ τις δεινὸς ἐραστής, ἀνίσταται πρὸς τὴν θέαν, καὶ πᾶσαν ἡλικίαν ἐγείρει· καὶ πατὴρ παιδὶ παραστὰς καὶ πρεσβύτης νέῳ ἥκει καὶ δείκνυσι, καὶ σκιρτῶσιν ἅμα τῇ θέᾳ. ἴσως μὲν οὖν δόξω μόνος παρὰ τοὺς ἄλλους ἐπὶ τηλικοῦτον ὄγκον πραγμάτων ἰέναι, καὶ τοσοῦτον εἶναί μοι θράσος, ὥστε καὶ θεάτρου μέσος ἀνέστηκα, καὶ τολμῶ τι λέγειν, κἂν ἀπειλῇ τις οὐ παύσομαι. τὸ δὲ οὐχ οὕτως ἔχει· ὅλη δὲ πόλις ἀνθ' ὧν εὖ πάσχει πρὸς ἀμοιβὴν κινεῖται δικαίαν· καὶ καθ' ἕκαστον ἄνδρα λέγειν οὐχ ἱκανὸν ἡγουμένη τὸν χρόνον, κοινῇ πάντες ψήφῳ τῇ τοῦ ῥήτορος ἀρκοῦνται φωνῇ. ὁ γὰρ ὑπὲρ πόλεως προβεβλημένος τῷ λόγῳ, μιᾷ γλώττῃ τὰς ἁπάντων ὑποκρίνεται γνώμας.

274. Procopius of Gaza, 29–30:

καὶ φαιδραὶ μὲν αἱ πόλεις, ἄλλη κατ' ἄλλα σεμνυνομένη· πᾶσαι δὲ κοινὸν προβέβληνται κόσμον, τὰς σὰς εἰκόνας ἐπ' εὐεργεσίαις ἱστῶσαι· . . . λόγοι δὲ τὰς σὰς εἰκόνας τιμῶσι, καὶ λόγων ἀγῶνες, καὶ διὰ τούτων αἱ Μοῦσαι. Ἀλλὰ τί ποτε ταύταις ἐπιγράψομεν; τί τῆς ἀξίας ἐχόμενον; ἢ πάντως ἐκεῖνα· "ἡ πόλις τὸν εὐεργέτην, δι' οὗ νῦν αὐχένα τε γαῦρον ἐπαίρω καὶ πόλις εἰμί;" ἀλλ' εἴη . . . τὰς δὲ πόλεις ἐπ' εὐτυχίαις στεφάνους πλέκειν, καὶ γραφὰς ἀνατιθέναι, καὶ ᾄδειν ὑμνούσας· ποιητῶν δὲ παῖδας καὶ ῥήτορας, ἀμφὶ σοὶ κινοῦντας τὴν γλῶτταν, εὐπορεῖν ἀεὶ καὶ τοῖς σοῖς τροπαίοις ἀβρύνεσθαι.

275. R. Delbrueck, *Spätantike Kaiserporträts von Constantinus Magnus bis zum Ende des Westreichs* (1933) 219–226. K. Weitzmann, ed., *Age of Spirituality* (1979) 29–30.

276. H. G. Niemeyer, *Studien zur statuarischen Darstellung der römischen Kaiser* (1968) 47–54, pl. 14–22.

277. A. Muñoz, *Il Codice purpureo di Rossano e il frammento Sinopense* (1907) pl. 13, Christ before Pilate; pl. 14, Christ and Barabbas. See also the important article by W. C. Loerke, "The Miniatures of the Trial in the Rossano Gospels," *Art Bulletin* 43 (1961) 176–182.

278. R. Delbrueck, *Die Consulardiptychen* (1929) Anastasius and Ariadne no. 16, 119f; cf. nos. 17, 19, 20, 21; Ostrogothic: no. 32; Justinian and Theodora on either side of Christ: no. 34.

306 Notes to Pages 71–74

279. *Cod. Just.*, 12, 3. On the giving of diptychs see Libanius ep. 1021; Symm. Epp. II, 81; V, 56; VII, 76; cf. Themistius, 224 bc, all quoted by Delbrueck, *Die Consulardiptychen* (1929), XXXIVff.

280. On Mamertinus speaking in 291 about gaining access to the presence of Diocletian and Maximian, see above at n. 52; cf. *Cod. Theod.*, 12, 8, 2.

281. Delbrueck, *Die Consulardiptychen*, nos. 1, 48 resp.; and W. F. Volbach, *Elfenbeinarbeiten der Spätantike und des früheren Mittelalters*, Römische-Germanisches Zentralmuseum zu Mainz (3rd ed. 1976) nos. 1, 48 resp.

282. Delbrueck, *Die Consulardiptychen*, 193f; K. Weitzmann, ed., *Age of Spirituality* (1979) 33–35.

283. Gnecchi, *I Medaglioni Romani* (1912) pl. 16, 1; 17, 1: coins of Valens.

284. Cf. H. P. L'Orange, *Studies on the Iconography of Cosmic Kingship in the Ancient World* (1953) 139ff and "Sol Invictus Imperator," *Symbolae Osloenses* 14, (1935) 86–114.

285. Cf. above, n. 232 on negative interpretations of such a view of the emperor.

286. *De Cer.*, 393, lines 9–10; 394, line 7; 395, line 7.

287. Procopius of Gaza *Panegyricus*, 1 (above, n. 273). *Pan. Lat.*, 3, 11, 4: Clamare omnes prae gaudio, iam sine metu vestri et palam manu demonstrare.

288. *Pan. Lat.*, 9, 19, 2: Felices qui te propius aspicerent, longius positi nominabant.

289. With the exception of the campaign against the Huns in 559 A.D., see E. Stein, *Histoire du Bas-Empire*, vol. 2 (1949) 539–540; 818–819 (on *De Cer.*, 497–498 Bonn).

290. Procopius *Aed.*, 1, 10–11–20; C. Mango, *The Brazen House. A Study of the Vestibule of the Imperial Palace of Constantinople*, Royal Danish Academy of Science and Letters, Arkaeologisk-kunsthistoriske Meddelelser (1959) 30ff.

291. See H. P. L'Orange, *Art Forms and Civic Life in the Later Roman Empire* (1965); note the portrayal of the audience, as rows of heads, in the circus scene of the mosaic from Gafsa, Tunis, National Bardo Museum: R. Bianchi Bandinelli, *Rome, The Late Empire* (1971) fig. 233 and pp. 251f; and C. M. D. Dunbabin, *The Mosaics of Roman North Africa, Studies in Iconography and Patronage* (1978) 92–93 and pl. 78.

292. Procopius of Caesarea, *Aed.*, 1, 10, 16–19:

ἐφ' ἑκάτερα μὲν πόλεμός τέ ἐστι καὶ μάχη, καὶ ἁλίσκονται πόλεις παμπληθεῖς, πὴ μὲν Ἰταλίας, πὴ δὲ Λιβύης· καὶ νικᾷ μὲν βασιλεὺς Ἰουστινιανὸς ὑπὸ στρατηγοῦντι Βελισαρίῳ, ἐπάνεισι δὲ παρὰ τὸν βασιλέα, τὸ στράτευμα ἔχων ἀκραιφνὲς ὅλον ὁ στρατηγός, καὶ δίδωσιν αὐτῷ λάφυρα βασιλεῖς τε καὶ βασιλείας, καὶ πάντα τὰ ἐν ἀνθρώποις ἐξαίσια κατὰ δὲ τὸ μέσον ἑστᾶσιν ὅ τε βασιλεὺς καὶ ἡ βασιλὶς Θεοδώρα, ἐοικότες ἄμφω γεγηθόσι τε καὶ νικητήρια ἑορτάζουσιν ἐπί τε τῷ Βανδίλων καὶ Γότθων βασιλεῖ, δορυαλώτοις τε καὶ ἀγωγίμοις παρ' αὐτοὺς ἥκουσι. περιέστηκε δὲ αὐτοὺς ἡ Ῥωμαίων βουλὴ σύγκλητος, ἑορτασταὶ πάντες. τοῦτο γὰρ αἱ ψηφῖδες δηλοῦσιν ἐπὶ τοῖς προσώποις ἱλαρὸν αὐτοῖς ἐπανθοῦσαι. γαυροῦνται οὖν καὶ μειδιῶσι τῷ βασιλεῖ νέμοντες ἐπὶ τῷ ὄγκῳ τῶν πεπραγμένων ἰσοθέους τιμάς·

Cf. Merobaudes *Carm.* I, MGH AA 14 (1905) 3 (ed. Vollmer), describing a mosaic ceiling in the palace in Ravenna in which members of the imperial family occupy the centre. See F. M. Clover, "Flavius Merobaudes, a Translation and Historical Commentary," *Transactions of the American Philosophical Society* 61 (1971) 11, 16–27; note 17–18 on the static quality of this mosaic.

293. Mango, *Brazen House*, 33–34.

294. This had become the obligatory reaction of subjects in relation to the deeds of their emperors; cf. Constantius II's address to the Roman Senate by Themistius (Dind. 18c):

> Χαίρειν ὑμᾶς εἰκός . . . καὶ τῷ πλήθει τῶν τρωπαίων εὐφραινομένους καὶ τῆς παρούσης εἰρήνης ἀσφαλῶς ἀπολαύοντας.

295. Procop. *Wars*, 7, 1, 1.

296. For the offering of wreaths to celebrate triumph in early Byzantium, see the protocol for the return of the emperor from a military expedition, *De Cer.*, 495–498 (Bonn). A general description of the reception of the emperor is followed by the specific example of the return of Justinian in 559 (cf. above, n. 289) who, however, was not presented with a wreath (line 16f: τῶν συγκλητικῶν καὶ τοῦ ἐπάρχου τῆς πόλεως ἐκεῖσε ἀπαντησάντων δίχα στεφάνων . . .); cf. below, n. 311.

297. Procopius *Wars*, 4, 9, 1ff.

298. No Gothic triumph, Procopius *Wars*, 7, 1, 1–4; Marcellinus *ad annum*, 540; Jordanes *Getica*, 60. The Vandal triumph: Procopius *Wars*, 4, 9, 3–12 passim:

> οὐ τῷ παλαιῷ μέντοι τρόπῳ, ἀλλὰ πεζῇ βαδίζων ἐκ τῆς οἰκίας τῆς αὐτοῦ ἄχρι ἐς τὸν ἱππόδρομον κἀνταῦθα ἐκ βαλβίδων αὖθις ἕως εἰς τὸν χῶρον ἀφίκετο οὗ δὴ ὁ θρόνος ὁ βασίλειός ἐστιν. ἦν δὲ λάφυρα . . . (10) ἀνδράποδα δὲ ἦν τοῦ θριάμβου Γελίμερ τε αὐτός, ἐσθῆτά πού τινα ἐπὶ τῶν ὤμων ἀμπεχόμενος πορφυρᾶν, καὶ τὸ ξυγγενὲς ἅπαν . . . ὡς δὲ ἐν τῷ ἱπποδρόμῳ Γελίμερ ἐγεγόνει καὶ τόν τε βασιλέα ἐπὶ βήματος ὑψηλοῦ καθήμενον τὸν τε δῆμον ἐφ᾽ ἑκάτερα ἑστῶτα εἶδε καὶ αὐτὸν οὗ ἦν κακοῦ περισκοπῶν ἔγνω, οὔτε ἀπέκλαυσεν οὔτε ἀνώμωξεν, ἐπιλέγων δὲ οὐκ ἐπαύσατο κατὰ τὴν Ἑβραίων γραφὴν "Ματαιότης ματαιοτήτων, τὰ πάντα ματαιότης." ἀφικόμενον δε αὐτὸν κατὰ τὸ βασιλέως βῆμα τὴν πορφυρίδα περιελόντες, πρηνῆ πεσόντα προσκυνεῖν Ἰουστινιανὸν βασιλέα κατηνάγκασαν. τοῦτο δὲ καὶ Βελισάριος ἐποίει ἅτε ἱκέτης βασιλέως σὺν αὐτῷ γεγονώς.

299. For triumph in the hippodrome, see also Priscian's panegyric on Anastasius, lines 171–173, Bonn, 522–523.

300. As it did, for instance, in the dialogue between Justinian and the factions recorded by Theophanes. See J. B. Bury, *History of the Later Roman Empire from the Death of Theodosius I to the Death of Justinian*, I (1923) 71ff.

301. In this context we may note that Constantinople, like earlier Rome, developed a precise topography of imperial *adventus*. For the protocol in general, see *De Cer.* (ed. Reiske), 495–497, and for specific arrivals, cf. above, n. 296.

302. See below at n. 317.

303. Procopius *Wars*, 4, 9, 4–9.

304. Procopius *Aed.*, 1, 2, 1ff. On the description of equestrian statues in Statius and Procopius, see P. Friedländer, *Johannes von Gaza, Paulus Silentiarius und Prokopius von Gaza* (1969) 64–65. The origin of Justinian's equestrian statue has produced much discussion. See most recently M. Vickers, "Theodosius, Justinian or Heraclius," *Art Bulletin* 58 (1976) 281, and M. Vickers, "Mantegna and Constantinople," *Burlington Magazine* 118 (1976) 680–687. On the star, see K.

Gantar, "Kaiser Justinian, 'jenem Herbststern gleich'," *Museum Helveticum* 19 (1962) 194–196 and 33 (1976) 119–121, with whose view, that the simile implies a criticism of Justinian, I agree. On Justinian "as Achilles," see M. P. Charlesworth, "*Pietas* and *Victoria*, the Emperor and the Citizen," *JRS* 33 (1943) 10.

305. Procopius *Aed.*, 1, 2, 10–12:

φαίη τις ἂν ποιητικῶς εἶναι τὸν ὀπωρινὸν ἐκεῖνον ἀστέρα. βλέπει δὲ πρὸς ἀνίσχοντά που τὸν ἥλιον, τὴν ἡνιόχησιν ἐπὶ Πέρσας, οἶμαι, ποιούμενος. καὶ φέρει μὲν χειρὶ τῇ λαιᾷ πόλον, παραδηλῶν ὁ πλάστης ὅτι γῇ τε αὐτῷ καὶ θάλασσα δεδούλωται πᾶσα, ἔχει δὲ οὔτε ξίφος οὔτε δοράτιον οὔτε ἄλλο τῶν ὅπλων οὐδέν, ἀλλὰ σταυρὸς αὐτῷ ἐπὶ τοῦ πόλου ἐπίκειται, δι' οὗ δὴ μόνου τήν τε βασιλείαν καὶ τὸ τοῦ πολέμου πεπόρισται κράτος. προτεινόμενος δὲ χεῖρα τὴν δεξιὰν ἐς τὰ πρὸς ἀνίσχοντα ἥλιον καὶ τοὺς δακτύλους διαπετάσας ἐγκελεύεται τοῖς ἐκείνῃ βαρβάροις καθῆσθαι οἴκοι καὶ μὴ πρόσω ἰέναι.

On this statue see J. Kollwitz, *Oströmische Plastik der theodosianischen Zeit* (1941) 7ff and esp. 12ff. On Justinian's equestrian statue in the hippodrome, commemorating a victory over Persians and another over the Huns, see Alan Cameron, "Some Prefects Called Julian," *Byzantion* 47 (1977) 42–64 at 42–46.

306. E.g., Toynbee, *Roman Medallions* (1944) pl. XX, 3; XLIV, 7. Late antique versions of this iconography appear on the Constantinian porphyry sarcophagus in the Vatican.

307. M. Restle, *Kunst und byzantinische Münzprägung von Justinian I bis zum Bilderstreit*, Texte und Forschungen zur byzantinisch-neugriechischen Philologie (1964) 147–149. K. Weitzmann, ed., *Age of Spirituality* (1979) 45–46.

308. Note also Procopius on Belisarius' consulship: *Wars*, 4, 9, 15–16. However, historical awareness of the Roman past under Justinian should not be exaggerated. For the ideas of Justinian on the subject, see A. M. Honoré, "Some Constitutions Composed by Justinian," *JRS* 65 (1975) 107–123, esp. 122–123. Justinian was not a devotee of classical culture; "His historical imagination reaches back a century, no more."

309. See above, n. 295.

310. Cf. Averil Cameron, *Corippus*, 2f; 7f.

311. See Liutprand of Cremona *Legatio* 9–10 (ed. Becker) and see *De Cer.*, 438 (Bonn), for the *adventus* of Nicephorus Phocas in Constantinople, before his accession. *De Cer.*, 495–508 describes various ceremonial arrivals, the last being the triumphal entry into Constantinople of Theophilus in 838 A.D.

312. Corippus, *In laudem Iustini* (henceforth, Corippus) I, 187–203:

> Itur in arcem
> obsequio comitante patrum. gratissima coniux
> subsequitur, non tunc solito stipata tumultu.
> incedunt media securam nocte per urbem
> (191–196) . . .
> limen ut Augustae sacro pede contigit aulae,
> omnia gallorum strepuerunt culmina cantu.
> exactam noctem primi sensere volucres,
> et laetum cecinere diem, alarumque dedere
> plausibus assiduis et acuta voce favorem.
> excubiae primum, quae summa palatia servant,
> imperium felix dominis intrantibus optant.

313. For which, cf. *Pan. Lat.*, 10, 32, 4.

314. Corippus, I, 295–301:

> Vox ingens facta est, plausus et gaudia surgunt,
> et fragor ex imis altum petit aethera terris,
> almaque discreto placuit concordia vulgo.
> laeta per Augustam pennis plaudentibus urbem
> Fama volans somnum populos inopina gravantem
> increpat, impellitque fores et limina pulsat,
> multiplicatque suas felix praenuntia linguas.

315. Corippus, I, 305–313:

> Et 'surgite, surgite' clamat,
> castigatque moras . . .
> (307–309) . . .
> accelerant, vacuantque domos, vicosque per omnes
> gaudentes currunt, et murmura prima moventur
> nondum clara metu, civemque interrogat omnem
> occurrens civis, rumorque per agmina serpit.

316. The words in brackets summarise Corippus I, 322–329. According to Malalas 175 (ed. Niebuhr, Bonn 1831), likewise, chariotracing was instituted to honour the sun, but the four colours stand for the four elements.

317. Corippus, I, 314–333:

> Solis honore novi grati spectacula circi
> antiqui sanxere patres, qui quattuor esse
> solis equos quadam rerum ratione putabant,
> tempora continui signantes quattuor anni,
> in quorum speciem signis numerisque modisque
> aurigas totidem, totidem posuere colores,
> et fecere duas studia in contraria partes,
> ut sunt aestivis brumalia frigora flammis.
> (322–329) . . .
> ipse ingens circus, pleni ceu circulus anni,
> clauditur in teretem longis anfractibus orbem,
> amplectens geminas aequo discrimine metas
> et spatium mediae, qua se via pandit, harenae.

318. Corippus, I, 338–344:

> Hunc veterum primi ritum non rite colebant,
> esse deum solem recta non mente putantes.
> sed factor solis postquam sub sole videri
> se voluit formamque deus de virgine sumpsit
> humani generis, tunc munere solis adempto
> principibus delatus honor munusque Latinis
> et iucunda novae circensia gaudia Romae.

See on this passage, Averil Cameron, *Corippus* 143–146. Cf. Salvian, *De Gubernatione Dei* 6, 24; 26: the circus games are offered to Christ; and 6, 85ff, circus games as a remedy for disasters and defeat.

319. Corrupt text at lines 346–347.

320. Corippus, I, 345–367:

Huc omnes populi, pueri iuvenesque senesque
dant agmina plausus
vox omnibus una,
mens eadem: nomen populis placet omnibus unum.
(349–355) . . .
. . . domini sic vulgus amore
undique conveniens . . .
'tu vincas, Iustine!' canunt, ingensque tumultus
crescit, . . .
. . . vox excitat omnes;
omnia Iustino praebent elementa favorem,
omnia congaudent, omnes clamore vocati
conveniunt proceres: lux sacra palatia complet.
(364–365) . . .
signa dedit manifesta deus, seque ipse probavit
Iustino claram regni imposuisse coronam.

321. Cf. MacCormack, *Historia* 21 (1972) 736–737 and cf. above at nn. 126ff.

322. J. P. Richter, *Quellen der byzantinischen Kunstgeschichte*, (1897) 13, 255–256, 271, and F. W. Unger, *Quellen der byzantinischen Kunstgeschichte* (1878) 146–147.

323. Imitated by Khusro I at Apamea: Procopius *Wars*, 2, 11, 31ff.

324. A. Pertusi, ed., *Giorgio di Pisidia, Poemi I. Panegyrici Epici*, Studia Patristica et Byzantina, 7 (1959) 77–81: *In Heraclium ex Africa redeuntem*.

325. George of Pisidia *In Heraclium*, 21f.

326. George of Pisidia *In Heraclium*, 39f.

327. George of Pisidia *In Heraclium*, 37f.

328. George of Pisidia *In Heraclium*, 76–85:

ὁ γὰρ πλάτος σοι καρδίας δωρούμενος,
ὡς πᾶσιν ἀρκεῖς μηδαμῶς στενούμενος,
δείξει κυβερνᾶν καὶ τὰ νῦν ἐκ τῆς ζάλης
πρὸς τὴν γαλήνην, ἣν ἔχεις, τὰ πράγματα,
ὅπως μερίμνης λοιπὸν ἐστερημένοι
τὸ ψυχικόν σου κάλλος ὡς ἐν εἰκόνι
ἐν ταῖς ἑαυτῶν ἐκτυποῦντες καρδίαις
ἀνεξάλειπτον ἱστορήσωμεν χάριν
δεικνύντες οἷον ἄνθος εὐλογημένον
ταῖς τῶν ἀκανθῶν συμπλοκαῖς ἐκρύπτετο.

329. George of Pisidia *In Heraclium*, 48ff.

330. George of Pisidia *In Heraclium*, 1–3:

Λόγος μὲν ὑμᾶς οὐ κατισχύει φράσαι,
αὐτοῦ τεθεικότος σε τοῦ Θεοῦ Λόγου,
ὑπερτετάχθαι τῶνδε τῶν ῥευστῶν λόγων.

331. On the chronology of the return of the Cross and of Heraclius' return to Constantinople, see A. Frolow, "La Vraie Croix et les expéditions d'Héraclius en Perse," *Rev. ét. byz.* (1953) 88–105, and V. Grumel, "La Réposition de la Vraie Croix à Jérusalem par Héraclius, le jour et l'année," *Polychordia*, Festschr. F. Dölger, *Byzantinische Forschungen*, 1 (1966) 139–149.

332. George of Pisidia *In Restitutionem S. Crucis* (ed. Pertusi, *Giorgio di Pisidia*,

225–30) 21–24; J. Gagé, "Σταυρὸς νικοποιός, la victoire impériale dans l'empire chrétien," *Rev. d'hist. et de philosophie religieuses* 13 (1933) 370–400; and cf. G. C. Picard, *Les trophées romains, contribution à l'histoire de la religion et de l'art triomphal de Rome*, Bibl. des éc. fr. d'Athènes et de Rome, 187 (1957) 494–508.

333. George of Pisidia *In Rest.*, 49–51.
334. George of Pisidia *In Rest.*, 52ff.
335. George of Pisidia *In Rest.*, 14, 66.
336. George of Pisidia, *Expeditio Persica* (ed. Pertusi, *Giorgio di Pisidia*, 84–136), I, 132–151, 248–52; II, 88–115.

337. J. Deer, "Das Kaiserbild im Kreuz," *Schweizer Beiträge zur allgemeinen Geschichte* 13 (1955) 48–112, reprinted in his *Byzanz und das abendländische Herrschertum* (1977) 11–44; A. Lipinsky, "La 'Croce gemmata' e il culto della Santa Croce nei monumenti superstiti e nelle raffigurazioni monumentali," *Felix Ravenna* (1960) 5–62; and K. G. Holum, "Pulcheria's Crusade of A.D. 421 and the Ideology of Imperial Victory," *Greek, Roman and Byzantine Studies* 18 (1977) 153–172.

338. Deer, "Das Kaiserbild," 98ff; Lipinsky, "La 'Croce gemmata'," 47f, suggesting Justin's sickness as a possible motive for the gift; and C. Belting-Ihm, "Das Justinuskreuz in der Schatzkammer der Peterskirche zu Rom," *Jahrbuch des römisch-germanischen Zentralmuseums Mainz* 12 (1965) 142–166. On the use of the cross (it is a *Handkreuz*, like the one carried by Bishop Maximian in the San Vitale imperial mosaic), see A. Lipinsky, "Crux Vaticana, Kaiser Justinus' II Kreuz," *Römische Quartalschrift* 63 (1968) 185–203.

339. E.g., Delbrueck, *Consulardiptychen*, no. 34, Justin, Constantinople 520 A.D. Cf. the parallel iconographies of nos. 16 (Clementinus, Constantinople 513 A.D.) and 32 (Orestes, Rome 530 A.D.), where the rulers frame the cross. On the unusual attitude and attire of the imperial couple on the cross, see C. Belting-Ihm "Das Justinuskreuz," 159ff, and A. Lipinsky, "Crux Vaticana," 193ff.

340. See Agapetus 63, *P.G.*, 86, 1184.
341. George of Pisidia, *In Rest.* 73. "ἐν σοὶ" refers, I think, to Heraclius, but Pertusi refers it to Golgotha: "La Croce su di te (Golgota)." See also his notes on lines 73ff. V. Grumel "La Réposition" (above, n. 331), 148, translates as I do.
342. George of Pisidia *In Rest.*, 73–103:

ὁ σταυρὸς ἐν σοὶ τοῖς ἐναντίοις νέα
κιβωτὸς ὤφθη τῆς δὲ κιβωτοῦ πλέον.
ἡ μὲν γὰρ ἄχρι τῶν βελῶν τοῖς βαρβάροις
πληγὴν ἐφῆκεν, ἡ δὲ τοῦ ξύλου τάσις
ἔμψυχα τούτοις ἐξαπέστειλεν βέλη.
Πάρθοι δὲ Πέρσας πυρπολοῦσι καὶ Σκύθης
Σκλάβον φονεύει καὶ πάλιν φονεύεται,
καὶ τοῖς ἑαυτῶν ἡματωμένοι φόνοις
πολλὴν ἔχουσι φύρσιν εἰς μίαν μάχην·
αὐτὸς δὲ σιγᾷς στέμμα καὶ σκῆπρον φέρων
ὥσπερ βραβευτὴς τῶν παλαιστῶν ἐν μέσῳ,
πολλοῖς παλαίσας, νῦν δὲ λύσας τὴν μάχην.
τῷ σῷ δὲ λοιπὸν προσβλέπουσι νεύματι
ἐξ ἀντιλόξου τῶν ἀγώνων οἱ μέσοι·
ὅπου δὲ νεῦσις, ἡ πάλη δίκην ἔχει.
(88–101) . . .

καὶ τῷ θεάτρῳ προσγελᾷς τῶν βαρβάρων
τοὺς πρὶν διώκτας εἰσορῶν ὑπηκόους.

On the date of the return of the Cross, 21 March 631 A.D., timed by Heraclius to coincide with the celebration of Holy Week, see V. Grumel, "La Réposition de la Vraie Croix," 139–149; cf. below, n. 343.

343. George of Pisidia *In Rest.*, 104–110:

> τούτων παρ' ἡμῖν τῶν ἀγαθῶν ἠγγελμένων
> εἰς καιρὸν εὐπρόσδεκτον, εἰς νικηφόρον,
> ὅτε προσελθὼν τοῖς τυράννοις τῶν τάφων
> ὁ τὴν καθ' ἡμᾶς οὐσίαν ἀναπλάσας
> ζωὴν ἐφῆκε τῷ νεκρῷ τοῦ Λαζάρου—
> ἔδει γὰρ, οἶμαι, τῇ νεκρῶν ἀναστάσει
> σταυροῦ γενέσθαι καὶ πάλιν μηνύματα—

344. George of Pisidia *In Rest.*, 111–116:

> ὅλη συνῆλθεν εἰς ἑαυτὴν ἡ Πόλις
> ὡς ψάμμος, ὡς ῥοῦς, ὡς ἄμετρα κύματα
> ποιοῦντα πολλάς σωματώδεις ἐκχύσεις.
> σπουδὴν γὰρ εἶχον, οἷα δορκὰς ἐν θέρει
> διψῶσα καὶ σφυζουσα, συντόμως φθάσαι
> τῶν σῶν, κράτιστε, συλλαβῶν τὰς ἰκμάδας.

345. George of Pisidia *In Rest.*, 1–8:

> Ὦ Γολγοθὰ σκίρτησον· ἡ κτίσις πάλιν
> ὅλη σε τιμᾷ καὶ καλεῖ θεηδόχον·
> ἐκ Περσίδος γὰρ ὁ βασιλεὺς ἀφιγμένος
> τὸν σταυρὸν ἐν σοὶ δεικνύει πεπηγμένον·
> κρότησον αὐτὸν τοῖς ἀοιδίμοις λόγοις·
> ἀλλ' εἴπερ οὐκ ἔχουσιν οἱ λίθοι στόμα,
> νέους προευτρέπιζε φοινίκων κλάδους
> πρὸς τὴν ἀπαντὴν τοῦ νέου νικηφόρου.

346. George of Pisidia *In Rest.*, 27–38:

> ὁ σταυρὸς ἦλθε βασιλικῶς δεδεγμένος
> λιταῖς, προσευχαῖς, δακρύοις, ἀγρυπνίαις,
> χωλοῖς ἐνάρθροις καὶ λαλοῦσιν ὀργάνοις,
> μέγα τρόπαιον τῷ βασιλεῖ συναρμόσας,
> ἐχθροὺς ποθοῦντας καὶ πλέον φοβουμένους·
> τῷ βαρβάρῳ γὰρ οὐ παροικεῖν ἤθελεν
> εἰ καὶ κολάζων τὴν ἁμαρτίαν τότε
> ἔκδημος εἰς γῆν ἣν δραμὼν ἀλλοτρίαν·
> ἀλλ' ἀντανῆλθε καὶ τὰ τέκνα συλλέγει
> ἐκ τῆς ἀειδοῦς καὶ νοθου παροικίας
> καὶ προσκυνεῖται καὶ πλέον δοξαεται,
> ὡς σοφρονίζων καὶ λυτρούμενος πλέον.

347. On the new and the old under Heraclius in terms of imperial titulature, see I. Shahîd, "The Iranian Factor in Byzantium under Heraclius," *DOP* 26 (1972) 295–320. Averil Cameron, "The Theotokos in Sixth Century Constantinople," *JTS* 29 (1978) 79–108, describes the new climate from another point of view. See also her "Images of Authority: Elites and Icons in Late Sixth-Century Byzantium," *Past and Present* 84 (1979) 3–35.

348. ἐθριάμβευσεν, Nicephorus, ed. de Boor, 22.

349. Note also the elephants in the funerary procession on the British Museum Consecratio Diptych, below, "*Consecratio*" at nn. 233ff. On the use of elephants in war and sometimes ceremony, see H. H. Scullard, *The Elephant in the Greek and Roman World* (1974) esp. 198–207.

350. Nicephorus, 22–23. For an earlier imperial precedent, cf. "The Feriale Duranum," ed. R. O. Fink, A. S. Hoey, and W. F. Snyder, "Feriale Duranum," *Yale Class. Stud.* 7 (1940) 79f.

351. εὐφημίας καὶ δόξης, Nicephorus 22; cf. Theophanes, ed. de Boor, 328.

352. Theophanes, 327, 24–328, 10:

> ὁ δὲ βασιλεὺς ἐν ἓξ ἔτεσι καταπολεμήσας τὴν Περσίδα, τῷ ζ ἔτει εἰρηνεύσας μετὰ χαρᾶς μεγάλης ἐπὶ Κωνσταντινούπολιν ὑπέστρεψε μυστικήν τινα θεωρίαν ἐν τούτῳ πληρώσας. ἐν γὰρ ἓξ ἡμέραις πᾶσαν τὴν κτίσιν δημιουργήσας ὁ θεός τὴν ἑβδόμην ἀναπαύσεως ἡμέραν ἐκάλεσεν· οὕτω καὶ αὐτὸς ἐν τοῖς ἓξ χρόνοις πολλοὺς πόνους διανύσας τῷ ἑβδόμῳ ἔτει μετ' εἰρήνης καὶ χαρᾶς ἐν τῇ πόλει ὑποστρέψας ἀνεπαύσατο. ὁ δὲ λαὸς τῆς πόλεως τὴν ἔλευσιν αὐτοῦ μαθόντες ἀκατασχέτῳ πόθῳ πάντες εἰς τὴν Ἱερείαν ἐξῆλθον εἰς συνάντησιν αὐτοῦ, σὺν τῷ πατριάρχῃ καὶ Κωνσταντίνῳ, τῷ βασιλεῖ καὶ υἱῷ αὐτοῦ, βαστάζοντες κλάδους ἐλαιῶν καὶ λαμπάδας, εὐφημοῦντες αὐτὸν μετὰ χαρᾶς καὶ δακρύων. προσελθὼν δὲ ὁ υἱὸς αὐτοῦ ἔπεσεν ἐπὶ τοὺς πόδας αὐτοῦ, καὶ περιπλακεὶς αὐτῷ ἔβρεξαν ἀμφότεροι τὴν γῆν τοῖς δάκρυσιν. τοῦτο θεασάμενος ὁ λαός, ἅπαντες εὐχαριστηρίους ὕμνους τῷ θεῷ ἀνέπεμπον· καὶ οὕτω λαβόντες τὸν βασιλέα σκιρτῶντες εἰσῆλθον ἐν τῇ πόλει.

Cf. George the Monk, ed. de Boor, 372. A. S. Proudfoot, "The Sources of Theophanes for the Heracleian Dynasty," *Byzantion* 44 (1974) 367–448 at 381; A. Pertusi, *Giorgio di Pisidia*, 292; 307, frag. no. 54 comes from the work Theophanes used. See also S. Spain Alexander, "Heraclius, Byzantine Imperial Ideology, and the David Plates," *Speculum* 52 (1977) 217–237, at 221–223; J. Trilling, "Myth and Metaphor at the Byzantine Court. A Literary Approach to the David Plates," *Byzantion* 48 (1978) 249–263; and K. Weitzmann, ed., *Age of Spirituality* (1979) 475–484. Cf. S. H. Wander, "The Cyprus Plates and the Chronicle of Fredegar," *DOP* 29 (1975) 345–346, on the "new David." An imperial *adventus* of the late seventh century may have been represented in a lost fresco from S. Demetrius, Thessalonica. See G. A. Soteriou and M. G. Soteriou, Ἡ βασιλικὴ τοῦ ἁγιοὺ Δημητρίου τῆς Θεσσαλονίκης (1952) 207–209, pl. 78–79; A. Grabar, *L'empereur dans l'art byzantin* (1936; 1971), 131; 234, n. 4, but compare J. D. Breckenridge, "The Long Siege of Thessalonika, Its Date and Iconography," *BZ* 48 (1955) 116–122.

II. CONSECRATIO

1. See Vollmer, "Laudationum funebrium Romanorum historia et reliquiarum editio," *Jhbb. f. class. Phil.* Suppl. 18 (1891) 445–528; "De funere publico Romanorum," *Jhbb. f. class. Phil.* Suppl. 19 (1892) 319–364. On the *laudatio funebris* by Augustus on Agrippa, see L. Koenen, "Die *laudatio funebris* des Augustus für Agrippa auf einem neuen Papyrus," *Zeitschrift für Papyrologie und Epigraphik* 5 (1970) 217–283; also, E. Malcovati, "Il nuovo frammento della *Laudatio Agrippae*," *Athenaeum* 50 (1972) 142–151. This *laudatio* has the old-fashioned Roman form of addressing the deceased ("tu"), not the audience. Cf. S. MacCormack, "Latin

Prose Panegyrics: Tradition and Discontinuity in the Later Roman Empire," *Revue des études augustiniennes* 22 (1976) 29–77 at 33–34.

2. See, for the Christian world, P. R. L. Brown, *Relics and Social Status in the Age of Gregory of Tours* (1977); for Islam, A. J. Wensinck, *The Muslim Creed* (1932), showing that the Muslim insistence on the absoluteness of Allah's being in effect precluded interventions by the living on behalf of the dead and vice versa (e.g., 118). Pious observances to the contrary within Islam appear to be clearly identifiable survivals of paganism, rather than resulting from theological concessions to daily practice: R. Kriss and H. Kriss-Heinrich, *Volksglaube im Bereich des Islam*, vol. 2 (1962) 208–209; also 207. For Judaism, see J. Neusner, *A History of the Jews in Babylonia*, vol. 4 (1969) 156–157; vol. 5 (1970) 287–289.

3. Shakespeare, *Julius Caesar*, Act III, Scene II.

4. See H. W. Ritter, *Diadem und Königsherrschaft. Untersuchungen zu Zeremonien und Rechtsgrundlagen des Herrschaftsantritts bei den Persern, bei Alexander dem Grossen und im Hellenismus* (1965); L. Cerfaux and J. Tondriau, *Un concurrent du christianisme: le culte des souverains dans la civilisation gréco-romaine* (1957); and P. Veyne, *Le pain et le cirque* (1976) 560ff.

5. On cults to Romans in the East, see L. Cerfaux and J. Tondriau, *Un Concurrent du christianisme: le culte des souverains dans la civilisation gréco-romaine* (1957) 278ff.; and F. F. Abbot and A. C. Johnson, *Municipal Administration in the Roman Empire* (1926) 270–276, 287. See also, for Italy, F. Taeger, *Charisma, Studien zur Geschichte des antiken Herrscherkultes*, vol. 2, (1960) 3ff, 141ff, and K. Hopkins, *Conquerors and Slaves* (1978) 200ff. On the egalitarianism of late republican aristocratic politics, see A. U. Stylow, *Libertas und Liberalitas. Untersuchungen zur innenpolitischen Propaganda der Römer* (1972) 20ff, 34. One strand of republican *libertas* is "die aristokratisch-egalitäre Freiheit mit ihrer Tyrannophobie." The Roman republican dislike of divinising a human being was inherited by the Christians; e.g., Socrates *H.E.*, 3, 23:

> Ζῆνα θεῶν ὕπατον, καὶ Ἀθηνᾶν τριτογένειαν
> Τιμᾶτε, βροτέων ἐν σώματι κρυπτὸν ἄνακτα
> Ὃν Ζεὺς ἀρίσταις γοναῖς ἔσπειρεν, ἀρωγὸν
> Εὐνομίης θνητοῖσιν Ἀλέξανδρον βασιλῆα.

Ταῦτα τὸ ἐν Πυθοῖ δαιμόνιον ἐχρημάτισεν. Ὃ καὶ αὐτὸ τοὺς δυνάμιας κολακεῦον ἐθεοποίει καὶ τοῦτο μὲν ἴσως κολακείᾳ ἐποίει.

6. Cicero *Ad Quintum fratrem*, 1, 1, 26–27; *Ad Att.*, 5, 21, 7: Nullos honores mihi nisi verborum decerni sino, statuas, fana, τέθριππα prohibeo.

7. Cicero *De re publica*, 6, 13:

> Omnibus qui patriam conservaverint, adiuverint, auxerint, certum esse in caelo definitum locum, ubi beati aevo sempiterno fruantur; nihil est enim illi principi deo, qui omnem mundum regit, quod quidem in terris fiat acceptius, quam concilia coetusque hominum iure sociati, quae civitates appellantur; harum rectores et conservatores hinc profecti huc revertuntur.

The Dream of Scipio was not an isolated statement about astral immortality. On Vergil and Manilius see J. Bayet, "L'immortalité astrale d'Auguste," *Revue des études latines* 17 (1939) 141–171, and see below, n. 8.

8. Plato, *Republic* 10, 13ff; *Favonii Eulogii Disputatio de Somnio Scipionis*, ed. A. Holder (1901) 1; Macrobius, *Commentarii in Somnium Scipionis*, ed. I. Willis (1970)

I, 1–2; II, 17; and W. H. Stahl, *Macrobius, Commentary on the Dream of Scipio* (1952) 11, 39. Cf. P. Boyancé, *Études sur le Songe de Scipion* (1936) and K. Büchner, *Somnium Scipionis, Quellen, Gestalt, Sinn*, Hermes Einzelschriften, 36 (1976).

9. The visionary quality of knowledge of the afterlife, and of contact between the living and the dead, emerges when Scipio, narrating his dream, is afraid to be awakened from it. To tell the dream, he has to dream it once more and says, Cicero, *De re publica* 6, 12: *St! quaeso . . . ne me e somno excitetis, et parumper audite cetera.* On the contradictions inherent in divinisation and *consecratio*, see E. Bickermann, "Consecratio," in *Le culte des souverains dans l'empire romain*, Entretiens Hardt, 19 (1972) 3–37 at 18: "The difference between the private veneration of a defunct emperor and the public cult of the same emperor as *divus* is essential and ineffaceable. . . . But even within the domestic cult the tomb and the apotheosis were incompatible."

10. Polybius, VI, 53f, with commentary by F. W. Walbank, *A Historical Commentary on Polybius*, vol. 1 (1957) 737f.

11. On *consecratio* and *damnatio memoriae*, see F. Vittinghoff, *Der Staatsfeind in der römischen Kaiserzeit* (1936).

12. S. Weinstock, *Divus Julius*, (1971) 346ff, 386ff; also, T. Mommsen, *Römisches Staatsrecht*, vol. 2, 2 (1877; 1952) 754–760.

13. Dio, 43, 14, 6; 21, 2, with Weinstock, *Divus Julius* (1971) 40, 53. On the inscription, D. Fishwick, "The Name of the Demigod," *Historia* 24 (1975) 624–628. See also A. D. Nock, "ΣΥΝΝΑΟΣ ΘΕΟΣ," *Harvard Studies in Classical Philology* 41 (1930) 1–62, reprinted in his *Essays on Religion and the Ancient World*, vol. 1 (1972) 202–251, at 202f. Perhaps an earlier depiction of this nature is referred to in Athenaeus XII, 536a: Demetrius Poliorcetes was represented in a painting in Athens ἐπί τῆς οἰκουμένης ὀχούμενος.

14. S. Weinstock, *Divus Julius* (1971) 40ff, 385ff.

15. *Ibid.*, 175f, 85.

16. As, for instance, in the late antique potpourri of the *origo gentis romanae*, the *liber de viris illustribus* and the *Caesars* of Aurelius Victor: see A. Momigliano, "Some observations on the '*origo gentis romanae*'," *JRS* 48 (1958) 56–73, reprinted in his *Secondo contributo alla storia degli studi classici* (1960) 145–176; and A. Momigliano, "Per una nuova edizione della '*origo gentis romanae*'," *Athenaeum* 36 (1958) 248–259, reprinted in his *Secondo contributo*, 177–190. O. Jahn, "Über die Subskriptionen in den HSS römischer Classiker," in *Ber. über die Verhandl. d. kgl. sächs. Ges. d. Wiss.* Leipzig, phil. hist. Cl., 3 (1851) 327–72, in part qualified by Alan Cameron, "Paganism and Literature in Late Fourth Century Rome," in *Christianisme et formes littéraires de l'antiquité tardive en Occident*, Entretiens Hardt, 23 (1977) 1–40.

17. Wissowa PW 4, 896ff. s.v. *Consecratio*; and cf. PW Suppl. 4, 816ff, Herzog-Hauser s.v. *Kaiserkult*.

18. Being a strictly Roman procedure, *consecratio* should be differentiated from other forms of ruler-cult, on which see (from among a vast literature, cf. above nn. 4, 5, 13) S. Eitrem, "Zur Apotheose," *Symbolae Osloenses* 10 (1932) 31–56; 11 (1932) 11–34; 15–16 (1936) 111–137. For the later empire, see L'Orange, "Sol Invictus Imperator," *Symb. Osl.* 14 (1935) 86–114, reprinted in his *Likeness and Icon* (1973) 325–344; also, E. Strong, *Apotheosis and After Life* (1915). In the East, the emperor-cult was a continuation of the cults of Hellenistic rulers; for

Egypt, cf. Blumenthal, "Der ägyptische Kaiserkult," *Arch. f. Papyrusforschung* 5 (1909–1913) 317–345. For the approximation of the emperor to various gods in portraiture, see L'Orange, *Apotheosis in Ancient Portraiture* (1947) 55f. See I. Scott Ryberg, *Rites of the State Religion in Roman Art*, Memoirs, American Academy in Rome, 22 (1955) 81ff, on the cult of *divi* and of the genius of living emperors.

19. Bickermann, "Die römische Kaiserapotheose," *Arch. f. Religionswissenschaft* 27 (1929) 31:

> Der jüngere Plinius . . . entrüstet sich über Domitians Versuche den Römern seine Verehrung aufzuzwingen. Und so wurde das Recht des Senats, nur nach eigener Wahl die überschwänglichste Adulation zu verleihen, einen Sterblichen den Unsterblichen einzureihen, zur letzten römischen Freiheit.

20. See below, n. 30.
21. See E. Strong, *Apotheosis and After Life* (1915) 222ff; E. M. Wightman, *Roman Trier and the Treveri* (1970) 239; on Hercules and the emperor, M. Simon, *Hercule et le christianisme* (1955) 130–143. For the ascent, see also M. J. Vermaseren, *Liber in Deum; l'apoteosi di un iniziato dionisiaco* (1976) 52ff. For the bust of a deceased private individual carried up by an eagle in Roman funerary art, where the imperial models were followed for this iconography, see W. Altmann, *Die römischen Grabaltäre der Kaiserzeit* (1905) 278ff. The origin of this iconography: below, n. 29.
22. Ovid *Met.*, 15, 745ff.
23. Ovid, *Met.*, 15, 760–761: Ne foret hic igitur mortali semine creatus,/ ille deus faciendus erat.
24. Ovid, *Met.*, 15, 868–870:

> Tarda sit illa dies et nostro serior aevo,
> qua caput Augustum, quem temperat, orbe relicto,
> accedat caelo faveatque precantibus absens.

25. E.g., *Pan. Lat.*, 9, 26, 1ff; 10, 38, 2.
26. *RIC*, II, 299.
27. The temple and altar *consecratio* coinages: *RIC*, I, 95: for Augustus, 14–22 A.D., temple, altar, eagle.
a. The temple alone: e.g., *RIC*, I, 42, for Caesar, DIVO IUL, temple; *RIC*, I, 117, for Augustus, DIVO AUG SC, temple with Caligula sacrificing; *RIC*, II, 123, for Titus, temple. *Consecratio* coins of Faustina the elder narrate the history of her temple: *RIC*, III, 69, 70, 73: temple with her statue, AED DIV FAUSTINAE or AETERNITAS; *RIC*, III, 73, DEDICATIO AEDIS, temple; *RIC*, III, 74, PIETAS, temple of Faustina, referring either to her *pietas* which merited the temple, or the *pietas* of Antoninus, who consecrated her; *RIC*, III, 60, temple, with statues of Augustus and Livia, restoration coinage of Antoninus Pius, 158–159 A.D., AED DIVI.
b. The Altar of Divus or Diva: *RIC*, II, 125, for Vespasian, DIVO VESP; *RIC*, III, 247, 314, for Sabina, PIETATI AUG; for Antoninus Pius DIVO PIO or DIVO PIO SC, all with altar; *RIC*, III, 273, 348, for Faustina II, CONSECRATIO or CONSECRATIO SC, altar; *RIC*, III, 247, for Antoninus Pius, eagle standing on altar CONSECRATIO; *RIC*, III, 397–398, 441, for Marcus Aurelius, eagle standing on altar CONSECRATIO; *RIC*, IV¹, 211–212, 239, for Septimius Severus, eagle standing on altar CONSECRATIO. The eagle and altar type with variations was also very frequent

during the second Tetrarchy: cf. below, at nn. 84ff. For the eagle as soul-bearer, see below at nn. 31, 50–51.

28. *RIC*, IV³, 131–132. Repeats of this combination were issued for other emperors: *RIC*, V¹, 118–119, Valerian; *ibid.*, 140; 147–148; 150, Carus; *ibid.*, 196, Numerian; *ibid.*, 203, Nigrinianus; *ibid.*, 234, Claudius Gothicus; *ibid.*, 240, Quintillus. See also *RIC*, VI, 256; VII, 311, eagle with outspread wings for Constantius I at Lugdunum and Rome.

29. Caesar: above, n. 13. The emperor enthroned over the sky: above, "*Adventus*" at n. 91, and below at n. 65. The emperor enthroned over the sky, or over a globe, and the translation of this imagery into Christianity: below at nn. 173ff.

30. Imperial gems: the cameo in Paris shows Germanicus on an eagle: G. M. A. Richter, *Engraved Gems of the Romans* (1971) no. 498; G. Bruns, *Staatskameen des 4. Jahrhunderts nach Christi Geburt*, Winckelmannsprogramm der archäologischen Gesellschaft zu Berlin, 104 (1948) 27, fig. 24: the cameo in Nancy showing, according to Bruns, Caracalla, seated on an eagle, crowned by Victoria and holding a cornucopiae. Baalbek: H. Seyrig, "La triade héliopolitaine et les temples de Baalbek," *Syria* 10 (1929) 315–356, at 336 with plate LXXXII, 1; see also 337–338, with fig. 2. For Syrian tombstones, see F. Cumont, "L'aigle funéraire des Syriens," *Rev. de l'hist. des religions* 62 (1910) 119–164, and "L'aigle funéraire d'Hierapolis et l'apothéose des empereurs," in his *Études Syriennes* (1917) 35–118. For the ascent to heaven of Ptolemy I, see G. Bruns, "Der grosse Kameo von Frankreich," *Mitteilungen des dtsch. arch. Inst.* 6 (1953) 71–115 at 82, quoting Theocritus Id., 17, 16–33.

31. For medallions, see J. M. C. Toynbee, *Roman Medallions* (1944) 101–102; also *RIC*, II, 305. For the regular coinage: *RIC*, II, 390 CONSECRATIO, for Sabina; *ibid.* 479 CONSECRATIO SC, for Faustina; *RIC*, III, 164, Marcus Aurelius; e.g., *RIC*, IV¹, 313; IV², 101, 110, 127, Augustae of the Severan house (cf. Gnecchi, II, 96, 1, Julia Domna on a swan: CONSECRATIO); the third century: *RIC*, IV¹, 239, Septimius Severus; *RIC*, V¹, 38, Valerian I; *RIC*, V¹, 117, with pl. 4, 66; 121, Valerian II.

32. E.g., Marcus, *RIC*, II, 397, 441; Severus, IV¹, 239.

33. E.g., Augustus, *RIC*, I, 95; Hadrian, *RIC*, II, 385; Pius, *RIC*, III, 247; Pertinax, *RIC*, IV¹, 94; 181; Severus, *RIC*, IV¹, 239; Valerian II, *RIC*, V¹, 117; Carus, *RIC* V², 138.

34. E.g., Sabina, *RIC*, II, 39; Marciana, *RIC*, II, 299; Marcus, *RIC*, III, 397.

35. Gnecchi, II, 43, 5.

36. Sometimes described as Aion, e.g., H. Schrade, "Zur Ikonographie der Himmelfahrt Christi," *Vortr. d. Bibl. Warburg* (1928–1929), 103f. See, on the monument as a whole, L. Vogel, *The Column of Antoninus Pius* (1973).

37. The relief in the Palazzo Conservatori, showing the empress Sabina carried up from her pyre by Aeternitas with Hadrian and the personification of the Campus Martius looking on, L. Vogel, *Column*, pl. 47, works on a similar basis. Cf. coin of Faustina II borne up by Victoria, *RIC*, III, 348.

38. According to C. C. Vermeule, *Roman Imperial Art in Greece and Asia Minor* (1968) 96f, 105, (fig. 40); it is Hadrian, who, however, is shown alive elsewhere on the monument.

39. Nyx according to Vermeule, *Roman Imperial Art*, 117.

40. See J. M. C. Toynbee, *Death and Burial in the Roman World*, (1971) 60–61,

and n. 244 on a sestertius and denarius of such a type of Aelius Verus. Chariot and pyre types were frequent for empresses: *RIC*, III, 164, Faustina I; also on medallions, Gnecchi, II, 56, 7; *RIC*, III, 350, Faustina II. CONSECRATIO medallions of Faustina I show the empress with flying cloak in a *biga* with Aeternitas (Gnecchi, 2, 56, 8), or in a *biga* alone (Gnecchi, II, 59, 4), or about to mount a *biga* (Gnecchi, II, 58, 2; cf. J. M. C. Toynbee, *Roman Medallions*, 101, where these issues are collected). This last also appears on the regular coinage. The type is repeated on the regular coinage for Faustina II, SIDERIBUS RECEPTA SC (*RIC*, III, 350).

41. *RIC*, III, 247, 314; Verus, *ibid.*, 333; Marcus, *ibid.*, 273; 397–8; Pertinax, *RIC*, IV^1, 181; Severus, *ibid.*, 292; Caracalla, *RIC*, IV^2, 127; 128; Valerian II, *RIC*, V^1, 117; Gnecchi, II, 116, 3, *biga*; Claudius Gothicus, *RIC*, V^1, 233–234; Nigrinianus, *RIC*, V^2, 203; cf. Toynbee, *Roman Medallions*, 61.

42. *RIC*, VI, 221.

43. See J. M. C. Toynbee, *Death and Burial*, 39–42; A. D. Nock, "Cremation and Burial in the Roman Empire," *Harv. Theol. Rev.* 25 (1932) 321–359, reprinted in his *Essays on Religion and the Ancient World*, vol. 1 (1972) 277–307.

44. Suetonius *Aug.*, 100.

45. See Weinstock, *Divus Julius*, pl. 30, 6; cf. pl. 28, 11, and 196, 379.

46. Tacitus *Agr.*, 1–3, 44–46, with the commentary of R. M. Ogilvie and I. Richmond, *Cornelii Taciti De Vita Agricolae* (1967).

47. See H. P. L'Orange, *Apotheosis in Ancient Portraiture*, 55ff, and L'Orange, "Sol Invictus Imperator, ein Beitr. zur Apotheose," *Symbolae Osloenses* 14 (1935) 86–114, reprinted in his *Likeness and Icon* (1973) 325–344.

48. According to M. P. Charlesworth, "Some Observations on Ruler Cult," *Harv. Theol. Rev.* 28 (1935) 32ff, Domitian introduced, as a test of loyalty, sacrifice before his own statue, a procedure which subsequently Pliny used in Bithynia under the *optimus princeps* Trajan. See also A. Alföldi, *Die monarchische Repräsentation*, 25ff, 38f, 79ff, 127ff, 213ff, etc., where the gradual emergence of ceremonial conduct and of insignia and attributes of the emperor is traced. Ceremonial and attributes were not necessarily objected to when first introduced, and the interpretation of them as in some way divine could be voluntary; thus Ovid regards Augustus' *corona civica* as an '*augurium*' of Iuppiter, *ibid.*, 129. W. Hartke, *Römische Kinderkaiser. Eine Strukturanalyse römischen Denkens und Daseins* (1951) 105f, rightly points out that imperial honours, to be acceptable, had to be conferred by others, not claimed by the emperor himself.

49. For rehabilitation, cf. J. Béranger, *Recherches sur l'aspect idéologique du principat* (1953) 274. As will be seen more clearly below, the function of the ceremonial of imperial funerals was to assist a smooth takeover of power, to provide a continuity from one emperor to the next, father to son. For this and other aspects of imperial funerals, there are parallels in the funeral of Herod as reported by Josephus, *Jewish Antiquities* 17, 188ff, and *Jewish War* 1, 665ff, although Herod was buried, not cremated. Also, there is, of course, no hint of *consecratio*. The sequence of events was preparations for the takeover of power, as part of the King's last wishes, which after his death were made public when his will was read; magnificent burial arranged by his son and successor Archelaus, with procession of the King's family, bodyguards and the army in battle-array; and, after this, the enthronement of the successor (subject to the approval of Augustus).

For the background, see A. Schalit, *König Herodes* (1969) 640–643. The sequence of events was exactly the same in sixth century Byzantium: below, at nn. 262, 278ff. I would like to thank Professor Yoram Zafrir for pointing out to me these passages in Josephus.

50. Dio, 75, 5, 5: περὶ τὴν πυρὰν πολιτικάς τε ἅμα καὶ πολεμικὰς διεξόδους διελίττοντες διεξῆλθον. This circling of the pyre was represented on the column base of Antoninus Pius. See L. Vogel, *The Column of Antoninus Pius*, (1973) 56ff.

51. There was some disagreement whether Severus' ashes, or his body, was brought to Rome: *H.A. Severus*, 24. The account of Herodian corroborates the former alternative, but the fact that doubt could occur shows what is well known from other evidence: that burial was becoming the norm, see above, n. 43. In an article which is still fundamental, E. Bickermann ("Die römische Kaiserapotheose," *Archiv für Religionswissenschaft* 27 (1929)) argued that a double funeral, as recorded for Pertinax and Severus, was the rule when the emperor was to be consecrated. E. Hohl, "Die angebliche 'Doppelbestattung' des Antoninus Pius," *Klio* 31 (1938) 169–185 disagreed completely. Bickermann repeated his original view in "Consecratio," in *Le culte des souverains dans l'empire romain*, Entretiens Hardt, 19 (1972) 19–27. This issue does not affect Bickermann's argument that essentially *consecratio* was a rite whereby the emperor's divinity was defined and reduced. This argument is taken up from a different standpoint here. Bickermann's view that it is the ceremony itself ["Bildzauber," *Arch. f. Relwiss.* 27 (1929) 15 and passim; cf. Entretiens Hardt, 19 (1972) 22–225], which, as understood at the time, achieved the transit from earth to heaven, deserves to be considered afresh in the light of anthropological research. See, e.g., Claude Lévi-Strauss, *Anthropologie structurale* (1958) 183–266.

52. Herodian 4, 2, 11:

ἀετὸς ἀφίεται σὺν τῷ πυρὶ ἀνελευσόμενος ἐς τὸν αἰθέρα, ὃς φέρειν ἀπὸ γῆς ἐς οὐρανὸν τὴν τοῦ βασιλέως ψυχὴν πιστεύεται ὑπὸ Ῥωμαίων.

53. *H.A. Pert.*, 14, 10f; cf. *Sev.*, 19, 3f.

54. *RIC*, V¹, 120–121.

55. Pliny *Panegyricus*, 10, 4f; 11, 1f; 89, 1f. See also Suetonius *Caligula*, 13; 15; 16, 3: gaining popularity by honouring the memory of Tiberius. On the dynastic aspect of *consecratio*, see W. den Boer, "Trajan's Deification," *Proceedings of the XIV International Congress of Papyrologists*, Oxford 24–31 July 1974 (1975) 85–90, discussing Pap. Giessen 33, where Apollo says,

"Having just mounted aloft with Trajan in my chariot, . . . I come to you, oh people, . . . to proclaim the new ruler Hadrian whom all things serve on account of his virtue and the genius of his divine father." (Cf. fig. 25.)

The link between *consecratio* and a legitimate accession could hardly be expressed more clearly. Divine election of Hadrian as emperor is also suggested in this papyrus. For divine election, see A. D. Nock, "A Diis Electa," *Harvard Theological Review* 23 (1930) 266–267, reprinted in his *Essays*, vol. 1 (1972) 264–265, on a coin of Hadrian PROVIDENTIA DEORUM.

56. *RIC*, IV³, 131–2.

57. In the wording of the inscription of the Arch of Constantine, cf. H. P. L'Orange and A. von Gerkan, *Bildschmuck*, 5f; fig. 15.

58. See H. P. L'Orange, *Apotheosis in Ancient Portraiture* (1947).

59. Cicero *De nat. Deor.*, 3, 50 cited by Lactantius *Div. Inst.* 1, 15, 6; see Béranger, *L'aspect idéol.*, 174. See also 194 on the *Somnium Scipionis*.

60. For Aurelian and Sol, see G. H. Halsberghe, *The Cult of Sol Invictus* (1972) 139f (coinage), 142ff, Roman temple and priesthoods; 152, coinage and Aurelian's titles, for which see also *RIC*, V, 1, 258, 299. For Diocletian, cf. below, n. 66.

61. *RIC*, IV, 1, 92ff, IMP CAE L SEP SEV PERT AUG and variants of this on obverses; 99, on reverses, DIVI M PII F PM TR P III COS II PP. See also 185, 187, 188.

62. W. Seston, "Jovius et Herculius ou l'épiphanie des Tétrarches," *Historia* 1 (1950) 257–266, and W. Seston, *Dioclétien et la Tétrarchie* (1946) 193ff; but see also the doubts expressed by N. Baynes in his review of this book, *JRS* 38 (1948) 109–113, at 111f.

63. *Pan. Lat.*, 3, 10, 5.

64. Cf. below, "*Accession*," at nn. 36ff, 140f, 175 etc.

65. Cf. below, at nn. 173ff, 185ff.

66. On the divine status of Diocletian, see W. Seston, *Dioclétien et la Tétrarchie*, Bibl. des écoles françaises d'Athènes et de Rome, 162 (1946) 193–210; on the end of the first Tetrarchy, G. S. R. Thomas, "L'Abdication de Dioclétien," *Byzantion* 43 (1973) 229–247, showing that Diocletian's retirement cannot be viewed as having been inbuilt as a feature of the Tetrarchic system from the beginning.

67. These words refer to Maximian, Constantine's father-in-law. The panegyric celebrates the marriage between Constantine and Maximian's daughter Fausta.

68. *Pan. Lat.*, 6, 14, 3f, 307 A.D.:

> O felix in imperio et post imperium felicior (audis enim profecto haec et vides), dive Constanti, quem curru paene conspicuo, dum vicinos ortus repetit occasu, Sol ipse invecturus caelo excepit! Quanto nunc gaudio potiris, quanta voluptate perfrueris, cum talem filium tuum, qui te primus patrem fecit, in imperii tui possessionem idem pater, idem socer, idem imperator induxerit! Haec est tua praeter omnes divos propria immortalitas quam videmus: filius similis adspectu, similis animo, par imperii potestate.

For the link between ascent in the solar chariot and succession of a son, see above, n. 55.

69. *Pan. Lat.*, 6, 3, 4.

70. *Luce perpetua*, cf. above, "*Adventus*" at nn. 54, 61ff.

71. Cf. Suetonius, *Caesar*, 81, 3, in a dream before his assassination: (Caesar) ipse sibi visus est per quietem interdum supra nubes volitare, alias cum Iove dextram iungere.

72. *Pan. Lat.*, 7, 7, 1:

> Dies me ante deficiat quam oratio, si omnia patris tui facta vel hac brevitate percurram. Cuius etiam suprema illa expeditio non Britannica tropaea, ut vulgo creditum est, expetivit, sed dis iam vocantibus ad intimum terrarum limen accessit. . . . ille tot tantisque rebus gestis . . . quod eloqui nemini voluit, iturus ad deos genitorem illum deorum ignea caeli astra refoventem prospexit Oceanum, ut fruiturus exinde luce perpetua iam videret illic diem paene continuum. Vere enim profecto illi superum templa patuerunt receptusque est consessu caelitum, Iove ipso dexteram porrigente. Quin immo statim sententiam rogatus cui imperium decerneret, dixit, ut decebat Constantium Pium; manifeste enim

sententia patris electus es, imperator. Quod quidem ita nos dicere cum veritas iubet, tum pietati tuae, ut video, gratissimum est. Sed cur tantummodo privatis tuis adfectibus blandiamur, cum omnium deorum fuerit illa sententia, et quidem iam pridem auctoritate perscripta, quamvis tunc pleno sit firmata consilio?

73. *Pan. Lat.*, 7, 7, 7; cf. 21, 4: Vidisti, *credo*, . . . Apollinem; *Pan. Lat.*, 7, 2, 1.

74. See F. Cumont, "La théologie solaire du paganisme romain," *Mémoires présentés par divers savants à l'Acad. des Inscr. et Belles Lettres*, 12, 2 (1923), 448–479; cf. his *Afterlife in Roman Paganism* (1922) 100f.

75. Pliny, *Panegyric*, 11, 2f; 89, 1f.

76. *Pan. Lat.*, 6, 2.

77. *Pan. Lat.*, 3, 11, 3: Atque haec quidem velut interioribus sacrariis operta veneratio eorum modo animos obstupefecerat. Cf. "*Adventus*," above, at nn. 51–52.

78. *Pan. Lat.*, 6, 3, 3f; 4, 1; 5, 1f; 7, 4, 1f.

79. *Pan. Lat.*, 7, 7, 3.

80. *Pan. Lat.*, 9, 25, 1f.

81. *RIC*, VI, 131, 217, 219, 256, 260, 263, 294, 325; *RIC*, VII, 180, 252, 310, 394, 429, 502.

82. Claudius as Constantine's ancestor: *Pan. Lat.*, 7, 2; P. Damerau, *Kaiser Claudius II Gothicus*, Klio Beiheft, 33 (1934) 81f; Claudius II as ancestor of the Constantinian house in the *H.A.*, J. Béranger, "Idéologie impérial dans l'*H. A.*, *Bonner Historia Augusta Colloquium 1972–1974* (1976) 35. It seems very probable that the Constantinian *memoria* issues for Constantius (below at nn. 90f) contain a deliberate reference to such issues for Claudius Gothicus. The Constantinian issues would thus suggest that the fictitious genealogy, which traced the family of Constantine back to Claudius, and for which the earliest literary evidence comes from the panegyric of 310 (*Pan. Lat.*, 7), was being contemplated as early as 307 A.D.

83. DIVO CONSTANTIO PIO *RIC*, VI, 131 London; 217 Trier; 260 Lugdunum; 325 Aquileia.

DIVO CONSTANTIO AUG, *RIC*, VI, 256; 260 Lugdunum; 294 Ticinum.

DIVUS CONSTANTIUS, *RIC*, VI, 219.

84. *RIC*, VI, 256, 306–307 A.D., eagle with outspread wings; *RIC*, VI, 261, 307–308 A.D., eagle standing on altar.

85. *RIC*, VI, 294, Ticinum 307–308 A.D., MEM DIVI-CONSTANTI or MEMORIA DIV-I CONSTANTI, eagle with outspread wings on domed shrine; *RIC*, VI, 326, Aquileia, 307–309/310 A.D., MEMORIA DI-VI CONSTANTI, eagle on altar enclosure.

86. *RIC*, VI, London, 131; Trier, 217; Lugdunum, 260, 263.

87. *RIC*, VI, 262.

88. For the remaining commemorative issues for Constantius I see below, and at n. 97.

89. The establishment of the cult of the *divus* by his successor was, up to the early third century, viewed as an act of imperial *pietas*; cf. above, at n. 55f. It is thus an aspect of *consecratio* by human verdict. On the temple of the gens Flavia at Hispellum—CIL 11, 5265—see J. Gascou, "Le réscrit d'Hispellum" *MEFR* 79 (1967) 609–659, esp. 647–656, stressing the "laïcisation du culte impérial." Rather than being incompatible with conclusions drawn here, this formulation

emphasises them. Both in the courtly milieu of coinage and panegyrics, and in the empire at large, we are dealing with the detachment of the imperial sanctity from the personal involvement of particular groups of people.

90. *RIC*, V¹, 236–237.

91. Commemorative issues for Claudius: *RIC*, V, 1, 236–7 MEMORIAE AETER-NAE, 233–4, CONSECRATIO; cf. *RIC*, V¹, 237, Ø DIVUS CLAUDIUS OPT IMP or DIVO CLAUDIO OPTIMO IMP, veiled, laureate head; R REQUIES OPTIMORUM MERITORUM (or abbreviations), veiled seated emperor raising right hand, sceptre in left. The reverses of these issues were repeated by Constantine to the last detail: *RIC*, VII, 180 Trier; 252 Arles; 294 Aquileia; 310 Rome; 429 Siscia; 502 Thessalonica. At the same mints the REQUIES OPTIMORUM MERITORUM types were issued with obverses for Constantius and Maximian, thus contradicting the panegyric propaganda about Maximian as *hostis publicus*: *Pan. Lat.*, 7, 14–20.

92. Cf. *RIC*, V¹, 233, 234.

93. *RIC*, VII, 377f, 381, 400, 403, 406.

94. DIVO ROMULO NV BIS CONS ROMAE Rome 309–310 A.D., *RIC*, VI, 377; DIVO ROMULO NV BIS CONS Ostia 309–312 A.D., *RIC*, VI, 400; Rome 310–11 A.D., *ibid.*, 381; IMP MAXENTIUS DIVO ROMULO NV FILIO, *RIC*, VI, 382 Rome; 404, 406 Ostia.

95. DIVO MAXIMIANO SEN AUG; DIVO MAXIMIANO PATRI MAXENTIUS AUG; IMP MAXENTIUS DIVO MAXIMIANO PATRI.

96. DIVO MAXIMIANO AUG; DIVO MAXIMIANO IUN AUG; DIVO MAXIMIANO SO-CERO MAXENTIUS AUG and IMP MAXENTIUS DIVO MAXIMIANO SOCERO.

97. IMP MAXENTIUS DIVO CONSTANTIO COGN; DIVO CONSTANTIO ADFINI MAX-ENTIUS AUG and IMP MAXENTIUS DIVO CONSTANTIO ADFINI.

98. *RIC*, VI, 518 and 294 respectively. For the image, cf. *RIC*, I, 95.

99. A. Grabar, *Martyrium I* (1946) 31ff; and cf. 144, 228–9, 278 with II (1972; 1943), pl. XV.

100. G. M. Hanfmann, *The Season Sarcophagus in Dumbarton Oaks* (1951) figs. 33, 65; see also F. Matz, "Das Problem des Orans und ein Sarkophag in Cordoba," *Madr. Mitt.* 9 (1968) 300–310, sarcophagi in Cordoba, Vatican, Hermitage, and in Capua, showing tomb with open door, between husband and wife orans; and B. Haarløv, *The Half-Open Door. A Common Symbolic Motif within Roman Sepulchral Sculpture* (1977).

101. Matz, "Das Problem," 305f.

102. For a funerary altar with open door from Alexandria, see W. Altmann, *Die römischen Grabaltäre der Kaiserzeit* (1905) 15; cf. 103, Victories opening double door on funerary altar from Rome, in Palazzo Barberini.

103. Matz, "Das Problem," 306.

104. B. Andreae, *Studien zur römischen Grabkunst* (1963) 34–35; see also W. N. Schumacher, "Hirt und 'Guter Hirt'," *Römische Quartalschrift für christliche Alter-tumskunde*, 34 Supplementheft (1977) 21–37.

105. Volbach, *Elfenbeinarbeiten*, no. 111; also no. 116. Perhaps the Munich ivory of resurrection and ascension, showing the tomb with closed doors, makes a deliberate statement *vis-à-vis* these two ivories with their iconography of open doors of pagan origin. See, on the Munich ivory, H. Schrade, "Zur Ikonographie der Himmelfahrt Christi," *Vortr. d. Bibl. Warburg* (1928–1929) 66–190, at 89–96. K. Weitzmann, ed., *Age of Spirituality* (1979) 502–504; cf. 504–505.

106. Cf. E. Nash, *A Pictorial Dictionary of Ancient Rome* (1968) s.v. Romulus Divus, Templum; P. Bruun, *Arctos, Acta Philol. Fennica*, N.S. 1 (1954) 21f; G. Lugli, *Stud. to D. M. Robinson*, vol. 2 (1953) 1211–1223. According to A. Frazer, "The Iconography of the Emperor Maxentius' Buildings in Via Appia," *Art Bulletin* 48 (1966) 385–392 at 388–391, the building on the coins is not the shrine in the forum, but, more probably, an evocation of the Maxentian mausoleum which formed part of a building complex of that emperor near the Via Appia.

107. *Pan. Lat.*, 2, 3–4; *Pan. Lat.*, 6, 14.

108. Cf. the QUIES AUGG legends issued for Diocletian in the years after 306 A.D.: *RIC*, VI, 39f, and Index II, s.v. QUIES AUG etc.

109. *RIC*, VI, 479, 482, 310 and 311 A.D.; 590, 311–313 A.D.: 682–685, 311–312 A.D. Constantine's takeover of Siscia was marked by issues to Claudius and Constantius, *RIC*, VII, 429, and of Thessalonica by issues to Claudius, Constantius and Maximian, *ibid.*, 502, but this is very little compared to the Western output.

110. This conclusion has been arrived at after surveying the provenance of all commemorative issues recorded in *RIC*.

111. Note the titulature of Sassanian kings as recorded by Ammianus, 17, 5, 3 quoting a letter of Sapor to Constantius II: Rex regum, Sapor, particeps siderum, frater solis et lunae. Cf. Ensslin, "Gottkaiser und Kaiser von Gottes Gnaden," *Sitzber. bayr. Akad.* 6 (1943) 14. Possibly the author of the panegyric of 291 was aware of such claims; see *Pan. Lat.*, 3, 13, 2.

112. Pliny *Panegyric*, 11, 1f.

113. Although, of course, the conflicts were known and understood. Cf. J. Straub, "Divus Alexander, Divus Christus," *Festschr. J. Quasten*, vol. 1, ed. P. Granfield and J. A. Jungmann, (1970) 461–73, reprinted in J. Straub, *Regeneratio Imperii* (1972) 178–194.

114. See. N. Baynes, "Eusebius and the Christian Empire," in his *Byzantine Studies and Other Essays* (1955) 168ff, and L. Delatte, *Les traités de la royauté d'Ecphante. Diotogène et Sthénidas* (1942); also R. Farina, *L'impero e l'imperatore cristiano in Eusebio di Cesarea* (1966). The Christian orientation of Eusebius is stressed by D. S. Wallace-Hadrill, *Eusebius of Caesarea* (1960) 168–189 (response to Baynes, 177f) and by G. F. Chesnut, *The First Christian Histories, Eusebius, Socrates, Sozomen, Theodoret and Evagrius*, Théologie historique, 46 (1977).

115. Eusebius *V.C.*, I, 20–22 passim:

> τὸ δε πᾶν αὐτῷ συνέπραττεν ὁ θεός, τῇ τοῦ πατρὸς διαδοχῇ προμηθούμενος αὐτὸν παρεῖναι . . . υἱοῖς θ' ἅμα καὶ θυγατράσι συνταξάμενος χοροῦ δίκην αὐτὸν κυκλοῦσιν, ἐν αὐτοῖς βασιλείοις ἐπὶ βασιλικῇ στρωμνῇ, τὸν κλῆρον τῆς βασιλείας νόμῳ φύσεως, τῷ τῇ ἡλικίᾳ προάγοντι τῶν παίδων παραδούς, διανεπαύσατο . . . αὐτῇ δ' ἁλουργίδι πατρικῇ Κωνσταντῖνος κοσμησάμενος τῶν πατρικῶν οἴκων προῄει, ὥσπερ ἐξ ἀναβιώσεως τὸν πατέρα βασιλεύοντα δι' ἑαυτοῦ δεικνὺς τοῖς πᾶσιν. εἶτα τῆς προκομιδῆς ἡγούμενος . . . τὸν πατέρα προύπεμπε . . . εὐφημίαις τε καὶ ὕμνοις οἱ πάντες τὸν τρισμακάριον ἐτίμων, ὁμογνώμονί τε συμφωνίᾳ τοῦ τεθνεῶτος ἀναβίωσιν τὴν τοῦ παιδὸς κράτησιν ἐδόξαζον, βοαῖς τ' εὐφήμοις τὸν νέον βασιλέα αὐτοκράτορα καὶ [σεβαστὸν] αὔγουστον εὐθέως ἐκ πρώτης ἀνηγόρευον φωνῆς. καὶ τὸν μὲν τεθνηκότα ἐκόσμουν αἱ βοαὶ ταῖς εἰς τὸν υἱὸν εὐφημίαις τὸν δὲ παῖδα ἐμακάριζον τοιοῦδε πατρὸς διάδοχον ἀποδειχθέντα. (translation after McGiffert).

116. Implied in Pliny *Panegyric*, 10, 4–6. Cf. above, n. 55.

117. These observations are the starting point of the article by A. Alföldi, "Die Ausgestaltung des monarchischen Zeremoniells am römischen Kaiserhofe," *Röm. Mitt.* 49 (1934) 3ff, reprinted in A. Alföldi, *Die monarchische Repräsentation im römischen Kaiserreiche* (1970).

118. *V.C.*, I, 3ff, 24, 28; II, 55 etc.; see also H. Dörries, *Das Selbstzeugnis Kaiser Konstantins*, Abh. d. Akad. d. Wiss. in Göttingen, Phil. Hist. Kl., 3, 34 (1954) 241–51, 262ff; cf. 281ff.

119. Churches: *V.C.*, III, 28ff and IV, 40; III, 41, 48, 50ff, 58. See also H. A. Drake, *In Praise of Constantine. A Historical Study and New Translation of Eusebius' Tricennial Orations* (1976) 70ff; and S. Spain Alexander, "Studies in Constantinian Church Architecture," *Rivista di archeologia cristiana* 47 (1971) 281–330, and 49 (1973) 33–44. Councils: *V.C.*, III, 6ff; III, 60; IV, 32–33, 41–46.

120. Eusebius *V.C.*, 1, 9.

121. Eusebius *V.C.*, IV, 67, echoed by Sozomen *H.E.*, 2, 34.

122. Herodian, 4, 1, 3:

οἵ τε προσαγορεύοντες τοὺς νέους αὐτοκράτορας παριόντες καὶ τὴν κάλπιν προσεκύνουν.

A Hellenistic precedent: Plutarch, *Demetrius* 53. Cf. Gregory Nazianzen *P.G.*, 35, 685 on the funeral of Constantius II, below, at nn. 196ff.

123. Eusebius *V.C.*, 4, 68.

124. Eusebius *V.C.*, 4, 63; cf. 71; 1, 9.

125. A. Kaniuth, *Die Beisetzung Konstantins des Grossen*, Breslauer Hist. Forsch., 18 (1941) 7–9. This division of the funerary ceremony into a secular and a Christian part was a temporary expedient. When Ambrose in his cathedral pronounced the *consolatio* for Theodosius, Honorius stood next to the sarcophagus, and the court and army, whom Ambrose specifically addressed, were present in the church: Ambrose *De ob. Theod.*, 3, 7, 11. On the Church of the Apostles, H. Koethe, "Das Konstantinsmausoleum und verwandte Denkmäler," *Jahrbuch des deutschen archäologischen Instituts* 48 (1933) 185–203; R. Krautheimer, "Zu Konstantins Apostelkirche," in *Mullus, Festschrift T. Klauser* (1964) 224–229, reprinted in his *Studies in Early Christian, Medieval and Renaissance Art* (1969) 27–34; and S. Spain Alexander, "Studies in Constantinian Church Architecture," *Rivista di archeologia cristiana* 47 (1971) 281–330, at 325–329, and *Riv. di arch. cr.* 49 (1973) 33–44, at 43–44. For the later history, P. Grierson, "The Tombs and Obits of the Byzantine Emperors (337–1043)," *DOP* 16 (1962) 1–63.

126. Eusebius *V.C.*, 4, 68. While lying in state, Constantine wore the diadem. This has a Hellenistic background; see H. W. Ritter, *Diadem und Königsherrschaft*, Vestigia, 7 (1965) 76–77.

127. Suetonius *Tiberius*, 22–23.

128. Suetonius *Claudius*, 45:

Mors eius celata est, donec circa successorem omnia ordinarentur; itaque et quasi pro aegro adhuc vota suscepta sunt et inducti per simulationem comoedi qui velut desiderantem oblectarent.

129. Libanius *Or.* 59, 48:

ἐπεὶ γάρ, ὅσον ἐδόκει τῷ κρείττονι, τὴν οἰκουμένην ὁ τῶνδε πατὴρ ἰθύνας αὖθις ἀπῆλθε συνεσόμενος τῷ τῇδε καταπέμψαντι, τοσούτου πράγματος συμβάντος οὐκ ἐκινήθη τὰ τῆς βασιλείας . . .

Cf. Theodoret *H.E.*, 1, 32. A very different version of these events appears in Philostorgius *H.E.*, 2, 16 and highlights the intensiveness of post-Constantinian imperial propaganda, which took the form that propaganda after an emperor's death generally took. Cf. above, notes 49 and 55. Libanius was also influenced by it. On his use of the *V.C.* in his *Or.* 59, see P. Petit, "Libanius et la *Vita Constantini*," *Historia* 1 (1950) 562–582.

130. Eusebius *V.C.*, 1, 9.
131. Eusebius *V.C.*, 1, 1:

> ὅπη γὰρ ἀτενὲς ἐμβλέψειεν, ἤν τε πρὸς ἕω ἤν τε πρὸς ἑσπέραν, ἤν τ' ἐπὶ γῆς αὐτῆς ὅλης ἤν τε πρὸς οὐρανὸν αὐτόν, πάντη καὶ πανταχοῦ τὸν μακάριον αὐτοῖς συνόντα βασιλέα ἐθεώρει (tr. McGiffert).

132. Eusebius *V.C.*, 1, 2:

> ἤδη δὲ καὶ πρὸς αὐταῖς οὐρανίαις ἁψῖσιν ἑαυτὸν ἐκτείνας, κἀνταῦθα τὴν τρισμακάριον ψυχὴν αὐτῷ θεῷ συνοῦσαν φαντάζεται . . . (tr. McGiffert).

133. Eusebius *V.C.*, 4, 64:

> αὐτὸς δ' ὅσον ἦν αὐτοῦ τῆς ψυχῆς νοερόν τε καὶ φιλόθεον τῷ αὐτοῦ θεῷ συναπτόμενος (tr. McGiffert).

134. *Pan. Lat.*, 6, 3, 3.
135. *Pan. Lat.*, 7, 7, 3.
136. Pliny *Panegyric*, 10, 4: [Nerva] quem di ideo caelo vindicaverunt . . . ; *Pan. Lat.*, 6, 3, 3: Ad deorum concilia translatus . . . ; 7, 7, 1: Dis iam vocantibus . . . ; 3: Receptusque est consessu caelitum . . . ; Pliny *Panegyric*, 11, 2: Sideribus patrem intulisti . . . ; 89, 2: Et tu pater Traiane, . . . si non sidera, proximam tamen sideribus obtines sedem; *Pan. Lat.*, 9, 25, 1: Gaudet e caelo, et iam pridem vocatus ad sidera. . . .
137. *Pan. Lat.*, 6, 14, 3.
138. Eusebius *V.C.*, 4, 69.
139. Eusebius *V.C.*, 1, 2. But Philostorgius, ὁ θεομάχος, according to Photius, does speak of a cult: *H.E.* 2, 17; cf. Theodoret *H.E.*, 1, 32. See on this question, I. Karyannopulos, "Konstantin der Grosse u. d. Kaiserkult," *Historia* 5 (1956) 341–357.
140. See Eusebius, *History of the Martyrs in Palestine*, ed. and tr. from Syriac into English by W. Cureton (1861) 21, 22–23. The martyrs enter heaven, and it is precisely in this respect that the martyrs themselves, according to Eusebius, felt themselves to be in a special position; by martyrdom they gained a crown which ordinary Christians would not gain. These passages are not in the shortened Greek version (VI, 7 and VII, 2 respectively). Cf. G. F. Chesnut, *The First Christian Histories* (1977) 157–158: "In a good many passages in Eusebius it seems to be assumed that when death came to each human being, his soul went immediately into God's presence without having to wait until the history of this world had run its course." But the passages cited all refer to Constantine, with one exception, *V.C.* 3, 46, which refers to Helena.
141. E. Diehl, *Inscr. Lat. Christ. Vet.*, vol. 2 (1961) caput 22, cf. 23; Venantius Fortunatus *Carm.*, 4, passim; H. Brandenburg, "Ein verschollener Mailänder Sarkophag," *Rivista di archeologia cristiana* 48 (1972) at 43–48. Cf. the Constantinian inscription in S. Peter's, Diehl, *Inscr. Lat. Christ. Vet.*, vol. 1 (1961) no. 1752.

142. See the prayer before death of S. Macrina, Gregory of Nyssa, ed. P. Maraval, *Vie de Sainte Macrine*, SC 178 (1971) § 24, 220ff; and B. Brenk, *Tradition und Neuerung in der christlichen Kunst d. ersten Jahrtausends* (1966) 19–36.

143. On Eusebius, see S. Calderone, "Teologia politica, successione dinastica e consecratio in età Constantiniana," in *Culte des souverains*, Entretiens Hardt, 19 (1972) 215–261.

144. This is one of the issues examined by E. Peterson, *Der Monotheismus als politisches Problem* (1935). The Byzantine resolution, based as it was on Eusebius, differed from the Western one, for which see Peterson, 96–100.

145. For continuities between heaven and earth in Augustan and later poetry, see K. Thraede, "Die Poesie und der Kaiserkult," in *Culte des souverains*, Entretiens Hardt, 19 (1972) esp. 283ff. Explicit statements of the type discussed here are lacking, however.

146. For the Byzantine view, see the Ἔκθεσις of Agapetus, *P.G.*, 86[1], 1164ff. and cf. I. Ševčenko, "A Neglected Byzantine Source of Muscovite Political Ideology," *Harvard Slavic Studies* 2 (1954) 141ff. In the West, the position was at times understood differently, e.g., Augustine *De civitate Dei*, 5, 25: the emperor was dependent on God, but did not, in this, differ from any other human being.

147. Grabar, *Christian Iconography, A Study of Its Origins* (1968) 35, 41ff; and P. Beskow, *Rex Gloriae, the Kingship of Christ in the Early Church* (1962) 11ff.

148. Grabar, *Christian Iconography*, xlii–1.

149. Eusebius *V.C.*, 4, 73, see below, at n. 159.

150. Eusebius *V.C.*, 4, 69, see below, at n. 173.

151. J. Maurice, *Numismatique Constantinienne*, vol. 2 (1911) 548.

152. *Ibid.*, 548, 607, 608, pl. 16, 17; 17, 25; 26.

153. G. Mazzini, *Monete Imperiali Romani*, vol. 5 (1958) 99, 101.

154. Cf. above, n. 91, for commemorative issues of Claudius II; and for *velatio* as a token of apotheosis, F. Matz, "Der Gott auf dem Elefantenwagen," *Akad. d. Wiss. u. d. Lit. Abhandl. Geistes- u. Sozialwiss. Kl.*, 1952 (1953) 725–729.

155. Maurice, *Numismatique*, 548 pl. 16, 17.

156. Cf. J. M. C. Toynbee in *JRS* 37 (1947) 135–144, and in *Studies to D. M. Robinson*, vol. 2 (1953) 261–277; and E. Kantorowicz, "ΕΥΝΘΡΟΝΟΣ ΔΙΚΗΙ," in his *Selected Studies* (1965) 1–6.

157. Pietas with children:

PIETAS AUGG, Gallienus, *RIC*, V[1], 83; Salonina, *RIC*, V[1], 109; 110; Postumus *RIC*, V[2], 363; *RIC*, VI, 374, PIETAS AUGG ET CAES N, Maxentius.

Pietas at altar:

RIC, V[1], 182, Gallienus, PIETAS AUG etc.; *RIC*, V[2], 268, Maximian, PIETAS AUG; 493, Carausius, PIETAS AUG etc. Under Constantine the imagery becomes blurred, and for PIETAS AUGUSTAE Fausta with a child is shown seated between Felicitas with cornucopiae and Pietas without attributes, *RIC*, VII, 203–204; cf. *ibid.*, 323; the *pietas* of the emperor is represented by the act of raising a female turreted figure, 612 PIETAS AUGUSTI N; 219 and 627, PIETAS AUGUSTI NOSTRI; cf. 54–55. For this motif in the context of *adventus*, cf. above, "*Adventus*" at nn. 67ff.

158. Aequitas, with AEQUITAS AUG or AUGG, is frequent in the third century, e.g., *RIC*, V[2], 34, Probus; 136, Carus; 166; 169, Carinus; 193, Numerian; 337, Postumus; 403, Tetricus; 526, Carausius; 559; 564, Allectus. Aequitas is always shown with scales and cornucopiae. Tetrarchic AEQUITAS AUGG issues are not recorded in *RIC*, but the figure of Aequitas with scales and cornucopiae appears

with UTILITAS PUBLICA *RIC*, VI, 465, and as Moneta, *ibid.*, see Index III. The third century issues could perhaps refer to accession, but are not dated; Carausius has the usual figure of Aequitas with AEQUITAS (or EQUITAS) MUNDI *RIC*, V², 517–518, PAS AUG 535 and FIDEM MILITUM NN 521. Perhaps these issues should be taken as shedding some light on the intended content of the posthumous issues for Constantine with the figure of Aequitas. The issues here mentioned demonstrate what can also be shown in other fields: that the disintegration of the classical tradition in imperial "*Bildsymbolik*" started before Constantine.

159. Eusebius *V.C.*, 4, 73:

Ἤδη δὲ καὶ νομίσμασιν ἐνεχαράττοντο τύποι, πρόσθεν μὲν ἐκτυποῦντες τὸν μακάριον ἐγκεκαλυμμένου τὴν κεφαλὴν σχήματι, θατέρου δὲ μέρους ἐφ' ἅρματι τεθρίππῳ ἡνιόχου τρόπον, ὑπὸ δεξιᾶς ἄνωθεν ἐκτεινομένης αὐτῷ χειρὸς ἀναλαμβανόμενον.

160. Cf. above, n. 55 on Pap. Giessen 30; the golden chariot on the pyre of Pertinax, Dio 75, 5, 3; the Antonine altar at Ephesus showing a consecrated emperor in the chariot of Helios, C. C. Vermeule, *Roman Imperial Art in Greece and Asia Minor* (1968) 107–109. Cf., for the empress, 117–119; the British Museum *consecratio* diptych, F. Volbach, *Elfenbeinarbeiten*, no. 56.

161. Grabar, "Recherches sur les sources juives de l'art paléochrétien," *Cahiers Arch.* 14 (1964) 53–57; cf. J. D. MacIsaac, "The Hand of God, a Numismatic Study," *Traditio* 31 (1975) 322–328. Cf. John of Damascus, *Exposition of the Orthodox Faith* I, 11: human beings cannot speak of God except by use of "images . . . derived from our own life." Hence, "God's hands mean the effectual nature of his energy."

162. See above, n. 21.

163. *Pan. Lat.*, 7, 7, 3, see above, n. 72, and Suet. *Cal.*, 57, 3, *consecratio* as *dextrarum iunctio* with Iuppiter. Note also the graphic expression, "Unless your heavenly right hand exact some justice," in an early third century inscription from Asia Minor addressed to the emperor, cited by R. Brilliant, *Gesture and Rank in Roman Art* (1963) 163.

164. W. F. Volbach, *Elfenbeinarbeiten der Spätantike und des frühen Mittelalters* (1976) no. 110; see also H. Schrade, "Zur Iconographie der Himmelfahrt Christi," *Vortr. Bibl. Warburg* (1928–1929), 89ff, 109–125; and S. H. Gutberlet, *Die Himmelfahrt Christi in der bildenden Kunst von den Anfängen bis ins hohe Mittelalter* (1935) 62–73. For a similar iconography—hand of God drawing Christ into heaven—on a marble reliquary casket from Ravenna, see P. Angiolini Martinelli, *Corpus della scultura paleocristiana, bizantina ed altomedievale di Ravenna*, ed. G. Bovini, (1968) no. 138.

165. See, for this transition, H. Schrade, "Zur Ikonographie der Himmelfahrt Christi," *Vortr. der Bibl. Warburg*, (1928–1929), 66–190, at 81ff, 97f; cf. S. H. Gutberlet, *Die Himmelfahrt Christi in der bildenden Kunst von den Anfängen bis ins hohe Mittelalter*, (1935) 73ff.

166. In my view this could be late third or early fourth century, but Deichmann, *Repertorium . . . Rom. Ostia*, no. 25c, dates it c. 335–365 A.D.

167. II Kings, 2. This scene also appears, without imperial elaborations as on the sarcophagus, in Byzantine MSS: J. Lassus, *L'illustration byzantine du Livre des Rois*, Bibl. cah. arch., 9 (1973) 22; pl. 31.

168. For these, see R. Sansoni, *I Sarcofagi paleocr. a porta di città*, Studi di anti-

chità cristiane, 4 (1969). For imperial ascent as departure, see above at nn. 35ff.

169. I would therefore date it later than the sarcophagus considered first (cf. above, n. 166), but Deichmann, *Repertorium*, no. 115, dates it to the last quarter of the third century. On the city gate, cf. above *"Adventus,"* n. 80.

170. Deichmann, *Repertorium*, no. 675, Grotto St. Peter's, Vatican; R. Sansoni, *I sarcofagi paleocr. a porta di città*, 3–19; cf. 83, 109–10; H. U. von Schoenebeck, *Der Mailänder Sarkophag und seine Nachfolge*, Studi di antichità cristiana, 10 (1935) esp. 19ff, 51ff; cf. 60, discusses the Paris and Milan sarcophagi; on the dates, see 115f.

171. *Sermo XL, De Elia, P.L.* 39, 1823–6 at 1825–6:

> Denique sicut Dominus, posteaquam multas virtutes exercuit, posteaquam passus est resurrexit et ascendit in coelum, ita et Elias post mirabilia quae per eum deus fecit, igneo curru elevatur ad coelum.

172. This development from a strictly biblical to an imperial manner of depiction is to be documented in similar fashion on sarcophagi showing Christ's entry into Jerusalem: cf. S. MacCormack, *Historia* 21 (1972) 743.

173. Eusebius, *V.C.*, 4, 69: ὑπὲρ ἀψίδων δ' οὐρανίων ἐν αἰθερίῳ διατριβῇ διαναπαυόμενον.

174. Eusebius, *V.C.* 1, 2, above, n. 132.

175. Dio 43, 14, 6; cf. above, at nn. 13 and 29.

176. *RIC*, II, 176; 180 cf. J. Carcopino, *REA* (1949) 266–267.

177. Gnecchi, 2, 45, 10.

178. *RIC*, III, 34.

179. Gnecchi, 101, 10.

180. Gnecchi, 156, 14; also on the regular coinage, *RIC*, V, 1.336.

181. Gnecchi, 157, 1.

182. Cf. Toynbee, *Roman Medallions*, 91f, pl. 47, 3.

183. Lactantius *De mort. pers.*, 48, 2:

> Ut daremus et Christianis et omnibus liberam potestatem sequendi religionem quam quisque voluisset, quo quicquid est divinitatis in *sede caelesti*, nobis atque omnibus qui sub potestate nostra sunt constituti, placatum ac propitium possit existere.

Cf. Themistius 188d: the highest god ὑπὲρ ἅπαν τὸ ὂν ἱδρυμένου, and Sidonius *Panegyric on Anthemius*, preface 1: Cum iuvenem super astra Iovem natura locaret.

184. *Pan. Lat.*, 2, 3, 3–4, 1:

> Sed longe illa maiora sunt quae tu impartito tibi imperio vice gratiae rettulisti: admittere in animum tantae rei publicae curam et totius orbis fata suscipere et oblitum quodammodo sui gentibus vivere et in tam arduo humanarum rerum stare fastigio, ex quo veluti terras omnes et maria despicias vicissimque oculis ac mente collustres ubi sit certa serenitas, ubi dubia tempestas, qui iustitiam vestram iudices aemulentur, qui virtutis vestrae gloriam duces servent, accipere innumerabiles undique nuntios, totidem mandata dimittere, de tot urbibus et nationibus et provinciis cogitare, noctes omnes diesque perpeti sollicitudine pro omnium salute transigere. Haec omnia cum a fratre optimo oblata susceperis, tu fecisti fortiter, ille sapienter.

185. *Pan. Lat.* 6, 14, 1:

> Te, pater, ex ipso imperii vertice decet orbem prospicere communem caelestique nutu rebus humanis fata decernere, auspicia bellis gerendis dare, compo-

nendis pacibus leges imponere. Te, iuvenis, indefessum ire per limites qua Romanum barbaris gentibus instat imperium, frequentes ad socerum victoriarum laureas mittere, praecepta petere, effecta rescribere.

This and the passage quoted at n. 184 are important statements of imperial theory in late antiquity and point to a reformulation of the problem of the mutual *securitas* of emperor and subjects, who could all too easily become a threat to each other; see H. U. Instinsky, *Sicherheit als politisches Problem des römischen Kaisertums* (1952), in connection with the emperor's *cura* for his subjects. The idea of *cura* was already voiced by Cicero when addressing Caesar, and by Pliny, but never before these Tetrarchic panegyrics was it so well integrated into the political and doctrinal framework of the empire. A related concept is the late antique Greek idea of imperial philanthropia; see H. Hunger, *Prooimion, Elemente der byzantinischen Kaiseridee in den Arengen der Urkunden*, Wiener Byzantinische Studien, 1 (1964) 143–154 and below, "Accession," n. 271.

186. Cf. P. Beskow, *Rex Gloriae* (1962) 12, n. 1; H. P. L'Orange, *Art Forms and Civic Life* (1967) 93. On the arch of Galerius see H. P. Laubscher, *Der Reliefschmuck des Galeriusbogens in Thessaloniki* (1975) at 69–78, and M. S. Pond Rothman, "The Thematic Organisation of the Panel Reliefs on the Arch of Galerius," *American Journal of Archaeology* 81 (1977) 427–454, esp. 444 and 453.

187. E.g., *RIC*, III, 250 Faustina II, SIDERIBUS RECEPTA SC, Diana standing with torch, crescent behind neck; or, Faustina in *biga* with veil billowing.

188. See A. Alföldi, *The Conversion of Constantine and Pagan Rome* (1948) 117, who regards the image as definitely pagan, incompatible with Christianity. In view of what is said of the dead emperor in Eusebius, and later in Byzantium, cf. below, at nn. 294ff, I am not so sure. The fact that the emperor was no longer shown in *art* seated on the globe, I would attribute to other reasons, outlined above, at n. 147. I would also suggest that the Senate would not commission a picture of an official nature which was intended to honour the emperor, but which at the same time offended against imperial policy. If it had been intended so to offend, I think Eusebius would not have reported it. In other words, in 337, this iconographic scheme was still acceptable in imperial art, although imperial art was now on the way to becoming Christian.

189. Deichmann, *Repertorium*, no. 680, 279ff; a similar iconographical scheme, Deichmann, *Repertorium*, no. 193, third quarter of the fourth century.

190. *Traditio legis*: Deichmann, *Repertorium*, no. 677, 1, third quarter of the fourth century; S. Costanza, Rome: Christ seated on the sphere amidst palm trees, *traditio legis* to Moses, according to A. Grabar, *The Beginnings of Christian Art* (1967) 188; *traditio legis* with Christ standing on the sphere in the Naples baptistry; A. Ferrua, *Atti. d. Pont. Acc.* ser. III, vol. 33 (1960–61) 216–219, mosaic in the catacomb of Domitilla, Christ seated on globe between Peter and Paul on thrones. For an interpretation of the image, see W. N. Schumacher, "*Dominus legem dat*," *Römische Quartalschrift* 54 (1959) 1–39 (16f and 26f on the sarcophagus of Junius Bassus). There are many examples of this image in later Christian art, e.g., Apse of S. Teodoro, Rome; triumphal arch of S. Lorenzo f.m. Rome (see G. Bovini, "Il Mosaico dell'arco trionfale di S. Lorenzo fuori le mura a Roma," in *XVIII Corso di cultura sull'arte Rav. e Biz.* [1971] 127–140); Basilica Euphrasiana, Parenzo (D. Talbot Rice, *Byzantine Art* [1968] fig. 142). On the ivory in Milan, see R. Delbrueck, *Bonn. Jhbb.* 151 (1951) 96f; Utrecht Psalter, Christ on globe, in man-

dorla, A. Grabar, *Christian Iconography*, (1968) fig. 145; eleventh-century Byzantine ivory, Florence, Mus. Naz., showing the Ascension with Christ on globe with stars, carried by two angels, J. Beckwith, *The Art of Constantinople*, (1961) fig. 147. Cf. C. Tolney, "The Visionary Evangelists of the Reichenau School," *Burlington Magazine* 69 (1936) 257–263, for a mediaeval development of this iconographical scheme.

191. Teaching Christ: Deichmann, *Repertorium*, no. 684, last quarter of the fourth century. Cf. no. 678, Christ holding crux gemmata, late fourth century; Christ giving the law: Deichmann, *Repertorium*, no. 28, last third of the fourth century; no. 58, late fourth century; nos. 200, 679, 724, all last quarter of the fourth century. The Christ in the apse of S. Vitale: M. Lawrence, "The Iconography of the Mosaics of S. Vitale," *Atti del VI Congresso Internazionale di Archeologia Cristiana, Ravenna 1962* (1965), 123–140, at 136–138; and now F. W. Deichmann, *Ravenna, Hauptstadt der spätantiken Abendlandes II, Kommentar II* (1976) 165–166 (emphasising the Second Coming as the dominant meaning). The Christ of Hosios David, Thessalonica, is thematically and iconographically related to the S. Vitale Christ; cf. R. F. Hoddinott, *Early Byzantine Churches in Macedonia and Southern Serbia, A Study of the Origins and Initial Development of East Christian Art* (1963) 173–179.

192. A similar iconographic scheme appears on a (Syrian?) silver platter in the Hermitage: the crux gemmata between two angels stands over the globe and the four streams of paradise. See A. Banck, "Monuments des arts mineurs de Byzance (IVᵉ–VIIᵉ siècle) au Musée de l'Ermitage," in *IX Corso di cultura sull'arte Rav. e Biz.* (1962) 109–123, at 113, 115, 118.

193. Cf. E. Sauser, "Das Paschamysterium in den sog. frühchristl. Passionssarkophagen," *Kyriakon, Festschr. J. Quasten* 2 (1970) 654–662.

194. Gregory Nazianzen *P.G.* 35, 685C.

195. Cf. above, n. 125.

196. Gregory Nazianzen *P.G.*, 35, 684BC.

> ὁ μέν γε παραπέμπεται πανδήμοις εὐφημίαις τε καὶ πομπαῖς καὶ τούτοις δὴ τοῖς ἡμετέροις σεμνοῖς, ᾠδαῖς παννύχοις καὶ δᾳδουχίαις, αἷς Χριστιανοὶ τιμᾶν μετάστασιν εὐσεβῆ νομίζομεν· καὶ γίνεται πανήγυρις μετὰ πάθους ἡ ἐκκομιδὴ τοῦ σώματος. . . . καὶ τοῦτο διεδόθη ταῖς τῶν πολλῶν ἀκοαῖς, ὅτι, ἐπειδὴ τὸν Ταῦρον ὑπερβάλλοι τὸ σῶμα πρὸς τὴν πατρῷαν αὐτῷ πόλιν διασωζόμενον . . . φωνή τις ἐκ τῶν ἄκρων ἔστιν οἷς ἐξηκούετο, οἷον ψαλλόντων τε καὶ παραπεμπόντων, ἀγγελικῶν οἶμαι δυνάμεων, γέρας τῆς εὐσεβείας ἐκείνῳ, καὶ ἀντίδοσις ἐπιτάφιος.

197. Gregory Nazianzen *P.G.* 35, 685AB:

> Ὡς δὲ πλησιάζοι τῇ μεγάλῃ και βασιλίδι πόλει, τί δεῖ λέγειν δορυφορίας τε τοῦ στρατοῦ παντὸς, καὶ τάξιν ἐνόπλιον, ὡς ζῶντι τῷ βασιλεῖ γινομένην, ἢ τῆς λαμπρᾶς πόλεως ἔκχυσιν, ὀνομαστοτάτην τῶν πώποτε γενομένων ἢ ἐσομένων;

198. Gregory Nazianzen *P.G.*, 35, 685BC. However, Julian merely supervised this funeral, just as Constantius II had supervised that of Constantine, Socrates *H.E.*, 3, 1. Removing the diadem appears to have been customary for such an occasion, Philostorgius *H.E.*, 6, 6.

199. Gregory Nazianzen *P.G.* 35, 688A:

Τῷ δὲ αἰσχρὰ μὲν τὰ τῆς ἐκστρατείας (ἠλαύνετο δήμοις καὶ πόλεσι, καὶ φωναῖς δημοσίαις καὶ βωμολόχοις, ὧν ἔτι καὶ νῦν οἱ πολλοὶ μνημονεύουσιν), ἀδοξοτέρα δὲ ἡ ἐπάνοδος. Τίς δὲ ἡ ἀδοξία; Μῖμοι γελοίων ἦγον αὐτόν, καὶ τοῖς ἀπὸ τῆς σκηνῆς αἴσχρεσιν ἐπομπεύετο. . . . καὶ τὴν ἄρνησιν, καὶ τὴν ἧτταν, καὶ τὸ τέλος ὀνειδιζόμενος. Καὶ τί γὰρ οὐ πάσχων κακῶν; τί δὲ οὐκ ἀκούων οἷς οἱ τοιοῦτοι νεανιεύονται, τέχνην τὴν ὕβριν ἔχοντες, ἕως ἡ Ταρσέων αὐτὸν ὑποδέχεται πόλις, οὐκ οἶδ' ὅπως καὶ ἀνθ' ὅτου τὴν ὕβριν ταύτην κατακριθεῖσα; Ἔνθα δὲ οἱ τέμενος ἄτιμον, καὶ τάφος ἐξάγιστος, καὶ ναὸς ἀπόπτυστος, καὶ οὐδὲ θεατὸς εὐσεβῶν ὄψεσι.

Socrates H.E., 3, 26 reports that, as precedent required, the arrangements for Julian's funeral were made by his successor Jovian. Gregory's interpretation of Julian's funeral is entirely his own. Julian was ultimately buried in the narthex of the Church of the Apostles, in a sarcophagus with a suitably Homeric inscription (quoting Iliad 3, 179), Zosimus 3, 34; cf. Greek Anthology 7, 747. A different version of the epitaph, Zonaras, 13, 13, 24 and Cedrenus Bonn, 1, 539: see P. Grierson, "The Tombs and Obits of Byzantine Emperors," DOP 16 (1962) 41; M. Di Maio, "The Transfer of the Remains of the Emperor Julian from Tarsus to Constantinople," Byzantion 48 (1978) 43–50. The site at Tarsus was already marked by the tomb of Maximinus, Philostorgius H.E., 8, 1.

200. Theophanes, ed. de Boor, 299.

201. Suetonius Augustus, 100.

202. Lar imperii virtutumque, Amm., 16, 10, 13; on the context, cf. above, "Adventus" at nn. 140ff. Julian to be buried in Rome, Amm., 25, 10, 5. See on this passage and Julian's ultimate burial, Grierson, "Tombs and Obits," DOP 16 (1962) 40–41.

203. Libanius Or., 18, 304:

Ἐπεὶ δὲ εἰκόνων ἐμνήσθην, πολλαὶ πόλεις ἐκεῖνον τοῖς τῶν θεῶν παραστήσαντες ἕδεσιν ὡς τοὺς θεοὺς τιμῶσι, καὶ τις ἤδη καὶ παρ' ἐκείνου, δι' εὐχῆς ἤτησέ τι τῶν ἀγαθῶν καὶ οὐκ ἠτύχησεν.

204. Libanius Or., 24, 40:

Λάβε πεῖραν, ὦ βασιλεῦ, τῆς γνώμης, ἅψαι τῆς βοηθείας, καὶ κεκτήσῃ τὴν τύχην. τοῦτό σοι δείξει γεωργουμένην τὴν Θρᾴκην, τοῦτο Θερμοπύλας ἀνοιγομένας, τοῦτο τοὺς ἀλωμένους ἐπανάξει, τοῦτο μεταποιήσει τὰ νῦν, τὰς φυγὰς καὶ τὰς διώξεις. . . . τούτων συνεφάψεται Ἰουλιανὸς πάντα καθιστὰς ῥάδια τοὺς μὲν ὀφθαλμοὺς τῶν στρατιωτῶν διαφεύγων τοῖς δὲ ἔργοις γνωριζόμενος.

(Cf. Libanius Or., 30 (Pro Templis), 40, where the successes of the time are attributed to the heroism of the dead Julian.) See on these two passages here cited, A. D. Nock, "Deification and Julian," JRS 47 (1957) 114–23, reprinted in his Essays, vol. 2, 832–846; D. Conduché, "Ammien Marcellin et la mort de Julien," Latomus 24 (1965) 359–380, discusses the views of Julian's death held by contemporaries, including the view of Libanius that he was murdered by a Christian.

205. See, e.g., Suetonius Augustus, 98 with Pan. Lat., 12, 12, 6; Nock, "Deification," 840.

206. Cf. above, "Adventus," at nn. 161 and 171f. Pagan hopes in Julian had their counterpart in Christian satisfaction at his death; cf. N. Baynes, "The Death of Julian the Apostate in Christian Legend," JRS 27 (1937) 22–29.

207. See above, "Adventus" at n. 176.

208. Libanius *Or.*, 30, *Pro Templis*. See esp. 9–10:

> ψυχὴ γάρ, ᾧ βασιλεῦ, τοῖς ἀγροῖς τὰ ἱερὰ προοίμια τῆς ἐν τοῖς ἀγροῖς κτίσεως
> γεγενημένα . . . καὶ τοῖς γεωργοῦσιν ἐν αὐτοῖς αἱ ἐλπίδες. . . .

Cf. J. Geffcken, *The Last Days of Greco-Roman Paganism*, tr. S. MacCormack (1978) 171f.

209. Libanius *Or.*, 18, 274f; *Or.*, 24, 6, 9ff, 17ff; cf. *Or.*, 17, 7; *Or.* 24, 8.

210. For Theodosius on the Frigidus, cf. W. Hartke, *Geschichte und Politik im spätantiken Rom, Klio*, 45 Beih. (1940) 104. On the rain-miracle as an event of religious import with imperial dimensions in Marcus Aurelius' own day, see H. Z. Rubin, "Weather Miracles under Marcus Aurelius," *Athenaeum* 57 (1979) 357–380.

211. *H.A. Marcus*, 24, 4 with Xiphilinus Dio, 71, 9. See Themistius *Or.*, 15, 191 ab, who saw the relief depicting the rain-miracle on Marcus' column; cf. W. Hartke, *Kinderkaiser*, (1951) 247ff. On pagan and Christian miracle in late antique historiography, see the excellent article by Lellia Cracco Ruggini, "The Ecclesiastical Histories and the Pagan Historiography: Providence and Miracle," *Athenaeum* 55 (1977) 107–126 (114, n. 37 on triumphal columns in Rome and Constantinople).

212. Eunapius *History*, frag. 26, C. Müllerus, *F.H.G.*, vol. 4 (1878) 25, quoted also by J. Bidez, *Vie . . . de Julien*, 329:

> Ἀλλ' ὁπότε σκήπτροισι τεοῖς Περσήϊον αἷμα
> ἄχρι Σελευκείης κλονέων ξιφέεσσι δαμάσσης,
> δὴ τότε σὲ πρὸς Ὄλυμπον ἄγει πυριλαμπὲς ὄχημα.
> ἀμφὶ θυελλείῃσι κυκώμενον ἐν στροφάλιγξι,
> λυσάμενον βροτέων ῥεθέων πολύτλητον ἀνίην.
> ἥξεις δ' αἰθερίου φάεος πατρώϊον αὐλὴν
> ἔνθεν ἀποπλαγχθεὶς μεροπήϊον ἐς δέμας ἦλθες.

Nock, "Deification and Julian," *Essays*, vol. 2 (1972) 845 and n. 52, regards this as given during Julian's lifetime. Straub, "Die Himmelfahrt des Julianus Apostata," *Gymnasium* 69 (1962) 310–326, at 322 and n. 5 (reprinted in his *Regeneratio Imperii* (1972) 172 and n. 59) regards it as posthumous. It is possible that this is the oracle referred to in Libanius *Or.*, 30 (*Pro Templis*), 41. See also Cumont, *Ét. Syr.* (1917) 104f.

213. II Kings, 2, 11, cf. 1; above, at nn. 165ff. The imagery of the ascent of Elias was alive in the late antique Near East; see J. B. Segal, *Edessa, "The Blessed City"* (1970) 92, citation from Philoxenus.

214. *H.A. Sept. Sev.*, 22, 1f:

> Signa mortis eius haec fuerunt: ipse somniavit quattuor aquilis et gemmato curru praevolante nescio qua ingenti humana specie ad caelum esse raptum; cumque raperetur, octoginta et novem numeros explicuisse, ultra quot annos ne unum quidem annum vixit. . . . cumque positus esset in circulo ingenti aereo, diu solus et destitutus stetit, cum vereretur autem, ne praeceps rueret, a Iove se vocatum vidit atque inter Antoninos locatum.

Severus' fear, *ne praeceps rueret*, recalls Suet. *Caligula*, 57. Caligula before his death dreamt that he was standing next to Iuppiter's heavenly throne but was kicked by Iuppiter and fell back to earth. Perhaps the author of the *H.A.* had this passage in mind. R. Syme, "Astrology in the *H.A.*," *Bonner Historia Augusta Col-*

loquium 1972–1974 (1976), 300, suspects the *H.A.* passage of being an invention of the author. It fits all the better into this present fourth-century context.

215. G. Bruns, *Staatskameen des 4. Jahrhunderts* (1948) 22f; figs. 17–18. D. Strong, *Roman Art* (Baltimore, 1976) fig. 246, also refers this cameo to Julian. A cameo now in Bucharest (Bruns, *Staatskameen*, 26, figs. 19–20; M. Gramotopol, "Le grand camée de Roumanie," *Latomus* 24 (1965) 870–885, identifies the figures as Julian and his wife Helena; K. Horedt, "Bemerkungen zur Deutung des Cameo Orghidan," *Latomus* 33 (1974) 673–675, suggests earlier dates) shows the same subject in an abbreviated form: the chariot has disappeared, and the city goddess (see Bruns, *Staatskameen*, 26 and n. 100) does not crown the emperor. This cameo is probably later than the one from Berlin. It has eliminated the chariot motif, and presents an image which, in the terms of Roman imperial art, was more conventional. An iconographic parallel appears on the Trier cameo, generally regarded as Constantinian: A. Alföldi, in W. Reusch, ed., *Aus der Schatzkammer des antiken Trier* (1959) 50–53; M. R. Alföldi, *Die konstantinische Goldprägung* (1963) 127–128.

216. F. Cumont, "L'aigle funéraire d'Hiérapolis," in *Et. Syr.* (1917) 35–118. See also E. R. Goodenough, *Jewish Symbols in the Greco-Roman Period*, vol. 8 (1958) 122–142, esp. 131ff, 136, for further examples.

217. H. P. L'Orange, *Studies on the Iconography of Cosmic Kingship in the Ancient World* (1953) 51f; cf. 64f, 80f.; cf. Cumont, "L'Aigle funéraire d'Hiérapolis," 91ff. Sassanian silver: L'Orange, *Cosmic Kingship*, figs. 52–53, 55.

218. E.g., on St. Mark's, Venice, L'Orange, *Cosmic Kingship*, 118f, fig. 86.

219. Sixth–eighth centuries: L'Orange, *Cosmic Kingship*, 128, fig. 91; S. H. Gutberlet, *Die Himmelfahrt Christi in der bildenden Kunst von den Anfängen bis ins hohe Mittelalter* (1935) 102–107; and A. Grabar, *Christian Iconography*, 134–135; cf. 112–113; K. Weitzmann, ed., *Age of Spirituality* (1979) 557.

220. L'Orange, *Cosmic Kingship*, 125, fig. 90; cf. Grabar, *Iconography*, 35, who relates the Rabbula miniature to Roman triumphal art. I think L'Orange's interpretation is more convincing. See also H. Schrade, "Himmelfahrt Christi," *Vortr. Bibl. Warburg* (1928–1929), 144ff; S. H. Gutberlet, *Die Himmelfahrt*, 50–62; cf. 42, a Monza ampulla, but without the wheels; and J. A. Leroy, *Les manuscrits syriaques à peintures conservés dans les bibliothèques d'Europe et d'Orient* (1964) 182–189 for a detailed discussion of this miniature and its context; K. Weitzmann, ed., *Age of Spirituality* (1979) 455, 495–496.

221. The ascent of Alexander as represented in Eastern imagery, in the West became an exemplum for pride: L'Orange, *Cosmic Kingship*, 118ff. A related use of the image showing Doeg the Edomite (I Samuel 22, 9ff) seated, facing backward on a throne supported by a simurgh, appears in the Corbie Psalter: J. Hubert, J. Porcher, and W. F. Volbach, *Europe in the Dark Ages* (1969) 195, fig. 205. Khusro II, another Western mediaeval exemplum for the sin of pride, was similarly shown on a throne chariot; see L. I. Ringbom, *Paradisus Terrestris*, (1958) 382f, 387ff (English summary 444f). A reminder of the old meaning of the throne chariot in a Christian Byzantine context appears in the Last Judgement scene at Torcello, where the mandorla in which Christ is seated is supported by two wheels. On Byzantine representations of the Ascension, see S. H. Gutberlet, *Die Himmelfahrt*, 117ff.

222. This is so even if we can no longer assume the existence of a "circle of Symmachus" or a vigorous intellectual climate in Rome during this period: Alan

Cameron, "Paganism and Literature in Late Fourth Century Rome," in *Christianisme et formes littéraires de l'antiquité tardive en Occident*, Entretiens Hardt, 23 (1977) 1–40. For pagan senatorial propaganda, see A. Alföldi, *Die Kontorniaten, ein verkanntes Propagandamittel der stadtrömischen heidnischen Aristokratie in ihrem Kampfe gegen das christliche Kaisertum*, Budapest, Magyar numismatikai Hársulat (1942–43) (revised and expanded, A. Alföldi, E. Alföldi, and C. L. Clay, *Die Kontorniat-Medaillons* (plates and catalogue 1976)); A. Alföldi, *A Festival of Isis in Rome under the Christian Emperors of the Fourth Century* (1937). For a modification, see S. Mazzarino, "La Propaganda senatoriale nel tardo impero," *Doxa* 4 (1951) 121–148. For *consecratio* in Rome see *P.W.* Suppl. 4, 815ff. (*Kaiserkult*), where it is stated that the senate consecrated emperors down to the fourth century, without always, however, citing the evidence. For what are, probably, the latest records, see Ioannes Bapt. de Rossi, *Inscr. Christ. Urbis Romae*, vol. 1 (1857–1861) 337–339, and the inscription on 338: *Martia Theudosium Dominorum Roma parentem aetherio divum venerans sacravit in orbe*. Ausonius still praises Gratian as *piissimus* for consecrating his father—*Gratiarum actio* 2—thus making a direct link with the ideology of the second century.

223. *Poli media stellantis in arce*, an expression resembling terms used for imperial *consecratio* elsewhere; cf. above, at n. 214 and the ἀψῖδες οὐράνιαι of Eusebius, above at n. 132; cf. below, at n. 225.

224. Claudian *VI cons.*, Praef. 11–26:

> Me quoque Musarum studium sub nocte silenti
>   artibus adsuetis sollicitare solet.
> namque poli media stellantis in arce videbar
>   ante pedes summi carmina ferre Iovis;
> (15–16) . . .
> Enceladus mihi carmen erat victusque Typhoeus:
>   his subit Inarimen, hunc gravis Aetna domat.
> quam laetum post bella Iovem susceperat aether
>   Phlegraeae referens praemia militiae!
> Additur ecce fides nec me mea lusit imago,
>   inrita nec falsum somnia misit ebur.
> en princeps, en orbis apex aequatus Olympo!
>   en quales memini, turba verenda, deos!
> fingere nil maius potuit sopor, altaque vati
>   conventum caelo praebuit aula parem.

225. Claudian *III cons.*, 163–184:

> Nec plura locutus,
> sicut erat, liquido signavit tramite nubes
> ingrediturque globum Lunae limenque relinquit
> Arcados et Veneris clementes advolat auras.
> hinc Phoebi permensus iter flammamque nocentem
> Gradivi placidumque Iovem; stetit arce suprema,
> algenti qua zona riget Saturnia tractu.
> machina laxatur caeli rutilaeque patescunt
> sponte fores. Arctoa parat convexa Bootes,
> australes reserat portas succinctus Orion
> invitantque novum sidus, pendentque vicissim
> quas partes velit ipse sequi, quibus esse sodalis

dignetur stellis aut qua regione morari.
O decus aetherium, terrarum gloria quondam,
te tuus Oceanus natali gurgite lassum
excipit et notis Hispania proluit undis.
fortunate parens, primos cum detegis ortus,
adspicis Arcadium; cum te proclivior urges,
occiduum visus remoratur Honorius ignem;
et quocumque vagos flectas sub cardine cursus,
natorum per regna venis, qui mente serena
maturoque regunt iunctas moderamine gentes,
saecula qui rursus formant meliore metallo.

226. Cf. Alan Cameron, *Claudian*, 208ff.

227. Santo Mazzarino, *Antico, tardoantico ed erà costantiniana*, vol. 1 (1974) 357ff. See also above, "*Adventus*" n. 182.

228. Claudian *III cons.*, 105–110:

> Iam libertate reducta,
> quamvis emeritum peteret natura reverti
> numen et auratas astrorum panderet arces,
> . . . .
> distulit Augustus cupido se credere caelo,
> dum tibi pacatum praesenti traderet orbem.

For the *adventus* of Honorius from the East, see above, "*Adventus*" at nn. 204f.

229. Claudian *IV cons.*, 428f.

230. Claudian *VI cons.*, 101f.

231. See below, at nn. 240ff.

232. The mention of *divi* by Sidonius is thus essentially mechanical: Sidonius *Carmen*, II, 210, 317ff; cf. *Carmen*, VII, 102f listing earlier emperors.

233. R. Delbrueck, *Die Consulardiptychen*, no. 59, 227f; W. F. Volbach, *Elfenbeinarbeiten der Spätantike und des frühen Mittelalters* (1976) no. 56; for the date, K. Wessel, "Eine Gruppe oberitalischer Elfenbeinarbeiten," *Jahrbuch des Instituts* 63–64 (1948–49) 111f. See also H. Schrade, "Himmelfahrt Christi," *Vortr. Bibl. Warburg* (1928–1929), 106ff. K. Weitzmann, ed., *Age of Spirituality* (1979) 70–71.

234. For the date of Macrobius, roughly contemporary with the ivory, see Alan Cameron, "The Date and Identity of Macrobius," *JRS* 56 (1966) 25–38.

235. Pyre surmounted by *quadriga*: *RIC*, III, 247, 398, 441, legend CONSECRATIO, commemorative issues for Antoninus Pius and M. Aurelius. Elephant *quadriga* for *consecratio*, H. H. Scullard, *The Elephant in the Greek and Roman World* (1974) 254ff and pl. XXIV f and g, for Augustus and L. Verus resp.; F. Matz, *Der Gott auf dem Elefantenwagen*, Akad. d. Wiss. u. d. Lit. Wiesbaden, Abhandl. geistes- u. Sozialwiss. Kl., 1952 (1953) 719–763, esp. 738ff.

236. Wessel, "Eine Gruppe," finds no solution to the identity of the charioteer; L'Orange, *The Iconography of Cosmic Kingship*, 60, rightly identifies the figure as the *Divus*.

237. Dio, 75, 4f; Herodian, 4, 1, 11f., above, at nn. 50ff.

238. Cf. Claudian *III cons.*, 105f, 163f; *IV cons.*, 428f. Macrobius *Somn.*, 1, 9–14.

239. F. Cumont, *Recherches sur le symbolisme funéraire des Romains* (1942) 87, 304, 373f, 487f.

240. On *consolationes* in Greece and Rome, see R. Kassel, *Untersuchungen zur*

griechischen und römischen Konsolationsliteratur, Zetemata, 18 (1958). J. Soffel, *Die Regeln Menanders für die Leichenrede*, Beitr. zur klass. Philologie, H. 57 (1974) 78–89, discusses Greek Christian funerary discourses. The tension between the overt rejection of pagan rhetorical rules on the one hand, and their observation for the sake of communicating a new Christian content (82ff on Gregory of Nyssa) applies to Ambrose also.

241. Ambrose *De Ob. Theod.* 3 with *Genesis* 50, 2f; see also, Herodian, 4, 1, 3f. For funerary processions and translations in general see E. Gabba and G. Tibiletti, "Una Signora di Treveri sepolta a Pavia," *Athenaeum* n.s. 38 (1960) 253–62; for triumphal aspects of the imperial funerary procession, Versnel, *Triumphus*, 123f.

242. Ambrose *De Ob. Theod.*, ed. Faller, 56:

> Nec vereare ne inhonorae videantur, quocumque accesserint reliquiae triumphales. Non hoc sentit Italia, quae claros spectavit triumphos, quae a tyrannis iterum liberata concelebrat suae libertatis auctorem: non hoc Constantinopolis, quae secundo ad victoriam principem misit, quem, cum vellet tenere, non potuit. Expectabat quidem in reditu eius triumphales sollemnitates et titulos victoriarum, expectabat totius orbis imperatorem stipatum exercitu Gallicano et totius orbis subnixum viribus. Sed nunc illi Theodosius potentior, nunc gloriosior redit quem angelorum caterva deducit, quem sanctorum turba prosequitur. Beata plane, quae paradisi incolam suscipis, et habitatorem supernae illius civitatis, augusto sepulti corporis tenebris hospitio.

The body of Theodosius was received in Constantinople and buried there by Arcadius, Socrates *H.E.*, 6, 1.

243. Above, n. 241; Dio, 75, 4f.

244. *Pan. Lat.*, 8, 8, 4, cf. above, "Adventus" at 58.

245. Ambrose *De Ob. Theod.*, 31, below, n. 257.

246. C. Mango, *The Homilies of Photius Patriarch of Constantinople* (1958) Homily 3, 84, 90ff; cf. Homily 4, 109; cf. MacCormack, "Roma and Constantinopolis," *CQ* 25 (1975) 149–150.

247. E.g., Gregory of Nyssa, encomium of St. Stephen; K. Baus, *Der Kranz in Antike und Christentum* (1940) esp. 144ff.

248. See A. Recheis, *Engel, Tod und Seelenreise. Das Wirken der Geister beim Heimgang des Menschen in der Lehre der alexandrinischen und kappadokischen Väter*, Temi e Testi, 4 (1958).

249. Ambrose *De Ob. Theod.*, 7–8:

> Desiluit equo princeps, et ante aciem solus progrediens, ait: 'Ubi est Theodosii deus?' Iam hoc Christo proximus loquebatur. Quis enim posset hoc dicere, nisi qui Christo se adhaerere cognosceret? Quo dicto excitavit omnes, exemplo omnes armavit, et iam certe senior aetate, sed validus fide. Theodosii ergo fides fuit vestra victoria: vestra fides filiorum eius fortitudo sit. Fides ergo auget aetatem. . . . Quid enim est fides nisi rerum earum quae sperantur substantia?

John Chrysostom knew Ambrose's *consolatio* for Theodosius and used this passage in his oration on an anniversary of the death of Theodosius: *P.G.*, 63, 491–494 at 491–492. The exegesis of the term *fides* in a political context was a recurring theme with Ambrose; cf. his *ep.* 40, 22, to Theodosius, in 388 A.D.

250. Note the interplay between *fides imperatoris* and *militum virtus, De Ob.*

Theod., 6. The latter reflects a much-repeated slogan on the coinage of this period—a pointer to Ambrose's ability to understand and utilise contemporary politics to propagate the Christian empire. Cf. *RIC*, VII, Index II, s.v. VIRTUS EXERCIT etc.; *RIC*, IX, Index V, s.v. VIRTUS EXERCITI. Ambrose *De Ob. Theod.*, 6–7:

> . . . Tantus imperator recessit a nobis, sed non totus recessit; reliquit enim nobis liberos suos, in quibus eum debemus agnoscere, et in quibus eum et cernimus et tenemus. Nec moveat aetas! Fides militum imperatoris perfecta aetas est; est enim perfecta aetas ubi perfecta est virtus. Reciproca haec, quia et fides imperatoris militum virtus est. Recognoscitis nempe, quos vobis Theodosii fides triumphos adquisiverit.

251. Ambrose *De Ob. Theod.*, 10: Ubi autem fides, ibi exercitus angelorum est.
252. Ambrose *De Ob. Theod.*, 11–12:

> Solvite filiis eius quod debetis patri . . . [filiis] imperatoris pii, imperatoris misericordis, imperatoris fidelis.

253. Ambrose *De Ob. Valent.*, 71–72:

> Huic ascendenti animae Gratianus frater occurrit et complexus eam . . . . Veni inquit, frater meus, exeamus in agrum, requiescamus in castellis, diluculo surgamus in vineas, hoc est, Venisti eo ubi diversarum virtutum fructus pro singulorum meritis deferuntur, ubi abundant meritorum praemia.

254. See F. Holmes Dudden, *The Life and Times of St. Ambrose*, (1935) 417–421.
255. *Augustae memoriae*: cf. above, at nn. 85ff, on the post-Tetrarchic MEMORIA issues.
256. *Luce perpetua*: for this image, see above, at n. 70.
257. Ambrose *De Ob. Theod.*, 31–32:

> In quam [requiem] festinavit intrare Theodosius, atque ingredi civitatem Hierusalem, de qua dictum est: Et reges terrae ferent gloriam suam in illam. Illa est vera gloria, quae ibi sumitur, illud regnum beatissimum, quod ibi possidetur, ad quod festinabat apostolus. . . . Absolutus igitur dubio certaminum fruitur nunc augustae memoriae Theodosius luce perpetua, tranquillitate diuturna, et pro his quae in hoc gessit corpore, remunerationis divinae fructibus gratulatur. Ergo quia dilexit augustae memoriae Theodosius dominum deum suum, meruit sanctorum consortia.

On the *principes Christiani* of the fourth century, cf. below, "Accession," n. 238.
258. Ambrose *De Ob. Theod.*, 39–40:

> Manet ergo in lumine Theodosius, et sanctorum coetibus gloriatur. Illic nunc complectitur Gratianum, iam sua vulnera non maerentem, quia invenit ultorem. . . . De quibus bene dicitur: Dies diei eructat verbum. Contra autem Maximus et Eugenius in inferno quasi nox nocti indicat scientiam, docentes exemplo miserabili quam durum sit arma suis principibus inrogare. De quibus pulchre dicitur, Vidi impium superexaltatum et elevatum super cedros Libani: et transivi et ecce non erat. Transivit enim pius de caligine saeculari ad lumen aeternum. . . . Nunc se augustae memoriae Theodosius regnare cognoscit, quando in regno est domini Iesu.

Cf. Eusebius *V.C.*, 1, 3; 27 and R. Farina, *L'impero e l'imperatore cristiano in Eusebio di Cesarea* (1966) 224ff.
259. E.g., *Pan. Lat.*, 3, 6–8.

260. Eusebius *V.C.*, 1, 23; cf. 47 (Tetrarchs); 1, 57, Galerius; 1, 38, Maxentius; 2, 18; cf. 2, 26ff., Licinius.

261. However, the identification of the enemy of the state with the enemy of religion, although not as explicit, started earlier. The usurper, enemy of the state, was also the enemy of the gods, because he disrupted the god-given order: see F. Burdeau, "L'empereur d'après les panégyristes latins," in *Aspects de l'empire romain* (1964) 39.

262. See Averil Cameron, *Flavius Crescontius Corippus, In laudem Iustini Augusti minoris* (1976) 10–14.

263. J. B. Bury, *History of the Later Roman Empire from the Death of Theodosius I to the Death of Justinian*, vol. 2 (1923) 70; Cameron, *Corippus* 5 with references to the panegyric.

264. Corippus *In Laud. Iust.*, 1, 1–3:

> Imperii culmen rerum non motibus ullis
> non armis sumptum, non ambitione potitum
> auspicio meliore cano.

265. Corippus *In Laud. Iust.*, 1, 31ff.

266. As he had been bidden by Justinian, according to Corippus *In Laud. Iust.*, 4, 332f.

267. Corippus *In Laud. Iust.*, 1, 130–153.

268. Corippus *In Laud. Iust.*, 1, 136.

269. Corippus *In Laud. Iust.*, 1, 138.

270. Corippus *In Laud. Iust.*, 1, 145–148:

> Te successorem statuens sibi. suscipe gaudens:
> in tua iura suum transmisit avunculus orbem.
> non te cognatum sanctissimus ille putavit,
> sed genitum. te iura vocant, te sustinet aula.

271. Corippus *In Laud. Iust.*, 1, 130.

272. Corippus *In Laud. Iust.*, 1, 173–180:

> Pedibus prostrata iacensque
> omnis turba simul 'pius es, miserere' perorat
> 'supplicibus, vir sancte, tuis: succurre periclis.
> omnia mox veniente die periisse videbis,
> si vacuam vulgus sine principe senserit aulam.
> (178) . . .
> Ipse tenere
> sceptra tuus moriens te iussit avunculus ore.

273. Corippus *In Laud. Iust.*, 1, 190–193:

> Incedunt media securam nocte per urbem
> fronte parum laeti, quamvis gaudente senatu
> imperium peterent, quamquam omnia tuta viderent.

274. Corippus *In Laud. Iust.*, 1, 208–211:

> Nam quis temptaret obesse,
> cum deus imperium sancto iam dixerat ore
> Iustino Sophiaeque dari, muroque potenti
> cinxerat atque armis totam caelestibus aulam?

275. Corippus *In Laud. Iust.*, 1, 236–247:

> . . . Suprema suae servans insignia vitae
> Iustinianus erat, non mutans morte colorem,
> sed solito candore nitens. quod vicerit orbem,
> mors veneranda viri signis monstravit apertis.
> ipse videbatur cunctis plangentibus unus
> effigie gaudere pia, diademate comptus
> purpureaque in veste iacens, requiescere somno
> credere quod posses, non duro funere, corpus.

276. Corippus *In Laud. Iust.*, 1, 263–271, cf. *Pan. Lat.*, 9, 24, 4–25, 1.

277. E.g., Suetonius *Nero*, 9; on Tiberius deflecting honour from himself to the dead Augustus, see M. P. Charlesworth, "The Refusal of Divine Honours," *PBSR* 15 (1939) 1–10.

278. Corippus *In Laud. Iust.*, 1, 257ff.

279. Corippus *In Laud. Iust.*, 2, 307–343.

280. Corippus *In Laud. Iust.*, 2, 137ff.

281. Corippus *In Laud. Iust.*, 1, 120–121.

282. Corippus *In Laud. Iust.*, 1, 276–281; 285–293:

> [Sophia] intextam pretioso murice vestem,
> Iustinianorum series ubi tota laborum
> neto auro insignita fuit gemmisque corusca.
> illic barbaricas flexa cervice phalanges,
> occisos reges, subiectasque ordine gentes
> pictor acu tenui multa formaverat arte.
> (281–284) . . .
> ipsum autem in media victorem pinxerat aula,
> effera Vandalici calcantem colla tyranni,
> plaudentem Libyam fruges laurumque ferentem.
> addidit antiquam tendentem brachia Romam,
> exerto et nudam gestantem pectore mammam,
> altricem imperii libertatisque parentem.
> haec ideo fieri vivax Sapientia iussit,
> ornatum ut propriis funus regale triumphis
> Augustum in tumulum fatalis duceret hora.

Compare this account to Procopius' description of the mosaic ceiling depicting Justinian's triumph, above "*Adventus*" at n. 292, and Averil Cameron, *Corippus*, *ad loc.*

283. Corippus *In Laud. Iust.*, 3, 13ff. The theme of triumph over the Orient goes back to Caesar and beyond, Vergil *Aeneid*, 1, 286–290:

> Nascetur pulchra Troianus origine Caesar,
> imperium Oceano, famam qui terminet astris,
> Iulius, a magno demissum homine Iulo.
> hunc tu olim caelo, spoliis orientis onustum
> accipies secura; vocabitur hic quoque votis.

284. Claudian *III cons.*, 210–211; *IV cons.*, 585ff.

285. Corippus *In Laud. Iust.*, 3, 31–36.

286. Corippus *In Laud. Iust.*, 3, 6.

287. Corippus *In Laud. Iust.*, 3, 8–10.

288. Corippus *In Laud. Iust.*, 3, 22; 42–43; 55.

289. Cf. Claudian *III cons.*, 126f; *IV cons.*, 580f; *VI cons.*, 543f. The theme of welcoming by a crowd has been treated in *adventus* as one of the main themes of imperial arrivals and appearances.

290. Corippus *In Laud. Iust.*, 3, 40–41:

> Omnis in exequias sexus convenit et aetas.
> Quis memorare potest tantae miracula pompae?

291. See Theophanes Continuatus (Bonn), 353, 4f: translation of the remains of Manuel from Chrysopolis to Constantinople, with singing, and candles. In the procession were senators and clergy. The body, in a cypress sarcophagus, was dressed in imperial robes.

292. Corippus *In Laud. Iust.*, 3, 59f. On Byzantine imperial funerals in the wider context of burial customs in general see J. Kyriakis, "Byzantine Burial Customs, the Care of the Deceased from Death to Prothesis," *The Greek Orthodox Theological Review* 19 (1974) 37–72.

293. Ambrose *De Ob. Theod.*, 32.

294. Corippus *In Laud. Iust.*, 1, 49–51:

> Quid fundis lacrimas? rerum quid gaudia defles?
> proice tristitiam: vivit pater, aethere vivit,
> et fruitur meliore die. succede labori.

295. Corippus *In Laud. Iust.*, 3, 31–5:

> Nos flemus tristes. . . .
> tu pater, angelicas inter, sanctissime, turmas
> laetus abes, positoque deum iam corpore cernis

(By contrast, Claudian *III cons.*, 163: Theodosius entered the sphere of the moon *sicut erat*, i.e., in the body)

> et frueris meliore die sub lumine solis
> nox cui nulla subit.

Cf. Evagrius *H.E.*, 2, 8 Bidez-Parmentier 57, describing the death of Marcian as πρὸς θεὸν ἐκδημίαν.

296. Corippus *In Laud. Iust.*, 4, 337–344:

> Vocor . . . alumne,
> et properat suprema dies, iussuque creantis
> a regnis in regna vehor. deus omne Latinum
> Iustino dedit imperium. . . .
>   . . . cum carne relicta
> spiritus ascendens claram penetraverit arcem,
> in medio procerum Iustini ad limina perge.
> invitato virum, nolit licet ille subire.

297. *Pan. Lat.*, 7, 7, 1ff (Constantius I); Eusebius *V.C.*, 1, 21 (Constantius I), and 4, 60–64 (Constantine); Claudian *III cons.*, 105–110 (Theodosius).

298. See, e.g., the funerary procession of Constantine Porphyrogenitus, in which the participants ᾄσμασι προπομπίοις τὴν ἔξοδον μεγαλύνοντες, Theophanes Continuatus 467, 19 (Bonn). For this and the following see O. Treitinger, *Die oströmische Kaiser- und Reichsidee* (1938; 1956) 155f.

299. *De Cer.* (Bonn), 1, 60:

ἔξελθε βασιλεῦ, καλεῖ σε ὁ βασιλεὺς τῶν βασιλευόντων καὶ κύριος τῶν κυριευόντων.
εἴσελθε βασιλεῦ, καλεῖ σε ὁ βασιλεὺς τῶν βασιλευόντων καὶ κύριος τῶν κυριευόντων.
ἀπόθου τὸ στέμμα ἀπὸ τῆς κεθαλῆς σου.

The calling of the emperor by God has a parallel in Leontius' Life of John the Almsgiver, who before his death dreamt that a eunuch in courtly dress delivered such a message to him. See A. J. Festugière, *Léontios de Néapolis, vie de Syméon le fou et vie de Jean de Chypre*, Inst. Fr. d'Arch. de Beyrouth, Vol. 95 (1974) *Vie de Jean* ch. 52, p. 403. The idea is also in Corippus, above at n. 296, with Averil Cameron, *Corippus, ad loc.*

300. Cf. above, at n. 146, and P. E. Schramm, "'Mitherrschaft im Himmel,' ein Topos des Herrscherkults in christlicher Einkleidung," *Polychronion, Festschr. F. Dölger* (1966) 480ff.

301. E.g., *Iliad*, 24, 258 Ἕκτωρ, ὃς θεὸς ἔσκε μετ' ἀνδράσιν; see L. Bieler, ΘΕΙΟΣ ΑΝΗΡ *Das Bild des "Gottlichen Menschen" in Spätantike und Frühchristentum.* (Vienna, 1935; Darmstadt, 1967), 9–13; also Themistius *Or.*, 7, 97b; 15, 193c, quoting the Delphic Oracle.

302. Agapetus, Ἔκθεσις § 63, *PG*, 86¹, 1184: ὁ μὲν Θεὸς οὐδενὸς δεῖται· ὁ βασιλεὺς δὲ μόνου Θεοῦ (cf. *Ann. Epigr.* 557 (1973): του εὐσεβ(εστάτου) καὶ φιλοχ (ρίστου) μετὰ θεοῦ/ ἡμῶν δεσπότου φλ(αουίου) Ἰουστινιανοῦ. . . .) This dictum is a variant on one of the Sentences of Sextus: ὁ μὲν Θεὸς οὐδενὸς δεῖται, ὁ δὲ πιστὸς μόνου Θεοῦ: H. Chadwick, *The Sentences of Sextus* (1959) 18 § 49; cf. 87, 166. Cf. the discussion of the pagan *mimesis theou* by rulers in relation to Eusebius, S. Calderone, "Teologia politica, successione dinastica e consecratio in età constantiniana," *Le culte des souverains*, Entretiens Hardt, 19 (1972) 237ff.

303. See J. D. Breckenridge, *The Numismatic Iconography of Justinian II*, Numismatic Notes and Monographs, 144 (1959) 22ff, 46ff. See also above at n. 193.

III. ACCESSION

1. See the excellent study, in part based on the coinage, by A. U. Stylow, *Libertas und Liberalitas, Untersuchungen zur innenpolitischen Propaganda der Römer* (1972).

2. See G. Wissowa, *Religion und Kultus der Römer* (1912; 1971) 146.

3. Tacitus *Hist.*, 1, 4.

4. Remitting taxes was one of the actions regularly praised in emperors; see below at n. 22 for Constantine. A remission of taxes by Trajan, with burning of the tax records, is depicted on one of the Plutei Traiani: E. Nash, *Pictorial Dictionary of Ancient Rome*, vol. 2 (1968) 176–178.

5. Ignaz Ziegler, *Die Königsgleichnisse des Midrasch beleuchtet durch die römische Kaiserzeit* (1903) 2. Contrast F. E. Brightman, "Byzantine Imperial Coronations," *JTS* 2 (1901) 359–392, where phase one of the imperial accession ceremonies (Augustus to Diocletian) is described as conforming more to the model of election by the Senate. Cf. H. U. Instinsky, *Bischofsstuhl und Kaiserthron* (1955) 32ff, on enthronement in the Curia.

6. Claudian *VI cons.*, 9–10; this is a *topos*. For an extended rendering of it, see Merobaudes *Panegyricus* II, 30–48 (ed. Vollmer, 8).

7. In 629 Heraclius assumed the title βασιλεύς, thus ending the ancient tension from a constitutional point of view. A revealing perspective on these issues is provided by I. Shahîd, "The Iranian Factor in Byzantium under Heraclius," *DOP* 26 (1972) 295–320. For divine election, see the fundamental article by A. D. Nock, "A Diis electa," *Harvard Theological Review* 23 (1930), reprinted in his *Essays*, vol. 1 (1972) 252–270, esp. 261ff, and J. Rufus Fears, *Princeps a diis electus. The Divine Election of the Emperor as a Political Concept at Rome*, American Academy in Rome, Papers and Monographs, 26 (1977).

8. See, on the dichotomy of election and dynasty, W. Sickel, "Das byzantinische Krönungsrecht bis zum 10. Jahrhundert," *BZ* 7 (1898) 511–557, at 512f and passim; and, from a different point of view, H. G. Beck, "Konstantinopel, zur Sozialgeschichte einer früh-mittelalterlichen Hauptstadt," *BZ* 58 (1965), reprinted in his *Ideen und Realitäten in Byzanz* (1972) 11–45, at 14: "Den fünf bis zehn deutschen Königsfamilien stehen annähernd dreissig byzantinische gegenüber." That is, it is possible in Byzantium to talk about dynasties, but at the same time, election *tout court* remained a method of choosing an emperor. For the second century, see also A. U. Stylow, *Libertas und Liberalitas*, 42.

9. Another representation of this type may have been the picture of Justin II designating Tiberius as Caesar, which was described by John of Ephesus *H. E. pars tertia*, 5 (tr. E. W. Brooks, (1936) 95):

> Quamobrem, cum tandem simulacra ambobus statuta sunt, angelus inter eos effictus est qui stabat et os ad aurem regis Iustini apponebat. itaque hoc fideliter ab omnibus acceptum est.

10. The *H.A.* presents a variety of formulations of the theme of election and succession of emperors, providing an insight into the diversity of concepts which still contributed to formulating imperial accessions in the late fourth century. See J. Béranger, "Idéologie impériale dans l'*H.A.*," *Bonner Historia Augusta Colloquium 1972–1974* (1976) 29–53, esp. 37 with n. 89, 43–45. Note the election of Tacitus, 49, stressing the role of the Senate, a then outmoded theme, which could, however, still be reflected in panegyric when an emperor was being praised for civilian virtues, Symmachus *Or.*, 2, 294.

11. See C. A. Bouman, *Sacring and Crowning* (1957); and R. Elze, *Die Ordines für die Weihe und Krönung des Kaisers und der Kaiserin*, Fontes Iuris Germanici antiqui in usum scholarum, 1960; see XXIIIff on the nature of these *ordines*. For Byzantium, below at nn. 372ff.

12. See, in general, H. Mattingly, "The Imperial Vota," *Proceedings of the British Academy* 36 (1950) 155–195, and 37 (1951) 219–268; for depictions of the *vota* of anniversaries in art, see I. Scott Ryberg, *Rites of the State Religion in Roman Art*, Memoirs, American Academy in Rome, 22 (1955) 131f; see also below, n. 25.

13. *RIC* IX, 17, 24, 31, 33, 76, 81, 217 with plate 11, 4.

14. But Theodosius avoided the celebration of the *vota*: Mattingly, *PBA* 37 (1951) 262–263. The *vota* coins of Honorius and his successors are a revival.

15. *Pan. Lat.*, 2, 3, 2: Illa lux divinum verticem claro orbe complectens.

16. But on the consular diptychs, it was only Constantius III who, shortly before he became emperor, ventured to let himself be represented with captives, as *triumphator*: W. F. Volbach, *Elfenbeinarbeiten*, no. 35 (plate 56). So it was appropriate that Rutilius in the newly discovered fragment of book II of his *De Red.*

should praise him as *Latii nominis una salus*. See M. Ferrari, "Frammenti ignoti di Rutilio Namaziano," *Italia Medioevale e Umanistica* 16 (1973) 15–30, at 28–30; cf. E. Cecchini, "Per il nuovo Rutilio Namaziano," *Rivista di filologia classica* 102 (1974) 401–403, for an expanded reading of the fragment.

17. *RIC*, IX, 277, 20; pl. 13, 5. For a related reverse iconography, showing VOTA PUBLICA TROBT, Gratian and the young Valentinian II (Gratian on the obverse), see A. Alföldi, *A Festival of Isis in Rome under the Christian Emperors of the Fourth Century* (1937) 53 and n. 155; pl. 10, 2.

18. For the emperors as SALUS ET SPES REIPUBLICAE compare the Constantinian issues with this reverse legend, showing Constantine enthroned frontally with Caesars at either side, *RIC*, VII, 328 (Rome 326 A.D.); 527 (Thessalonica 335 A.D.); 577, 583 (Constantinople 330 and 335–336 A.D. respectively). Iconography and legend are related to the issue here described, but the *vota* legend is absent.

19. *Pan. Lat.*, 4, 2, 2–3, 1:

> Det igitur mihi, Caesar invicte, hodiernae gratulationis exordium divinus ille vestrae maiestatis ortus ipso quo illuxit auspicio veris illustrior, cui dies serenus atque, ut celebrantes sensimus, ultra rationem temporis sol aestivus incaluit, augustiore fulgens luminis claritate quam cum originem mundi nascentis animavit, siquidem tunc inter illa rerum tenera primordia moderatus dicitur ne noceret ardentior, nunc certasse creditur ne maiestate vestra videretur obscurior. O felix beatumque ver novo partu, iam non amoenitate florum nec viriditate segetum nec gemmis vitium nec ipsis tantum favoniis et luce serenata laetum atque venerabile quantum ortu Caesarum maximorum!

20. Claudian *IV cons.*, 170ff.
21. Cf. above, "*Adventus*" at nn. 56ff.
22. *Pan. Lat.*, 8, 13, 1–4; 6:

> Quinque annorum nobis reliqua remisisti! O lustrum omnibus lustris felicius! O lustrum quod merito hanc imperii tui aequavit aetatem! Nobis ergo praecipue te principem di immortales creaverunt, quibus singulis haec est nata felicitas, ex quo tu imperare coepisti. Quinquennalia tua nobis, etiam perfecta, celebranda sunt. Illa enim quinto incipiente suscepta omnibus populis iure communia, nobis haec propria quae plena sunt. Praeclara fertur Catonis oratio de lustri sui felicitate. Iam tunc enim in illa vetere re publica ad censorum laudem pertinebat, si lustrum felix condidissent, si horrea messis implesset, si vindemia redundasset, si oliveta larga fluxissent. Quid ergo nos convenit gratulari de hoc indulgentiae tuae lustro, lustro quo, licet illa frugum cessarit ubertas, fecisti tamen ut omnia largiora videantur fuisse quam fuerint? . . . Hoc nobis est ista largitio, quod Terra mater frugum, quod Iuppiter moderator aurarum: quidquid illi parcius dederant, nobis tamen ex beneficio tuo natum est.

23. See above, "*Adventus*" at nn. 145f.
24. See also Eusebius *L.C.*, 6, 5–6 and *V.C.*, 4, 40 (cf. 68, for the proclamation of the Caesars as Augusti).
25. Eusebius *L.C.*, 3, 1; 2–5 passim:

> ὁ δὲ . . . . προσθήκας αὐτῷ μακρῶν περιόδων τῆς βασιλείας προστίθησιν, . . . παρέχει τε παντοίας ἑορτὰς ἐκτελεῖν σὺν πολλῇ ῥαστώνῃ τῆς μοναρχίας, ἐφ' ἑκάστῃ περιόδῳ δεκαετοῦς πανηγύρεως, ἕνα τινὰ τῶν αὐτοῦ παίδων ἐπὶ τὴν τοῦ βασιλικοῦ θρόνου κοινωνίαν προχειριζόμενος καὶ ὥσπερ εὐθαλεῖ καὶ ἀκμαίῳ φυτῷ χρόνων αὐξήσεις δωρούμενος. . . . οὕτω δῆτα χρόνων ἅμα καὶ παίδων αὐ-

ξήσεις βασιλεῖ τῷ θεοφιλεστάτῳ θεὸς αὐτὸς ὁ παμβασιλεὺς δωρούμενος, ἀκμάζουσαν αὐτῷ καὶ νεαρὰν τὴν κατὰ τῶν ἐπὶ γῆς ἐθνῶν ἡγεμονίαν ὥσπερ ἄρτι φύειν ἀρχομένην καθίστησιν. . . . εἶθ' ὑπὸ μίαν ζεύγλην βασιλικοῦ τεθρίππου τέτταρας ὑποζεύξας αὐτὸς αὐτῷ οἷά τινας πώλους τοὺς ἀνδρειοτάτους καίσαρας, ἡνίαις τε αὐτοὺς ἐνθέου συμφωνίας τε καὶ ὁμονοίας ἁρμοσάμενος, ἄνωθεν ὑψηλῶς ἡνιοχῶν ἐλαύνει, ὁμοῦ τὴν σύμπασαν ὅσην ἥλιος ἐφορᾷ διϊππεύων, αὐτός τε τοῖς πᾶσιν ἐπιπαρὼν καὶ τὰ πάντα διασκοπούμενος.

κἄπειτα τῆς οὐρανίου βασιλείας εἰκόνι κεκοσμημένος, ἄνω βλέπων, κατὰ τὴν ἀρχέτυπον ἰδέαν τοὺς κάτω διακυβερνῶν ἰθύνει. . . .

Tr. H. A. Drake, *In Praise of Constantine* (1976) 86–87, with commentary 159–160. See also Socrates *H.E.*, 1, 38, who here follows Eusebius and notes the same connection between Constantine's decennial anniversaries and the successive nominations of his sons as Caesars. In short, the two authors explicitly associate the *vota* with accessions.

26. *V.C.*, 4, 40.

27. E.g., Pliny *ep.*, 10, 52–3, 102–103.

28. See R. O. Fink, A. S. Hoey, and W. F. Snyder, "The Feriale Duranum," *Yale Classical Studies* 7 (1940) 1–221, and M. Grant, *Roman Anniversary Issues* (1950).

29. E.g., *Pan. Lat.* 2, 1, 1f; 3, 1, 1f; 4, 2, 2, where the serenity and beauty of the day of Constantius' accession is stressed.

30. John Lydus *De Mens.*, 4, 10; cf. Wissowa, *Religion und Kultus*, 448, cf. 381–383. On the pagan character of these celebrations in the fourth century, see A. Alföldi, *A Festival of Isis in Rome under the Christian Emperors of the Fourth Century* (1937) 12–14, 42–58, esp. 47ff.

31. See below, at nn. 396ff; cf. n. 467.

32. For the expression of this aspect of Christianity in rhetorical theory, see G. L. Kustas, *Studies in Byzantine Rhetoric* (1973) 30ff.

33. Nonetheless, different nuances could still be brought to bear at different times; thus, see below at nn. 456ff. on the imperial mosaics of San Vitale.

34. W. Seston, *Dioclétien et la Tétrarchie*, Bibl. des éc. fr. d'Athènes et de Rome, 162 (1946) is fundamental to the issues here discussed. On Hercules, and his juxtaposition with Iuppiter in an imperial context, see also M. Simon, *Hercule et le christianisme* (1955) 131–142 with 77–118.

35. Cf. Fink, "Feriale Duranum," *Yale Class. Stud.* 7 (1940) 102–112.

36. *Pan. Lat.*, 2, 1, 4: Hoc die quo immortalis ortus dominae gentium civitatis . . . . celebratur.

37. *Pan. Lat.*, 2, 1–2.

38. *Pan. Lat.*, 2, 1, 3.

39. *Pan. Lat.*, 2, 3, 1.

40. *Pan. Lat.*, 2, 2, 2f.:

Quis enim dubitat . . . Italia quidem sit gentium domina gloriae vetustate, sed Pannonia virtute? An divinam generis tui originem recensebo, quam tu non modo factis immortalibus, sed etiam nominis successione testaris?

41. *Pan. Lat.*, 2, 3, 3. The exercise of *cura* by the emperor is an ancient theme in Roman imperial theory: see J. Béranger, *Recherches sur l'aspect idéologique du principat*, Schweizer Beitr. zur Altertumswiss., 6 (1953) 186–217.

42. The reference is to Vergil *Aeneid*, 8, 184–279. See also K. Latte, *Römische Religionsgeschichte* (1960) 213–221 on the Roman background.

43. *Pan. Lat.*, 2, 2, 1:

> Quare si nunc Romae omnes magistratus et pontifices et sacerdotes iuxta parentes urbis et statores deos Herculis templa venerantur, quia partam aliquando ex victoria praedam a flumine Hibero et conscio occidui solis oceano ad pabula Tyrrhena compulerit et in Palatino iugo venturo tibi reliquerit vestigia, quanto tandem studio nos hic convenit, qui te praesentem intuemur deum toto quidem orbe victorem, sed nunc cum maxime in eadem occidentis plaga non pastorem trino capite deformem, sed prodigium multo taetrius opprimentem, quidquid spiritus et vocis habeamus, omne id in laudibus tuis non occupare modo, sed, si res poscat, absumere?

44. H. P. L'Orange, "Ein tetrarchisches Ehrendenkmal auf dem Forum Romanum," *Römische Mitteilungen* 53 (1938) 1–34, reprinted in his *Likeness and Icon* (1973) 131–157, at 137f, 143ff; and H. Kähler, *Das Fünfsäulendenkmal für die Tetrarchen auf dem Forum Romanum*, Mon. Artis Rom., 3 (1964) 6 and passim. Cf. G. Wissowa, *Religion und Kultur der Römer* (1912; 1971) 561f; K. Latte, *Römische Religionsgeschichte* (1960) 41f, and, for the military aspect, A. von Domaszewski, *Abhandlungen zur römischen Religion*, (1909; 1975) 16–18. On other representations of this rite in art, see I. Scott Ryberg, *Rites of the State Religion in Roman Art*, Memoirs, American Academy in Rome, 22 (1955) 104ff.

45. *Pan. Lat.*, 3, 2, 1; 3, 7.

46. *Pan. Lat.*, 3, 3, 4.

47. *Deum imperii nostri veneremur auctorem*: Letter of Honorius to Aurelius, Bishop of Carthage: *P.L.*, 48, 397a.

48. *Pan. Lat.*, 3, 3, 6.

49. *Pan. Lat.*, 3, 2, 4.

50. *Pan. Lat.*, 3, 3, 9–4, 1.

51. Menander, ed. Spengel, 370, 21ff.

52. *Pan. Lat.*, 4, 4.

53. See F. J. Dölger, "Das Sonnengleichnis in einer Weihnachtspredigt des Bischofs Zeno von Verona," *Antike und Christentum* 6 (1940–1950) 1–56. The image was widespread. See also Gregory of Nyssa *P.G.*, 46, 560a.

54. For the image of the chariot, cf. Eusebius *LC*, 3, 4, with H. A. Drake's note (*In Praise of Constantine* [1976]). See also the further exegesis bringing in the dimension of time, *LC*, 6, 5–6 and 8ff; above, n. 25.

55. *Pan. Lat.*, 4, 4, 1f:

> Et sane praeter usum curamque rei publicae etiam illa Iovis et Herculis cognata maiestas in Iovio Herculioque principibus totius mundi caelestiumque rerum similitudinem requirebat. Quippe isto numinis vestri numero summa omnia nituntur et gaudent: elementa quattuor et totidem anni vices et orbis quadrifariam duplici discretus oceano et emenso quater caelo lustra redeuntia et quadrigae solis et duobus caeli luminibus adiuncti Vesper et Lucifer. Sed neque sol ipse neque cuncta sidera humanas res tam perpetuo lumine intuentur quam vos tuemini, qui sine ullo fere discrimine dierum ac noctium illustratis orbem . . .

56. *Pan. Lat.*, 4, 3, 1:

O tempus quo merito quondam omnia nata esse credantur, cum eodem nunc confirmata videamus! O Kalendae Martiae, sicuti olim annorum volventium, ita nunc aeternorum auspices imperatorum!

57. Cf. above, *"Adventus,"* at nn. 83ff. and at n. 123. For portraiture on the coinage see also *RIC*, V¹, pl. 5, 78f; 6, 83–92; Aurelian, *RIC*, V¹, 7, 97–108; pl. 8, 9–passim. Probus, *RIC*, V², pl. 1–5. An important work touching on this question is R. Delbrueck, *Die Münzbildnisse von Maximinus bis Carinus* (1940).

58. A. D. Nock, "The Emperor's Divine Comes," *JRS* 37 (1947) 102–116, reprinted in *Essays on Religion and the Ancient World*, vol. 2 (1972) 653–675.

59. E.g., Toynbee, *Roman Medallions*, pl. 9, 2 with 174, 184, 214. We see in this context, as elsewhere, that the panegyrists could very skilfully pick up empire-wide themes, like that of Hercules on the coinage, and work them into a context that fitted local conditions and interests.

60. E.g., *RIC*, V², 24, 285–286 A.D.

61. Or AUGG: *RIC*, V², 255–256; cf. 25 undated CONCORDIA MILITUM: Diocletian receiving a victory from Iuppiter.

62. *RIC*, V², 250, 288.

63. Heraclea, 292–295 A.D., Antioch, 293 A.D., both CONCORDIA MILITUM, *RIC*, V², 289, 294; IOVI CONSERVATORI Tripoli, 285–290 A.D., *RIC*, V², 295.

64. At Ticinum, Rome, Siscia: *RIC*, VI, 283, 355, 358, 465.

65. At Heraclea, Cyzicus, Antioch, Alexandria: *RIC*, VI, 531–532, 580–581, 621–622, 667, 670, 675.

66. K. Baus, *Der Kranz in Antike und Christentum* (1940) 143–157, and T. Klauser, *"Aurum Coronarium,"* in *Ges. Schriften* (1974) 292–309.

67. *RIC*, VI, 379, 578, 457, 167.

68. Description of the relief: H. P. Laubscher, *Galeriusbogens*, 64–69.

69. Above, *"Adventus"* at nn. 61ff.

70. *Pan. Lat.*, 3, 6–12; M. P. Charlesworth, *"Pietas* and *Victoria*, the Emperor and the Citizen," *JRS* 33 (1943) 1–10.

71. *Pan. Lat.*, 4, 6, 1:

Statim itaque Gallias tuas, Caesar, veniendo fecisti. Siquidem illa celeritas, qua omnis ortus atque adventus tui nuntios praevertisti, cepit oppressam Gesoriacensibus muris pertinacem . . . manum piraticae factionis.

72. This imagery has a ceremonial background, which, however, did not enter the Byzantine accession ceremonial. See H. U. Instinsky, *Bischofsstuhl und Kaiserthron* (1955) 31–35, on the enthronisation of Pertinax in the Curia. Note the civilian context. The gold multiple described below, by contrast, shows the emperors in military dress. On the transition from civilian to military imperial imagery and ideology, see A. Alföldi, "Insignien und Tracht der römischen Kaiser," in *Die monarchische Repräsentation im römischen Kaiserreiche*, 161–186 (originally published in *Röm. Mitt.* 50 (1935) 43–68).

73. Gnecchi, 5, 7 (on Concordia, cf. *Pan. Lat.*, 2, 9). A similar motif with a different legend, VIRTUS AUGUSTOR, Gnecchi 4, 4; 5, had appeared under Carinus, showing two emperors standing, facing each other, one crowned by Sol, the other by Hercules. The legend of this latter piece, like other legends including FIDES MIL, emphasises the important link there existed between the emperor's performance in war and the legality of his rule. This was a practical point which

was by no means forgotten. The legitimate emperor, according to official propaganda, including panegyrics, was made by success, among other requirements which were less easy to identify. For Tetrarchic parallels to the VIRTUS AUGUSTOR multiple, see *RIC*, V², 251, 254, 290, 293, where also the later image of the enthroned emperors overshadowed by the wings of Victory (plate 50) is forecast, but complete frontality not yet achieved.

74. But cf. Gnecchi, 71, 6, Marcus Aurelius and Venus; reverse, Capitoline Triad enthroned frontally.

75. See on this development in imperial art, R. Brilliant, *Gesture and Rank in Roman Art* (1963) 163ff, and H. P. L'Orange, *Art Forms and Civic Life* (1965). On the arch of Galerius, above, "*Consecratio*," at nn. 185ff.

76. *Pan. Lat.*, 6, 14, 1; cf. "*Consecratio*" at nn. 185ff. *Pan. Lat.*, 4, 4; cf. above at n. 19.

77. *Pan. Lat.*, 6, 10.

78. *Pan. Lat.*, 6, 8, 2.

79. Wissowa, *Religion und Kultus* (1912; 1971) 338ff; cf. 448, n. 3. MacCormack, "Roma, Constantinopolis, the Emperor, and His Genius," *CQ* 25 (1975) 131–150.

80. See C. Koch, "Roma Aeterna," in *Religio, Studien zu Kult und Glauben der Römer* (1960) 142–175.

81. *RIC*, V¹, 103, 114, 358; *RIC*, V², 32, 62.

82. Except for Carausius, *RIC*, V², 497, 545, 549.

83. *RIC*, VI, 372; cf. 409; *RIC*, VII, 165, n. 22; 166 with 713.

84. J. M. C. Toynbee, *Roman Medallions*, pl. XXXVII, 3–8 *Roma* and *Constantinopolis*; pl. V, 3; VII, XXXVII, 2; XLIX, 2 *Roma*; pl. XXXVII, 9; XXXVIII, 1–4; XLVIII, *Constantinopolis*. Where capitals are shown singly, frontality is incomplete. See also "*Adventus*," n. 135.

85. *Pan. Lat.*, 6, 7, 6:

> Ut enim ille qui omnes aquas caelo et terris praebet Oceanus semper tamen in motibus suis totus est, ita tu potes imperium, Maximiane, donare, non potes non habere.

See, for the concept of the inalienability and indivisibility of dominion, be it divine or imperial, E. Peterson, *Der Monotheismus als politisches Problem* (1935) esp. 45–46.

86. *Pan. Lat.*, 6, 12, 1f. The image occurs in a related context in Claudian, who applies it to Theodosius, *IV cons.*, 49ff.

87. *Pan. Lat.*, 6, 12, 4: Inhaesit tibi ingenita maiestas.

88. *Pan. Lat.*, 6, 2, 1.

89. *Pan. Lat.*, 6, 2.

90. *Pan. Lat.*, 6, 3, 3.

91. *Pan. Lat.*, 6, 5, 3. Cf. Camille Jullian, *Histoire de la Gaule*, Vol. 7 (1926) 99–104.

92. *Qui te amant*: *Pan. Lat.*, 7, 2, 1. For Claudius Gothicus, see "*Consecratio*," n. 81.

93. *Pan. Lat.*, 6, 3, 4ff; 7, 4, 2ff.

94. *Pan. Lat.*, 9, 4.

95. *Pan. Lat.*, 7, 21, 6; cf. 7, 17 and above "*Adventus*," at nn. 111, 112.

96. *Pan. Lat.*, 7, 2, 3.

97. *Pan. Lat.*, 7, 4, 1.

98. *Pan. Lat.*, 7, 2, 2; 3, 1.

99. *Vetus illa imperatoriae domus praerogativa*: *Pan. Lat.*, 7, 2, 4.

100. *Non fortuita hominum consensio; non repentinus aliquis favoris ventus*: *Pan. Lat.*, 7, 3, 1.

101. *Omisso ambitu et suffragatione*: *Pan. Lat.*, 7, 2, 5.

102. *RIC*, VII, 467, 471–2, 374, etc., SOLI INVICTO COMITI, Constantine crowned by Sol, 320–322 A.D. Ticinum, 320–321 A.D.: *RIC*, VII, 375; Aquileia 320 A.D.: *RIC*, VII, 397; Sirmium 320 A.D.: *RIC*, VII, 468; Antioch 324–325 A.D.: *RIC*, VII, 685, SOLI COMITI AUG N, Sol handing Victory on globe to Constantine. Arles and Thessalonica, 317 A.D.: *RIC*, VII, 245; 500, FELICITAS PERPETUA SAECULI, Sol handing Victory on globe to Constantine. Ticinum 316 A.D.: *RIC*, VII, 368, SOLI COMITI CONSTANTINI AUG, Sol handing Victory on globe to Constantine. See also the related images, the emperor crowned by Victoria or presented with a victory on globe by her: Ticinum 316 A.D.: *RIC*, VII, 369, VICTORIOSO SEMPER. Same date and place *RIC*, VII, 368–369, VICTOR OMNIUM GENTIUM. Thessalonica 317 A.D.: *RIC*, VII, 500, VICTORIA AUGUSTORUM. *Ibid.*, VICTORIA CONSTANTINI AUG. 316 A.D.: *RIC*, VII, 368, RECTOR TOTIUS ORBIS, Constantine holding the zodiac crowned by Victoria. 326–330 A.D.: *RIC*, VII, 555, SALUS ET SPES REIPUBLICAE, Constantine crowned by Victoria, receiving victory on globe from turreted woman. *RIC*, VII, 374; 713f, GLORIA ROMANORUM, Constantine receiving a globe from Victoria.

103. *Pan. Lat.*, 7, 2, 2; 7, 4.

104. *Pan. Lat.*, 7, 8, 2:

> Universus in te consensit exercitus, te omnium mentes oculique signarunt et, quamquam tu ad seniores principes de summa re publica quid fieri placeret rettulisses, praevenerunt studio quod illi mox iudicio probaverunt. Purpuram statim tibi, cum primus copiam tui fecit egressus, milites utilitati publicae magis quam tuis adfectibus servientes iniecere lacrimanti. Neque enim fas erat diutius fieri principem consecratum.

105. The underlying thought here is that power should not be claimed by the emperor on his own behalf (cf. Augustine *De Civ. Dei*, 5, 19 on *dominationis cupiditas*), but bestowed on an individual unwilling to rule, whose exercise of power will therefore not be a tyranny. See J. Béranger, *Recherches sur l'aspect idéologique du principat*, Schweizer Beitr. zur Altertumswissenschaft, 6 (1953) 137–169, "Le refus du pouvoir."

106. Instinsky, "*Consensus universorum*," *Hermes* 75 (1940) 265–278.

107. Another example of this new use of the term *consecratus* is in Amm., 16, 10, 12: Nec in trabea socium privatum asscivit [Constantius], ut fecere principes consecrati.

108. *Pan. Lat.*, 7, 8, 2.

109. *Pan. Lat.*, 7, 2, 3.

110. *Pan. Lat.*, 7, 8, 3.

111. *Pan. Lat.*, 7, 4, 1.

112. Cf. above, "*Consecratio*" at nn. 113ff.

113. Camille Julian, *Histoire de la Gaule*, vol. 7 (1926) 3–98; cf. 110–115.

114. νόμος φύσεως: Eusebius *V.C.*, 1, 21.

115. *Ibid.* Eusebius' attitude, so far removed from the views of the earlier empire, became normative. Cf. Theodoret *H.E.*, 5, 25: Theodosius τοῖς υἱοῖς τὴν βασιλείαν διένειμε, with Claudian *III cons.*, 105–110, also on Theodosius.

116. Eusebius *V.C.*, 1, 22.

117. Eusebius *V.C.*, 1, 24.

118. *Ibid.* For the ceremonial aspects of victory on the coinage see above, n. 102; on the background to Eusebius' political theology, see E. Peterson, *Der Monotheismus als politisches Problem* (1935) 63f, 71ff, 78–84.

119. See F. Vittinghoff, *Der Staatsfeind in der röm. Kaiserzeit,* (1936).

120. *Pan. Lat.*, 9, 4 with *Pan. Lat.*, 12, 31.

121. Eusebius *V.C.*, 1, 6; 2, 3, etc.

122. Cf. J. Gagé, "Σταυρὸς νικοποιός, la victoire impériale dans l'empire chrétien," *Rev. d'hist. et de philosophie religieuses* 13 (1933) 370ff. For Constantine, see also Eusebius *H.E.*, ed. Bardy, 9, 9, 11:

> τούτῳ τῷ σωτηριώδει σημείῳ, τῷ ἀληθεῖ ἐλέγχῳ τῆς ἀνδρείας τὴν πόλιν ὑμῶν
> ἀπὸ ζυγοῦ τοῦ τυράννου διασωθεῖσαν ἠλευθέρωσα, ἔτι μὴν καὶ τὴν σύγκλητον
> καὶ τὸν δῆμον Ῥωμαίων τῇ ἀρχαίᾳ ἐπιφανείᾳ καὶ λαμπρότητι ἐλευθερώσας
> ἀποκατέστησα,

the inscription on the statue of Constantine in Rome (312 A.D.)

123. *Pan. Lat.*, 7, 14f.

124. Ticinum 315 A.D.: *RIC*, VII, 62; 364, and n. 36, SALUS REIPUBLICAE; K. Weitzmann, ed., *Age of Spirituality* (1979) 66.

125. See *RIC*, VII, 364, n. 36, and 62.

126. Cf. above, "*Consecratio*" at nn. 145f.

127. Cf. J. Deer, "Der Ursprung der Kaiserkrone," *Schweizer Beitr. zur allg. Geschichte* 8 (1950) 51–87, reprinted in his *Byzanz und das abendländische Herrschertum* (1977) 11–41.

128. Eusebius *V.C.*, 1, 22.

129. As implied in *Anon. Val.*, 64. See E. Stein, *Histoire du Bas-Empire*, Vol. 2 (1949) 47, n. 1, and M. McCormick, "Odoacer, Emperor Zeno and the Rugian Victory Legation," *Byzantion* 47 (1977) 212–222.

130. *De Cer.*, 93 (ed. Reiske) 428 cd. But contrast the proclamation of Julian as Augustus, Amm. 20, 4, 17–18, and of Hypatius during the Nika riot, Procopius *Wars*, 1, 24, 24. Cf. Averil Cameron, *Corippus*, Commentary on 2, 86f.

131. *Pan. Lat.*, 9, 26, 4f.:

> Fac igitur ut, quod optimum humano generi dedisti, permaneat in aeternum, omnesque Constantinus in terris degat aetates. Quamvis enim, imperator invicte, iam divina suboles tua ad rei publicae vota successerit et adhuc speretur futura numerosior, illa tamen erit vere beata posteritas ut, cum liberos tuos gubernaculis orbis admoveris, tu sis omnium maximus imperator.

132. I believe the speech to be genuine; cf. *Pan. Lat.*, 10, 37, 5: *Constantine Caesar incrementum maximum boni publici*, with Vergil *ecl.*, 4, 49: Cara deum suboles, magnum Iovis incrementum.

133. See Galletier, ed., *Pan. Lat.*, 2, 149; *Pan. Lat.*, 10, 3, 4ff.

134. *Pan. Lat.*, 9, 36, 5; cf. 10, 4, 5 *imperator optime*; 10, 3, 1 *Constantine maxime.*

135. *Pan. Lat.*, 10, 2.

136. Cf. *Pan. Lat.*, 6, 13–14; 7, 21, 4; 9, 26.

137. *Pan. Lat.*, 10, 4.

138. Eusebius *V.C.*, 4, 40; Libanius *Or.*, 59, 10–11; 22, 27–28; Julian *Or.*, 1, 10 (Bidez 14a); Themistius, 44ab; cf. 46d ff. and 2b.

139. Compare Nazarius *Pan. Lat.*, 10, 2 with Eusebius *L.C.*, 3, 1–4; 6, 1–2; *V.C.*, 1, 9; 4, 40.

140. Eusebius *V.C.*, 1, 2; 4, 68, and above, n. 25.

141. τὰ πανταχοῦ πάντα στρατόπεδα: Eusebius *V.C.*, 4, 68, 2. For an examination of the role of Constantius II during this period, see J. W. Leedom, "Constantius II, Three Revisions," *Byzantion* 48 (1978) 132–145.

142. See H. U. Instinsky, *Bischofsstuhl und Kaiserthron* (1955) 26f, esp. 35–37. Cf., on the other hand, Socrates *H.E.*, 1, 28 and 29, where the succession of Constantine's sons is explained with reference to Constantine's will and arrangements made during his lifetime.

143. Libanius, ed. Foerster, vol. 4, 201f.

144. Libanius *Or.*, 59, 13. The phrase is also used by Themistius *Or.*, 1, 2b.

145. See P. Petit, "Libanius et la *Vita Constantini*," *Historia* 1 (1950) 562–582.

146. Julian *Or.*, 1, 5 (Bidez 6c f.)

147. Julian *Or.*, 1, 7 (Bidez 8d f.)

148. Julian *Or.*, 3, 2 (Bidez 51b f.)

149. Themistius *Or.*, 1, 4bc; 6b, etc.

150. Gnecchi, 12, 1; *RIC*, VII, 576; Toynbee, *Roman Medallions*, 198. I prefer Bruuns' date 330 A.D. to Toynbee's 333 A.D.; the latter date would suggest that one of the Caesars was not represented, which is unsatisfactory, whereas, if the multiple is dated to 330 A.D., all the ruling emperors are shown. Also see Baus, *Der Kranz in Antike und Christentum* (1940) 203f, and M. R. Alföldi, *Die konstantinische Goldprägung*, (1963) 136f, catalogue no. 148, fig. 214.

151. See R. Brilliant, *Gesture and Rank in Roman Art* (1963) 181–188, and pl. 4, 64.

152. For this and related images see J. D. MacIsaac, "The Hand of God, a Numismatic Study," *Traditio* 31 (1975) 322–328, and A. Grabar, "Un Médaillon en or provenant de Mersine en Cilicie," *DOP* 16 (1951) 27–49.

153. M. R. Alföldi, *Goldprägung*, 93; Eusebius *V.C.*, 4, 66f. The dead Constantine is honoured as though still alive and wears diadem and purple.

154. Toynbee, *Roman Medallions*, 198; Gnecchi, 10, 2; *RIC*, VII, 580; Alföldi, *Goldprägung*, cat. 448, fig. 247, p. 118.

155. *RIC*, VII, 328; Toynbee, *Roman Medallions*, 198, n. 43.

156. *RIC*, VII, 626, n. 160 and 631.

157. *RIC*, VII, 583. Similar types and legends, Alföldi, *Goldprägung*, pl. 16, 17, 20; 108f, 112f.

158. Constantine's pre-eminent position is shown on two rarer types, showing him seated, handing a phoenix on a globe to a standing prince GLORIA SAECULI VIRTUS CAESS, *RIC*, VII, 283, n. 5; 328; or handing a simple globe to a prince GAUDIUM REI PUBLICAE, *RIC*, VII, 178.

159. Gnecchi, 9, 11 and 14, gold multiples of Constans, SALUS ET SPES REI PUBLICAE, three cuirassed emperors of equal height standing frontally with spear and shield; FELICITAS PERPETUA VOT V, three emperors enthroned. Gnecchi, 30, 2, showing a difference in rank between the three emperors: FELICITAS PERPETUA VOT V, three emperors enthroned, the central one nimbate and taller.

160. *RIC*, VII, 650 with pl. 22; also, Constantius II Caesar, Gnecchi, 32, 2; 3: three or four emperors under an arch; Constantius II Augustus, Gnecchi, 31, 14; 32, 1, two emperors under an arch; Gallus, Gnecchi, 33, 12, two emperors under an arch; Legends all FELICITAS ROMANORUM. Cohen, vol. 8, 51, 63, Julian Augustus, Victoria or Julian under arch, VICTORIA ROMANORUM, exergue SIRM; Jovian: Gnecchi, 34, 3, one emperor under an arch, GLORIA ROMANORUM. Further GLORIA ROMANORUM specimens: Cohen, vol. 8, 74, 4 Jovian: emperor under arch; parallel iconographies: Gnecchi, 34, 6, Valentinian I; Gnecchi, 35, 1, also in *RIC*, IX, 279, 29, Valens; Gnecchi 35, 3, *RIC*, IX, 279, 31, Valens. The latter two issues: 367–375 A.D.

161. Gnecchi, 36, 7, Theodosius GLORIA ROMANORUM; cf. Gnecchi, 36, 8.

162. See E. Baldwin Smith, *Architectural Symbolism of Imperial Rome and the Middle Ages* (Princeton, 1956) 140ff, with the earlier literature; O. von Simson, *Sacred Fortress. Byzantine Art and Statecraft in Ravenna* (1948) 82. See also J. G. Deckers, "Die Wandmalerei des tetrarchischen Lagerheiligtums im Luxor," *Römische Quartalschrift* 68 (1973) 1–34; R. Fellmann, "Le Camp de Dioclétien à Palmyre," *Mélanges Paul Collart* (1976) 173–191; but consult also G. de Francovich, *Il palatium de Teodorico a Ravenna e la cosidetta ‹architettura di potenza›. Problemi d'interpretazione di raffigurazioni architettoniche nell'arte tardoantica e altomedioevale* (1970).

163. See "*Adventus*" at n. 51; cf. Themistius, 2c.

164. See Procopius *Wars*, 1, 5, 2; 7 cf. 1, 6, 13; 1, 11, 2ff; 1, 21, 17ff; 1, 23 for Byzantine awareness of the difficulties of the Sassanian succession. On the position in Byzantium, H. G. Beck, "Senat und Volk von Konstantinopel," *Bayer. Akad. d. Wiss. Phil. Hist. Kl.* SB (1966), reprinted in his *Ideen und Realitäten in Byzanz* (1972) is fundamental. See also W. Sickel, "Das byzantinische Krönungsrecht bis zum 10. Jhdt.," *BZ* 7 (1898) 511–557.

165. *Pan. Lat.*, 11, 27, 5; cf. the commentary of H. Gutzwiller, *Die Neujahrsrede des Konsuls Claudius Mamertinus vor dem Kaiser Julian* (1942) *ad loc.*

166. Cf. Libanius *Or.*, 12, 27ff.

167. Libanius *Or.*, 12, 59:

> ἀλλὰ τίς δὴ λόγος ἀληθέστερος; θεὸς μὲν ἐξώρμησεν ἐκείνους οὐδὲν προεσκεμμένους, ἀλλ' ἔφθασε τὸν λογισμὸν ἡ φωνή. θεοῦ δὲ τοῦτο. πρόσταξις ἧκεν ἀδελφὴ τῆς προτέρας προστιθεῖσα θαλαττίῳ χλαμύδος βαφῇ λιθοκόλλητον ταινίαν φέρουσάν τι καὶ αὐτὴν καρποῦ θαλαττίου. ὁ δὲ ἔβλεπε πρὸς οὐρανόν, καὶ ἦν ὁμοίως ἥ τε δόσις ἥ τε λῆψις ἄμφω βουλῇ δαιμόνων.

Libanius' accounts of Julian's accession are not altogether consistent with each other; see P. Petit, "Recherches sur la publication et la diffusion des discours de Libanius," *Historia* 5 (1956) 479ff.

168. Amm., 15, 8.

169. Amm., 15, 8, 9:

> Dicere super his plura conantem, interpellans contio lenius prohibebat arbitrium summi numinis id esse non mentis humanae velut praescia venturi proclamans.

170. Amm., 20, 4, 14ff; 5, 10. See also J. Bidez, *La vie de l'empereur Julien* (1930) 183ff; J. Szidat, *Historischer Kommentar zu Ammianus Marcellinus Buch XX–XXI, Teil I, Die Erhebung Julians*, Historia Einzelschriften, 31 (1977) 84ff, 149ff, and the

excellent account in G. W. Bowersock, *Julian the Apostate* (Cambridge, Mass., 1978) 46ff.

171. Initially, coronation with a necklace was suggested, and Julian rejected this: Ammianus, 20, 4, 17. During the Nika riot, Hypatius was crowned with a necklace: Procopius *Wars* 1, 24, 24. Alföldi regards the coronation with a torque as of non-Roman origin, and as not a mere emergency resort: *Insignien*, 170ff. Shield-raising was practised by the Germans in the first century A.D.: Tacit. *Hist.* 4, 15, 1; cf. Szidat, *Historischer Kommentar*, 152ff; see also C. Walter, "Raising on a Shield in Byzantine Iconography," *REB* 33 (1975) 133–175, esp. 157ff, reprinted in his *Studies in Byzantine Iconography* (1977), no. 12. But according to W. Ensslin, "Zur Torqueskrönung und Schilderhebung bei der Kaiserwahl," *Klio* 35 (1942) 268–298, at 273ff, Julian's elevation on the shield and crowning were emergency resorts. Julian *Letter to the Athenians*, 284d: he did not want to accept the acclamation by the soldiers, or the crown, στέφανον; but later, pressed by the soldiers, he took the torque, μανιάκην, and put it on his head. In short, the torque did duty for the diadem. On this *Eigenkrönung*, see Szidat, *Historischer Kommentar*, 157. A. Selem, "L'atteggiamento storiografico di Ammiano nei confronti di Giuliano dalla proclamazione di Parigi alla morte di Costanzo," *Athenaeum* 49 (1971) 89–110, compares this text to the account of Ammianus.

172. Libanius *Or.*, 13, 33:

> Ἄγαμαι δὲ τῶν στρατιωτῶν ἐκείνων, οἳ στεφανούμενόν σε τοῖς τροπαίοις ὁρῶντες οὐκ ἤνεγκαν μὴ περιθεῖναι τὸν ἐκ λίθων στέφανον.

173. Julian *Letter*, 284b–285a; cf. *ep.* 51, to the Jews (Wright), urging the Jews to pray for his rule to God: τῷ καταξιώσαντι στέψαι με τῇ ἀχράντῳ αὐτοῦ δεξιᾷ, and ep. 21 (ep. 60 Bidez) to the Alexandrians . . . : ἡμῶν, οὓς οἱ θεοὶ πάντες, ἐν πρώτοις δὲ ὁ μέγας Σάραπις ἄρχειν ἐδικαίωσαν τῆς οἰκουμένης. And see, with this, L. Budde, "Julian-Helios-Sarapis und Helena-Isis," *Archäologischer Anzeiger* (1972) 630–642, on a pottery lamp.

174. Amm., 20, 5, 10:

> Nocte tamen, quae declarationis Augustae praecesserat diem, iunctioribus proximis rettulerat imperator, per quietem aliquem visum, ut formari Genius publicus solet, haec obiurgando dixisse: 'Olim Iuliane vestibulum aedium tuarum observo latenter, augere tuam gestiens dignitatem, et aliquotiens tamquam repudiatus abscessi: Si ne nunc quidem recipior, sententia concordante multorum, ibo demissus et maestus. Id tamen retineto imo corde, quod tecum non diutius habitabo.'

This passage has an almost exact parallel in Suetonius *Galba*, 4: among the omens of his empire is a dream in which Fortuna tells Galba that she has visited him, is impatient with waiting and will pass to another unless he admits her. For Julian, cf. Ammianus, 25, 2, 3: the *genius publicus* departs from him.

175. See G. Dagron, "L'empire romain d'orient au IVᵉ siècle et les traditions politiques de l'Hellénisme," *Travaux et mémoires* 3 (1968) 62ff; see also J. Geffcken, *Kaiser Julianus* (1914) esp. 45ff, and his *The Last Days of Greco-Roman Paganism* (tr. S. MacCormack) (1978) 136ff. F. Dvornik, "The Emperor Julian's Reactionary Ideas on Kingship," in *Late Classical and Medieval Studies in Honour of A. M. Friend* (1955) 71–81.

176. In the occasion of this panegyric, accession, *adventus*, and consulship

overlap, as emerges from Socrates *H.E.*, 3, 26: after burying Julian, Jovian reached Dadastana: Ἔνθα καὶ Θεμίστιος ὁ φιλόσοφος μετὰ τῶν ἄλλων συγκλητικῶν ἀπαντήσας (the technical term for an official welcome, above "*Adventus*" at n. 258) τὸν ὑπατικὸν ἐπ' αὐτοῦ (scil. Jovian) διεξῆλθε λόγον, ὃν ὕστερον καὶ ἐν Κωνσταντίνου πόλει ἐπὶ τοῦ πλήθους ἐπεδείξατο. The official nature of the oration is emphasised by its being repeated before the people of Constantinople.

177. Themistius 64b:

> Ἀλλὰ βούλει γνῶναι τὴν παρὰ φιλοσοφίας συντέλειαν; νόμον ἔμψυχον εἶναί φησι τὸν βασιλέα, νόμον θεῖον ἄνωθεν ἥκοντα ἐν χρόνῳ τοῦ δι' αἰῶνος χρηστοῦ, ἀπορροὴν ἐκείνης τῆς φύσεως, πρόνοιαν ἐγγυτέρω τῆς γῆς, ἁπανταχοῦ πρὸς ἐκεῖνον ὁρῶντα, πανταχοῦ πρὸς τὴν μίμησιν τεταμένον, ἀτεχνῶς διογενῆ καὶ διοτρεφῆ, καθάπερ Ὅμηρος λέγει, κοινωνοῦντα τῷ θεῷ καὶ τῶν λοιπῶν ἐπικλήσεων, ξένιον, ἱκέσιον, φίλιον, ἐπικάρπιον, ἑάων δοτῆρα, δικαιοσύνης χορηγὸν, ῥαστώνης ταμίαν, πρύτανιν εὐδαιμονίας. ταύτας εἰσφέρουσι τὰς εἰσφορὰς φιλόσοφοι βασιλεῦσιν οἱ μὴ ψευδώνυμοι.

On the circumstances of the election, see 65 c–d: it occurred οὐκ ἐν σχολῇ, οὐκ ἐν εἰρήνῃ, οὐδέ ἐνδιδόντος τοῦ καιροῦ θεραπείας καὶ προσαγγελίας καὶ δεκατισμούς, ἀλλ' ὡς ἐν ἀκμῇ τῆς Ἐνυοῦς ἐν τοῖς ξίφεσιν, ἐν τοῖς δόρασι φέροντες τὰς ψήφους . . .

178. This is an important concept; see G. Dagron, "L'empire romain d'orient au IVe siècle et les traditions politiques de l'Hellénisme," *Travaux et mémoires* 3 (1968) 127–138. For Byzantium, see H. Hunger, *Prooimion, Elemente der byzantinischen Kaiseridee in den Arengen der Urkunden* (1964) 117–122.

179. Themistius, 65c ff.

180. Themistius, 65b.

181. Note the neat phrase 65c: the soldiers acclaimed κληρονόμον τῆς ἀλουργίδος τὸν κληρονόμον τῆς ἀρετῆς.

182. Themistius, 73b. On the election of Valens, see Amm., 26, 2, 6–10, Valentinian's speech before the army asserting his own right to make the choice, which the soldiers assented to. The event crystallised thinking on the nature of imperial power and the right of the senior emperor to elect his colleague. See Philostorgius *H.E.*, 8, 8 and Theodoret *H.E.*, 4, 5: it was for the soldiers to elect Valentinian, but once elected, he says: ἐμὸν λοιπόν, οὐκ ὑμέτερον τὸ περὶ τῶν κοινῶν διασκοπεῖσθαί πραγμάτων.

183. See E. Kantorowicz, *The King's Two Bodies* (1957) 296–8. For the documentation of the actual phrase see Hans Walther, *Proverbia sententiaeque Latinitatis Medii Aevi. Lateinische Sprichwörter und Sentenzen des Mittelalters in alphabetischer Abordnung* 5 (1967) 919.

184. Themistius, 73c–74a:

> μὴ γὰρ οἴεσθε, ὦ γενναῖοι, τοὺς στρατιώτας κυρίους εἶναι τηλικαύτης χειροτονίας, ἀλλ' ἄνωθεν αὐτὴ κάτεισιν ἡ ψῆφος, ἄνωθεν ἡ ἀνάρρησις τελειοῦται—τοῦτο δέ φησιν Ὅμηρος ἡ τοῦ Διὸς βουλή—ταῖς τῶν ἀνθρώπων διακονίαις. τοὐντεῦθεν οὖν ὑμέτερον δεῖξαι τῷ θεῷ τοὺς στρατιώτας διακονήσαντας. ὡς εἰ μὲν τῷ κράτει μόνῳ θαρσοίητε, δόξετε ἀκριβῶς παρὰ τῶν ὅπλων εἰληφέναι τὴν δυναστείαν, εἰ δὲ τῷ κατ' ἀρετὴν ὑπερέχειν, ἐκ τοῦ οὐρανοῦ φανήσεσθε προβεβλημένοι. τοῦτο γὰρ τῆς ἐκεῖθεν χειροντονίας σημεῖόν ἐστιν, οὐ χρυσοῦς ἀετὸς οὐδὲ γράμματα πολυτίμητα οὐδὲ φλήναφοι, ἀλλὰ γνώμη πρὸς ἐκεῖνον

ὁρῶσα καὶ πρὸς τὸν ἐκείνου ϛῆλον συντεταμένη. . . . ἥ τε γὰρ παρὰ τοῦ πλήθους ἀνάρρησις τὸ ἔντιμον ἔχει, ἥ τε παρ' ἑνὸς τοῦ κρατοῦντος·ἄμφω ταῦτα ἐφ' ὑμῶν συνδεδράμηκε.

Cf. elsewhere Themistius' emphasis on philanthropia as a godlike quality: e.g., Or. 7, on the victory over Procopius.

185. Themistius Or. 9, 120cd.

186. Themistius Or. 9, 123bc, 124b ff., referring to the honours Valentinian II gained by his descent; 124d ff., the election.

187. Symmachus Or. 1, 1f.

188. Symmachus Or. 1, 11f. For the unfavourable circumstances of Jovian's election according to Themistius, see above, n. 177.

189. Cf. E. Kantorowicz, "Oriens Augusti—Lever du Roi," DOP 17 (1963) 119–177, esp. 119–135.

190. Symmachus Or., 1, 7:

> Urgeor, Auguste venerabilis, ut mihi tamquam aliquod lumen astrorum post privatas exuvias iam purpuratus in oratione nascaris. sentio divinae lucis adflatum, ut ferme adsolet, cum iubar emicat et mundi splendor aperitur. aut cum solis emergente purpura ruborem ducit aurora, tandem rogatus exorere sideri novo similis, quod in rediviva diei erumpentis officia perfusum sacris undis adtollit oceanus! procedat imperii candidatus insignis suis armis ante quam publicis, nam semper enituit, qui electioni omnium solus occurrit. Galea diademate, sceptris pila mutentur: auri praemium ferri labore meruisti; haec in te mutari sola potuerunt, nam quod spectat ad mores, unum hoc tibi fortuna addidit, ut plura curares.

191. But cf. the emphasis on official splendour by R. MacMullen, "Some Pictures in Ammianus Marcellinus," Art Bulletin 46 (1964) 435–455.

192. Symmachus Or., 3, 5:

> Si quis mihi Zeuxis discoloribus ceris haec comitia spectanda digereret, si quis Apelleus imitator illud caeleste iudicium verisimili adflatu artis animaret, viserent posteri vix credenda miracula. hinc Augustum, inde legiones et inter hos medium regni inpuberem candidatum; anceps diu utrimque certamen et cunctis alacri favore plaudentibus patrem sero cedentem. turmas supplices, cuneos ambientes digna tabula saeculis, digna pictura temporibus quibus magis utiles videmus eligi quam volentes!

193. Themistius Or., 15, 191ab; cf. W. Hartke, Römische Kinderkaiser, (1951) 247. On awareness of ancient art in general, C. Mango, "Antique Statuary and the Byzantine Beholder," DOP 17 (1963) 55–75.

194. Amm., 27, 6, 10–11:

> Nondum finita oratione, dictis cum assensu laeto auditis, . . . milites aliųs alium anteire festinans, tamquam utilitatis et gaudiorum participes, Gratianum declararunt Augustum . . . Quo viso maiore fiducia Valentinianus exultans, corona indumentisque supremae fortunae ornatum, filium osculatus . . .

195. Amm., 26, 4, 3:

> Universorum sententiis concinentibus—nec enim audebat quisquam refragari—Augustum pronuntiavit, decoreque imperatorii cultus ornatum, et tempora diademate redimitum, in eodem vehiculo secum reduxit.

Cf. Philostorgius H.E., 8, 8.

196. Amm., 15, 8, 17.

197. For Valentinian II, see the brief account, Amm., 26, 1, 5.

198. Amm., 25, 5, 7–8:

Quod si gravis quidam aequitatis spectator, in ultimo rerum spiritu factum criminatur improvide, nauticos idem iustius incusabit, si amisso perito navigandi magistro, saevientibus flabris et mari, clavos regendae navis cuilibet periculi socio commiserunt. His ita caeco quodam iudicio fortunae peractis . . .

R. von Haehling, "Ammians Darstellung der Thronbesteigung Jovians im Lichte der heidnisch-christlichen Auseinandersetzung," in *Bonner Festgabe Johannes Straub* (1977) 347–358, regards Ammianus' report of Jovian's accession as biased against this emperor; a more balanced view is D. Conduché, "Ammien Marcellin et la mort de Julien," *Latomus* 24 (1965) 359–380, at 363ff. See also Themistius' account of Jovian's election, above, n. 177.

199. Amm., 26, 6, 12–19; 9, 1–10.

200. Amm., 26, 1, 5:

Ut aptus ad id quod quaerebatur . . . Valentinianus, nulla discordante sententia, numinis adspiratione caelestis electus est.

201. Amm., 26, 2, 2f.

202. E.g., Gnecchi, 18, 1 and *RIC*, IX, 116, 1.

203. *RIC*, IX, 16, 367–375 A.D.

204. Trier, *RIC*, IX, 21, 375–378 A.D., Valens, Gratian, Valentinian II; 24, 378–383 A.D., Gratian, Valentinian; on issues for Gratian, one emperor is smaller; for Theodosius, they are of equal size. *RIC*, IX, 68, Arles, Maximus 383–388 A.D.; 76f. Milan, Gratian, Valentinian II, Theodosius, 383–388 A.D.; 98 Aquileia, the same emperors, 378–83 A.D.; no. 40, 383–388 A.D., Valentinian II, Theodosius, Arcadius; *RIC*, IX, 145 no. 2, Siscia, Valentinian I, 364–367 A.D.; 159, Sirmium, Gratian, Valentinian II, Theodosius, 378–383 A.D.; two emperors, one smaller; 180, 34 Thessalonica, Gratian, Theodosius, Valentinian II, 378–383 A.D.; 2, London, 383–388 A.D., Theodosius.

205. Thessalonica, Gratian, Valentinian II, Theodosius, 378–383 A.D., *RIC*, IX, 179f, and 182, n. 41.

206. May 19, 387 A.D., O. Seeck, *Regesten der Kaiser und Päpste . . . 311–476 n. Chr.* (Stuttgart, 1919) 272: should the VICTORIA AUGG of Valentinian II, *RIC*, IX, 182, 41 be reclassified to a later period?

207. Trier 383–8 A.D., *RIC*, IX, 28; Milan, 79, no. 15; Aquileia, 105, no. 52. Cf. *Année épigraphique* 186 (1969–70), inscription from Monte Regole, Italy, 361–364 A.D., Bono reip na[to] d. n. Fl. Cl. Juliano PF victori ac triumphatori semp Aug M(ilia) LXXXV.

208. Claudian *IV cons.*, 121ff.

209. R. Delbrueck, *Spätantike Kaiserporträts* (1933) 179–182, pl. 79.

210. Cf. Themistius, 189c.

211. Claudian *IV cons.*, 47. On the rehabilitation of Theodosius the elder as *auctor* of the Theodosian dynasty, and the urban Roman context, see D. Vera, "Le statue del senato di Roma in onore di Flavio Teodosio e l'equilibrio dei poteri imperiali in età teodosiana," *Athenaeum* 57 (1979) 381–403.

212. *Pan. Lat.*, 12, 5.

213. *Pan. Lat.*, 12, 6, 1.

214. Themistius *Or.*, 14, 182b:

προήγαγε δὲ σε εἰς τὴν ἁλουργίδα οὐκ ἀγχιστεία γένους, ἀλλ' ἀρετῆς ὑπεροχὴ, οὐδὲ οἰκειότητος ἐγγύτης, ἀλλὰ ῥώμης ἀπόδειξις καὶ ἀνδρείας. καὶ σοφῶς Γρατιανὸς καὶ πολιᾶς, οὐ νεότητος ἐπαξίως, ὅτι μὴ τὸν οἰκειότατον ἄριστον, ἀλλὰ τὸν ἄριστον ὑπέλαβεν οἰκειότατον. καὶ καλῶς ἑαυτοῦ πεποίηται ψῆφον, ἣν προλαβὼν ὁ καιρὸς ἐψηφίζετο.

(Cf. 182c–d).

215. Themistius, 181a f.
216. Themistius, 182a.
217. Cf. above, "*Adventus*" at n. 95f; Themistius' oration is an early indicator of the emergence of the Senate and people of Constantinople in imperial elections, which is traced by H. G. Beck, "Senat und Volk von Konstantinopel," *Bayer. Akad. d. Wiss. Phil. Hist. Kl.*, SB (1966), in his *Ideen und Realitäten in Byzanz* (1972). On the political formation of Constantinople see G. Dagron, *Naissance d'une capitale, Constantinople et ses institutions de 330 à 451* (1974). Cf. Socrates *H.E.*, 3, 11, after his accession Julian opened the temples:

θυσίας δὲ ἐπετέλει τῇ Κωνσταντίνου πόλεως Τύχῃ δημοσίᾳ ἐν τῇ βασιλικῇ, ἔνθα καὶ τὸ τῆς Τύχης ἵδρυται ἄγαλμα.

Cf. above, n. 174.

218. Themistius, 188c.
219. Themistius *Or.*, 19.
220. Themistius *Or.*, 15, 189b. On the emperor's imitation of God in Christian terms, see R. Farina, *L'impero e l'imperatore cristiano in Eusebio di Cesarea* (1966) 107ff. Cf. "*Consecratio*," nn. 268–269.
221. *Od.*, 19, 109–114, cited by Plato, *Republic* 2, 6.
222. Themistius, 188c–189a:

Καὶ γὰρ τὴν ἀρχὴν ἐφεξῆς ταξιαρχοῦντα καὶ στρατηγοῦντα τῷ τῆς βασιλείας στεφάνῳ Γρατιανὸς ἀνεκήρυξεν. ἀλλ' εὖ τοι γίνωσκε, ὦ χρηστὲ, ὡς οὔτε κάλλος οὔτε μέγεθος οὔτε ὠκύτης οὔτε ἀλκὴ τὸν ἀγαθὸν ποιεῖ βασιλέα, εἰ μὴ τι ἴνδαλμα φέροι ἐν τῇ ψυχῇ τῆς πρὸς τὸν θεὸν ὁμοιώσεως. τοὐντεῦθεν οὖν καὶ αὐτοὶ ζητῶμεν καὶ τὸν ποιητὴν παρακαλῶμεν διδάσκειν ἡμᾶς ὅπως ἄν τις χαμαὶ βαδίζων καὶ σάρκα ἠμφιεσμένος ἔχειν τὸ ἴνδαλμα νομισθείη τοῦ ὑπὲρ τῆς ἄκρας ἁψῖδος καὶ ὑπὲρ ἅπαν τὸ ὂν ἱδρυμένου. ἀκούωμεν τοίνυν αὐτοῦ· οὐ γὰρ εἰς μακρὰν ἡμᾶς ἀνακαλεῖται, ὁπόθεν οἴεται γνωματεύειν τὸν θεοειδῆ βασιλέα·

Ὥστε τευ, φησί, βασιλῆος ἀμύμονος, ὅστε θεουδὴς
εὐδικίας ἀνέχῃσι· φέρῃσι δὲ γαῖα μέλαινα
πυροὺς καὶ κριθάς· βρίθῃσι δὲ δένδρεα καρπῷ,
τίκτει δ' ἔμπεδα πάντα, θάλασσα δὲ παρέχει ἰχθῦς
ἐξ εὐηγεσίης· ἀρετῶσι δὲ λαοὶ ὑπ' αὐτοῦ.

ἡ δίκῃ οὖν καὶ ἡ εὐδικία τὸ ἔργον τῆς τέχνης ταύτης ἐστί, καὶ ἐντεῦθεν τὸ θεοείκελον καὶ θεοειδές. καὶ κινδυνεύει ὁ θεῖος Πλάτων παρ' Ὁμήρου αὐτὸ μεμαθηκέναι. καὶ γὰρ ἐκεῖνος τὴν δικαιοσύνην μετὰ φρονήσεως ὁμοίωσιν λέγει πρὸς τὸν θεόν.

223. αὐτάρκης σὺ σεαυτῷ, Themistius, 189d.
224. Themistius, 193c.
225. Themistius, 225d:

Ἥκεις, ὦ Λυκόεργε, ἐμὸν ποτὶ πίονα νηόν,
Ζηνὶ φίλος καὶ πᾶσιν Ὀλύμπια δώματ' ἔχουσι.

δίζω ἠὲ θεὸν μαντεύσομαι, ἢ ἄνθρωπον.
ἀλλ' ἔτι καὶ μᾶλλον θεὸν ἔλπομαι, ὦ Λυκόεργε.

226. Themistius, 227c–228a:

> ἆρα διστάσεις καὶ ἐπισκέψῃ πότερον θεὸς ἢ ἄνθρωπος εἰσελήλυθεν ἡμῖν εἰς
> τὸν νεών, καὶ οὐκ ἀποφανῇ θαρραλεώτερον ἢ περὶ τῆς ψάμμου ὁπόσῃ ἐστὶν ἐν
> τῇ γῇ, τούτῳ τῷ βασιλεῖ προσήκειν τῆς ἄνωθεν προσηγορίας; . . . ἅτε νόμῳ ἐμ-
> ψύχῳ ὄντι καὶ οὐκ ἐν γράμμασιν ἀμεταθέτοις καὶ ἀσαλεύτοις. διὰ τοῦτο γάρ, ὡς
> ἔοικε, βασιλείαν ἐκ τοῦ οὐρανοῦ κατέπεμψεν εἰς τὴν γῆν ὁ θεός, ὅπως ἂν εἴη
> καταφυγὴ τῷ ἀνθρώπῳ ἀπὸ τοῦ νόμου τοῦ ἀκινήτου ἐπὶ τὸν ἔμπνουν καὶ ζῶντα.

227. This possibly concerns the rioters in Antioch in 387; see Hardoin's note
in Dindorf's edition of Themistius, 637; cf. Browning, "The Riot of A.D. 387 in
Antioch. The Role of the Theatrical Claques in the Later Empire," *JRS* 42 (1952)
13–20, reprinted in his *Studies in Byzantine History, Literature and Education* (1977).

228. Proverbs, 21, 1; the idea was also articulated in a purely Greek tradition—Pindar *Pyth.*, 4, 272–274: It is easy to shake a city, but hard to build it:

εἰ μὴ θεὸς ἀγεμόνεσσι κυβερνατὴρ γένηται—

and in Christianity at this time: Theodoret *H.E.*, 4, 3, letter by Athanasius to
Jovian on the faith of Nicea:

> οὕτω γὰρ ἀληθῶς καὶ τὴν καρδίαν ἔχοις ἐν χειρὶ Θεοῦ, καὶ τὴν βασιλείαν μετ'
> εἰρήνης πολλαῖς ἐτῶν περιόδοις ἐπιτελέσαις.

229. Themistius, 229ab:

> πεπίστευκε γὰρ εὖ ποιῶν τῷ λόγῳ τοῦ 'Ασσυρίου, ὅς τὴν καρδίαν τοῦ βασι-
> λέως λέγει ἐν τῇ τοῦ θεοῦ παλάμῃ δορυφορεῖσθαι, ἥν οὐχ οἶόν τε γράμμασι
> θανατηφόροις ἑαυτὴν συνεπιδοῦναι, ἀλλ' ἀνάγκη τὸν ἐκεῖνα τὰ γράμματα γρά-
> φοντα εὐχερῶς ἐξολισθαίνειν τῆς χειρὸς τῆς ἀεὶ χορηγούσης ζωήν. ἄνωθέν τοι,
> βασιλεῦ, ἡ πολιτεία τὸ τῆς θειότητος ὄνομα ὑμῖν ἐπεφήμισεν . . . ὅτι μόνῳ θεῷ
> καὶ βασιλεῖ ἐν ἐξουσίᾳ ἐστὶ ζωὴν ἐπιδοῦναι.

Cf. Themistius, 230a.

230. *Pan. Lat.*, 12, 3, 1–2:

> Det igitur mihi sermonis huius auspicium ille felicitatis publicae auspex dies
> qui te primus inauguravit imperio. Nam ut divinis rebus operantes in eam caeli
> plagam ora convertimus a qua lucis exordium est, sic ego vota verborum quae
> olim nuncupaveram soluturus id oratione mea tempus aspiciam quo Romana lux
> coepit.

A. Lippold, "Herrscherideal und Traditionsverbundenheit im Panegyricus des
Pacatus," *Historia* 17 (1968) 228–250, analyses this panegyric in terms of the concepts which traditionally were used to validate an emperor's accession (230f)
and dominion.

231. *Pan. Lat.*, 12, 3, 5–6:

> In integro itaque rem totam esse faciamus et in quodam orbis terrarum comitio
> quaeri putemus quisnam sit ille qui debeat tantam molem subire et nutantia Ro-
> manae rei fata suscipere. Nonne is omnium suffragiis hominum tributim cen-
> turiatimque legeretur, cui felix patria, cui domus clara, cui forma divina, cui
> aetas integra, cui militarium civiliumque rerum usus contigisset?

232. *Pan. Lat.*, 12, 4ff.

233. *Pan. Lat.*, 12, 11, 1–2:

> Argumento est dies ille communis boni auctor quo tu, cum ad suscipiendam rem publicam vocabaris, oblatum imperium deprecatus es; nec id ad speciem tantumque ut cogi videreris, sed obnixe et diu et velut impetraturus egisti. Quippe aberat causa fingendi. Non enim te princeps solus et domi et tanquam temptaret ambibat, sed publice et in comitio et ut aliud iam facere non posset, prorsus ut, nisi imperium adfectu simplici noluisses, potueris velle securus.

Cf. J. Béranger, *Recherches sur l'aspect idéologique du principat* (1953) 137–169.

234. *Pan. Lat.*, 12, 11, 4f.

235. *Pan. Lat.*, 12, 12, 1f.

236. *Pan. Lat.*, 12, 11, 4, on Arcadius. Claudian, *IV cons.*, 121–127, on Honorius:

> Hoc nobilis ortu
> nasceris aequaeva cum maiestate creatus
> nullaque privatae passus contagia sortis.
> omnibus acceptis ultro te regia solum
> protulit et patrio felix adolescis in ostro,
> membraque vestitu numquam violata profano
> in sacros cedidere sinus.

(Cf. Claudian *III cons.*, 8ff) and see also Claudian *IV cons.* 379–380:

> Nostro nec debes regna favori,
> quae tibi iam *natura* dedit.

237. Claudian *IV cons.*, 18f. The other sources are quoted in A. Lippold, *Theodosius der Grosse und seine Zeit* (Stuttgart, 1968) 138, n. 2.

238. On Honorius born in the palace, see Claudian *IV cons.*, 121ff. An extended dynastic statement of the Christian empire was made in the next generation in visual terms by Galla Placidia. The depiction of her salvation from shipwreck in San Giovanni Evangelista comprised portrait busts in medallions of members of the houses of Valentinian and Theodosius: see R. Farioli, "Ravenna paleocristiana scomparsa," *Felix Ravenna* 83 (1961) 5–88, esp. pp. 41–50 on S. Giovanni Evangelista; and now, F. W. Deichmann, *Ravenna, Hauptstadt des spätantiken Abendlandes, Kommentar* 1 (1974) 107–123, where the hypothesis that these medallions covered the entire Christian empire back to Constantine is disproved (115). Cf. Ausonius, *gratiarum actio* 11, Gratian to Ausonius, palmatam tibi misi in qua divus Constantius *parens noster* intextus est.

239. Claudian *VI cons.*, 361–493.

240. Claudian *VI cons.*, 524ff.

241. Delbrueck, *Consulardiptychen*, no. 2, text 91f; Volbach, *Elfenbeinarbeiten*, no. 35.

242. E.g., the fifth century Western diptych of Roma and Constantinopolis, Delbrueck, *Consulardiptychen*, 38; Volbach, *Elfenbeinarbeiten*, 38 and below, at nn. 308f.

243. Rutilius Namatianus *De red.*, 1, 47ff.

244. Themistius, 189bc:

> . . . ἰοὺ ἰοὺ ὁπόσα λέγει ἀγαθὰ ἀκολουθεῖν ἡ Καλλιόπη· εὐθηνεῖσθαι μὲν αὐτῷ τὰ λήια, εὐθηνεῖσθαι δὲ τὰ δένδρα καὶ τὰς ἀμπέλους, τίκτεσθαι δὲ πολλὰ μὲν ζῷα, πολλοὺς δὲ ἀνθρώπους, ἅπαντα ἔμπεδα καὶ βιώσιμα· δωροφορεῖν δὲ οὐ

μόνον τὴν γῆν τοὺς καρποὺς, ἀλλὰ καὶ τὴν θάλασσαν τοὺς ἰχθύας. βαβαὶ, ὁπόση δύναμις τῆς εὐδικίας, ἧς διικνεῖται τὸ κέρδος οὐ μόνον εἰς τὰ ἀρχεῖα καὶ τὰ δικαστήρια, ἀλλὰ καὶ εἰς τὰ ζῷα καὶ εἰς τὰ φυτὰ καὶ τὰ σπέρματα καὶ τὰ ἔμβρυα.

Cf. 180cd, delivered in 379:

ἡβᾶν δὲ αὖθις ὑπέλαβον, ἡνίκα ἐπυθόμην ἐν γράμμασι παρὰ τοῦ κρατίστου τῶν ἡμετέρων ζακόρων ὄψεσθαι τὴν χρυσῆν γενεὰν ἐπανήκουσαν, ὄψεσθαι ἡμᾶς βασιλείαν ὁλόκληρον καὶ ἀρτίπουν, λάμπουσαν τοῖς κάλλεσιν ἀμφοτέροις, τοῖς τε ψυχῆς καὶ τοῦ σώματος.

245. Themistius, 189a f.; cf. Amm., 22, 10, 6. 'Personified Justice' was a frequently used political concept; see E. Kantorowicz, "ΣΥΝΘΡΟΝΟΣ ΔΙΚΗΙ," in his *Selected Studies* (1965) 1–6.

246. Claudian *IV cons.*, 98–99:

Illi iustitiam confirmavere triumphi
praesentes docuere deos.

247. Claudian *IV cons.*, 135–153.
248. Claudian *IV cons.*, 172–183:

Tenebris involverat atra
lumen hiems densosque Notus collegerat imbres.
sed mox, cum solita miles te voce levasset,
nubila dissolvit Phoebus pariterque dabantur
sceptra tibi mundoque dies: caligine liber
Bosphorus adversam patitur Calchedona cerni.
nec tantum vicina nitent, sed tota repulsis
nubibus exuitur Thrace, Pangaea renident
insuetosque palus radios Maeotia vibrat.
nec Boreas nimbos aut sol ardentior egit:
imperii lux illa fuit; praesagus obibat
cuncta nitor risitque tuo natura sereno.

249. The two wreaths: Themistius, 181d f.; cf. above, "*Adventus*" n. 132. Earth and sea, Themistius 207b; cf. above at n. 73 for Diocletian.

250. Themistius, 182d: βασιλέα δὲ βασιλεὺς ἀναδεῖ καὶ οὐκ ἐλαττοῦται διδοὺς, ἀλλὰ προσλαμβάνει. Cf. above, n. 25 on Eusebius.

251. Themistius, 188c:

καὶ γὰρ τὴν ἀρχὴν ἐφεξῆς ταξιαρχοῦντα καὶ στρατηγοῦντα τῷ τῆς βασιλείας στεφάνῳ Γρατιανὸς ἀνεκήρυξεν.

252. Claudian records that Honorius, like Julian and other emperors after him up to Phocas, was raised on the shield (*IV cons.*, 174): see Ensslin, "Zur Torqueskrönung und Schilderhebung," *Klio* 35 (1942) 268–290; Ostrogorsky, "Zur Kaisersalbung und Schilderhebung," *Historia* 4 (1955) 246–256, at 252f. In later Byzantine art, the shield is sometimes shown with stars upon it (see H. P. L'Orange, *Studies on the Iconography of Cosmic Kingship* (1953) fig. 76) and may have served as a replacement for the starry globe upon which the consecrated emperor was enthroned before the empire became Christian.

253. Claudian *III cons.*, 110: Tibi pacatum praesenti traderet orbem.
254. Claudian *III cons.*, 111ff.
255. Claudian *IV cons.*, 565ff; for *VI cons.*, see above, "*Adventus*," at nn. 184ff.

256. *Pan. Lat.*, 7, 7, 5:

> Iam tunc enim caelestis suffragiis ad salutem rei publicae vocabaris, cum . . .
> repentinus tuus adventus inluxit, ut non advectus cursu publico, sed divino
> quodam curriculo videreris.

257. Kantorowicz, "Oriens Augusti," *DOP* 17 (1963) 119ff; Claudian *III cons.*, 131.

258. Not everyone will agree. See E. Kitzinger, "A Marble Relief of the Theodosian Period," *DOP* 14 (1960) 17–42, reprinted in his *The Art of Byzantium and the Medieval West, Selected Studies* (1976) 1–31.

259. Claudian *IV cons.*, 214ff.

260. E.g., *RIC*, IX, 179, 33, and pl. 10, 3 GLORIA REIPUB, for Theodosius.

261. E.g., *RIC*, IX, pl. 11, 7–9.

262. Gnecchi, 19, 11; 20, 1.

263. See R. Delbrueck, *Kaiserporträts*, 222ff, and above, "*Adventus*" at n. 275.

264. R. Delbrueck, *Consulardiptychen* (1929), 235–242; cf. J. Ramón Mélida, *El Disco de Teodosio*, Real Academia de la Historia (Madrid, 1930) and Kurt Weitzmann, ed., *Age of Spirituality* (1979) 74–76. On Hadrianic coins, TELLUS STABIL, see P. L. Strack, *Untersuchungen zur röm. Reichsprägung d. 2. Jhdt.* vol. 2 (Stuttgart, 1933), 182–184; pl. 4, 275; Gnecchi, 145, 12.

265. Sidonius *ep.*, 4, 8.

266. G. Mathew, *Byzantine Aesthetics* (1963) 38–47, 82–91.

267. Philo, *Questions and Answers on Exodus* (tr. from Armenian, Loeb, Philo Supplement, 2) 2, 102 on Exodus 27, 3. I would like to thank Eunice Maguire for this reference.

268. For the conferment of offices by the emperor, see A. Grabar, *L'empereur*, 88f, 149, where the image is traced back to the second century REX DATUS coinages, and for late antiquity see W. C. Loerke, "The Miniatures of the Trial in the Rossano Gospels," *Art Bulletin* 43 (1961) 171–195, at 177–178.

269. For a Constantinian antecedent of this iconography of emperor and palace, see H. Fuhrmann, "Studien zu den Konsulardiptychen und verwandten Denkmälern I," *Röm. Mitt.* 54 (1939) 161–175 and above, n. 162. Cf. D. Brown, "The Arcuated Lintel and Its Symbolic Interpretation in Late Antique Art," *American Journal of Archaeology* 46 (1942) 389–399, with Suetonius *Caesar* 81, 3, on the *fastigium* of Caesar's house.

270. For the potential savagery of imperial victory, see *Pan. Lat.*, 7, 8.

271. Themistius *Or.*, 15; see G. Downey, "Philanthropia in Religion and Statecraft in the Fourth Century," *Historia* 4 (1955) 199–208; L. J. Daly, "The Mandarin and the Barbarian: The Response of Themistius to the Gothic Challenge," *Historia* 21 (1972) 351–379; cf. above, "*Consecratio*," n. 185. Contrast the attitude of Synesius, in his *De Regno*, 3–4, 9–10, 15.

272. Cf. A. Momigliano, *Alien Wisdom. The Limits of Hellenization* (1975) 63, on the sculptures of Pergamon, "a monument to human pain made somehow more tolerable to contemplate because embodied in barbarians." A similar aesthetic sensitivity is operative in late antique works where Romans are separated from barbarians by registers.

273. Toynbee, *Roman Medallions*, 225–6; *RIC*, VII, 580; 583 GAUDIUM AUGUSTI NOSTRI; A. Alföldi, "Zur Erklärung der konstantinischen Deckengemälde in Trier," *Historia* 4 (1955) 131–150 expounds the public *laetitia* of the Roman Em-

pire, its occasions (anniversaries, etc.) and imagery comprising the images mentioned here, as well as the frequently involuntary nature of such rejoicings. See also F. Matz, "Ein römisches Meisterwerk, der Jahreszeitensarkophag Badminton-New York," *JB DAI*, Ergänzungsheft 19 (1958) 45ff. on Hellenistic and second-century Roman antecedents.

274. *RIC*, VII, 490 and 520, 165; cf. 627, 161.

275. *RIC*, VII, 561ff, esp. 564 and n. 3.

276. *RIC*, VII, 54–55; cf. above, n. 273.

277. E.g., Gnecchi, 2, 72, 1; 87, 3–5; 111, 6; 121, 6; 122, 3; cf. Toynbee, *Roman Medallions*, 90. For an analysis of seasons imagery in imperial art see G. M. A. Hanfmann, *The Season Sarcophagus in Dumbarton Oaks* (1951) 163–184. Cf. *Pan. Lat.*, 4, 4, 1f, above at n. 55.

278. *RIC*, VII, 366, 41–42; pl. 9.

279. *RIC*, VII, 396, 31 and 388; Gnecchi, 6, 6.

280. *Pan. Lat.*, 8, 13, 6.

281. Themistius, 189a ff. Cf. Sidonius *Carm.*, 7, 600–3: felix tempus nevere soreres/ imperiis . . . tuis et . . ./fulva . . . saecula. The newly elected Leo I was acclaimed χρυσέους αἰῶνας βασιλεύουσα εὐτυχὴς εἴη ἡμῖν ἡ βασιλεία σου: *De Cer.*, 412, 15 (Bonn).

282. *RIC*, II, 372, 277–278, 441, no. 791; 445, no. 835. Related iconographies appear on the mosaic from Sentinum now in Munich and the Buffalo Seasons Sarcophagus, G. M. A. Hanfmann, *The Season Sarcophagus in Dumbarton Oaks* (1951) figs. 108, 110.

283. Gnecchi, pl. 54, 7; cf. 86, 8–10, Commodus; see above, n. 264 and C. L. Clay, "Nilus and the Four Seasons on a New As of Septimius Severus," *Numismatic Chronicle* 7, 10 (1970) 71–87, 81ff, on Terra Mater.

284. Cf. eternal spring in Vergil *Georgics*, 2, 149. The tomb of the Haterii also has three seasons only, shown in Hanfmann, fig. 130. On Ge with seasons, at Bēth Govrin, see *Revue Biblique* (1922) 259ff, pl. 8–10; spring and summer are inscribed, while winter (?) is not. The seasons here are three in number. I would like to thank Eunice Maguire for this reference. See also, for photograph of the entire floor, M. Avi-Yonah, *Encyclopaedia of Archeological Excavations in the Holy Land* (1975) 196.

285. E.g., on the *consecratio* relief of Antoninus and Faustina, above, "*Consecratio*" at n. 36.

286. Cf. Tellus in the exergue of a gold multiple of Valens, showing an *adventus*, Gnecchi, 16, 1, cf. 17, 1 and Toynbee, *Roman Medallions*, pl. 10.

287. Delbrueck, *Consulardiptychen*, no. 1; Volbach, *Elfenbeinarbeiten*, no. 1.

288. Toynbee, *Roman Medallions*, pl. 49, 2. On the history of this concept see C. Koch, "Roma Aeterna," in his *Religio, Studien zu Kult und Glauben der Römer* (1960) 142–175.

289. Rutilius, *De red.* 1, 139–40:

> Illud te repararat quod cetera regna resolvit,
> Ordo renascendi est crescere posse malis.

Cf. Sidonius *Carm.*, 5, 63–64:

> Tua nempe putantur
> Surgere fata malis et celsior esse ruina.

290. Sidonius *Carm.*, 7, 123ff. On the cultural background of this kind of poetry, and on Sidonius' training and erudition see A. Loyen, *Sidoine Apollinaire et l'esprit précieux en Gaule aux derniers jours de l'empire* (1943) esp. 11ff. Culture and erudition are not, however, the only factors that should be brought to bear on Sidonius the panegyrist, who viewed the world with more realistic eyes than his imagery would lead the modern reader to suppose. On the panegyrics, see A. Loyen, *Recherches sur les panégyriques de Sidoine Apollinaire*, Bibl. de l'École des Hautes Études, 285 (1942). On Sidonius himself, see Philip Rousseau, "In Search of Sidonius the Bishop," *Historia* 25 (1976) 356–377.

291. Sidonius *Carm.*, 7, 489ff.

292. Sidonius *Carm.*, 7, 501–510:

> Testor, Roma, tuum nobis venerabile nomen
> et socium de Marte genus (vel quicquid ab aevo,
> nil te mundus habet melius, nil ipsa senatu),
> me pacem servare tibi vel velle abolere
> quae noster peccavit avus, quem fuscat id unum
> quod te, Roma, capit; sed di si vota secundant,
> excidii veteris crimen purgare valebit
> ultio praesentis, si tu, dux inclite, solum
> Augusti subeas nomen. Quid lumina flectis?
> invitum plus esse decet.

See, on the non-Roman context of this speech before a Visigothic assembly of nobles, C. Sanchez-Albornoz, *Estudios Visigodos* (1971) 158ff.

293. Sidonius *Carm.*, 7, 538–543.

294. Sidonius *Carm.*, 7, 577–580:

> Concurrunt *proceres* ac *milite* circumfuso
> aggere composito statuunt ac *torque* coronant
> castrensi maestum donantque *insignia regni*;
> nam prius induerat solas de principe curas.

For the use of the torque among the Visigoths, and others, see A. Odobescu, *Le trésor de Pétrossa* (Paris, 1889–1900) 219ff, plate between 356 and 357.

295. Sidonius *Carm.*, 7, 585ff.

296. Sidonius *Carm.*, 5, 13ff. On the circumstances of this panegyric, see A. Coville, *Recherches sur l'histoire de Lyon du Vme au IXme siècle* (1928) 56ff.

297. Sidonius *Carm.*, 5, 53ff.

298. Sidonius *Carm.*, 5, 386–388:

> Postquam ordine vobis
> ordo omnis regnum dederat, *plebs, curia, miles,*
> et *collega* simul.

299. Cf. H. Meyer, "Der Regierungsantritt des Kaisers Majorianus," *BZ* 62 (1969) 5–12.

300. Sidonius *Carm.*, 5, 1–6:

> Concipe praeteritos, respublica, mente triumphos:
> imperium iam consul habet, quem *purpura* non plus
> quam *lorica* operit, cuius *diademata* frontem
> non luxu sed lege tegunt, meritisque laborum
> post palmam *palmata* venit; decora omnia regni
> accumulant *fasces* et princeps consule crescit.

For the imperial attire described here, see plate 61 and above at n. 287 on the consular diptych showing Honorius; the consular diptych of Ariadne, fig. 52 and below, at n. 454; also H. Stern, *Le Calendrier de 354* (1953) 152ff.
301. Sidonius *Carm.*, 2, 30–31:

> Salve sceptrorum columen, regina Orientis,
> orbis Roma tui.

Cf. *Carm.*, 2, 436ff.
302. Themistius *Or.* 14. Note especially the words 182a:

> προσήκει γὰρ δήπου τῷ βασιλεῖ τῶν πόλεων συνᾴδειν τοὺς βασιλεύσαντας τῶν ἀνθρώπων. καὶ τῶν γε δυοῖν μητροπόλεων τῆς οἰκουμένης . . . μᾶλλον ἄν σοι φαίην ἁρμόττειν τὴν ἡμετέραν.

303. Sidonius *Carm.*, 2, 210ff.
304. Sidonius *Carm.*, 2, 13–22:

> Hic est, o proceres, petiit quem Romula virtus
> et quem vester amor; cui se ceu victa procellis
> atque carens rectore ratis res publica fractam
> intulit, ut digno melius flectenda magistro,
> ne tempestates, ne te, pirata, timeret.
> te prece ruricola expetiit, te foedere iunctus
> adsensu, te castra tubis, te curia plausu,
> te punctis scripsere tribus collegaque misit
> te nobis regnumque tibi; suffragia tot sunt
> quanta legit mundus.

305. Sidonius *Carm.*, 2, 1–8 (translation after W. B. Anderson):

> Auspicio et numero fasces, Auguste, secundos
> erige et effulgens trabealis mole metalli
> annum pande novum consul vetus ac sine fastu
> scribere bis fastis; quamquam diademate crinem
> fastigatus eas umerosque ex more priorum
> includat Sarrana chlamys, te picta togarum
> purpura plus capiat, quia res est semper ab aevo
> rara frequens consul.

306. Cf. A. Alföldi, *Die monarchische Repräsentation*, 150ff, and R. Delbrueck, *Consulardiptychen*, no. 38.
307. Servius *Comm. in Verg. Aen.*, 1, 4 (ed. Thilo and Hagen).
308. Delbrueck, *Consulardiptychen*, no. 38; Volbach, *Elfenbeinarbeiten*, no. 38; K. Weitzmann, ed., *Age of Spirituality* (1979), 173–175.
309. Sidonius *Carm.*, 5, 18f, 14f.
310. Sidonius *Carm.*, 2, 433–434. Cf. the less differentiated Roma and Constantinopolis on the diptych of Magnus, Constantinople, 518 A.D., Delbrueck, *Consulardiptychen*, no. 22; Volbach, *Elfenbeinarbeiten*, nos. 23–24; cf. Basilius, Rome 480 A.D., Delbrueck, *Consulardiptychen*, no. 6; Volbach, *Elfenbeinarbeiten*, no. 5, Roma with fasces, helmet and long hair, for which cf. Sidonius *Carm.*, 5, 14–15.
311. For Valentinian III, IMP XXXII COS XVII PP or VIRTUS ROMANORUM or VOT XXX MULT XXXX, see Cohen, vol. 8, 210, 4; 214, 33; 215, 42.
312. Cohen, vol. 8, 215, 46.
313. Cohen, vol. 8, 222, 9.

314. Cohen, vol. 8, 232, 13.

315. F. F. Kraus, *Die Münzen Odovacars und des Ostgotenreiches in Italien* (1928) pl. 7, pl. 14–15.

316. J. B. Bury, *A History of the Later Roman Empire from Arcadius to Irene* vol. 2 (1889) 36, n. 1; John of Ephesus *H.E.*, 3, 14, (tr. Brooks) (1936) 104.

317. Cohen, vol. 8, 197, 7; Gnecchi 20, 2; Toynbee, *Roman Medallions* pl. 49, 2. Versions of this image with different legends recurred for most emperors of the fifth century in East and West: Cohen, vol. 8, 210, 3 GLORIA ROMANORUM, Valentinian III; cf. 211, 9 SALUS REIPUBLICAE Valentinian III and Theodosius II enthroned; 221, 2 VICTORIA AUGG, Avitus; 225, 12 VOTIS MULTIS, Leo and Majorian; 230, 2–5 etc., SALUS REIPUBLICAE, Anthemius and Leo standing frontally; W. Wroth, *Catalogue of the Coins of the Vandals, Ostrogoths and Lombards in the British Museum* (1911) (hereafter, Wroth), pl. 4, 5–6 Justin and Justinian enthroned frontally: on the obverse, DN IUSTIN ET IUSTINI PP AUG. On the topics of imperial enthronement, coronation and imperial Christian symbolism, see F. Gerke, "L'iconografia delle monete imperiali dall'augusta Galla Placidia alla fine dell'Impero d'Occidente," *XIII Corso di cultura sull'arte Rav. e Biz.* (1966) 163–204.

318. Delbrueck, *Kaiserporträts*, 211f.

319. On the basis of the evidence cited by Delbrueck, *Kaiserporträts*, and *De Cer.*, Bonn 1, 43, 218–9. For similar scenes in Byzantine art, see C. Walter, "The Coronation of a Co-Emperor in the *Skyllitzes Matritensis*," *Actes du XIVᵉ Congrès international des études Byzantines* 2 (Bucarest, 1975) 453–458, reprinted in his *Studies in Byzantine Iconography* (1977).

320. J. M. Wallace-Hadrill, *Early Germanic Kingship in England and on the Continent* (1971) 9ff. For Theodoric, Rome and Italy, see also P. Llewellyn, *Rome in the Dark Ages* (1971) 21–51 with bibliography; P. Courcelle, *Histoire littéraire des grandes invasions germaniques* (1964) 206ff; O. von Simson, *Sacred Fortress. Byzantine Art and Statecraft in Ravenna* (1948) 71ff; and in general, W. Ensslin, *Theodorich der Grosse* (1947).

321. Ennodius *panegyricus*, 14, 29, 48. On the date of this panegyric, 507 A.D., J. Sundwall, *Abhandlungen zur Geschichte des ausgehenden Römertums* (1919; 1975), 41–44.

322. Ennodius *pan.*, 31, 92, 59, 71.

323. M. Wes, *Das Ende des Kaisertums* (1967) 163.

324. Ennodius, ed. Vogel *pan.*, 14, p. 205:

> Par te, inclyte domine, laus respicit donati diadematis et defensi. Si te illarum rector partium non amavit, perculsus praefuit reipublicae: si dilexit, obnoxius; usus es in tuorum fide meritorum teste purpurato.

325. Ennodius *pan.*, 11.

326. Ennodius *pan.*, 43.

327. Wes, *Das Ende*, 185ff, and A. D. Momigliano, "Gli Anicii e la storiografia latina del VI seculo D.C.," *Secondo contributo alla storia degli studi classici* (1960) 231–53; and Jordanes *Getica*, 79–81, 314.

328. Ennodius *pan.*, 78f; Cassiodorus, in *Cassiodori Senatoris Variae* (MGH, AA) ed. T. Mommsen, *Cassiodori orationum reliquiae* (ed. L. Traube), 467, 473, 483. On the educational background, P. Riché, *Éducation et culture dans l'occident barbare* (1972) 62ff, 96ff; on the occasions of Cassiodorus' two panegyrics, Sundwall,

Abhandlungen, 230; 296, and Traube in Cassiodorus, 463, with nn. 1 and 3. Cassiodorus and to a lesser extent Ennodius were not unique in creating an idiom of panegyric for barbarian rulers. On Venantius Fortunatus, see J. Szövérffy, "A la Source de l'humanisme chrétien médiéval: 'Romanus' et 'Barbarus' chez Vénance Fortunat," *Aevum* 45 (1971) 77–86.

329. Ennodius *pan.*, 17f, 30, 85; cf. 48; 56f, 60 and 69, 74ff; Cassiodorus, 467.
330. Ennodius *pan.*, 93; Cassiodorus *Or.*, 1.
331. Ennodius *pan.*, 80:

> Agis ut prospera merearis adipisci, sed potitus universa adscribis auctori. exhibes robore, vigilantia, prosperitate principem, mansuetudine sacerdotem.

See further, E. Kantorowicz, *Laudes regiae. A Study in Liturgical Acclamations and Medieval Ruler Worship* (Berkeley and Los Angeles, 1946) 47, 57, n. 148; 112f; cf. 124, and, for analogies to the juxtaposition of *princeps* and *sacerdos*, below n. 384.
332. W. Ensslin, *Zur Frage nach der ersten Kaiserkrönung durch den Patriarchen und zur Bedeutung dieses Aktes im Wahlzeremoniell* (1947). See H. Hunger, *Prooimion, Elemente der byzantinischen Kaiseridee in den Arengen der Urkunden* (1964) 84–154.
333. For the emperor as Moses, see O. Treitinger, *Die oströmische Kaiser- und Reichsidee* (1938; 1956), 130ff; Theodosius II as David and Moses, Socrates *H.E.*, 7, 22, *PG*, 67, 788bc. Moses receiving the law is shown next to Justinian's procession in San Vitale; for this and the priestly privileges of the Byzantine emperor, see O. von Simson, *Sacred Fortress*, 29f; cf. Treitinger, *Kaiser*, 124ff.
334. Ennodius *pan.*, 48.
335. Ennodius *pan.*, 56.
336. Cassiodorus, 468; *Pan. Lat.*, 11, 16; Ausonius, *gratiarum actio*, 3.
337. See Traube's introduction in *Cassiodori . . . Variae* (n. 328, above), 463, n. 3.
338. Cassiodorus, 475–476. See also Procopius *Wars*, 5, 11, 5; 7, 2, 11f; 18; 3, 1; 8, 33, 6 for the election of Vitigis, Totila and Teia by the Goths.
339. Ennodius *pan.*, 88ff:

> Solus es meritis et natura compositus, cuius magnanimi iussa sectentur. origo te quidem dedit dominum, sed virtus adseruit. sceptra tibi conciliavit splendor generis, cuius si deessent insignia, eligi te in principem mens fecisset. sed nec formae tuae decus inter postrema numerandum est, quando regii vultus purpura ostrum dignitatis inradiat. exhibite, Seres, indumenta, pretioso murice quae fucatis, et non uno aeno bibentia nobilitatem tegmina prorogate. discoloribus gemmis sertum texatur, et quem vehementior vipera custodit lapis adveniat. quaecumque ornamenta mundo obsequente transmissa fuerint, decorata venerandi genio corporis plus lucebunt. statura est quae resignet prolixitate regnantem; nix genarum habet concordiam cum rubore; vernant lumina serenitate continua; dignae manus quae exitia rebellibus tribuant, honorum vota subiectis. nullus intempestive positum iactet, quia quod agunt in aliis dominis diademata, hoc in rege meo operata est deo fabricante natura. illos faciunt tot divitiarum adiumenta conspicuos, sed hunc edidit simplex et indemutabilis figura meliorem. quid! cultu laborent qui cupiunt peregrinam obtinere pulcritudinem.

340. Cf. P. E. Schramm, *Herrschaftszeichen und Staatssymbolik*, vol. 1 (1954) 219–233, and figs. 13–19.

341. Cf. Propertius, 1, 2.
342. Wroth, 57–58.
343. Wroth, 67ff.
344. Wroth, 69, 62f, Rome.
345. Wroth, 74, 16.
346. Wroth, 79, 11.
347. Wroth, 102f.
348. Wroth, 103, 104, 105.
349. Wroth, 106f.
350. Agnellus *Lib. Pont.*, 94 (Holder-Egger).
351. Cf. A. H. M. Jones, "The Constitutional Position of Odoacer and Theoderic," *JRS* 52 (1962) 126–130.
352. Wroth, 46ff.
353. Anastasius and monogramme of Theodoric: Wroth 50f.

Justin I and monogramme of Athalarich: Wroth 63, 27; 64, 30f; 66, 46f. Justin I and DN ATHALARICHUS REX: Wroth 63, 28f; 64, 35f; 67, 57f.

Justinian and monogramme of Theodahad: Wroth 72, 1f; 74, 1f; Justinian and DN THEODAHATUS REX: Wroth 73, 3f; 74, 16f.

Justinian and DN VVITIGES REX: Wroth 77, 1f; 79, 11f; note also, for Vitigis, the issues showing, as usual, the Byzantine emperor, in this case Justinian, on the obverse, and on the reverse the monogramme of Theodoric: Wroth 78, 7f. These issues may be viewed as an attempt, in troubled times, at proclaiming the continuance of the dynasty of Theodoric.

Justinian and monogramme of Matasuntha: Wroth 80–81.

Justinian and DN BADVILA REX (Totila): Wroth 86. See further the antiquarian issues under Totila, commemorating the golden age of Ostrogothic kingship during the period of Anastasius and Theodoric: Wroth 86ff passim, and similarly under Teia, Wroth 95f.

354. Wroth, 75, 19ff.
355. Wroth, 88, 23; 89, 24; 91, 38.
356. Wroth, 93–94; Alföldi, *Die Kontorniaten* (1942) catalogue, e.g., nos. 351–352, 355, 361, 363, 380, 389, 405f, with victory acclamations to charioteers.
357. P. E. Schramm, *Herrschaftszeichen, loc. cit.* (above, n. 340).
358. See E. Dyggve, *Ravennatum Palatium Sacrum. La basilica ipetrale a cerimonie* (1941) 4ff; 22, to be consulted with G. de Francovich, *Il palazzo de Teodorico a Ravenna e la cosidetta ‹architettura di potenza›* (1970) and F. W. Deichmann, *Ravenna, Hauptstadt des spätantiken Abendlandes, Kommentar* 1 (1974) 141–145.
359. G. Bovini, *XIII Corso di cultura sull'arte Rav. e Biz.* (1966) 51–81; cf. below, n. 368.
360. The hand of one of the figures, making the gesture of acclamation, may still be seen on one of the columns, see fig. 55.
361. Deichmann, *Ravenna* (n. 380), 141 and 145; cf. Nordström, *Ravennastudien* (1953) 57. The owner of the palace is thus shown in its pediment and in its main entrance, while the city goddess appears in her own gate: ruler and city are juxtaposed. There is an iconographic analogy for Theodoric in the pediment of his palace and Ravenna in her gate: it is Roma in the pediment of the Templum Urbis on the Ephesian Arch of S. Maria Maggiore, see N. Brodsky, *L'iconographie oublié de l'arc Ephésien de Sainte-Marie Majeure à Rome* (1966) 66f.

362. Sidonius *Carm.*, 2, 1ff; 5, 1ff; and cf. Rome enthroned in majesty, 13ff; 7, 3–10; 578–580; cf. *Pan. Lat.*, 3, 11, Diocletian and Maximian in the palace of Milan; Claudian, *IV cons.* 565ff, etc.

363. *Pan. Lat.*, 7, 4, 1: Sacrum istud palatium non candidatus imperii, sed designatus intrasti confestimque te illi paterni lares successorem videre legitimum, and Eusebius *VC*, 1, 22 on Constantine; Amm., 15, 8, 17: Susceptusque denique ad consessum vehiculi, receptusque in regiam (Julian), and Amm., 21, 10, 1, a crowd at Sirmium acclaimed Julian and led him to the palace; Claudian *VI cons.*, 25–38 on Honorius resident in the palatium in Rome; cf. 640ff.

364. Cassiodorus *Variae*, ed. Mommsen, 7, 5, 1:

> Formula Curae palatii: Haec nostrae sunt oblectamenta potentiae, imperii decora facies, testimonium praeconiale regnorum: haec legatis sub ammiratione monstrantur et prima fronte talis dominus esse creditur, quale eius habitaculum comprobatur.

365. Agnellus *Lib. Pont.* ed. Holder-Egger 86, MGH, Script. Rer. Lang.

366. C. O. Nordström, *Ravennastudien* (1953) 46–54, and S. K. Kostof, *The Orthodox Baptistery of Ravenna* (1965) 76–82. The image of the empty throne has antecedents in pagan sepulchral and triumphal art; see J. W. Salomonson, *Chair, Sceptre and Wreath. Historical Aspects of Their Representation on Some Roman Sepulchral Monuments* (1956).

367. Agnellus *Lib. Pont.*, 70–71, on the negotiations preceding the formal welcome of the bishop Maximian, appointed by Justinian. Cf. H. Kruse, *Studien zur offiziellen Geltung des Kaiserbildes.* . . . (1934) 32–34.

368. The dates of the different mosaics in S. Apollinare Nuovo have been clarified definitively by G. Bovini, "Antichi rifacimenti nei mosaici di S. Apollinare Nuovo di Ravenna," *XIII Corso di cultura sull'arte Rav. e Biz.* (1966) 51–81. It is clear that C. O. Nordström, *Ravennastudien* (1953) 79 (cf. Deichmann, *Ravenna, Geschichte und Monumente* (1969) 199 and figs. 257–60) was right in regarding not only the Palatium and Classis compositions, but also the enthroned Christ and Theotokos, as Ostrogothic. These mosaics therefore provide important evidence about the nature of Ostrogothic kingship as formulated under Theodoric, for they showed the ruler on earth, Theodoric, juxtaposed to the ruler of heaven, exactly as was done for Late Roman and Byzantine emperors.

369. On the date, C. A. Trypanis, *Fourteen Early Byzantine Cantica* (1968) 17ff, and see S. MacCormack, "Roma, Constantinopolis, the Emperor, and His Genius," *CQ* 25 (1965) 131–150, on the relationship between ruler and capital and its pagan and Christian context. On my interpretation of the narthex mosaic in S. Sophia (p. 150), contrast N. Oikonomides, "Leo VI and the Narthex Mosaic of Saint Sophia," *DOP* 30 (1976) 153–172 at 170–171.

370. See Hunger, *Prooimion*, 63ff. and below, at nn. 395ff and 401.

371. See also the analysis, starting from different premises, by Nordström, *Ravennastudien*, 83ff.

372. J. B. Bury, "The Ceremonial Book of Constantine Porphyrogennetos," *EHR* 22 (1907) 209–227 at 211–213; H. G. Beck, "Senat und Volk von Konstantinopel," *Bayer. Akad. d. Wiss. Phil. Hist. Kl. SB* (1966) 11. See also, on the period here under discussion, in the wider context of Rome and Byzantium, F. E. Brightman, "Byzantine Imperial Coronations," *JTS* 2 (1901) 359–392; W. Sickel,

"Das byzantinische Krönungsrecht bis zum 10. Jhdt.," *BZ* 7 (1898) 511–557, and Aikaterine Christophilopoulou, Ἐκλογή, ἀναγόρευσις, καὶ στέψις τοῦ βυζαντίνου αὐτοκράτορος (1956). Brightman, 368, takes the accession of Leo as a turning point, using evidence from *De Cer.* as a guideline, as is also done here, while Christophilopoulou begins with Marcian.

373. Philostorgius records an accession of this type, which is of considerable theoretical interest, *H.E.*, 3, 22.

374. Leo II and Justinian, *De Cer.*, 94; 95; Leo I, Anastasius and Justin I, *De Cer.*, 91–93. *De Cer.*, 93 reveals that the accession of Justin I was controversial, an impression which is amply confirmed by Evagrius, *H.E.*, 4, 1–3. Thus, the account of *De Cer.*, 93 shows how, in such a situation, the effect of ceremonial can serve to acquire and register *consensus*, and to validate events, even if only retrospectively. Cf. below, n. 423.

375. Amm., 20, 4, 18: Abstractum sibi torquem, quo ut draconarius utebatur; cf. above, nn. 170–171.

376. On Justin, see Averil Cameron, *Corippus*, Commentary, 154ff (on Corippus *Laus . . . Iustini* 2, 84ff, taking in also the accounts in *De Cer.*), with the other literature, which is not repeated here. On shield-raising, see now C. Walter, "Raising on a Shield in Byzantine Iconography," *Rev. des études byzantines* 33 (1975) 133–175, where the literary evidence also is presented and discussed. On Byzantine, compared to mediaeval Western, coronations, J. Nelson, "Symbols in Context," *Studies in Church History* 13 (1976) ed. D. Baker, 97–119.

377. Hauck, in P. E. Schramm, *Herrschaftszeichen und Staatssymbolik*, vol. 1 (1954) 145f.

378. Thus it was a significant occasion when, to face the rebelling populace of Constantinople, Anastasius appeared in the hippodrome not wearing the diadem; E. Stein, *Histoire du Bas-Empire*, vol. 2 (1949) 177–178.

379. See Alan Cameron, *Porphyrius the Charioteer* (1973) 248–252; for a view over a longer time-span, Alan Cameron, *Circus Factions. Blues and Greens at Rome and Byzantium* (1976) 157–192; and in a wider context, G. Dagron, *Naissance d'une capitale, Constantinople et ses institutions de 330 à 451* (1974) 314–347.

380. See Ensslin, *Zur Frage nach der ersten Kaiserkrönung durch den Patriarchen*, (1947) (shortened version in *BZ* 42 (1943–1949) 101–115, 369–372).

381. Treitinger, *Kaiser*, 13ff, 26ff, "der Kaiser bedurfte der kirchlichen Krönung in Byzanz nie" (27–8), 34–43; and Ostrogorsky's review of *Kaiser*, *BZ* 41 (1941) 211–223. By comparing the Byzantine situation to the West, J. Nelson, in her "Symbols in Context," *Studies in Church History* 13 (1976) ed. D. Baker, 97–119, overcomes these impasses and impossibilities.

382. See W. Sickel, "Das byzantinische Krönungsrecht bis zum 10. Jahrhundert," *BZ* 7 (1898) 511–557 at 513ff; also J. Deer, "Der Ursprung der Kaiserkrone," *Schweizer Beiträge zur allgemeinen Geschichte* 8 (1950) 51–87, reprinted in Deer, *Byzanz und das abendländische Herrschertum* (1977), on the interrelation between insignia and ceremonial.

383. J. Meyendorff, "Justinian, the Empire and the Church," *DOP* 22 (1968) 43–60.

384. On the role of Constantine, with respect to the church, cf. above, "*Adventus*" at n. 144; J. Straub, "Kaiser Konstantin als ἐπίσκοπος τῶν ἐκτός," *Studia Patristica* 1 (1957) 678–695, reprinted in his *Regeneratio Imperii* (1972) pp. 119–133,

and J. Straub, "Konstantin als κοινὸς ἐπίσκοπος," *DOP* 21 (1967) 37–55, reprinted in *Regeneratio Imperii*, pp. 134–158. On Marcian, see A. Grillmeir, S.J. and H. Bacht, S.J., *Das Konzil von Chalkedon; Geschichte und Gegenwart*, vol. 2 (1959) 525, with 103–107. On Anastasius, see Procopius of Gaza *Panegyricus*, 4 (Bonn); cf. Socrates *H.E.*, 7, 23, *PG*, 67, 785A: Theodosius discussed the Scriptures with bishops ὡς ἱερεὺς πάλαι καθεστώς.

385. Agapetus *PG*, 86¹, § 1, Col. 1164; §15, col. 1169:

> Τιμῆς ἁπάσης ὑπέρτερον ἔχων ἀξίωμα, βασιλεῦ, τίμα ὑπὲρ ἅπαντας τὸν τούτου σε ἀξιώσαντα Θεόν, ὅτι καὶ καθ' ὁμοίωσιν τῆς· ἐπουρανίου βασιλείας, ἔδωκέ σοι τὸ σκῆπτρον τῆς ἐπιγείου δυναστείας. . . .
> Ὑπὲρ πάντα τῆς βασιλείας τὰ ἔνδοξα, τῆς εὐσεβείας τὸ στέμμα τὸν βασιλέα κοσμεῖ. ὁ γὰρ πλοῦτος ἀπέρχεται, καὶ ἡ δόξα μετέρχεται. τὸ δὲ κλέος τῆς ἐνθέου πολιτείας ἀθανάτοις αἰῶσι συμπαρεκτείνεται, καὶ λήθης ἐπέκεινα τοὺς ἔχοντας ἵστησι.

386. The point is noted by Reiske, *De Cer.*, Commentary, 412.

387. *De Cer.*, 411: καὶ οὕτω φανεὶς τῷ δήμῳ, παρὰ πάντων τῶν' ἀρχόντων κατὰ τάξιν προσεκυνήθη. . . .

388. *De Cer.*, 428. For the late sixth century we have some additional information about the ceremonial of coronation from the Guidi Chronicle, tr. Th. Nöldeke, "Die von Guidi herausgegebene syrische Chronik," *Wien. Akad. d. Wiss. SB Philos. hist. Kl.* 128 (1893) IX Abh., 16:

> Der König (i.e., Khusro II) nahm ihn [Theodosius son of Maurice] mit grossen Ehren auf und gebot dem Katholikos dass er ihn in die Kirche führe, und dass nach römischer Sitte die Kaiserkrone auf den Altar gelegt und ihm sodann aufs Haupt gesetzt werde.

389. On early examples of this phrase and its significance see H. U. Instinsky, "Consensus universorum," *Hermes* 75 (1940) 265–278.

390. Or, possibly, Marcian, see O. Treitinger, *Oströmische Kaiser- und Reichsidee*, 87.

391. Procopius *B.P.*, 1, 24, 19ff.

392. See, e.g., Socrates *H.E.*, 5, Prologue: Church and state are joined by συμπαθεία τις, so that what disturbs one disturbs the other; emperors convoke synods, and the church depends on emperors. The absence of differentiation emerges even in Socrates' vocabulary, since he juxtaposes not the neat entities church and state but τὰ δημόσια and τὰ τῶν ἐκκλησιῶν. See also Socrates *H.E.*, 7, 22 and 23 (*P.G.*, 67, 788b; 792a) of the people in the hippodrome on two different occasions: ὅλη μὲν ἡ πόλις μία ἐκκλησία ἐγένετο.

393. Θεὲ φιλάνθρωπε: note the parallel with Themistius, above, nn. 177, 226–229.

394. Entry into the palace has been met with earlier as one of the actions of claiming sovereignty: e.g., above, nn. 223–224. N. 269 on the Missorium of Theodosius; nn. 358 and 361 on the Palatium mosaic in S. Apollinare Nuovo.

395. *De Cer.*, 410–411:

> εἰσάκουσον, ὁ Θεὸς, σὲ παρακαλοῦμεν. ἐπάκουσον, ὁ Θεός. Λέοντι ζωή. εἰσάκουσον, ὁ Θεός. Λέων βασιλεύσει. Θεὲ φιλάνθρωπε, Λέοντα βασιλέα τὸ πρᾶγμα τὸ δημόσιον αἰτεῖ. ὁ στρατὸς Λέοντα βασιλέα αἰτεῖ. Λέοντα οἱ νόμοι ἐκδέχονται. Λέοντα τὸ παλάτιον ἐκδέχεται. αὗται εὐχαὶ τοῦ παλατίου· αὗται ἐντεύ-

ξεις τοῦ στρατοπέδου. αὖται εὐχαὶ τῆς συγγκλήτου· αὖται εὐχαὶ τοῦ λαοῦ. Λέοντα ὁ κόσμος ἀναμένει. Λέοντα ὁ στρατὸς ἐκδέχεται· τὸ κοινὸν καλὸν, Λέων, ἐλθέτω. τὸ κοινὸν ἀγαθὸν, Λέων, βασιλεύσει. εἰσάκουσον, ὁ Θεὸς, σὲ παρακαλοῦμεν.

These acclamations are extraordinarily similar to those recorded, over 500 years later, for the accession of Nicephorus Phocas, *De Cer.*, 1, 96, 439 (Bonn). The separate enumerations of communalty, army, senate, laws and palace as desiring the new emperor are particularly striking. On the enumeration of people, senate and army at accessions in late antique Constantinople, see H. G. Beck, "Senat und Volk von Konstantinopel," *Bayer. Akad. d. Wiss. Phil. Hist. Kl.* SB (1966) 10–15. See also *Theodosian Code, Gesta Senatus* 5, with *H.A.* Probus 11, 6ff.

396. *De Cer.*, 411:

Λέων αὔγουστε, σὺ νικᾷς, σὺ εὐσεβής, σὺ σεβαστός· ὁ Θεός σε ἔδωκεν, ὁ Θεός σε φυλάξει· τὸν Χριστὸν σεβόμενος ἀεὶ νικᾷς· πολλοὺς χρόνους Λέων βασιλεύσει· χριστιανὸν βασίλειον ὁ Θεὸς περιφρουρήσει.

Cf. *Theodosian Code, Gesta Senatus* 5: Adclamatum est . . . Deus vos nobis dedit, deus vos nobis servet.

397. *De Cer.*, 411–412.

αὐτοκράτωρ Καῖσαρ Λέων νικητὴς ἀεὶ σεβαστός· ὁ Θεὸς ὁ παντοδύναμος καὶ ἡ κρίσις ἡ ὑμετέρα, ἰσχυρώτατοι συστρατιῶται, αὐτοκράτορά με τῶν τῶν Ῥωμαίων δημοσίων πραγμάτων εὐτυχῶς ἐξελέξατο. Παρά πάντων ἐκράγη. Λέων αὔγουστε, σὺ νικᾷς· ὁ σὲ ἐκλεξάμενος σὲ διαφυλάξει· τὴν ἐκλογὴν ἑαυτοῦ ὁ Θεὸς περιφρουρήσει· εὐσεβὲς βασίλειον ὁ Θεὸς φυλάξει· καὶ εὐσεβὴς καὶ δυνατός.

Cf. for Justin, *De Cer.*, 429–430.

398. *De Cer.*, 424:

Κύριε, ἐλέησον· υἱὲ Θεοῦ, σὺ αὐτὸν ἐλέησον. Ἀναστάσιε αὔγουστε, τούμβηκας· εὐσεβῆ βασιλέα ὁ Θεὸς φυλάξει· ὁ Θεός σε ἔδωκεν, ὁ Θεός σε φυλάξει.

For the divine election of Anastasius, see also John of Nikiu *Chronicle*, 89, 9, p. 122 (tr. R. H. Charles (1916)).

399. *De Cer.*, 429–430:

ἄφθονα τῇ οἰκουμένῃ. ὡς ἔζησας, οὔτω βασίλευσον· ἄφθονα τῇ πολιτείᾳ· βασιλεῦ οὐράνιε, σῶσον τὸν ἐπίγειον. Ἰουστῖνε αὔγουστε, σὺ νικᾷς· τοῦ νέου Κωνσταντίνου πολλὰ τὰ ἔτη· ἡμεῖς δοῦλοι τοῦ βασιλέως.

400. E.g., Marcian's letter informing Pope Leo of his accession, Leo *ep.*, 73 *PL*, 54, 899. Cf. C. Mango and I. Ševčenko, *BZ* (1972) 380, inscription of Anastasius: Ο ΨΗΦΩ Θ(ΕΟ)Υ ΤΩΝ ΟΛΩΝ ΚΡΑΤΩΝ ΑΝΑΣΤΑΣΙΟΣ ΕΥΣΕΒΗΣ ΑΥΤΟΚΡΑΙΤΩΡ.

401. *De Cer.*, 439: ὑπόδεξαι τὸν θεόστεπτον Νικηφόρον. Although the account of this accession belongs to the tenth, not the sixth, century (Bury, *EHR* 22 (1907) 211), it shares numerous features with the late antique accounts. Cf. above, n. 395.

402. *De Cer.*, 410; 425; 427. These acclamations express the consensual aspect of the coronation ceremony. See on this E. Shils, "The Meaning of the Coronation," *Center and Periphery, Essays in Macrosociology* (1975) 135–152.

403. *De Cer.*, 417, 422.

404. *De Cer.*, 426, ὁ τῆς θείας λήξεως.

405. *De Cer.*, 426:

ὁ δεσπότης ἡμῶν, ὡς ἄνθρωπος, ἐτελεύτησεν· δεῖ οὖν ἡμᾶς πάντας κοινῇ βου-
λεύσασθαι, καὶ τὸν τῷ Θεῷ ἀρέσκοντα καὶ τῇ πολιτείᾳ συμφέροντα ἐπιλέξασθαι.

This interpretation is at variance with J. Nelson, "Symbols in Context," *Studies in Church History* 13 (1976) ed. D. Baker, 107 and n. 43. My argument about the links between imperial funerals and accessions has been that any 'stand-in' such as the patriarch was not required between one reign and the next. The ceremonial in itself creates the desired coherence.

406. C. Halm, *Rhetores Latini Minores*, 556–557.

407. *De Cer.*, 425, 430.

408. Priscian *Panegyric* (Bonn), 38f; Procopius of Gaza, *Panegyric* (Bonn), 6–7.

409. Priscian *Panegyric* 1–7:

> Accipe Romanum clementi pectore carmen,
> accipe, quod soleo caelesti reddere regi,
> munere pro vitae, pro pulchro lumine solis.
> namque deum sentis placari carmine tantum,
> quem sequeris, princeps animo iustissime recto,
> *qui tibi regna dedit*, cui debes omnia soli
> prospera, quae bellis pariter vel pace tulisti.

410. Procopius of Gaza *Panegyric*, 5:

> δόγμα τι θεῖον ὡς ἀληθῶς ἐπὶ σοὶ τὴν ψῆφον ἐκίνει· καὶ ὥσπερ ἐκ μιᾶς
> γνώμης ὁ δῆμος ἅπας ἐβόα· μεγάλη βουλὴ προσετίθετο. βασιλὶς ἐπένευεν· ἡ δὲ
> ψῆφος ἐφέρετο.

411. See on Corippus and George of Pisidia, T. Nissen, "Historisches Epos und Panegyrikos in der Spätantike," *Hermes* 75 (1940) 298–325; on Corippus, Averil Cameron, *Corippus* (1976) 2f, 7f. On epic tendencies and *ekphrasis* in Claudian, Alan Cameron, *Claudian*, 254–279; an excellent survey is presented by L. Previale, "Teoria e prassi del panegirico bizantino," *Emerita* 17 (1949) 72–105; *Emerita* 18 (1950) 340–366. On description, *ekphrasis*, see also P. Friedländer, *Johannes von Gaza, Paulus Silentiarius und Prokopius von Gaza, Kunstbeschreibungen justinianischer Zeit* (1969; 1912 and 1939), esp. 1–23. See further, above p. 279 n. 26.

412. Corippus *De Laud. Iust.*, 1, 32ff. See throughout Averil Cameron's commentary in her *Corippus*, 1966.

413. Corippus *De Laud. Iust.*, 1, 115ff.

414. Corippus *De Laud. Iust.*, 1, 148: Te iura vocant, te sustinet aula.

415. Corippus *De Laud. Iust.*, 1, 187ff.

416. Corippus *De Laud. Iust.*, 1, 226ff.

417. Corippus *De Laud. Iust.*, 1, 345–367:

> Hunc omnes populi, pueri, iuvenes, senesque
>   dant agmina plausus
>   vox omnibus una,
> mens eadem: nomen populis placet omnibus unum.
> ales ut exustos cum phoenix innovat artus,
> a busto recidiva suo. . . .
> (351–352) . . .
> sic decus imperii, sanctum sic iota resurgens

exortum est de fine suo, seniumque reponens
nominis erecti Iustino in principe vivit
Iustinianus apex; domini sic vulgus amore
undique conveniens. . . .
'tu vincas Iustine' canunt, ingensque tumultus
crescit, et Augusta luctus discessit ab aula
laetitia veniente nova. vox excitat omnes.
omnia Iustino praebent elementa favorem,
omnia congaudent, omnes clamore vocati
conveniunt proceres: lux sacra palatia complet.
(364–365) . . .
signa dedit manifesta deus, seque ipse probavit,
Iustino claram regni imposuisse coronam.

On the harmony between the elements, the nobles, the palace and God in procuring the imperial election see above at notes 394–395. On lines 353f. see Cameron, *Corippus* p. 148.

418. Corippus *De Laud. Iust.*, 2, 1ff. On Justin's prayer to God, and Sophia's to the Virgin, see Cameron, *Corippus* (1976) 149ff, and also her "The Theotokos in Sixth Century Constantinople," *JTS* 29 (1978) 79–108, esp. 82ff.

419. καὶ παραχρῆμα Λέων. . . . ἠνέχθη: *De Cer.*, 411; cf. 418–421, 423, 426–429, 431–432.

420. Corippus *De Laud. Iust.*, 3, 79, cf. 1, 181, 250; the circus passage: 1, 314ff, with commentary, *ad loc.*, in Averil Cameron, *Corippus*, 143ff. *Anthologia Latina* 1, 197 likens the Circus Maximus in Rome to the vault of heaven; translated in D. R. Dudley, *Urbs Roma, A Source Book of Classical Texts on the City and Its Monuments* (London, 1967) 213, along with other texts on the Circus Maximus.

421. Corippus *De Laud. Iust.*, 2, 165ff. Cf. above, n. 389.

422. Corippus *De Laud. Iust.*, 1, 361; 2, 92ff.

423. Corippus *De Laud. Iust.*, 2, 86ff. On the unusual location of Justin's coronation, inside the palace, see Averil Cameron, *Corippus*, 156ff. This is another instance of ceremonial being used to cover over somewhat unusual circumstances; cf. above, n. 374, on Justin I, and above, at nn. 170ff and 198 on Julian and Jovian.

424. Corippus *De Laud. Iust.*, 2, 105–112:

cruraque puniceis induxit regia vinclis,
Parthica . . . tergora . . .
. . .
lectaque pro sacris . . . plantis
quis solet edomitos victor calcare tyrannos
Romanus princeps et barbara colla domare.
Augustis solis hoc cultu conpetit uti,
sub quorum est pedibus regum cruor . . .

On the imperial shoes, see A. Alföldi, "Insignien und Tracht," reprinted in his *Die monarchische Repräsentation im römischen Kaiserreiche* (1970) 183f, and *ibid.*, 143ff, on the emperor's exclusive right to wear triumphal costume. Other particulars in Averil Cameron, *ad loc.*

425. Corippus *De Laud. Iust.*, 2, 118–127:

Caesareos umeros ardenti murice texit
circumfusa chlamys, rutilo quae ornata metallo
principis exerta vincebat lumina dextra.
aurea iuncturas morsu praestrinxit obunco
fibula, et a summis gemmae nituere catenis,
gemmae, quas Getici felix victoria belli
praebuit atque favens dominis Ravenna revexit,
quasque a Vandalica Belisarius adtulit aula.
signa triumphorum, pie Iustiniane, tuorum
sospite Iustino mundumque regente manebunt.

426. Corippus *De Laud. Iust.*, 2, 130–136:

Armati manibus sacrati circulus auri
inpositi in collo imperium sublime dicavit,
quod faciens ter, ter dextram cum munere tendens
'Augusti, Iustine, locum tibi confero' dixit.
'ast ego te iubeo' princeps ait 'esse tribunum'.
felix Armatus, primus qui verba loquentis
audiit et primus sollemnia dona recepit.

427. Corippus *De Laud. Iust.*, 2, 145–158:

Nunc maximus orbis
communis benefactor adest, cui subdita reges
colla parant, nomenque tremunt et numen adorant.
adstitit in clipeo princeps fortissimus illo
solis habens specimen. lux altera fulsit ab urbe;
mirata est pariter geminos consurgere soles
una favens eademque dies. mea carmina numne
mensuram transgressa suam? mirabere forsan,
quod dixi geminos pariter consurgere soles.
nec vacuis verbis nec inanibus ista figuris
ore feres prolata meo, si dicta rependis.
mens iusti plus sole nitet: non mergitur undis,
non cedit tenebris, non fusca obtexitur umbra.
lux operum aeterno lucet splendore bonorum.

428. Cf. E. Kantorowicz, "*Oriens Augusti—Lever du Roi*," *DOP* 17 (1963) 119–177.

429. Corippus *De Laud. Iust.*, 2, 173. See, on the underlying concepts of this expression, H. U. Instinsky, "Kaiser und Ewigkeit," *Hermes* 77 (1942) 313–355.

430. See E. Stein, "Post-Consulat et αὐτοκρατορία," *Mélanges Bidez* (1934) 869–912, reprinted in E. Stein, *Opera Minora Selecta*, ed. J. R. Palanque (1968) 315–358.

431. Corippus *De Laud. Iust.*, 1, 62–65.

432. Corippus *De Laud. Iust.*, 2, 146–147.

433. Corippus *De Laud. Iust.*, 2, 178–189:

'super omnia regnans
regna deus regnum nobis concessit avitum,
et patrium diadema dedit, curasque regendi
imposuit rerum genitor, quas ipse creavit.
laudamus factoris opus, regemque tremendum

suspicimus. grates agimus gratesque fatemur.
ipsius est quodcumque sumus . . .
(185: lacuna)
pluribus ex membris animal componitur unum,
sed caput est quod membra regit, deus erga creator
componens hominem (lacuna)
omnibus ut membris caput imperet.

434. Whereas in the West, there were the different coronation orders: C. A. Bouman, *Sacring and Crowning* (1957); P. E. Schramm, *Kaiser, Könige und Päpste; gesammelte Aufsätze zur Geschichte des Mittelalters*, vol. 2 (Stuttgart, 1968) Abschnitt 3, on Frankish and Anglo-Saxon *ordines*; cf. J. Nelson, "The Problem of King Alfred's Anointing," *Journ. of Eccl. Hist.* 18 (1967) 145–163. Also: E. Kantorowicz, *Laudes Regiae* (1958), and J. Nelson, "Symbols in Context," in *Studies in Church History* 13 (1976) ed. D. Baker, 97–119. For the later Byzantine ceremonial, E. Stein and G. Ostrogorsky, "Die Krönungsordnungen des Zeremonienbuches," *Byzantion* 7 (1932) 185–233, reprinted in E. Stein, *Opera Minora Selecta*, ed. J. R. Palanque (1963) 255–304; G. Ostrogorsky, "Zur Kaisersalbung und Schilderhebung im spätbyzantinischen Krönungszeremoniell," *Historia* 4 (1955) 246–256. A. Christophilopoulou, Ἐκλογὴ . . . (1956) covers the entire Byzantine period.

435. See on the occasion and the texts, Averil Cameron, "An Emperor's Abdication," *Byzantinoslavica* 37 (1976) 161–167.

436. Theophanes, 252 (de Boor).

437. Theophylact Simocatta *Hist.*, 3, 11 (Bonn 136) ἰδέ, ὁ θεὸς ὁ ἀγαθύνων σε. τοῦτο τὸ σχῆμα ὁ θεός σοι διδῶσιν, οὐκ ἐγώ, repeated, like the rest of this account, in Theophanes 248f (de Boor). The other detailed contemporary account where Justin is inspired by an angel, is in John of Ephesus, *H.E.*, 3, 5, tr. (Latin) E. W. Brooks (1936).

438. Simocatta *Hist.*, 3, 11, (Bonn 137), followed by Theophanes, 248 (de Boor):

μὴ εἰς ἔχθραν ὁμοιωθῇς ἐμοί· ἐγὼ γὰρ ὡς ἄνθρωπος εἰσωδιάσθην (καὶ γὰρ πταιστὸς ἐγενόμην) καὶ ἀπέλαβον κατὰ τὰς ἁμαρτίας μου. ἀλλὰ δικάσομαι τοῖς ποιήσασί μοι τοῦτο ἐπὶ τοῦ βήματος τοῦ Χριστοῦ. μὴ ἐξεπαιρέτω σε τοῦτο τὸ σχῆμα ὡς ἐμέ. οὕτω πρόσχες πᾶσιν, ὡς σεαυτῷ. γνῶθι τί ἧς καὶ τί εἶ νῦν. μὴ ὑπερφανήσῃς καὶ οὐχ ἁμαρτάνεις. οἶδας τί ἤμην καὶ τί ἐγενόμην, καὶ τί εἰμί. ὅλοι οὗτοι τέκνα σού εἰσι καὶ δοῦλοι.

439. Simocatta *Hist.*, 3, 11 (Bonn 137), cf. Theophanes, 249:

ἐὰν θέλῃς, εἰμί· ἐάν μὴ θέλῃς, οὐκ εἰμί. ὁ θεὸς ὁ ποιήσας τὸν οὐρανὸν καὶ τὴν γῆν, πάντα ὅσα ἐπελαθόμην εἰπεῖν σοι, αὐτὸς ἐμβάλῃ εἰς τὴν καρδίαν σου.

For the subjects as the emperor's slaves, cf. above, n. 399. Cf. Themistius on a related topic, the heart of kings in the hand of God, above at n. 228.

440. καλὸν ἐντάφιον ἡ βασιλεία ἐστί: Procopius *BP*, 1, 24, 37, with T. Nöldeke, "Die von Guidi . . . Chronik," *SB Wien* 178 (1893) Abh. 9, 15.

441. Pertusi, ed., *Giorgio di Pisidia*, 77–81; cf. above, "*Adventus*" at nn. 324ff. On George of Pisidia's vocabulary and poetic technique see J. D. C. Frendo, "The Significance of Technical Terms in George of Pisidia," *Orpheus* 21 (1974) 45–55. On his epic characteristics, see above, n. 411. On the changed role of classical culture in Byzantium at this time, see Averil Cameron, "Images of Author-

ity: Elites and Icons in Late Sixth-Century Byzantium," *Past and Present* 84 (1979) 3–35, at 24–29.

442. Theophanes, 299, lines 9f. Before this Heraclius was crowned with a στέμμα from a church of the Theotokos in Cyzicus: Theophanes, 299, lines 3f. The στέμμα could have been an object resembling the votive crowns of Visigothic Spain: J. Fontaine, *L'Art préroman hispanique* (La Pierre-qui-Vire, 1973) 246f.

443. George of Pisidia *In Heraclium ex Africa redeuntem*, 8; 25, 53, 81, 72, 76f, resp. Cf. *Exped. Pers.* 1, 35–50, 76–81, 221f.

444. I. I. Tolstoi, *Les Monnaies byzantines* (1912–14) (?: no publisher given) Arcadius pl. 3, 78–79; 81; 83–85; 87–89; Eudoxia Arcadii pl. 3, 136; 138–141; Eudoxia Theodosii pl. 6, 86; 88–91; Pulcheria pl. 6, 36; pl. 7, 30–31; 33–35; 37; Verina pl. 9, 53–55; Zenonis pl. 11, 94; see K. G. Holum, "Pulcheria's Crusade of A.D. 421–422 and the Ideology of Imperial Victory," *Greek, Roman and Byzantine Studies* 18 (1977) 153–172, on Pulcheria's coins.

445. See P. Courcelle, "Le serpent à face humaine dans la numismatique impériale du Vᵉ siècle," in *Mélanges A. Piganiol*, Vol. 1 (1966) 343–353. See also Cohen, vol. 8, Valentinian III, no. 24; P. Courcelle, *Histoire littéraire des grandes invasions germaniques* (1964) 351, pl. 5; serpent solidi issued 425 onwards.

446. A. Grabar, "Recherches," *Cahiers archéologiques* 14 (1964) 53–57, and in greater detail, "Un médaillon en or provenant de Mersine," *DOP* 6 (1951) 27–49, at 34ff; K. Weitzmann, ed., *Age of Spirituality* (1979) 72–74.

447. For which cf. H. P. L'Orange, *Iconography of Cosmic Kingship* (1953) 88–89.

448. Ivories: J. Beckwith, *Early Christian and Byzantine Art*, (1970) figs. 163b, 173, 176; cf. fig. 222 Roger II of Sicily. Coinage: e.g., Wroth 2, pl. 52, 1; 53, 2; 54, 10–11. For the use of this iconography in churches at a later date, see Robert of Clari, *The Conquest of Constantinople*, tr. E. Holmes McNeal (New York, 1936; 1964) 56.

449. On Justin and Justinian, see A. R. Bellinger, *Catalogue of the Byzantine Coins in the Dumbarton Oaks Collection and in the Whittemore Collection*, vol. 1 (1966) 56ff and pl. XII; Justinian alone, Wroth 1, pl. 8, 3; 8; Bellinger, *Catalogue*, 136ff; pl. XXXV.

450. This being a regular obverse of Justin II's base metal coinages: Bellinger, *Catalogue*, 204ff; 221ff, etc. and pl. L–LIX; Wroth 1, 77f; pl. 11, 8–12, 14.

451. Bellinger, *Catalogue*, 320, and pl. LXX; cf. 373f, and pl. LXXX. Wroth 1, pl. 19, 22, 23.

452. Bellinger, *Catalogue*, 373–375 and pl. LXXX. Wroth 1, pl. 20, 1; cf. Heraclius, Wroth 1, 195f, pl. 23, 8f passim.

453. P. Grierson, *Catalogue of the Byzantine Coins in the Dumbarton Oaks Collection and in the Whittemore Collection*, Vol. 2, 1 (1968) 162, 168, 174, 176, etc., pl. II–V; Wroth, 1, 165f, pl. 20, 9; 21, 5; 7; 22, 1–2; 4–5.

454. Delbrueck, *Consulardiptychen*, nos. 50 and 52; Volbach, *Elfenbeinarbeiten*, nos. 51 and 52. Cf. K. Weitzmann, ed., *Age of Spirituality* (1979) 31–32.

455. For instance, on the column-base of Arcadius, and on the Barberini diptych, above, "*Adventus*" at nn. 225, 285.

456. For the imperial mosaics, see the masterly exegesis by G. Rodenwaldt, "Bemerkungen zu den Kaisermosaiken in San Vitale," *J. d. I* 59–60 (1944–45) 88–110. For the late antique artistic context of Ravenna, J. Kollwitz, "Ravenna

zwischen Orient und Occident," *Atti del VI Congresso Internazionale di Archeologia Cristiana, Ravenna 1962* (1965), 383–402. See now F. W. Deichmann, *Ravenna, Hauptstadt des spätantiken Abendlandes 1, Geschichte und Monumente* (1969) 226–227 with *Ravenna. . . . 2, Kommentar 2* (1976) 3, 6–7 (the dedicatory inscription of Julius Argentarius and its date); 48–49, 188–195 (the date of the structure and of the mosaics).

457. The offering at the accession: *De Cer.* (Bonn), 91, 413 (Leo I); 92, 425 (Anastasius). Cf. A. Grabar, "Quel est le sens de l'offrande de Justinien et Theodora sur les mosaïques de Saint Vital?" *Felix Ravenna* (1960) 63–77 with the older literature. For an exhaustive discusson of the San Vitale imperial mosaics with the literature, now see F. W. Deichmann, *Ravenna, Hauptstadt des spätantiken Abendlandes 2, Kommentar 2* (1976) 180–187.

458. E. Stein, *Hist. du Bas-Empire*, vol. 2, 459; Justinian, Nov. 47, 537 A.D.; note the preface!

459. Cf. above at n. 443; George of Pisidia, *In Her. ex Afr. red.* 8–9:

> ἡμᾶς δὲ τῶν ψυχικῶν κινημάτων
> τὴν ἔνθεον φρόνησιν ὑμνεῖν εὐπρεπές.

Cf. *In Rest. S. Crucis* 43–6.

460. On this iconography see F. Cumont, "L'adoration des mages et l'art triomphal de Rome," *Atti della Pontificia Accademia Romana di Archeologia* Ser. 3, Mem. 3 (1932–1933) 81–105.

461. For an empress' humility, see Gregory of Nyssa, *Funerary Oration for Flacilla*, *P.G.* 46, 884b ὑποηλὴ ταπεινοφροσύνη, and below, n. 466.

462. On the significance of Theodora's niche, see F. W. Deichmann, *Ravenna, Kommentar 2* (1976) 182. The prophet niches in S. Apollinare Nuovo, F. W. Deichmann, *Bauten und Mosaiken von Ravenna* (1958) pl. 100–107; niches of the bishops of Ravenna in S. Apollinare in Classe, *ibid.* pl. 394–400 with *Kommentar 2* (1976) 262, cf. 271; for the date, 245–246. Both in S. Apollinare Nuovo and in S. Apollinare in Classe, crowns are suspended from the centre of the niches, above the heads of the personages standing beneath—whereas Theodora is already crowned with the imperial diadem. The niches in S. Apollinare in Classe also contain curtains, which may perhaps be viewed as a hint at the life after death. See, on a Ravenna sarcophagus, cross between curtains under conch-type niche, flanked by two crosses under arch: G. Valenti Zucchini and M. Bucci, *Corpus della scultura paleocristiana bizantina ed altomedioevale di Ravenna*, ed. G. Bovini (1968) no. 31b. A sarcophagus with a similar symbolic structure, showing, in the centre, curtains drawn aside under a pediment, is now in Cleveland (the space behind the curtains has been cut away for later use of the sarcophagus as a reliquary altarfront): M. Lawrence, "Two Ravennate Monuments in American Collections," in *Studies in Art and Literature for Belle da Costa Greene*, ed. D. Miner (1954) 132–142, and fig. 100. The departed were shown under conch-type niches already in paganism: e.g., R. Schindler, *Führer durch das Landesmuseum Trier* (1977) 104f, pl. 327 and 334, third century funerary monuments. For a Ravenna-type iconography of S. Peter under such a niche, and holding the cross over the four streams of Paradise (cf. the fountain in the Theodora mosaic, below n. 465) see W. F. Volbach, *Elfenbeinarbeiten* no. 164, and K. Weitzmann, ed., *Age of Spirituality* (1979) 539–540, commenting on the unusualness of the iconography.

463. This is chronologically possible but tight. San Vitale was dedicated in 547 (above, n. 457); Theodora died in June, 548, *PW*, II, 5 (1934) col. 1787; Stein,

Hist. du Bas-Empire, vol. 2 (1959) 589, n. 4. The mosaic decorations need not have been complete at the time of dedication. Such a monument to Theodora after her death would not be incompatible with other evidence. For the inscription commemorating her at Sinai, see I. Ševčenko, "The Early Period of the Sinai Monastery in the Light of Its Inscriptions," *DOP* 20 (1966) 255–264 at 262, no. 4; for Justinian's homage to her after his triumphal entry into Constantinople in 559, *De Cer.*, 497, line 19; he lit candles in the Church of the Apostles εἰς τὸ μνῆμα τῆς δεσποίνης. See also Paul the Silentiary, *Ekphrasis of S. Sophia,* 58–65 (ed. P. Friedlander in *Johannes von Gaza, Paulus Silentiarius und Prokopius von Gaza* (1969), 228–229.

464. On the curtain in the iconographies of Ravenna, see above, n. 462. See also the third-century sarcophagus in the Musée du Bardo, Tunis: in the centre, the deceased stands in front of a door covered by a curtain, flanked by the four Seasons: R. Bianchi Bandinelli, *Rome, The Late Empire. Roman Art AD 200–400* (1971) 222 (Bianchi Bandinelli suggests a fourth-century date for this work, *ibid.*). For the symbolism of the door in life and afterlife, see above, "*Consecratio*" at nn. 93ff, and plates 37–40. Even though on the Bardo sarcophagus the curtain is not being held aside for the deceased, I would suggest that the imagery is analogous to that of the curtain and doorway on the Theodora mosaic. (I would like to thank Eunice Maguire for drawing my attention to the Bardo Sarcophagus.)

465. Fountains of "living water" in the Mausoleum of Galla Placidia: F. W. Deichmann, *Ravenna, Kommentar,* I (1974) 83–84, with biblical passages, referring such fountains to the *refrigerium* of the dead. See also, on the paradisal significance of fountains in the atrium of a church (if indeed Theodora's whereabouts should be viewed as the atrium of a church), F. Muthmann, *Mutter und Quelle. Studien zur Quellenverehrung im Altertum und im Mittelalter* (Basel, 1975) 384.

466. See Gregory of Nyssa, *Funerary Oration of Flacilla,* P.G. 46, 877–892, with K. G. Holum, *Theodosian Empresses: Women and Imperial Dominion in Late Antiquity* (in press).

467. On Sophia—Wisdom, see Corippus *Laus Iustini,* Preface 22–25; Panegyric of Anastasius 34; book I, 9; III, 148; IV, 280. I, 291, Sapientia—Sophia exercises the virtue of *pietas* by preparing Justinian's funeral; II, 198 Sophia as σύνθρονος with Justin, cf. below, n. 468. Acclamations to Justin and Sophia, II, 168ff; 310–11; cf. III, 71; 83–84. Theodora and Sophia, IV, 270–273.

468. See Kantorowicz, "ΣΥΝΘΡΟΝΟΣ ΔΙΚΗΙ," in his *Selected Studies* (1965) 1–6.

469. See above "*Adventus*" at nn. 328, 343; cf. George of Pisidia *Heraclias,* 1, 201: χαῖρε, στρατηγὲ κοσμικοῦ γενεθλίου. Cf. *Exped. Pers.,* 1, 17f.

470. See J. Kollwitz, *Oströmische Plastik der theodosianischen Zeit* (1941) 145–152 and notes.

471. *De Cer.,* 411; 424: ὁ Θεός σε ἔδωκεν, ὁ Θεός σε φυλάξει.

472. *De Cer.,* 430: βασιλεῦ οὐράνιε, σῶσον τὸν ἐπίγειον.

EPILOGUE

1. E.g. M. Weber, *Die Stadt, Wirtschaft und Gesellschaft* (1925); and E. Durkheim, *Les formes élémentaires de la vie religieuse, le système totémique en Australia,* 2nd ed. (Paris, 1925).

2. Themistius *Or.* 13. This speech is entitled after a now-lost platonizing dialogue of Aristotle.

3. See F. Klingner, *Römische Geisteswelt* (1961); F. Schneider, *Rom und Romgedanke im Mittelalter* (Munich, 1926); and W. Rehm, *Der Untergang Roms im abendländischen Denken* (1930; 1966).

4. Themistius, 81c.

5. *Pan. Lat.*, 3, 11, 3.

6. Horace, *Ars Poetica*, 361; cf. C. O. Brink, *Horace on Poetry, the Ars Poetica* (Cambridge, 1971), Commentary, *ad loc.*

7. Cicero *De Republica*, I, 25; cf. E. Shils, "Consensus," *Center and Periphery, Essays in Macrosociology* (1975) 164–181.

PLATES

All plates are discussed in the text. At the same time, they have been arranged so as to tell their own story and to allow the reader to approach this visual evidence to some extent independently of the text.

THE FIGURE OF THE EMPEROR

Many strands of artistic tradition and political theory combined to give the visual representation of any given emperor its own cast and its own style. At each accession, an image of the new emperor, part reality, part ideal, had to be formulated. The examples of imperial images which follow present some of the many options which were available in late antique imperial portraiture.

PLATE 1 Divine inspiration and imperial power: portrait of Gallienus. Rome, Terme Museum. (Photo: DAI, Rome)

PLATE 2 The countenance of the military emperor. Porphyry head of a Tetrarch from Egypt. London, British Museum.

PLATE 3 The Tetrarchs at San Marco, Venice. The group depicts an imperial encounter, and in this context expounds some of the most potent slogans of the Tetrarchic period: imperial concord and solicitude for the defense and well-being of the empire. (Photo: DAI, Rome)

PLATE 4 Divine inspiration and imperial authority: portrait of a prince of the family of Constantine. Rome, Conservatori. (Photo: DAI, Rome)

PLATE 5 *'Principes clausi'* or *'tranquillitas nostra'*? Portrait head of Arcadius. Istanbul, Archeological Museum. (Photo: DAI, Rome)

PLATE 6   The emperor Honorius in the panoply
of the military emperor: but in his case, the insignia outweighed the reality. Diptych of Probus,
Rome, 406 A.D. Aosta, Collezione dell' Accademia
di Sant' Anselmo. (Photo: Alinari)

PLATE 7   *Sollicitudo nostra:* the careworn majesty of the emperor as leader
of an army. Portrait statue of an un-
known late antique emperor. Barletta.
(Photo: Alinari)

ADVENTUS

In late antiquity, the depiction of *adventus* changed away from a repertoire of images which were deeply rooted in the pagan classical world
and were capable of depicting the emperor as a companion of the gods
or inspired by them. Instead, there emerged an imagery of hierarchy,
which placed Christ, the emperor, and the emperor's subjects, each into
an apportioned place.

PLATE 8   Ancient ceremonies: The monument erected in Rome to
celebrate Diocletian's Vicennalia and the Decennalia of his Caesars in
303. Decennalia Base, Roman Forum. *Top*: One of the most venerable
rites of the Roman state, the purificatory sacrifice of a bull, a sheep
and a pig, the *suovetaurilia*. *Bottom*: An emperor, crowned from behind
by Victoria and the Genius Senatus, pours the preliminary libation in
the presence of attendants and of Mars, Roma and the sungod.

PLATE 9

a. The Arras Medallion, minted at Trier; gold, actual size. Imperial victory and *adventus*: Constantius I is welcomed by the personification of the city of London, 296 A.D. Arras. (Photo: Ashmolean Museum, Oxford, from electrotype)

Obverse: FL VAL CONSTA-NTIUS NOBIL CAES.

Reverse: R-EDDITOR LUCIS AETERNA-E LON PTR.

b. Gold multiple minted at Trier, actual size. Constantius I 'restores' a kneeling downcast province. Ashmolean Museum, Oxford.

Obverse: FL VAL CONSTANTIUS NOB CAES

Reverse: PIETAS AUGG

PLATE 10   Practical and theoretical foundations of Tetrarchic rule
were translated into images on the Arch of Galerius at Thessalonika.
South pillar, north face. (Photo: DAI, Rome)
    From the top down:
    Galerius celebrates a ceremonial arrival; he is greeted by the citizens
of a town, and by the town's divinity, who waves from a temple.
    Galerius is crowned by an eagle for victory in personal combat
against a Sassanian general.
    The concord of the four Tetrarchs is represented in a scene of cosmic
dominion, in the centre of which Diocletian and Maximian are enthroned over personifications of sky and earth respectively.

PLATE 11   The emperor and his divine companion: the Ticinum Medallion; gold, actual size. Bibliothèque Nationale, Paris.
    Obverse: INVICTUS CONSTANTINUS MA-X AUG. Constantine side-by-
side with the sungod.
    Reverse: FELIX ADVENTUS AUGG NN SMT. The imperial arrival.

PLATES 12 AND 13   Imperial events in a cosmic setting: Constantine's departure from Verona with the setting moon, and his *adventus* in Rome with the rising sun. Arch of Constantine, Rome. (Photo: DAI, Rome)

PLATES 14 AND 15   The culmination of *adventus*: the emperor and
his subjects. Constantine on the Roman Forum addresses the citizens
of Rome and distributes largesse. Arch of Constantine, Rome. (Photo:
DAI, Rome)

PLATE 16   Movement transformed into tranquillity: an arrival of Constantius II. *Largitio*
bowl. Leningrad, Hermitage.

PLATES 17 AND 18   The eternal presence: emperor and subjects in Constantinople. Obelisk base of Theodosius, Istanbul.

17. Imperial victory is depicted by means of gestures of ceremonious submission: Persians (left) and northern barbarians (right) bring offerings.

18. The imperial family presides at chariot races. The relief lastingly defines in stone what would be a regular sight in the very place where the relief was displayed.

19. East side: Senators offer the *anrum coronarium*.

20. South side: The Roman provinces bring gifts.

PLATES 19, 20, AND 21 The column base of Arcadius (Freshfield drawings). Protected by symbols of Christ's victory, the emperors Arcadius and Honorius confront mankind. Library of Trinity College, Cambridge, reproduced by courtesy of the Master and Fellows.

21. West side: Conquered enemies make their submission.

PLATE 22   The Barberini Diptych. The traditional imagery of *adventus* is integrated within a cosmic hierarchy where emperor and empire mediate between Christ in the clouds of heaven, and subjected barbarians. Paris, Louvre. (Documentation photographique des musées nationaux)

PLATE 23   *Roma et Renovatio*. Gold multiple, minted in Constantinople, three-fourths actual size. Formerly, Paris, Bibliothèque Nationale. (from an electrotype, photo British Museum)

Obverse: D N JUSTINI-ANUS P P A-UG.

Reverse: SALUS ET GL-RIA ROMANO-RUM CONOB. An *adventus* of Justinian depicted in the idiom of the Roman past.

PLATE 24   Heavenly and terrestrial power comprised in one single symbol: busts of Christ as Pantokrator, with busts of Justin II and Sophia on the cross which the imperial couple sent to Rome. Rome, Vatican. (Photo: DAI, Rome)

PLATE 25   *Adventus* and *Parousia*. Christ enters Jerusalem (central panel, bottom), and is enthroned over the personified heaven (central panel, top). Sarcophagus of Junius Bassus, Rome, Vatican, 359 A.D. (Photo: DAI, Rome)

CONSECRATIO

Unlike the imagery of *adventus*, that of *consecratio* and of the imperial afterlife formed no continuous evolution. Rather, images which were parallel or analogous to each other were explored simultaneously. The diversity of these images reflects diversity and conflicts in pagan beliefs about the imperial afterlife which were only resolved in Christianity.

PLATE 26   On the wings of eagles: A solar deity is supported on two eagles. Limestone plaque from Baalbek. Berlin (East), Staatliche Museen, Preussischer Kulturbesitz.

PLATE 27   The apotheosis of an emperor on a chariot supported by wreathbearing eagles. Late antique cameo. Berlin (West), Staatliche Museen, Preussischer Kulturbesitz.

PLATE 28 From the Campus Martius in Rome, Antoninus and Faustina depart to eternity on the wings of a personification of time and the cosmos. Column base of Antoninus Pius. Rome, Vatican. (Photo: DAI, Rome)

PLATE 29 An emperor of the second century A.D. (Trajan?) ascends to the above in the chariot of the sungod. Slabs I and K of the Antonine Altar at Ephesus. Vienna, Kunsthistorisches Museum.

PLATE 30 Imperial motifs enter Christian art. Over the waves of the River Jordan, the prophet Elias ascends to heaven in a chariot. Christian sarcophagus. Rome, Vatican. (Photo: DAI, Rome)

PLATE 31 The elaboration of Christian art: Elias ascends to heaven in a chariot, while his disciple Elisha receives the master's cloak with the courtly gesture of veiled hands. Beneath the chariot are Adam and Eve with the serpent, while the background is decorated with a city gate. Christian sarcophagus, Sant' Ambrogio, Milan. (Photo: DAI, Rome)

PLATE 32 Ascent to the gods: Minerva assists in the apotheosis of Hercules, who rises to heaven in a chariot. The scene is framed by the zodiac. Igel Monument. (Photo: Marburg)

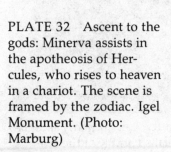

PLATE 33 Constantine as a charioteer is welcomed to heaven by the hand of God. Bronze coin minted at Alexandria, two times enlarged. Washington, D.C., Dumbarton Oaks.
Obverse: DV CONSTANT-NUS PT AUGG
Reverse: SMALA

PLATE 34 The Resurrection and Ascension of Christ, who is welcomed to heaven by the hand of God. Ivory plaque. Munich, Bayerisches Nationalmuseum.

PLATE 35   Solidus minted at Trier, 310/313 A.D.; two times enlarged. Vienna, Kunsthistorisches Museum, Münzkabinett.

Obverse: DIVUS CONSTANTIUS. Head of Constantius.

Reverse: CONSE-CRATIO. Three-tiered pyre, surmounted by emperor in chariot.

PLATE 36   The ascent of a divinized emperor on a Roman ivory diptych of c. 430 A.D. The emperor rises from the pyre as a charioteer in heroic nudity, while also being carried to the celestial sphere by windgods. London, British Museum.

PLATE 37 Cinerary urn: two victories standing under palm trees open the gate to the other world. Rome, Vatican.

PLATE 38 Sarcophagus of a married couple: they stand on either side of a door which is ajar, each with a friend, and make gestures of farewell. Cordoba, Alcazar. (Photo: DAI, Rome)

PLATE 39   Bronze coin, minted at Ostia, commemorating Maximian,
one and one-half times enlarged. Washington, D.C., Dumbarton Oaks.
Obverse: DIVO MAXIMIANO SEN AUG. Veiled head of Maximian.
Reverse: AETERNA MEMORIA MOSTS. Shrine with a half open door.

PLATE 40   Ivory plaque from a casket, showing the tomb of the res-
urrected Christ with the doors ajar. London, British Museum.

PLATE 41   Bronze multiple of Alexander Severus and Iulia Mamaea,
actual size. Paris, Bibliothèque Nationale.
   Obverse: IMP SEVERUS ALEXANDER AUG IULIA MAMAEA AUG MATER
AUG. Busts of Alexander Severus and Julia Mamaea facing each other.
   Reverse: TEMPORUM FELICITAS. Alexander Severus enthroned on a
starry globe. He holds the circle of the year, from which emerge the
four Seasons. Felicitas stands at the left, and Victoria, at the right,
crowns the emperor.

PLATE 42   Christ en-
throned on a globe over the
four streams of paradise. Divine life and human life, celestial and terrestrial dominion are joined together in
one single image. Ravenna,
San Vitale. (Photo: DAI,
Rome)

ACCESSION

Before the ceremony of coronation emerged as indispensable to a legitimate imperial accession in mid-fifth-century Constantinople, the emperor's rise to power was validated by other ceremonies, such as *adventus*, and by the vows taken annually for his safety. At the same time, in art, the emperor's legitimate majesty could be depicted in a civilian context by images of enthronement, and in a military context it could be depicted by showing him crowned for victory or with the soldiers who had elected him. Such images, and the ceremonies and ideas which underlay them, not only survived the emergence of the early Byzantine ceremonial of coronation, but also contributed to the formulation of this ceremonial and the portrayal of the imperial majesty in visual art at that time.

PLATE 43   Intaglio of the early fifth century, signed by the engraver Romulus, from the Western Empire. Two men, the one on the left marked out as an emperor by the diadem he wears, are crowned with laurel wreaths by figures of Victory, while themselves investing a junior emperor with wreath and chlamys. This very unusual image depicts both the ancient idea of coronation for victory, and the late antique one of coronation for accession, which later remained unexpressed in the more regular iconographies of late antique imperial art. Leningrad, Hermitage.

PLATE 44   Gold multiple, minted in Rome, actual size. Budapest, Magyar Nemzeti Múzeum.

Obverse: IMP C M AUR VAL MAXIMIANUS PF AUG. Maximian wearing the lionskin of Hercules.

Reverse: PERPE-TUA CONCORDIA AUGG PR. Diocletian and Maximian enthroned are crowned by Iuppiter (left) and Hercules (right), respectively.

PLATE 45   Gold multiple, minted in Constantinople, one-third actual size. Vienna, Kunsthistorisches Museum, Münzkabinett.

Obverse: FL IUL CONSTANTIUS NOB CAES.

Reverse: GAUDIUM R-OMANORUM MCONS. Constantine, standing between two sons, who are crowned by Virtus (left) and Victoria (right), is himself crowned by the hand of God from a cloud.

PLATE 46   Bronze coin, minted in Constantinople, one and one-half times enlarged. Washington, D.C., Dumbarton Oaks.

Obverse: D N ARCAD-IUS PF AUG. Arcadius, wearing the imperial diadem, is crowned with a circlet by the hand of God.

Reverse: GLORIA RO-MANORUM CONC. Arcadius in military dress with captive.

PLATE 47   Gold multiple, minted in Constantinople, actual size. The Hague, Kon. Penning Kabinet.

Obverse: CONSTANTI-NUS MAX AUG. Constantine, wearing the imperial diadem.

Reverse: SALUS-ET SPES REIPUB-LICAE CONS. Constantine, nimbate, enthroned between two sons.

PLATE 48   Solidus, minted at Constantinople, two and one-half times enlarged. Washington, D.C., Dumbarton Oaks.

Obverse: D N VALENTINI-ANUS P F AUG.

Reverse: VOTA-PU-BLICA CONS. Valentinian I and Valens nimbate, enthroned as consuls, with two captives at their feet.

PLATE 49   Solidus, minted in Antioch, two and one-half times enlarged. Washington, D.C., Dumbarton Oaks.
   Obverse: DN VALENTINI-ANUS PF AUG. Bust of Valentinian.
   Reverse: SPE-S RP VOT V MULT X ANTI. Valentinian I and Valens enthroned on either side of the young Gratian, son of Valentinian. The
legend acclaims the emperors as "hope of the state" and also notes the
vows which have been paid for their fifth anniversary, and are anticipated for their tenth.

PLATE 50   Solidus, minted at Milan, two and one-half times enlarged. Washington, D.C., Dumbarton Oaks.
   Obverse: DN THEODO-SIUS PF AUG. Bust of Theodosius.
   Reverse: VICTOR-IA AUGG COM. Theodosius and Valentinian II, nimbate, are enthroned, overshadowed by the wings of Victoria.

PLATE 51   Silver multiple, minted in Ticinum, twice enlarged. Munich, Staatliche Münzsammlung.

Obverse: IMP CONSTANT-INUS PF AUG. Constantine armed and wearing a helmet, which displays, over his forehead, the Chi Rho.

Reverse: SA-LUS REI-PUBLIC-AE. Constantine addressing his soldiers from a platform.

PLATE 52   *Largitio* bowl of Valentinian I. The emperor is depicted at the head of his soldiers. Geneva, Musée d'Art et d'Histoire.

PLATE 53   Silver coin minted at Cyzicus, one and one-half times enlarged. Vienna, Kunsthistorisches Museum, Münzkabinett.
   Obverse: CONSTANTINUS IUN NOB C. Head of Constantine II.
   Reverse: FELICITAS ROMANORUM SMK. Constantine the Great standing under an archway, betokening the palace, with three sons.

PLATE 54   The Palace of Theoderic, Sant' Apollinare Nuovo, Ravenna. Before the Justinianic alterations of this mosaic, it probably showed Theoderic in the central archway and dignitaries of his court in the flanking ones. On the third column from the left can still be seen the hand and lower arm of one of these personages. (Photo: Anderson)

PLATE 55   The Missorium of Theodosius, commemorating, according to the inscription, the tenth anniversary of his accession. Theodosius is enthroned between his two imperial colleagues. The composition joins into one image expressions of majesty which elsewhere appear in isolation: enthronement in the palace with soldiers in attendance, the imperial act of bestowing office on a kneeling dignitary, and the universal dominion which is betokened by the reclining figure of Earth in the exergue. Madrid, Real Academia de la Historia. (Photo: DAI, Rome)

PLATE 56   An overmighty subject, Constantius before he became Emperor as Constantius III, is portrayed in an imperial position, above subject barbarians. The top register displays the imperial cities with their emperors: on the left Rome with Honorius, on the right Constantinople, who affectionately places her hand on the shoulder of her young emperor Theodosius II. Consular diptych of the Western Empire, early fifth century. Halberstadt, Domschatz.

PLATE 57   The personifications of the two imperial cities, Rome and Constantinople, in their regalia. The majesty of these two cities complemented and validated that of the emperors who ruled over them and vice versa. Ivory diptych of the Western empire, fifth century A.D. Vienna, Kunsthistorisches Museum.

PLATE 58 Large bronze, minted in Constantinople, one and one-half times enlarged. Washington, D.C., Dumbarton Oaks.

Obverse: DN IUSTI-NUS PP AUG. The emperor Justin II, and his consort Sophia enthroned together. Where formerly the emperor might have shared his majesty with one of the two imperial cities personified as a woman, he now shares it with his empress.

Reverse: M ANNO III CON.

PLATE 59 Solidus, minted in Ravenna, two times enlarged. Washington, D.C., Dumbarton Oaks.

Obverse: DN GALLA PLA-CIDIA PF AUG. The empress Galla Placidia crowned by the hand of God.

Reverse: SALUS REI-PUBLICAE RV COMOB. Victory inscribes the Chi Rho on a shield which formerly would have displayed the vows for the emperor's safety.

PLATE 60   Gold multiple of Galla Placidia, minted in Ravenna, actual size. Paris, Bibliothèque Nationale.
   Obverse: DN GALLA PLA-CIDIA PF AUG. Bust of Galla Placidia wearing diadem and chlamys, with the Chi Rho displayed on her sleeve.
   Reverse: SALUS REI-PUBLICAE RV COMOB. Galla Placidia nimbate, enthroned frontally.

PLATE 61   An early Byzantine empress surrounded by symbols of triumph and majesty which were derived from imperial Rome: eagles with a garland of laurel, and the aedicula which stands for the entrance of the palace. But her insignia are early Byzantine: diadem, pearl-edged embroidered chlamys, sceptre and cross bearing orb. Imperial diptych of c. 500 A.D. Florence, Bargello. (Photo: Anderson)

PLATE 62 The empress Theodora with her retinue in an architectural setting of Christian and transcendental majesty. Ravenna, San Vitale. (Photo: DAI, Rome)

PLATE 63 The emperor Justinian with his dignitaries, the supporters and exponents of his terrestrial dominion. Ravenna, San Vitale. (Photo: DAI, Rome)

BIBLIOGRAPHY

Classical and late antique sources are cited from the standard editions. Editions or translations with commentary appear in this bibliography under the name of the modern author. Some works incidental to the main themes of this book, although cited in the notes, have been omitted from the bibliography.

Abbott, F. F., and A. C. Johnson. *Municipal Administration in the Roman Empire.* Princeton, 1926.

Alexander, S. Spain, "Studies in Constantinian Church Architecture." *Rivista di archeologia cristiana* 47 (1971): 281–330 and 49 (1973): 33–44.

Alföldi, A. "Die Ausgestaltung des monarchischen Zeremoniells am römischen Kaiserhofe." *Mitteilungen des Deutschen Archäologischen Instituts*, Römische Abteilung 49 (1934): 3–118. Reprinted in his *Die monarchische Repräsentation im römischen Kaiserreiche.* Darmstadt, 1970.

——. "Insignien und Tracht der römischen Kaiser." *Mitteilungen des Deutschen Archäologischen Instituts*, Römische Abteilung 50 (1935): 3–158. Reprinted in his *Die monarchische Repräsentation im römischen Kaiserreiche.* Darmstadt, 1970.

——. *A Festival of Isis in Rome under the Christian Emperors of the IVth Century.* Budapest, 1937.

——. *Die Kontorniaten, ein verkanntes Propagandamittel der stadtrömischen heidnischen Aristokratie in ihrem Kampfe gegen das christliche Kaisertum.* Budapest, 1942–43. Revised and expanded with plates and catalogue by A. Alföldi, E. Alföldi and C. L. Clay, *Die Kontorniat-Medaillons.* Berlin and New York, 1976.

——. *The Conversion of Constantine and Pagan Rome.* Oxford, 1948 (1969).

——. "Der grosse römische Kameo der Trierer Stadtbibliothek." *Trierer Zeitschrift* 19 (1950): 41–44. Reprinted in W. Reusch, ed. *Aus der Schatzkammer des antiken Trier.* Trier, 1959, pp. 50–53.

——. "Zur Erklärung der konstantinischen Deckengemälde in Trier." *Historia* 4 (1955): 131–150.

Alföldi, M. R. *Die konstantinische Goldprägung. Untersuchungen zu ihrer Bedeutung für Kaiserpolitik und Hofkunst.* Mainz, 1963.

———. "Die Sol *comes* Münze vom Jahr 325." In *Mullus, Festschrift T. Klauser.* Münster, 1964, pp. 10–16.

Alföldy, G. "The Crisis of the Third Century as Seen by Contemporaries." *Greek, Roman and Byzantine Studies* 15 (1974): 89–111.

Altmann, W. *Die römischen Grabaltäre der Kaiserzeit.* Berlin, 1905.

Andreae, B. *Studien zur römischen Grabkunst.* Mitteilungen des deutschen archäologischen Instituts, Römische Abteilung, 9. Ergänzungsheft. Heidelberg, 1963.

Angiolini Martinelli, P. *Corpus della scultura paleocristiana, bizantina ed altomedievale di Ravenna.* Edited by G. Bovini. Rome, 1968.

Baldwin Smith, E. *Architectural Symbolism of Imperial Rome and the Middle Ages.* Princeton, 1956.

Banck, A. "Monuments des arts mineurs de Byzance (IVᵉ–VIIᵉ siècle) au Musée de l'Ermitage." *IX Corso di cultura sull'arte Ravennate e Bizantina.* Bologna (1962): 109–123.

Bastien, P. and C. Metzger. *Le trésor de Beaurains (dit d'Arras).* Numismatique romaine, 10. Wetteren, 1977.

Baumstark, A. "Orientalisches in den Texten der abendländischen Palmenfeier." *Jahrbuch für Liturgiewissenschaft* 7 (1927): 148–153.

Baur, P. C., O.S.B. *Johannes Chrysostomus und seine Zeit.* Munich, 1930.

Baus, K. *Der Kranz in Antike und Christentum.* Theophaneia, 2. Bonn, 1940.

Bayet, J. "L'immortalité astrale d'Auguste." *Revue des études latines* 17 (1939): 141–171.

Baynes, N. "The Death of Julian the Apostate in Christian Legend." *Journal of Roman Studies* 27 (1937): 22–29.

———. "Eusebius and the Christian Empire." In his *Byzantine Studies and Other Essays.* London, 1955, pp. 168–172.

———. *Constantine the Great and the Christian Church.* Edited by H. Chadwick. London, 1972.

Becatti, G. *La colonna coclide istoriata: problemi storici, iconografici, stilistici.* Rome, 1960.

Beck, H. G. "Konstantinopel, zur Sozialgeschichte einer früh-mittelalterlichen Hauptstadt." *Byzantinische Zeitschrift* 58 (1965). Reprinted in his *Ideen und Realitäten in Byzanz.* London, 1972.

———. "Senat und Volk von Konstantinopel." *Bayer. Akad. d. Wiss. Phil. Hist. Kl.* Sitzungsberichte, 1966. Reprinted in his *Ideen und Realitäten in Byzanz.* London, 1972.

———. "Antike Beredsamkeit und byzantinische Kallilogia." *Antike und Abendland* 15 (1969): 91–101. Reprinted in his *Ideen und Realitäten in Byzanz.* London, 1972.

Beckwith, J. *The Art of Constantinople: An Introduction to Byzantine Art, 330–1453.* London, 1961.

———. *Early Christian and Byzantine Art.* Harmondsworth, 1970.

Bellinger, A. R. *Catalogue of the Byzantine Coins in the Dumbarton Oaks Collection and in the Whittemore Collection*, I. Washington, D.C., 1966.

Belting-Ihm, C. "Das Justinuskreuz in der Schatzkammer der Peterskirche zu

Rom." *Jahrbuch des römisch-germanischen Zentralmuseums Mainz* 12 (1965): 142–166.

Benoît, F. *Sarcophages paléochrétiens d'Arles et de Marseille.* Supplément à *Gallia*, 5 (1954).

Béranger, J. *Recherches sur l'aspect idéologique du principat.* Schweizer Beiträge zur Altertumswissenschaft, 6. Basel, 1953.

———. "Idéologie impériale dans l'*H.A.*." *Bonner Historia Augusta Colloquium 1972–1974* (1976): 29–53.

Beskow, P. *Rex Gloriae. The Kingship of Christ in the Early Church.* Stockholm, 1962.

Bianchi Bandinelli, R. *Rome, the Late Empire. Roman Art AD 200–400.* London, 1971.

Bickermann, E. "Die römische Kaiserapotheose." *Archiv für Religionswissenschaft* 27 (1929): 1–34.

———. "Consecratio." In *Le culte des souverains dans l'empire romain.* Entretiens Hardt, 19. Geneva, 1972, pp. 3–37.

Bidez, J. *La vie de l'empereur Julien.* Paris, 1930.

Binneboessel, R. "Studien zu den attischen Urkundenreliefs d. 5. und 4. Jhdts." Dissertation, Leipzig, 1932.

Blockley, R. C. "The Panegyric of Claudius Mamertinus on the Emperor Julian." *American Journal of Philology* 43 (1972): 437–450.

Blumenthal, F. "Der ägyptische Kaiserkult." *Archiv für Papyrusforschung* 5 (1909–1913): 317–345.

Boer, W. den. "Trajan's Deification." *Proceedings of the XIV International Congress of Papyrologists*, Oxford, 24–31 July 1974 (London, 1975): 85–90.

Born, L. K. "The Perfect Prince According to the Latin Panegyrists." *American Journal of Philology* 55 (1934): 20–35.

Bouman, C. A. *Sacring and Crowning. The Development of the Latin Ritual for the Anointing of Kings and the Coronation of an Emperor before the Eleventh Century.* Groningen, 1957.

Bovini, G. "Antichi rifacimenti nei mosaici di S. Apollinare Nuovo di Ravenna." *XIII Corso di cultura sull'arte Ravennate e Bizantina.* Bologna, 1966, pp. 51–81.

———. "Il Mosaico dell'arco trionfale di S. Lorenzo fuori le mura a Roma." *XVIII Corso di cultura sull'arte Ravennate e Bizantina.* Bologna, 1971, pp. 127–140.

Bowersock, G. W. *Greek Sophists in the Roman Empire.* Oxford, 1969.

Boyancé, P. *Études sur le Songe de Scipion.* Bibliothèque des Universités du Midi, 20. Paris, 1936.

Brandenburg, H. "Ein verschollener Mailänder Sarkophag." *Rivista di archeologia cristiana* 48 (1972): 43–78.

Breckenridge, J. D. "The Long Siege of Thessalonika, Its Date and Iconography." *Byzantinische Zeitschrift* 48 (1955): 116–122.

———. *The Numismatic Iconography of Justinian II.* Numismatic Notes and Monographs, 144. New York, 1959.

Brenk, B. *Tradition und Neuerung in der christlichen Kunst des ersten Jahrtausends.* Wiener Byzantinische Studien, 3. Vienna, 1966.

Brightman, F. E. "Byzantine Imperial Coronations," *Journal of Theological Studies* 2 (1901): 353–392.

Brilliant, R. *Gesture and Rank in Roman Art.* Memoirs of the Connecticut Academy of Arts and Sciences, 14. New Haven, 1963.

Brodsky, N. *L'iconographie oublié de l'arc Ephésien de Sainte-Marie Majeure à Rome.* Paris, 1966.

Brown, D. F. "The Arcuated Lintel and Its Symbolic Interpretation in Late Antique Art." *American Journal of Archaeology* 46 (1942): 389–399.

Brown, P. R. L. *Religion and Society in the Age of St. Augustine.* London, 1972.

———. *Relics and Social Status in the Age of Gregory of Tours.* The Stenton Lecture, 1976. Reading, 1977.

———. *The Making of Late Antiquity.* Cambridge, Mass., 1978.

Browning, R. "The Riot of A.D. 387 in Antioch. The Role of the Theatrical Claques in the Later Roman Empire." *Journal of Roman Studies* 42 (1952): 13–20. Reprinted in his *Studies in Byzantine History, Literature and Education.* London, 1977.

Bruns, G. *Der Obelisk und seine Basis auf dem Hippodrom zu Konstantinopel.* Istanbuler Forschungen, 7. Istanbul, 1935.

———. *Staatskameen des 4. Jahrhunderts nach Christi Geburt.* Winckelmannsprogramm der archäologischen Gesellschaft zu Berlin, 104. 1948.

———. "Der grosse Kameo von Frankreich." *Mitteilungen des deutschen archäologischen Instituts* 6 (1953): 71–115.

Bruun, P. "The Consecration Coins of Constantine the Great." *Arctos, Acta Philol. Fennica* N.S. 1 (1954): 19–31.

———. "Constantine's *Dies Imperii* and *Quinquennalia* in the Light of the Early Solidi of Trier." *Numismatic Chronicle* 7 (1969): 177–209.

———. "Notes on the Transmission of Imperial Images in Late Antiquity." In *Studia Romana in honorem Petri Krarup.* Odense, 1976, pp. 121–131.

Budde, L. "Julian-Helios-Sarapis und Helena-Isis." *Archäologischer Anzeiger* (1972): 630–642.

Büchner, K. *Somnium Scipionis, Quellen, Gestalt, Sinn.* Hermes Einzelschriften, 36. Wiesbaden, 1976.

Bütler, H. P. *Die geistige Welt des jüngeren Plinius. Studien zur Thematik seiner Briefe.* Heidelberg, 1970.

Bullough, D. "*Imagines Regum* and Their Significance in the Early Medieval West." In *Studies in Memory of David Talbot Rice.* Edited by G. Robertson and G. Henderson. Edinburgh, 1975, pp. 223–276.

Burdeau, F. "L'empereur d'après les panégyriques latins." In F. Burdeau, N. Charbonnel, and M. Humbert. *Aspects de l'empire romain.* Paris, 1964, pp. 1–60.

Bury, J. B. *A History of the Later Roman Empire from Arcadius to Irene.* London, 1889.

———. "The Ceremonial Book of Constantine Porphyrogenetos." *English Historical Review* 22 (1907): 209–227.

———. *History of the Later Roman Empire from the Death of Theodosius I to the Death of Justinian* (A.D. 395 to A.D. 565). London, 1923.

Calderone, S. "Teologia politica, successione dinastica e consecratio in età constantiniana." In *Le culte des souverains dans l'empire romain.* Entretiens Hardt, 19. Geneva, 1972, pp. 215–261.

Cameron, Alan. "Wandering Poets, a Literary Movement in Byzantine Egypt." *Historia* 14 (1965): 470–509.

———. "The Date and Identity of Macrobius." *Journal of Roman Studies* 56 (1966): 25–38.

———. *Claudian, Poetry and Propaganda at the Court of Honorius.* Oxford, 1970.

———. *Porphyrius the Charioteer.* Oxford, 1973.

———. *Circus Factions. Blues and Greens at Rome and Byzantium.* Oxford, 1976.

———. "Some Prefects Called Julian." *Byzantion* 47 (1977): 42–64.

———. "Paganism and Literature in Late Fourth Century Rome." In *Christianisme et formes littéraires de l'antiquité tardive en Occident.* Entretiens Hardt, 23. Geneva, 1977, pp. 1–40.

Cameron, Averil. *Flavius Crescontius Corippus, In Laudem Iustini Augusti minoris.* London, 1976.

———. "An Emperor's Abdication." *Byzantinoslavica* 37 (1976): 161–167.

———. "The Theotokos in Sixth Century Constantinople." *Journal of Theological Studies* 29 (1978): 79–108.

———. "Images of Authority: Elites and Icons in Late Sixth-Century Byzantium," *Past and Present* 84 (1979): 3–35.

Catafygiotu Topping, E. "Romanos on the Entry into Jerusalem, a *Basilikos Logos.*" *Byzantion* 47 (1977): 65–91.

Cecchini, E. "Per il nuovo Rutilio Namaziano." *Rivista di filologia classica* 102 (1974): 401–403.

Cerfaux, L. and J. Tondriau. *Un concurrent du christianisme: le culte des souverains dans la civilisation gréco-romaine.* Bibliothèque de Théologie, 3, 5. Tournai, 1957.

Chadwick, H. *The Sentences of Sextus.* Cambridge, 1959.

Charlesworth, M. P. "Some Observations on Ruler Cult, Especially in Rome." *Harvard Theological Review* 28 (1935): 5–44.

———. "The Virtues of a Roman Emperor." *Proceedings of the British Academy,* 23 (1937): 105–133.

———. "The Refusal of Divine Honours." *Papers of the British School at Rome* 15 (1939): 1–10.

———. "*Pietas* and *Victoria,* the Emperor and the Citizen." *Journal of Roman Studies* 33 (1943): 1–10.

Chesnut, G. F. *The First Christian Histories, Eusebius, Socrates, Sozomen, Theodoret and Evagrius.* Théologie historique, 46. Paris, 1977.

Christol, M. "La *pietas* de Constance Chlore: l'empereur et les provinciaux à la fin du IIIe siècle." *Bulletin de la société française de numismatique* 30, 10 (1975): 858–861.

Christophilopoulou, Aikaterine. Ἐκλογή, ἀναγόρευσις, καὶ στέψις τοῦ βυζαντίνου αὐτοκράτορος. Athens, 1956.

Clay, C. L. "Nilus and the Four Seasons on a New As of Septimius Severus." *Numismatic Chronicle* 7 (1970): 71–87.

Clover, F. M. "Flavius Merobaudes, a Translation and Historical Commentary." *Transactions of the American Philosophical Society* 61 (1971).

Cohen, H. *Description historique des monnaies frappées sous l'empire romain.* 2nd ed. vols. 7 and 8, Paris, London, 1888 and 1892.

Collins-Clinton, J. *A Late Antique Shrine of Liber Pater at Cosa.* Leiden, 1977.

Conduché, D. "Ammien Marcellin et la mort de Julien." *Latomus* 24 (1965): 359–380.

Courcelle, P. *Histoire littéraire des grandes invasions germaniques.* Paris, 1964.

———. "Le serpent à face humaine dans la numismatique impériale du Vᵉ siècle." *Mélanges A. Piganiol*. Vol. 1. Paris, 1966, pp. 343–353.

Coville, A. *Recherches sur l'histoire de Lyon du Vᵐᵉ au IXᵐᵉ siècle*. Paris, 1928.

Cracco Ruggini, L. *Simboli di battaglia ideologica nel tardo ellenismo*. Pisa, 1972.

———. "The Ecclesiastical Histories and the Pagan Historiography: Providence and Miracles." *Athenaeum* 55 (1977): 107–126.

Cumont, F. "L'aigle funéraire des Syriens." *Revue de l'histoire des religions* 62 (1910): 119–164.

———. "La théologie solaire du paganisme romain." *Mémoires présentés par divers savants à l'Académie des Inscriptions et Belles Lettres* 12, 2 (1923): 448–479.

———. "L'aigle funéraire d'Hiérapolis et l'apothéose des empereurs." In his *Études Syriennes*. Paris, 1917, pp. 35–118.

———. *Afterlife in Roman Paganism*. New Haven, 1922.

———. "L'adoration des mages et l'art triomphal de Rome." *Atti della Pontificia Accademia Romana di Archeologia*, Serie 3, Memoria 3 (1932–33): 81–105.

———. *Recherches sur le symbolisme funéraire des Romains*. Paris, 1942.

Dagron, G. "L'empire romain d'orient au IVᵉ siècle et les traditions politiques de l'hellénisme. Le témoignage de Thémistios." *Travaux et Mémoires* 3 (1968): 1–242.

———. *Naissance d'une capitale, Constantinople et ses institutions de 330 à 451*. Paris, 1974.

Daly, L. J. "The Mandarin and the Barbarian: The Response of Themistius to the Gothic Challenge." *Historia* 21 (1972): 351–379.

Damerau, P. *Kaiser Claudius II Gothicus. Klio*, Beiheft 33. Leipzig, 1934.

Decker, D. de. "La politique religieuse de Maxence." *Byzantion* 38 (1968): 472–562.

Deckers, J. G. "Die Wandmalerei des tetrarchischen Lagerheiligtums im Ammon-Tempel von Luxor." *Römische Quartalschrift* 68 (1973): 1–34.

Deer, J. "Der Ursprung der Kaiserkrone." *Schweizer Beiträge zur allgemeinen Geschichte* 8 (1950): 51–87. Reprinted in his *Byzanz und das abendländische Herrschertum*. Sigmaringen, 1977, pp. 11–44.

———. "Das Kaiserbild im Kreuz." *Schweizer Beiträge zur allgemeinen Geschichte* 13 (1955): 48–112. Reprinted in his *Byzanz und das abendländische Herrschertum*. Sigmaringen, 1977, pp. 125–177.

Deichmann, F. W. *Repertorium der christlich-antiken Sarkofage I, Rom und Ostia*. Wiesbaden, 1967.

———. *Frühchristliche Bauten und Mosaiken von Ravenna*. Baden-Baden, 1958.

———. *Ravenna, Hauptstadt des spätantiken Abendlandes*. Vol. 1: *Geschichte und Monumente*. Wiesbaden, 1969; vol. 2, 1 and 2: *Kommentar*. Wiesbaden, 1974 and 1976; *Plananhang*. Wiesbaden, 1976.

Delatte, L. *Les traités de la royauté d'Ecphante. Diotogène et Sthénidas*. Paris, 1942.

Delbrueck, R. *Die Consulardiptychen und verwandte Denkmäler*. Berlin, 1929.

———. *Antike Porphyrwerke*. Berlin, 1932.

———. *Spätantike Kaiserporträts von Constantinus Magnus bis zum Ende des Westreichs*. Berlin, 1933.

———. *Die Münzbildnisse von Maximinus bis Carinus*. Berlin, 1940.

———. "Das fünfteilige Diptychon in Mailand (Domschatz)." *Bonner Jahrbücher* 151 (1951): 96–107.

Demougeot, E. *De l'unité à la division de l'empire romain.* Paris, 1951.

Deschamps, G. and G. Cousin. "Inscriptions du Temple de Zeus Panamaros." *Bulletin de correspondance hellénique* 12 (1888): 82–104.

Deubner, L. *Attische Feste.* Berlin, 1932. Edited by B. Doer. Hildesheim, 1966.

Dill, S. *Roman Society in Gaul in the Merovingian Age.* London, 1926.

Dinkler, E. *Der Einzug in Jerusalem. Ikonografische Untersuchungen im Anschluss an ein bisher unbekanntes Sarkofagfragment.* Arbeitsgemeinschaft für Forschung des Landes Nordrhein-Westfalen, Geisteswissenschaften, Heft 167. 1970.

Dölger, F. J. "Das Sonnengleichnis in einer Weihnachtspredigt des Bischofs Zeno von Verona." *Antike und Christentum* 6 (1940–50): 1–56.

Dörries, H. *Das Selbstzeugnis Kaiser Konstantins.* Abh. d. Akad. d. Wiss. in Göttingen. Phil. Hist. Kl., 3, 34. 1954.

Dohrn, T. *Die Tyche von Antiocheia.* Berlin, 1960.

Doignon, J. "Le Monogramme cruciforme du sarcophage paléochrétien de Metz représentant le passage de la mer rouge: un symbole de triomphe sur la mort dans le cadre d'une iconographie aulique d'inspiration constantinienne," *Cahiers Archéologiques* 12 (1962) 65–87.

Domaszewski, A. von. *Abhandlungen zur römischen Religion.* Leipzig, 1909 (New York, 1975).

Downey, G. "Philanthropia in Religion and Statecraft in the Fourth Century after Christ." *Historia* 4 (1955): 199–208.

———. "The Christian Schools of Palestine, a Chapter in Literary History." *Harvard Library Bulletin* 12 (1958): 297–319.

Drake, H. A. *In Praise of Constantine. A Historical Study and New Translation of Eusebius' Tricennial Orations.* University of California Publications, Classical Studies, 15. Berkeley, 1976.

Dudden, F. Holmes. *The Life and Times of St. Ambrose.* Oxford, 1935.

Duval, Y. M. "L'éloge de Théodose dans la *Cité de Dieu* (V, 26, 1). Sa place, son sens et ses sources." *Recherches augustiniennes* 4 (1966): 135–179.

Dvornik, F. "The Emperor Julian's Reactionary Ideas on Kingship." In *Late Classical and Medieval Studies in Honour of A. M. Friend.* Princeton, 1955, pp. 71–81.

Dyggve, E. *Ravennatum Palatium Sacrum. La basilica ipetrale a cerimonie.* K. danske vid. sel., Arch.-kunsthist. medd., 3. Copenhagen, 1941.

Edbrooke, R. O. "The Visit of Constantius II to Rome in 357 and Its Effect on the Pagan Roman Senatorial Aristocracy." *American Journal of Philology* 97 (1976): 40–61.

Ehrenberg, V. "Athenian Hymn to Demetrius Poliorcetes." In his *Aspects of the Ancient World, Essays and Reviews.* Oxford, 1946, pp. 179–198.

Eitrem, S. "Zur Apotheose." *Symbolae Osloenses* 10 (1932): 31–56; 11 (1932): 11–34; 15–16 (1936): 111–137.

Elze, R. *Die Ordines für die Weihe und Krönung des Kaisers und der Kaiserin.* Fontes Iuris Germanici antiqui in usum scholarum. Hanover, 1960.

Ensslin, W. "Zur Torqueskrönung und Schilderhebung bei der Kaiserwahl." *Klio* 35 (1942): 268–298.

———. "Gottkaiser und Kaiser von Gottes Gnaden." *SB der bayerischen Akad. d. Wiss. Phil. Hist. Kl.,* 6. 1943.

———. *Theodorich der Grosse.* Munich, 1947.

————. *Zur Frage nach der ersten Kaiserkrönung durch den Patriarchen und zur Bedeutung dieses Aktes im Wahlzeremoniell.* Würzburg, 1947. Shortened version in *Byzantinische Zeitschrift* 42 (1943–1949): 101–115; 369–372.

Farina, R. *L'impero e l'imperatore cristiano in Eusebio di Cesarea.* Zürich, 1966.

Farioli, R. "Ravenna paleocristiana scomparsa." *Felix Ravenna* 83 (1961): 5–88.

Fears, J. Rufus. *Princeps a diis electus. The Divine Election of the Emperor as a Political Concept at Rome.* American Academy in Rome, Papers and Monographs, 26. 1977.

Fellmann, R. "Le Camp de Dioclétien à Palmyre." In *Mélanges d'histoire ancienne et d'archéologie offerts à Paul Collart.* Paris, 1976, pp. 173–191.

Férotin, D. M. *Le Liber Ordinum en usage dans l'église wisigothique et mozarabe d'Espagne.* Monumenta Ecclesiae Liturgica, 5. Paris, 1904.

Ferrari, M. "Frammenti ignoti di Rutilio Namaziano." *Italia Medioevale e Umanistica* 16 (1973): 15–30.

Ferrua, A. "*Qui filius diceris et pater inveniris*: Mosaico novellamente scoperto nella catacomba di S. Domitilla." *Atti della Pontifica Accademia* ser. III, *Rendiconti* 33 (1960–1, [1961]): 209–224.

Festugière, A. J. "L'expérience religieuse du médecin Thessalos." *Revue biblique* 48 (1939): 45–77. Reprinted in his *Hermétisme et mystique païenne.* Paris, 1967, pp. 141–180.

Fink, R. O., A. S. Hoey, and W. F. Snyder. "The Feriale Duranum." *Yale Classical Studies* 7 (1940): 1–221.

Fishwick, D. "The Name of the Demigod." *Historia* 24 (1975): 624–628.

Fontaine, J. "Vienne carrefour du paganisme et du christianisme dans la Gaule du IVᵉ siècle." *Bulletin de la société des amis de Vienne* 67 (1971): 17–36.

Francovich, G. de. *Il palatium di Teodorico a Ravenna e la cosidetta ‹architettura di potenza›. Problemi d'interpretazione di raffigurazioni architettoniche nell'arte tardoantica e altomedioevale.* Rome, 1970.

Frazer, M. "The Iconography of the Emperor Maxentius' Buildings in Via Appia." *Art Bulletin* 48 (1966): 385–392.

Frendo, J. D. C. "The Significance of Technical Terms in George of Pisidia." *Orpheus* 21 (1974): 45–55.

Freshfield, E. H. "Notes on a Vellum Album Containing some Original Sketches of Public Buildings and Monuments, Drawn by a German Artist who Visited Constantinople in 1574." *Archeologia* 72 (1921–1922): 87–104.

Friedländer, P. *Johannes von Gaza, Paulus Silentiarius und Prokopius von Gaza, Kunstbeschreibungen von justinianischer Zeit.* Hildesheim, New York, 1969 (Berlin, 1912 and Rome, 1939).

Frolow, A. "La Vraie Croix et les expéditions d'Héraclius en Perse." *Revue des études byzantines* 11 (1953): 88–105.

Fuhrmann, H. "Studien zu den Konsulardiptychen und verwandten Denkmälern." *Mitteilungen des deutschen archäologischen Instituts, Römische Abteilung* 54 (1939): 161–175.

————. "Die Konsulardiptychen und verwandte Denkmäler II, tönerne Missoria aus der Zeit der Tetrarchie." *Mitteilungen des deutschen archäologischen Instituts, Römische Abteilung* 55 (1940): 92–99.

Gabba, E. and G. Tibiletti. "Una Signora di Treveri sepolta a Pavia." *Athenaeum*, n.s. 38 (1960): 253–262.

Gärtner, H. "Einige Überlegungen zur kaiserzeitlichen Panegyrik und zu Ammians Charakteristik des Kaisers Julian." *Akad. d. Wiss. u. Lit. Mainz Abh. Geistes u. Sozialwiss. Kl.*, 10. 1968.

Gagé, J. "La théologie de la victoire impériale." *Revue historique* 13 (1933): 1–43.

———. "Σταυρὸς νικοποιός, la victoire impériale dans l'empire chrétien." *Revue d'histoire et de philosophie religieuses* 13 (1933): 370–400.

Galletier, E. *Panégyriques latins*, vols. 1–3. Paris, 1949–1955.

Gantar, K. "Kaiser Justinian, 'jenem Herbststern gleich'." *Museum Helveticum* 19 (1962): 194–196 and 33 (1976): 119–121.

Gascou, J. "Le réscrit d'Hispellum." *Mélanges d'archéologie et d'histoire, École Française de Rome* 79 (1967): 609–659.

Geffcken, J. *Kaiser Julianus*. Leipzig, 1914.

———. *The Last Days of Greco-Roman Paganism*. Translated by S. MacCormack. Amsterdam, 1978.

Gerke, F. "L'iconografia delle monete imperiali dall'augusta Galla Placidia alla fine dell'Impero d'Occidente." *XIII Corso di cultura sull'arte Ravennate e Bizantina*. Bologna, 1966, pp. 163–204.

Gnecchi, F. *I Medaglioni Romani*. Vols. 1–3. Milan, 1912.

Gnilka, C. "Götter und Dämonen in den Gedichten Claudians." *Antike und Abendland* 18 (1973): 144–160.

———. "Dichtung und Geschichte im Werke Claudians." *Frühmittelalterliche Studien*, 10 (1976): 96–104.

Goffart, W. "The Date and Purpose of Vegetius' 'De re militari'." *Traditio* 33 (1977): 65–100.

Goodenough, E. R. *Jewish Symbols in the Greco-Roman Period* 8. New York, 1958.

Grabar, A. *L'empereur dans l'art byzantin*. Strasbourg, 1936 (London, 1971).

———. *Martyrium*. Paris, 1943 and 1946 (London, 1972).

———. "Un médaillon en or provenant de Mersine en Cilicie." *Dumbarton Oaks Papers* 6 (1951): 27–49.

———. "Quel est le sens de l'offrande de Justinien et Theodora sur les mosaïques de Saint Vital?" *Felix Ravenna* 3, 30 (81) (1960): 63–77.

———. "Recherches sur les sources juives de l'art paléochrétien." *Cahiers archéologiques* 14 (1964): 53–57.

———. *The Beginnings of Christian Art*. London, 1967.

———. *Christian Iconography, a Study of Its Origins*. Princeton, 1968; London, 1969.

Gramotopol, M. "L'apothéose de Julien l'apostat et de Flavia Helena sur le grand camée de Roumanie." *Latomus* 24 (1965): 870–885.

Grant, M. *Roman Anniversary Issues*. Cambridge, 1950.

Grierson, P. "The Monetary Reforms of Abd-al-Malik." *Journal of the Economic and Social History of the Orient* 3 (1960): 241–264.

———. "The Tombs and Obits of the Byzantine Emperors (337–1043)." *Dumbarton Oaks Papers* 16 (1962): 1–63.

————. *Catalogue of the Byzantine Coins in the Dumbarton Oaks Collection and in the Whittemore Collection* 2, 1. Washington, D.C., 1968.

Grumel, V. "La Réposition de la Vraie Croix a Jérusalem par Héraclius, le jour et l'année." *Byzantinische Forschungen* 1 *Polychordia*, Festschrift F. Dölger. Amsterdam, 1966, pp. 139–149.

Guarducci, M. "Teodosio 'rinovatore' di Corinto, in una epigrafe greca di Kenchreai." In *Le Monde grec, pensée, littérature, histoire, documents, hommages à Claire Préaux*. Brussels, 1975, pp. 527–534.

Guillou, A. "Demography and Culture in the Exarchate of Ravenna," in his *Studies on Byzantine Italy*, London, 1970.

Gussone, N. "Adventus Zeremoniell und Translation von Reliquien. Victricius von Rouen, *de laude Sanctorum*." *Frühmittelalterliche Studien* 10 (1976): 125–133.

Gutberlet, S. H. *Die Himmelfahrt Christi in der bildenden Kunst von den Anfängen bis ins hohe Mittelalter*. Strasbourg, 1935.

Gutzwiller, H. *Die Neujahrsrede des Konsuls Claudius Mamertinus vor dem Kaiser Julian*. Basler Beitr. zur Geschichtswiss., 10. 1942.

Háarløv, B. "A Contribution to the Iconography of the Emperor Gallienus." In *Studia Romana in honorem Petri Krarup septhagenarii*. Odense, 1976.

————. *The Half-Open Door. A Common Symbolic Motif within Roman Sepulchral Sculpture*. Odense, 1977.

Habicht, C. *Gottmenschtum und griechische Städte*. Zetemata, 14. Munich, 1970.

Halsberghe, G. H. *The Cult of Sol Invictus*. Leiden, 1972.

Hamberg, P. G. *Studies in Roman Imperial Art with Special Reference to the State Reliefs of the Second Century*. Copenhagen, 1945.

Hanfmann, G. M. A. *The Season Sarcophagus in Dumbarton Oaks*. Cambridge, Mass., 1951.

Hari, R. "Une image du culte égyptien à Rome en 354." *Museum Helveticum* 33 (1976): 114–121.

Hartke, W. *Geschichte und Politik im spätantiken Rom*. Klio, 45 Beiheft. 1940.

————. *Römische Kinderkaiser. Eine Strukturanalyse römischen Denkens und Daseins*. Berlin, 1951.

Haynes, D. E. L. "A Late Antique Portrait Head in Porphyry." *Burlington Magazine* 118, 829 (June 1976): 350–357.

Heinzelmann, M. *Bischofsherrschaft in Gallien, zur Kontinuität römischer Führungsschichten vom 4. bis zum 7. Jahrhundert. Soziale, prosopographische und bildungsgeschichtliche Aspekte*. Beihefte der Francia, 5. Munich, 1976.

Heitsch, E. "Die griechischen Dichterfragmente der römischen Kaiserzeit," I and II, *Abh. d. Akad. d. Wiss. in Göttingen, Phil.-Hist. Kl.* 49 (1961) and 58 (1964).

Hirschfeld, O. "Die römische Staatszeitung und die Akklamationen im Senat." *SB der Berliner Akademie* (1905): 930–948. Reprinted in his *Kleine Schriften*, Berlin, 1913 (New York, 1975), pp. 682–702.

Hitti, P. K. *The Origins of the Islamic State, being a Translation from the Arabic . . . of the Kitâb Futûḥ al-Buldâh of al Imâm abu-l 'Abbâs Aḥmad ibn Jâbir al Balâdhuri*. New York, 1916 (Beirut, 1966).

Hohl, E. "Die angebliche 'Doppelbestattung' des Antoninus Pius." *Klio* 31 (1938): 169–185.

Holum, K. G. "Pulcheria's Crusade of A.D. 421 and the Ideology of Imperial Victory." *Greek, Roman and Byzantine Studies* 18 (1977): 153–172.

———. *Theodosian Empresses: Women and Imperial Dominion in Late Antiquity* (in press).

Holum, K. G. and G. Vikan. "The Trier Ivory, *Adventus* Ceremonial and the Relics of Saint Stephen." *Dumbarton Oaks Papers* 33 (1979): 113–133

Honoré, A. M. "Some Constitutions Composed by Justinian." *Journal of Roman Studies* 65 (1975): 107–123.

Hopkins, K. *Conquerors and Slaves*. Cambridge, 1978.

Horedt, K. "Bemerkungen zur Deutung des Cameo Orghidan." *Latomus* 33 (1974): 673–675.

Hubert, J., J. Porcher, and W. F. Volbach. *Europe in the Dark Ages*. London, 1969.

Hunger, H. *Prooimion, Elemente der byzantinischen Kaiseridee in den Arengen der Urkunden*. Wiener Byzantinische Studien, 1. Vienna, 1964.

Instinsky, H. U. "*Consensus universorum.*" *Hermes* 75 (1940): 265–278.

———. "Kaiser und Ewigkeit." *Hermes* 77 (1942): 313–355.

———. *Sicherheit als politisches Problem des römischen Kaisertums*. Baden-Baden, 1952.

———. *Bischofsstuhl und Kaiserthron*. Munich, 1955.

Jahn, O. "Über die Subskriptionen in den HSS römischer Classiker." *Berichte über die Verhandlungen der königlichen sächsischen Gesellschaft der Wissenschaften*. Leipzig, phil. hist. Cl. 3 (1851): 327–372.

Jeffreys, M. "The Nature and Origin of Political Verse." *Dumbarton Oaks Papers* 28 (1974): 143–195.

Jerphanion, G. de. "L'ambon de Salonique, l'arc de Galère et l'ambon de Thèbes." *Atti della Pontificia Accademia Romana di Archeologia* Serie 3, Memoria 3 (1932–33): 107–132.

Jones, A. H. M. "The Constitutional Position of Odoacer and Theoderic." *Journal of Roman Studies* 52 (1962): 126–130.

Jullian, C. *Histoire de la Gaule*. Vols. 7 and 8. Paris, 1926.

Kähler, H. *Zwei Sockel eines Triumphbogens im Boboligarten zu Florenz*. Winckelmannsprogramm der archäologischen Gesellschaft zu Berlin, 96. 1936.

———. *Das Fünfsäulendenkmal für die Tetrarchen auf dem Forum Romanum*. Monumenta Artis Romanae, 3. Cologne, 1964.

———. "Der Sockel des Theodosiusobelisken in Konstantinopel." *Acta ad archaeologiam et artium historiam pertinentia* 6 (1975): 45–55.

Kalavrezou-Maxeiner, Ioli. "The Imperial Chamber at Luxor." *Dumbarton Oaks Papers* 29 (1975): 227–251.

Kaniuth, A. *Die Beisetzung Konstantins des Grossen*. Breslauer Hist. Forsch., 18. 1941.

Kantorowicz, E. "The 'King's Advent' and the Enigmatic Panels in the Doors of Santa Sabina." *Art Bulletin* 26 (1944): 207–231. Reprinted in his *Selected Studies*. Locust Valley, 1965, pp. 37–64.

———. *The King's Two Bodies, a Study in Mediaeval Political Theology*. Princeton, 1957.

———. "Oriens Augusti—Lever du Roi." *Dumbarton Oaks Papers* 17 (1963): 119–177.

———. "*Puer exoriens*: On the Hypapante in the Mosaics of S. Maria Maggiore."

In *Perennitas: P. Thomas Michels, O.S.B. zum 70. Geburtstag.* Edited by H. Rahner, S. J. and E. von Severus, O.S.B. Münster, 1963, pp. 118–135. Reprinted in his *Selected Studies.* Locust Valley, 1965, pp. 25–36.

———. "ΣΥΝΘΡΟΝΟΣ ΔΙΚΗΙ." *American Journal of Archaeology* 57 (1953): 65–70. Reprinted in his *Selected Studies.* Locust Valley, 1965, pp. 1–6.

Karyannopulos, I. "Konstantin der Grosse und der Kaiserkult." *Historia* 5 (1956): 341–357.

Kassel, R. *Untersuchungen zur griechischen und römischen Konsolationsliteratur.* Zetemata, 18. 1958.

Keil, J. "Ephesos und der Etappendienst zwischen der Nord- und Ostfront des Imperium Romanum." *Anzeiger der österr. Akad. d. Wiss. Phil. hist. Kl.* 12 (1955): 159–170.

Kempen, C. *Procopii Gazaei in Imp. Anastasium Panegyricus.* Dissertation, Bonn, 1918.

Kitzinger, E. "The Cult of Images in the Age before Iconoclasm." *Dumbarton Oaks Papers* 8 (1954): 83–149. Reprinted in his *The Art of Byzantium and the Medieval West, Selected Studies.* Bloomington, London, 1976, pp. 90–156.

———. "A Marble Relief of the Theodosian Period." *Dumbarton Oaks Papers* 14 (1960): 17–42. Reprinted in his *The Art of Byzantium and the Medieval West, Selected Studies.* Bloomington, London, 1976, pp. 1–31.

Klauser, T. "*Aurum Coronarium.*" In his *Gesammelte Arbeiten zur Liturgiegeschichte, Kirchengeschichte und Christlichen Archaeologie.* Jahrbuch für Antike und Christentum Ergänzungsband, 3. Münster, 1974, pp. 292–309.

Klingner, F. *Römische Geisteswelt.* Munich, 1961.

Koch, C. "Roma Aeterna." In his *Religio, Studien zu Kult und Glauben der Römer.* Nuremberg, 1960.

Koenen, L. "Die *laudatio funebris* des Augustus für Agrippa auf einem neuen Papyrus." *Zeitschrift für Papyrologie und Epigraphik* 5 (1970): 217–283.

Koethe, H. "Das Konstantinsmausoleum und verwandte Denkmäler." *Jahrbuch des deutschen archäologischen Instituts* 48 (1933): 185–203.

Kollwitz, J. *Oströmische Plastik der theodosianischen Zeit.* Berlin, 1941.

———. "Ravenna zwischen Orient und Occident." *Atti del VI Congresso Internazionale di Archeologia Cristiana, Ravenna 1962.* Vatican, 1965, pp. 383–402.

Kostof, S. K. *The Orthodox Baptistery of Ravenna.* New Haven, London, 1965.

Kraus, F. F. *Die Münzen Odovacars und des Ostgotenreiches in Italien.* Halle, 1928.

Krautheimer, R. "Zu Konstantins Apostelkirche." In *Mullus, Festschrift T. Klauser,* Münster, 1964, pp. 224–229. Reprinted in his *Studies in Early Christian, Medieval and Renaissance Art.* New York, 1969, pp. 27–34.

———. "The Beginning of Early Christian Architecture," *Review of Religion* 3 (1939): 127–148. Reprinted in his *Studies in Early Christian, Medieval and Renaissance Art.* New York, 1969, pp. 1–20.

Kriss, R. and H. Kriss-Heinrich. *Volksglaube im Bereich des Islam* 2. Wiesbaden, 1962.

Kruse, H. *Studien zur offiziellen Geltung des Kaiserbildes im römischen Reiche.* Studien zur Geschichte und Kultur des Altertums 19, 3. Paderborn, 1934.

Kustas, G. L. *Studies in Byzantine Rhetoric.* Thessalonike, 1973.

Kyriakis, J. "Byzantine Burial Customs, the Care of the Deceased from Death to Prothesis." *The Greek Orthodox Theological Review* 19 (1974): 37–72.

Labrousse, M. *Toulouse antique, des origines à l'établissement des Wisigoths.* Bibl. des éc. fr. d'Athènes et de Rome, 212. 1968.

La Piana, G. *Le rappresentazioni sacre nella letteratura bizantina dalle origini al sec. IX.* Grottaferrata, 1912 (London, 1971).

Lassus, J. *L'illustration byzantine du Livre des Rois.* Bibl. cahiers archéologiques, 9. Paris, 1973.

Latte, K. *Römische Religionsgeschichte.* Munich, 1960.

Laubscher, H. P. *Der Reliefschmuck des Galeriusbogens in Thessaloniki.* Berlin, 1975.

Lawrence, M. "Columnar Sarcophagi in the Latin West." *Art Bulletin* 14 (1932): 102–185.

———. "Two Ravennate Monuments in American Collections." In *Studies in Art and Literature for Belle da Costa Greene.* Edited by D. Miner. Princeton, 1954, pp. 132–142.

———. "The Iconography of the Mosaics of S. Vitale." *Atti del VI Congresso Internazionale di Archeologia Cristiana, Ravenna 1962.* Vatican, 1965, pp. 123–140.

Leroy, J. A. *Les manuscrits syriaques à peintures conservés dans les bibliothèques d'Europe et d'Orient.* Bibl. arch. et hist., 77. Paris, 1964.

Lévi-Strauss, Claude. *Anthropologie structurale.* Paris, 1958.

Lipinsky, A. "La 'Croce gemmata' e il culto della Santa Croce nei monumenti superstiti e nelle raffigurazioni monumentali." *Felix Ravenna* Ser. 3, 81 (1960): 5–62.

———. "Crux Vaticana, Kaiser Justinus' II Kreuz." *Römische Quartalschrift* 63 (1968): 185–203.

Lippold, A. "Herrscherideal und Traditionsverbundenheit im Panegyricus des Pacatus." *Historia* 17, (1968): 228–250.

Loerke, W. C. "The Miniatures of the Trial in the Rossano Gospels." *Art Bulletin* 43 (1961): 171–195.

Loli, M. *Il sarcofago paleocristiano di Catervio nel duomo di Tolentino.* Bologna, 1971.

L'Orange, H. P. "Sol Invictus Imperator. Ein Beitrag zur Apotheose." *Symbolae Osloenses* 14, 1 (1935): 86–114. Reprinted in his *Likeness and Icon, Selected Studies in Classical and Early Mediaeval Art.* Odense, 1973, pp. 325–344.

———. "Ein tetrarchisches Ehrendenkmal auf dem Forum Romanum." *Mitteilungen des deutschen archäologischen Instituts, Römische Abteilung* 53 (1938): 1–34. Reprinted in his *Likeness and Icon, Selected Studies in Classical and Early Mediaeval Art.* Odense, 1973, pp. 131–157.

———. *Apotheosis in Ancient Portraiture.* Oslo, 1947.

———. *Studies on the Iconography of Cosmic Kingship in the Ancient World.* Instituttet for sammelignende Kulturforskning. Oslo, 1953.

———. *Art Forms and Civic Life in the Later Roman Empire.* Princeton, 1965.

L'Orange, H. P., and A. von Gerkan. *Der spätantike Bildschmuck des Konstantinsbogens.* Berlin, 1939.

Loyen, A. *Recherches historiques sur les panégyriques de Sidoine Apollinaire.* Bibl. de l'École des Hautes Études, 285. Paris, 1942.

———. *Sidoine Apollinaire et l'esprit précieux en Gaule aux derniers jours de l'empire.* Paris, 1943.

Lugli, G. "Edifici rotondi del tardo impero in Roma e suburbio." In *Studies to D. M. Robinson* 2. Saint Louis, 1953, pp. 1211–1223.

Lumpe, A. "Ennodiana." *Byzantinische Forschungen* 1. In *Polychordia, Festschrift Franz Dölger*. Amsterdam, 1966, pp. 200–210.

Maas, P. "Metrische Akklamationen der Byzantiner." *Byzantinische Zeitschrift* 21 (1912): 28–51.

McCail, R. C. "P. Gr. Vindob. 29788C." *Journal of Hellenic Studies* 98 (1978): 38–63.

MacCormack, S. "Change and Continuity in Late Antiquity, the Ceremony of *Adventus*." *Historia* 21 (1972): 721–752.

———. "Roma, Constantinopolis, the Emperor, and His Genius." *Classical Quarterly* 25 (1975): 131–150.

———. "Latin Prose Panegyrics: Tradition and Discontinuity in the Later Roman Empire." *Revue des études augustiniennes* 22 (1976): 29–77.

McCormick, M. "Odoacer, Emperor Zeno and the Rugian Victory Legation." *Byzantion* 47 (1977), 212–227.

MacIsaac, J. D. "The Hand of God, a Numismatic Study." *Traditio* 31 (1975): 322–328.

MacMullen, R. "Some Pictures in Ammianus Marcellinus." *Art Bulletin* 46 (1964): 435–455.

Maehler, H. "Menander Rhetor and Alexander Claudius in a Papyrus Letter." *Greek, Roman and Byzantine Studies* 15 (1974): 305–312.

Maguire, H. "Truth and Convention in Byzantine Descriptions of Works of Art." *Dumbarton Oaks Papers* 28 (1974): 113–140.

Malcovati, E. "Il nuovo frammento della *Laudatio Agrippae*." *Athenaeum* 50 (1972): 142–151.

Mango, C. *The Brazen House. A Study of the Vestibule of the Imperial Palace of Constantinople*. Royal Danish Academy of Science and Letters, Arkaeologisk-kunsthistoriske Meddelelser. Copenhagen, 1959.

———. "Antique Statuary and the Byzantine Beholder." *Dumbarton Oaks Papers* 17 (1963): 55–75.

Mathew, G. "The Character of the Gallienic Renaissance." *Journal of Roman Studies* 33 (1943): 65–70.

———. *Byzantine Aesthetics*. London, 1963.

Matthews, J. F. "Gallic Supporters of Theodosius." *Latomus* 30 (1971): 1073–1099.

Mattingly, H. "The Imperial Vota." *Proceedings of the British Academy* 36 (1950): 155–195 and 37 (1951): 219–268.

Mattingly, H., E. A. Sydenham, and others. *The Roman Imperial Coinage*. 1; 2; 3; 4, 1, 2, 3; 5, 1, 2; 6; 7; 9. London, 1923–1967.

Matz, F. "Der Gott auf dem Elefantenwagen." *Akad. d. Wiss. u. d. Lit. Abhandl. Geistes- u. Sozialwiss. Kl.*, 1952. Wiesbaden, 1953, pp. 719–763.

———. "Ein römisches Meisterwerk, der Jahreszeitensarkophag Badminton-New York." *Jahrbuch des deutschen archäologischen Instituts*. Ergänzungsheft. 1958.

———. "Das Problem des Orans und ein Sarkophag in Cordoba." *Mitteilungen des deutschen archäologischen Instituts Madrid* 9 (1968): 300–310.

———. *Die dionysischen Sarkophage* 3. Berlin, 1969.

Maurice, J. *Numismatique Constantinienne*. Vols. 1–3. Paris, 1908–1912.

Mazzarino, S. "La propaganda senatoriale nel tardo impero." *Doxa* 4 (1951): 121–148.

———. *Antico, tardoantico ed erà constantiniana*. Dedalo Libri, 1974.

Mazzini, G. *Monete imperiali Romani*. Vols. 1–5. Milan, 1957–1958.

Merten, E. *Zwei Herrscherfeste in der Historia Augusta. Antiquitas.* Reihe 4. Beitr. zur H.-A.-Forschung, 5. Bonn, 1968.

Meslin, M. *Les Ariens d'Occident 335–430.* Patristica Sorbonensia, 8. Paris, 1967.

———. *La fête des Kalendes de Janvier dans l'empire romain.* Coll. Latomus, 115. Brussels, 1970.

Meyer, H. "Der Regierungsantritt des Kaisers Majorianus." *Byzantinische Zeitschrift* 62 (1969): 5–12.

Miescher, R. "A Late Roman Portrait Head." *Journal of Roman Studies* 43 (1953): 101–103.

Millar, F. *The Emperor in the Roman World.* London, New York, 1977.

Miller, D. A. "Royauté et ambiguïté sexuelle." *Annales; économies, sociétés, civilisations* 26 (1971): 639–652.

Momigliano, A. "Gli Anicii e la storiografia latina del VI seculo D.C." *Rendiconti accademia dei Lincei, classe di scienze morali, storiche e filologiche,* Ser. 8, vol. 11, fasc. 11–12, 279–297. Reprinted in his *Secondo contributo alla storia degli studi classici.* Rome, 1960, pp. 231–253.

———. "Some Observations on the '*origo gentis romanae*'," *Journal of Roman Studies* 48, (1958): 56–73. Reprinted in his *Secondo contributo alla storia degli studi classici.* Rome, 1960, pp. 145–176.

———. "Per una nuova edizione della '*origo gentis romanae*'," *Athenaeum* 36 (1958): 248–259. Reprinted in his *Secondo contributo alla storia degli studi classici.* Rome, 1960, pp. 177–190.

———, ed. *The Conflict between Paganism and Christianity in the Fourth Century.* Oxford, 1964.

———. *Alien Wisdom. The Limits of Hellenization.* Cambridge, 1975.

Mommsen, T. *Römisches Staatsrecht,* 2, 2. Leipzig, 1877. (Basel, 1952.)

Müller-Wiener, W. *Bildlexikon zur Topographie Istanbuls.* Tübingen, 1977.

Muñoz, A. *Il Codice purpureo di Rossano e il frammento Sinopense.* Rome, 1907.

Nash, E. *A Pictorial Dictionary of Ancient Rome.* London, 1968.

Naumann, R. "Theodosiusbogen und Forum Tauri in Istanbul." *Istanbuler Mitteilungen* 26 (1976): 117–142.

Nelson, J. "Symbols in Context." D. Baker, ed. *Studies in Church History* 13 (1976): 97–119.

Neusner, J. *A History of the Jews in Babylonia.* Leiden, 1965–1970.

Niemeyer, H. G. *Studien zur statuarischen Darstellung der römischen Kaiser.* Monumenta Artis Romanae, 7. Berlin, 1968.

Nilsson, M. *Griechische Feste von religiöser Bedeutung mit Ausschluss der Attischen.* Leipzig, 1906.

———. "Die Prozessionstypen im griechischen Kult." *Jahrbuch d. Kaiserlich deutschen archeologischen Instituts* 31 (1916): 309–339.

Nissen, T. "Historisches Epos und Panegyrikos in der Spätantike." *Hermes* 75 (1940): 298–325.

Nock, A. D. "ΣΥΝΝΑΟΣ ΘΕΟΣ." *Harvard Studies in Classical Philology* 41 (1930): 1–62. Reprinted in his *Essays on Religion and the Ancient World.* Vol. 1. Oxford, 1972, pp. 202–251.

———. "A Diis Electa." *Harvard Theological Review* 23 (1930): 251–274. Reprinted in his *Essays on Religion and the Ancient World.* Vol. 1. Oxford, 1972, pp. 252–270.

———. "Cremation and Burial in the Roman Empire." *Harvard Theological Review*

25 (1932): 321–359. Reprinted in his *Essays on Religion and the Ancient World*. Vol. 1. Oxford, 1972, pp. 277–307.

———. "The Emperor's Divine Comes." *Journal of Roman Studies* 37 (1947): 102–116. Reprinted in his *Essays on Religion and the Ancient World*. Vol. 2. Oxford, 1972, pp. 653–675.

———. "Deification and Julian." *Journal of Roman Studies* 47 (1957): 114–123. Reprinted in his *Essays on Religion and the Ancient World*. Vol. 2. Oxford, 1972, pp. 832–846.

Nöldeke, T. "Die von Guidi herausgegebene syrische Chronik." *Wien, Akad. d. Wissenschaften, Sitzungsberichte, Philos. hist. Kl.* 128 (1893). 9 Abhandlung.

Nordström, C. O. *Ravennastudien: ideengeschichtliche und ikonographische Untersuchungen über die Mosaiken von Ravenna*. Stockholm, 1953.

Oehler, K. "Der *consensus omnium* als Kriterium der Wahrheit in der antiken Philosophie und der Patristik." *Antike und Abendland* 10 (1961): 103–129.

Ostrogorsky, G. "Zur Kaisersalbung und Schilderhebung im spätbyzantinischen Krönungszeremoniell." *Historia* 4 (1955): 246–256.

Paschoud, F. *Roma Aeterna, étude sur le patriotisme romain dans l'Occident latin à l'époque des grandes invasions*. Bibliotheca Helvetica Romana, 7. Rome, 1967.

———. "Zosime 2, 29 et la version païenne de la conversion de Constantin." *Historia* 20 (1971): 334–53. Reprinted in his *Cinq études sur Zosime*. Paris, 1975, pp. 24–62.

Pertusi, A. (ed.). *Giorgio di Pisidia, Poemi I. Panegirici Epici*. Studia Patristica et Byzantina, 7. Ettal, 1959.

Peterson, E. Εἰς Θεός. *Epigraphische, formgeschichtliche und religionsgeschichtliche Untersuchungen*. Göttingen, 1926.

———. "Die Einholung des Kyrios." *Zeitschrift für systematische Theologie* 7 (1930): 682–702.

———. *Der Monotheismus als politisches Problem*. Leipzig, 1935.

Petit, P. "Libanius et la *Vita Constantini*." *Historia* 1 (1950): 562–582.

———. "Recherches sur la publication et la diffusion des discours de Libanius." *Historia* 5 (1956): 479–509.

Picard, G. C. *Les trophées romains, contribution à l'histoire de la religion et de l'art triomphal de Rome*. Bibl. des éc. fr. d'Athènes et de Rome, 187. 1957.

Pichon, R. *Les derniers écrivains profanes*. Paris, 1906.

Piganiol, A. *L'empire chrétien*. Edited by A. Chastagnol. Paris, 1972.

Polara, I. *Publii Optatiani Porfyrii Carmina*. Turin, 1973.

Pond Rothman, M. S. "The Thematic Organisation of the Panel Reliefs on the Arch of Galerius." *American Journal of Archaeology* 81 (1977): 427–454.

Popović, V. and E. L. Ochsenschlager. "Der spätkaiserliche Hippodrom in Sirmium." *Germania* 54 (1976): 156–181.

Préaux, J. "Securus Melior Felix, l'ultime *Orator Urbis Romae*." In *Corona Gratiarum, Miscellanea Patristica, Historica et Liturgica Eligio Dekkers O.S.B. XII Lustra Completenti oblata*, 2. Bruges-Gravenhage, 1975, pp. 101–121.

Previale, L. "Teoria e prassi del panegirico bizantino." *Emerita* 17 (1949): 72–105 and 18 (1950): 340–366.

Proudfoot, A. S. "The Sources of Theophanes for the Heracleian Dynasty." *Byzantion* 44 (1974): 367–448.

Recheis, A. *Engel, Tod und Seelenreise. Das Wirken der Geister beim Heimgang des Menschen in der Lehre der alexandrinischen und kappadokischen Väter.* Temi e Testi, 4. Rome, 1958.

Restle, M. *Kunst und byzantinische Münzprägung von Justinian I bis zum Bilderstreit.* Texte und Forschungen zur byzantinisch neugriechischen Philologie. Athens, 1964.

Rice, D. Talbot. *Byzantine Art.* Harmondsworth, 1968.

Richard, M. "ΑΡΟ ΦΩΝΗΣ." *Byzantion* 20 (1950): 191–222. Reprinted in his *Opera Minora.* Vol. 3. Leuwen, 1977. no. 60.

Riché, P. *Éducation et culture dans l'occident barbare VIe–VIIIe siècles.* 3rd ed. Paris, 1972.

Richter, G. M. A. *Engraved Gems of the Romans.* London, 1971.

Richter, J. P. *Quellen der byzantinischen Kunstgeschichte.* Vienna, 1897.

Ringbom, L. I. *Paradisus Terrestris, Myt, Bild och Verklighet.* Acta Societatis Scientiarum Fennicae, N.S.C., I. Helsingfors, 1958.

Ritter, H. W. *Diadem und Königsherrschaft. Untersuchungen zu Zeremonien und Rechtsgrundlagen des Herrschaftsantritts bei den Persern, bei Alexander dem Grossen und im Hellenismus.* Vestigia, Beiträge zur alten Geschichte, 7. Munich, 1965.

Rodenwaldt, G. "Zur Begrenzung und Gliederung der Spätantike." *Jahrbuch des deutschen archäologischen Instituts,* 59–60 (1944–1945): 81–87.

———. "Bemerkungen zu den Kaisermosaiken in San Vitale." *Jahrbuch des deutschen archäologischen Instituts* 59–60 (1944–1945): 88–110.

Rousseau, P. "In Search of Sidonius the Bishop." *Historia* 25 (1976): 356–377.

Rumpf, A. *Stilphasen der spätantiken Kunst.* Arbeitsgemeinschaft für Forschung des Landes Nordrhein-Westfalen, Geisteswissenschaften, Abh. 44. 1957.

Ryberg, I. Scott. *Rites of the State Religion in Roman Art.* American Academy in Rome, Memoirs, 22. 1955.

Salomonson, J. W. *Chair, Sceptre and Wreath. Historical Aspects of Their Representation on Some Roman Sepulchral Monuments.* Dissertation, Groningen. Amsterdam, 1956.

Sanchez-Albornoz, C. *Estudios Visigodos.* Rome, 1971.

Sansoni, R. *I sarcofagi paleocristiani a porta di città.* Studi di antichità cristiane, 4. Bologna, 1969.

Sauser, E. "Das Paschamysterium in den sogenannten frühchristlichen Passionssarkophagen." *Kyriakon. Festschrift J. Quasten* 2. Münster, 1970, pp. 654–662.

Schalit, A. *König Herodes.* Berlin, 1969.

Schefold, K. *Die Griechen und ihre Nachbarn.* Berlin, 1967.

Schoenebeck, H. U. von. *Der Mailänder Sarkophag und seine Nachfolge.* Studi di antichità cristiana, 10. Vatican, 1935.

Schrade, H. "Zur Ikonographie der Himmelfahrt Christi." *Vorträge der Bibliothek Warburg* (1928–1929): 66–190. Leipzig, 1930.

Schramm, P. E. *Herrschaftszeichen und Staatssymbolik.* Schr. Mon. Germ. hist., 13. Stuttgart, 1954–1955.

———. "'Mitherrschaft im Himmel,' ein Topos des Herrscherkults in christlicher Einkleidung." *Polychronion, Festschrift F. Dölger.* Heidelberg, 1966, pp. 480–485.

Schumacher, W. N. *"Dominus legem dat,"* Römische Quartalschrift 54 (1959): 1–39.
———. "Hirt und 'Guter Hirt'," *Römische Quartalschrift*, 34. Supplementheft (1977).
Scott, W. *Hermetica.* Vol. 2. Oxford, 1925, pp. 461–482. (On Treatise 18.)
Scullard, H. H. *The Elephant in the Greek and Roman World.* London, 1974.
Seitz, K. *Die Schule von Gaza, eine literargeschichtliche Untersuchung.* Dissertation, Heidelberg, 1892.
Selem, A. "L'atteggiamento storiografico di Ammiano nei confronti di Giuliano dalla proclamazione di Parigi alla morte di Costanzo." *Athenaeum* 49 (1971): 89–110.
Seston, W. *Dioclétien et la Tétrarchie.* Bibl. des écoles françaises d'Athènes et de Rome, 162. 1946.
———. "Jovius et Herculius ou l'épiphanie des Tétrarches." *Historia* 1 (1950): 257–266.
Ševčenko, I. "A Neglected Byzantine Source of Muscovite Political Ideology." *Harvard Slavic Studies* 2 (1954): 141–179.
———. "The Early Period of the Sinai Monastery in the Light of Its Inscriptions." *Dumbarton Oaks Papers* 20 (1966): 255–264.
Seyrig, H. "La triade héliopolitaine et les temples de Baalbek." *Syria* 10 (1929): 315–356.
Shahîd, I. "The Iranian Factor in Byzantium under Heraclius." *Dumbarton Oaks Papers* 26 (1972): 295–320.
Shils, E. "The Meaning of the Coronation." In his *Center and Periphery, Essays in Macrosociology.* Chicago, 1975, pp. 135–152.
———. "Consensus." In his *Center and Periphery, Essays in Macrosociology.* Chicago, 1975, pp. 164–181.
Sickel, W. "Das byzantinische Krönungsrecht bis zum 10. Jahrhundert." *Byzantinische Zeitschrift* 7 (1898): 511–557.
Simon, M. *Hercule et le christianisme.* Strasbourg, 1955.
Simson, O. von. *Sacred Fortress. Byzantine Art and Statecraft in Ravenna.* Chicago, 1948.
Skeat, T. C. *Papyri from Panopolis.* Chester Beatty Monographs, 10. Dublin, 1964.
Soffel, J. *Die Regeln Menanders für die Leichenrede in ihrer Tradition dargestellt, herausgegeben, übersetzt und kommentiert.* Beitr. zur klass. Philologie, 57. 1974.
Soteriou, G. A. and M. G. Soteriou. Ἡ βασιλικὴ τοῦ ἁγίου Δημητρίου τῆς Θεσσαλονίκης. Athens, 1952.
———. "Heraclius, Byzantine Imperial Ideology, and the David Plates." *Speculum* 52 (1977): 217–237.
Stahl, W. H. *Macrobius, Commentary on the Dream of Scipio.* New York, 1952.
Stein, E. "Post-Consulat et αὐτοκρατορία" *Mélanges Bidez.* Brussels (1934): 869–912. Reprinted in his *Opera Minora Selecta.* Edited by J. R. Palanque. Amsterdam, 1968, pp. 315–358.
———. *Histoire du Bas-Empire.* Edited by J. R. Palanque. Vols. 1 and 2. Paris, 1949 and 1959.
Stein, E. and G. Ostrogorsky. "Die Krönungsordnungen des Zeremonienbuches." *Byzantion* 7 (1932): 185–233. Reprinted in E. Stein, *Opera Minora Selecta.* Edited by J. R. Palanque. Amsterdam, 1968, pp. 255–304.

Stern, H. *Le Calendrier de 354, étude sur son texte et ses illustrations.* Institut français d'archéologie de Beyrouth. Paris, 1953.

Stertz, S. A. "Pseudo Aristides ΕΙΣ ΒΑΣΙΛΕΑ." *Classical Quarterly* n.s. 29 (1979): 172–197.

Straub, J. *Vom Herrscherideal in der Spätantike.* Stutttgart, 1939 (Darmstadt, 1964).

———. "Konstantins Verzicht auf den Gang zum Kapitol." *Historia* 4 (1955): 297–313. Reprinted in his *Regeneratio Imperii, Aufsätze über Roms Kaisertum und Reich im Spiegel der heidnischen und christlichen Publizistik.* Darmstadt, 1972, pp. 100–118.

———. "Kaiser Konstantin als ἐπίσκοπος τῶν ἐκτός." *Studia Patristica* 1 (1957): 678–695. Reprinted in his *Regeneratio Imperii.* Darmstadt, 1972, pp. 119–133.

———. "Die Himmelfahrt des Julianus Apostata." *Gymnasium* 69 (1962): 310–326. Reprinted in his *Regeneratio Imperii.* Darmstadt, 1972, pp. 159–177.

———. "Konstantin als κοινὸς ἐπίσκοπος." *Dumbarton Oaks Papers* 21 (1967): 37–55. Reprinted in his *Regeneratio Imperii.* Darmstadt, 1972, pp. 134–158.

———. "Divus Alexander, Divus Christus." In *Festschrift J. Quasten.* Vol. 1. Edited by P. Granfield and J. A. Jungmann. Münster, 1970, pp. 461–473. Reprinted in J. Straub, *Regeneratio Imperii.* Darmstadt, 1972, pp. 178–194.

Stroheker, K. F. *Der senatorische Adel im spätantiken Gallien.* Tübingen, 1948.

Strong, E. *Apotheosis and After Life.* London, New York, 1915.

Stylow, A. U. *Libertas und Liberalitas, Untersuchungen zur innenpolitischen Propaganda der Römer.* Munich, 1972.

Sundwall, J. *Abhandlungen zur Geschichte des ausgehenden Römertums.* Helsinki, 1919 (New York, 1975).

Sutherland, C. H. V. "The Intelligibility of Roman Imperial Coin Types." *Journal of Roman Studies* 49 (1959): 46–55.

Swift, J. "The Anonymous Encomium of Philip the Arab." *Greek, Roman and Byzantine Studies* 7 (1966): 267–289.

Syme, R. "Astrology in the *H.A.*" In *Bonner Historia Augusta Colloquium 1972–1974* (1976), pp. 291–309.

Szidat, J. *Historischer Kommentar zu Ammianus Marcellinus Buch XX–XXI, Teil I, Die Erhebung Julians.* Historia Einzelschriften, 31. 1977.

Szövérffy, J. "A la source de l'humanisme chrétien médiéval: 'Romanus' et 'Barbarus' chez Vénance Fortunat." *Aevum* 45 (1971): 77–86.

Taeger, F. *Charisma, Studien zur Geschichte des antiken Herrscherkultes.* Vols. 1 and 2. Stuttgart, 1957 and 1960.

Thomas, G. S. R. "L'abdication de Dioclétien." *Byzantion* 43 (1973) pp. 229–247.

Thraede, K. "Die Poesie und der Kaiserkult." In *Le culte des souverains dans l'empire romain.* Entretiens Hardt, 19. 1972, pp. 273–303.

Tolney, C. "The Visionary Evangelists of the Reichenau School." *Burlington Magazine* 69 (1936): 257–263.

Tolstoi, I. I. *Les Monnaies byzantines.* N.p., 1912–14.

Toynbee, J. M. C. *The Hadrianic School.* Cambridge, 1934.

———. *Roman Medallions.* Numismatic Studies, 5. New York, 1944.

———. "Roma and Constantinopolis in Late Antique Art from 312–365." *Journal of Roman Studies* 37 (1947): 135–144.

———. "Roma and Constantinopolis in Late Antique Art from 365–Justin II." In *Studies Presented to D. M. Robinson*, 2. Saint Louis, 1953, pp. 261–277.

———. "Christian Paintings in S. Maria in Stelle near Verona." In *Kyriakon, Festschrift J. Quasten*, 2. 1970, pp. 648–653.

———. *Death and Burial in the Roman World*. London, 1971.

Treitinger, O. *Die oströmische Kaiser- und Reichsidee nach ihrer Gestaltung im höfischen Zeremoniell. Vom oströmischen Staats- und Reichsgedanken*. Jena, 1938 (Darmstadt, 1956).

Trilling, J. "Myth and Metaphor at the Byzantine Court. A Literary Approach to the David Plates." *Byzantion* 48 (1978): 249–263.

Trypanis, C. A. *Fourteen Early Byzantine Cantica*. Wiener Byzantinische Studien, 5. Vienna, 1968.

Unger, F. W. *Quellen der byzantinischen Kunstgeschichte*. Vienna, 1878.

Valenti Zucchini, G. and M. Bucci. *Corpus della scultura paleocristiana bizantina ed altomedioevale di Ravenna*. Edited by G. Bovini. Rome, 1968.

Vera, D. "I rapporti fra Magno Massimo, Teodosio e Valentiniano II nel 383–384." *Athenaeum* 53 (1975): 267–301.

———. "Le statue del senato di Roma in onore di Flavio Teodosio e l'equilibrio dei poteri imperiali in eta teodosiana." *Athenaeum* 57 (1979), 381–403.

Vermaseren, M. J. *Liber in Deum; l'apoteosi di un iniziato dionisiaco*. Leiden, 1976.

Vermeule, C. C. *Roman Imperial Art in Greece and Asia Minor*. Cambridge, Mass., 1968.

Versnel, H. S. *Triumphus. An Enquiry into the Origin, Development and Meaning of the Roman Triumph*. Leiden, 1970.

Veyne, P. *Le pain et le cirque. Sociologie historique d'un pluralisme politique*. Paris, 1976.

Vickers, M. "The Hippodrome at Thessaloniki." *Journal of Roman Studies* 62 (1972): 25–32.

———. "Theodosius, Justinian or Heraclius." *Art Bulletin* 58 (1976): 281.

———. "Mantegna and Constantinople." *Burlington Magazine* 118 (1976): 680–687.

Viljamaa, T. *Studies in Greek Encomiastic Poetry of the Early Byzantine Period*. Commentationes Humanarum Litterarum Societatis Scientiarum Fennicae, 48, 4. Helsinki, 1968.

Ville-Patlagean, E. "Une image de Salomon en basileus byzantin." *Revue des études juives. Historica Judaica*, 4th series, 1 (121) (1962): 9–33.

Vittinghoff, F. *Der Staatsfeind in der römischen Kaiserzeit*. Neue deutsche Forschungen. Alte Geschichte 2. Berlin, 1936.

Vogel, L. *The Column of Antoninus Pius*. Cambridge, Mass., 1973.

Volbach, W. F. *Elfenbeinarbeiten der Spätantike und des frühen Mittelalters*. Römische-Germanisches Zentralmuseum zu Mainz. 3rd ed., 1976.

Vollmer, F. "Laudationum funebrium Romanorum historia et reliquiarum editio." *Jahrbücher für classische Philologie*, Supplement 18 (1891): 445–528.

———. "De funere publico Romanorum." *Jahrbücher für classische Philologie*, Supplement 19 (1892): 319–364.

Walbank, F. W. *A Historical Commentary on Polybius* I. Oxford, 1957.

Wallace-Hadrill, D. S. *Eusebius of Caesarea*. London, 1960.

Wallace-Hadrill, J. M. *Early Germanic Kingship in England and on the Continent.* Oxford, 1971.

———. "Raising on a Shield in Byzantine Iconography." *Revue des études byzantines* 33 (1975): 133–175, reprinted in his *Studies in Byzantine Iconography.* London, 1977.

Walter, C. "The Coronation of a Co-Emperor in the *Skyllitzes Matritensis.*" *Actes du XIVᵉ Congrès international des Études Byzantines* 2. (Bucarest, 1975) 453–458, reprinted in his *Studies in Byzantine Iconography.* London, 1977.

Wander, S. H. "The Cyprus Plates and the Chronicle of Fredegar." *Dumbarton Oaks Papers* 29 (1975): 345–346.

Weinstock, S. *Divus Julius.* Oxford, 1971.

Weitzmann, K. *The Monastery of Saint Catherine at Mount Sinai. The Icons* I. Princeton, 1976.

Weitzmann, K., ed. *Age of Spirituality. Late Antique and Early Christian Art, Third to Seventh Century.* New York, 1979.

Wensinck, A. J. *The Muslim Creed.* Cambridge, 1932.

Wes, M. *Das Ende des Kaisertums im Westen des römischen Reiches.* Gravenhage, 1967.

Wessel, K. "Eine Gruppe oberitalischer Elfenbeinarbeiten." *Jahrbuch des deutschen archäologischen Instituts* 63–64 (1948–9): 111–160.

Wightman, E. M. *Roman Trier and the Treveri.* London, 1970.

Williams, G. *Change and Decline. Roman Literature in the Early Empire.* Berkeley, 1978.

Willis, W. H. "Greek Literary Papyri and the Classical Canon." *Harvard Library Bulletin* 12 (1958): 5–34.

Wissowa, G. *Religion und Kultus der Römer.* Munich, 1912 (1971).

Wistrand, E. "A Note on the *geminus natalis* of Emperor Maximian." *Eranos* 62 (1964): 131–145. Reprinted in his *Opera Selecta.* Stockholm, 1972, pp. 427–441.

Wlosok, A. *Laktanz und die philosophische Gnosis.* Abh. d. Heidelberger Akad. d. Wiss. phil. hist. Kl., 2. 1960.

Worrell, W. H. *The Coptic Manuscripts in the Freer Collection.* New York, London, 1923.

Wrede, H. "Zur Errichtung des Theodosiusobelisken in Istanbul." *Istanbuler Mitteilungen* 16 (1966): 178–198.

Wroth, W. *Catalogue of the Coins of the Vandals, Ostrogoths and Lombards and of the Empires of Thessalonica, Nicaea and Trebizond in the British Museum.* London, 1911 (Chicago, 1966).

Ziegler, I. *Die Königsgleichnisse des Midrasch beleuchtet durch die römische Kaiserzeit.* Breslau, 1903.

INDEX OF ANCIENT AUTHORS AND TEXTS

Brief or incidental references have been omitted.

INDEX OF NAMES AND SUBJECTS*

This index does not attempt to reiterate information given in the table of contents. For authors cited, also consult Index of Ancient Authors and Texts.

*I would like to thank Christine Boynton for her generous help in compiling this index.

Designer: Sandra Drooker
Compositor: G & S Typesetters
Text: 10/13 Linotron 202 Palatino
Display: Linotron 202 Palatino
Printer: Maple-Vail Book Mfg. Group
Binder: Maple-Vail Book Mfg. Group